THE
BIBLE
DIGEST

THE
BIBLE
DIGEST

by

CHARLES W. SLEMMING, D.D.

Complete in One Volume

KREGEL PUBLICATIONS
Grand Rapids, Michigan 49501

Published by Kregel Publications, a Division of Kregel, Inc., P.O. Box 2607, Grand Rapids, Michigan 49501.

Library of Congress Catalog Card No. 68-27671

ISBN 0-8254-3706-7

Originally published in three volumes, in 1960 by The Bible Testimony Fellowship, London, England.

First American Edition 1968
Second Printing 1971

DEDICATED TO THE MEMORY OF

LYDIA M. CROOK

CONTENTS

PREFACE

Of the many methods used today for the study of the Bible there are two which must remain fundamental. They are known as Biblical Analysis and Biblical Synthesis. All other methods are subsidiary to these and are but methods of approach. Analysis is the act of breaking down. Synthesis is the art of putting together.

Before man manufactures an article, or an inventor produces a new material, or a construction engineer builds a highway or an edifice, all of the materials must go to the chemist's laboratory, there to be broken down to find exactly their consistency and their ability to stand up to whatever pressure, wear, or tear may be put upon them. If they can stand that test, the materials are adapted for man's use. This is called *analysis*. In the breaking down of such materials chemists have discovered that they are a combination of ingredients. These have been separated into by-products which, in turn, are put together in new combinations and are called synthetics.

Biblical analysis and synthesis are similar. THE BIBLE DIGEST comes as a handbook to Bible study presenting these two approaches. Each book of the Bible is introduced in such a way as to make known the human author and the period in which he was writing. Afterward, the text of the book is dealt with in brief form, giving pertinent facts concerning it and bringing insights into the practical life of the people of God then and now.

The first half of the Old Testament contains stories of the lives of patriarchs, as Abraham, Isaac, Jacob, Joseph; of kings, as David and Solomon; of prophets, as Samuel, Elijah and Elisha. It also contains the wonderful Exodus story, with descriptions of the sufferings and triumphs of God's people. All of these are used as examples of faith. God's people were able to live godly lives in their day and exercise their influence on others because of a faith that ever saw the future. Our lives may be patterned accordingly "for the hope that is set before us."

The Poetical Books are quite distinctive, and deal with philosophy, worship, and wisdom. Apart from the Book of Job, which reasons suffering philosophically, most of the other writings come from the pens of David and Solomon. While there is lack of continuity in the Psalms and Proverbs yet, nevertheless, there is an analysis which we have attempted to set forth.

The Minor Prophets are *minor* only insofar as the size of each book is concerned. They certainly are *minus* in most Christian reading and thought. Some even consider that these books do not belong to the present dispensation. While this is true historically, it is not true spiritually or morally. They contain many warnings we would do well to heed, and many lessons we could well afford to learn. This section of the Bible should prove valuable in these present days because the messages delivered to the nations then are as up-to-date with our present history, and our social, economic, and moral problems, as any writings could be. These books are a fascinating study as they are read in connection with the happenings in the Middle East at this time.

I have not entered into much detail where the Gospel narrative is concerned, because most persons are well acquainted with the text, and the Lord spoke in a simple language readily understood by the people. Most of it is also a record of the things which He did.

The Epistles are more profound as they deal largely with the subject of doctrine. In many instances we have sought to give a cameo, or keyhole picture, of the city concerned and the prevailing conditions of the time, because those conditions were apt to creep into the local church and influence its behaviour. This "keyhole picture" creates a background to each Epistle which often makes it much easier to understand why the Apostle wrote certain things. This, in turn, aids us in interpretation.

For twenty-five years and more my wife and I have been traveling giving lectures on these subjects, as well as others. These travels have taken us throughout the British Isles, the whole of the United States of America, across Canada, and into every State of Australia and New Zealand, as well as to Europe and Jamaica. We have received many testimonies of blessing that has come to the persons reached, and not a few have been challenged to a fuller life and to a new desire to study the Word of God for themselves.

As with the Word of God, so with our lives. If we would have the Bible do in our lives and with our lives the very best, then we must study it. We must find out what it is, and what it contains (analysis), then allow it to take a new form and, instead of being an abstract code of laws, etc., its truths will now build into the fibre and character of our lives (synthesis). Our whole being will adjust itself to the doctrines and examples of the Bible and the Christ of the Bible. Thus we will become Spirit-filled, Christ-controlled, Bible-loving Christians.

We are exhorted to study to show ourselves approved unto God. We are bidden to search the Scriptures and are instructed to compare Scripture with Scripture.

This work has been written in the language of the layman, avoiding technical matters but seeking always to apply the truth to the everyday life of the Christian, so that the Bible might work itself out in the everyday lives of men and women today.

To all who possess this book, we would commend the *Bible Digest Charts** which have been prepared to give a pictorial and panoramic view of each book of the Bible. These charts have been designed in harmony with this particular work and based on the same analysis. They will prove to be invaluable in studying the Bible and in equipping oneself for Christian endeavour.

It is my prayer that THE BIBLE may captivate our hearts and that we may capture the spirit and purpose of both the Bible and its Author, God Himself.

Yours because His,

C. W. SLEMMING.

*62 Bible Charts presenting a pictorial outline of each book of the Bible. Kregel Publications, Grand Rapids, Michigan 49501.

THE BIBLE

THE WORD OF GOD

" There is none like that; give it me." (I SAMUEL xxi. 9)

THE AUTHOR

Whilst there were many penmen referred to as " authors ", there was but one true Author — God Himself. When Scripture is compared with Scripture and the Book is read as a whole instead of piecemeal we see continuity, oneness, accord, things which would immediately destroy the theory that the Bible only "contains" the Word of God. The Book, from cover to cover, is stamped with the authority of Divine Authorship. Note the constant repetition of such expressions as — " The Lord spake saying ", " The Lord said unto ", " The Word of the Lord came unto ", " Jesus saith unto them ", " The servant of Jesus Christ ", and many similar statements. Such phrases are to be found in every section of the Bible, such as The Pentateuch, The Judges, The Prophets, The Gospel, The Epistles, giving evidence that the whole Bible is the Word of God. God is doing the speaking ; man, as the servant of God, is only doing the recording. The Bible IS the Word of God. " God, Who at sundry times and in divers manners spake in time past unto the fathers by the prophets, hath in these last days *spoken* unto us by His Son " (Heb. i. 1). " For the prophecy came not in old time by the will of man : but holy men of God *spake* as they were moved by the Holy Ghost " (II Peter i. 21).

THE BOOK

One of the most impressive things that it is possible for a person to witness takes place at the Coronation of a British Monarch. Millions of people were privileged to see this in 1953 through the medium of television.

In royal attire and with regal dignity Queen Elizabeth II sat in Westminster Abbey, that ancient building, sacred with the memories of great people of past ages and now alive with the vast assemblage of great people of the present generation. These included Rulers from all parts of the world, Lords, Peers, and Dukes, Earls and Barons, with their wives, Diplomats and

Representatives of the Governments of the world, all of them wearing their costly robes of rank or office, whilst the ladies shone with the adornments of fabulous jewellery and coronets.

From the altar, filled with gold plate and bejewelled symbols, dignitaries of the Church in their elaborate vestments carried and presented to the Queen the Orb, Sceptre, Spurs, Ring, Swords and other regalia of the Sovereign's rights, powers and privileges, consummating with the anointing oil from the ampulla which dates back to before 1399, and the crowning with the imperial state crown containing 3,093 jewels which include the Black Prince's ruby and the Star of Africa, part of the Cullinan diamond.   In the midst of this wealth and splendour there was presented to Her Majesty, with these profound words, a simple copy of The Holy Bible.   " I present to you the *greatest* thing this world affords. Here is wisdom.   Here are the lively oracles, here is the Royal Law ".

Amidst the grandest pomp and ceremony the world knows, before the largest gathering of Nobles and Rulers, and surrounded by the greatest collection of wealth, the Bible is acclaimed " The greatest thing this world affords " — and no one can challenge it.

Greater in position than kings and queens.

Greater in power than diplomats and governments.

Greater in honour than the awards of the world.

Greater in wealth than gold and diamonds.

Greater in its past than all history.

Greater in its claims than all the authority of the Church.

This Book is the property of Queen and subject.   It is the wisdom of the wise and of the ignorant.   It is the revelation of God to man, the only Book that will lead man to God.

It is the rarest gem, the surest compass, the firmest foundation, the highest hope, the widest invitation, and the greatest assurance — the only revelation of man's salvation.

The highest achievements of man's mind and making fall into nothingness, and the greatest things in God's creation fade into insignificance before this Book, because this Book is the Word of God.   It is declared that heaven and earth shall pass away, but the Word of the Lord abideth for ever.

This is the Book we have to study — " Search the Scriptures ", " Meditate therein day and night ".

This is the Book we have to make known — " Preach the Word in season, out of season ".

This is the Book we have to obey — " Be ye doers of the Word and not hearers only ", " To obey is better than sacrifice ".

If this Book is all that it claims to be, then man is blessed indeed who adjusts his life according to its precepts. If this Book is the treasure it is claimed to be, then no man can despise it without doing himself irreparable harm.

A UNIVERSAL TESTIMONY

Everything bears testimony to the authority of the Scriptures as the Word of God. On one occasion when the Jews were criticising the conduct of Christ Himself, He gave them four witnesses to His authority. They were (1) The Father ; (2) John the Baptist ; (3) His works ; (4) The Scriptures. These four witnesses embrace four realms. (1) The Father — Divine. (2) John the Baptist — Human. (3) His works — the present. (4) The Scriptures — the past. These create an all-embracive or Universal Witness. This witness can be applied to the Scriptures. We have the testimony of

(1) God, or the witness of the Creator.
(2) Man, or the witness of the Creature.
(3) Science, or the witness of the Creation.
(4) The Bible, or the witness of Credence.

(1) *God — or the witness of the Creator.* God has permitted His Name and Character to be inscribed in every part of this Book. It is a Divine Revelation, however and wherever you look at it, externally or internally, historically or doctrinally.

" In the beginning GOD " (Gen. i. 1).

" All Scripture is given by inspiration of GOD " (II Tim. iii. 16).

" Holy men of God spake as they were moved by the Holy Ghost " (II Peter i. 21).

" All things were made by Him ; and without Him was not anything made that was made " (John i. 3).

" For in HIM we live, and move, and have our being " (Acts xvii. 28).

" Through faith we understand that the worlds were framed by the Word of GOD, so that things which are seen were not made out of things which do appear " (Heb. xi. 3).

" From everlasting to everlasting Thou art GOD " (Psalm xc. 2).

" Seeing HE giveth to all life and breath and all things " (Acts xvii. 25).

Much more of the evidence of Divine approval will be seen as the Book is approached from the other angles.

(2) *Man — or the witness of the Creature.* Many great men of the past and present have borne testimony to the Word of God through their experience. Many scientists have verified the Word of God through investigation. Many archaeologists have proved the Word of God through discovery. Many saints have enjoyed the Word of God through reading and obedience. Many infidels have attacked the Word of God without disproving it. Every age and every realm of life could stand up and bear witness. A few have been chosen at random that would represent a good cross-section from every walk of life.

Sir Walter Scott, the Novelist, when dying, asked his son-in-law to read from the Book. " What book ? " said Lockhart. Scott replied : " There is but one Book — the Bible ".

William Gladstone, the English Statesman, called it " The impregnable rock of Holy Scripture ". He said he knew only 95 really great men — 90 of these were believers in the Bible.

John Adams, a United States President, said : " So great is my veneration for the Bible that the earlier my children begin to read it, the more confident will be my hopes that they will prove to be useful citizens and respectable members of society ".

Queen Victoria considered the Bible as the secret of her nation's greatness.

Thomas Carlyle wrote : " There never was a Book like the Bible and there never will be any other such Book ".

Charles Dickens, the author, said that the most pathetic story in all literature was of the prodigal son.

Daniel Webster, America's outstanding lawyer, said : " The greatest legal digest was the sermon on the Mount ".

Coleridge quoted the Beatitudes as the richest passage in literature.

Six-hundred-and-seventeen British Scientists on one occasion signed a document that no scientific discovery had proved any discrepancy in the Bible.

Now take one testimony to the contrary : —

Voltaire, the infidel, said : " Twelve men started Christianity, but one man will destroy it and I will be that one man. Within one hundred years only a few odd Bibles will be found in Museums ". Those hundred years have passed. At an auction sale the whole of Voltaire's works (91 volumes) were sold for 10/0d. ($1.41-), whilst the British Government purchased a portion of the Bible — the Codex Siniaticus — for £250,000 ($700,000.00-), the greatest price ever paid for a book.

Hundreds of such testimonies could be cited as MAN continues to bear his testimony to the Word of God.

(3) *Science — or the witness of Creation.* What a witness is creation to the authority and accuracy of God's Word! As has already been stated, true science has never found anything to conflict with the Bible. So much is being discovered that one is almost at a loss to know what to choose. Here is a testimony to the Word of God from the leading realms of Science : —

History. Archaeological research ever confirms the recorded History of the Bible, whether it concerns the Flood of Noah's day or the question of whether Moses knew writing, or that the Hittites ever existed. We have the Rosetta Stone, the Tell-el-amarna tablets, the Codices, etc. History is the past re-told as prophecy is the future fore-told. Therefore the Bible is the beginning and end of all *History.*

Astronomy. The heavens are measured by millions of miles, and the heavenly bodies are counted by the billions. "The sweet influences of the Pleiades", of which the Psalmist speaks, are 300 billion miles away. The sun that rules the day is approximately 93 million miles away from the earth. Yet, whilst so inconceivably vast, it is by this planetary system that time is measured to the minutest degree, so that the length of the year is 365 days 5 hours 45 minutes 48 seconds, for these heavenly bodies never vary in their course or momentum. Surely a testimony to the truth of the Book which says : "He meted out heaven with the span" (Isaiah xl. 12). "The heavens declare the glory of God and the firmament sheweth forth His handiwork . . . night sheweth knowledge" (Psalm xix. 1-2). "Lift up your eyes on high, and behold Who hath created these things that bringeth out their host by number : He calleth them all by names by the greatness of His might, for that He is strong in power; not one faileth" (Isaiah xl. 26). Remember, the writers of that day were not equipped with the modern precision instruments of to-day.

From the astronomer's telescope we turn to the microscope of *Chemistry.* From the heavens to the earth, to the composition of matter, here we learn everything is made up of two or more of ninety-two component parts (although this figure has recently been slightly increased). As all computations of figures are based on ten digits, and all English literature is built up of twenty-six letters, so matter is made of millions of different combinations of these component parts. Air is made of two — oxygen and nitrogen. Water is made of two — called H_2O. The soil is made of sixteen. Can this be attributed to chance or to evolution ? Surely, behind all the composition of matter, made of that wonderful atom, there must be a " Supreme Being ". Chemistry bears its evidence and testimony to the Word of God. " God created the heavens and the earth ", " He holdeth the world together ", " And comprehended the dust of the earth in a measure ". He comprehended the dust of the earth so minutely that all matter is well balanced for the good of man.

Biology. Man is made of bone, flesh, blood, skin, muscle, nerve ; of heart, brain, lungs, kidneys ; of sight, hearing, smelling, and much, much more. All of these in turn are made of millions of cells, tissues, etc. And this man, with all animal and vegetable life, continues to produce after his kind. Biologists can define all of these things, but cannot produce anything. They cannot create life, a testimony to the Word of God which says : " Whose seed is in itself ", " In Him we live and move and have our being ".

Physics. The study of heat, sound, light, electricity, testifies to light independent of the sun, and God created the light on the first day and the sun on the fourth day. Moses and Job knew the laws of Physics. Who taught them ? God.

Logic. In this realm we could not conceive that metal and glass could take upon themselves certain shapes by chance, and then, by the same mysticism of chance, these shapes and pieces come together to form a perfect time-keeping watch. This would be called illogical. Logic says that a master-mind and a skilled hand must be behind such a formation. True — and the world is a perfect time-keeping orbit in a perfect time-keeping universe, with day and night, heat and cold, seedtime and harvest, summer and winter, tides and moons, never varying. This proves a Master-mind and a skilled hand. The Bible declares these things in portions of Scriptures such as Genesis viii. 22.

Likewise the Bible, with its many books, and many writers, over a period of many years, has a prophetic time-keeping accuracy which must cancel out any suggestion of chance. It has been said that if we were to put together

    (1)   The Magna Charta
    (2)   The History of Plato
    (3)   The songs of Wesley
    (4)   The writings of Carl Marx
    (5)   The religion of Buddha
    (6)   The theories of George Bernard Shaw
    (7)   The prophecy of Mother Shipton

they would make a volume of utter confusion ; yet, in one volume, called the Bible, we have

(1) The law of Moses
(2) The history of Israel
(3) The psalms of David
(4) The writings of the prophets
(5) The gospel of Jesus
(6) The theology of Paul
(7) The revelation of John,

and together they make for perfect harmony and accord. Each can be blended harmoniously into the other. Surely, logic can testify to the accuracy of Scripture !

Law. This is all based on the Mosaic law.

Art. In painting, poetry, music, etc., it turns to the Bible for its inspiration.

Geology, Philosophy, Scholarship, all in turn bear their witness. Science in every department declares everywhere and every day that the Bible is true.

(4) *The Bible — or the witness of Credence.* This Book speaks for itself.

Its Formation. The Bible contains two volumes, the Old and New Testaments. These comprise 66 books, 39 in the Old Testament and 27 in the New Testament. There are 1,189 chapters (929 O.T. and 260 N.T.) ; 31,173 verses ; 773,693 words ; 3,536,489 letters. This was the first Book ever printed, as well as being the smallest and largest volume ever put into print. It has several times been hand-written, the last time in Chicago in 1949. The centre verse of the Bible is Psalm cxviii. 8 ; the longest verse Esther viii. 9 ; the shortest John xi. 35.

These sixty-six books were written by about forty different earthly writers, coming from every walk of life and belonging to all levels of human society. They included kings and statesmen, professional men and labourers, fishermen and farmers, priests and prophets, shepherds and scribes. None of these men could confer with the other for few of them met. Moses wrote at Sinai, kings and prophets in Palestine, exile prophets in Babylon and Persia, Paul in Asia and Europe, John in Patmos, whilst between the writers there was not only distance but 1,600 years of time. Yet there remains the evidence of One Author for there is continuity of thought, harmony of purpose, perfection of detail and lack of contradiction, permitting us to compare Scripture with Scripture. We more perfectly understand the writings of the one by comparing

them with the writings of another. Such a statement could not
be made about any two books written in the secular world.

We often compare Genesis with Revelation, Leviticus with
Hebrews, Old Testament with New Testament, New Testament
with Old Testament. We see Old Testament prophecies wonderfully fulfilled in the New Testament times and often forget that
the writers knew not each other and were not always conscious
themselves of the significance of their writings and utterances.

In dealing with formation it should be noted that the structure
of the Book is more than human. The balance of the Old Testament is 17 Historical books, 5 Poetical books, and 17 Prophetical
books. The Jew divides his Scriptures into The Law, the Prophets,
and The Writings. The last 17 books are divided into what are
called the Major and Minor Prophets. These terms have nothing
to do with the character of the prophets themselves, nor with the
quality of their message. It merely designates the longer books
from the shorter ones.

In the New Testament practically the whole is Doctrinal.
There are 4 Gospels, 1 Historical book (Acts), 21 Epistles, and 1
Prophetical book. The Epistles are themselves classified into
Pauline Epistles, written by Paul, and the General Epistles, written
by James, Peter, John and Jude.

The Pauline Epistles divide into 9 Church Epistles, addressed
to Churches, and 4 Pastoral Epistles, written to Pastors. The
Book of Hebrews stands on its own addressed to a people — the
Hebrews, wherever they might be.

Its Preservation. Looking now at the External, or material,
side of this amazing Book, we learn that *holy men wrote as they
were moved.* Whether one thinks of Moses on the Mount, or Paul
in prison, or John on Patmos, or any other writer, they were
ordinary men — men subject to like passions as we are, but men
who were yielded to God. God, by His Spirit, inspired these men
to write, robbing none of them of their own personality, so that
Moses is different in style from David, and David different from
Isaiah, and Isaiah different from Paul. Down through the ages
God has enabled men to expound His Word, some through
writing and others through preaching, each in his own style and all
making their own contribution.

In the early days Scribes copied these Scriptures in a meticu-
lous fashion, taking fifteen years. The Scriptures then only
included the first five books of the Bible, known to us as The
Pentateuch and known to the Jew as his Torah. The reason for
so long a period was that he copied one letter at a time, checking

each letter from five scrolls. Three more years were spent by other Scribes checking and, if necessary, correcting. This kept the Hebrew writing in such pure form.

Scholars translated mainly from the Hebrew and the Greek into other languages. Wycliff, Tyndale, Coverdale, and others, translated the Book into the English language, and today it is still being translated so that already it is in more than a thousand languages and dialects, and scholars continue to bring it to people who as yet have not heard its message in their tongue.

Inventors printed. At the time when scholars were engaged in their translating, a German boy, by the name of Johan Gutenburg, was playing with some letters cut out from lino. Accidentally he dropped one into a vessel of dye standing before the fire. He took it out with his hand but it was so hot he dropped it quickly. It fell on to a parchment also before the fire. When he picked it up again a J was indelibly printed on the parchment. The story tells that his mother left an imprint on the boy's anatomy ! But the imprint on his mind proved the more lasting for, in after years, he continued to meditate on that imprint on the parchment and, as a result of his meditation, he invented what was known as " movable type ". Thus the Bible had an increased circulation through the medium of printing. Recently a Gutenburg Bible sold for a very large sum of money.

History of the English Bible. This is a great and fascinating story and can only be summarised here thus :

The Manuscripts. The originals are lost. The oldest and most valuable in existence are called Codices, three of which are the

Codex Alexandrinus ⎫
Codex Sinaiticus ⎬ both in the British Museum.

Codex Vaticanus, in the Vatican at Rome.

From the Manuscripts came

The Versions. The most important of these are the Vulgate, Syriac, Samaritan, and Septuagint.

From the Versions came

The Translations.

1381 Wycliff translated from the Latin Vulgate.
1525 Tyndale translated at Worms.
1535 Coverdale translated from Tyndale and the Vulgate.
1537 Matthews translated from Tyndale and Coverdale.
1539 Taverner's Translation.

1539   The Great Bible, or The Chained Bible of Henry
        VIII.
1560   The Geneva Bible.
1568   The Bishops Bible.
1582   The Douay, or Rheims. The Bible of the Roman
        Catholic Church.
1611   King James, or The Authorised Version.
1885   The Revised Version.
1901   American Standard.

All of these are the foundation of the Bible as we now know it.
Although translations are continually being brought to the market
not one of them is looked upon as that which is fundamental. To
each there is a following of a group of people who accept them
for their value as modern language.

Throughout all of this change the Book has remained distinct
from all other books, has maintained the stamp of Divine Revelation and continued to be the Word of God which is the power of
God unto salvation.

Its Revelation. From the external we turn to the internal,
from the material to the spiritual, or its message. Comparing the
two Testaments the following comparisons would be of interest : —

OLD TESTAMENT	NEW TESTAMENT
The Scriptures of Israel, an earthly people with earthly promises and blessings.	The Scriptures of the Church, a spiritual people with heavenly promises.
Outward ceremonies to control inward principles.	Inward principles to control outward actions.
Reformation.	Regeneration.
Continual sacrifices.	One sacrifice for sin.
Types and shadows.	Anti-types and substance.
Bondage.	Liberty.
Law.	Grace.
Ends with a curse.	Ends with a blessing.
Pentateuch — Israel's foundation.	Gospel — the Church's Founder.
History — Israel's legislation.	Acts — the Church's Foundation.
Poetical — Israel's aspiration.	Epistles — the Church's Faith.
Prophetical — Israel's expectation.	Revelation — the Church's Future.

The Bible begins with God. The Eternal introduces man as a perfect creation, records the entrance of sin into the world with its tragic results, after which it outlines the history of a nation, established in Abram and finding its way into the slavery of Egypt. God emancipates these people through the Passover, leads them into the Wilderness of Sinai, and there gives to them a Law. According to His promise He leads them into a land which was to be their own, and a royal throne is established. As a result of continued sin, this nation becomes divided into two kingdoms, and eventually one kingdom is carried into Assyria and the other banished to Babylon. After seventy years Judah returns from Babylon and is later dispersed throughout the world, whilst other nations, known as Gentiles, govern world affairs. During this time the New Testament history comes into being. Christ is born in Bethlehem and makes His way to Calvary to become the Emancipator, the Redeemer of mankind. This divides the world into two classes, the believer and the unbeliever. The Saints make up the Church of Christ, which is now in the world. Soon the Lord will come back again to take from the world that Church, thus completing its history.

Then the history of the Jewish nation will operate again as these scattered people are brought back to their land — Palestine. Here they will enjoy a thousand years of peace, known as the Millennium, after which there will come a day of reckoning for all men. This will mean blessing for all who have acknowledged and served the Lord, but damnation for all God-rejectors. So the Book closes.

This is the story we study in all its detail as we now travel through the books of the Bible.

GENESIS

MAN CREATED

" And God said, Let us make man in our image, after our
likeness . . . So God created man in His own image, in the
image of God created He him . . . And God blessed them,
and God said unto them, Be fruitful, and multiply, and
replenish the earth . . . "   (Gen. i. 26-28)

INTRODUCTION

Truth is not fully obtained by surface reading. It is often underlying. A Judge has to listen to all the statements made, then put one and one together to obtain his evidence. Man has to read the Word of God as a whole, then compare Scripture with Scripture to obtain the Divine Revelation. Did He not say that He spake in parables that they seeing should not see, and hearing they might not hear nor understand (Matt. xiii. 13). He also said : " I thank Thee, O Father, Lord of Heaven and earth, because Thou hast hid these things from the wise and prudent, and hast revealed them unto babes " (Matt. xiii. 25).

Let us read therefore between the lines before we read the lines.

It is to be observed that the first book of the Bible has known more abuse, suffered more opposition, received more challenge, and endured more criticism than any other book. There must be a reason for this. Attack of this nature always comes from the enemy, and with intent to destroy. If Satan would dispose of this book, we ought to hold tenaciously to it. If he hates it, then we should love it. If it does him untold harm, it should do us that amount of good.

Why does Satan use all of his forces to bring discredit to the book of Genesis ? Because it records his fall and his final doom, and also tells of a relationship that has been established between God and man which he does not want man to know, for his desire is that man should serve him.

Consider, firstly, the negative side of this book.

WHAT GENESIS IS NOT. The enemy seems somewhat satisfied that he has done this book material harm by his constant attack upon the creation story. He takes man back to protoplasm, unfolds and evolves it, and believes he has explained beginnings, and has dealt with cause and effect. At least he is satisfied that he has man believing this theory of evolution. But all of this reasoning and attack are merely falling on a decoy, or a camouflage. Main issues have been missed, for there remains unassailed and undefined the great incomprehensible statement " In the beginning God ". This statement is ahead of, and above, all theories, beyond all science, biology, geology, physiology, and everything else of man's reasoning.

Genesis is not a scientific treatise. By that we mean it was not written as such. Nonetheless it remains perfectly scientific. Science is ever finding out ; it is never complete. Science today is in conflict with science of fifty years ago, so we cannot wonder if it differs from science of six thousand years ago. The Bible never contradicts itself. It never has to be changed fundamentally to bring it up to date. Some people have tried to change it, but have not succeeded because the Bible, as we know it, never becomes obsolete as a result of their reasonings. Others have sought to bring the language up to date in modern translations but these should never alter the fundamental truths.

Genesis is not myth. Myth is always opposite to fact. So much has been proved that we can rely on that which has not been defined in so many words. Mythology contains a great amount of impurity. Genesis maintains a very high standard of morals.

Genesis is not imagination. Nothing suggests that an individual, or individuals, sat down to write what might have happened. The book speaks with much certainty and remains positive throughout.

WHAT GENESIS IS. This brings us to the positive side which shows that *Genesis is a revelation,* and a Divine Revelation at that. The Lord revealed the past to Moses as He revealed the future to John. This would make Genesis to be Apocalyptic. Moses lived more than two thousand four hundred years after the creation that he narrates. Genesis is in perfect harmony with the rest of the Bible.

One of the wonderful things about the book is that it deals with more subjects over a longer period of time than any other book in the Bible.

PURPOSE

If the book is a Divine Revelation the question arises — what does it reveal, or, what was the purpose that God had when He inspired a holy man to write this book ?

If one were to answer this question without due consideration, the most likely answer would be that it was to give us a record

of the beginning of things, to tell the story of creation ; but, upon
further reflection, this cannot be because these beginnings are told
in a very summary fashion, in not more than eleven chapters,
whilst thirty-nine chapters are given to one man and his descendants, and that in great detail. This is out of all proportion —
eleven chapters to the immense subject of the world of nature
and the beginning of the human race, given in the most abridged
form, and thirty-nine chapters concerning a family in all the fullest
detail !

The first section tells of *man created in Adam*. The second
section shows *man called in Abram*. From this we discover that
the theme of the book from chapter one to chapter fifty is MAN, or
the creature comes before the creation. This would suggest that the
theme of the book of Genesis is MAN and his relationship with
his God. In the first section, *man created in Adam*, the relationship is of a creature toward a Creator. In the second, *man called
in Abram*, the relationship is of a son toward a Father. These
are the only two relationships that can exist between God and man,
and the emphasis (39 chapters) is on the Family Relationship.
Might it be expressed this way ? God made the world for man,
and then made man for Himself. No wonder the Psalmist said :
" When I consider Thy heavens, the work of Thy fingers, the
moon and the stars, which Thou hast ordained ; what is man,
that Thou art mindful of him, and the son of man, that Thou
visitest him ? For Thou hast made him a little lower than the
angels, and hast crowned him with glory and honour " (Psalm viii.
3-5).

The book is one of Generation. The first three verses give us
Generation, Degeneration, and Regeneration. The second division
of this book commences with the words : " Now these are the
generations ". The book of generations gives the

Generations of the heaven and the earth	Chs.	2-4
Generations of Adam	Chs.	5-6
Generations of Noah	Chs.	6-9
Generations of the sons of Noah	Chs.	10-11
Generations of Shem	Ch.	11
Generations of Terah	Ch.	11
Generations of Ishmael	Ch.	25
Generations of Isaac	Chs.	25-35
Generations of Esau	Chs.	36-37
Generations of Jacob	Chs.	37-50

The theme throughout is the Family.

The Hebrew word "Toledoth", translated "generations", refers to effect rather than cause, to descendants more than to ancestry, to result rather than origin, although the book remains one of origin. The thing first declared is carried out to its final results. This idea of result rather than origin can be seen clearly in the fact that there are no generations of Abram, the most important person. They are the generations of Terah, but it was not Terah who mattered. He was the cause. Everything centres in and around Abram, the result.

In this book of generations, or the Seed Book of the Bible, we not only have the beginning of the world and man, but almost everything begins here. For example, there is a record of the beginning of time, the universe, man, sin, marriage, death, languages, rain, science, travel, etc.

The book is also to be seen as one of

PROGRESS

It starts with great expectation and ends with bitter disappointment. It commences with life and concludes with death. The opening statement is "In the beginning God", and the final words are "A coffin in Egypt". What a contrast! What a tragedy!! The same applied to a nation. Great promises were made to Abram, great expectations were looked for from his descendants, but all ended in a coffin in Egypt.

Life is the same. The new-born babe becomes the hope and ambition of parents. They watch it grow, mature, advance. Hopes soar higher and higher, but it ends in a coffin in the Egypt of this world. "Egypt" may be a great place for art and culture, progress may be amazing, invention bewildering, pleasure abundant, and such is this world in which we find ourselves. But how does this life end — in a coffin!

The coffin is not the end of *all* things. It is the end of Genesis, and Genesis is "beginnings". So the coffin is only the end of the beginning. Genesis is the prelude to the whole Bible. Time is the prelude to an eternity. The coffin only marks the end of Time. Man then enters eternity. Where that is spent depends upon our decisions whilst in time. Therefore, the most important thing is to know now whether one is a creature related to a Creator, or whether a son related to the Father.

The whole subject might be looked upon as a drama. The world is but the stage upon which the drama is to be enacted. The centre figure is man, who is representative of all humanity. On to the stage come two suitors, each seeking to obtain man's love and loyalty. The first to appear asks for man's devotion and obedience because He is his Creator. He claims He made man for Himself. He promises him all that will be for his good and an eternal life in His presence. The second suitor enters and demands man's sympathy and submission. He claims that he has a right to him because he is the god of this world, and man in coming into the world has stepped into his domain. He promises pleasure, prosperity, success, and all for which man could wish in this life. He says nothing about the life to come. The drama continues with man divided in his decision as to what he considers the right course, and concludes with part of the human family yielding to God and finding everlasting life, and part allowing Satan to have his way, thus leading them into a lost eternity. When the drama of Time ends man moves into eternity one way or the other, which way depending upon his own decision as to eternal things.

When the dramatic season has ended the stage is usually torn down, wanted no more. When God has finished with this earth He is going to burn it up, but man will live on for ever. Says Peter : " The heavens shall pass away with a great noise and the elements shall melt with fervent heat, the earth also and the works that are therein shall be burned up. Seeing then that all these things shall be dissolved, what manner of persons ought ye to be " (II Peter iii. 10-11).

POINTS OF INTEREST IN THE CONTENTS

(1) *Creation*. It has already been stated that the creature, man, is more important than the creation. It must now be observed that as to the subject of creation there is only one verse, and that contains only one statement. " In the beginning God created the heaven and the earth ". This gives the Scientist and the Geologist all the millions of years that they like to talk about because " In the beginning " is just a dateless past. How God created and what He created in that world we do not know. Many people have thought of the whole chapter as dealing with creation, but this is not so. It is a chapter of re-creation. Verse 1 is the statement of creation, or generation. Verse 2 is chaos, or degeneration, and verse 3 onwards is regeneration. Verse 2 cannot belong to creation because one cannot create without form unless it were energy, and neither can one create a thing and call it void. The fact is that the earth became void. This condition may be appreciated from other Scriptures. Job said concerning God : " Which removeth the mountains, and they know not ; which overturneth them in His anger. Which shaketh the earth out of

her place, and the pillars thereof tremble. Which commandeth the sun, and it riseth not ; and sealeth up the stars " (Job ix. 5-7). Says Isaiah : " Behold, the Lord maketh the earth empty, and maketh it a waste, and turneth it upside down, and scattereth abroad the inhabitants thereof" (Isaiah xxiv. 1). "For thus saith the Lord that created the heavens : God Himself that formed the earth and made it ; He hath established it, He created it not in vain, (margin : " a waste "). He formed it to be inhabited " (Isaiah xlv. 18).

The question may be asked — What would cause the earth to become chaotic if God created it perfect ? The answer which has been given is that, when God created the earth, He elected that one of His created angelic beings should have the oversight of that earth. He chose one by the name of Lucifer and set him upon that holy mountain (read Ezekiel xxviii. 11-19). In this honoured position Lucifer became very proud, then ambitious, then rebellious, claiming that he would ascend into heaven and be equal with God. But Lucifer was a created being and God was the Creator, and God knows no equal. As a result God cast him out of that beautiful earth and, in so doing, God turned that world upside down, and so it became without form and void (read Isaiah xiv. 4-15). In this condition the earth could have remained for thousands or millions of years. This would explain the coal fields, the oil fields, the caves with their wonders, and all the other things belonging to the geological world. It also explains how Satan (Lucifer) became the god of this world.

From Genesis i. 3 onwards the chapter is not given to creation but to re-creation. God is putting into order that which He had earlier thrown into disorder. In this connection it must be noted that two words are used in the Hebrew. One is " Bara ", only used four times and translated " created ". These are in verses 1, 21, and 27. God created the heaven and the earth. God created whales, and God created man. In every other instance the word " Asah " is used and is translated " made ", and means " reconstructed or made out of material already in existence ". The two words are used together in summarising : " And God blessed the seventh day, and sanctified it ; because that in it He had rested from all His work which God *created* and *made*" (Genesis ii. 3).

(2) *Man.* (Ch. i.) We have learned that he is the most important subject in this world of creation, but he is more. Man was made for fellowship with God. Therefore he was made in the likeness and image of God. Man was created an immortal

creature and also a moral creature. Evolution is contrary to all of this and is false. In fact it is already an exploded theory. Man was the climax and the apex of all God's creative energy, not the lowest. The physical form of man was made from dust and returns to dust, not from a jelly to a jelly. The moral part of man has ever been infinitely above the animal. There is nothing that is common to both.

(3) *The Fall*. (Ch. iii.)   The question is often asked — why did God permit Satan to become a tempter, and why did God allow sin to come into the world if He knew that it would bring such a curse ?   The answer to this perplexing question is that it was necessary.   Man had been created a free-will agent.   The " Will " is something that no ape nor any other creature possesses, but what use is the will if there is no medium of exercise.   It would be as worthless as a £5 note, or a $20.00 bill, in the pocket of a cold and hungry man if that man were living in the midst of a desert without the facilities to spend that money.   He may be rich in cash and yet die from cold.   The tree in the midst of the garden and the commandment " Thou shalt not " became the mediums whereby that will was exercised as man made his own choice to obey or disobey.   If man, and his wife, had obeyed, their reward would have been to partake of the second tree of the garden — the Tree of Life ; but because they failed they were expelled from the garden, and the Tree of Life was guarded by cherubim with flaming sword.   That Tree of Life has been transplanted from the Eden of earth to the Eden above, and still remains the reward for the overcomer.   This is made known to us in Rev. ii. 7 : " To him that overcometh will I give to eat of the Tree of Life, which is in the midst of the paradise of God ".

This means we should dwell less on The Fall and more on The Recovery, less on the degeneration of the human heart and more on the regeneration offered by the Lord Who died to redeem us from death.

(4) *Cain and Abel*. (Ch. iv.)   It is usually suggested that the sacrifice of Cain was rejected and that of Abel accepted because of the nature of their offerings, that one represented works and the other faith, or works versus blood, but this can hardly be true. If a farmer offers produce and a shepherd offers sheep surely they are equal in that both offer the results of their labours. So often the question of blood is raised when it should be the question of sin.   There is no mention of sin in the narrative up to this point. The book of Leviticus names five offerings, only one of which is

called a Sin Offering. In the Cain and Abel story the word " offering " is " Minchah " in the Hebrew, and is the same word from which is derived Meal Offering in Leviticus ii. The Meal Offering was never offered for sin and, incidentally, was the only offering that had no blood in it. The word " Minchah " means " the gift of an inferior to a superior ". The same word " Minchah " is translated "present " in the story of Jacob and Esau. " Then thou shalt say, They be thy *servant* Jacob's; it is a present (Minchah) sent unto my lord Esau " (Gen. xxxii. 18). The whole idea, therefore, is that these two men were offering a gift in acknowledgment of the God they worshipped. This makes it an act of worship rather than an act of repentance. In the light of these circumstances, it appears that " Cain brought of the fruit of the ground ". This statement gives no indication that Cain made any choice. He brought the fruit that may have been first to hand. In the next verse Abel brough*t firstlings* of his flock. That suggests a choosing of the best, " and the fat thereof ". Eastern people loved the fat. It was to them the choicest part of the animal. Quality came into Abel's offering.

We learn from this that it was not the nature of the offering that mattered but the quality, and the quality revealed the condition of heart of the offerer. Therefore " The Lord had respect unto *Abel* and to his offering. But unto *Cain* and to his offering He had not respect ". The lesson is that God accepted Abel first, then his offering, and He rejected Cain because of his offering. In other words, God accepted the offering because of the Offerer, and not the Offerer because of the offering.

Christian, do not look at your service, look at yourself. If *you* are acceptable to God your service is bound to be right because it rests on motive. Some have quoted verse 7, " sin lieth at the door ", as meaning a sin offering lieth at the door. This is not so. In the Hebrew the word " lieth " is " coucheth ", and a lamb does not couch. The thought is of a wild animal couching ready to spring. If thou doest not well then sin, like a wild animal, is couching at the door of your heart ready to spring on you and make you its victim, for unto thee is its desire BUT thou shouldest rule over it (sin). This is shown in the margin of any reference Bible.

(5) *Cain's Wife.* (Ch. iv.) Many of the problems here are caused by misquotation. Believing that Cain went down to the land of Nod and found a wife, men have asked the question — Where did Cain get his wife ? — assuming that he found her

amongst another race of people not mentioned in the Bible. The
fact is that Cain " dwelt in the land of Nod on the East side of
Eden, and Cain *knew* his wife ". There is no suggestion that he
found her there. He took his wife with him. Cain married his
own sister, for Adam " begat sons and daughters " (Gen. v. 4).
Nothing was wrong about that in the beginning. It was when the
human family had increased sufficiently, and the continuance of the
practice of marrying close relatives would have weakened the stock,
that God gave the law in Lev. xviii. forbidding such marriages.
Until a law is given there is no law to break, " for where no law
is, there is no transgression " (Rom. iv. 15).

(6) *The Sons of God and the Daughters of Men.* (Ch. vi.)
Two questions arise — were the sons of God the sons of Seth who
married the daughters of Cain, or were they the fallen angels who
had intercourse with human beings ? To those who believe the
first, that the righteous line of Seth married the ungodly line of
Cain, it must be pointed out that the result of these marriages
was that their offspring were " mighty men which were of old,
men of renown ". This means that their offspring were a supernatural race of giants instead of the natural race, the race from
which Christ should come. Do godly men marry ungodly women
to-day ? Yes ! Do ungodly men marry godly women to-day ?
Yes ! As a result, do they produce unnatural offspring ? The
answer is No ! As their offspring was unnatural so these marriages
must have been different. These Sons of God refer to some beings
created by God. They were angels — see Job i. 6 ; ii. 1 ; xxxviii.
7 ; II Peter ii. 4 ; and Jude vi. These were angels who kept not
their first estate but fell with Satan and Satan is using them to
populate the world with a supernatural race and thus make extinct
the natural race. To do this he would prevent " the seed of the
woman ", who was to bruise his head, from coming into the
world, and thereby he would prevent his own destruction.

Some would say this cannot be because angels are non-sex,
they are not given to marriage, but the Scripture says " . . . they
neither marry, nor are given in marriage ; but are as the angels in
heaven " (Mark xii. 25). " In heaven " is not out of heaven.
When these angels lost their first estate they lost their heavenly
condition.

There are many who will not accept this interpretation, but
some confirmation can be found in the realm of mythology. All
mythology is built upon fact and is usually a distortion of truth.
" In Greek and Roman mythology the story is told of the love of

Jupiter for the beautiful women of the earth which resulted in the birth of such stalwart heroes as Hercules thereby arousing the wrath of Juno ". Such mythology gives proof that the story of the Bible as here told must have been believed in those early days.

As a result of these conditions the world was filled with wickedness so that God decided He would destroy the world with

(7) *The Flood.* (Chs. 6-9) Before effecting this destruction God must save the human race and thereby His promise of redemption. Noah was instructed, therefore, by God to build an Ark and to take into it those few righteous souls who would afterwards multiply and replenish the earth.

The eighth chapter gives us the indication of the length of the year. Many have supposed that the years must have been considerably shorter to account for the longevity of man's life, but this was not so. Chapter viii. 5 speaks of a tenth month. The adding of forty days (vs. 6) and seven days (vs. 10) and other seven days (vs. 12) give eleven full months. Verse 14 states that there are at least 27 days in a month, so the little balance that is not mentioned may be very readily assumed thus showing the year to be the same then as now. Life shortened sharply after the Flood, dropping from nine hundred years' average to one hundred and twenty years' average. This means that the Flood had something to do with the shortening of life. It must be borne in mind that rain is not mentioned in the world's early history, but the earth was watered with a mist (Gen. ii. 5-6). When rain came it brought mud, mud brings germ, germ brings disease, disease brings death, and behind all of this is sin, the cause of the Flood. Most of our ailments are caused by weather conditions and climatical changes.

(8) *Tower of Babel* (Ch. xi.) is the next important fact in the book. Man had but one tongue and language. The people planned to build a tower and make for themselves a name. There is nothing wrong in building a tower. It was the purpose for which it was built that brought upon them the wrath of God. History shows that their purpose was to establish for themselves a religion independent of God. This man has been doing ever since. God stopped the building by scattering the people. The building God fused into solid rock by fire and the jagged formation still stands today, known as Birs Nimrod, so rock-hard that man cannot break it down. It stands as a testimony of God's indignation towards false religion. Later man made another attempt and built the Tower of Bel in the days of Nebuchadnezzar. Babel

warns us that "Thou shalt worship the Lord thy God and Him only shalt thou serve".

(9) *Call of Abram*. (Ch. xii.) This chapter commences the second section of the book. It also commences the Dispensation of Promise and the beginning of the nation of Israel. " Get thee out . . . and I will . . . I will . . . I will ". Most of the promises of God are conditional, and the condition is ofttimes obedience. Says Hebrews xi. 8 : " By faith Abraham . . . obeyed ; and he went out, not knowing whither he went ", but what blessings came to that life, and such can be ours if we also obey Him. At the beginning this obedience was not complete, and neither were his blessings. Verse 1 of chapter xii. commences " Now the Lord *had* said . . . ". The past tense means that this was not the first call. In that earlier call God had said : " Get thee out of thy country, and from thy kindred, and from thy father's house ". The first part he obeyed as they went forth from the land of Ur of the Chaldees (xi. 31), but partial obedience is not obedience. It is doing a thing only to the extent that it pleases ourselves, not God. God said, " And from thy kindred ", but Abram's kindred travelled with him as far as Haran, and there they dwelt. His father was prepared to leave the city but not prepared to leave the country, so the kindred became a hindrance to progress. God took the father away, then called Abram again, but still he had not left his father's house, for he took Lot, his brother's son, who became a thorn in the flesh. So another separation took place bringing complete obedience. Then come the words, " And the Lord said unto Abram, *after that Lot was separated from him,* Lift up now thine eyes, and look . . . For *all* the land which thou seest, to thee will I give it, and to thy seed for ever " (Read xiii. 14-18).

(10) *Melchizedek*. (Ch. 14) This priest of the most high God came out to meet and to bless Abram after his battle with Chedorlaomer. Christ, we are told, was a Priest after the order of Melchizedek, principally because it was the order of an endless life. This is explained in the Epistle to the Hebrews where we learn that it was an unchanging Priesthood, but in this chapter we discover that it was also a Unique Priesthood in that Christ and Melchizedek were the only two Priests who could claim kingship, and both had a Universal Priesthood. The Levitical priesthood was limited to the Nation of Israel, but Melchizedek appeared to Abram and blessed him before Levi was born or Israel established — Universal because there was no division. In Christ there

is neither Jew nor Gentile. We are one. The division has been made good and so the Priestly work in Christ became Universal again.

(11) *Abram.* (Ch. xv.) In this chapter Abram suffered a further testing and came through triumphantly, with God as his shield for the present and his exceeding great reward for the future. God established His covenant with this father of the faithful.

Man has ever been a creature of doubts and unbelief. God had promised to Abram a son, but Abram was old and his wife well stricken in years. God had promised but Abram and Sarai felt that God had got Himself into a corner and they must help Him out of His difficulty, and so the suggestion that Abram should make use of Sarai's handmaid. The result — Ishmael was born. Instead of getting God out of a difficulty, Abram put himself right into one. Ishmael, the son of the bondwoman, became a source of constant irritation and strife. So many of the problems we face along the road of life are self-imposed, and yet we want to blame God. Abram may have his way and obtain his Ishmael, but God still has His way and provides His Isaac, the gift of His grace.

Here Abram's name was changed to Abraham, " the father of a great multitude ".

Isaac arrived fifteen years later than Ishmael. With that age difference Ishmael was found mocking Isaac, the Son of Promise, with the result that both Ishmael and his mother, Hagar, were expelled from their home by Sarah, which thing was a grief to Abraham. This incident was taken up as an allegory by Paul when writing to the Galatians concerning Law and Grace. Ishmael, the son of the bondwoman, represented Law, whilst Isaac, the son of the freewoman and of promise, stood for Grace. These two things cannot dwell together. When Christ comes into the heart with all the blessings of the Divine Life, then that which is of the flesh must take its departure.

In the meantime God revealed His friendship with Abraham by showing to him what He was about to do with Sodom, and Abraham showed his intimacy with God by pleading for mercy in the behalf of any righteous souls within that city.

(12) *Abraham and Isaac.* (Ch. xxii.) Although God had renewed His Abrahamic Covenant in Isaac, He now puts Abraham to the greatest test of his life by bidding him to offer his only son as a sacrifice. Abraham is unflinching in his faith in God, and his son is given back to him out of the jaws of death.

(13) *Death of Sarah*. (Ch. xxiii.)   Although God had said
to Abraham " All the land that thou seest will I give to thee and
to thy seed ", and Abraham had believed God in this promise,
yet, when Sarah died, he did not even possess six feet of land in
which he could bury his wife. Abraham had to bargain for a piece
of ground and then purchased it from the children of Heth. There
they buried Sarah, Abraham, Isaac, Jacob, and Joseph.

(14) *Isaac*. (Ch. xxiv.). " Abraham was old " — the blessings of God now continued in the person of Isaac. In this chapter
is the wonderful story of Isaac and Rebekah. Abraham sent his
servant to another country to find a wife for his son, Isaac. In
an interesting way the servant was led to the right person, and
Rebekah, when asked, " Wilt thou go with this man ? ", responded in the affirmative. She travelled in the company of the
servant. Rebekah and Isaac met in the fields and he took her to
his mother's tent. A spiritual application has often been drawn
from this delightful story. The Holy Spirit is in this world, a
far-off country, seeking a Bride for His Master's Son. He convicts
the world of sin, righteousness, and judgment. He seeks to win
and woo a people for the Lord. In the company of the Holy
Spirit, the Paraclete, we journey until the Lord will come out
into the clouds to receive us unto Himself and take us to His
Father's House, where there are many mansions prepared for
us. Isaac had two sons

(15) *Jacob and Esau*. (Chs. xxv-xxvii.) In a quarrel between
these two brothers the blessing passed from Esau, the firstborn,
to Jacob. A forsaken birthright can mean a stolen blessing so
often. We have a right to New Birth. If we do not lay hold of
it then we shall lose every other blessing in life. The Devil will
see that we are robbed.

(16) *Jacob's Ladder*. (Ch. xxviii.) The Abrahamic Covenant
was renewed in Jacob as he watched the angels ascending and
descending. Note the use of the ladder for, contrary to all of the
traditions of men, angels have no wings. Jacob called this place
Bethel, or " The House of God ", and there he vowed a vow
promising that, if God would prosper him and bring him back,
then he would serve the Lord. God did prosper him. He gave him
two wives, twelve sons, and much cattle.

(17) *Jacob's Twelve Sons*. (Chs. xxix-xxx.) They were all
born to him in these two chapters (at least eleven of them —
Benjamin's birth is in xxxv. 18). What a study these twelve men

make, and what a history as the twelve men become twelve tribes
creating that great Nation of Israel which has played, and will yet
play, a prominent part in the history of the world !

The struggle between the women for priority, the meanings
of the twelve names, the characters of the twelve men, are all
worth consideration.

(18) *Jacob's Return.* (Ch. xxxi.) Jacob's life was not transformed yet. He was still driving hard bargains and doing deceitful
things. Here he bargained with Laban and, by cunning, gained
most of the cattle and then fled, taking everything with him. Laban
pursued Jacob and a further quarrel ensued resulting in

Mizpah. This incident has been badly misinterpreted. The
word is seen in many places as a motto, as a keepsake, on cards
and brooches, and is often exchanged by friends when they part
from each other, understanding the word to mean " The Lord
watch between me and thee, when we are absent one from
another ". That, of course, is the meaning, but these were not
the words of parting friends but of distrustful enemies. The story
tells that two hard-bargaining men, neither trusting the other, set
up a heap of stones and each promised the other that they would
not pass that barrier to do the other harm (vs. 52). Then, still
not being sure of each other's confidence, Laban said, " The Lord
watch between me and thee when we are absent one from another.
If thou shalt afflict my daughters, or if thou shalt take other wives
beside my daughters, no man is with us ; see, God is witness
betwixt me and thee " — or, when I cannot keep my eye on you,
remember God does !

In this same chapter God appeared to Jacob but, instead
of introducing Himself as the God of Abraham and of Isaac, He
declared Himself, " I am the God of Bethel . . . where thou vowedst
a vow unto me ". God is a Covenant-keeping God. Not only
does He keep His Word but He requires that, when man promises
to do anything for God or promises in the Name of God, those
vows must be kept. The safest way is to " Swear not ", but to
let our yea be yea and our nay, nay — just a plain yes or no !

(19) *Israel.* (Ch. xxxii.) This chapter sees the end of Jacob
as God met him face to face at Peniel. Jacob was broken and
then made into a new and worthy vessel. He was knighted on the
battle-field and came out of it an Israel, a prince with God and
with man. In the next chapter he is reunited with his brother. A
few incidental things and some generations bring one to the last
prominent character in Genesis.

(20) *Joseph* (Chs. xxxix-xlviii.)   Joseph is one of the
most beautiful Old Testament characters who represent Christ in
type, one of the very few men without a BUT in his life. Like Jesus,
he was despised by his brethren but the darling of his father's
heart.   He knew temptation but did not yield.   He went down
into Egypt.   His words were not believed.   Although man brought
him down into prison and he was caused to suffer wrongfully,
yet God exalted him to Pharaoh's right hand.   There he became
the salvation of his people as he provided them corn in Egypt.   He
married a Gentile bride, and later saw his brethren come to
acknowledge him and bend the knee before him. God gave him two
sons which caused him to forget all the sorrow of the past.

All of these things are to be seen in the life of Christ, and
in the end He is going to stand before His Father and say :
" Behold, I and the children which God hath given Me "   (Heb.
ii. 13).

(21) *Patriarchal Blessings* (Chs. xlviii-l.)   The book ends
with Jacob blessing the sons of Joseph, then bestowing his patriarchal blessings upon his twelve sons.*

The forty-ninth chapter can be read in conjunction with Deut.
xxxiii. where Moses bestows his blessing upon the twelve tribes,
and with the stones on the Breastplate of the High Priest in Exodus
xxviii.

This wonderful book, that covers a history of 2,400 years
and begins with the creative power of God demonstrated in
Creation, ends with a great mourning because of the death of
Jacob, then records the death of Joseph, and closes with the words
" A coffin in Egypt " — the great anti-climax that has become the
lot of man as a result of sin.   The joy is that this is only the end
of Genesis, and not the end of the Bible story.

EXODUS

MAN REDEEMED

"Thou in Thy mercy hast led forth the people which Thou hast redeemed; Thou hast guided them in Thy strength unto Thy holy habitation." (EXODUS xv. 13)

INTRODUCTION

We have learned from the book of Genesis that things did not continue as they began, so that holiness was lost to sin, freedom to bondage, and life to death. Although God had manifested His Grace in calling out a people in Abraham, yet the people had failed to respond, thus the sufferings in Egypt.

Exodus is a sequel to Genesis, hence the conjunction " Now " as the first word. In Genesis the earth rises out of darkness. In Exodus Israel emerges out of Egypt.

The theme of the book might readily be " Out of the bondage of the flesh into the liberty of the Spirit ", particularly the first part. This is why it is known as " The outgoings ", which is the meaning of the word "Exodus ". Genesis ended with a coffin, the symbol of death, for in Adam all die, yet beyond that coffin is the Exodus of resurrection. " So in Christ shall all be made alive ". Christ, Who is greater than Moses, came to lead us out of the bondage of sin and of death into newness of life. The latter Moses could not do. He never led them in because he sinned. Jesus never sinned, therefore He could finish the work that God had given Him to do and lead us in.

Exodus divides into two main sections :

(1) Historical — Chs. i-xix. (2) Legislative — Chs. xx-xl. These sections break down again and again into an analysis.

HISTORICAL

The book opens with the names of the children of Israel, thus linking with the story of Genesis ; then tells how God was blessing these people even as He had promised Abraham, Isaac and Jacob, for they were fruitful and increasing abundantly. Then it was that a Pharaoh came to the throne who " knew not Joseph ". One wonders why this Pharaoh did not know him for, had it not been for Joseph, he would never have come to the throne, for there would have been no Egypt. Seven years of famine against which no preparation had been made would have liquidated that nation. There seems to be but one answer. He did not know Joseph because he did not want to know him! This is what is called wilful ignorance, a thing that God will not tolerate. Men try to do these things today. They will never enter a Church. They will not open the Bible, and then think they can go their own way, enjoy their pleasures and in the end plead ignorance, but wilfulness is inexcusable at any time.

If Pharaoh could claim no knowledge of Joseph then he could claim no knowledge of Joseph's God and thereby not recognise God's people. That is exactly what he wanted, and that is what God resisted.

(1) *Bondage.* (Chs. i-iii.)   The privileged people became a persecuted people. Their hardships were constantly increasing. Their male children were being cast into the river. It would seem that God had forsaken them and left them to their own fate, and so the people complained. We would say — not without cause! Rightly so — but, whilst they murmured against God, they were not aware that God was moving toward them inasmuch as their deliverer was already born and, although he was under the same condemnation of death, God was opening the way and Moses was being prepared. How true this is today! Whilst many of God's people murmur against their lot in this life and watch the increase of evil and corruption on every hand, wondering whether God has forsaken this present world, He, Who was once born under the cloud of judgment when again an edict had been issued that all male children should be slain (Matt. ii. 16), is now standing upon the very threshold of heaven ready to come in the fulness of His power to take from this world His own.

Moses. (Chs. ii-iii.)   These chapters recount the birth of the deliverer — Moses, the son of Amram and Jochebed. This is the story that has fascinated us from our childhood. Although he came as the deliverer he was in need of deliverance, having been born under an edict of the king that required all male children to be slain. Necessity being the mother of invention Jochebed made an ark of bulrushes and slipped it into the river to hide Moses from the vengeance of the king. There Pharaoh's daughter discovered him and, through the intervention of this woman and of Miriam, his sister, Moses found his way into the king's palace.

Years passed quickly, during which Moses was trained in all the art of the Egyptians. The day came when he became conscious of his life's work, that he must deliver his people from their bondage. At first he made the same mistake that many of us make. He tried to fulfil his task in his own way and with his own strength. This always spells defeat and failure. He slew the Egyptian, then began to handle two others who strove together. When he learned his failure he fled to the land of Midian and there, leading the sheep to the backside of the desert and in the place of quietude, God met him and gave him his *divine call*.

(2) *Deliverance.* Moses wanted to deliver his people. God told him that He was going to deliver them (iii. 8) and Moses was going to help God only through the medium of submission and obedience. That is the only way any of us will be able to serve the Lord.

The burning bush that was unconsumed, which had attracted Moses' attention, was but an emblem of that great people whom God had called out to Himself in the promises that He had made to Abraham, to Isaac, and to Jacob. God's people may burn in the fire of persecution not only then, but again and again in their long history, but no such fire could ever destroy them. Well has God fulfilled His promise to His people as declared to Moses in the burning bush and quoted by Isaiah : " O Israel, Fear not : for I have redeemed thee, I have called thee by thy name ; thou art Mine. When thou passest through the waters, I will be with thee ; and through the rivers, they shall not overflow thee : when thou walkest through the fire, thou shalt not be burned ; neither shall the flame kindle upon thee. For I am the Lord Thy God, the Holy One of Israel, thy Saviour " (xliii 1-3).

The call is later followed by *his Commission* as in chapter **iv**. he is commanded to go and appear before Pharaoh. God was making known to Moses the futility of his own power that he had been seeking to exercise, by causing his rod to become a serpent and his hand to become leprous. Both serpents and leprosy are dangerous, yet Moses had not the power to change their natures. Many things that we possess can appear as innocent as Moses' rod and hand, and yet can become agencies of destruction. God is showing to Moses, and to us, how that, in a life of submission, He will control such things.

Moses was of the opinion that he had no power of control over his tongue. It was his complaint, not his excuse. God was angry with Moses for this evidence of doubt, and permitted Aaron to act as his mouthpiece. God could have handled that tongue but He did not. He used a substitute — Aaron. In the light of this, notice that Moses' great sin which kept him out of the land of promise was " that he spake inadvisedly with his lips (Ps. cvi. 33). No wonder James has so much to say about that unruly, uncontrollable member! (James iii.).

Burdens increased. (Ch. v.)   What a testing for the people, but how much more for Moses!   God had promised deliverance (iii. 8) but instead of relief they were receiving an increase in the burdens.   The supply of straw was taken away but the output of the bricks had to remain the same.   An interesting interpretation is to be found on this matter.   It has usually been conceded that the straw was put inside the bricks as binding material, thus creating reinforcement.   If this were so the children of Israel might have produced their quota of bricks by leaving the straw out or using it very sparingly.   Of course this would weaken the brick and it would crumble in time.   But the suggestion is that the straw mentioned was " teban ", the very short straw or the dust of the threshing floor.   This was used not for binding but for dusting the moulds to prevent the clay sticking to the sides.   Without this teban a brick would have to be made again and again because it would not come out of the mould cleanly but, clinging to the mould, would twist or break.   This would slow up production considerably.

In chapter vi. God renewed His promises of deliverance with seven " I will's ", four of which are used in connection with the four cups on the Passover Table.   These promises were " *I will* bring you out ", " *I will* rid you out of their bondage ", " *I will* redeem you ", " *I will* take you to Me for a people ", " *I will* be to you a God ", " *I will* bring you in ", " *I will* give it you for an inheritance ".

The Ten Plagues (Chs. vii-xii.) These plagues were not sent merely to inconvenience man or to afflict his body.   This happened but it was consequential.   The full purport of the plagues was a deliberate attack by God against the religious system of the Egyptian people.

The basis of their religion was to worship anything that suggested life, because they had a horror of death.   Anything that was associated with death was an abomination.   In the art of Egypt can be found a design called the egg and arrow, or the egg and dart — the egg the symbol of life, and the arrow the symbol of death.   They worshipped

The Nile.   It became a sacred river because it was the source of their life.   Egypt knew no rainfall.   It depended upon the melting snows of the mountains of North Africa which flowed into the

Nile. The Nile overflowed its banks at the Nile Delta. When the water subsided the seed was cast into the alluvial soil left behind and so the life of the nation was sustained. The crocodile and certain fish became sacred because they lived in the same river. Consequently God turned the waters of this river into blood so that their source of life became the source of death, and their religion could not prevent nor reverse what Jehovah had done.

The Frogs also were sacred. These could live in two elements, in water or on dry land. This gave the idea of the transmigration of spirits from one form to another or from one realm to another which became part of their worship. The magicians claimed to have the same power to produce frogs. That might be difficult to prove when there were so many but, even so, they only added to the calamity, which was no help. The trouble was that they could not remove them and, being the sacred animal, no one was permitted to kill a single frog.

Lice and Flies. Concerning the third and fourth plagues, there has been a great deal of reasoning amongst scholars, none of which is too weighty in its evidence, so we will be satisfied to accept it as it has come to us as lice and flies, even though they might have been mosquitoes and beetles. What is to be learned is that the Egyptians, in their quest for life, worshipped so many forms of nature, and God touched them all.

The first two plagues were associated with water, the third came from the dust (earth), and the fourth attacked them from the element of the air. The first two were announced — the lice came unannounced. The first two the magicians sought to imitate with their treachery, the third they could not, and so submitted to the fact that this was God's doing. However, Pharaoh was not submitting his pride. In the first three there is nothing to intimate that Israel did not meet some of the inconvenience ; in the fourth the land of Goshen was immune. God was making His power more marked each time.

As to the lice, this would particularly hurt the pride of the Egyptian priests, as they were exceedingly particular about the matter of cleanliness. They constantly washed and shaved. Now with the rest they were covered with vermin.

The flies have been considered to be a winged beetle. We do know that the beetle was sacred to Ra the Sun God, and that the scarab was a worshipped beetle. If so, then again they would not be permitted to kill them, even though they plagued the people and corrupted the land.

Murrain on the cattle. The cow was a sacred animal worshipped by the people because it suckled its young. It was, therefore, a sustainer of life.

Hail and Darkness were in opposition to Isis and Osiris, or Sun and Moon worship, whilst the plague of

Locusts was against Serapes, a god who was supposed to keep the land free from these creatures. To sum up these plagues, they were against the

NILE .... a source of life.

FROGS .... a symbol of life.

SUN AND MOON ..... givers of life.

ANIMALS .... the cults of life.

ENBALMING was practised as a preservation of the body for the future life.

Then came God's great and final blow to this system.

The Death of the Firstborn. (Ch. xii.) From the king on the throne to the captive in the dungeon, the firstborn of the family and the firstborn of their cattle died. Thus God proved the weakness of the gods of Egypt, and then was ready to demonstrate His own right and power for His people and against their enemies.

Pharaoh tried to compromise with God, only to learn that such compromise brought further trouble. So it is with man today. God is a jealous God and has a right to claim complete obedience and perfect submission. For such yieldedness there is unending blessing and victory.

The Passover (Ch. xii.) This was the end of their slavery and the beginning of a new life of freedom. " This month shall be unto you the beginning of months ; it shall be the first month of the year to you " (xii. 2). They had to take *a lamb* (vs. 3), which became *the lamb* (vs. 4), which in turn became *your lamb* (vs. 5). This declared a close identity with the sacrifice that was to be made. The blood of this lamb had to be applied to the door frame of the house. It was not sufficient to see the blood or recognise the blood. It had to be applied blood. How true today! Many would be prepared to acknowledge Calvary as a historical event. Many would be glad to recognise the right of the Church and its teachings, so long as the doctrines do not become too personal and interfere with their lives. Again, the blood was on the side posts and the upper post, but none on the threshold. The Blood is above as protection, not below to be trampled upon ; above and without, protection beneath and within, feasting and fellowship, all of which were enjoyed through obedience.

So far-reaching was this event that brought redemption to a whole nation that God caused this feast to become commemorative and required that it should be observed annually. At the same time God so ordained it that it became a type of the greater redemption which was to be made through the death of the Lamb of God, so that Paul told the Corinthians " Christ our Passover was slain for us ".

(3) *Discipline. The Exodus* (Ch. xii.) That night they moved out in haste. The Egyptians were so pressing that the children of Israel should leave immediately that two things happened which must be noted. Firstly, it would appear that they did not eat unleavened bread in Egypt. The dough was still in the kneading troughs when they carried them out (vs. 34) ; and, secondly, the Egyptians were so insistent that they were willing to give the Israelites anything for which they asked. Thus they spoiled the Egyptians (vs. 36), and they went out a rich people. The reason for these two things was (1) the dough did not contain leaven, and leaven is a type of sin. This was not eaten in Egypt, the place of sin, but was carried out to be eaten the next day at Succoth, the beginning of a new experience. (2) God enriched His people with the spoils of Egypt that they might have that which they could give back to God for the building of the Tabernacle.

It was on the fifteenth day of the month of Abib, in the year 1491 B.C., on the morrow after the Passover, they moved forward, probably between one-and-a-half and two million people. This number is assessed by the fact that there were six-hundred-thousand, or more than half a million, men on foot, to which must be added the men too old to march, plus all the women who would probably number more than the men, plus all the children, plus the mixed multitude. This mixed multitude would include Egyptians who had recognised the power of Jehovah and seen the weakness of their own gods, and other nationals in Egypt who would have become alarmed at the calamities that had befallen that nation.

Though there were so many, and in spite of the haste with which they moved out, this was no panic, no rout of the people, but a well-organised mass evacuation. This is gathered from a statement in chapter xiii verse 18 : " And the children of Israel went up harnessed out of the land of Egypt ". The word " harnessed " means " rank upon rank, or file upon file, in military formation ", suggesting that there must have been captains over thousands and captains over hundreds and captains over fifties and captains over tens (Deut. i. 15).

When these people stepped out of Egypt into this new life with God, they stepped into a well-ordered life. Thus it should be with the child of God. Christian life is disciplined life. "Let all things be done decently and in order" (I Cor. xiv. 40).

We will journey with the children of Israel in this new experience that became theirs after 430 years in Egypt and, as we do, remember that Paul said "Now these things happened unto them for ensamples; and they are written for our admonition" (I Cor. x. 11).

Their first resting place was

Succoth (xii. 37), the name meaning "booths" or "temporary dwelling place". The name Succoth became an immediate reminder to them that although they were out of Egypt, this was not their dwelling place. They were constantly reminded of the same thing. The Feast of Tabernacles became an annual feast through which they must remember that they were pilgrims and strangers, that they moved toward a land that was to be theirs. Do we not need to remind ourselves of the same fact that this world does not belong to us or we to it? We journey toward our eternal Home, and must lay up our treasures there.

As previously stated, it was at Succoth where they ate the unleavened bread, not in Egypt. Leaven is a type of sin and Egypt represents the world. From this they have come away, so now they ate the unleavened bread. This feast was to be observed for seven days every year. Seven being the number of completion, meant the complete life was to be separated unto the Lord. This they must not only observe but teach their children through succeeding generations. As a further demonstration of this life of sanctification the first-born of both man and beast had to be separated unto the Lord as a token of the whole life and family.

From Succoth the people moved forward to

Etham (xiii. 20), which is referred to as "the edge of the wilderness", or the edge of the unknown. This is the place where we become conscious that this world holds nothing for us. It is a barren land and we are pilgrims and strangers in it seeking another country. It was here at Etham that God gave to them the symbol of His Presence in the form of a pillar of cloud by day and a pillar of fire by night to lead them in the way. It is at such places we learn to sing: "I'd rather walk in the dark with God than go alone in the light". From Etham He led them to

Pi-Hahiroth, Migdol, and Baal Zephon (iv. 2). These places were in the territory of the Red Sea. They found themselves hemmed in by sea and mountains. When the Egyptians heard that the Israelites were entangled in the contour of the land, they pursued them with the intent to annihilate. Is this what is meant by following the Lord ? Does He find pleasure in entangling His people as the spider seeks to catch the fly ? No! No!! Man's extremity is always God's opportunity. Man is complaining about his defeat, but God is campaigning for his victory. It was here that the symbol of God's Presence became a Pillar of Light to light the path that God had made across the sea which He had parted that His people might go over on dry ground. But the very same Pillar that gave light and guidance to Israel became the Pillar of Darkness and Confusion to the enemy. The Bible is like that. To those who believe the Word of God it is both chart and compass for the journey of life. It is a lamp to our feet and a light to our path, but to the unbelieving heart God's Word is confusion and contradiction.

Crossing the Red Sea (Ch. xiv.) Thus it was that " By faith they passed through the Red Sea as by dry land ; which the Egyptians assaying to do were drowned " (Heb. xi. 29).

It must be borne in mind that every one of these moves was a gigantic undertaking. We see pictures of a narrow channel across the Red Sea with a couple of hundred people crossing it, but there were one and a half to two million people, with tents and possessions, with flocks of sheep and herds of cattle, horses and asses, and all the other paraphernalia.

On reaching safely the other side and witnessing the destruction of their enemy they found themselves on the *right side of the sea* (Ch. xv.) Here Moses taught them to sing a song of triumph and to give thanks to God. This is a good practice for God's people. Whenever we have seen the Hand of God working on our behalf, meeting us in our needs, delivering us out of our problems, we would do well to raise our song of praise. This song is no doubt the one referred to in the book of Revelation as the Song of Moses because, basically, it is the same as the Song of the Lamb. The theme of both is Redemption — in the Old Testament it was redemption by power, the song of the New Testament is Redemption by Blood.

Marah (xv. 23-26) This journey was one of singing and sighing. One day they rejoiced, the next day they murmured, only to be rejoicing again the following day. Is this not typical of the Christian experience ? It is one of constant change, so that we

are compelled to say : " Change and decay in all around I see,
but Thou Who changest not, abide with me ".

Yesterday they were singing at the shore of the Red Sea,
to-day they are murmuring at Marah. Their complaint was that
the waters were bitter, but God showed to Moses a tree which he
had to cast into the waters, with the result they were made sweet.
We all meet bitter experiences along the way and have our disappointments. Next time you have such an experience look away
to the Lord and He will show you a tree called Calvary, which
is able to sweeten every bitter experience that may be ours.

Elim (Ch. xv. 27) — the place of twelve wells and seventy
palm trees. This was an oasis in the desert, a place of refreshing,
and again they would rejoice. Nothing is said about their stay
here, but one might readily imagine that some would have desired
to remain at such a place. There are many Christians to-day who,
so soon as they arrive at an Elim of blessing are ready to settle,
feeling they have all that they could desire ; but we must never
be in a hurry to settle. This is not our home and there is always
much land to be possessed. Next came the

Wilderness of Sin (Ch. xvi.), and more complaints. This time
it was food, but again God intervened and sent manna* which
became their constant supply for the forty years of pilgrimage.
It never failed them so long as they complied with the instructions
God gave. The manna was a type of the Lord Jesus Christ, Who
once said : " I am the Bread of Life. Your fathers did eat manna
in the wilderness, and are dead. This is the Bread which cometh
down from heaven, that a man may eat thereof, and not die "
(John vi. 48-50). As manna sustained the children of Israel
throughout a desert journey, so the Lord will sustain His people
by His Word throughout the whole of the journey of this life.

Rephidim (Ch. xvii.) Two important things happened here.
Firstly, the people were without water and again they were complaining. These people never seemed to learn the lesson of trust
from past experiences. But then, who are we to point a finger at
them for we are no better than those who were before us ! Moses
was bidden to go and smite the rock, and forthwith water flowed
abundantly. It is interesting that this incident should follow the
giving of Manna, for He Who is the Bread of Life is also the Water
of Life and to that end He was smitten. Without water man
cannot live, and without Christ we are spiritually dead. He Who

* See chapter on Manna in Author's book, *Made According to Pattern*

once cried : " I thirst " is saying : " If any man thirst let him
come unto Me and drink ".
> " I tried the broken cisterns, Lord,
> But ah ! The waters failed.
> E'en as I stooped to drink they fled
> And mocked me as I wailed ".
> " I came to Jesus and I drank
> Of that life-giving stream,
> My thirst was quenched, my soul revived,
> And now I live in Him ".

The other incident was war with Amalek. As long as Moses
upheld his hands in intercession Israel prevailed — as soon as the
hands fell, Amalek prevailed. So Aaron and Hur upheld the hands
of Moses until the going down of the sun, bringing to Israel a
complete victory. Sometimes, when things are going hard, we
feel that we are right in the front line of the battle and our lot is
as hard as any lot can be. On such occasions if we were to look
around the valley of this world and see the battle some other people
have to fight, we would cease from our own murmurings and climb
the hill of prayer and engage in the ministry of intercession which
would strengthen the other man in his struggle and, at the same
time, increase our own sense of gratitude to God for His goodness
to us.

The historical section closes with a visit of Jethro, Moses'
father-in-law, who became concerned about the amount of responsibility that Moses carried and suggested that it should be shared by
elders. Moses submitted to Jethro's suggestion without consultation with God on the matter, and the result was that, later on, the
suggestion became a failure. There are always those who would
be kind to us and relieve us of the duties that God has given to us.
We should yield nothing of our Divine Commission until we are
sure that God Himself is relieving us.

The children of Israel had now reached Sinai where they
halted for twelve months. This leads into the second section of
the book.

LEGISLATIVE

This is of vital importance — in fact, it is very fundamental,
for here we have the giving of the Law of God. Up to this time
the Law of God had been unwritten.

Sinai (Ch. xix.) Here is given one of the few pictures of the
awesomeness of the presence of a Holy God. It is descriptive of

His Majesty, His Power, and His Holiness. It is a fearful thing to fall into the Hands of a Holy God. David said : "He uttered His voice, the earth melted " (Psalm xlvi.). At Sinai the mountain trembled and was on fire ; boundaries must be set to keep man at a distance. At Sinai God gave the Law to Moses, and through Moses to the people.

The Law was given three times, the first time

Orally. "And God spake all these words, saying " (xx. 1), but so awful was the sight and so alarming the experience that the people trembled (margin) and said to Moses, " Speak thou with us, and we will hear ; but let not God speak with us, lest we die " (xx. 19). How Christians of to-day need to learn that God is a Holy God and that His Majesty and Power demand our respect and humiliation. Most of us are too glib in speaking of God and in our relationship to Him.

There was no written Law until chapter xxxi. Then it was that God gave them two tables of stone upon which it was

Written. This was after the instructions for the building of the Tabernacle. " And He gave unto Moses, when he had made an end of communing with him upon Mount Sinai, two tables of testimony, tables of stone, written with the finger of God " (xxxi. 18). Whilst Moses was receiving this Law, the people were saying: " . . . as for this Moses, the man that brought us up out of the land of Egypt, we wot not what is become of him ", so they made for themselves a golden calf (chapter xxxii.). Moses returned from the top of the mount carrying the tables of stone with him. Hearing the shout of the people as they said : " These be thy gods, O Israel, which have brought thee up out of the land of Egypt " (xxxii. 8), he read on the tables : " Thou shalt have no other gods before Me " and, looking down the mountain side, he saw the golden calf. Again he read : " Thou shalt not make unto thee any graven image, or any likeness of any thing that is in heaven above, or that is in the earth beneath, or that is in the water under the earth ". Thereupon he cast the two tables of stone to the ground and broke them because the Law written thereon was already broken. Once again Moses climbed the mountain and for the third time God gave him the ten commandments.

Written on two other tables (xxxiv. 1-4), these were those placed inside the Ark of the Covenant.

The Law as given to Moses was threefold — Moral Law, Civil Law, and Ceremonial Law. The first controlled the individual life of the people, the second the national life of the people, and the third the religious life, which means that God gave Laws to control all phases of life.

Moral Law, or the ten commandments. This was the law that controlled the individual life. Note the repetition of the words THOU (thirteen times) and THY (fifteen times) in ten commandments. Men have a relationship with God, with their neighbour, and with themselves, and it is the first essential of moral life to know these things and do them.

These commandments divided themselves into sections, possibly represented by the two stones. The first four showed man's duty to God, and the other six man's duty to man. The Lord Himself bore this truth out when He said to the lawyer : " Thou shalt love the Lord thy God with all thy heart, and with all thy soul, and with all thy mind. This is the first and great commandment (first stone of four), And the second is like unto it. Thou shalt love thy neighbour as thyself (the second stone of six). On these *two* commandments hang *all* the law and the prophets " (Matt. xxii. 37-39).

Civil Law. This was related to the nation, and had to do with social affairs. Upon these very laws is based the legislation of Britain and the United States, the laws of justice and equity, the protection of the innocent, the punishment of the evil-doer, human rights and property rights, human relationship and international relationship. Maybe one would be more correct and honest if it were said that our laws *were* based upon the Mosaic law, for alas ! we are moving far from some of these laws when we see the easy divorce to-day and the lack of corrective measures meted out to the evil-doer, so that in places delinquency and mob crime are causing fear. Parents are obeying children, instead of children obeying parents, whilst the sanctity of the Lord's Day is lost to trading, sport and pleasure. Do not these things declare plainly the need of getting back to the Bible, which was the foundation of the greatness of our Countries ?

Ceremonial Law concerned the religious life and is far more detailed in the book of Leviticus. So far as Exodus is concerned it is confined to the matter of the Tabernacle and the Garments of the High Priest. As the Author has dealt with these subjects in detail elsewhere* it will suffice here to say that the Tabernacle was ordained, designed and occupied by God Himself. " And let them make Me a Sanctuary, that I may dwell among them "

---

* See Author's books, *Made According to Pattern* for a complete study of the Tabernacle, and *These are the Garments* for a description and application of the Priestly Robes.

(xxv. 8). It was God's desire to be in the midst of His people then as it is His desire to dwell in their hearts now, for the New Testament teaches us that our bodies are the temples of the Holy Ghost. Every part of the Tabernacle, every piece of furniture, every measurement, every colour, and all materials, have wrapped up in them Divine truths concerning the Lord and His Church. Likewise all the details of the Garments of the High Priest in chapter xxviii declare the wonderful attributes of the One Who became our Great High Priest and Who is now seated at the right Hand of the Majesty on high, making intercession for us.

From these laws let us learn that we cannot please ourselves. No! Not even under Grace. We have to please Him Who hath called us. He is the Supreme Controller of our lives. Therefore He has instructed us how to live morally, socially, and spiritually.

The closing chapters declare that Moses built the Tabernacle according to the pattern that was showed him in the Mount. When Moses had obeyed God in all things, then the glory of the Lord came down and rested on the Mercy Seat, and the pillar of cloud and fire rested upon the Tabernacle as an outward evidence of an internal Presence, and by it His people were ever led. We too will know His leadership and enjoy in life the tokens of His Presence when He reigns within the heart, and that indwelling will be ours when we learn submission and obedience.

LEVITICUS

MAN WORSHIPPING

*" And they brought that which Moses commanded before the
tabernacle of the congregation ; and all the congregation drew
near and stood before the Lord. And Moses said, This is the
thing which the Lord commanded that ye should do ; and the
glory of the Lord shall appear unto you "*. (LEV. ix. 5-6)

INTRODUCTION

Leviticus is the third book of the Pentateuch, and therefore
the central book of the five books of Moses. It deals primarily
with sacrifice, which was the centre of all Hebrew worship. The
book is, therefore, an important one. Somewhere near the centre
of this book is the 16th chapter with its record of the great Day
of Atonement, that day of humiliation when the High Priest with
blood made an atonement for the sins of the people, which was
a type of the Lord Jesus Christ, the great High Priest, Who, laying
aside His glory, came down to this world to make an atonement
(or better, redemption) for the sins of the world. This picture
in the centre of the central book of the Pentateuch places the
suffering Christ at the heart of the Law — the One Who came
not to destroy the Law but to fulfil it. Chapterwise, Leviticus iv.
is the middle of the Pentateuch and that deals wholly with the Sin
Offering.

In Genesis God spoke from heaven,
In Exodus God spoke from the Mount,
In Leviticus God spoke from the tabernacle,

a picture of God making a constant approach toward man with
a desire to enjoy communion and fellowship with him.

Another interesting feature of the book is —
Genesis covers a history of 2,400 years.
Exodus covers a history of 360 years (*circa*).
Leviticus covers a history of 30 days, or one calendar month.

This causes one to state that the book of Leviticus is more expressly the Word of God than any other part of the Word of
God. This is not a statement of denial — all Scripture is given
by inspiration of God. But, under Divine Inspiration, it can be
seen that

In Genesis Moses was a historian, collecting his material.
In Exodus Moses was a historian, collecting his material.
In Leviticus Moses became a stenographer, taking dictation.

This may be better appreciated when it is realised that, in the Jewish Scroll of the Law, known to the Jew as his Torah, there are no names to these books. The Jew was content to use the first word of each book as the designation of the book, thus —

Genesis	.....	.....	Bereshith	.....	.....	" In the beginning "
Exodus	.....	.....	Ve-elleh Shemoth	.....	" These the names "
Leviticus	.....	.....	Vay-yikra	.....	.....	" And He called "
Numbers	.....	.....	Vay yedabar	.....	....	" And He spake "
Deuteronomy	....		Elleh Had-debharim	" These are the words "

So, the name of this third book of the Bible in Hebrew is Vay-yikra — " And He called ". Not only is Vay-yikra the first word but it occurs at least fifty times throughout the book. All the chapters, save one, are the words of God to Moses.

Keywords. All books of the Bible have a keyword, or a key phrase. If the right key is found then the book can be unlocked and the secrets and the treasures discovered. A few keywords at random are : —

Genesis .... Beginning	Exodus .... Redemption
Numbers .... Service	Deuteronomy ..... Obedience
Matthew .... Kingdom	Mark .... Straightway
Hebrews .... Better	Jude .... Kept

Leviticus has two keywords because the book divides into two main sections.

The theme of the book of Leviticus as a whole is " God's great demand for holiness and His provision for it ". The book then divides into two at chapter xvi. The first part concerns *The way to God through sacrifice* (Chs. i-xvi.). This embraces the five Offerings and the Priesthood. The keyword is Atonement. The second part tells of *The walk with God through separation* (Chs. xvii-xxvii.). This covers the seven Feasts of Jehovah with some miscellaneous Laws. The keyword here is Holiness.

Atonement is mentioned 45 times.
Holiness (or holy) is mentioned 87 times.
Blood is also found 87 times.

Leviticus is often referred to as the commentary on Hebrews, whilst Hebrews is spoken of as the commentary on Leviticus. This is discovered from the two expressions of comparison —

Leviticus ..... " The shadow of good things to come ", **and**
Hebrews __. " Better things than these ".
There cannot be shadow without substance, yet shadows very
inadequately reveal the beauty or the detail of the substance.
So Leviticus speaks of blood, hope, promises, sacrifices, etc.,
whilst Hebrews tells of better blood, a better hope, better promises,
a better sacrifice, etc.

EXPOSITION

(1) THE WAY TO GOD THROUGH SACRIFICE (Chs. i-vii.)

The Offerings. A person cannot walk *with* God until he has
walked *to* God. So the order here is natural, but more than this
must be learned. When one has walked to God through sacrifice
he has only just begun his walk with God through separation. It
is not sufficient to accept God's gift of salvation and then sit down.
Christianity is more than an acceptance. It is an experience, a
life, a continuance in Divine things, a submission to the Will of
God as we die to self and live for Him.

The sacrifice of the Lord Jesus Christ was so perfect, so
complete, that no one sacrifice of any ceremonial order could
begin to portray its sufficiency. Therefore God ordained that five
Offerings should be observed, each one giving a different aspect
of the One Offering. These Offerings are detailed in the first five
chapters, with two more chapters giving the Laws concerning the
Offerings. The five Offerings were Burnt Offering, Meal Offering,
Peace Offering, Sin Offering, and Trespass Offering. This is not
the order in which they were observed because the Peace Offering
was last. Peace comes as a result of fulfilling the rest. Here they
are listed under two major headings — the first three were voluntary and called Sweet Savour Offerings, the other two were com-
pulsory.

Much is to be learned from all the minute detail which cannot
be included in this work,* but each Offering can be studied under
the same analysis.

The NATURE of each Offering showed that the

Burnt Offering was according to *possession* — herd, flock, or
birds. The more man possesses the more God requires.

Meal Offering differed according to *property* — and was
prepared in the oven, in the pan, or on the griddle.

Sin Offering varied according to *position* — a priest, the whole
congregation, the ruler, or a commoner. It is to be noted that
the Offering of the Priest was equal to the Offering of the whole

*See Author's book *A Living Sacrifice.*

congregation when it sinned. The reason for this is ably expressed
by one of the old divines, for it was Trapp who said : " When a
teacher sins he teaches sin ".

Trespass Offering depended on the *practice* of the sinner.
All the various trespasses are enumerated.

Peace Offering was common to all.

The OFFERER'S WORK in most instances was his identification with the Offering. This could be in the laying on of his
hands, or in slaying the Offering, or in confessing his sin upon it.
We have to identify ourselves with the death of the Lord, for only
as we recognise His death on our behalf shall we be recognised
with Him in His glory.

The PRIEST'S WORK. In the Burnt Offering, Sin Offering,
and Trespass Offering, the blood had to be sprinkled at the altar
of sacrifice. In the Meal Offering the Priest took a handful of
the flour, which was a memorial of the whole, and burnt it on
the altar ; whilst in the Peace Offering he took the breast and the
shoulder and waved them before the Lord.

The Offerings were then to be divided between God and the
Priests and the People.

GOD'S PORTION. In each Offering God had a portion
which was always burned so that it could not be taken back.
God had the *first* portion, and this He still requires from all of
His people. Much that we give to the Lord we take back, inasmuch as we give our tithes and offerings and then take them back
to pay the ministry and to maintain the Church, paying the electric
bill, the heating and cleaning, etc. This, of course, is right. As
in these Offerings made to the Lord only the portion became
His, likewise in all of our Christian activity, service, and giving,
only a handful truly becomes the Lord's because we have no
share in it — that handful is our true heart worship. " The true
worshippers shall worship the Father in spirit and in truth ; for the
Father seeketh such to worship Him. God is a Spirit, and they that
worship Him must worship Him in spirit and in truth " (John iv.
23 - 24).

The PRIEST'S PORTION. In every instance the Priest had
a portion, for the Scripture teaches that a labourer is worthy of his
hire. " Even so hath the Lord ordained that they which preach
the Gospel should live of the Gospel " (I Cor. ix. 14). Therefore
in the *Burnt Offering,* which was a whole Burnt Offering, the
Priest had the skin, the part that was not burned. The skin was
the evidence of a sacrifice made. It was with such a skin that

our foreparents were clothed when they sinned. It is by His
Sacrifice that we are clothed as priests unto God. In the *Meal
Offering* the Priests had all but the handful. They had also a
portion of the *Sin Offering* and *Trespass Offering*. In the case of
the *Peace Offering* they had the shoulder which denoted strength,
and the breast which was the symbol of love and affection.

The OFFERER'S PORTION. In four of the Offerings it
was nothing. The only one in which they shared was the Peace
Offering. In this God and Priest and people rejoiced together.
We have no part in our salvation except to accept the peace that
comes as a result.

The SYMBOLISM, or how these things apply to the believer.
This can be summarised thus :

Burnt Offering ..... The consecration of self.
Meal Offering ..... The consecration of our gifts.
Sin Offering ..... The expiation of our sin.
Trespass Offering Restitution and Restoration.
Peace Offering ..... Reconciliation.

TYPICAL TEACHING, or how these Offerings show forth
the One True Offering, Christ Jesus :

Burnt Offering ..... Christ giving Himself as a whole Burnt
Offering upon the Cross. (Ephes. v. 2 ;
Heb. ix. 14).
Meal Offering ..... Christ as the corn of wheat (John xii. 24).
Bruised in the Mill of Calvary, He became
the Bread of Life for His people.
Sin Offering ..... Christ is our Sin Offering (2 Cor. v. 21 ;
1 Pet. ii. 24).
Trespass Offering Christ is our Trespass Offering (Col. ii.
13-14 ; 2 Cor. v. 19).
Peace Offering ..... Christ is our Peace Offering (Rom. v. 1 ;
Col. i. 20).

The PRIESTHOOD (Chs. viii-x.) Whilst God had ordained
the Offerings and required that man should obey them, man still
was without direct communication with God, therefore the Priesthood was a most important function of the old economy. In fact,
the same is true of the new order, for man still is without direct
access to God. The one great difference is that our Mediator
is no longer of an earthly order. There is now one Mediator
between God and men, the Man Christ Jesus. Hence dependence
upon His priestly and intercessory work at the right Hand of the

Father is as important as our dependence upon His finished work
as the Great Sin Offering at Calvary.

Exodus xxix. should be read in connection with these three
chapters. Aaron was cleansed, clothed, and consecrated, then
commissioned. The consecration was a unique ceremony. The
ram of consecration was slain and its blood taken and put on the
right ear, the thumb of the right hand, and the great toe of the
right foot. The symbolism of these things would be that the
right ear anointed by blood denotes a yielding of the senses.
Through the ear comes the word. From there it passes to the
heart for acceptance ; then by way of the mind to the other
members for action. The anointed thumb is full identity. In
making legal statements the law requires a thumb impression for
identity. There are no two thumb prints alike. No person can
act by proxy here. The man and his ministry are becoming one.
The great toe denotes his standing with God. The great toes give
to man his poise. Without them he has lost his balance and cannot
stand. The dictionary tells us that equilibrium is equality of
weight, power, force, etc. These things have become consecrated
in this surrendered life.

This is followed by the commission, which is the greater
portion of the book.

Cannot some parallel of this be seen in the life of the Lord
before He took upon Himself His priestly ministry ? The washing
would take place as He came to the Jordan and was baptised —
clothed with the mantle of the Holy Spirit as He came up out of
the water — after which He was led into the wilderness for His
peculiar three-fold consecration. The tempter touched His appetite,
His eyes, His mind — the lust of the flesh, the lust of the eyes,
and the pride of life. These have been referred to as the three
avenues through which all temptations must come. Christ consecrated every one of them in victory. The account of the temptation
in Matt. iv. 1-11 is followed by the statement : " Now when Jesus
had heard that John was cast into prison, He departed into
Galilee " — that is, from His temptation straight into His public
ministry, His commission.

In a measure this is the progress of the child of God. Having
been cleansed from sin by the Blood of Christ and clothed with
His righteousness, we are to consecrate ourselves to the Lord and
to His service. Are we not all called to be priests unto God ?

In the performance of his ministry, Aaron had to offer a sin
offering for himself firstly (ix. 8), and then he made the offering
for the people (ix. 15). This is an order that is maintained right

through the Word of God, and is still maintained to-day. Our own relationship with God must be established before we can deal with the relationship of others. Our own life must be surrendered before we can minister to the need of others.

In the life of the flesh it is always others first.

In the life of the Spirit it is always ourselves first.

Before we can be concerned with the heart, life, or service of others, is our heart right with God ? Is our life fully yielded ? Is our service God-honouring ? If this relationship is not right, then the next chapter (x.) may be the consequence. The sons of Aaron offered strange fire and, as a result, perished before the Lord. For, says the Lord, " I will be sanctified in them that come nigh Me, and before all the people I will be glorified " (x. 3).

This incident is followed by some Laws of holiness. The priest (or the servant of God) must refrain from certain indulgencies and practices because " Ye may put difference between holy and unholy, and between unclean and clean " (x. 10). Example and precept go hand in hand.

LAWS OF PURITY (Chs. xi.-xv.)   This is the part of the book which is so uninteresting and causes so many not to ponder or even read the book.   In principle God is showing to His people how very easy it is to become contaminated by the things that are around, and such contact is dangerous to the physical well-being. It was necessary, therefore, to be well informed of these physical dangers so that man might continue to maintain his own health and also that he might not become the carrier of trouble to other people, either by contagion or infection.   Through that which was physical God spoke to them as to their spiritual life.   We must always be on guard against the contagions and infections of sin which, like a cancer, a leprosy, a disease, not only deprive us of spiritual health and vigour, but can be passed on by us to the cursing of some other soul.   If we have a firm grip of the principles that are included in this teaching then we may get much out of the detail of these chapters.

One thing must always be maintained in our study, and that is right balance and right relationship, that will not cause us wrongly to divide the Word of Truth.   In some portions of Scripture, such as that before us now, some people cannot see any spiritual truth, but against this there are always those who want to spiritualise everything they read until there is nothing practical left ; but God teaches spiritual truths through material experiences. Therefore both must be seen and known. The danger of being unbalanced one way or the other can be serious. If leprosy is spiritualised and is considered to be a type of sin, which is perfectly right and proper, that does not alter the fact that leprosy is still leprosy and, as such, can be a potential danger to the physical life.

This point must be made because so many people have spiritualised the Old Testament until to them there is no Old Testament left. The argument of so-called Christians in the Church today is, " I am not under law, I am under grace ". This is true, but grace has not annihilated law. Grace does not permit one to behave as though law never existed. " For when the Gentiles, which have not the law, do by nature the things contained in the law, these, having not the law, are a law unto themselves " (Rom. ii. 14). Yet again the Apostle says, " Do we then make void the law through faith ? God forbid ; yea, we establish the law " (Rom. iii. 31).

As Christians our attitude toward these things should be not how much less, but how much more.

In this 11th chapter of Leviticus God gave sundry laws concerning food. If these things were good for the people of God under law, how much *more* must they be good for the people of God today ? It is now a recognised fact that most of our food has been abused, either poisoned by fertilizers or the life destroyed by processing and storage.

We speak of dietetics, sterilization, isolation, sanitation, and ventilation, as modern scientific approaches to a healthy life, overlooking the fact that all these sciences were commanded by God in the book of Leviticus, and man is only being brought back to principles of life from which he has departed. We would do well to study this book, find out where our departures have been, and find our way back to those divine principles which are unalterable.

In this section the matters involved are food restriction, child birth, diagnosing leprosy, cleansing, and issues, each of them containing some good sound commonsense for healthy living and for holy living.

THE DAY OF ATONEMENT (Ch. xvi.) This is the heart of the book, the heart of the Bible, and the heart of the Gospel, for without the shedding of Blood there is no remission for sin. Once in the year, on the tenth day of the seventh month, the High Priest laid aside all his robes of beauty and glory and, wearing a plain white coat, he entered into the ritual of this particular Day.

Two goats were chosen, one to become a scapegoat and the other a sacrificial goat. The first was taken into the wilderness and lost after that the sins of the people had been imputed to it by the laying on of hands. The other was killed and its blood carried by the High Priest into the Holy of Holies, there to be sprinkled seven times upon the Mercy Seat, signifying a perfect acceptance with God, and then sprinkled seven times before the Mercy Seat, a token of a perfect standing before God. This having been done, Aaron came out to the great concourse of people there gathered and, lifting up his hands, declared : " Ye are clean from all your sin ". At the same time the carcases of the beasts of the sin offering were burned outside the Camp. As this was a day of humiliation, when the people must afflict their souls, the High Priest wore plain white garments (xvi. 4).

This is important to note because so many people have taught that the bells were upon the hem of the garment of the High Priest to indicate to the people outside that he was still alive after he had passed beyond the Veil. This is not so, as this was the only day in the year that the High Priest did not have the bells upon his person. The bells were upon the hem of the Robe of the Ephod, but that garment, with the others, had been laid aside for the linen coat. The bells rang in the Holy Place, where the daily intercessions took place at the Golden Altar, not in the Holy of Holies, which was only entered once a year.

The truth to be learned from this Day of Atonement is that once, in the end of the age, the Lord laid aside all the glory that He had with the Father in a past eternity and, in a plain white robe of humanity, He stepped down to this earth and with His own Blood paid the price of man's redemption. Bearing our sins in His Body upon the Tree, our sins were imputed to Him — His righteousness imputed to us.

When the work of that day was finished, the High Priest put on the glorious robes he had temporarily laid aside and continued his daily ministrations, and again the bells began to ring.

Jesus, having finished the work that God had given Him to do, returned to the glory, and the bells of His intercession may now be heard by the believing heart — He maketh intercession for us.

(2) THE WALK WITH GOD THROUGH SEPARATION
(Chs. xvii-xxvii.)

It has been stated that the 16th chapter is the heart of the book, so with it the first section is concluded. " The way to God through sacrifice" now becomes "The walk with God through separation", a walk that is so beautifully outlined in the seven Feasts of Jehovah.

Before considering the main issue of this section there are some miscellaneous laws.

LAWS OF HOLINESS (Chs. xvii-xxii.)   These are threefold — for the people, for the Priests, and for the Offerings.

(a) *The People*. If the people were to live lives that were to glorify the Lord, if they were to be a separated people, then they must meet certain requirements.   They must appreciate the *value and the importance of the blood*.   The life is in the blood and God alone is the Creator of life.   Therefore man must not shed blood.   Blood was required upon the altar for sin.   Jesus later was to shed His Blood for the remission of sin.   Thus blood was to be looked upon as a holy thing, and what is holy must not become commonplace.   A law was established, therefore, requiring one place for the offering of the sacrifice — the door of the Tabernacle.   Added to this was a further demand that *blood should never be eaten*.

Chapter xviii. concerns *Marriage*. This ought to help many people who appear to be confused concerning Cain's wife.   The only way a race could increase that has commenced with one family would be to marry in the family.   This was in order whilst the stock remained strong, but when the time came that the human stock began to weaken by close marriage, and, at the same time, the population had become large enough to meet the demands without close association, then God in His wisdom said : "Thou shalt not", and foolish is the man who seeks to defy an all-wise Creator in his desire to satisfy the lusts of the flesh.

This is followed by a chapter of *sundry laws* which could be summed up by the maxim : "Take care of the little things, the big things will take care of themselves".

Then followed some weightier matters in the realm of moral behaviour, as *adultery* and *immorality*, matters in which we are badly losing out today in the Church as well as in the nation.

(b) *The Priests*. These had to watch their marriage relationships and their physical fitness.

(c) *The Offerings*. God does not accept anything.   He requires the best and has a right to the best.   The offering therefore had to be without blemish, and had to be of a certain age. Malachi reproved the people of his day for failing God in this respect.

The FEASTS OF JEHOVAH.* These are all catalogued in the 23rd chapter and detailed in other parts of the Scriptures. The Feasts were seven in number and were observed over a period of seven months. The seven are grouped into three major Feasts, known as Passover, Pentecost, and Tabernacles.

The Jews had to go up to Jerusalem three times in the year to keep the Feasts.

The Feasts were :

Passover	On the 14th day of the 1st month.
Unleavened Bread	On the 15th day of the 1st month.
Firstfruits	On the 16th day of the 1st month.
Pentecost	On the 6th day of the 3rd month.
Trumpets	On the 1st day of the 7th month.
Atonement	On the 10th day of the 7th month.
Tabernacles	On the 15th to the 22nd days of the 7th month.

The period between Firstfruits and Pentecost, which was seven weeks, is sometimes referred to as the Feast of Weeks.

Then, too, there was the weekly Sabbath (vs. 3).

Seven is the number of completion, and these seven Feasts reveal the complete walk of the believer.

(1) *Passover.* This was observed according to Exodus xii. to commemorate Israel's deliverance from Egypt. In type it is a picture of the work accomplished by the Lord in delivering man from sin through His death on the Cross. Hence Paul says : " Christ, our passover is sacrificed for us ". Having walked to Christ through sacrifice, we are naturally brought into *Salvation,* and so have begun our Christian walk.

(2) *Unleavened Bread.* No leaven was to be found in any of their dwellings. It had to be removed completely from the Camp. This was done the day before the eating of the Passover. The day set apart for its removal was called, therefore, the day of preparation. The Feast continued for seven days, declaring that the complete life from the time we met Christ, our Passover, must be a life free from the leaven of sin. The Emmaus walk is the picture of walking with the Lord, the Holy One, Who has bidden us to be holy even as He is holy. It is the life of *separation,* abstaining not only from evil but also from all appearances of evil. Sin must be out of our lives and out of our dwellings. As

* See Author's book *Your Reasonable Service.*

this Feast was a continuation of the Passover, even so separation is a part of and a continuation of salvation.

(3) *Firstfruits.* This was on the 16th day, so again is very closely associated with the Feast that preceded it. No harvest was allowed to be reaped until the first sheaf had been presented to the Lord. Therefore, on this day, three men, accompanied by the priest and certain elders of the City, went out to the neighbouring fields, and cut three sheaves of grain from three separate fields. Processionally they returned to the City, where the priest presented the sheaves to the Lord. It was then that harvesting began.

The Lord has always required firstfruits, not only of the harvest, but also of man and beast, and of all our possessions. He asked also for the first day of the week. Christ Himself became the Firstfruits of them that sleep, with the promise " As I live ye shall live also ".

The requirement of the Lord still holds today, so that He is asking that we should give the best of our lives to Himself. This is called *Consecration.* Separation is separation *from* the world — consecration is separation *to* the Lord.

(4) *Pentecost.* For the seven weeks following Firstfruits no Feast was observed because everyone was busy gathering the harvest. Then came what was known as Harvest Home. Fifty days had to be numbered from the day of the waving of the sheaf till they offered a new wave offering, two loaves of two-tenth deals of fine flour. The Feast was called Pentecost because the word Pente means Fifty.

After Jesus rose as the Firstfruits from the dead He was seen for forty days, and then He ascended on high. Before that ascension He bade His disciples Go, tarry at Jerusalem, until they be endued with power from on high. These disciples met in prayer for ten days ; forty and ten make fifty, so we read in Acts ii. " Now when the day of Pentecost was fully come ". Thus the Holy Spirit descended fifty days after the presentation of the Lord Who became the Representative of the great harvest of believers who will be caught up to meet the Lord at the great Harvest Home.

The difference between a sheaf as offered at Firstfruits and a loaf as waved at Pentecost is that a sheaf comprises many separate grains of corn. A loaf of bread is the same grains consolidated into one body. Even so, on the day of Pentecost in Acts ii., one hundred and twenty individual disciples were fused into one body, now known as the Church.

In our Christian walk the consecrated life has to be fully yielded until it becomes Spirit-possessed by a baptism of the Holy

Spirit such as the early Church knew : " For the promise is unto
you, and to your children, and to all that are afar off, even as
many as the Lord our God shall call " (Acts ii. 39). " Ye shall
receive power after that the Holy Spirit is come upon you ".

Following Pentecost there was no other Feast for a period of
three months ; then three Feasts were observed in the seventh or
Sabbatic month. Bearing in mind that this, in the first analysis,
is Jewish history, after Pentecost there came a casting off of that
nation. " He came unto His own (Israel), but His own received
Him not, but to as many as received Him to them gave He the
power to become the children of God " (the Church). This three
months of silence is, therefore, the period of the Church when
Israel has been temporarily laid aside. The thought is confirmed
when it is seen that all the Feasts prior to this gap are historical
events belonging to the past, and that the three Feasts yet to come
are all prophetic, having still to be fulfilled after the Church has
gone.

The first of these future events is

(5) *The Feast of Trumpets,* celebrated on the first day of the
seventh month. These trumpets, which were two in number and
were made of silver (Num. x. 2), had several uses, but in principle
they were for the calling together of the assembly of Israel for
walk, work, or worship. According to the various sounds of these
trumpets so Israel responded. In this present period these people
are scattered over the face of the earth, buried in the graveyard of
the nations, but, when the trumpet shall sound, they will hear it
and respond, and there will be a regathering after this long period
of dispersion.

This event is wonderfully described in prophetic language in
Ezekiel xxxvii, where the Prophet saw a valley of dry bones and
was asked as to the possibility of such bones living again. Twice
he was bidden to prophesy, or, to use the language of this Feast,
twice he was bidden to blow the trumpet. On the first prophesying
the bones came together and became a valley of dead corpses.
Upon the second prophesying they stood up a living army.
Ezekiel was then told that the incident represented the regathering
of Israel. So upon the first blowing of the trumpet the nation will
be regathered, or brought together again, in the land of Palestine,
their rightful home ; but, says the Word of the Lord, they will
go back in unbelief, dead in trespasses and sin. Then will come
the second blowing of the trumpet when they shall behold Him
Whom they pierced, and say, " Blessed is He that cometh in the
Name of the Lord ". And it shall come to pass that a nation

shall be born in a day, and Israel will stand up a living army, to become the head of the nations and not the tail.

Applying the Feast of Trumpets to the Christian walk, it is the man of God who has been endued with the Holy Spirit who will be able to take up the trumpet of the Word of God and bear a clear *Testimony* of truth and faith.

(6) *The Day of Atonement.* This has already been considered in the 16th chapter. An added thought is that Atonement spells out AT-ONE-MENT, and as a result of that day's ministry the nation was brought into a place of at-one-ment with God when all the sin of a year had been atoned. At the present moment this world and the Church are full of discord and maladjustment, but all of these things will be rectified at the Coming of the Lord when He will complete the work of Redemption as we shall be delivered from the presence of sin and given a spiritual body which will be in harmony with our spiritual life.

(7) *The Feast of Tabernacles* was the final Feast and the longest in duration, for it lasted eight days. On this occasion every man left his permanent abode to dwell in booths as described. In so doing they were to remind themselves of the days when in the desert they dwelt in tents with no established residence, and also that even now they were only pilgrims, for there remaineth *yet* a rest for the people of God. God has planned a Millennial Rest and a security His people have not yet known.

For the Christian walking with God this is not our home. We are pilgrims and strangers in this world, moving toward a City Whose Builder and Maker is God, an eternal Home, for ever with the Lord.

CIVIL LAWS (Chs. xxiv-xxvii.) The concluding chapters deal with a few civil laws which are preceded by nine verses that reflect back to the Tabernacle of the book of Exodus. In these verses the people were commanded to supply the oil for the seven-branched candlestick and to provide the twelve cakes which were to be placed weekly upon the Table of Shewbread. Might this not be a reminder that we, as the people of God, are responsible for making provision for the continual needs of the Church ?

The Civil Laws covered such subjects as :

Punishment for the blasphemer.

Life for a life — or, Capital Punishment.

The Sabbatic Year, which included resting the land for resuscitation, which does more than all chemicals.

The Year of Jubilee — the fiftieth year which God ordered to be the year of liberation and emancipation for the people. As a result of this law Palestine has ever remained a land in which properties can only be purchased on lease. There can never be freehold property because " The land shall not be sold for ever : for the land is Mine " (xxv. 23).

Blessings and Cursings according to obedience or disobedience, would be meted out upon the land.

The book closes with God's requirements concerning vows and dedicated things which, in the eyes of the Lord, are binding upon us. The subject of vows might be summarised in the words of the Preacher : " Be not rash with thy mouth, and let not thine heart be hasty to utter anything before God : for God is in heaven, and thou upon earth : therefore let thy words be few . . . When thou vowest a vow unto God, defer not to pay it ; for He hath no pleasure in fools ; pay that which thou hast vowed. Better is it that thou shouldest not vow, than that thou shouldest vow and not pay " (Eccles. v. 2-5).

NUMBERS

MAN SERVING

*"Now all these things happened unto them for ensamples:
and they are written for our admonition, upon whom the
ends of the world are come."* (1 COR. X. 11)

INTRODUCTION

This book concerns the pilgrimage of God's people in the
wilderness. Its theme is that of Service and Walk, and is a strict
continuation of the book of Exodus.

It covers a period of thirty-eight years ten months (*cf.* Num.
i. 1 with Deut. i. 3). The Levites are predominant in their service
as the Priests were in Leviticus in worship.

The book takes its name from two numberings of the nation.
The first is recorded in chapter i. and took place at Mount Sinai
when 603,550 men from twenty years old and upward were numbered. The second numbering took place on the plains of Moab
and is recorded in chapter xxvi. The total in this census was
601,730 men, showing a difference of less than 2,000. When it is
remembered that of all who came out of Egypt, a company of
possibly 2,000,000 people, only two entered the Promised Land,
we learn that the second generation went in almost as strong as
the first generation that came out. In spite of all the sin, failure,
and rebellions on the part of these people — an opposition that
kindled the wrath of God — yet the nation went in. God will
have His way. His purposes will be fulfilled, if not in one generation then in the next. If we fail God in our day then He uses
someone else, and we shall be the losers of the blessings.

We are told that this *generation* did not enter in because of
their unbelief but, according to His promise, the *nation* entered
in through the abundance of His Grace.

The book is divided into four main sections :

(1) PREPARATION FOR THE JOURNEY —
    THE ENCAMPMENT AT SINAI

(2) DISAFFECTION ON THE JOURNEY
    FROM SINAI TO KADESH

(3) INTERRUPTION OF THE JOURNEY —
KADESH TO KADESH

(4) CONTINUATION OF THE JOURNEY —
FROM KADESH TO THE PLAINS OF MOAB

(1) PREPARATION FOR THE JOURNEY — THE ENCAMP-
MENT AT SINAI

(a) *Age Limits.* Israel was at Sinai with the newly erected Tabernacle in their midst. Everything was put into an order that made it possible for the nation to recommence their journeyings after being encamped for a full year at Sinai.

It was here that the first numbering of the men took place. There is an enrolment in Heaven in the Lamb's Book of Life of all who have been redeemed by the Blood of the Lamb.

Not only was there a numbering of all men for the army of Israel, but there was an exemption. These were the Levites who had been set apart for the ministry of God. These had to be registered when only one month old (iii. 15), but engaged in the service of the Lord from 30 to 50 years of age (iv. 3). The difference between these groups of people was that army life required strength, tenacity, and courage, such as would be found in the age group of 20 and upwards, but the ministry needed experience, maturity and understanding, which come to man when he is 30. Added to these qualifications was energy but, unlike the others, this is not progressive but at a certain time in life begins to wane. As a result a retirement age of 50 is mentioned. The picture is one of God asking for the best portion of life to be used in His service.

(b) *Order of Camp.* The Tabernacle always had a central position in the Camp as the Lord should always have a central position in our lives. The Camp had to pitch afar off — God's Holiness and Majesty must always be respected. It is only through the Blood of the Cross that we have the right, and that also by invitation, to draw nigh to God.

Three tribes were to pitch on each side, every one in his respective place as ordained by God. Between the twelve tribes and the Tabernacle were the tents of Jehovah's servants — the Levites. This tribe divided into three families — the Kohathites, the Merarites, and the Gershonites. They occupied three sides of the Tabernacle whilst to the front were the tents of Moses, Aaron and Hur.

The next two chapters (iii & iv.) describe the specific duties of each of these families. Everything was in order, for God is not a God of confusion. In the service of Christ there is neither choosing nor self-will. Says Paul : " But every man hath his proper gift of God, one after this manner, and another after that " (1 Cor. vii. 7).

(c) *Laws.* The next five chapters contain some legal institutions, such as *Quarantine for the unclean* (Ch. v.). Anything that would defile was to be put outside the Camp. What blessing would come to the Church if we would excommunicate all the defiling elements that are to be found in our memberships today !

Restitution enjoined (Ch. v.) This might be summed up in the simple words — strict honesty with our property.

Trial for Jealousy (Ch. v.). In this instance it would be strict honesty in our personal relationships.

Law of the Nazarite (Ch. vi.) These people, by being set apart to the Lord's service, took upon themselves certain vows by which they were obligated to abide throughout the days of their consecration. Might we learn that it is no light matter to pledge ourselves to any particular work. If we do, the Lord will bind us to it. Too many people run in and out of the Lord's work, taking a Sunday School class, joining a choir, becoming a member of some Committee or Council, and then attending only when it suits their convenience. This is dishonouring to the Lord and damaging to the Church. The Lord is going to hold such responsible for their conduct.

The Priestly Blessing (Ch. vi.) These well-known words seem to appear in the most unlikely place. They are like an oasis in the desert, like a planet in the heavens : " The Lord bless thee, and keep thee : the Lord make His face shine upon thee, and be gracious unto thee : the Lord lift up His countenance upon thee, and give thee peace ".

(d) *Provision for Service.*

The Princes' Offering (Ch. vii.) They gave six wagons which were used for the transportation of the Tabernacle in their journeyings. Their other gifts were in connection with the dedication of the altar.

The Voice from the Mercy Seat (Ch. vii. 89) We fail to hear the Voice of God because we fail to dedicate to Him. The one follows the other.

Cleansing the Levite (Ch. viii.) Prior to this God had required that all the firstborn should be His. Now He was going to accept a tribe as representative of all the tribes instead of a child to represent a family. " For they (the Levites) are wholly given unto Me from among the children of Israel ; instead of such as open every womb, even instead of the firstborn of all the children of Israel, have I taken them unto Me " (viii. 16).

Age Limit for Service (Ch. viii.) In chapter iv. it was pointed out that the service of the Levite was rendered between the age of 30 and 50 years. This does not suggest complete retirement at 50. There is no retirement from the Lord's service. In this eighth chapter, verse 25, an explanation is given : " And from the age of 50 years they shall cease waiting upon the service thereof, and shall serve no more : But shall minister with their brethren in the Tabernacle of the congregation, to keep the charge, and shall do no service ". This means that at the age of 50 they ceased to do the heavier work of erection and conveyance of the building, and the slaying of beasts, and took the position of oversight, instructing the younger brethren in the work.

Young ministers today are our Church builders as they pioneer in new housing communities and on the Mission Field, whilst the older men, who have had their field day, become Church stabilizers as they establish the saints in their most holy faith, and work more in an advisory capacity.

Passover to be kept (Ch. ix.) This was probably the last time they kept the Passover whilst in the wilderness because, after this, their wanderings began and we know that the Feast went into abeyance because it had to be re-established as soon as they entered the Promised Land (see Jos. v.).

A further provision was made for the man who, through uncleanness or anything beyond his control, was unable to keep the Feast at the appointed time. He could observe the Feast on the 14th day of the second month, instead of the 14th day of the first month.

The Sinai period closes with this chapter.

The Pillar of Cloud (Ch. ix.) The pillar of cloud and of fire which had been given to them at the Red Sea now hovers above the newly constructed Tabernacle. The Lord instructed Moses that this was to become their emblem of guidance as again they renewed their journeyings. Whether the Pillar moved by day or by night, or whether it tarried for two days or a month or a year, they had to obey. The matter of personal convenience should never come under consideration. One may have to move in the middle of the night, or one may desire to move earlier from a given area, or stay longer in pleasant surroundings, but cannot because he is under command.

It is a dangerous thing for any one of us to make a move until we are sure that we have the Will of God in the matter, and that He has bidden us go forward.

As a second witness of His Will they had to make and use *Two Silver Trumpets* (Ch. x.), which summoned the people to journey or to go out to war or to assemble for their worship.

The Lord has given us the Pillar of His Holy Spirit to lead us in the way, and the Trumpet of His Word, the two trumpets suggesting Old and New Testaments, and the silver its redemptive message. May we ever be guided by both.

(2) DISAFFECTION ON THE JOURNEY — FROM SINAI TO KADESH

The Camp was now ready to move forward. Again we are reminded that God is a God of order for, as surely as every tribe had a place in the Camp, so they had a position on the march. Judah, Issachar, and Zebulun led the way ; then the six wagons, the gifts of the princes, followed carrying the Tabernacle. Three more tribes, Reuben, Simeon, and Gad, made the first half of the host. The family of the Kohathites had a central position as they carried the furniture of the Tabernacle, which included the Ark of the Covenant, upon their shoulders. The remaining six tribes followed in order — Ephraim, Manasseh, Benjamin, Dan, Asher, and Naphtali. The Pillar of cloud was before them and the Ark of the Covenant in the midst of them, both symbols of the Presence of God.

The closing verses of chapter x. give a record of the first move, which would be typical of all their moves as they journeyed from place to place. "And they departed from the Mount of the Lord three days journey : and the Ark of the Covenant of the Lord went before them in the three days journey, to search out a resting place for them. And the cloud of the Lord was upon them by day, when they went out of the camp " (x. 33-34).

Journeyings (Chs. xi-xiv.) These four chapters concern progressive journeyings, as against wanderings both purposeless and purposeful that came later. In these same chapters is to be seen both sedition and apostasy. They commence with the first of eight murmurings that came from ungrateful people. Israel murmured concerning the way, their food, their leaders, giants, the land, the priesthood, thirst and provision — but, who are we to point the finger at them ? We are no better than they, always grumbling, never thankful, yet these things were written for our admonition.

Murmuring concerning the way (Ch. xi.)   Although God
was leading they were dissatisfied, thus kindling the displeasure
of the Lord in which He sent fire into their midst. Oh, to learn to
be submissive!

Murmuring concerning their food (Ch. xi.)   God was
miraculously providing them with manna every morning. It had
never failed them. It was satisfying to them, but they murmured
again, saying : " Who will give us flesh to eat ? " They longed for
the fish, the cucumbers and melons, the leeks, onions and garlic of
the old life in Egypt. Once more God's anger was kindled and
He said : " . . . the Lord will give you flesh, and ye shall eat it.
Ye shall not eat one day, nor two days, nor five days, neither ten
days, nor twenty days ; but even a whole month until it come
out at your nostrils and it be loathsome unto you : because that
ye have despised the Lord . . . " (xi. 18-20).

Manna has always been used as a type of the Word of God,
that food for our souls which He has promised should never fail
us. But the Church today has tired of that Word and cried out,
" Give us flesh to eat, give us some of the food of the old land,
the philosophies of men, a social gospel, advanced education,
propaganda, the logic of this world ", and God, in His anger and
because of His jealousy for His Word, has permitted men to feed
upon all this materialism and liberalism until it is beginning to
become loathsome to them, for only then will man appreciate
the value and beauty of His Word.

The pressure of this murmuring people began to weigh heavily
upon Moses, so that he cried out to God, saying : " Have I
conceived all this people ? Have I begotten them, that Thou
shouldest say unto me, Carry them in thy bosom, as a nursing
father beareth the suckling child . . . I am not able to bear all
this people alone, because it is too heavy for me ". (xi. 12-14).

Seventy Elders appointed (Ch. xi.)   God's reply to Moses
was : " Gather unto Me seventy men of the elders of Israel ".
One seems to sense a rebuff here. Back in the eighteenth chapter
of Exodus, when Moses was carrying a heavy burden, Jethro, his
father-in-law, had suggested that Moses should appoint some able
men to share in the carrying of this great load, and Moses did
so. The question arises — What became of those elders ? Maybe
the answer is to be found in Exodus xviii. 24 : " So Moses
hearkened to the voice of his father-in-law, and did all that he had
said ". The failure was that Moses obeyed the voice of man instead of consulting God. Now that Moses does come to God
His reply is : " Gather unto *Me* seventy men ", or ' Moses, if

you had consulted me at the time Jethro made his suggestion, I
would have agreed to it then and you could have had this help all
along'. How many burdens we carry along life's way because
we fail to share them with the Lord! How pungent with truth is
the hymn : —

> " What a Friend we have in Jesus,
> All our sins and griefs to bear ;
> What a privilege to carry
> Everything to God in prayer.
> Oh, what peace we often forfeit,
> *Oh, what needless pain we bear,*
> *All because we do not carry*
> *Everything to God in prayer."*

Murmuring concerning leaders (Ch. xii.)   How slow we are
to learn our lessons! Again these people were complaining, this
time concerning the leadership. Moses had married an Ethiopian
woman. Aaron and Miriam, his brother and sister, did not seem
pleased with this new relationship, so together they chided Moses,
questioning his right of leadership and suggesting that any of them
had the right to lead (xii. 1-2). Moses did not retaliate but,
evidently, submitted to their rebukes for, at this juncture, the
meekness of Moses is made known in verse 3, as God stepped
in to defend His servant. God called these three people to the
Tabernacle and there declared, in no uncertain words, that leadership is not the prerogative of anyone who has a desire for it, but
belongs to a person to whom God reveals Himself and with whom
He will speak mouth to mouth. Then to Aaron and Miriam He
said : " Wherefore then were ye not afraid to speak against my
servant Moses ?"

How bold we would be in our ministry if we were as assured
of our calling and as aware of the Lord fighting for us and reproving our opponents as Moses was assured.

God even went farther, for Miriam was put forth from the
presence of the Lord, smitten with leprosy. Aaron, one of the
guilty party, appealed to his brother for mercy, and Moses, in
turn, pleaded with God. But God refused the request, saying
that she must go into quarantine.

Two lessons are to be learned here. Firstly, some people
see an act of injustice on the part of God inasmuch as Aaron and
Miriam were partakers in the same sin. One was punished with
leprosy and the other was allowed to go unpunished — that
suggests partiality. It is an exceedingly dangerous thing to charge

a Just God with injustice. To do so is to rob Him of His Holiness. There are many instances such as this one where, on the surface, there appears to be an injustice. The safe policy in such a situation is to blame oneself for a faulty understanding of the narrative, not to charge God with injustice. If we read the account a second time it might be seen that a great amount of guilt rested upon the shoulders of Aaron, so that, not only had he wronged Moses, but he had also wronged his sister. Realising this, do you not think that Aaron must have had a very guilty conscience, and, if so, do you not think that he would have readily changed places with Miriam and taken the leprosy instead ? There are two kinds of punishment. One is physical, which was the lot of Miriam, the other is moral, with that awful sense of responsibility about which one can do nothing. That was Aaron's, and the question can be asked, ' Which is the greater punishment to take ? ' God must remain just.

The other lesson is in the words of verse 15 : " And the people journeyed not till Miriam was brought in again ". The sin of an individual can halt the advancement of a whole nation, and can bring to a standstill the progress of the Church of God today.

The twelve Spies (Ch. xiii.) The reason why these spies came back with unbelief was because they went with it ! God had told the nation to " go in and possess the land ". Such instruction from God needs no investigation, only obedience. It may be said that the Lord commanded to send the spies, but this is one of the many instances where we must obey the Lord and compare Scripture with Scripture. Read Deut. i. 22-23 and 32-33, then come back to Numbers i. 1-3, and it will be seen that the people said : " We will send men before us ", and Moses said : " The saying pleased me well and I took twelve men of you, one of a tribe . . . Yet in this thing ye did not believe in the Lord your God ". The picture becomes one of the Lord submitting to what these rebellious people demanded, and that to their undoing.

The choice of Saul as king, because of popular request, is another instance. We ofttimes bring problems into our own lives because we keep telling the Lord what we want and how He should do it for us, instead of saying : " Thy will be done ". Abram tried to help God instead of believing God, and the result was Ishmael, the thorn in the flesh. Rachael demanded a second son and died in childbirth. Thus was Benjamin born. In the story here forty days of searching brought forty years of wandering.

How easy it is for us to believe the evil report even though the reporters have no proof of their statements. The ten never brought back one giant to prove there were giants, whilst the two brought back of the fruit of the land only to have their evidence rejected. This shows how much unbelief was in their hearts.

Israel's Revolt (Ch. xiv.) This unbelief led to open revolt. The people threatened to stone Moses and to appoint a captain who would take them back to Egypt. In turn God said that He would send a pestilence, and would disinherit these people and establish another nation in Moses. Then comes one of those beautiful intercessory prayers of Moses, seeking pardon for the people who were ready to destroy him, and reminding the Lord of His long-suffering and mercy. God listened to Moses, and, instead of destroying that nation, declared that He would destroy only that generation, all except Joshua and Caleb, who would lead the next generation into the Land of Promise.

In verse 4 they charge the Lord for bringing them out to destroy their wives and children. Too many people try to hide behind their children and seek excuse for their failure in spiritual things, but God will never accept such cowardice. He says: " The soul that sinneth IT shall die ; the children shall not die for the parents nor the parents for the children ". In this instance the parents had sinned. Therefore the parents should die, but the children shall be the generation that shall inherit. Parents, do not blame your family for neglected spiritual exercises ! Children, do not rest on the faith and the works of your parents ! ! It is YOU with whom God deals.

In verse 40 they tried to defy God by not accepting His punishment. Contrary to His command they sought to move forward. " They presumed to go up unto the hill top ; nevertheless the ark of the covenant of the Lord, and Moses, departed not out of the camp " (vs. 44), but instead of moving forward God drove them backward. Without His leadership we are defeated before we begin.

This brings to an end their journeyings. The next part of the story is an :

(3) INTERRUPTION OF THE JOURNEY — KADESH TO KADESH

For years they moved in circles only to come back to the same place. Christian, is this a picture of your life ? How much progress have you made in spiritual things in the past five years, during this last year ? Must you confess that you have not

advanced ?   Are you concerned ?   The possible answer is —
Disobedience.   Somewhere along the way the Lord said to you :
" Go in and possess ", or " Do this ", or " Go there " — and
you replied :   " Lord, I am not able ".   If this be true, then there
is no more progress until you obey the Lord in that thing.

Laws of Sundry Offerings (Ch. xv.)   A chapter of laws is
interjected here in relationship to their Offerings which were to
be observed when they reached the Land which was yet a long way
off.   It is difficult to see why this chapter should be given at this
time unless it was to encourage them in the fact that they would
eventually take possession of the Land.

Sabbath breaker stoned.   Why should a man be punished
for gathering sticks on the Sabbath Day ?   One sin leads to another.
Why should he want to gather sticks ?   Obviously to light a fire,
but Exodus xxxv. 3 says :   " Ye shall kindle no fire throughout
your habitation upon the Sabbath Day ".   A little thing, says
someone, but disobedience of the expressed Will of an Almighty
God can never be little.   If we had taken care of the so-called
" little " things relating to the Lord's Day, we should not be
desecrating it today with sports, public functions, cinemas and
open stores, drawing thousands of people away from our churches
and the sound of the Gospel.   Christians would not be using
the Lord's Day as their day, and spending it in worldliness instead
of worship.

Murmuring concerning the Priesthood — Aaron's Rod (Chs.
xvi. and xvii.)   The sixth of the people's great murmurings was
against the Priesthood.   God had chosen Aaron to be the High
Priest.   The congregation said that Moses had chosen him so
again they rose up against Moses.   Korah and his companions
organised a rebellion and the people quickly joined.   God would
have destroyed them, but once more Moses interceded.   As a
result of this uprising, Korah, Dathan, and Abiram, and many of
their families, died from an earthquake that God sent.   Two
hundred and fifty princes, who had associated themselves with
these men and had claimed the right of priesthood, died from a
fire that broke out from their censers.   God also sent a plague
which destroyed a further fourteen thousand seven hundred.   All
of this judgment was because they questioned the Word of God.
Judgment did not break the rebellion.   God then commanded that
twelve rods should be brought by the twelve princes of the twelve
tribes.   Each rod was to bear the name of the owner, because the
one that budded, brought forth blossoms, and yielded almonds,
would designate the man of God's choice. Thus it was that Aaron's

rod budded. That rod, which was accepted by Israel as a sign of a God-chosen Priesthood, was taken and placed in the Ark of the Covenant.

A dead stick breaking into new life, bearing the blossom of beauty and the almond of fruitfulness, became the sign of a God-chosen Priesthood. The Aaronic Priesthood was never questioned again.

The same sign can be found in Christ Who alone rose from the dead and became the firstfruits of them that sleep. In His Resurrection Life He became our God-chosen High Priest. The believer, who was once dead in sin as a dry stick and has now received the bud of Divine Life, should be showing forth the fragrance of a Christian life and bearing the fruit of the Spirit. Such a Christian reveals that he, too, is a God-chosen Priest, called to intercede for others.

Service of the Priests and Levites (Ch. xviii.)　Men who are separated for Divine Service can have no part in the world and yet they still live in it. So it becomes necessary that, inasmuch as they serve the people in God's behalf, the people must serve them.

This is followed by some laws of purification in chapter xix.

The Death of Miriam (Ch. xx.)　Only one verse records the fact, but few women have their death recorded at all. Miriam played a prominent part in the life of Moses, right from the day she was appointed as his protector when, as a babe, he lay in an ark among the flags, until the unfortunate day when she exceeded her privilege and was smitten with leprosy.

Murmurings concerning Thirst (Ch. xx.)　Once more they were murmuring, for they were without water. But the question may be asked, Why were they without water ? At this time they were at Kadesh. In Exodus xvii. they were crying for water at Rephaim and God bade Moses meet Him at Horeb, there to strike the rock from which the water flowed freely. Might one suggest that this water became a river and, therefore, a constant supply, even as the Manna was unfailing ? This suggestion would come from the fact that, when Paul was reminding the people of Corinth of God's faithfulness to Israel, he stated : " And did all drink of the same spiritual drink for they drank of that Spiritual Rock that followed them, and that Rock was Christ " (I Cor. x. 4). The supply which came from the source followed, meaning the water. If so, then to be without water now suggests that the people had moved away from the supply. Is this not often our trouble — not the failure of the supply but our wandering ?

Might not the Psalmist suggest the same thought : "So that it went ill with Moses for *their sakes*" (Ps. cvi. 32).

That be as it will, the more important lesson is that the people were without water and they were chiding Moses. God told Moses to "Take the rod and gather thou the assembly together . . . and speak ye unto the rock before their eyes". We know that Moses struck the rock twice. Many Preachers have said that Moses was forbidden entrance to the Promised Land because he thus broke a type. The rock should only have been smitten once. Others tell us that Moses never entered the Land because here he lost his temper. Let us be careful with our interpretations. If Moses were deprived of the privilege of entering in because he lost his temper once in forty years whilst leading a rebellious people, then we may begin to doubt our admission into heaven, for most of us have lost our tempers more than once for much smaller things.

No! Moses did not take a big punishment for a little sin. Read what the narrative says. "Hear now, ye rebels ; must WE fetch you water out of this rock" (vs. 10). God told Moses to speak to the rock, but instead he spoke to the people and, in doing so, claimed for himself the power to produce the water. As a result, God spoke to Moses saying : "Because ye believed me not, to sanctify Me in the eyes of the children of Israel, THERE-FORE ye shall not bring this congregation into the Land which I have given unto them" (vs. 12). This was no small sin. It was something very grievous, and alas ! we ofttimes commit the same sin. God does a work through us, or answers our prayer. Then we tell everyone what WE have done. Many a testimony meeting is a self-appraisement before others instead of a God-honouring ministry. It must not be overlooked that Aaron was a participant in the act, and he, too, died before they reached the Land. How many possessions have we lost because we have failed to acknowledge God ? The thought is borne out in Psalm cvi. 33. "Because they provoked his spirit, so that he spake unadvisedly with his lips". This is no suggestion of lost temper.

(4) CONTINUATION OF THE JOURNEY — KADESH TO THE PLAINS OF MOAB

This move forward commenced at Chapter xx. 22. "And the children of Israel, even the whole congregation, journeyed from Kadesh, and came unto Mount Hor".

Refused by the Edomites (Ch. xx.) Prior to this move and in preparation for it, they sent to the king of Edom for permission to pass through his land, with the promise that they would keep to the king's highway and not touch any of his property ; but the king refused permission.

Edom was a brother to Israel, inasmuch as the Edomites descended from Esau and the Israelites from Jacob. Jacob and Esau had come to terms of reconciliation but, evidently, they had not been accepted by the descendants. The request of Moses was reasonable, and the refusal of Edom was without any reason. The Church ofttimes has to apply to the world for certain privileges, but the world is not always so anxious to comply. Because we are not of the world the world finds itself rather fearful of our presence although they never give a reason. The reason is usually obvious.

Death of Aaron (Ch. xx.) Miriam, Aaron, and Moses, all die in the same year, the year before Israel entered the Promised Land. All had rendered long service to the nation, but all of them had sinned. Aaron had shared in the tragedy at Meribah and could not enter the Land any more than could Moses. Aaron was the first of the long line of men who held the priestly office. There is something significant in that Aaron and Eleazer, his son, were commanded to come to Mount Hor. God caused that the holy garments should be taken from Aaron and placed upon his son before death took place. When Aaron died it was the man, not the office. The office had already been transferred. This was a reminder to the people, and us, that the priestly office is a continuous office. God takes His man, but His work goes on.

Murmuring concerning Provision — The Brazen Serpent (Ch. xxi.) The way they now travelled was hard and rugged. The margin of our Bible states that the words " much discouraged " (vs. 4) should read " impatient ", and when people become impatient tempers get frayed and everything goes wrong. They complained, therefore, about their provision, no bread, and no water. This was not strictly true. God was still supplying them with Manna and with water. It was a general spirit of dissatisfaction and complaining, when they were actually the receivers of God's abundant blessings. It was this rebellious spirit that brought the plague of fiery serpents from the Lord which, in turn, brought repentance from the people. Since their faith in God had wavered their trust in God must be proved. Hence God bade that a serpent of brass should be set upon a pole and those who looked should live. They were surrounded by serpents ! They wanted to be rid of serpents, but God told them to make another serpent ! There was nothing

logical in this requirement of God. Thus it became the look of
faith. If man would be free from his sin, he must accept by faith
the finished work of the One Who became sin upon the Cross of
Calvary.

Journeyings (Ch. xxi.) The balance of this chapter records
further journeyings. As far as Pisgah all went well. Thereafter
they began to meet their enemies. Sihon, king of the Amorites
and Og, king of Bashan, sought to obstruct their passage, but
Israel warred against these nations and God gave them the victory.

Balaam and Balak (Ch. xxii.) Balak, king of the Moabites,
came next but he, being afraid, hired Balaam to curse these people.
However, God caused Balaam only to utter words of blessing. But
Balaam had a covetous eye on the reward that Balak was offering.
He became responsible, therefore, for the sensuous feast of Baal
Peor recorded in the opening verses of Num. xxv. and confirmed
in xxxi. 16. There are always those who will sell themselves and
their people for some small earthly reward.

Blessing came out of this tragedy for Phinehas, of the tribe of
Levi, took a javelin and dealt with certain offenders, wherefore
God turned back His wrath and Israel was saved. Because of
this action God established the priesthood in the family of this man
and bestowed upon it His continued peace.

Israel numbered (Ch. xxvi.) This is the second census
referred to at the beginning of this chapter. God has a registration of the names of all believers recorded in the Lamb's Book of
Life.

Joshua chosen (Ch. xxvii.) God's work ever goes on. He
always has His man for the hour of need .

Feasts and Offerings (Chs. xxviii. and xxix.) Two chapters
are given to remind Israel of their obligations toward the Lord in
the matter of the Ceremonial Law. Man is ever forgetful, but God
is ever reminding.

Vows unto the Lord (Ch. xxx.) The Word of God has a
great deal to say about vows which we must reserve for later
comment. Sufficient here to learn that vows are serious things
and are binding when they are made to, or before, or in the Name
of, the Lord. Such vows cannot be broken without punishment.

We are also taught the responsibility that belongs to the head
of a family, and the relationships that should be recognised in each
family — parents and their responsibility, children and their submission, husbands and wives and their mutual obligations.

War with the Midianites (Ch. xxxi.) In this war of almost
extermination God meted out vengeance upon a people because of

the wrong they had done Israel earlier. The wheels of God's justice may move slowly, but they move surely. A valuable lesson of the chapter is that the man who remains behind with the stuff should share in the spoils of war with those who fight in the battle. The Lord Himself is entitled to recognition and a share of the spoils of victory, for victory is of the Lord.

The inheritance of the two and a half tribes (Ch. xxxii.) Reuben and Gad, with half of Manasseh, were not prepared to go all the way with the people of God. As soon as they saw something that appealed to the flesh they were anxious to stake their claims, having only selfish desires. When reproved for this action they consented to go ahead and fight with their brethren as long as their reward was secure. Should we not watch our conduct lest selfish desire prevents us from advancing with our brethren ?

In the closing chapters of Joshua we shall learn that this selfish attitude almost brought to them the loss of their association and relationship. Our petty, selfish desires ofttimes rob us of great spiritual inheritances.

Itinerary of Journey (Ch. xxxiii.) As the people came to the conclusion of their years of travel and prepared themselves to enter the Land, a survey of their journeys was put on record. Surveying of this kind is always good because each place reminds a person of some experience. We do it after a vacation or a trip somewhere, and to do it with life is to call to remembrance the Grace of God.

The Land (Ch. xxxiv.) " When ye be come into the Land ". God was telling Moses beforehand just where and how the land was to be divided before they had even entered it, and certainly had not begun to conquer it. The future is ever in God's Hands and He alone will distribute the rewards in the life to come. It is also a picture of assurance and faith. God divides the Land as though it were already in their possession.

The Cities (Ch. xxxv.) Having divided the Land into territorial possessions the Lord now distributes the Cities. Levi, not being counted with the twelve because separated unto the Lord for holy things, received no inheritance. Each tribe, therefore, had to give so many Cities — forty-eight in all. This caused that the sons of Levi were scattered over the whole Land, thus distributing the ministry of the Lord amongst the people. Out of these forty-eight Cities, six were set apart as

Cities of Refuge for the manslayer. Christ is the great Refuge for all sinners who will flee to Him.

The names of these Cities are significant :
Kedesh means Holy Place for the Unclean.
Shechem means Shoulder for the Weary.
Hebron means Fellowship for the Homeless.
Bezer means Stronghold for the Helpless.
Ramoth means Exalted for the Hopeless.
Golan means Separated for the Tempted.

The book concludes with an interesting incident which established a new Law of

Inheritance (Ch. xxxvi.)   A man named Zelophehad had five daughters.   In chapter xxvii. they had claimed a right to inherit from their father because he had no sons.   This had been granted. Now the question arose : What would happen if, having inherited property, they married men of other tribes ?   Properties would move from family to family and tribe to tribe, until the tribes would cease to have individual identity.   So the Lord established a law that the daughters could inherit but if they did, and afterwards desired marriage, they could only marry a man of their own tribe.

Might this not remind us that, when we become Christians and thereby inheritors with the saints in light, marriage should be to and with those of like precious faith.

It is not convenient to be receivers of Divine Grace and become partakers of the world and its lusts.

DEUTERONOMY

MAN CONTINUING

" But continue thou in the things which thou hast learned and hast been assured of, knowing of Whom thou hast learned them."   (II Tim. iii. 14)

INTRODUCTION

This book is the fifth and final of the Pentateuch. In recent years the Mosaic authorship has been challenged by the critics but against their assertions it can be stated that Moses wrote this book. The evidence is overwhelmung, and the Scriptural references numerous.

The name "Deuteronomy" is not good. We have already made the point that these are not the Hebrew names, but those given by the English translators. "Deuteronomy" is derived from two Greek words — "Deuteros" meaning "second", and "Nomos" meaning "Law", thus making this book to be the second law. This is not good because it would suggest that the first Law had failed, or not met its objective, so that a second Law was required to take the place of the first. Of course, this is not so. The book, instead of being a second law, is actually a reiteration of the original Law to a second generation. The Hebrew name for this fifth book is "Elleh Had-debharim" meaning "These are the words."

The third verse of chapter i. : " In the fortieth year, in the eleventh month, on the first day of the month ", gives the time element, which was immediately before this generation entered the Promised Land. This would indicate the purpose of the book. The previous generation, who had been the recipients of the Law, had perished — all save Joshua and Caleb — necessitating that the Law be given again to this new generation which was now ready to possess the Promised Land.

It is not just a mere recapitulation of the Law, nor a verbatim report, but something deeper. It has been said that it reviews the past with its eyes on the future. It is a repetition to a new generation with no amendments so far as the Moral Law was concerned, but with certain adjustments to the Civil Law and Ceremonial Law caused by the changing conditions as these people moved from a nomad life in the desert to a more settled and established life in the Land.

If there is one lesson above all others to be learned from the book of Deuteronomy it is that, whilst social life may ever be changing, thus requiring adjusted laws, the moral life never changes. In these modern days our young people ever want to remind us that they live in a different world from that of their parents, hoping thereby to find the means of escape from some religious obligation. We would remind young people, and also their elders, that it is quite true that the youth of today lives in a different world from the one of our youth, BUT it is only the social world that is different. The moral world is exactly the same. Sin is still sin. The requirements of God never vary. He is the same yesterday, and today, and forever, in His demands for holiness as He is in the supplies of His Grace. As the Lord repeated the Moral Law by word to the second generation so He would repeat it to every succeeding generation.

The keyword of the whole book is " Obedience ". Moses realised that the new generation was no better than their fathers. He reminded them, therefore, of the many failures of the past because of their disobedience, and exhorted them to obey God at every turn of the way. This would be the only path of blessing in all the future.

The book has several unusual and important features, one of them being that every quotation made by the Lord when He was tempted of the Devil in the wilderness is found in these chapters.

There are three divisions to the book, each of them being an address delivered by Moses. They are :

The Past	.....	Historical	.....	A Review.
The Present	.....	Legislative	.....	A Repetition.
The Future	.....	Prophetical	.....	A Revelation.

(1) THE PAST — HISTORICAL — A REVIEW (Chs. i.-iv.)

This was delivered from the plains of Moab, from whence Moses reviewed God's dealings with the people over the past forty years. In verse 5 we read : " On this side Jordan, in the land of Moab, began Moses to declare this Law, saying . . . ". The word " declare " means " To dig in " or " to go deep ". This generation must know the full truth and its implications. " Ye have dwelt long enough in this mount ". Chapter one takes them from Horeb, or Sinai, to Kadesh. Moses detailed much, including their desire to spy out the Land and his submission to their request, the return of the two spies with the evidence of the fruitfulness of this territory, and the rebellion because they were more prepared to receive the evil report, causing the anger of God to be kindled against them, bringing upon that generation thirty-eight years of wandering during which all but two perished.

Three times Moses mentioned that they were responsible for the act that kept him out of the Promised Land (i. 37 ; iii. 26 ; iv. 21). This was a great grief to Moses.

In chapters two and three he reviewed the journey from Kadesh to Mount Pisgah, reminding them of their disobedience on the one hand, and God's faithfulness in subduing their enemies, on the other hand.

From journeying experiences he turned to moral obligations in chapter four. It is another call to obedience. God had given them a Law. He had appeared to them at Sinai. He had brought them out of an iron furnace. Now God asked — What other nation on the earth had received such privileges ? Who else had heard the Voice of God and lived ? Who else had seen such signs and wonders ? In return for all of this He asked two things — (1) Loyalty, that they would not make any graven image or worship any other god, for He is a Jealous God ; and (2) Testimony, they were to teach their sons, and their sons' sons — in other words, all succeeding generations.

Whilst this was all review of the past, yet Moses warned them that, even though they were about to possess the Land, if they should fail in these things, then He would take away their privileges. " I call heaven and earth to witness against you this day, that ye shall soon utterly perish from off the land whereunto ye go over Jordan to possess it ; ye shall not prolong your days upon it, but shall be utterly destroyed. And the Lord shall scatter you among the nations, and ye shall be left few in number among the heathen . . . " (iv. 26-27).

We, too, must bear in mind that many of the promises of God are conditional. The Lord can only continue to bless us as we are yielded to Him and submissive to His Will in a life of full surrender and of testimony.

The section closes with the setting apart of the first three Cities of Refuge which were on the east side of Jordan, places where the manslayer, the man who killed his neighbour unwittingly, might flee for refuge. These Cities gave no sanctuary for the murderer. Jesus is the Great Refuge. " The Name of the Lord is a strong tower ; the righteous runneth into it, and is safe " (Prov. xviii. 10).

> " Oh, safe to the Rock that is higher than I,
> My soul in its conflicts and sorrows would fly ;
> So sinful, so weary, Thine, Thine would I be,
> Thou blest Rock of Ages, I'm hiding in Thee."

We do a great deal of killing. We kill time. We destroy opportunities, we make of non-effect the promises of God. We give service that yields no fruit, we break hearts by our lack of charity, we allow men to go to Hell because we fail to tell them of the Love of God. If these things are done by us ignorantly, then we thank the Lord that He is our City of Refuge. But, alas! We cannot too often claim ignorance. If we do it might prove to be wilful ignorance or carelessness on our part, and God is going to hold us responsible for our misconduct, work, opportunity and privilege, that we have murdered.

(2) THE PRESENT — LEGISLATIVE — A REPETITION (Chs. v.-xxv.)

(a) MORAL LAW (Chs. v.-xi.) It has been stated that the Moral Law knows no change. This Law is repeated in chapter five without amendment. There is also a reminder of the Holiness and Severity of a Just God, a peep into His august Majesty, and a glimpse of His mighty Power, as the circumstances in which the Law was given were also repeated. " These words the Lord spake unto all your assembly in the mount out of the midst of the fire, of the cloud, and of the thick darkness, with a great voice : *and He added no more*" (v. 22). So fearful were the people that they requested that God should not speak lest they should die. They would willingly obey Moses if God would make known His Laws to him. God commended them in their decision and longed that they would always be as submissive.

Do you not think that we in the Church today have lost the sense of His Holiness and His Majesty ? We speak of Him in a light way at times and ever fail to recognise His Majesty. We are more inclined to tell God what we want, and almost give Him our commands as though He were our servant, instead of learning to bow before Him with a consciousness of our unworthiness, and pray " Thy Will be done ", or, " Lord, what wilt Thou have me to do ? ".

Love to God enjoined (Ch. vi.) This chapter opens with three words — Commandments, Statutes, and Judgments, all of which were to be taught. The difference between them is that Commandments control the Moral life, Statutes are basic to Civil life, and Judgments are meted out according to our relationship

with the first two. An example may be found in Exodus xv. 26.
The Lord promised that if His people would obey His Commandments and keep His Statutes He would free them from the diseases
that befell the Egyptians. A review of Israel's history shows that
every sickness that befell them was a judgment because they failed
Him morally. So far as the Statutes were concerned which related
to food, exercise, sterilisation, isolation, sanitation, etc., the people
never failed and never suffered. The Jew is still particular about
these same things.

In the classic words of verses 4-9 the Law is

(1) Personal   ..... THOU shalt love the Lord Thy God.

(2) Family   ..... Teach them diligently unto THY
                           CHILDREN.

(3) Communal   ....   When thou WALKEST BY THE WAY.

The Law was to be a sign upon their hand and as frontlets
between their eyes. Between the eyes is the seat of the mind,
or the intellect — meaning, they must know the Law. On the
hand is the symbol of action — they must do it. The same
requirement of God belongs to us today. Be not hearers only
but doers of the Word. If the Law of God is not on hand and
forehead, the Mark of the Beast may be !

Israel was then warned of the danger of forgetting God's
goodness. " Then beware lest thou forget the Lord, which brought
thee forth out of the land of Egypt, from the house of bondage "
(vi. 12). It is so easy to remember the Lord when things are
adverse and trials press sore — so easy to forget when things are
prosperous and the larder is full and we are enjoying good health.
Success can be man's worst enemy !

There is also the responsibility of teaching our children the
things of the Lord. We should ever be in a position to satisfy
the enquiring mind.

National Separation (Ch. vii.) Moses then proceeded to
remind this generation that they must have no relationship with
the nations round about them. They were to remain a holy and
a separated people. " . . . The Lord thy God hath chosen thee
to be a special people unto Himself . . . " (vii. 6). Are not
Christians a chosen people to the Lord, and should we not be
separated from the world ? Paul tells us not to be unequally
yoked with unbelievers.

In verse 7 the Lord told them, and us, the reason for His
interest — not because of what we are but because of what He

is. He is loving and He is faithful. He did for them, and does for us, " for His Name's sake ".

Call to Obedience (Ch. viii.) Three things are to be noted in this chapter. (1) There was a reminder of God's provision and His protection whilst they were in the desert (vs. 1-5). (2) There was a promise of an abundant supply when they came into the Land (vs. 7-10). (3) There was a warning that prosperity could bring forgetfulness with a sense of self-satisfaction. This in turn would bring a pride of heart which could cause them to perish (vs. 11-20).

Reminder of Rebellions (Ch. ix.) Moses continued by reminding them of their stubbornness. He took their minds back to

> Horeb where they made a golden calf for worship.
>
> Taberah where their murmurings kindled the anger of God.
>
> Masseh where they complained for lack of water.
>
> Kibroth where they despised the Manna.
>
> Kadesh, the scene of unbelief that resulted in forty years of wandering.

What a history !

It is against this background that the Lord said to them : " Not for thy righteousness, or for the uprightness of thine heart, dost thou go to possess their land ; but for the wickedness of these nations the Lord thy God doth drive them out from before thee, and that He may perform the word which the Lord sware unto thy fathers, Abraham, Isaac, and Jacob " (vs. 5). From this we learn that the child of God has no merit. Everything comes to us "for His Name's sake ", and because of His faithfulness to His declared Word.

In the light of this condition chapter x. becomes an exhortation to obedience, summed up in verses 12-13 : " And now, Israel, what doth the Lord thy God require of thee, but to fear the Lord thy God, to walk in all His ways, and to love Him, and to serve the Lord thy God with all thy heart and with all thy soul ; To keep the commandments of the Lord, and His statutes, which I command thee this day for thy good ? "

Call to Obedience (Ch. xi.) Chapter xi., which concludes the Moral Law, again required submission to God's Will and obedience to His Word, the result of which was going to bring the people a land of prosperity, fruitful seasons, and plentiful supply. But if, in their prosperity, they forgot God and served other gods, then the supply would be cut off immediately. He, therefore, bade them abide closely to His Word, hide it in the heart, bind it on the hand, keep it in the mind, write it on the door posts and upon the gates, pass it on to the children. All of this seems to sum up — keep that Word always before you, never allow it to take a back place.

Oh, to hear the Word of God foremost in every action of life today, to allow it to be the finger-post that says : " This is the way, walk ye in it " ! Our relationship with the Word of God is established in verses 26-28 : " Behold, I set before you this day a blessing and a curse ; a blessing if ye obey the command- ments of the Lord your God . . . and a curse, if ye will not obey the commandments of the Lord your God ".

(b) CEREMONIAL LAW (Chs. xii-xvi.)

One place for Worship (Ch. xii.). Moses had been brought up in a land of idolatry. The people were surrounded by idolatrous nations, and the same sinful tendency was in their hearts. From the beginning of time man has always wanted to see what he wor- shipped. Therefore idols of any kind were to be destroyed and idolatrous worship overthrown. Having overthrown false gods there could still be a desire to set up holy places and sacred sites within the realm of Jehovah worship. So God established one place. " But unto the place which the Lord your God shall choose out of all your tribes to put His Name there, even unto His habita- tion shall ye seek, and thither thou shalt come " (vs. 5). This was understandable in those days, but does not apply today when the Church of Jesus Christ is worldwide. Hence it was that He said: " Woman, believe me, the hour cometh when ye shall neither in this mountain nor yet at Jerusalem worship the Father . . God is a Spirit, and they that worship Him must worship Him in spirit and in truth " (John iv. 21-24). Seeing we can no longer gather in one place geographically, God would have us gather in one place morally, and that is around the one and only revelation of Himself — the Bible. To abide here would deliver many souls from the " idols " of men's reasonings, theories and philosophies, and save them much sorrow of heart because of spiritual wandering.

Blood forbidden (Ch. xii.) God has put a dignity and a sacredness upon blood, for the life is in the blood. Life is some- thing man cannot create. God is the source of all life. Jesus said, " I am the Life ". Blood being the sacred thing it is, God required it for sin, " for without the shedding of Blood there is no remission for sin ". Not only was this the requirement of God but, later, it became the provision of God when He gave His only begotten Son. Jesus shed His Blood on Calvary so that now " The Blood of Jesus Christ, God's Son, cleanseth us from all sin ". The world rebels against this, only because they have no part in it. Nonetheless it remains eternal truth.

Idolaters and Abettors to Die (Ch. xiii.) When God gave to Moses the ten commandments, the first two were, " Thou shalt have no other gods before Me " and, " Thou shalt not make unto thee any graven image ", to which commandments He added a postscript — " For I am a jealous God ". This same jealousy for His Divine Right is manifested in this chapter, when He declared that, not only idolaters, but also those who enticed men to worship other gods, should be put to death. Any City responsible for, or allowing, idolatry was also to be punished. In the light of God's severe judgment and His declared attitude toward this sin, ought we not to be very careful lest we be entangled with any of the cults and isms of those who fail to accept the Divinity of Christ, and who worship according to their own interpretations! To worship Mary, to pray to the saints, to bow before an altar, to confess to men, are all contrary to the declared revelation of a jealous God.

Food restrictions (Ch. xiv.) May we quote from the Rev. J. Orr, M.A., B.D., in the *Pulpit Commentary* : " The symbolic traits observable in certain animals may have had to do with their rejection. We can see reason in the exclusion of creatures of cruel and rapacious habits, of those also in whose dispositions we trace a reflection of the human vices. It may be pushing the principle too far to seek recondite meanings in the chewing of the cud (meditation) and the dividing of the hoof (separation and walk) or in the possession of fins and scales in fishes (organs of advance and resistance). But a law impregnated with symbolism could scarcely reckon as clean a filthy and repulsive creature like the sow. The accursed serpent, the treacherous fox, the ravenous jackal, even had they been suitable for food in other respects, could scarcely on this principle have been admitted. The reptile tribes generally, and all tribes of vermin, were similarly unclean by a kind of natural brand. A lesson of seeing in the natural a symbol of the moral. Nature is a symbolic lesson book, daily open to our inspection.

" The distinction once ordained, and invested with spiritual significance, observance of it became to the Jews a sign and test of holiness. The general lesson taught is that of sanctification in the use of foods. Holiness, indeed, is to be carried into every sphere and act of life. Eating, however, is an act which, though on its animal side related to the grossest part of us, is yet, on the spiritual side, of serious religious import. It is the act by which we supply oil to the flame of life. It has to do with the maintenance of those vital functions by which we are able to glorify God in the body. There is thus a natural sacredness about food, and it is to be received and used in a sacred fashion. That it may be " clean " to us, it is to be " sanctified by the Word of God and prayer ", being ' received with thanksgiving of them which believe and know the truth ' (1 Tim. iv. 3-5). It is to be remembered, too, that in the sphere of the higher life, if not in the lower, clean and unclean are distinctions of abiding validity. Intellect, heart, spirit, etc. — the books we read, the company we keep, the principles we imbibe ".

Tithing (Ch. xiv.) In this chapter it relates to the field because they were mostly an agricultural people, but we must appreciate that the " seed " of our future prosperity is in our income and that our " field " is the office, the shop, the factory, the place of our livelihood. God expects that from our increase we shall set apart a tithe for the Lord. " And the Levite that is within thy gates ; thou shalt not forsake him ". One knows of some churches that are so missionary minded, and boast so much about their missionary budget, that they forget the preacher within their own gates ! Some of us have been the victims of this forgetfulness. Both must come within the practical interests of the child of God.

The Year of Release (Ch. xv.) This release came every seven years when the debtor was released. This portion of the law could suffer much abuse if not properly understood. If it were a matter of all debts being cancelled two dangers would be created. The first, many unscrupulous people would seek to borrow all they could in the sixth year against the cancellation of the seventh year. This, in turn, would create the second danger, that of the rich man becoming wise and lending nothing in the sixth year because of no return. This would make it difficult for the poor and honest man who really needed to borrow. But such is not the law. The word " release " in the Hebrew comes from a word that means " to leave, to let lie fallow ", and is used only here and in Exodus xxiii. 11. " But the seventh year thou shalt LET IT REST and lie still ". The thought is that the debt was not cancelled but allowed to rest for that year.

As God required that in this year the land was to rest, that no harvest was to be taken from it, this might prove a little hard upon the poorer people who, with lower incomes, might not be able to meet their commitments. In these circumstances the rich people must not press their due but allow them to " rest " also, so that they could be made good at a later date. Honesty is a principle of Scripture, so the poor man is not totally relieved. He is expected to pay his way and not to owe any man anything. On the other hand, the Bible teaches us to be long-suffering with the poor and generous in our liberality, remembering that God has been long-suffering with us and forgiven us our debts.

Sanctification of the Firstborn (Ch. xv.) Just another reminder that firstfruits of everything belong to God. Man was not permitted to trade with, nor profit by, anything that belonged to God. The firstborn of the animal had to be sanctified to the Lord. Later it would become a Love Feast but, in the meantime, the bullock was not to be worked nor the sheep sheared. No compromise, says God, but absolute honesty. Oh, that we might learn so to live !

The Great Feasts (Ch. xvi.) A reminder to this new genera-tion now coming into the Land that three times in the year they must go up to the place of God's choosing to keep the Feasts — Passover, Pentecost, and Tabernacles. These three journeys embraced all seven Feasts. We must not fail to discharge our spiritual duties and responsibilities at all times.

Judges and Justice (Ch. xvi.). Here is again a plea for honesty. It is to be exercised in moral conduct as well as in material possessions. Bribery of any kind is condemned.

Groves Forbidden (Ch. xvi.) The section which concerned their religious life commenced in chapter xii. with one place for worship, and the forbidding of idols. It closes with the very same command.

(c) JUDICIAL LAW (Chs. xvii-xxvi.)

Sundry Laws (Chs. xvii-xxv.) These Laws can only be summarised. It would take a volume to enter into the detail. Nothing is left to chance. The weak man and the wronged person are protected and provided for ; whilst the evil-doers and the un-scrupulous are dealt with according to their conduct. The standard of these laws is high, and the Christian under Grace ought not to fall short of God's standard. It is of special interest to note the little things for which God makes provision — the neighbour's landmark — the battlements — the unequal yoke — borrowed goods. We have a slogan that says : " Take care of the pence and the pounds will take care of themselves ". In the language of the Christian the maxim would be : " Take care of the little things of conduct, the big things will take care of themselves ".

Is this not where we fail — those little details that make or mar
our testimony ?   The little foxes that spoil the vine !

Other details included in these Laws relate to war, siege,
murder, manslaughter, prisoners, inheritance, firstborn, stubbornness, humanity, adultery, fornication, uncleanness, fugitives,
divorce, pledges, man-stealers, leprosy, lending, hire, justice,
charity, immodesty, unjust weights, etc., etc.

In fact these Laws were the foundation of the legal system
of both Great Britain and the United States. Unfortunately one
says they *were*, because in recent years we have begun to move
away from many of them as we abolish Capital Punishment, sanc-
tion divorce, overlook adultery and fornication, by calling it sex
appeal, whilst our nations morally and spiritually decline as a
result.

Firstfruits (Ch. xxvi.)   Moses came back to this subject
again and again. " When thou art come into the land which the
Lord thy God giveth thee " (vs. 1).   This is different from the
Feast of Firstfruits of Leviticus.   There they brought a sheaf and
waved it before the Lord.   Here they brought the first of all the
fruit of the earth, and put it in a basket, and set it down before
the altar.   The Feast of Firstfruits was an annual Feast ordered
by God.   It was a memorial and acknowledged God's right to
everything.

Personally one would question the evidence of this offering
of Deut xxvi. being an annual thing.   This is not the first of the
harvest, but the first of all the fruit of the earth upon Israel's
possession of the Promised Land, the reason for this particular
ceremony being an acknowledgment of their own unworthiness
to be the possessors of anything.   " A Syrian ready to perish was
my father, and he went down into Egypt, and sojourned there
with a few . . .   And the Lord brought us forth out of Egypt with
a mighty hand . . . and hath brought us into this place, and hath
given us this land . . . And now, behold, I have brought the firstfruits of the land, which thou, O Lord, hast given me " (Ch. xxvi.
5-11).   The Feast of Firstfruits in Leviticus seems to be the recognition of God and His rights, the firstfruits of the land seem to be
a confession of man's own unworthiness.   As they gave the first
of the fruit when they entered the Land so also they gave the
first City — Jericho — when they entered.   (See comment on
Josh. vi. 17-18).

Tithing (Ch. xxvi.)   Once every three years they had to
check their giving and make confession to God that they had
fulfilled His commands and discharged their responsibilities in

relationship with their tithes, which were used for the maintenance of the Levites, who had no other inheritance ; also in the provision for the poor, the widow, and the stranger. When all was in order God and man entered into a covenant for future blessing.

(3) THE FUTURE — PROPHETICAL — A REVELATION (Chs. xxvii-xxx.)

This section is really a demonstrated ratification. It is one thing for God to give a Law and for Moses to pass it on to the people. It is another thing for the people to accept a Law and its responsibilities. Man sometimes tries to hide behind an idea that if a thing is not accepted, it cannot be used as a basis of reward or punishment. God, therefore, had all the people gathered together, whilst on Mount Ebal and Mount Gerizim great stones were covered with plaster and the Law inscribed thereon. (Not an uncommon thing in those days). An altar was then erected of whole stones which had never been tooled. This was according to Exodus xx. 25.

The nation was then divided. Representatives of six tribes stood on Mount Girizim to bless the people. These were Simeon, Levi, Judah, Issachar, Joseph, and Benjamin, all sons of Rachael and Leah, the lawful wives of Jacob. On Mount Ebal were the representatives of the other six tribes who were to utter the curses. These were Gad and Asher, the sons of Zilpah, a handmaid, Dan and Naphtali, the sons of Bilhah, also a handmaid, Zebulun, the youngest son of Leah, and Reuben, the man who forfeited his birthright.

Before these mountains were the Ark of the Covenant and the Priests (Joshua viii. 33).

Starting with Ebal, the mount of cursing for disobedience, the Laws were read one at a time, with the declaration of judgment for disobedience, and Law by Law all the people were to say Amen. Likewise was there a declaration of blessing for obedience. Thus were these Laws ratified.

The conclusion of this setting forth of the Law is marked by the words of Moses : " See, I have set before thee this day life and good, and death and evil ; . . . I call heaven and earth to record this day against you, that I have set before you life and death, blessing and cursing : therefore choose life, that both thou and thy seed may live " (Ch. xxx. 15-19).

(4) CONCLUSION (Chs. xxxi.-xxxiv.)

These chapters record the resignation of Moses from that long life of successful leadership and faithful ministry toward a rebellious and a murmuring generation of people. It includes his last words to Israel, his last song of praise to God, his last blessings bestowed upon the twelve tribes, and then his death.

His last words (Ch. xxxi.) These were words of exhortation and challenge to the people to be strong and of a good courage, to press forward to complete victory. He then encouraged his successor, Joshua, assuring him that he was about to take the people across the Jordan into the Land of Promise. He wrote the Law and delivered it to the priests to carry with them. The whole emphasis of these concluding words of Moses is the importance of the Word of God, a Word that must go with them, be read by them, and obeyed in all succeeding generations.

Moses' Song (Ch. xxxii.) This song commenced with praise to God, He Who is stable in His character — the Rock, perfect in His works, just in all His ways, and true in all His dealings. His blessings were continually poured out upon His people in delivering, leading and providing. It moved on to the faithlessness of the people who provoked Him to jealousy by turning to other gods, thus bringing forth the vengeance of God. But at the last His mercy will override His anger !

At the end of this song God bade Moses climb Mount Nebo, for there he must die because of his failure at Meribah. Nonetheless whilst he could not enter the Land, the Lord was going to grant him the privilege of seeing it.

Before climbing the mountain Moses farewelled the people as he bestowed his final benediction in the form of

Blessing the Twelve Tribes (Ch. xxxiii.) Beautiful are these meditations which must be read with the blessings bestowed upon the sons of Jacob before they enlarged to become tribes. (See Gen. xlix.). After the individual blessing there came a collective benediction that many of us have sought to claim in our day and generation for the comfort of its security. " The eternal God is thy refuge and underneath are the everlasting arms " (Ch. xxxiii. 27).

The book concludes with what is possibly an appendix, as it is an account of

The Death of Moses (Ch. xxxiv.) There seems something tragic about this chapter as we watch an old warrior, 120 years of age, yet still full of vigour " for his eye was not dim, nor his natural force abated ", climbing Mount Nebo to die a lonely death. But death is tragic at any time and in any circumstances. Death is diametrically opposed to life. God is the source of life and sin is the cause of death. It is, therefore, something that is unnatural.

Then, when we think of the solitary figure climbing alone, we are moved with compassion. But is not death always a lonely thing ? The death chamber may be full of friends, weeping, praying, comforting, but alone man slips out of this life. We brought nothing into the world and we take nothing out. What a consolation to know the companionship of the Saviour at such an hour !

But, surely, this was a punishment too severe for the nature of the offence compared with the faithfulness of the service rendered by Moses ? This is where we must be very careful, and pray : " Lord, guard Thou the words of my lips ". So soon as we suggest that a punishment is too severe we find ourselves charging God with a miscarriage of justice, and this cannot be, for He is Just and Holy. What do we mean by too great a punishment ? What was the punishment ? God took from him no eternal reward. His salvation was not affected. What was it that he lost ? Just one earthly desire, that was all — the desire to enter the Land. But do any of us see the fulfilment of all our desires ? I think not.

All that really happened was that an old warrior, who had engaged in a long battle and had suffered many heartbreaks because of the failures of the people he had led, and had seen many victories for his Master, entered into his well-earned rest, and received his crown of reward, a few days earlier than he had expected — that is not punishment ! Of course, there was the tinge of human disappointment, but then he had sinned against God. Someone still may reason against it and say — Surely God could have forgiven him ? Yes, and He did, but we must realise that even sin can be relative and can change its dimension according to relationships. We sometimes say — the greater the privilege the greater the responsibility — that is relative. Watch your shadow ! Here it is small and insignificant, there it is large and forbidding It just depends on the relationship of the light with the substance. The drop of oil that falls on the engineer's overalls whilst he works, scarcely costs him a thought. But let that same drop of oil fall on the bride's dress on the morning of her wedding and it would be a tragedy of the first order — just relative !

Even so, what may be termed a failure on the part of some ordinary person becomes a great offence in the life of a man like Moses. Christian worker, watch that conduct of yours. You are a leader. You tell other people what God expects. You tell them what they ought to do. Precept and practice must go together. Failure on your part may prove disastrous to that weaker brother's faith.

The last thought from the end of the life of this mighty servant of God is — so near, and yet so far! He led them out but was unable to lead them in. That privilege became the lot of another man — Joshua.

Moses never finished, but the world is full of unfinished symphonies — songs unfinished, books without a conclusion, objectives not accomplished, work not completed. I trust that when I reach the end of life and the Lord calls me to my reward I shall still have the longing to preach one more sermon, to write one more book, to bring a blessing to one more soul, to serve my Master one more day. It would be a tragedy to be finished rather than to be unfinished. May we ever have the desire that, when life's journey comes to an end, our service rendered for the Master shall be so well done that, like Moses, we shall leave the unfinished task in such a way that it will be easy for our successor to pick it up, so that the work will go on unhindered by our removal, as it did with Joshua.

JOSHUA

MAN POSSESSING

"Every place that the sole of your foot shall tread upon, that have I given unto you." (JOSHUA i. 3)

"And truly, if they had been mindful of that country from whence they came out, they might have had opportunity to have returned. But now they desire a better country, that is, an heavenly: wherefore God is not ashamed to be called their God: for He hath prepared for them a City."
(HEB. xi. 15-16)

INTRODUCTION

Leaving behind the Pentateuch one moves on into the second section of the Bible, and yet it is not a section.

J. Sidlow Baxter points out that this book is not strictly a continuation of the Pentateuch. It is more an introduction to the books yet to come, and yet there is a sense in which it is a continuation, not in principle but in narrative. Yet again there is a sense in which the book stands alone, a link between the past and the future, between Law and History. It stands in a similar position to that of the Acts of the Apostles in the New Testament. Neither the Pentateuch nor the Gospel were written as history, although they contain histories. The first gives the origin of the Hebrew religion — the second the beginning or the foundation of the Christian faith. History is used to illustrate meaning and origin. Joshua begins the history of the Nation. Acts commences the history of the Church. In both cases it is Faith and Practice.

THE MAN

Joshua had been aide-de-camp to Moses over the years. He is introduced soon after the Children of Israel started their journey from Egypt, when Moses instructed him to fight against Amalek whilst he went to the mountain top to pray for victory (Exodus xvii. 9). Joshua accompanied him to the top of Sinai when God gave the tables of stone (Exodus xxiv. 13), and returned with him at the time the people made the golden calf

99

(Exodus xxxii. 17). He ministered in the Tabernacle (Exodus xxxiii. 11 ; this was prior to the Tabernacle Moses built with which we are familiar and prior to the establishment of the Priesthood). He was also one of the twelve spies which went to Jericho (Num. xiii. 8). With Caleb, he was one of the only two of that generation who entered the Promised Land. A man who knew both Moses and Moses' God. A man who had been faithful in small things, now God was going to make him ruler over much.

Joshua introduced the land God had promised to Abram, the land to which Moses had led the people, the land that now lies before them for possession.

THE BOOK

It opens with God's commission to Joshua. "Moses My servant is dead ; now therefore arise". That is when most of us want to sit down and give up in despair. They had looked to Moses for guidance for years, now he had gone. Once before he had taken his departure from them and gone to the top of Sinai for forty days, and they had cried : "We wot not what has become of Moses", but he returned from Sinai with new inspiration and more insight. Now he had gone to the top of Nebo, never to return. The people could have said 'If ever we needed Moses it is now! This is where our battles are really beginning. We give up, we cannot go on without him'. Many a person has sunk into this dismay when some leader has been taken from their midst. They want to sit and mourn their loss. They want to spend their time in talking of the past — what it used to be. God would challenge you — "Moses, My servant, is dead ; now therefore arise, go over this Jordan, thou, and all this people, unto the land which I do give to them, even to the children of Israel". God may remove His workers but the work must go on. God may take His Moses, but the God of Moses is still with us to lead through whatever servant He may choose.

The book divides itself into three parts. Graham Scroggie names them :

1) Entering the Land   Chapters i. - v.

2) Conquering the Land   Chapters vi. - xii.

3) Possessing the Land   Chapters xii. - xxiv.

This is an important analysis and in itself should have a great impact. Many people have entered into salvation which comes by an act of faith in the finished work of Christ. But are we conquering ? The Christian experience is one that is beset with problems and difficulties. We are Christ's but we are still living in this world even though we are not of it. Satan is still the god of this world, so there are still enemies to subdue, and the greatest enemy is self. We should be dead to self — but are we? Have we conquered our love for this world, and its cares and riches which, like the thorns in the parable of the Sower, can choke the seed as soon as it springs up?

Then we must possess. When we possess we can give the instructions. The Land becomes subservient to us. Are you possessing your spiritual inheritance? Are all the promises yea and amen to you? Are you enjoying the fruit of the Spirit? Are you using the gifts of the Spirit? Do you know the peace of God that passeth all understanding? Is yours a life of complete surrender to Him and of complete victory for Him? If not, you have not yet possessed your possessions. This is vital because, unless we learn this life of victory as revealed in Joshua, we may find ourselves falling into a life of Anarchy as declared in Judges. Anarchy is " every man doing that which is right in his own eyes ", and, obviously, that belongs to the person who is not doing that which is right in the eyes of the Lord.

(1) ENTERING THE LAND (Chs. i-v.)

The first two chapters of this section are given to

Preparation (Ch. i.) This is an essential to accomplishment. Years of preparation had to precede D-Day if the invasion of Europe were to be a success. Years of preparation are spent in the drawing office of the architect before the foundations of a great building are laid or the keel of a mighty ocean-going liner is laid. Years pass whilst we wait for that new highway, not because the authorities are indifferent to the need, but because the surveyors are at work, the plans are being made, the materials are being prepared.

The Lord has gone to prepare a place for us such as eye hath not seen nor ear heard. Not only the place for us, but there must be some preparation of us for the place. All our testings and trials here are the preparing of the gold, silver, and precious stones for reward there.

Firstly, there was the preparation of the leader. Twice Joshua was commanded to be strong and of a good courage. He needed strength of faith and courage of action. He must trust the Divine Leader to Whom he must always be subservient. This Joshua proved when put to the test in chapter v. As he stood before Jericho a man stood by him with a drawn sword. Not

knowing the stranger the Captain immediately made the challenge
— 'Who goes there?' — or, "Art thou for us, or for our
enemies?"; to which came the unexpected reply of "Nay". "I
am not for you, you are for me. Joshua, you are not the Captain
in this battle. This is not going to be your strategy but the Lord's
supremacy" — and straightway Joshua yielded as he fell on his
face to the earth, and did worship, and said : "What saith my
Lord unto His servant ? "

Joshua is also encouraged to have, to hold, and to keep, the
Book of the Law. This was to be his regulations. He must
meditate therein day and night. We, as the servants of God, have
with our commission the Bible as our book of regulations, and
must abide by the instructions therein. Joshua accepted his responsibility unwaveringly and entered into his task whilst the people
accepted Joshua.

Secondly, the army had to be prepared. This was done in
the form of a reconnaissance. Maintaining the morale of an army
is important. Joshua sent two spies to Jericho, who returned
declaring that the morale of the people in the City had collapsed.
This strengthened the hands of Israel and they were ready to go
forward.

In the City of Jericho was found one woman with faith in
God. It was not a faith that could save a City but it was a faith
that could bring salvation to her soul and, wherever God finds
that faith, He responds to it, independent of race or colour. Rahab,
like Ruth, found her way into the life of Israel. She is mentioned
as a heroine of faith in Hebrews xi., showing that the grace of
God bringeth salvation to all men.

With all preparation made, now comes

D-Day (Ch. iii.) — crossing the Jordan. The Ark of the
Covenant led the way by two thousand cubits, or three quarters
of a mile. We may share with the Lord in service as "workers
together with God", but we can never share in leadership. That
is His alone. A distance was between the Ark and the people
in travel, as a vail was between them in encampment. The Holiness of God must always be recognised and His Majesty acknowledged.

When the children of Israel left Egypt one stroke of the rod
of Moses and the waters parted — a picture of salvation. But
when they came to entering Canaan it was a step by step walking
into the water, and so the waters parted. This is the walk of
faith. God has never promised to remove all obstacles, thus
making life to become plain sailing, but He has promised to give

us grace to meet the problems, and ofttimes it is the act of obedience that becomes the fulcrum that removes the thing we often fear.

Upon entering the Land the Pillar of cloud and fire that had led them in the wilderness was withdrawn. The Ark which had been in the midst of the twelve tribes was moved to the front and now led. As we move on in experience God may at times change His method of leading, but He never fails to lead. Not only did the Pillar cease to go before, but the Manna that had come so regularly every day of those forty years ceased. " And the manna ceased on the morrow after they had eaten of the old corn of the Land ; neither had the children of Israel manna any more " (v. 12). The manna did not cease the day before but the morrow after, so creating an overlap that took them in. The Manna of God's Word will not only be our portion unto death, but through death and into His Presence where we shall eat of " hidden manna ". (This last statement is application, not interpretation. One is not suggesting that Canaan represents heaven. It does not. There are no battles to be fought in heaven, no enemies to subdue. Heaven is rest and reward, not service and struggle).

Gilgal (Chs. iv. and v.). These chapters are a reminder not to forget to set up our memorials as a testimony to God's goodness. " Lest we forget ". " Gilgals " need not be erected in stones. We sometimes read autobiographies which are men's Gilgals. They mark God's goodness and stand there as an encouragement to someone else who may be walking the same rugged way. Let us put on record, by deed or testimony, what God has done for us. It may help another saint in like circumstances.

Reference has been made to two things that ceased upon entering the Land — the pillar of guidance and the manna. These chapters tell of two things that were re-established : (1) Circumcision ; (2) Passover. These had gone temporarily into abeyance because in the desert neither had been practical, but now they are practical the people must not be neglectful of God's requirements. Let us be watchful that the emergencies of life which cause temporary changes do not become permanent steps toward a condition of backsliding.

If one cannot read his Bible when very sick that is no excuse not to read it as soon as he is well enough. Because a Government compels a person to work on a Sunday because of a war, or a national emergency, that gives him no permission to do such things when the emergency has passed. It may be right to take an animal out of the ditch if he fall into it on the Sabbath Day, but that does not give permission to push the animal in so that it may be taken out. We must ever watch our conduct.

(2) CONQUERING THE LAND (Chs. vi-xii.)

This is a series of glorious victories and yet with some defeats because of failure caused by disobedience on the part of the people. *Jericho* (Ch. vi.) — the City they had spied out thirty-eight years earlier. Then they said the walls were to heaven and the inhabitants giants. True, it was a strong City, but unbelief always exaggerates. " We be not able " was their cry, but here it is right before them. God never removes these tests of faith. He will increase the faith but not lessen the test. Not only did the fortification still stand as formidable as ever, but their inability was still the same. They were about to learn that God was going to fight this battle, and He could and would have fought it before if they had allowed Him. Beloved, it is true, it always will be true — we be not able, but faith is well able. Let us stand still and see the salvation of God.

" And ye shall compass the city, all ye men of war, and go round about the city once. Thus shalt thou do six days. And seven priests shall bear before the Ark seven trumpets of ram's horns ; and the seventh day ye shall compass the city seven times, and the priests shall blow with the trumpets " (vs. 3 and 4). But this was not logical. Of course not — if it were, men could explain it, but if it were illogical and it worked, then men must give glory to God. The whole of the life of the Spirit operates that way. Obedience is victory.

The marching around this city so many times should not create a problem. It only covered seven acres. It was really an outpost, or a fortification. This was revealed when Prof. John Garstang unearthed Joshua's Jericho a few years ago. It was also revealed that the whole of the City had been burned with fire. This is not only in accord with Scripture (vi. 24), but was according to the requirement of God. In verse 17 the statement is " And the city shall be accursed, even it, and all that are therein, to the Lord ". The word " accursed " is corrected in the margin to its Hebrew meaning, " devoted ". The way men would devote a thing to God would be to offer it upon the altar of sacrifice. When we realise that this was the first city that God had given them, we can see that God was requiring that they should devote the very first city to Himself ; then the rest would be the portion of the people. It is but another example of God asking for the firstfruits, for a tithe of all we possess, firstborn of man and beast,

firstfruits of harvest, first day of the week, the first of our money
and possessions.

Ai (Chs. vii. and viii.) This was the place of defeat, a place
of many spiritual truths. Why were the people defeated ? Most
of us appreciate that it was because of secret sin — the stolen
and hidden garment, gold and silver. But it was even more.
This sin was not in Joshua, the Captain. It was not committed by
one of the Officers, but by one ordinary common soldier. Yet
it brought defeat to the whole army of Israel. Have you ever
thought that one secret sin in the life of one ordinary member of
the Church can bring defeat to the whole Church of Jesus Christ ?
When there is lack of victory and accomplishment in the Church,
when souls are not being saved, it is easy to look to the leaders
and wonder whether there is fault with minister or deacons, when
the cause may be in you because you have a secret sin, and God
is going to search you out.

Another lesson is one of selfish misappropriation. God had
said : " And the city shall be devoted, even it, and all that are
therein, to the Lord " (vs. 17). This man, therefore, took that which
belonged expressly to the Lord. Shall a man rob God ? God
has required certain things of us. He asks for worship, for obedience, for a day in seven. He asks for a surrendered life, for
tithes and offerings, and many other things. To steal these things
secretly or openly, to take the *Lord's* Day and use it for *our*
pleasure, to take the *Lord's* money and use it for *our* comfort, is
to bring defeat to the whole work of God. When the sin was
removed the blessing of the Lord returned.

Gibeon (Ch. ix.) Moving forward in conquest Joshua was
caught off guard. The Gibeonites, hearing of the successes of
Israel and fearing that they would succumb to this people, played
a role of deception. They came to Joshua posing to be a people
who had come a very great journey. Their request was that
Joshua should make a league with them that they might live.
Whilst Joshua had a suspicion that they might be neighbours and
raised that question with them, yet he failed to consult God on
the matter but bound himself and the nation to these people by
a vow — " he sware unto them " (vs. 15). He learned afterwards
that he had been deceived. How often we make the same mistake
of not consulting God in prayer.

The Church has many enemies within her midst, false cults,
isms, and creeds, that ought to have been destroyed but, instead,
we are giving them room, and in many instances even offering
them fellowship. Let us beware of all the unions, counsels, and

organisations that men are seeking to establish for what they call
a united front in the Church. The Lord said : " Come ye out
from among them and be ye separate ".

We have already learned that vows can be dangerous things
(see Leviticus). This Joshua was yet to learn.

Beth-Horon (Ch. x.)   The story here is so well known, how
the Lord wrought one of His mightiest miracles in causing the sun
to stand still in the heavens whilst a battle was fought to a
victorious conclusion, but it has not always been noticed that this
miracle was not performed for God's people Israel, but for the
deceitful Gibeonites.   When Adonizedec heard of the league made
between the Gibeonites and Israel he thought to destroy Gibeon
before this link became too strong.   Therefore he gathered four
other kings into an alliance to fight against Gibeon.   Gibeon, who
had feared being overwhelmed by Israel, was now the victim of
another powerful army.   They appealed for help from Israel and
Israel must give it because they were under an obligation to help
by virtue of the vow they had established.   So again we are taught
that vows must be honoured before anything else.

The chapter concludes with the conquering of twelve other
kings, thus completing victory over the south.

Joshua's military strategy seems to have been the one used
by Generals in modern warfare.   He drove a wedge, split the
enemy into two, captured the cities of the south firstly, then turned
to the North, and so on to

Meon (Chs. xi. and xii.)   He found the north a stiffer proposition, but one by one the enemy was subdued as God had
promised, until at last all of the country had been taken and
thirty-one kings had been subdued.   " And the land rested from
war " (xi. 23).

(3) POSSESSING THE LAND (Chs. xiii-xxiv.)

This is a great essential.   We have had to keep an army of
occupation in Germany, in Japan, and other places where there
has been conquest, otherwise the enemy would rise again for further
war.   In the Christian life whilst God, in Christ, has brought us
into a new life and bidden us conquer, yet it must be remembered
that our great enemy, Satan, although subdued, is still alive, still
active, and longs to rise again.   Therefore we must possess.   We
must lay hold of the promises of God and allow them to be fulfilled
in our lives.   We must live in the fulness of His life.   God has
given us a Book.   Of what value is it if it remains a closed Book ?

" Now Joshua was old and stricken in years ; and the Lord
said unto him, Thou art old and stricken in years, and there re-

maineth yet very much land to be possessed " (xiii. 1). We shall
never have possessed everything so long as we remain in this life.
Even down to old age, the incentive should remain — to possess.
East of Jordan (Ch. xiii.)   The two and a half tribes had
made a request for their inheritance, and it had been granted by
Moses in the days before they crossed the Jordan. Whilst it was
granted to them it was on the understanding that they could not
take possession until they had fought with the rest of their brothers
and all the territory had been conquered. That day had now come,
so Reuben, Gad, and Manasseh returned to their possessions.

West of Jordan (Chs. xiv-xix.)   This was divided by lot.
Judah was the first to receive. He had always had first place.
He led in the journeyings — now he leads in possession. Caleb
belonged to this tribe, and he made a special request. He reminded
Joshua that when he was forty years old he was one of the spies
who went in from Kadesh Barnea to spy out the Land, and that
at that time he was not swayed by the unbelief of the ten but that
" I wholly followed the Lord my God. And Moses sware on that
day, saying, Surely the land whereon thy feet have trodden shall
be thine inheritance and thy children's for ever . . . I am this day
fourscore and five years old. As yet I am as strong this day as I
was in the day that Moses sent me : . . . Now therefore give me
this mountain " (xiv. 8-12). Some of the promises of God are
for us to possess in our youth. Some of them we cannot claim
until the time of old age but, when the time comes and the promises
mature, let us. like Caleb, claim them and they will be ours.

Caleb, in his desire for inheritance, offered his daughter as
a reward to the man who would accept his challenge and take
Kirjath Sepher. Othniel did this and received his reward — Achsah.
She in turn made a request of her father. She had land but she
wanted springs of water. She, too, received her request — " Ask
and ye shall receive ". God has offered His only begotten Son
to men as a reward of faith, and Jesus has requested for us springs,
the waters of blessing and the waters of His Holy Spirit, to make
fruitful our spiritual inheritance — all things are yours, only
believe !

The next divisions went to the children of Joseph — Ephraim
and Manasseh (Chs. xvi. and xvii.), Benjamin (Ch. xviii.), Simeon,
Zebulun, Issachar, Asher, Naphtali, Dan (Ch. xix.).

After each tribe had received, then came some allocations
within the tribes. Joshua received a small portion of rough territory within his own tribe — Ephraim. Here he built up Timnath-
serah, and quietly spent his remaining days.

The Cities of Refuge (Ch. xx.)   Six cities were set apart for
the manslayer. Three were on each side of Jordan. They were
well distributed so that the man who slew his neighbour unwittingly
might flee and find refuge from the avenger of blood. The cities
were Kedesh, Shechem, Hebron, Bezer, Ramoth, and Golan. No
sanctuary could be provided for the murderer. He was wilful
in his crime and must die according to law.

From a casual reading of the death of Jesus it would appear
that the Jewish nation took Him and crucified Him in cold-blooded
murder. They refused to accept His teaching. They listened to
the voice of their rulers. They shouted in unison : " Away with
Him, crucify Him ", and again : " His Blood be upon us and upon
our children ". For the murderer there was no sanctuary. Therefore the whole nation would be under the condemnation of death.
But God in His mercy delivered them from the guilt of murder
by charging them with an act of manslaughter, the Lord saying :
" Father, forgive them : they know not what they do " (Luke
xxiii. 34). Peter established the same fact of ignorance when he
told them : " And now, brethren, I wot that through ignorance
ye did it, as did also your rulers " (Acts iii. 17). Paul, in turn,
confirmed their position : " Which none of the princes of this
world knew : for had they known it, they would not have crucified
the Lord of glory " (1 Cor. ii. 8).

As a manslayer this nation has been persecuted through the
years, but God has provided for her a ' city of refuge ' against
the final judgment. This is found in Isaiah xxvi. 20 : " Come,
my people, enter thou into thy chambers, and shut thy doors about
thee : hide thyself as it were for a little moment, until the indignation be overpast ".

The Cities of Levi (Ch. xxi.)   These were claimed by the
children of Levi after all the tribes had received their portions.
Levi had no inheritance in the Land, having been separated for
the work of the ministry. Those tribes who did receive gave from
their allocation cities for this one tribe. As soon as we receive
from the Lord there comes a giving back of a portion to the Lord.
The family of the Kohathites received twenty-three cities from
Judah, Simeon, Benjamin, Ephraim, Dan, and the half tribe of
Manasseh. The family of the Gershonites received thirteen cities
from Issachar, Asher, Naphtali, and the half tribe of Manasseh.

The family of the Merarites received twelve cities from
Reuben, Gad, and Zebulun. In all there were forty-eight cities.
The people who are set apart by God for service in holy things

have to be maintained by those to whom they minister. This is the teaching of both the Old and the New Testament.

The Levites were thus scattered throughout the twelve tribes so that their ministry was enjoyed by all, and also they were near to hand to minister to the people according to their need. The Church of the New Testament, which found its inception in Jerusalem, was soon scattered by persecution, so that they went everywhere preaching the Word. The *greatest* blessings of the Christian life are not found in the fellowship of the Church within but in the testimony and service of the life without.

(4) CONCLUSION (Chs. xxii-xxiv.)

The two and a half tribes return (Ch. xxii.)

The Land was now conquered and possessed, therefore the two and a half tribes, who had made an early claim on the east side of Jordan, might return. Having obeyed the Lord's command by helping their brethren in the conquest of the Land, they could now enjoy their own inheritance. So Joshua blessed them and they went their way. Upon reaching the river Jordan they had to cross it, for their inheritance was on the other side. Now they realised that they had made a mistake earlier. They had been in too much of a hurry. They had requested that this good pasture should be theirs. As they crossed the river a fear struck them. Maybe in the process of time this river might be looked upon as a boundary line, that everything and everyone east of it might become alienated. They had decided too quickly and had not exercised sound judgment. This often happens. The first little blessing and some Christians say — ' This is enough, we are satisfied ', and the desire to go forward in spiritual things is insulated so that there comes a loss in spiritual power and possession.

Reuben, Gad, and Manasseh, fearing this possible severance from their own people, decided that something must be done. They conceived the idea that, if they built an altar on the east bank of the Jordan, which would be identical with the altar on the other side, then it would be a token of the fact that they were of the same faith. This they did but, when their brethren heard of it, they immediately prepared for war, saying : " What trespass is this that ye have committed against the God of Israel, to turn away this day from following the Lord, in that ye have builded you an altar, that ye might rebel this day against the Lord ? " (xxii. 16).

The two and a half tribes replied that there was no intention of rebellion. They had not erected the altar for worship. They never intended to offer a sacrifice, nor yet to kindle a fire. The only purpose of its existence was : " that it may be a witness between us, and you, and our generations after us, that we might do the service of the Lord . . . that your children may not say to our children in time to come, Ye have no part in the Lord " (xxii. 27). When Israel learned the facts, the war, which almost broke out between them, was averted. A tragedy almost hit the nation in the form of civil war because of the hasty judgment of brethren who failed to enquire and thereby find out the facts.

Beloved, is it not true that we sometimes make quick decisions on hearsay and judge our brethren in the Church, or in some organisation or denomination, without knowing the truth, ofttimes creating enmity and war within our own ranks when there should be a unity of the Spirit ?

The last two chapters are occupied with

A Farewell (Chs. xxiii. and xxiv.)   Joshua in his old age gathered together the elders, heads, judges and officers, to give them words of encouragement and exhortation. He reminded them of God's faithfulness and of what they had already possessed, assuring them that God would continue to give if they would continue to obey the law of God and keep themselves free from the contamination of the nations round about and their idolatrous worship. He concluded his exhortation with the words that have become precious to so many of us : " And, behold, this day I am going the way of all the earth : and ye know in all your hearts and in all your souls, that not one thing hath failed of all the good things which the Lord your God spake concerning you ; all are come to pass unto you, and not one thing hath failed thereof " (xxiii. 14).

Again Joshua gathered the elders (Ch. xxiv.), this time to give them a brief history of the past from the days of Terah, the father of Abram, when they were back in Mesopotamia, through the lives of Abram, Isaac, Jacob, Esau, Moses and Aaron, their deliverance out of Egypt and God's faithfulness in the desert, how He brought them into the Promised Land and subdued their enemies, establishing them in the Land. What a long history in a few verses !

How far can you go back in your testimony of the Lord's goodness ? Like Joshua we could go back to those days before the Lord called, whilst we were still in the world of sin. God was true to His Word then. " When we were dead in trespasses and sin Christ died for us ". He brought us out of the world into a new life. We could name the men whom God has brought into our lives in blessing and for spiritual leadership. We could tell of our journey through this world that became hostile and desert-like to us and of His faithfulness, and then of the way He led us into our spiritual possessions, building us up in our most holy faith and causing us to " Grow in grace and in the knowledge of our Lord and Saviour, Jesus Christ ", until we found ourselves in that life of fellowship and victory which is ours today, so that with confidence we can say : " As for me and my house we will serve the Lord " (xxiv. 15).

The people of Israel who had wandered from the Lord res-ponded to this challenge of Joshua. They agreed that God had been faithful and that they would serve Him, but Joshua said, ' No, not whilst there is any sin in your life '. God is holy and He is jealous and will accept no half-hearted yielding. He will accept no words of the lips unless the heart goes with the words they say. The people endorsed the challenge with a full surrender, and said : " Nay, but we will serve the Lord . . . and His voice will we obey ". Then was

The Covenant renewed, and a stone was set up by Joshua under an oak tree. The people bore witness to the covenant there made with God. If you, reader, have only been using your lips in your promises to God, know right now that it is all worthless and you have no victory, no joy, and no communion with a holy God until you know heart-surrender, which means complete surrender of all you are and have. Read this last chapter of Joshua again.

The death of Joshua. " And it came to pass after these things, that Joshua the son of Nun the servant of the Lord, died ", as all the servants of the Lord have died, but the work of the Lord goes on. Not only did Israel serve the Lord during Joshua's ministry but, as a result of this renewal of the covenant to which Joshua had challenged the people immediately before his death, the people went on serving the Lord for that generation.

The Burial of Joseph. When Joseph died, as is recorded in the last chapter of Genesis, he requested of his people that he should not be buried in Egypt. The day would come when God would deliver them from their bondage, when He would bring them to their own Land. Joseph's desire had been that they should bury him in that Land. The people complied with his wishes and, when he died, they embalmed him and put him in a coffin in Egypt. When Israel left Egypt at the exodus they took that coffin with them. For forty years they carried it through the wilderness. As they fought their way to victory in the Land of Promise they carried that coffin, and now that they were established they buried the bones of Joseph (for his body had long since disintegrated) in the same place as many of his forbears.

JUDGES

MAN IN REBELLION

*" In those days there was no king in Israel : every man did that
which was right in his own eyes."* (JUDGES xxi. 25)

INTRODUCTION

Moses had led the people out of Egypt and across the wilderness. It became Joshua's responsibility to lead them into the Land, and then to allocate to each tribe its own inheritance. The people being thus settled, Joshua's ministry was complete and the Lord had taken him home. The book of Joshua ended with God's people in blessing.

We are now introduced to the next period of Israel's history. "Now after the death of Joshua" (i. 1). God then elected to govern His people through the medium of Judges, hence the name of the book. These Judges were more than judicial. The word in the Hebrew language is wide in its meaning and suggests "To defend and deliver" as well as "to avenge and punish". This means that these men (and women) were deliverers as well as Judges.

The book as a whole reveals on the one side "The utter failure of Israel", and on the other side "The persistent grace of God".

The main portion of the book relates to *seven great apostasies,* followed by a period of *confusion and anarchy,* in which every man was doing that which was right in his own eyes, with no respect for law or order and no recognition of leadership, Divine or otherwise.

We have, therefore, as a study of the book —

Seven great apostasies, which brought to the people
Seven severe servitudes, when they became subjected to
Seven heathen nations, until they repented and God granted
Seven wonderful deliverances.

113

In this book are found a moral condition and a Divine patience that have remained in varying degrees throughout the history of mankind. The record is an amazing description of life as we find it in our own generation.

Scofield points out that "In the choice of the Judges is illustrated Zechariah's great words : ' Not by might, nor by power, but by My Spirit, saith the Lord of Hosts ' " (Zech iv. 6). This is true as it is noticed that

Othniel had no ability.

Ehud wielded a dagger.

Shamgar had an ox-goad.

Barak was favoured by a storm.

Gideon had to operate with three hundred men.

The source of the strength and ability of these men is found in the fact that of Othniel (iii. 10), Gideon (vi. 34), Jephthah (xi. 29), and Samson (xiv. 6 and 19), it is said : " And the Spirit of the Lord came upon him ".

God never has chosen men because of their exceptional wisdom nor their military might, their political ability, their skilful leadership, their scientific genius, nor yet their noble birth. God has always chosen very ordinary men — a shepherd from the flock, as Moses, David, or Amos — a plowman as Shamgar or Elisha — fishermen like Peter, John and Andrew — a mill-hand as David Livingstone — or the cobbler whose name was William Carey — and thousands more like them. " For ye see your calling, brethren, how that not many wise men after the flesh, not many mighty, not many noble, are called : but God hath chosen the foolish things of the world to confound the wise ; and God hath chosen the weak things of the world to confound the things which are mighty ; and base things of the world, and things which are despised, hath God chosen, yea, and things which are not, to bring to nought things that are : that no flesh should glory in His presence " (1 Cor. i. 26-29).

It has been pointed out that this Book is a *book of human character* — Ehud, Shamgar, Deborah, Barak, Gideon, Abimeleck, Jothan, Jephthah, Manoah, Samson, Micah, Benjamin, Othniel, Heber, Sisera, Jael. You may find every one of these characters in the world today.

Again, the Book is a *book of society*. For thousands of years Society has been on the brink of dissolution yet it never dissolves ; disputes, collisions, contentions, wars, never cease, and yet, amidst them all, there is constant progress. Society is always coming to the point of ruin yet always escaping it. Might is always rising above right, and yet right is ever prevailing.

With this as an introduction, we will survey the history. The nation was passing through a transitional period, a period always fraught with many dangers. They had no supreme leader, as Moses or Joshua had been. They had no king or central government, as the other nations around, for God was their King and His Law their governing factor, but the people were coming short in their relationship with their God.

His Laws were being rejected in an open rebellion. As a result of their idolatry and sin God was allowing the nations round about to attack them. Sometimes these were bands of plunderers, sometimes armies of soldiers, but these nations were increasingly becoming a menace to Israel. If there is one verse that will sum up the character of this book it is the unalterable Law of any nation at any time, " Righteousness exalteth a nation ; but sin is a reproach to any people " (Prov. xiv. 34).

The first two chapters concern a few battles with the enemy. Some of it is repetition of information already given by Joshua.

The first battle was against the Canaanites. These people had not been conquered nor their land possessed in the advances of Israel. Joshua tells this in his seventeenth chapter, for at the twelfth verse he says : " Yet the children of Manasseh could not drive out the inhabitants of those cities ; but the Canaanites would dwell in that land. Yet it came to pass, when the children of Israel were waxing strong, that they put the Canaanites to tribute ; but did not utterly drive them out ". It is true in Christian experience that some things remain in our lives as enemies that are not subdued in our early experience with the Lord, for reasons that we cannot always tell. But the day does come when the Lord does give us the victory. It could be our thorn in the flesh that maybe is caused to remain until we can learn how to be humble before the Lord. These Canaanites of Bezek were in the northern part of the territory. After this victory they fought them in the south. Othniel was the man who gained this victory. It has already been considered in Joshua xv.

However, the chapter goes on to relate that they did not complete all of their victories. They permitted certain of the people to remain in their midst. This was to be their undoing. The Lord reminded them that He had told them to make no league with the inhabitants of the Land but to throw down their altars (ii. 2). They had failed to do this and the Lord reproved them for not obeying His voice. This failure in not destroying

the altars became a stumbling block to the next generation (ii. 10),
who worshipped Baalim (ii. 11), and Baal (ii. 13), and Ashtaroth
(ii. 13). Their disobedience became the downfall of their children.
Maybe we would be more truthful if we were more honest and
confessed that our disobedience has become the downfall of our
children. We live in an age when youth is far removed from
God. We cannot altogether blame youth. We have permitted
things to remain in the world and to come into the Church which
we should have destroyed. These are the conditions that lead
us into the main section of the book at ii. 14-15. " And the anger
of the Lord was hot against Israel, and He delivered them into the
hands of spoilers that spoiled them, and He sold them into the
hands of their enemies round about, so that they could not any
longer stand before their enemies. Whithersoever they went out
the hand of the Lord was against them for evil, as the Lord had
said, and as the Lord had sworn unto them and they were greatly
distressed ".

Against this declaration of His judgment for sin the next
verse (16) is a display of His mercy toward the sinner. " Nevertheless the Lord raised up Judges which delivered them out of
the hand of those that spoiled them ". This mercy was spurned
again and again, as declared in the next verse (17). " And yet
they would not hearken unto their Judges ". The result was a
continual deterioration so that the last Judge, Samson, who was
the man most favoured, proved to be little better than those he
judged, ending his life in tragic disappointment. This brings us
to

The Seven Great Apostasies and the Judges (Chs. iii-xvi.)

The first enemy was MESOPOTAMIA. " Therefore the
anger of the Lord was hot against Israel, and He sold them into
the hand of Chushan-rishathaim, king of Mesopotamia ; and the
children of Israel served Chushan-rishathaim eight years " (iii. 8).
In the bitterness of their experience the children of Israel cried
unto the Lord, and He, Who is plenteous in mercy, heard their
cry and raised up a deliverer.

OTHNIEL (Ch. iii. 9-11) We are told very little about this man
other than " he was the son of Kenaz, Caleb's younger brother ",
but we have met him previously. Both in Joshua xv. 17 and
Judges i. 13 we learn that, when Caleb offered his daughter as a
reward to the man who would capture Kirjath-sepher, Othniel
accepted the challenge, captured the city and won his bride. The
man who could fight a battle to win a bride could be trusted to

fight a battle to save a nation. He did, and under his leadership
the nation enjoyed peace for forty years.

The name Othniel means " Lion of God ". He proved
worthy of his name. The only qualities this man had were, he
was *good* and he was *brave*. God is wanting good and brave men
today, men whom He can trust. Christian, if you have these
qualities God can use you to help bring peace on earth. Your
name is Christian. Are you a good representative of that name ?

Judgeship was not hereditary as is kingship so, when Othniel,
the first of the twelve Judges, died, there was no one to succeed
him. As a result of this the nation drifted back into sin until
God lifted another rod of chastisement. This time it was
MOAB with Eglon as its king. For eighteen years Israel served
this enemy. Eglon was demanding much from Israel. Every year
they had to bring a present to the king, probably of crops and
taxes. Again, in their distress, Israel repented and cried unto
the Lord, and once more He heard their cry and raised up another
deliverer,

EHUD (Ch. iii. 15-30)   This man was a son of Gera of the tribe
of Benjamin. The only characteristic about Ehud was that he
was left-handed. This might be considered against a man, especially
if he is to captain an army. Maybe it was not such a handicap
as one might think. It was a peculiarity that belonged to the tribe
of Benjamin which can be gathered from Ch. xx. 15-16. " And
the children of Benjamin were numbered at that time . . . among
all this people there were seven hundred chosen men left-handed ;
every one could sling stones at an hair breadth and not miss ".
This is an extraordinary statement when we remember that the
name Benjamin means " Son of my right hand ".

It was Ehud's peculiarity or his weakness that became his
strength and brought to his nation a victory. He was the man
who had to deliver to the king of Moab the present he required.
Before doing so Ehud made for himself a dagger and, being left-
handed, he placed it upon his right thigh. It is usually the habit
of authorities to examine a man for arms before he goes into
the presence of a king, and this was probably done but, naturally,
they would look to the left side for any such weapon. So it was
that Ehud entered into the presence of the king. After presenting
the gift to Eglon he asked for a private interview. Then he laid
hold of his dagger with his left hand and, with a powerful thrust,
slew the king and delivered Israel. Under this man's leadership
Israel had peace for eighty years.

Ehud carried both a present and a dagger. The present came first, then the fatal blow. There is something here that has a parabolic truth. We should come before men bringing to them the gift of eternal life. This is our privilege, but we should also carry with us the warning dagger of eternal damnation. We have not been given a one-sided message. It is one of life and death. We must teach love and judgment, heaven and hell. Says Paul : " For we are unto God a sweet savour of Christ, in them that are saved, and in them that perish. To the one we are a savour of death unto death ; and to the other the savour of life unto life " (2 Cor. ii. 15-16).

One verse only (iii. 31) is used to describe the next period. The PHILISTINES were the enemy who were attacking the people of God. There was no suggestion that they possessed them. We are told that

SHAMGAR (Ch. iii. 31) delivered Israel. What a wonderful battle that was. A ploughman was at work in the fields, engaged in his normal agricultural pursuits and, whilst following his oxen, a group of soldiers appeared. They may have been an advance guard, but they were making an attack on Israel. Shamgar considered the situation. Loyalty to his people surged in his veins — patriotism, that something we cannot define yet know so well, moved him to action. The only thing he possessed right there was the ox-goad that was in his hand, the implement with which he goaded on his animals. No one with any stretch of imagination would consider it a weapon of warfare. No armament council would ever approve its use in battle. But Shamgar knew that ox-goad. He knew its weight. He had handled it often and with it he moved forward with such a surprise attack that he scattered the Philistines and slew six hundred of them.

Modern Science and advanced education and all the pride of modern man will not give approval to the Word of God, yet that Word alone has the ability to solve the problems of society and bring us victory. Of course, no soldier could have fought the Philistines with an ox-goad. It was the right implement in the hand of the right man that accomplished such a notorious victory. The Bible in the hands of a politician or an educator will accomplish nothing. They know not how to handle it ; but the Bible in the hand and heart of a fully surrendered child of God, who knows the Book, loves the Book, and allows the Holy Spirit to interpret that Book, can drive back the enemy and bring deliverance to sin-sick souls.

In chapters four and five the nation was again doing evil in the sight of the Lord, so that the Lord sold them into the hand of Jabin, king of the CANAANITES for further chastisement. Things became very difficult during the twenty years that they oppressed Israel. It ceased to be safe on the highways. Caravans no longer travelled, so that people went on foot through the by-ways (v. 6). Seemingly the nation had neither shield nor spear for their protection (v. 8), whilst the Canaanites had nine hundred chariots of iron. In these circumstances Israel again cried to God for help (iv. 3), and the Lord intervened. This time He gave them a woman —

DEBORAH (Ch. iv. and v.). She was both a judge and a prophetess. Not able to lead the armies of Israel into battle, being a woman, she commissioned Barak to be the Captain and assured him of victory, but he declined declaring : " If thou wilt go with me then I will go, but if thou wilt not go with me then I will not go " (iv. 8).

Some people have referred to Barak as a coward who wanted the moral support of a woman. Somehow that is hard to accept. Would it not rather be that he was a man who was conscious that, like so many other men in Israel at that time, he was out of touch with God, had lost the ability to pray and to seek the Lord's guidance and counsel. Therefore he requested the presence of this prophetess to give him spiritual advice. It is an awful experience to feel that God has left you, because you have left Him. It leaves a man shorn of all strength and with a consciousness of utter weakness. Saul knew this. Deborah agreed to go, but informed the Captain that the coming victory would not be to his honour, but that it would go to a woman.

The battle lined up in that great Old Testament battlefield — the valley of the Kishon, also known as the Esdraelon Plain, and the Valley of Megiddo. It is a flat stretch between two mountain ranges with the River Kishon trickling its way through as an innocent stream, until a storm bursts. Then the waters come off the mountains on either side and the river quickly overflows its banks. This is what happened in this story. Deborah prayed, the clouds gathered, the storm broke, and the children of Israel turned from the defensive to the offensive, and won a glorious victory. Sisera, the captain of the armies of Jabin, fled on foot when his chariot, like the others, bogged in the flood. As he fled, climbing to higher ground, he came to the tent of Heber. Heber was away but his wife, Jael, offered the fugitive sanctuary at his request. Instead of being satisfied with her promised protection in THE tent (iv. 18 and iv. 20), he crept into HER tent (iv. 22), thus risking the life of the woman at the hand of her own husband for, should he return and find a man in HER tent, it would suggest some unholy relationship that would cause the husband to slay both, according to the law of Deut, xxii. 22. To save her own life and her own character Jael killed Sisera on that day of victories.

Chapters four and five of Judges must be read together, for much of the detail of the battle of chapter four is found in the song of chapter five.

For forty years Deborah governed the nation.

Back into sin, and God raised another enemy, the MIDIAN-ITES. They came in bands and plundered the land, carrying away harvests, cattle, tents, etc. For seven years they plundered until the land was greatly impoverished. Again Israel cried to the Lord and again He answered. One of the number was threshing his wheat in secret to hide it from the Midianites, when the Angel of the Lord appeared to him and addressed him as : "Thou mighty man of valour " — and so the story of

GIDEON (Chs. vi-viii.) Who of us is not familiar with this story of Gideon and his three hundred ! Of the battle that was won, not by might, nor power, nor skill, but by a faith and an obedience to the command of God !

The symbols of that victory were :

A Trumpet	.....	Testimony.
A Pitcher	.....	Self to be broken.
A Torch	.....	The flame of God's Spirit.
A Shout	.....	" The Sword of the Lord and of Gideon " which is the Sword of the Spirit.

Before Gideon entered into this battle he was very anxious to be sure that he was in the Will of God, as we should all be. He put God to the test, firstly with the wet fleece and then with the dry fleece, and God responded to Gideon's requests. He always will if we conscientiously seek His Will. John says : " Try the spirits whether they are of God " (1 John iv. 1). The Lord speaking through Malachi said : " Prove me now " (Mal. iii. 10).

Again the nation enjoyed forty years of peace under the leadership of Gideon. Then came those tragic words : " And it came to pass, as soon as Gideon was dead, that the children of

Israel turned again, and went a-whoring after Baalim, and made
Baal-berith their god. And the children of Israel remembered
not the Lord their God . . . " (viii. 33-34).

The period became one of CIVIL WAR, during which time
ABIMELECK (Ch. ix.), the son of Joshua, slew all of his brethren
save one, Jotham, and sought to reign. It was a period of fighting
one against another as different men sought authority. The
struggles occupy all of chapter nine.

Two other judges followed this period of Civil War, about
whom we know nothing. They were

TOLA (Ch. x.), who judged Israel for twenty-three years.

JAIR (Ch. x.), who judged Israel for twenty-two years.

The three men together covered a period of forty-eight years.
These years ended in a struggle against still another nation, the
AMMONITES, who distressed Israel. Again Israel cried for
mercy confessing that they had sinned, but these confessions are
often so false and selfish that they have no real sense of guilt. The
Lord reminded them, therefore, that they had done this many
times and He had intervened, only to see them forsake Him again
and again for other gods. Now He refused, and bade them seek
deliverance from the gods they served.

In these circumstances the people showed their earnestness
by forsaking their gods and serving the Lord so that His mercy
went out toward them.

At this time Israel had no leader, no one who would lead
them in battle. They had badly deteriorated through this period.
There was one strong man in their midst but the people had abused
him so that he had fled from them. He was an illegitimate child,
but that was no fault of his and neither was it his sin that he should
be thus treated. He had already come into the world at a dis-
advantage. Now in their need they sought out this man whose
name was

JEPHTHAH (Ch. xi.), and they promised that they would reinstate
him in their society if he would fight for them as their leader.
Jephthah accepted their invitation. Firstly, he appealed to Ammon
to withdraw but, when the king refused, Jephthah prepared for
battle. At this point he made the tragic mistake of his life. "And
Jephthah vowed a vow unto the Lord, and said, If Thou shalt
without fail deliver the children of Ammon into mine hands, then
it shall be, that whatsoever cometh forth of the doors of my house
to meet me, when I return in peace from the children of Ammon,

shall surely be the Lord's, and I will offer it up for a burnt offering" (30-31). As we know, this proved to be his daughter.

Man may reason as he will in seeking to justify Jephthah, but let the Word of God be true. Jephthah should never have made such a rash vow without first weighing up all the possibilities because he should have been aware of the law which said : " If a man vow a vow unto the Lord, or sware an oath to bind his soul with a bond ; he shall not break his word, he shall do according to all that proceedeth out of his mouth " (Num. xxx. 2). " I will offer it up for a burnt offering " were the words that proceeded from this man's mouth, so how could a continuance of virginity, as suggested by some, satisfy a holy God Who pronounced this law ? To those who say that God did not approve of human sacrifice we would give hearty agreement, but God did not approve either act. This man was in a dilemma. Whatever he did would displease God but, seemingly, God put more importance on a vow taken in the Name of the Lord than human sacrifice, for " Thou shalt not take the Name of the Lord thy God in vain for the Lord will not hold him guiltless that taketh His Name in vain ". In the light of this we should appreciate more the words of David when he said " Lord, guard Thou the words of my lips ", and why the New Testament says : " Let your yea be yea, and your nay nay ".

There are always people who cannot bear to see others obtaining success. They never desire to enter into activity that might cost them something but, if that particular project proves a success without them, then their jealousy seeks to turn a triumph into a tragedy. This is what the men of Ephraim sought to do with Jephthah, but did not prevail. Jephthah judged Israel for only six years and died.

The next twenty-five years saw three more judges of whom we know nothing.

IBZAN (Ch. xii.), of Bethlehem, ruled for seven years.

ELON (Ch. xii.), of Zebulon, ruled for ten years.

ABDON (Ch. xii.), the son of Hillel, ruled for eight years.

Throughout this period Israel fell back into sin again and God delivered them into the hands of the PHILISTINES. For forty years they were thus dominated, until God gave to them their last judge,

SAMSON (Chs. xiv-xvi.), the man who had the greatest opportunity but proved to be the biggest disappointment. Numerous are the warnings and the lessons of this life, but as we are surveying the book of Judges and not studying the life of Samson one must only summarise.

Samson was dedicated to God before birth. He was favoured with a spiritual upbringing and the most congenial environment. He knew the things God required of men and the things that God hated ; yet in these things he became wilful, refusing to listen to the advice of his seniors.

The salient points of this man's downward life are :
1) A desire for women.
2) Marrying women of other countries, forbidden by God.
3) Sporting with Divine favours, using them for his amusement instead of God's service.
4) Although strong physically he was weak morally, so that he could keep no secret when women began to influence him.

(These things all happened in Timnath in chapter fourteen).

In chapter fifteen he again fooled with his privileges and, in so doing, angered the Philistines who, knowing his weakness, used Delilah to find the secret of his strength. Little by little he yielded until that tragic moment when he declared to his enemy, and the enemy of God's people, his Nazarite vow, thus allowing them to shave off that hair which he had promised should never be cut.

Young people, watch those promises you have made to the Lord. Cherish those spiritual gifts that God has given to you. The world will try and make you yield a principle here and another there but, remember, your life is not your own. You have already given it to the Lord and, in return, He is blessing that life. Every time you yield a point to the enemy so surely he will cut off a lock of your blessings, until you can become devoid of the Lord's gifts, the Spirit's power, and life's joys.

Whilst God was gracious in bringing to Samson a measure of restoration in his last days, yet he died tragically. With eyes put out, the mighty man of the past was led in by a boy to the amusement of those out of whom he had obtained his amusements.

We learn from the life of Samson that :
Religious life can be spurned.
Life is real and must be taken seriously.
The gifts of God are for use, not for abuse.
The seriousness of the unequal yoke.

Samson was a man who :
Failed his God.
Disappointed his parents.
Fooled himself.

Thus ended the twenty years of Samson's leadership and more than four hundred years of the Judges which, like all other periods where man is concerned, ended with failure.

CONFUSION AND ANARCHY (Chs. xvii-xxi.)

A steady decline had been taking place until we see a nation given over entirely to its own desires. God was not in their thoughts. The incidents of these last chapters are only examples picked out to describe what the life of the nation was as a whole.

Two things are mentioned in the closing chapter which always happen to the nation that forgets God. They are superstition and immorality. The first is seen in

MICAH'S IDOLATRY (Chs. xvii. and xviii.)   It is a picture of a people who try to show a pretence of religion and worship and yet, at the same time, act contrary to the revealed Will of God. This man set up his own house of gods and also ordained his own priesthood, all with the intent of trading within the realm of religion and making for himself a profitable income. This man's house became a centre of irregular worship, of soothsaying, and divination, that met the desires of the superstitious people.

GIBEAH'S IMMORALITY (Chs. xix. and xx.)   Several times in these closing chapters we are told that there was no king in Israel. Seeing that at this particular time in Israel's history no kingdom had ever been established, no throne ever set up, and no king ever appointed, it must be appreciated that the expression must have a broader basis of understanding. The terms would mean that the nation was without a leader of any kind, no king, judge or prophet, nor did it possess a government. Anarchy prevailed where every man was doing that which was right in his own eyes. There does not even appear to be a moral code of guidance. Men were selfish, seeking only to fulfil the desires of the flesh, hence this monstrous wickedness here recorded. Sin of this kind does not suddenly hit a man and catch him at some unguarded moment. This comes as a result of a steady, constant moving away from the Lord, sometimes unmarked, unnoticed, but, nonetheless, a sliding away. We need to watch that first step back, that first act of disobedience. The step to Joppa took

Jonah a long way down. It brought this nation into a place of gross immorality.

In seeking to deal with this sin the tribes sent to Benjamin, in whose territory Gibeah was, that they should deliver the guilty men for punishment. Instead Benjamin identified themselves with the crime by refusing to produce the criminals. War was declared, brethren against brethren — civil war — producing a tremendous loss of life on both sides. Things became so serious that a tribe was almost obliterated, not only by loss in battle but also because they pledged themselves not to marry the women of Benjamin.

However, a way of escape was found and the tribe was saved. With this the book of Judges closes a long and sad history. It remains a constant testimony of the fact that the heart is deceitful above all things and desperately wicked. It should teach us to turn our eyes away from ourselves — doing that which is right in our own eyes — and to get our eyes upon Jesus and to look into His wonderful face.

It is easy for us to close this book and with some comment or other say : " And that ends the Judges " — but it does not ! The Bible maintains a wonderful continuity that so many people miss because of their spasmodic and piecemeal way of reading. The next book opens with the words : " Now it came to pass in the days when the Judges ruled " (Ruth i. 1), so history continued. Moving on to the next book again we are introduced to Samuel, who was both a Judge and a Prophet. His ministry was somewhat different from that of his predecessors. Samuel has sometimes been referred to as the last Judge. In one sense this is true. He was the last to exercise his judgeship to the good of the nation, but he was not the last Judge. " And it came to pass, when Samuel was old, that he made his sons judges over Israel. Now the name of his firstborn was Joel ; and the name of his second, Abiah ; they were judges in Beer-sheba. And his sons walked not in his ways, but turned aside after lucre, and took bribes, and perverted judgment " (1 Sam. viii. 1-3).

It was as a result of the failure of these sons in exercising their office that the people demanded a king. When Saul was elected as king and the monarchy was established, then it was that Samuel relinquished his authority as a judge, but he never yielded his calling as a prophet.

Thus we learn that the period of history known as the " Period of the Judges " extended from the termination of the great leaders,

Moses and Joshua, to the commencement of the Kingdom in the days of Saul.

RUTH

THE GREAT LOVE STORY

*" Love suffereth long, and is kind; love envieth not; love
vaunteth not itself, is not puffed up, doth not behave itself
unseemly, seeketh not her own, is not easily provoked,
thinketh no evil; rejoiceth not in iniquity, but rejoiceth in
the truth; beareth all things, believeth all things, hopeth all
things, endureth all things. Love never faileth ... And now
abideth faith, hope, love, these three; but the greatest of these
is love."* (1 COR. xiii. 4-13)

INTRODUCTION

The book before us is one loved by everybody because it is
one of the loveliest love stories. In human affection this story,
and that of David and Jonathan, will ever transcend all others.

This little book of only four chapters finds itself between the
book of Judges and that of Samuel, both of which are full of wars
and intrigues, conflicts and conquests. Thus the book, with the
gentler side of life, comes as a relief from those hard and stern
things.

Instead of hatred there is love.

Instead of army life there is family life.

Instead of battlefields there are cornfields.

Instead of attacking and counter-attacking there are love,
courtship and marriage.

Oases are always to be found in the desert, tranquility in
the midst of the world's turmoil, the balm of God's peace where
the storms of sin assail.

This is one of two books that holds the name of a woman
as its title. J. Sidlow Baxter points out that the only two books
named after women were named for good women. Both women
married, both marriages affected the human race and yet each
was the reverse to the other.

Ruth, a *Gentile*, married into a *Jewish* family and thereby
came into the line of David, and through it all Gentiles have been
blessed.

Esther, a *Jewess,* married a *Gentile* monarch and through that
marriage brought deliverance to the Jewish nation and became
their salvation.

The story is occupied with three women who have been
described as

Ruth — the sacrificing woman.
Naomi — the sensible woman.
Orpah — the sensitive woman.

They have been summed up in this fashion — " And now abideth
Orpah, Naomi, Ruth, these three, but the greatest of these is
Ruth ".

The book concerns the subject of the Kinsman Redeemer
and, therefore, is a beautiful outline of Redemption and the
Restoration that comes as a result. J. Sidlow Baxter in his book,
Explore the Book, gives the following in connection with the
meaning of the names :

' The story opens at Bethlehem, the name of which means
' House of Bread ' (Beyth = house ; lechem = bread). The first-
mentioned figure is Elimelech, whose name means ' My God is
King ' or ' My God is my King ' (Eli = my God ; melech = king).
This Israelite, along with his wife Naomi, whose name means
' Pleasantness ', or ' favour ', leaves Bethlehem in the land of
Israel, because of famine, and seeks succour in the alien land
of Moab. The names of their two sons, whom they take with
them are Mahlon (joy, or song) and Chilion (Ornament, or perfectness). Under testing they forsake the place of covenant standing,
and resort to an expedient involving compromise. In Moab,
Elimelech (my God is my King) dies ; so do Mahlon (Song) and
Chilion (Perfectness). After ten tragic years Naomi, the pathetic
remnant, returns ; but instead of being Naomi (Pleasantness, Sweetness, Favour), she is, by her own testimony, Mara (Bitterness).

Now if this is not a striking type-picture of Israel we are much
deceived. Israel as originally constituted in Canaan was a
Theocracy. God was Israel's King. Israel was Elimelech — and
could say " My God is my King ". Israel was married, as it were,
to Naomi — pleasantness, favour, and blessing ; and Israel's offspring were Mahlon and Chilion — song and perfectness. But,
under testing, Israel compromised and went astray, leaving the
early allegiance to Jehovah. Elimelech died. No longer could
Israel say with a perfect heart before the Lord — ' My God is
my King '. Mahlon and Chilion passed away too — the ' song '
of praise and the ' ornament ' of devout godliness died off ; while
eventually Naomi, the once ' favoured ' and ' pleasant ' returns,

a sorry remnant, ' empty ' and ' bitter ', as in the days when the remnant returned, under Ezra and Nehemiah.

But from the point of Naomi's return, Ruth (' comeliness ') takes the prominent place ; and Ruth is a type of the Church. The type-picture is made up of three scenes — (1) Ruth in the harvest field ; (2) Ruth in the threshing floor ; (3) Ruth in the home of Boaz.

The book can be analysed according to its chapter divisions into a group of different headings depending on the approach one seeks to make or the type of meeting one might have to address. Here are four approaches :

(1) Backsliding (Ch. i.) Return (Ch. ii.) Restoration (Ch. iii.) Fruitfulness (Ch. iv.).

(2) Ruth deciding (Ch. i.) Ruth serving (Ch. ii.) Ruth resting (Ch. iii.) Ruth rewarded (Ch. iv.).

(3) A wise choice (Ch. i.) Humble industry (Ch. ii.) Accepting advice (Ch. iii.) Highly exalted (Ch. iv.).

(4) In Moab (Ch. i.) In Bethlehem (Ch. ii.) Into Israel (Ch. iii.) Into the Royal line (Ch. iv.).

Here the book will be outlined according to the first of these groups.

(1) BACKSLIDING (Ch. i. 1-18)

One is not surprised at the way in which the narrative is introduced. " Now it came to pass in the days when the judges ruled, that there was a famine in the land ". We are still in the period of history that belonged to the judges. There is a great deal of continuity in the books of the Bible.

God had four sore punishments that He declared He would mete out upon the God-rejector and the idolater — war, famine, pestilence, and death. These He used again and again, but especially famine — a famine in Egypt, a famine in the days of David, Samaria had a sore famine. Ahab was punished thus and there are many, many other instances not only in Bible history but throughout secular history.

So it was because of the sins of Israel during the time of the Judges that God sent this famine.

Of the family of Elimelech we know nothing prior to this story. This man Elimelech, his wife Naomi, and their two sons Mahlon and Chilion, instead of accepting this punishment as something that God had sent and repenting the cause, they sought to flee from the punishment. They feared death but in running from it ran straight into it, in that all three men died in the land of their escape. This family could not run away from God any more than could Adam or Jonah. God has a way of pursuing us. We tell children that the quickest way out of trouble is to confess, but how slow we are to practise what we preach!

The whole of Elimelech's trouble was that he moved to the land of Moab without seeking to find out whether it was the Will of the Lord. To be out of the Will of the Lord is a condition of backsliding.

Moab may be all right for some people but it is not the place for the children of God. It was a land of idolatry. It was a foreign place. It represents the world. The parents might be strong in faith; probably they could go to Moab and remain steadfastly true, they could be a testimony, but what about their children? It was a natural thing for boys to become interested in girls; marriage, and future life, came into their thinking, but the Lord had forbidden His people to inter-marry with the nations that were round about. Would this not become a problem? Would it not be a temptation for these boys to seek marriage without considering whether they were Israelites or not? Yes, it worked just that way!

This brings home a tremendous lesson. There are many things that may appear safe to a strong Christian, but we have responsibility and influence. Parents have great and grave responsibilities toward their offspring. They must never by their conduct expose their children to unnecessary temptation.

So long as this family remained in Moab there could be no blessing. Elimelech died, his two sons who had each married Moabite women also died, leaving three widows. It would be a tragic picture in the East where widows were blamed for their widowhood and were sadly despised and neglected.

This leads us into the second part of the story.

(2) RETURN (Chs. i. 6 - ii. 23)

In these bitter circumstances Naomi decided to return to Bethlehem — the House of Bread. In so doing she revealed to what extent she had backslidden, for verse 6 tells us : " Then she arose with her daughters-in-law; that she might return from the country of Moab; for she had heard in the country of Moab how that the Lord had visited His people in giving them bread ". Her reason for return was not because of any repentance of heart, nor because she was seeking the Lord, but there was bread. It was with selfish intent.

For a time these three sad figures travelled together, until Naomi made a decision. It was that her daughters-in-law should return to their country and their people and that she should travel alone.

Consider these three women as they stood at the crossways of life, each making their own decision as to their future, for they are representative of the whole human race and where it journeys. Firstly there was

NAOMI — *the sensible woman.* She had decided to return. At the moment her motive was wrong. She had painted a very black picture of the future for her daughters-in-law — no prospects, no home, no husbands — nothing! But evidently she felt that Bethlehem with its difficulties was better than Moab with its supplies so far as she was concerned. This was a step in the right direction. As yet she was still blaming God as she said : " The Almighty hath dealt very bitterly with me ". She never blamed herself nor her husband. She never confessed that sin was bitter. God had indeed emptied her but not in judgment, rather in love because He knew that it was her only way back. She would journey alone, her daughters-in-law might return to their homes and start life again. But in these decisions Naomi was making some mistakes. She was right to return, but she was wrong in blaming God, she was wrong in sending these girls back to an idolatrous country after all that she and her sons had told them about Israel and about the Love of Jehovah, the only true God. They had talked enough about their God that Ruth had already pledged her love to Him as we are yet to learn.

Another mistake that Naomi made was that her grief was causing her to forget the true facts of life. Israel had a law given by God in which poor persons did not lose permanently their inheritance. The year of Jubilee brought back to them what they might have forfeited temporarily. Also there was the law of the Kinsman Redeemer. A near kinsman could buy back any sold property and restore it to a widow. If there were no family he could marry the widow so that the name should not die out from Israel (See Deut. xxv. 5-10). Naomi had a kinsman, a man of wealth and influence, but she had forgotten all about him as she painted her hopeless future and bade the girls return. When one loses their contact with God they lose so much else. David learned that when he prayed : " Restore unto me the joy of Thy salvation, and uphold me with Thy free Spirit. THEN will I teach trans-

gressors Thy ways ; and sinners shall be converted unto Thee ".
(Ps. li. 12-13).

Naomi had made her decision. She was returning to her
people, her country, and, we trust, her God. The other two
had to make their decisions as everyone else has to do in life.
Decisions are often big. They are usually hard. They are nearly
always important, but they are always personal. Others may
counsel, advise, warn, or encourage, but the final decision is
personal. It is so with salvation. No one can decide between
life and death, between heaven and hell, but you yourself.
The second character was

ORPAH — *the sensitive woman.* She just comes into the picture
and then quickly disappears out of it, never to be heard of again.
The picture is a sad one, and yet representative of so many.
Outwardly this woman showed signs of wanting to follow Naomi.
In fact she had started on the journey, but she was so easily discouraged. She had a divided heart. She wanted to go with Naomi
and Ruth, but she also longed for her native home. This woman
was not a backslider, she was undecided. She comes and goes
like so many more. They want to, they ought to, but they do
not. Orpah teaches just three things that are exceedingly vital.
They are :

(1) It is possible to go a long way toward Christianity and
yet not be a Christian. She had learned about the God of Israel.
She had agreed that all was truth. She knew she should yield
her life to Him. She had started on the journey BUT she could
not make a complete break with the old life. She wept, she kissed,
she returned — a professor.

(2) It is possible to deceive ourselves and to think that all
is right when, in truth, all is wrong with our souls. Orpah did
not want to be a hypocrite. She thought she was in earnest. Ruth
and she had walked together, talked together, wept together,
decided together ; in fact, she thought they had all things in
common, until that moment on the way to Bethlehem she had
to make a personal decision. How easy to be carried along on
the wave of some other person's enthusiasm and to discover that
ours has been a passion instead of a principle, an earthly love
instead of a heavenly devotion. Yes, there was a love for God,
but the love for Moab was greater. This is profession, but not
possession. It is a condition of self-deception and, alas, there
are thousands of people who call themselves Christians who are

travellers with Orpah. There will come a rude awakening one day — one can only trust not too late.

(3) Our Christianity profits only as we pursue it to its end. Instead of sailing the ocean of time in the boat of Christian faith, people get caught in the tide of a religious interest, only to be cast off further down-stream. Felix trembled, Balaam prophesied, Herod heard gladly, Judas sat at the table, Orpah journeyed, but none of them enjoyed the blessings of Ruth, who went all the way out of Moabitish idolatry into the fulness of the blessings of Israel, out of obscurity into an honour that shall be hers for all time.

The third character was

RUTH — *the sacrificing woman.* Her position, environment, and opportunities were exactly the same as those of Orpah. Let not a person say 'It depends entirely on one's circumstances'. It does not. Circumstances may have some influence, but it depends upon one's personal decision. So it was here, and thus it usually is. Samson had everything in his favour and went the wrong way. Ruth, at this moment of time, had nothing in her favour and she went the right way. Her decision was made in those immortal words which came after Orpah's decision and return, and after she was advised to go back also. " And Ruth said, Entreat me not to leave thee, or to return from following after thee, for whither thou goest, I will go ; and where thou lodgest, I will lodge ; thy people shall be my people, and thy God my God : where thou diest, will I die, and there will I be buried : the Lord do so to me, and more also, if aught but death part thee and me " (16-17). " So they two went until they came to Bethlehem " — a definite decision followed by immediate action. What had this woman to gain by following her mother-in-law ? From what she had been told and for all she knew, absolutely nothing. This is one of the greatest pictures that we have of disinterested love. She did not love for what she could or would get out of it. She loved for the sheer joy of loving. She sacrificed everything to love a sad and lonely woman, a love that could only be broken by death. What did she lose ? Nothing ! But gained everything that both time and eternity could give her.

We have spoken of a Kinsman Redeemer and of a restoration of the properties of her deceased husband but about this she knew nothing whatever.

Life in Bethlehem began as Naomi had said, a dark and hard experience. Verse 19 tells us that " when they were come to Bethlehem, that all the city was moved about them ". This expression does not hold the same connotation that we would give it. We would possibly interpret this as the whole city was excited about their arrival, or that it was moved with sympathy, but alas! this is not true. It means the whole city " gossipped " concerning them ; then, having learned the true facts, quickly cooled off. Those who need sympathy mostly are usually those who get the least. The world only smiles on prosperity. Thus it was that Ruth had to resort to the lot of the lowest and poorest of the people — to the task of gleaning. God had commanded that when men reaped the harvest they should remember the poor. " And when ye reap the harvest of your land, thou shalt not wholly reap the corners of thy field, neither shalt thou gather the gleanings of thy harvest. And thou shalt not glean thy vineyard, neither shalt thou gather every grape of thy vineyard ; thou shalt leave them for the poor and stranger ; I am the Lord your God " (Lev. xix. 9 -10).

Ruth was humiliating herself in the midst of a gossipping community that she might make provision for Naomi as well as for herself. As a stranger she went gleaning amongst strangers, and ii. 3 says : " And her hap was to light on a part of the field belonging unto Boaz, who was of the kindred of Elimelech ". Was it hap or was it God ? He has promised that a cup of cold water given in the name of a disciple should not lose its reward. Then can the Lord allow a sacrifice and a love such as this woman was displaying to go unrewarded ?

When Boaz saw the stranger he enquired of his servants as to who she was. He told her to remain in his fields and to follow his reapers. To make it easier for her to glean he bade his men to allow handfuls of barley to fall on purpose. He also told her that she could drink of the water that his servants had drawn, at the same time instructing his men to give her all the protection she should need. All of this was because Boaz had heard of the love this girl had given to her mother-in-law. At least one person had appreciated the qualities of a stranger.

On her return to her mother-in-law she made known to her the exploits of the day. As a result the forgetful mind of Naomi was quickened to remember that this very man was a kinsman, one who, if he would, could bring them

(3) RESTORATION (Ch. iii.)

And thus it was. One often meditates the sacrificing character of Ruth, but Naomi was just as unselfish. It was in the interest of these daughters-in-law that she decided to return alone. Now she gave motherly advice as she watched with interest a love that was developing between Ruth and Boaz. Boaz was undoubtedly attracted to this maiden, but pressed no issue because he was conscious that he was so much older and she might not want his companionship. Naomi told Ruth to abide in these fields and await events. Here is an incident that has puzzled and confused so many minds. At the instruction of her mother-in-law, Ruth went down to the threshing floor, dressed in her best that she might become an attraction to the man. Then, after he had settled down to sleep, she was to go and uncover his feet, there to lay herself down. When he awakened with alarm finding a woman at his feet, it would seem that with an impudence she bade him cover her with his skirt. On first reading, this certainly appears to be an act that, to say the least, does not display prudence — in fact, it savours that which might suggest something immoral. Yet from the rest of the story we cannot believe this was so, hence an explanation.

The act was a delicate one and could not have been carried out except with reservations. Naomi was sure of Boaz, his noble character, his steadfast loyalty, and his honour at all times. Naomi was also sure of Ruth, her purity, love, loyalty, and sweetness of character. Thus she could suggest that she go and lay at his feet, a symbol of subjection to him and of his right to protect her as a near relative and as a kinsman redeemer of Elimelech, knowing that both would appreciate the meaning of the act and neither would take advantage of the situation.

Although Boaz became alarmed when he awakened to find a woman at his feet, he was consoled immediately when he learned that the woman was Ruth. Ruth quickly explained her conduct. Unfortunately our Authorised Version has not used the best words in its translation, which has somewhat caused the embarrassment. The rendering should be : " I am Ruth, thine handmaid, and thou hast spread thy wings over thine handmaid ; for thou art a near kinsman " (iii. 9). Earlier Boaz had said to Ruth : " The Lord recompense thy work, and a full reward be given thee of the Lord God of Israel, under Whose wings thou art come to trust " (ii. 12). Now she returned the salutation to him by saying in effect, ' Not only have I come under the gracious wings of the Lord God and enjoy His blessings, but you, too, have stretched out your wings for my protection, for you know that you are my kinsman. I am here to ask you whether you are willing to complete that work '. She was wanting to come completely under his care. She had observed that his interest had been more than casual, that his affections were warm toward her and her love was certainly toward him. Quickly he responded to her overture. It was what he was wanting but, as before stated, his age caused him to be slow in proposing. This can be gathered from his reply to her proposal. " Blessed be thou of the Lord, my daughter ; for thou hast shown more kindness in the latter end than at the beginning, inasmuch as thou followedst not young men, whether poor or rich ".

If this were a question of love only it would have been settled there and then, but she had raised the question of the kinsman. Two things were required of him for the sake of the dead. (1) " If brethren dwell together, and one of them die, and have no child, the wife of the dead shall not marry without unto a stranger : her husband's brother shall go unto her, and take her to him to wife, and perform the duty of a husband's brother unto her " (Deut. xxv. 5). (2) " If thy brother be waxen poor, and have sold away some of his possession, and if any of his kin come to redeem it, then shall he redeem that which his brother sold " (Lev. xxv. 25). There was an obligation related to posterity and one to possession.

Boaz, being the honourable man he was, did not allow his love to come before duty, for there was another man who was more closely related to Ruth, and therefore he must have the first privilege to redeem both Ruth and her husband's inheritance. If he would not, then Boaz assured Ruth that he would, and also it should be done in the morning without any delay. Ruth returned to her mother-in-law with her mission successfully carried out and with six measures of barley as a gift from Boaz.

The same morning Boaz was found at the City gate, the place where all business was legally transacted in the presence of witnesses.

Boaz found the kinsman, gathered ten elders to act as witnesses, and then declared his business. It concerned buying the property that had once been Elimelech's, but must remain in the family or, at least, the tribe. Naomi must sell this land to deliver herself from poverty. This unnamed man was the man with the first right of purchase. Therefore he was offered the inheritance, the redemption of which he was prepared to make. Boaz intimated that there was a clause in the contract that required the purchaser of the land to buy with it Ruth, the Moabitess, who, through her marriage to a son of Elimelech, had become the future heir of the property. She, being a widow without child, must be received as a wife of the purchaser so that seed might be raised in the name

of the deceased in order that his name should not die out in Israel.
The would-be purchaser found himself in the position where
he could not accept the terms. If he did it might mar his own
inheritance. A suggestion has been made that this man was
possibly a widower with a sizeable family. This family would
receive his inheritance in due course, but, if he married this woman
and his family were enlarged still more, the division of his inheritance among so many would mar it, or cause it to fritter away
in so many small pieces. Whatever may have been the reason,
there was one and, because of it, he declined his privilege and
offered it to Boaz as the next kinsman. Boaz gladly accepted.
And now in the presence of the elders of the City the contract was
drawn up and legally sealed according to the custom of the day.
So the man drew off his shoe and handed it to Boaz, saying :
" Buy it for thee ". This act could suggest ' I forfeit my right to
you ; therefore I give you my shoe for I have no right, nor
privilege, to walk on that property : it is yours '.

Thus the Moabitess, who had once lost her all in the death
of husband and, later, forfeited everything that could have become
hers that she might cherish her mother-in-law in her need and her
age, became the inheritor of great blessing in Israel. No one who
has so willingly given ever became a loser. What we give to the
Lord is only lent because He rewards us so abundantly. " Give,
and it shall be given unto you ; good measure, pressed down, and
shaken together, and running over, shall men give into your bosom.
For with the same measure that ye mete withal it shall be measured
to you again " (Luke vi. 38).

To the Jew a woman had one great office, and that was to bear
children. Nothing was more degrading as being childless. That
was why Sarah gave Hagar to her husband, and why she later
hated her. That was why Rachel and Leah contested with each
other. That was why Rachel cried : " Give me children or I
die ". Hannah was mistaken as a drunken woman in the Temple
when, with passion, she was pleading with God to give her a son,
and others reveal the same longings. If a woman should bear a son
and he died in infancy, she would have the child's likeness graven
on her hand where she might ever remind herself that she had
at least borne a child, and which she could show to her friends
if they should begin to despise her. It was because of this custom
that Isaiah said : " But Zion said, The Lord hath forsaken me,
and my Lord hath forgotten me. Can a woman forget her sucking
child, that she should not have compassion on the son of her
womb ? Yea, they may forget, yet will I not forget thee. Behold,

I have graven thee upon the palms of my hands; thy walls are continually before Me " (Isa. xlix. 14-16).

In the light of this the greatest congratulations one could give to a bride in those days was such as they conferred upon Ruth at that time. " The Lord make the woman that is come into thine house like Rachel and like Leah, which two did build the house of Israel; and do thou worthily in Ephratah, and be famous in Bethlehem; and let thy house be like the house of Phares, whom Tamah bare unto Judah, of the seed which the Lord shall give thee of this young woman " (iv. 11-12).

(4) FRUITFULNESS (Ch. iv. 13-22)

These blessings of the Lord were granted to Ruth in a measure that the well-wishers never dreamed. Ruth bare a son, and called his name Obed, and everyone rejoiced with Naomi, saying: " Blessed be the Lord, which hath not left thee this day without a kinsman, that his name may be famous in Israel. And he shall be unto thee a restorer of thy life, and a nourisher of thine old age; for thy daughter-in-law, which loveth thee, which is better to thee than seven sons hath borne him " (iv. 14-15). The language was flowery, congratulatory, and commonplace. What they did not know was that it was prophetic — " that His Name may be famous in Israel ".

Obed became the father of Jesse, Jesse became the father of David, and Jesus, the Messiah, was great David's greater Son.

Thus the book closes with a genealogy that links this family up with the birth of Christ, the One Who became the Restorer of many lives.

How often is the wrath of man turned into the praise of Jehovah! How often man proposes but God disposes! ! Elimelech moved out of Bethlehem into Moab to save his life. In that he failed, but out of it God brought into the Royal line a Gentile and, in so doing, reminded us that in His death He would bring in many Gentiles, so that in Christ there should be neither Jew nor Gentile, but that we should be one.

I SAMUEL

THE GREAT TRANSITION

*"For this child I prayed; and the Lord hath given me my
petition which I asked of Him; Therefore also I have lent
him to the Lord; as long as he liveth he shall be lent to the
Lord. And he (they) worshipped the Lord there."*

(1 SAMUEL i. 27-28)

INTRODUCTION

This first of the two books named after the great Seer of
Israel covered a transitional period between the Judges and the
Monarchy. Transitions are always dangerous periods and this
was no exception. The transition can be seen when one realises
that Samuel was a judge and a prophet, the last judge, not the
first prophet, and not a king. He was in between. In time he
surrendered his position as judge in favour of the king, but he
never yielded his prophetic office. Further, up to this point the
priest had played a prominent part in the life of the people and
the prophet a small part. From now on the priesthood that had
become a corrupted thing was replaced by the prophetic office
which became a voice of authority. It is to be noted that the
king and the prophet became two offices that supplemented each
other. The difference between these two offices would be that the
king represented the earthly throne and kingdom but the prophet
was the representative of the King of kings Who sat upon the
heavenly throne. As a result there was no succession to the
prophet. It was not hereditary. God raised up a man from any
class among the people, a man who would be after His own heart
to be His mouthpiece. Hence the prophet had more authority
than the king. The Church to-day ought to be using its authority
as the representative of the Divine Throne, opposing all that the
politician seeks to establish which may be contrary to the revealed
Will of God or opposed to the laws of God. To read the Old
Testament intelligently one must ever place them side by side.
In the compilation of our Bible all the kings are put together in
these next six books ; and most of the prophets are together in the
prophetical section which follows the Poetical books. Our Bible,

therefore, sets the books out in groups, but we should study them in chronological order.

In this vital period of transition Samuel was of the opinion that they were rejecting him when the people demanded a king, but God made it known that He was the One Who was being rejected. Most dissatisfactions in the world, which cause such international upheavals, come about as a result of men refusing the only One Who can give real peace and satisfaction — He Who is the King of kings and Lord of lords.

Four leading characters dominate the book of Samuel — Eli, Samuel, Saul, and David. These in turn introduce three major offices — Priest, Prophet, and King, and remind us of the Lord Jesus Christ, in Whom all of these offices found their consummation, the only One Who was Prophet, Priest and King.

We shall divide the book into a study of these four men.

THE DAYS OF ELI (Chs. i-vi.)

Although the book is divided into the lives of four men there is necessarily a great deal of overlapping.

Samuel's early days. Elkanah was a man with two wives, a habit that appears to have been permissible in those days. Abram, Jacob, Moses, David, Solomon, all had plurality of wives. Permission is discovered by a law established concerning such. " If a man have two wives, one beloved, and another hated, and they have borne him children, both the beloved and the hated . . . " (Deut. xxi. 15). Such were the circumstances in this family, except when the story opens the beloved wife had not borne any children to her husband. The woman was greatly distressed because, although her name, Hannah, meant " gracious ", and she was the recipient of much love and grace from her husband, yet she had borne no fruit to her husband, whilst the other wife had. We, who have so wondrously received love and favour from the Lord, should be bearing fruit to His honour and glory. If we are not, then we should be greatly exercised concerning it. In her bitterness of soul Hannah went to the Temple and poured out her complaint before the Lord, promising the Lord that, if He would grant her a son, she would give him back to the Lord.

The unnamed mother of Samson was told to give her child back to the Lord when he was born. Both women did so, but what a difference in the lives of the two men. One was full of self and became a disappointment and a failure. The other was ever obedient and died an honourable man. Both of these men were Nazarites from the womb. Samson " began " to deliver

Israel. Samuel continued to the end of life. This picture does not support the household salvation that some people desire to read into the New Testament.

As this woman, Hannah, poured out her soul before the Lord and prayed through to victory, we get our first introduction to Eli, the priest, and with him the corrupted priesthood of that day, a picture that is sad and tragic from the very beginning. A man who was kind but exceedingly weak, his spiritual life was as blunted in its alertness as his moral powers were toward his sons, for here we meet a priest who cannot discern between a woman in passionate prayer from one who might be intoxicated with liquor. He reproved Hannah for being drunken so that she had to explain that she was praying.

The disciples were charged with being drunk on the Day of Pentecost, but that verdict came from the world outside; a priest should know differently.

Hannah was offering to consecrate this life to the Lord at a time when the Lord was looking for a consecrated life. So God gave to Hannah and Hannah gave back to God.

Samuel at Shiloh. For a time Hannah returned home and reared the child until he was old enough to be given to the Lord in a physical sense. Then she fulfilled her vow and brought the child to the Temple and, explaining to Eli that she was the woman he had reproved but whom God had honoured by giving to her this son, she now gave him to the service of God. Neither was her gift a grudging one, with a regret that she had made such a vow. She gave him with that spontaneous prayer of thanksgiving recorded in the first two verses of chapter two.

This prayer is followed by a further description of the condition of the priesthood. Not only was Eli dull in his discernment, but his two sons, who were priests, were living evil lives. They were dishonest in the Holy things, making merchandise out of the sacrifices. They were also immoral in their practices, and Eli was not strong enough in character to correct the wrong, and so it continued unmolested. Hence God must step in and deal with the situation. So comes the well-known and well-loved story of chapter three, with the young child, Samuel, ministering before the Lord, doing duties that should have been performed by the two sons. The first verse tells us that the Word of the Lord was precious in those days, which should read "rare", indicating that the Lord's voice was not often heard. It was not surprising, therefore, that, when God spoke to the child, Samuel made immediate response to what he thought was Eli's voice.

" Hush'd was the evening hymn,
 The temple courts were dark,
 The lamp was burning dim
 Before the sacred Ark ;
 When, suddenly, a Voice divine
 Rang through the silence of the shrine.

 The old man, meek and mild,
 The priest of Israel, slept ;
 His watch the temple child,
 The little Levite, kept ;
 And what from Eli's sense was sealed
 The Lord to Hannah's son revealed ".

Alexander McLaren puts this scene into a beautiful parabolic picture thus — The dim-eyed priest slept, the lamp was burning low, the little lad was keeping night vigil, whilst the sons, whose responsibility it was to keep the Temple charge, were away indulging in a sinful life. So darkness hung over the whole nation, the spiritual eye of the priest was dim, the order seemed to be growing old and decrepit, but the lamp of God had not altogether gone out. The child was the hope of a new day.

In the failure of one voice God was raising up a new voice, that of the prophet. Thus it was that, through the child Samuel, God made known the judgment that He would mete out upon Eli and his family. The judgment was not delayed, for it came to them in the next chapter.

Fall of the Theocracy. Chapters iv-vi. outline the fall of the Theocracy. Israel went to war against the Philistines, and this at their own charges. God had not instructed them to war, neither had the Philistines declared the war. Here the children of Israel were getting out of the Will of God. The result is obvious. They were defeated, as man always is when away from the Lord's leading. With their realisation of defeat a suggestion was made that they bring the Ark of the Covenant into the battle because the presence of the Ark always meant victory. So they sent to Shiloh, where the Ark was, and it was carried down to the battlefield on the shoulders of Hophni and Phinehas, the sons of Eli. The old man, anxious for the Ark, sat at the gate of the City to await news. But, surely, victory is secure ! Not at all. When the over-confident army saw the Ark coming into their midst they raised a mighty shout, a shout that echoed across the valley to be heard by the Philistines. A watchman in the enemy camp climbed the watchtower to find the reason for the shout and he discerned the Ark of God going into the camp.

This brought dismay to the Philistines. They had heard about that Ark, how it parted the river Jordan, how it had been carried around the walls of Jericho victoriously. They knew that it represented the God of Israel. Said they : " God is come into the camp . . . And they said, Woe unto us ! For there hath not been such a thing heretofore " (iv. 7). The Philistine army would have surrendered. They, too, believed the Ark meant sure victory for Israel. But the captain thought otherwise and, having encouraged the men, he bade them " Quit yourselves like men and fight ", with the result that the Philistines gained another victory. Israel was defeated, the Ark was lost to the Philistines, and the two priests were slain. A messenger fled back to Shiloh to carry the sad tidings. When Eli heard that the Ark of God had been taken, he fell backwards off his seat, broke his neck, and died.

Israel defeated, the Ark lost, Eli the High Priest dead, and the successors to the priesthood dead also. The priestly order had ended, and so the judgment God pronounced against this family was quickly fulfilled.

The question is naturally being asked — but, surely, the presence of the Ark should have brought victory ? Had not God promised it ? Yes ! When the Ark led the way — but here Israel had gone to war and, when things went wrong, they brought down the Ark to make God become their servant and deliver them out of the crisis into which they had brought themselves.

Beloved, we often do the same thing to our sorrow. God is our Master, not our servant. God goes before to instruct us, He will never follow behind to be instructed by us. Let us be sure that we have right relationships with God.

The Glory of the Lord had departed from Israel. There had been complete national failure on the part of the people. This was put on record when the wife of Phinehas, who at that time gave birth to a son, named him Ichabod, which name means : " The glory of the Lord hath departed ".

The Philistines, aware of the sacredness of the Ark of the Covenant, and not anxious to kindle the wrath of Jehovah, treated their trophy of victory with great reverence. They placed it in the house of their god, Dagon, at Ashdod, not knowing that Jehovah will not share His worship with another ; that He is a jealous God ; neither did they know that God and mammon cannot dwell together. In the morning, when they came to worship, Dagon was on the ground. With a sense of fear they replaced their god and worshipped, but the next day he had fallen again and was broken in pieces. The presence of God always means the overthrow of idolatry.

In this same city a plague of emerods broke out amongst the men and a plague of mice mowed down the corn in the fields, and so the Ark was moved from Ashdod to Gaza, to Askelon, to Gath, and to Ekron (vi. 17), and in each city the same plagues broke out, demanding its removal. After seven months of suffering the Philistines decided to return the Ark of God to its rightful place.

Not being certain whether the plagues were an evidence of God's judgment, or whether they were a coincidence hitting the same cities in which the Ark was established, a test was suggested. The test was a very unnatural thing. Nonetheless God responded to it because the Lord likes to be proved. Through Malachi He said : " Prove me now herewith, saith the Lord of Hosts " (Mal. iii. 10), whilst John says : " Beloved, believe not every spirit, but try the spirits whether they are of God " (1 John iv. 1).

A new cart was built, a trespass offering was prepared two oxen that had never borne a yoke before were selected, everything was done reverently ; but the oxen were mothers that had young, and mother-love is very strong. The babies were to be tied up nearby and the mothers harnessed to the cart to carry away the Ark. If, when the young ones cried, a natural thing, the mothers turned to them, also a natural thing, then it was not of God, but if these mothers ignored their offspring and moved straight toward Bethshemesh, then it would be accepted that this was the judgment of God. Thus it was, and the Ark returned.

On its way back the men of Bethshemesh rejoiced to see it. They lifted the Ark from off the cart and broke up the cart for fuel. Then they slew the oxen for a sacrifice of burnt offering. But someone of the company looked into the Ark and drew down the judgment of God in a great slaughter. Our Authorised Version tells us that fifty thousand and seventy men perished. Men may question the authenticity of that number, but a truth remains that God meted out judgment in no uncertain way. But why such a slaughter ? One cannot tell whether the person who lifted that Mercy Seat did it out of curiosity as to what was inside, or out of concern that the Philistines had not desecrated it by removing any of the contents. Could it be that it was here that the pot of Manna and Aaron's Rod were removed, because there were only the two tables of law in the Ark when Solomon carried it into the Temple ? (2 Chron. v. 10). Be that as it may, when the Mercy Seat was lifted mercy was taken away from a law that was inside, a law which man could not keep, and so the company was exposed to the ministry of death.

As a result of this tragedy the people of Bethshemesh would not touch the Ark, but sent to the men of the next town, Kirjath-jearim, to come and take it away. They did so, and brought it to the house of Abinadab, and sanctified Eleazer, his son, to care for the Ark. There it remained for twenty years, whilst Abinadab enjoyed the blessing of the Lord, as will anyone who gives the Lord His rightful place in the home and the family.

THE DAYS OF SAMUEL (Ch. vii.)

Although only one chapter, it covers a long period of time. There were the twenty years of verse two during which time not only was the Ark of the Covenant away from Shiloh, but the people were away from God and were serving idols. Samuel faithfully ministered all through this period bidding the people to turn back to God. At last repentance came, and Samuel gathered the people to Mizpeh to pray with them as well as for them.

The pouring out of the water was a declaration of their helpless condition. The thought is better seen in the words of the woman of Tekoah who, when pleading with the king, said : " For we must needs die, and are as water spilt on the ground, which cannot be gathered up again " (2 Sam. xiv. 14).

Whilst they were confessing their helplessness the Philistines closed in for battle, but Israel was encouraged to trust in the Lord. Samuel, instead of taking up arms against the Philistines, offered a lamb as a burnt offering. God intervened with a storm that drove the enemy back. Israel pursued and smote them so that the Philistines troubled Israel no more during the life of Samuel. It was in commemoration of this event that Samuel set up the stone which he called Ebenezer, a name that has been familiar with the Church of God ever since. " Hitherto hath the Lord helped us ". Oh, that we might have a trust in God that would help us to know the experience of the Lord's help more than the meaning of the word !

So it was that the prophet moved from place to place in circuit, judging Israel, until he began to increase in years. His sons were not walking in the footsteps of their father, but were perverting judgment. As a result of this the people demanded a change. So came

THE DAYS OF SAUL (Chs. viii-xv.)

The demand for a king. The people were demanding a king like the other nations. This greatly grieved Samuel, because he thought they were rejecting him ; but the Lord told him that their sin was more serious. They were not rejecting the prophet but refusing the Lord, Who was their unseen King, Samuel only being His representative.

Samuel, at the Lord's bidding, discouraged them, telling the people what a king would demand from them. But they insisted, saying : " Nay, but we will have a king over us ".

There has been debate as to whether the choice that was made was God's choice or the people's choice. It would appear that God chose Saul, although God insisted that David was the man after His heart, and David was His choice. The answer is that, whilst God found the man, the people chose him. They said that they wanted a man who would lead them in battle. God said in effect — ' I know exactly what you are seeking. It is a man of strength and courage, a man who outwardly looks good and able. You are not concerned with his moral, intellectual, or spiritual qualities, only his physique. I know the man and I will find him for you ' — nations usually get the leaders they deserve !

Election of Saul. Saul, the son of Kish, was head and shoulders above everyone else, but a man who, seeking his father's asses, was soon ready to give up. It was the persistence and the ingenuity of his servant, who found the quarter of a shekel reward, who brought Saul into the presence of Samuel. Samuel made known to Saul that the people were seeking a king and he was the man they wanted, and so Saul was anointed privately as king by Samuel, who, at the same time, assured him that his lesser mission was over — the asses were found.

Saul was given certain instructions and told that, "when these signs are come unto thee, that thou do as occasion serve thee ; for God is with thee " (x. 7). The signs were fulfilled, the Spirit of the Lord came upon him, and he became another man. This was Saul's great opportunity if only he had submitted and become obedient but, alas, this was not to be.

At the appointed time Samuel came down to Mizpeh for the public anointing of the king. Again he reminded the people that their act was one of rebellion. One by one the tribes were presented until Benjamin was taken. This would suggest that things were out of line with Divine purpose. Was not Judah the Royal tribe from which kings should come ? From tribe to family and family to man until Saul, the son of Kish, was announced as the appointed king, but they could not find him. He had hidden himself among the stuff. When they brought him out there he stood head and shoulders above the people : and with one accord the people shouted "God save the king". How blind people become to facts when they make up their mind. His hiding was a display of his moral weakness which they failed to see because they were preoccupied with his physical strength. Yes, this was the man of their choosing.

What a difference between the call of Saul, the son of Kish, and Saul of Tarsus! The first was readily accepted by the people, but not so ready himself to accept the responsibility, he hid himself. The second said with boldness : "I was not disobedient to the heavenly vision", although the people were slow in recognising him as an apostle of Jesus Christ.

The kingdom established. The next chapter tells of a plot on the part of Nahash which was bringing trouble to Israel. News came to Saul, who quickly and courageously dealt with the matter, bringing his first victory to Israel, and thereby he confirmed his leadership with the people and established himself.

Samuel's Farewell. Chapter twelve is a sad scene. The old, grey-haired prophet was about to relinquish his office as judge. The king was established and there was not room for both, so Samuel gathered the people and bore testimony to them of his own faithfulness from his childhood up, and also of the faithfulness of God from the time He brought them out of Egypt until the establishment of their first king. He told them that if they and their king would fear the Lord and obey Him all would be well — if not, then the judgment of the Lord would fall upon them.

Whilst Samuel had relinquished his office as judge in favour of the king yet he never surrendered his prophetic office. To prove this to the people, he made a prophetic utterance, asking God to give a sign of His power by sending rain and thunder in the time of the harvest, an unheard of thing in Palestine. It came, and the people confessed repentance and faith, but it was very shallow. The faith that rests only in signs and wonders soon disappears in the realities of life ; the repentance that is caused by a thunderstorm is soon forgotten when the sun shines. Modern battlefields prove this. Oh, for a deep work of grace in our hearts !

Saul's Wars. The next three chapters deal with Saul's wars, his disobedience and his rejection. In these chapters we do not see just mistakes on the part of Saul or an occasional disobedience, but a persistently rebellious heart that creates a consistent decline.

It reveals the true character of the man. His first testing and failure were at Gilgal, the place of his anointing. The untrained army that he had so recently used he sent back home, all save three thousand experienced men. These he divided into two groups, two thousand under his leadership, and one thousand with Jonathan, his son. These could hold certain strong points. He planned a campaign without God. He did not want Him, he wanted to exercise his own strategy. However, Jonathan trusted God and God gave Jonathan the victory to the undoing of Saul. Samuel, feeling that Saul desired to be an autocrat, put him to the test. He had said : " And thou shalt go down before me to Gilgal ; and, behold, I will come down unto thee, to offer burnt offerings, and to sacrifice sacrifices of peace offerings : seven days shalt thou tarry, till I come to thee, and show thee what thou shalt do " (x. 8). The seven days were running out, the people were running away. Was Samuel not coming ? Therefore Saul offered the offerings, which was not within his domain or prerogative. Immediately afterward Samuel arrived, right at the last hour but nonetheless on time. Saul tried to excuse himself, but excuses never justify disobedience, and so the first indication of his doom was made known.

In chapter fifteen God bade Saul fight against the Amalekites because they had been the enemies of Israel in the past. His instructions were —" utterly destroy all that they have and spare them not ; but slay both man and woman, infant and suckling, ox and sheep, camel and ass " (xv. 3). The order was plain, but Saul used his own discretion and destroyed what he considered the vile, and spared what he considered the best. God told Samuel of His anger, and Samuel went to meet Saul. Saul met Samuel with a pretence that he had obeyed, but Samuel replied : " What meaneth then this bleating of the sheep in mine ears, and the lowing of the oxen which I hear ? " (xv. 14). Partial disobedience is no different from complete disobedience. Then we only obey so far as it pleases us. That is God-rejection. All the excuses in the world, all the fine platitudes we make, will not suffice for " Behold, to obey is better than sacrifice, and to hearken than the fat of rams " (xv. 22).

In the first rebellion God said : " Thy kingdom shall not continue ". Now He said : " The Lord He hath also rejected *thee* from being king " (xv. 23).

Although we leave Saul for David so far as the divisions of the book are concerned, the steady decline of this character is still to be observed.

With so many of us it is not a matter of open rebellion as it is of constant disobedience that brings us into that slow unnoticed slipping back which robs us of so much blessing here and will rob us of much reward in the hereafter.

THE DAYS OF DAVID (Chs. xvi-xxxi.)

This is a story of Divine choice. Samuel did not want to anoint David. He was fearful of the consequences, but God assured him that He had rejected Saul.

Samuel, by command, went to the house of Jesse to find the new king. A sacrifice was prepared, the sons of Jesse were sanctified, and one by one, beginning at the eldest, seven sons passed before the prophet. They were fine men of good build and muscle, tall and handsome, but of each God said ' No ', assuring Samuel that He did not consider the outward appearance. That is man's judgment, and the nation already had failed there in the choice of their first king. Now God was making the choice and " . . . the Lord looketh on the heart " (xvi. 7). But God had refused every one of them. Had Samuel been deceived ? In his bewilderment Samuel enquired of Jesse whether or not all his sons were present. There was one missing, but he was the youngest and only a shepherd, a despised son never privileged to attend this ceremony ; but God has a way of taking the despised things of the world to bring to nought the things which are (1 Cor. i. 28). God sees the heart. God had also seen the faithful and brave lad, tending, leading and defending those sheep, dealing with the lion and the bear, when no one was looking. He that is faithful in little things can be ruler over much. So David was brought from the sheepcotes and there, before his brethren, was anointed future king of Israel. Let us ever be faithful in the little things, for God still works in the same way, and still finds His man in the obscure places.

God now showed His displeasure toward the selfish and disobedient king as He began to withdraw His Spirit from him, so that Saul became troubled in mind, restless and irritable. Saul's servants sought to quieten his mind by supplying soothing music. How many people today seek the medical profession or the psychiatrist or some drug or a pleasure to soothe a restlessness which they think is mental or physical when, if they were honest, they would confess it is spiritual. Why do men flee from God instead of to God, when He begins to convict them of sin ?

David was not only a good shepherd, he was also a skilful musician and a sweet singer. God's over-ruling now brought him into the royal court, that he might obtain some preparation for his future ministry, for he was chosen out of the thousands of Israel to play before the king.

The scene changes at chapter seventeen to the much-loved story of the battle between David and Goliath, a story that reveals the fear that was in the hearts of Israel, and the confidence that David had in his God. David had been used to the quiet place out on the grassy slopes with the sheep, but also with his God. The man of the quiet place — the place of communion — is always the man of strong faith. The Israelites measured the giant by cubits, and his strength by armour and arms and, as a result, trembled. David measured the same man by the God he served, and had confidence. Faith is the victory that overcomes the world.

The farther Saul moved away from David the nearer Jonathan, Saul's son, moved toward him, until one of the strongest loves between man and man was established. It is a beautiful picture. It was Jonathan who ever moved toward David. It must be that way always. The prince can always step down to the commoner, when the commoner cannot move up to the prince. The latter would be presumption. It is Jesus Who always moves toward the sinner. We love him because he *first* loved us. Jonathan surrendered to David everything he had.

His robe was the yielding of his royal rights.

His garments were his earthly comforts.

His sword would symbolise his bodily protection.

His bow kept his enemy at a distance.

His girdle was his very strength.

A lack of wisdom on the part of the people increased the hazards of David's life as they sang: "Saul hath slain his thousands and David his ten thousands ". From now on Saul not only hated David but was afraid of him. The once brave man now became fearful, cautious, calculating, and envious, whilst David continued to increase in wisdom, strength, and popularity.

When Samuel said the kingdom should be taken from Saul and given to another, Saul must often have wondered who the other person was. Now he was realising the fact but, instead of submitting to what was obviously the inevitable, he was resisting with an increasing hatred, not only toward David, but also toward his own son.

This resentful spirit grew into a spirit of murder as Saul sought the life of David. It is an awful picture of soul tragedy.

Jonathan's love had so grown, and realising what God was doing and how the throne was changing, and that he would not be able to succeed his father, he gladly resigned himself to what was happening, saying to David : " Thou shalt be king and I will be next unto thee ". What a comparison of natures!

The next five chapters tell of " love for hatred ". David never retaliated, never sought vengeance, never allowed anyone else to try and carry out a revenge for him. To the contrary he warned everyone not to touch the Lord's anointed. David knew that the God Who exalts is the One Who also abases.

In chapter twenty, David, sensing danger, asked leave of absence from the king's table through Jonathan. Jonathan, in seeking to protect David, not only learned to what extent Saul hated David, but he also learned that his own love for David was endangering his own life at the hand of his father. Out in the fields David and Jonathan made a covenant with each other, displayed the strength of their love as the two men kissed and wept exceedingly with each other, and then parted.

So the intrigue went on, as David lived a life of exile, being pursued at Nob, Gath, Adullam, Keilah, Ziph, and Engedi. Every one of these names brings to our minds a host of truth.

The death of Samuel is recorded in chapter twenty-five, followed by the story of the selfish Nabal, who refused to meet David and his men in their need, even though David had done much in protecting Nabal's own men. An intervention on the part of Abigail, Nabal's wife, prevented David from taking vengeance on this man. Nabal died, and David took Abigail, the widow, to be his wife.

Saul was still pursuing David for his life. David came into Saul's tent whilst he slept and had the opportunity of destroying Saul, but did not. He took Saul's spear and cruse of water as an evidence to Saul that he could have taken his life as easily as he took the spear, but he preferred to exchange love for hatred and leave judgment to God.

David, not trusting Saul's repentance, sought sanctuary with the Philistines. The Philistines gave to David Ziklag, where he dwelt for sixteen months. During these days the Philistines declared war on Israel and Saul was afraid. The once brave man had become a coward. It was the realisation that the Lord was no more with him. In his need he had gone to Samuel, but Samuel was now dead. This brings us to the last and the darkest hours of this tragic life, when the man who, in his earlier days had abolished witchcraft in every form from the nation, resorted to it for himself in the consciousness of soul loneliness, a picture which for ever condemns spiritism. Saul sought the witch of Endor. He asked this woman to call up the spirit of Samuel. When she was assured that her own life would be protected from the law of the land which forbade the practice, she was prepared to meet the request of the " stranger ", and called up the spirit of Samuel. When Samuel appeared she was the person who was scared, and announced that her client must be Saul.

Why was this woman so surprised and so frightened when she did what she promised to do ? The obvious thing is that hers was a life of deception. She promised to speak to Samuel, but she never expected to do so. His appearance was not her doing, it became her undoing. How is this explained ? This woman, like others who ply in her business of deceit, had a " familiar spirit " ; that is, one evil spirit with which she was familiar, who always came at her bidding and posed to be any person she wanted. Instead of the familiar spirit coming at this time, God worked a miracle and raised up the true spirit of Samuel, not only to the condemnation of this witch and of Saul, but to the condemnation of spiritism in all time, including our present day, when this devilish deception is still practised upon people who have lost loved ones. Is spiritism real ? Yes, but it is deception nonetheless, and is of the Devil.

Samuel pronounced the judgment of God that befell Saul the next day, and reminded him that his tragedies were all the result of his disobedience. This has ever been and ever will be so. Let us assure ourselves that we are fully obedient to His revealed Will, for only therein is our peace and blessing.

When the Philistines prepared for the war in which was fought the tragic battle of Gilboa, David was in the army of the Philistines. Fortunately for all concerned he was advised to return. This was well for David, otherwise some may have wondered whether he might have been responsible for the death of Saul. It was also well for the people of Ziklag for, whilst the army was away to do battle with Israel, the Amalekites took advantage of the situation and ransacked Ziklag, carrying away the inhabitants, which included the wives of David. David sought the mind of the Lord through Urim and Thummim, and was instructed to pursue. Thus all that was lost was restored by David.

At the same time the Philistines met in combat with Israel. In the engagement Saul was wounded. Fearing the conduct of the enemy he requested that his armour-bearer slay him, but he would not. Therefore Saul took his own life. In so doing his armour-bearer did the same. Saul's three sons, including Jonathan, died in this same battle, and Israel was defeated.

Next day the Philistines found the bodies of the slain and took the head of Saul, parading it around their cities, whilst his armour was put into the house of their god and his body fastened to the city wall, with those of his sons. Thus they abused Saul. The men of Jabesh-gilead delivered the bodies and buried them.

So ended the life of a man who set out amidst the shout of " God save the king ", with all the promise of a noble reign, but ended a God-forsaken man who, full of fear and with a sense of intense loneliness, died on the battlefield of Mount Gilboa.

Like the ship that sets out on its maiden voyage amidst the shouts of the people, with its bands and its excited and dancing passengers ; it is the pride of its owners but, after years of ocean travel, of battling the storms of the seas, and maybe the toll of war, it is pulled into the breakers' yard by the little puffing, fussing tugs — the one-time pride of the ocean doomed to destruction.

Man in all his pride can thus end life, whilst the soul that is obedient to the Lord can enter victoriously into the joy of his Lord. So this book of Samuel compares the life without God and the life with God.

II SAMUEL

THE REIGN OF DAVID

" I have made a covenant with my chosen, I have sworn unto
David my servant, Thy seed will I establish for ever and build
up thy throne to all generations."   (PSALMS lxxxix. 3-4)

INTRODUCTION

Whilst the first book of Samuel has a great deal to record concerning David, it all belonged to his early life. David had not yet come to the throne. This second book is occupied entirely with the reign of David For seven and a half years he reigned over Judah from Hebron, and for thirty-three years he was king over all Israel, his throne being established in Jerusalem. Therefore he occupied the throne for forty years.

This reign may be divided into three phases :

    (1)   David's Triumphs (Chs. i-ix.).

    (2)   David's Troubles (Chs. x-xxi.).

    (3)   David's Testimony (Chs. xxii-xxiv.).

The outstanding events in this glorious reign were :

    (1)   Twice crowned king — Judah and Israel.

    (2)   Captured Jebus for his Capital City.

    (3)   Brought up the Ark of the Covenant.

    (4)   Desired to build a Temple.

    (5)   Faced a family disruption.

    (6)   Committed two major sins.

    (7)   Final Restoration.

(1)   DAVID'S TRIUMPHS (Chs. i-ix.)

The book is a strict continuation of that which has gone before. David therefore was still at Ziklag, where he was at the time of the battle of Gilboa, and where he had just gained an overwhelming victory against the Amalekites. His courage was his salvation for, at that time, everything seemed against him, when news came that changed the whole of the circumstances of his life — Saul was dead. The only thing that stood between David and the throne had been removed. The throne was now David's, but there was no rush for it ; instead, the evidence of a deep sorrow of heart for Saul and Jonathan, and a swift judgment on the man who had falsified the account of their deaths in the hope of a reward. By these actions David made it clear to the nation and to his enemies that he was in no way a participant in the tragedy of Mount Gilboa in order that he might gain that throne. What a mercy it was for David that he had responded to the request of Achish not to go into this battle !

Whilst one would not belittle for a single moment the undoubtedly real sorrow of heart that was David's, yet there was an act of diplomacy, both in his slowness to move to the throne, and in his sorrow of heart, in the light of all the evidence of an enmity that existed between Saul and David.

Thus David lamented the deaths of Saul and Jonathan, and what a lamentation it was, both beautiful and pathetic, especially concerning Jonathan — " . . . O Jonathan, thou wast slain in thine high places. I am distressed for thee, my brother, Jonathan: very pleasant hast thou been unto me : thy love to me was wonderful, passing the love of women. How are the mighty fallen, and the weapons of war perished ! " (i. 17-27).

David crowned king of Judah. The men of Judah came and anointed David king over the house of Judah. David's first act was to reward the men of Jabesh-Gilead for their burial of Saul. He had been quick to punish the man who had posed as Saul's slayer, and just as quick to reward those who had performed this burial at great risk to themselves ; in fact, a twofold risk. They imperilled their lives at the hands of the enemy in securing the bodies. They also risked misunderstanding, and maybe death, at the hand of their new king, because such an act could have been interpreted as one of loyalty toward Saul, which could spell disloyalty toward David.

David soon learned that he had another claimant to the throne. Abner, Saul's cousin, although aware that God had elected David, stubbornly resisted and sought out the only surviving son of Saul, a weakling by the name of Ishbosheth, and set him up as a puppet king. David did nothing about it, but submitted to reign at Hebron and await God's time. Sometimes definite action is needed, sometimes we can afford to wait, especially when we are sure that we are in the Will of God. This is a beautiful picture of submission. This is the man who could write : " Wait on the Lord and keep His way, and He shall exalt thee to inherit the land : when the wicked are cut off, thou shalt see it " (Ps. xxxvii. 34). One of the hardest lessons that some of us have to learn is to wait.

Two kings reigning led to civil war amongst the people. Abner was ever seeking to defend the family of Saul, whilst Joab, as a faithful servant of David, constantly opposed Abner. This continued for the seven years and more that David reigned over Judah, but David was ever increasing in strength whilst the house of Saul was constantly weakening.

Abner, who opposed David and set up Ishbosheth as king, was reproved by Ishbosheth because he had committed sin with Rizpah, one of Saul's concubines. Abner was so displeased with Ishbosheth that he revolted against him and joined ranks with David, promising him that he would bring the whole house of Israel on to his side. David accepted the person of Abner and his promised help, to the annoyance of Joab, his commander. Joab then sought Abner and slew him. David, in lamenting for Abner, made it known that this death was not with his approval.

With Abner dead, Ishbosheth, the weakling, became fearful, as did all Israel. Now two of Ishbosheth's own captains came and slew their master, whilst he lay on his bed, and took his head and brought it to David, again thinking that they would be rewarded, but he reminded them of the man who tried to gain his favour by killing Saul, and how he punished him. These men would be dealt with accordingly for slaying a righteous man upon his bed.

David crowned king of all Israel. The death of Ishbosheth brought to an end this civil war between the North and the South. At last the elders of Israel came to the place where they realised that

    (1)   David was their bone and their flesh.
    (2)   David was the victorious captain during Saul's reign.
    (3)   David had been ordained of the Lord.
    (4)   David should be king of all Israel.

Some people are slow to learn the things that are obvious. Selfishness is usually the veil that blinds.

Captured Jebus and made it his Capital City. David, now being king of all Israel, must show himself kingly. Hebron was his centre when king over Judah, but it is far south. He must have a new Capital City. It must be a stronghold. Jebus was the place. It was strategically and beautifully situated, and had never been captured in the days when Joshua took possession of the Land. It had such a natural defence that the Jebusites were confident that it would never be captured. When David began to interest himself in the city the Jebusites jeered at him. Verse six has been interpreted that, as an act of defiance, the Jebusites put blind men and lame men on the wall, saying that even these could protect this city, so come and take it if you can! But pride goes before a fall, and over-confidence is always a dangerous attitude, especially when there is a David at hand. The city received its water supply from without, so that a conduit conveyed the water under the city wall and into the citadel. David offered promotion to the man who would climb through the watercourse. A volunteer was soon forthcoming and the city was captured from within by Joab, and became known as the city of David, or Jerusalem. Let not the world brag about its strength and scorn the Church of God. God is able to reveal the overlooked watercourse of faith which can bring to naught the mighty.

The Philistines, incensed by David coming to the throne, made an attack. David enquired of the Lord, and, with the Lord's approval, fought the Philistines. This, of course, meant victory. The Philistines made a second attack. David did not take things for granted but, for the second time, he prayed, and so a second victory.

Brought up the Ark. Having established his Capital City, David decided that the place which was to be the centre of his government should be the place of his worship. If David as king was to reign successfully from Jerusalem, then the King of kings should also reign at the same place. Therefore he planned to bring up the Ark of the Covenant. Prior to the Ark being taken by the Philistines, Shiloh had been its home, but since its return it had spent twenty years in the house of Abinadab in Gibeah. David was doing the right thing, but he did it the wrong way.

David made a new cart, as did the Philistines, to bring the Ark back, but, as it travelled over a rough cobbled area of a threshing floor, the Ark rocked from side to side and looked as though it might fall from the cart. Uzzah, seeing the position, put out his hand to steady the Ark, and died on the spot. David was both displeased and afraid. He would take the Ark no farther, so withdrew it from its journey, and placed it in the house of Obed-Edom. There the Ark abode for three months, during which time Obed-Edom enjoyed the blessing of the Lord.

The question naturally arises — Why did God judge so severely a man who was performing a noble act? The tragedy

has to be laid at the feet of David.   It may have been right for
the Philistines to convey the Ark on a new cart, but it was wrong
for David so to do, because God had instructed that the Ark was
always to be carried on the shoulders of the priests, by means of
the staves.   The Philistines had no sanctified priests, but Israel
had.   If the priests had carried the Ark it could never have toppled.
The second mistake was that the Ark represented the God of
Israel, and God is very well able to protect Himself.   When a man
tried to steady the Ark it was like a poor puny creature trying to
uphold the Creator, which was somewhat an act of presumption.

Obed-Edom gave the Ark a place of honour in his home so
that every member of his family was blessed.   If we give the Lord
His rightful place in our lives, our home, our business, we, too,
will know the same riches of His Grace.

When David learned of Obed-Edom's blessing he realised that
he had made a mistake, so once again he sought to bring the Ark
up to Jerusalem, but this time he did it the right way.   He brought
down the priests, who bore it on their shoulders, whilst he danced
before the Ark.   It was placed in the tabernacle that David had
prepared for it, so that once more the Ark was in the midst of the
people.

Desired to build a Temple.   David was rejoicing in the
blessings that God had brought into his life and was anxious to
acknowledge God as the Giver of every perfect gift.   Therefore he
made known to Nathan, the prophet, what was in his heart, as he
said :   " See now, I dwell in an house of cedar, but the Ark of
God dwelleth within curtains ".   David desired to build a house
for God, one worthy of the Name of God — truly, a noble gesture.
God did not approve, however, for David had been a man of war,
and how could he build a house for the God of all peace !   God
had been content to dwell in a tabernacle and to move with His
people, but He had promised to David an establishment of his
family and of his throne and that a son of his should succeed him.
Now He would permit that that son should build a house to the
Name of God.   Instead of David becoming jealous and rebellious
because he could not have his way, as many of us do, humbly
he thanked God, confessed his own unworthiness, and then set to
work to prepare material, that he might make it easier for the next
man to do what he could not do.   What a lesson — and most of
us need to learn it !

The next chapter (viii.) records a series of successes that David
secured over his enemies.   The surrendered and submissive life
is always the life of victory.   Yet, whilst David was a great warrior

and stern in his judgment, he was always kind of heart and gracious in spirit as the ninth chapter reveals.

"And David said, Is there yet any that is left of the house of Saul, that I may show him kindness for Jonathan's sake?" This was a dangerous thing to do, and contrary to all custom. As can be seen repeatedly in the Old Testament, when the throne changed from one family to another, the new family slew all who lived of the old dynasty, lest there should come an uprising to bring the throne back again. (See I Kings xv. 29 ; I Kings xvi. 11 ; II Kings xi. 1).

A young man was found, Mephibosheth, the son of Jonathan, a man who was lame on both his feet. David sent for him, restored to him all the land that had belonged to Saul, and appointed servants to till the ground for him. What grace! David also instructed that Mephibosheth should sit at the king's table. This last act could have been a precaution rather than an honour. "To eat at my table" could mean that he would always be under the king's observation, so that he would not be able to take an advantage of David's goodness to secure the throne for himself.

The term "I am a dead dog" is just the usual type of flowery language of the Easterner and is meaningless.

It must be borne in mind that this offer was not made to Mephibosheth because of Mephibosheth, or because the king particularly loved him or trusted him. The display of grace was for "Jonathan's sake" (vs. 1). It was that name which David sought to honour. God does not love us because of what we are or who we are, nor because He can trust us more than others. Every blessing, every grace, every privilege that is ours, is granted for Jesus' sake. Let us never look for our merits. We have none. We must always see His.

(2) DAVID'S TROUBLES (Chs. x-xix.)

After displaying his kindness to Mephibosheth, chapter ten shows him extending another friendly overture, this time towards the king of Ammon, but a man who has no kindness in his own heart can never see it in another. The attitude of the king of Ammon was, therefore, one of suspicion — What did David want? What was behind this? This is so often the world's attitude toward the Church and the things of the Lord. The Ammonites abused the messengers of David in such a way as to suggest that they were ready to fight. They gathered others with them. David, seeing the ugly situation, speedily gathered his men and made the first attack. Sometimes, like David, we have to wait patiently for God ;

sometimes, like David, we have to accept the challenge and make the attack.

David's sins. One of the two major sins of David's life occupies chapters eleven and twelve. God-fearing and obedient as David was, a man of noble character and of fine integrity, yet there were some failings. Perfection is not the lot of man upon earth, and the heart is deceitful above all things and desperately wicked.

Here God put His finger right on to an ugly spot in this life. David already had several wives, and now he fell for another woman. Upon enquiry he learned that she was the wife of one, Uriah by name, but, instead of turning from the lust that was in his heart, he continued and fell into a gross sin, the result of which was that the woman was found to be with child. David sought to deliver himself from this responsibility, but was not successful. Therefore he instructed Joab to put Uriah into the front of the battle, in a place where there would be little opportunity for survival. So it was that Uriah died at the hand of the enemy but at the command of David. With Uriah out of the way, David married the widow, Bathsheba, and felt that he would be recognised as the legal father of the child. God was very displeased with this conduct and His displeasure must be made known to David. Therefore God sent to him Nathan, the prophet, with a parable. It concerned a poor man with an only lamb which he kept as a pet and from which he derived a deal of comfort and companionship. There was also a wealthy man with flocks of sheep, who had a visitor call on him. In entertaining his friend he would not kill one lamb of his flocks. Instead he took the poor man's lamb and slew it for his feast. The kindly, generous David, who was always ready to defend the man who was wronged, upon hearing the story, demanded immediate restitution. Imagine his surprise when Nathan said : " Thou art the man ".

Is it not strange that he could send a man to the front of the battle and have him slain to order by the hand of another that he might " lawfully " steal his wife and yet see no sin in his action ? How is it we can always see the splinter in our brother's eye and fail to realise that there is a beam in our own eye ?

That is the story of Bathsheba. Well might we pray — Oh, that we may see ourselves as others see us ! The fact is that we do see ourselves reflected in other people but fail to recognise our likeness.

When God pointed out to David his sin he immediately acknowledged his guilt and accepted his punishment. Here is where we are ofttimes slow. We try to excuse ourselves, or justify our action, and thereby fall into further sin. Confession is the sure way out.

God must punish, so that the child born of Bathsheba died. David hoped against hope that God's mercy would rise above His judgment. Therefore he did much praying and fasting, but it was not to be.

One does, however, find a display of God's mercy. It was David's sin, but Bathsheba had to be a partaker in his punishment in that she lost her child. God made this up to Bathsheba in permitting her to be the mother of the one who would succeed David on the throne — Solomon.

David's next trouble was a domestic one and concerned his son, Absalom, who is the principal character in the next six chapters.

It commenced with an injustice committed by Absalom's brother, Amnon, toward his sister, Tamar. Sin is a treacherous thing and often hides like a skeleton in the cupboard and comes out always at an inopportune moment. Here it was the sin of immorality committed by a brother toward a sister. What could David do about it? They were his children, but then he had committed a similar sin, and his had included murder. The sinning parent always produces the delinquent child because where there is no point of example there is no power to discipline.

For two years Absalom waited his opportunity for revenge upon his brother. At a feast of the king's sons, which Absalom had planned, he commanded his servants to kill Amnon. Then Absalom fled for his own life. Rumour came to David that all of his sons had died. This, however, was soon disproved. David mourned for his son, Amnon, but Absalom spent three years in exile until David began to long for him, for he, too, was as a lost son.

David was in a difficult position. As a king he must administer the law — that meant banishment — and Absalom must remain in exile. David was also a father and longed for his son. Joab laid hold of this situation to secure a return for Absalom. Therefore he sought out the woman of Tekoah, who was to feign herself as one who was in distress and so gain an entry into the presence of the king with a plea for mercy which, when granted by the king, was converted into a liability of the king toward his son, Absalom. Joab obtained his objective and Absalom was permitted to return to his house but not allowed to see the king. After two more years of separation, again with Joab's help, Absalom and David met.

At this particular time David was not being seen too much in public. After the great sin he had committed concerning Bathsheba and Uriah, the evidence is that he was filled with remorse. Joy went out of his life and the palace seems to have been his hiding place. Undoubtedly this was the period in his life which caused him to pray the prayer recorded in the fifty-first Psalm, in which he confessed his sin, asking God to create in him a clean heart, and said : " Restore unto me the joy of Thy salvation ".

Absalom took advantage of this situation and, whilst the king continued in his self-imposed exile, he moved amongst the public, seeking to win their loyalty. He also sat at the gate of the city, making promises of justice if he were the leader, kissing the hands of the men as he blinded them with fair words. After four years of flattery and promises and pointing out the king's failures, the critical hour came. Absalom asked leave to sacrifice at Hebron. Rebellion in a family is bad enough but, when it is done under the guise of religion, it is infinitely worse. How much of this unholy practice goes on to-day ? So it was that father and son parted, neither knowing that it was the last parting nor yet the tragic consequences that were just ahead.

Absalom had taken two hundred men with him. All were supposed to be his friends, yet none of them knew anything of the plot that was on hand. Wicked men love to use the innocent. If these men had been loyal to their king they would never have become the friends of Absalom. Many Christians become involved in the things of the world that could never have been if only they had been true and steadfast in their loyalty to the Lord. Let us watch our friendships. We cannot make friends with the world and remain a friend of the Lord. The devil loves to see it that way.

The last plan in the plot was to take Ahithophel, David's counsellor. So a treacherous son and a traitor friend joined hand in hand. Is this " Mine own familiar friend in whom I trusted," about whom David wrote in Psalm xli. 9, a man " which did eat of my bread, hath lifted up his heel against me ? "

From Hebron the trumpet sounded at the command of Absalom, and the nation, once so loyal to David, followed the traitor. How very gullible is the public, and how deceitful the heart! Judas could change, Peter could fall, Paul and Barnabas could dissent. How we need to watch lest we also fall into temptation.

On hearing the news, David flew from Jerusalem with his few faithful servants who had pledged their loyalty. These servants were made up of some foreigners. They included men from Gath, where David had killed Goliath. They were faithful when the nation proved faithless, reminding one of the faithlessness of that nation whom the Lord called " His Own ". They forsook Him. They said : " Away with Him ! Crucify Him ! " " But as many as received Him, to them (the foreigners — the Gentiles) gave He power to become the sons of God ". In turn that Church fails Him in the last days, except for the faithful few who are ready to be recognised with Him in His rejection. The testimony of their loyalty is heard in words like : " And the king's servants said unto the king, Behold, thy servants are ready to do whatsoever my lord the king shall appoint " (xv. 15), or Ittai saying : " . . . As the Lord liveth, and as my lord the king liveth, surely in what place my lord the king shall be, whether in death or life, even there also will thy servant be " (xv. 21).

David was so cast down, conscious that this was the result of his own sin, that he had no spirit to fight or to retaliate. Even when Shimei followed alongside and cursed, he accepted his punishment from God (xvi. 10). The only thing that David did was to send Hushai into the ranks of Absalom with the intent that he might upset the councils of the traitor friend, Ahithophel. This worked out to the advantage of David. Ahithophel took his own life.

In chapter xviii. David regained some strength morally and numerically. He numbered his people and divided them into three companies and sent them out to battle under the hands of Joab, Abishai, and Ittai. At the people's request David himself did not go into the battle, but he gave orders that no harm should come to Absalom.

The story is well known of how the battle went against the rebellious army so that they were scattered, and fled. The handsome and proud Absalom, whilst riding on his mule, had his head tangled in the branches of a great oak. The mule moved on, leaving Absalom suspended in mid-air. Instead of taking the usurper as a prisoner, which in any case would be correct procedure, particularly so in this instance, as the king had given orders that the young man's life should be spared, Joab, in defiance of orders given by the supreme commander, took three darts and thrust them into the heart of Absalom, and he died.

Thus ended another tragic battle in the life of David. Absalom in his pride, and having no children, had already prepared his own sepulchre, known as Absalom's pillar, but he was never buried therein. As a traitor a heap of stones placed over him was all that marked his untimely burial. Pride goes before a fall.

The chapter closes with that beautiful ode of lamentation that fell from the lips of David : " O my son Absalom, my son, my son Absalom ! Would God I had died for thee, O Absalom, my son, my son . "

The question might readily arise in many minds as to why such an ode for such a traitor. The people at that time had the same question in their minds. Joab reproved the king for displaying a grief over one dead traitor and forgetting the loyalty of all his faithful followers, as he said : " For this day I perceive that if Absalom had lived, and all we had died this day, then it had pleased thee well " (xix. 6). But there was a very deep reason for this lamentation, with the emphasis on " my son ". David felt that Absalom had wronged him only because he had been wronged in the first place. He was a spoiled child. Unpunished sin always becomes an uncontrollable giant later. If David had trained the child he would have been a disciplined man. Many parents have suffered grief in their later years and have gone to the grave with a guilty conscience and a sad heart because they have had to reap the fruit of seed sown in early days, the seed of a spoiled child. Let us watch our family responsibility and thereby enjoy good family relationship.

A turn in events took place in chapter nineteen as David was reinstated. He returned to Jerusalem with great joy, surrounded by a company of well-wishers. Three men sought and obtained an interview. Firstly came Shimei, the man who had cursed the king when he was in exile. He confessed his sin and was forgiven. Secondly, Mephibosheth, who had not followed the king in his wanderings, came to plead his innocence and was accepted. Then came Barzillai, and his purpose was to conduct the king safely over Jordan. David was anxious to reward him for service rendered, and offered him full provision. Barzillai, being an old man of four-score years, felt that he would be a burden rather than an asset, and declined the king's charity, requesting that it should be bestowed upon a substitute, one by the name of Chimham. David agreed, and so the journey continued.

Whilst the king was received with thanksgiving by the men of Judah there was a dissension. Israel was not sure, so Sheba led a revolt. He was supported by Amasa in an act of disobedience. David quickly gathered together the men of Judah and both Amasa and Sheba died.

Three successive years of famine struck the land of Israel, causing David to enquire the reason of the Lord. God informed David that it was because Saul had slain the Gibeonites. There appears to be no other record than this concerning the slaughter, but the crime was heinous. It was true that these people were alien, but they had appealed to Joshua for protection, and it had been granted under oath (Jos. ix. 15). God would not allow vows to be broken without punishment. Saul had evidently defied the law of God in this respect, and had slain the people who should have been protected. We must conclude that the nation had not protested against the king's conduct. Therefore God was punishing the nation with famine, year after year, until the nation had righted its wrong. Seeing the Gibeonites were the people who had received the injustice, they should have the right to decide what retribution should be made.

They asked for the lives of seven sons of the man who was responsible for the massacre. To this David gave his assent. So seven sons of Saul were taken, Mephibosheth, the son of Jonathan, being spared because of an oath that existed between David and Jonathan. Two sons of Rizpah and five sons of Michal were given to the Gibeonites, who hanged them in Gibeah.

This story recounts one of the most heroic vigils of all time. The mother of two of these men, Rizpah by name, took up a lonely vigil over these dead bodies, allowing neither bird by day nor wild beast by night to touch them. How long did Rizpah maintain her lonely watch ? We can only guess, but we are told "from the beginning of harvest (which would be about April of our year) until water dropped upon them out of heaven ". Palestine knows no rainfall between late April and early October, which would suggest a five-month vigil. David, hearing of the devotion of this woman, took the bones of these men and, with those of Saul and Jonathan, gave them proper burial. This act of Rizpah revealed another failing on the part of either David or the Gibeonites, or both, for Deut. xxi. 22-23 says : "And if a man have committed a sin worthy of death, and he be to be put to death, and thou hang him on a tree : His body shall not remain all night upon the tree, but thou shalt in any wise bury him that day ; (for he that is hanged is accursed of God ;), that thy land be not defiled, which the Lord thy God giveth thee for an inheritance ".

A couple of more wars with the Philistines end the chapter.

(3) DAVID'S TESTIMONY (Chs. xxii-xxiv.)

David then entered a period of blessing. It commenced with a song of thanksgiving that is typical of so many of his psalms. One almost thinks it is a chapter which has lost its place in the book.

A list of David's mighty men and what they did is then given — lives devoted and sacrifices made, not readily forgotten in this world nor in the world to come. There are names written in heaven; there are also the " other books " which record the works that we have performed for great David's greater Son.

The last chapter records the second of David's two great sins. This time it was numbering the children of Israel, an act contrary to the revealed mind of God. Joab warned David of his mistake, but David accepted no warning and went ahead with his plan, until it was too late. As the total figure was brought to David so his heart smote him with guilt and he confessed his foolishness, but the sin had been performed. David was told to choose the punishment that must be inflicted :

    (1)   Seven years of famine in the land.

    (2)   Fleeing before his enemy for three months.

    (3)   Three days of pestilence in the land.

David was wise enough to cast his burden on the Lord, and allowed Him to make the choice, trusting that the Lord would show forth His mercy. God sent the pestilence, and also His mercy as the pestilence reached the city of Jerusalem. " It is enough : stay now thy hand ! " said God to the destroying angel.

David, who was always ready to take his own punishment, told the Lord that he had done the sinning — why should these sheep suffer ? What had they done ? Fundamentally, the sin was not David's ; instrumentally it was. In the first verse of the chapter God's anger was kindled against Israel. It was the nation which must be punished. God moved David, so that David became the instrument.

David purchased the threshing floor of Araunah, the site where God stopped the punishment, and there he built an altar and offered offerings that were accepted by God.

The book ends abruptly because the narrative continues in the next book. We shall end our lives abruptly here to find a continuation in the life that is to come.

I KINGS

THE ESTABLISHMENT AND DECLINE OF THE KINGDOM

*" And he (David) charged Solomon his son, saying, I go the
way of all the earth : be thou strong therefore, and shew
thyself a man : And keep the charge of the Lord thy God,
to walk in His ways, to keep His statutes, and His commandments, and His judgments, and His testimonies, as it is written
in the law of Moses, that thou mayest prosper in all that thou
doest, and whithersoever thou turnest thyself : That the Lord
may continue His Word which He spake concerning me,
saying, If thy children take heed to their way, to walk before
Me in truth with all their heart and with all their soul, there
shall not fail thee (said He) a man on the throne of Israel."*
(1 KINGS ii. 1-4.)

INTRODUCTION

For many years these two books of Kings were one. The
Septuagint Translators were the first to divide the book into two
parts, their only purpose being for easiness of reference.

Whilst the books are recognised as being historical, and that
in relationship to a nation and its kings, yet it should be appreciated
that the character of the books must be different from any other
book of history as, for example, a history of the kings of England.
It has been said that

(1) The records would be those of pious Jews who would see
everything in relation to religion rather than politics. The historians
of Israel were mostly prophets. If Jeremiah were the author of
the books of the Kings, as many think, this would be appreciated.

(2) Divine Inspiration would guide these men to write concerning these kings, not so much in their relationship to their
subjects as in relationship to the Invisible Ruler of Israel.

The statement has also been made that " Hebrew antiquity
does not know the secular historian ". As a result of this the king
and the prophet have an equal prominence in this Old Testament
history. It will be noted that, from the end of the reign of Solomon,
the voice of the prophet was prominent to the end of the Old
Testament.

It is discovered, therefore, that the object of the books is to show the rise, the glories, and the decline of the Hebrew kingdom according to the people's acceptance or rejection of their God, and that the people's relationship with God was so often dependent on the attitude of their reigning monarch.

The two books cover a period of four hundred and fifty years from the ascension of Solomon to the captivity of Jehoiachin.

The first book divides equally into two parts :

(1) The History and reign of Solomon (Chs. i-xi.).

(2) The History of the kingdoms of Judah and Israel (Chs. xii-xxii.).

A further division gives :

(a) The death of David.

(b) The life and reign of Solomon.

(c) The building of the Temple.

(d) The disruption of the Kingdom.

(e) The ministry of Elijah.

The two principal characters are :

Solomon, the king.

Elijah, the prophet.

(1) THE HISTORY AND REIGN OF SOLOMON (Chs. i-xi.)

(a) THE DEATH OF DAVID. The book is a strict continuation of 2 Samuel and opens with the death of David.

The opening verses are a little puzzling to most of us. Seemingly, there was a practice in those early days, under med:cal advice, whereby the life of an older person could be prolonged through the warmth of the body of a young maiden, and apparently the young breath helped to sustain life, but at the expense of the health of the maiden (quoted from *Pulpit Commentary*).

Adonijah, David's eldest son, realising that his father's life was near an end, felt that, as the eldest son, he had a right to the throne, but was conscious that it was not coming to him legally. Therefore he conceived a scheme whereby he might obtain it by guile. Gathering some admirers around him, including Abiathar, the priest, he established himself as king at Enrogel.

Nathan, the prophet, quickly reacted to the situation by sending Bathsheba, the mother of Solomon, into the presence of David, enquiring of David whether he was aware of the conduct of Adonijah, or whether he had withdrawn his promise that Solomon should reign. Whilst she was in the king's presence Nathan came to confirm her story.

David strengthened himself for the occasion and ordered the proclamation of Solomon as king. "Adonijahs" respect neither age, infirmity, principle, nor anything else. They are always ready to assert their selfish authority. The Christian must be bold and quick in action to defend the right against the would-be usurper.

Behind the conduct of this selfish authority of Adonijah is a solemn word to all parents, and, remember, all Scripture is written for our admonition. It is the sixth verse of this first chapter : "And his father had not displeased him at any time in saying, Why hast thou done so ? . . . " It is another of the many evidences of the results of bad training. He had never been reproved as a child. He had always had his own way ; of course, he expected it now — but it was too late. Absalom had rebelled before him, again because of bad training. Absalom's heap of stones never spoke to this man. He was too selfish to see anything but self.

David then gave to Solomon a charge to walk in the ways of God and to keep His statutes, also to deal with the enemies of the throne according to their desert.

So David died, after reigning for forty years — Israel's greatest king.

(b) THE LIFE AND REIGN OF SOLOMON. Solomon, having come to the throne, was quickly put to the test by another sly move on the part of Adonijah, who made a second bid for the throne. Through the medium of Solomon's mother he sought the king's permission to marry Abishag, the young maiden who had ministered to David in his last days. It was a move toward that throne by marriage, with intent to dethrone Solomon. The king, seeing that so long as Adonijah lived the throne would be endangered, ordered his execution. Joab, who had shared in Adonijah's sins, shared also in his judgment and died for his disloyalty. Abiathar was exiled, his life being spared because he was a priest and had carried the Ark of the Covenant.

David's other enemy, transferred to Solomon's care, was Shimei. He was bidden to build a house in Jerusalem and to remain there. So long as he did he would live. Shimei accepted the conditions, but in time failed to abide by them, and died as a result.

Chapter three moves right into Solomon's life as it says : "And Solomon made affinity with Pharaoh, king of Egypt, and took Pharaoh's daughter . . . ". This calls for an overall picture.

Such shows the tragedy of polygamy. Many wives mean quarrellings and wranglings for favour. This would be imbibed by the children, who would be reared in a morally unhealthy environment, with a hatred each for the other, in a luxury which was harmful to mental ability, and with a lack of parental influence which was revealed in after life, and is seen in Adonijah, Absalom, Rehoboam, as well as Solomon, who failed completely because of polygamy.

Solomon had three visions in his life :

(1) In his youth   — His ascension   — To encourage
(2) In his success   — The Temple Dedication — To warn
(3) In his decline   — His idolatry   — To condemn

God brought him three enemies :

(1) Rezon   —   In Syria.
(2) Hadad   —   The Edomite.
(3) Jeroboam   —   The son of Nebat.

His three great sins were :

(1) Polygamy   —   Many wives.
(2) Polytheism —   Many gods.
(3) Pleasure   —   Many indulgences.

These together spell Declension.

Solomon began his reign very well, showing himself kingly before his enemies and godly before the people. " Solomon loved the Lord, walking in the statutes of David his father " (iii. 3). At the time when he made the great sacrifice of a thousand burnt offerings at Gibeon, the Lord made His first appearance to Solomon. It was a great occasion. God came to him, saying : " Ask what I shall give thee ? " Some may say — surely, he had enough ! But evidently not, or God would not have offered him such a choice. What a privilege, say others ! But is it not our privilege as well ? " Ask and it shall be given you " is the Lord's promise. James tells us that we have not because we ask not (iv. 2-3). Our trouble is that we fail to lay hold of our privileges, or we abuse our privilege by asking amiss. Solomon showed wisdom in asking for wisdom. This, too, could be ours, for James encourages us in this virtue, saying : " If any of you lack wisdom, let him ask of God, that giveth to all men liberally, and upbraideth not : and it shall be given him " (James i. 5).

The particular wisdom given to Solomon is seen in his books of Wisdom — Proverbs, Song of Solomon, and Ecclesiastes, to which are added his 1,005 songs (iv. 32).

His gift of wisdom was quickly demonstrated when two women came to him claiming one baby.

The next chapters tell of the wealth and prosperity of this great king. His princes and officers are listed, the abundance of his household, the extent of his wisdom, and his alliance with Hiram, king of Tyre.

(c) THE BUILDING OF THE TEMPLE. Knowing that "Hiram was ever a lover of David" Solomon sent to him telling of the desire of David to build a house unto the Name of the Lord his God, and making known how God had not permitted David to build but had promised that his son should. Solomon told of his intent to erect that building, and requested Hiram's help in supplying the material and craftsmen. Hiram agreed to this and terms were arranged.

So began the building of the most magnificent Temple ever constructed for the worship of God, details of which cannot be dealt with in a digest. Fundamentally it was an enlargement and elaboration of the Tabernacle, which is the more profitable study.

Maybe the subject could be summarised thus :

The Preparation. This included making the plans and gathering the material, the fir and the cedar, the huge costly stones, the gold and the brass. There must always be preparation before building. God planned His Church in eternity and began to build it on earth at Pentecost. Buildings are planned and preparations made long before man sees any evidence of construction, and hearts must know something of the preparation of the Holy Spirit if men are to witness the building of Christian character and see the Church established on earth.

The Building. Sufficient to say that the best of man's intellect, the costliest of material, the greatest of man's skill, and the finest of workmanship, tell us that nothing short of the best is good enough for God. Then followed

The Dedication. When Solomon began to pray he was on his feet (viii. 22). When he finished he was on his knees (viii. 54). The sense of the Presence of God will always humble the believer as he becomes sensitive to his unworthiness.

The order of this building is beautiful — Preparation, Realisation, Dedication — We desire, God gives, we give back.

Besides the Temple Solomon also built his own palace, the house of the forest of Lebanon, the house of Pharaoh's daughter, and the porch of judgment.

After these great accomplishments, when Solomon was at the height of his fame, God appeared to him for the second time, this time with a word of warning. It is in chapter nine. Maybe two statements from verses 4 and 6 would sum up the nine verses : " If thou wilt walk before Me as David thy father walked . . . But if ye shall turn from following Me ". How we all need such a reminder from time to time, and especially when a measure of success comes our way.

Twenty years of his reign were behind him at this point, and twenty years of reign were yet to be. Solomon was still building, and his navy was still bringing wealth to him.

It was at this time that he was visited by the queen of Sheba. This royal personage had heard a great deal of the fame of Solomon. She had heard more than she could believe. She did the wisest thing that any sceptic can do. She took a journey to find out for herself. This brought from her lips the well known words : " Howbeit I believed not the words, until I came, and mine eyes had seen it : and, behold, the half was not told me : Thy wisdom and prosperity exceedeth the fame which I heard " (x. 7).

If only we would come personally to the Word of God and look for ourselves into the " depth of the riches both of the wisdom and knowledge of God " (Rom. xi. 33) we, too, would have to declare that the half has never yet been told.

Having learned so much about the glory of Solomon, chapter eleven commences with that unpleasant word of the reverse — BUT. " But Solomon loved many strange women " — seven hundred wives and three hundred concubines. It would have been tragic if the narrative had told us that he loved many women, but that word " strange " turns tragedy into disaster. Apart from the daughter of Pharaoh, an Egyptian, there were Moabites, Ammonites, Edomites, Zidonians, Hittites. These were the heathen nations with whom the Lord had forbidden marriage. God had a reason why He forbade these marriages — the thing that happened right here. They turned his heart away from the Lord to other gods, a polygamy that led to a polytheism. As a result God was angry with Solomon and, for the third time, appeared to him, on this occasion in condemnation. He had turned from God, God would turn the kingdom from him. So came the first step in the decline of the kingdom. Turning from God means decline in any life, irrespective of any kind of past success or present popularity.

Because of David and God's promises to him, the judgment
was to be delayed until the next generation but, for the moment,
God was going to punish Solomon with three enemies :

Hadad   — the Edomite, one of the king's seed.

Rezon   — the king of Syria.

Jeroboam — the son of Nebat, about whom we shall read
much, for he was the man who led the
revolt that rent the kingdom in twain.

This chapter, which began with " But king Solomon loved
many strange women ", ends with the death of Solomon, recorded
in only three verses.

This was another outstanding life that ended sorrowfully
because of turning away from God — Samson, Saul, Solomon.

(2) HISTORY OF THE KINGDOMS OF JUDAH AND
ISRAEL (Chs. xii-xxii.)

(d) THE DISRUPTION OF THE KINGDOM. The throne
being hereditary, all Israel went to Shechem to make

Rehoboam, the son of Solomon, king, but God had already
declared otherwise. A remnant of the kingdom would remain in
the family for David's sake, who walked in the fear of the Lord,
but the major part would be taken away because of Solomon, who
walked not in the ways of the Lord.

Jeroboam, speaking on behalf of the congregation of Israel,
sought from the new king some relief from the heavy taxation that
had been imposed on them for the building up of the nation and
the fabulous buildings of Solomon. Rehoboam consulted the older
men, who agreed that this must be done. He then consulted the
younger men, who advised an increase in the burdens. Rehoboam
followed the foolish advice of the inexperienced men to his undoing.
A revolt took place. Ten tribes followed Jeroboam and only two
tribes remained with Rehoboam, the son of Solomon. So we
have the divided kingdom that has remained until this day and
will continue until the fulfilment of Ezekiel's prophecy in Ezk.
xxxvii. 15-28.

The ten tribes have been known as the House of Israel and
the two tribes (Judah and Benjamin) as the House of Judah. Here
begins the chequered history of the nation under the kings — some
good, some evil.

Jeroboam, fearing that if the people went to Jerusalem for
their worship and their feast days, they might desire to return to
Rehoboam and the House of David, established two golden calves
and altars, one in Dan in the extreme North, and the other in

Bethel, and bade all the people worship at the one or the other. Thereby idolatry was established in the land.

One day, as Jeroboam was at the altar in Bethel engaged in his idolatrous worship, God sent a prophet to him to prophesy against the altar and to tell of God's coming judgment on idolatry in the days of Josiah, who would re-establish the worship of God and would burn the bones of the false priests upon their own false altars. The fulfilment of this prophecy is recorded in 2 Kings xxiii. 20. As a sign that he was declaring the truth, the prophet said that this altar in Bethel would be rent and the ashes poured forth, and so it was. Jeroboam put forth his hand to lay hold on the prophet and, as he did, God withered it. At the request of the king God restored the hand. The king desired to reward the prophet, and so invited him home for a meal, but God had warned him not to eat or drink in that place. Therefore he refused and went on his way. Whilst resting, he was met by another prophet (not a prophet of the Lord) who bade him come home to eat and drink. After a first refusal he went, and thereby disobeyed the Word of the Lord, and on his return was slain by a lion.

This should be a reminder to us that life is full of temptations, even for the servant of the Lord, and that there are many false prophets and false spirits abroad in these last days. We must know, therefore, the Word of the Lord on the one hand, and try the spirits on the other hand. Does not the Word of the Lord through Peter fit into this story ? " But there were false prophets also among the people, even as there shall be false teachers among you, who privily shall bring in damnable heresies, even denying the Lord that bought them, and bring upon themselves swift destruction " (2 Pet. ii. 1).

Jeroboam showed no signs of repentance even after this warning from God, but increased his evil ways. However, evil men have a way of running to the Lord when they are in personal distress. Jeroboam had a son, Abijah, who fell sick and, being anxious as to the boy's future, he told his wife to disguise herself and to go to Ahijah, the prophet of the Lord, and enquire as to whether the child should live. But men cannot deceive God. God informed the prophet of the guise, and he was ready to pronounce the judgment of God upon Jeroboam and the whole of his house. So Jeroboam, king of Israel, died after twenty-two years of evil reign, and Nadab, his son, reigned in his stead. He only reigned for two years and then the throne was taken from that family.

The narrative leaves the House of Israel and turns to the House of Judah, to the remnant that was left with Rehoboam who, for seventeen years, reigned in Jerusalem. It is the same sad story of God rejection and the setting up of images and groves. As a punishment God allowed Shishak, king of Egypt, to war against Jerusalem and to carry away some of the wealth that Solomon had accumulated. Shishak carried away the shields of gold, Rehoboam replaced them with shields of brass. This deterioration was typical. They had substituted the gold of a pure religion for the tarnished brass of idolatry, which involves not only a loss of faith, but of morals, of character, of power, of wealth, of everything that is worthwhile. Our faith is our foundation. Keep it pure. Keep it in God, and we are rich ; lose it and we have lost everything.

Rehoboam was succeeded on the throne by *Abijam*. He not only followed Rehoboam to the throne, but he also followed him in all his evil ways. God only allowed him to remain on the throne so that it could come to his son and thus remain in the family of David, as God had promised. So Abijam reigned for three years and died, and *Asa,* his son, reigned in his stead.

Asa was a good king. His heart was right with God. He reigned for forty-one years, that was a year longer than either Saul, David, or Solomon, and yet little is recorded ; in fact, nothing other than his constant war with Baasha, king of Israel. He died in old age with disease in his feet. There are many Christians like Asa. Good men, without a doubt, but they are belligerent, so aggressive in fighting their brethren that they come to the end of life without accomplishing anything. They never have a constructive policy — just diseased feet that trample down the other people.

Again we return to Israel to read that *Nadab* reigned for two years, *Baasha* for twenty-four years, *Elah* for two years, *Zimri* for seven days, and *Omri* for twenty-two years, each man doing that which was evil in the eyes of the Lord, walking in the ways of Jeroboam, until it is recorded that : " Omri wrought evil in the eyes of the Lord, and did worse than all that were before him " (xvi. 25). Even here the deterioration had not stopped, because Omri had a son who stepped lower still, for we are led into the infamous reign of *Ahab.* He is introduced to us with this condemnation : " And Ahab the son of Omri did evil in the sight of the Lord above all that were before him. And it came to pass, as if it had been a little thing for him to walk in the sins of Jeroboam the son of Nebat, that he took to wife Jezebel the daughter of Ethbaal king of the Zidonians, and went and served Baal and worshipped him " (I Kings xvi. 30-31).

Here we are introduced to another era.

(g) THE MINISTRY OF ELIJAH. It was at this point that the voice of the prophet became pronounced. The king had failed as an example of godly leadership, so now the king and prophet rule together. The king ruled the people, but God would rule the king through the prophet. Both men wielded an influence over the nation, one for evil and the other for good. The balance of this book concerns Ahab, the king, and Elijah, the prophet. The voice of the prophet prevailed over the voice of the king, for it was both powerful and effective. The following chapters give some wonderful pictures of the prophet, a witness for God in the midst of the sins of his day.

Elijah was the prophet of fire, the man who denounced kings, who pronounced judgments, and was so different in his ministry from the Elisha who followed him.

Six outstanding events are recorded out of this amazing life.

Elijah at the Brook Cherith.

The Widow of Zarephath.

Raising the Widow's son.

Elijah on Mount Carmel.

Elijah at Horeb.

Naboth's vineyard.

He is introduced standing before the wicked Ahab announcing a three-year drought because of sin ; after this he was ushered away to the *Brook Cherith,* where God commanded the ravens to feed him, whilst he drank from an ever-dwindling brook. There is no limit to the Lord's ways and means of providing for His people, both naturally and supernaturally. The brook may run dry and fail, but the Lord can never fail in the constancy of His supply. Would it not be wonderful if we could all learn that fact. We get so concerned with our diminishing supply that we forget to look up to the immeasurable sky and to the steadfast mountains from whence cometh our help.

Zarephath. The Lord bade His servant to leave his long exile, go to a place called Zarephath in Zidon, and dwell there. Here he would enjoy the company and the hospitality of a widow woman. The name " Zarephath " means " the place of furnaces ". Scholars tell us that there is evidence that at one time a smelting and refining business had been carried on in this locality, from whence it evidently got its name. Little did either Elijah or the widow know that God was about to put them both into the furnace of trial. However, we rejoice in that they both came out as refined gold and as purified silver. Firstly, there was Elijah who, when he arrived at the city, found his hostess a poor woman

gathering sticks — not very encouraging, to be sure ! He asked for
water. That was a cheap enough commodity. Not at all ! There
was a drought so that water was in very short supply. He had
just moved from Cherith for water. This was test number one
for the widow, but there was no hesitancy on her part.

Then he asked for bread, and the whole truth was revealed.
This woman had a son to support, and they had been reduced
to the last handful of meal and the last drop of oil, and beyond
these there was nothing because of the famine. Her few sticks
were to kindle the fire in order to bake this last cake, and die.
Now both prophet and widow went into the furnace of testing.
A strong healthy well-fed man had to say to a starving woman,
with a hungry son : " Make me thereof a little cake first, and
bring it unto me, and after make for thee and for thy son. For
thus saith the Lord God of Israel, The barrel of meal shall not
waste, neither shall the cruse of oil fail, until the day that the
Lord sendeth rain upon the earth. And she went and did according to the saying of Elijah ; and she, and he, and her house, did
eat many days " (xvii. 13-15).

Could I do that if I were in the prophet's room ? Could I
do that if I were in the widow's need ? Truly the place of furnaces,
but faith rose to the occasion and God never fails.

The Widow's son. One would have thought that this woman
had proved herself, but " God moves in a mysterious way His
wonders to perform ". In return for this generous hospitality
God took her child from her, and she complained. Elijah took
the body of the child to his room and interceded with God,
stretching himself upon the child. God answered his prayer, and
the child was raised from death and returned to the sorrowing
mother. Thus were Elijah and his ministry confirmed as being of
God.

Mount Carmel. After three years of drought for the nation
and three years of exile and provision for the prophet, God sent
Elijah back to Ahab the king.

Ahab, who was more concerned about his horses than he
was about his subjects, divided the land between himself and his
servant Obadiah, that they might search for grass. This Obadiah
was a God-fearing man who had helped to save some of the
prophets of the Lord from the hand of Jezebel. As they were
engaged in their search Elijah met Obadiah and bade him go and
tell Ahab that " Behold, Elijah is here ". Obadiah was not willing
to obey until assured by Elijah that he would really meet the

king. Thus the two men came face to face after three years of hide and seek.

Elijah suggested a means whereby the true God, Jehovah or Baal, might be proved. Ahab accepted the challenge. The people of Israel were gathered to the top of Mount Carmel, also four hundred and fifty prophets of Baal and four hundred of the groves (xviii. 19). Elijah challenged the people : " How long halt ye between two opinions ? If the Lord be God, follow Him : but if Baal, then follow him ". It is to be noted that the people had no answer, which was a confession of their guilt and an evidence as to which way the conflict would end. Elijah stood alone and gave the advantage to Baal and his four hundred and fifty prophets, who called all day for him to send down fire. They used all of their religious ritual, but without success.

After this, when the sun had fallen in the sky, with no suggestion of solar fire, Elijah repaired the altar of the Lord that was broken down. Elijah was offering no new thing, but was calling the people back to the old altar, to the old faith. He then drenched the altar with water.

Some people ask about this water, seeing they were at the end of a three-year drought. The well is still on Mount Carmel, it is still giving water, it has never failed. It is called Elijah's well. Of course, a well on a mountain will not supply the needs of towns in the valley.

Then came the glorious victory as Elijah prayed and the fire came down, whilst the people cried : " The Lord, He is the God. The Lord, He is the God ". The prophets of Baal, who had been leading the people away from God, were slain by Elijah.

Elijah told Ahab to return with speed because there was the sound of abundance of rain.

The next scene is very different. It is

Mount Horeb — from elated victory to dejected defeat. Jezebel, upon hearing of the death of the prophets of Baal, declared that Elijah would be as they within twenty-four hours. So Elijah arose and went for his life. It has often been remarked that the courageous Elijah, who stood and defied kings, fled like a coward from the woman, Jezebel. Such remarks are uncharitable and certainly not good interpretation, because they are not in harmony with the character of the man, nor yet in accord with the narrative.

The Scripture tells us that he " came to Beersheba, which belongeth to Judah, and left his servant there. But he himself went a day's journey into the wilderness, and came and sat down under a juniper tree : and he requested for himself that he might

die : and said, It is enough ; now, O Lord, take away my life ; for
I am not better than my fathers " (xix. 3-4). That does not sound
like a frightened man fleeing from a woman who has declared that
she would kill him. He was not afraid to die. He was prepared
to die right there in a lonely wilderness, but it does sound like
the language of a very disappointed man, as he says : " . . . for
I am not better than my fathers ".

Elijah thought a great victory had been gained on Mount
Carmel, the result of which would be a national revival, and that
God would have been acknowledged from the throne downwards.
Instead it was increased opposition. Jezebel had expressed her
feelings and Elijah fled as a disappointed man into solitude, where
he could think this through with God. This has ofttimes been a
preacher's reaction, although the world and, at times, the Church
never knows it.

As an evidence of this condition of soul the text shows no
reproof for cowardice but, firstly, a meal was supplied by God
for his physical exhaustion after the battle, and then He took him
on to Horeb to show him that God has more than one way of
gaining victories and winning the hearts of men. Sometimes it is
in the wind, the earthquake, and the fire, the Mount Carmel
experience — but not always. God has a way of using the still
small voice.

One has watched a nation living under the stress and strain
of war, air-raids, food shortage, and every other calamity, without
a sense of their need of God except in a superficial way. In fact,
the evidence was a slow but persistent moving away from God.
Then came the voice of the humble servant of the Lord — a man
with a message : " The Bible says ", and the nation begins to fall
on its knees.

God had to show to Elijah that He had other servants and
other ways, seven thousand who had not bowed the knee to Baal.

Could it be that the " still small voice " was the introduction
to the ministry, the quiet ministry, of Elisha, for the chapter closes
with the call of the new prophet.

Elisha was actively engaged in his farming pursuits when the
passing Elijah cast his prophetic mantle upon him. God always
calls busy men. The man who is faithful in the little things is the
man who can be ruler over much ; Moses, David, and Amos, with
the sheep, Elisha behind the plow, Peter and John mending nets,
and Carey mending shoes, Livingstone from the loom of Blantyre.

What a story is the call of Elisha ! " He left the oxen and
ran " — no delay. He returned to burn his yokes and sacrifice

his oxen — full surrender. " Then he arose, and went after Elijah and ministered unto him " — appreciating the company of a good man.

Chapter twenty deals with war between Benhadad, the king of Syria, and Ahab, king of Samaria. Samaria was besieged, but God delivered not once, but twice. However, Ahab failed God in destroying the enemy to his own undoing. This is followed by the well-known story of

Naboth's Vineyard. Although Ahab had extensive possessions, he coveted a property belonging to one by the name of Naboth. Sending for him, the king offered an exchange of land or a handsome price, assuring Naboth that he intended to have the vineyard to turn it into a garden of herbs. Naboth refused the proposition with the words : " The Lord forbid it me, that I should give the inheritance of my father unto thee ". This was more than the king expected. Therefore he went back to his palace much displeased, and sulked over his disappointment. Jezebel, finding the king in this condition, enquired the reason and learned that he had been frustrated by Naboth, who had refused to sell him his vineyard. This wicked woman, who was really dominating the king and the nation at the time, took the situation in hand, asking the king as to who was reigning, he or Naboth. She assured the king that she would secure the property. She did. By foul means she had Naboth murdered, and then instructed Ahab to take possession of the vineyard as Naboth was no longer alive. Without asking questions as to the cause of this man's death, Ahab went down to take possession and to make his plans of conversion into a kitchen garden. God had witnessed this atrocious act, and instructed Elijah to go down and meet Ahab. He would be found in Naboth's vineyard taking possession of it. Thus Ahab and Elijah, who had not seen each other from the day of Mount Carmel, which was seven years earlier, were brought face to face, when Elijah pronounced God's judgment upon the wicked king.

An explanation of this story is required, as some have put the responsibility of the crime upon the shoulders of Naboth because he was stubborn instead of co-operative with the king. They suggest that the king's offer was fair, and that it would matter little to Naboth whether he had this piece of land or another.

It must be borne in mind that the land was divided into tribes and then into families. Nonetheless the land remained the Lord's. In Lev. xxv. 33 it states : " The land shall not be sold for ever : for the land is Mine ". As a result of this law, land was always sold on a fifty-year lease, so that in the year of Jubilee the land returned to the original landlord, which is the record of Lev. xxv. This would mean that King Ahab was wanting to buy away from Naboth his inheritance. To sell to Ahab would mean selling to Jezebel, and she was a Zidonian. This was the reason of Naboth's refusal. He was a man faithful to his trust.

The book concludes with the battle that brought to an end twenty-two years of an evil reign. Ahab solicits the help of Jehoshaphat, king of Judah, to war against Syria, because the man, who greedily wanted Naboth's vineyard, had not learned his lesson, and now wanted Ramoth-Gilead, even although Micaiah, the man of God, warned him. It may appear that Micaiah was on the side of Ahab from casual reading, although Ahab did not recognise any friendship. The answer is that the remarks of Micaiah were sarcastic. If read that way the narrative becomes clear.

In the battle Ahab died according to the word of Elijah in Ch. xxi. 19.

The last two kings are mentioned as far as the history of the kings goes in this first book. Jehoshaphat reigned twenty-five years in Judah and died. Ahaziah, the son of Ahab, reigned two years in Israel and died.

II KINGS

MAN'S DISRUPTION

" Because thou servest not the Lord thy God with joyfulness,
and with gladness of heart, for the abundance of all things:
Therefore shalt thou serve thine enemies which the Lord shall
send against thee, in hunger, and in thirst, and in nakedness,
and in want of all things: He shall put a yoke of iron upon
thy neck, until He have destroyed thee. The Lord shall
bring a nation against thee from far, from the end of the
earth, as swift as the eagle flieth; a nation whose tongue
thou shalt not understand."   (DEUTERONOMY xxviii 47-49)

INTRODUCTION

This book, which is a strict continuation of 1 Kings, still
deals with the two characters, the king and the prophet. The
three centuries it covers is the period from Elijah's translation to
the Babylonian captivity.

The book teaches on the one hand God's steadfastness, and
on the other hand man's disruption. It reveals an ever-repeated
fact that the heart is deceitful above all things and desperately
wicked.

Except for Saul and David, all the kings of Judah and Israel
are recorded in these joint books.

The book can be analysed thus — the first seventeen chapters
contain the contemporary history of Israel and Judah, the last
eight chapters record the decline and fall of Judah; or it can be
divided at chapter eight: (1) The Prophet; (2) The Kings. The
book will be treated according to this second division.

(1) THE PROPHET

(a) ELIJAH'S FINAL MINISTRY. The first two chapters
bring to a conclusion the ministry of Elijah. Ahaziah, the king,
had met with an accident and, being concerned as to whether he
should recover, he sent his servants to enquire of Baal-zebub, a
heathen god. Elijah met these servants on the way and bade
them return to their master and tell him he would surely die. The
king enquired of his servants from whence they secured their
information. When they described the man, Ahaziah recognised

that it was Elijah, the prophet. Therefore he sent a captain with fifty men to instruct Elijah to come down. Instead of going, the prophet called down fire from heaven. The reason for this was that the prophet knew that there was no repentance in the heart of the king but, rather, he hoped that he might persuade or bribe the prophet to reverse the judgment. A second fifty were sent with the same result. As to the injustice that appears, one is left to conclude that these men were one with the king in his sin. Notice the hard commands they gave the prophet : " Come down " (vs. 9). " Come down quickly " (vs. 11). The world has no right to order a servant of the Lord who takes his instructions from his Master. It was because these men were in opposition to God that Elijah called down fire from heaven and consumed these two bands. When the third captain came with his fifty, it was without command. He came with humility and with a desire for mercy. Therefore he obtained mercy and gained his mission without even asking.

Thus man should never dictate to God, but, rather, confess his unworthiness and seek divine grace. To such the Lord has promised : " Before they call I will answer and whilst they are yet speaking I will perform ".

Elijah returned with this captain to the king, not to compromise, but to confirm the judgment already declared, and so it was that Ahaziah died as a God-rejector.

(b) ELIJAH'S TRANSLATION. This servant of the Lord, who had three times called down fire from heaven, was now caught up to heaven in a chariot of fire, with horses of fire. The man, who was here today and somewhere else tomorrow, who was moved so mysteriously by the Lord that Obadiah said : " And it shall come to pass as soon as I am gone from thee, that the Spirit of the Lord shall carry thee whither I know not " (1 Kings xviii. 12) was now caught up to heaven in a whirlwind. Elijah had lived a remarkable life, much of it in exile. He had performed many very unpleasant tasks during his ministry. Now he had a remarkable exit.

Referring to a remarkable life, there is an interesting study in comparing this life and ministry with that of John the Baptist. Christ linked these two names together several times, in such a way as to make them appear as one character. For example, on one occasion He said of John : " If ye had received it, this is Elias that was for to come " (Matt. xi. 14). He is also one of the two witnesses of Revelation xi.

The person who was called upon to succeed him was a totally different character. God so often brings opposites together.

Elijah was fiery.   Elisha was friendly.

Elijah came in judgment.   Elisha came in grace.

Elijah was despotic.   Elisha was domestic.

Elijah was adamant.   Elisha was diplomatic.

God is teaching that His work is done in many ways and by many people ; also that He is not always in the storm and the earthquake, but often in " the still small voice ".

In the record of Elijah's departure, the two men journeyed together. Several times Elijah bade Elisha to tarry, but he refused to be parted from his master. Several times he was told by others that he was going to lose his master, to which he replied : " Yea, I know it ; hold ye your peace ". What a picture of determination and loyalty ! He was aware of the loss that was coming, but he would not accept it one moment before he had to, neither was he going to lose any further blessing that might come from Elijah. It is a great privilege for a student if he can be an assistant to a real man of God.

The honour that came to Elisha and Timothy has come to many through the history of the Church. One would say to young people today — value the company of the older saint of God, obtain all you can from the experience of your minister, establish a close fellowship with him as far as is possible. It is going to mean much in the years to come. Said Jacob to the angel : " I will not let thee go unless thou bless me ". These might readily have been the words of Elisha.

Underscore in your Bible those statements in chapter two : " So they went down " (vs. 2). " So they came to Jericho " (vs. 4). " And they two went on " (vs. 6). " And they two stood by Jordan " (vs. 7). " So that they two went over on dry ground " (vs. 8). Christian companionship is one of God's precious gifts.

The result of Elisha's persistence was " Ask what I shall do for thee before I be taken away from thee ". What would be your answer ? Would it be something material, such as : " Please, sir, leave me your library ", or would it be something spiritual ? " Let a double portion of thy spirit be upon me ". Elisha was not asking for a double amount of blessing or twice as much success. The " double portion " was the lot of the firstborn. It was an inheritance. It was the law (Deut. xxi. 15-17). In verse 17 of that Scripture it is stated : " But he shall acknowledge the son of the hated for the firstborn, by giving him a double portion of

all that he hath : for he is the beginning of his strength ; the right
of the firstborn is his ". Elisha was asking, therefore, for the
privilege of being Elijah's successor. He was asking that the prophetic mantle might be his. He had already bidden farewell to
his parents. He had already surrendered his plough and oxen,
which would be his earthly gain.

It was because of this that Elijah said : " Thou hast asked a
hard thing ". This was not within the power of Elijah to give.
Only God can choose His men, but faith was rewarded, the
surrendered life was acknowledged for, when Elijah was translated,
Elisha was there to be the recipient of the mantle that fell, not
only from his earthly master — Elijah — but also from his
Heavenly Master, the Lord Himself. It is one thing to receive
the mantle of office, it is another thing to receive the power of a
Divine Call.

Elisha returned to the Jordan alone, carrying the mantle —
was he alone ? Smiting the waters with that mantle, he cried :
" Where is the God of Elijah ? ", to discover that He was right
there waiting to be proved. Where is the God of Elijah ? Is that
our cry ? Beloved, He still lives, all power is His in heaven and
earth. It is for us to strike by faith the waters of our difficulties,
to step forward in His Name, and see Him work.

When the Lord took His departure from this world, the
garment of His Holy Spirit fell upon His followers, those who
would be His witnesses. How can we know that that power is
ours ? In the same way that Elisha knew — he used it.

From his experience beyond Jordan Elisha came back to serve
his Lord in this vale of tears.

When one receives the power of the Holy Spirit there is no
need for one to declare it. The Sons of the prophets (the qualified
men, the men who might have had a considered claim for this
office, the men who had been by-passed by the Lord in favour of
a farmer) witnessed the scene at Jordan. They recognised the
enduement and came out to meet Elisha and to bow in submission
to it. Why did God choose a farmer's son instead of one of those
theological students ? Because God chooses men of full surrender
whoever they may be.

The next chapters are given to

(c) ELISHA'S MINISTRY. The ministry of the prophet
had precedence over the king. We are familiar with the miracles
of Jesus, but God wrought some great miracles through this

surrendered life. In fact, we may summarise the whole of this ministry by what God did through Elisha more than by what He said through him. Many of these instances were miracles.

(1) *Dividing the waters of Jordan* (ii. 14) This we have already considered and learned that faith without works is dead, and that power is proved by practice.

(2) *Healing the poisoned waters* (ii. 19-22). The situation of the city was pleasant, but the whole was being spoiled by bad water which was causing the land to become non-productive. The prophet commanded the men to bring him a new cruse and to put salt therein. This he took to the spring, or the source of the water supply, and the waters were healed. Elisha knew that to cure the flow one must touch the source.

The world that God has made is a beautiful place, but its moral life has been corrupted and men have become barren as a result of sin. Many have tried, and are still trying, to remedy the situation by casting into the stream all of their social salves — better conditions, social improvements, psychiatry, prison reforms, etc. Most of these are carried away with the stream. The source of all corruption is the heart, which is deceitful above all things and desperately wicked. We need to take the salt of the Gospel, which is found in the new cruse of the New Testament, and apply it to the hearts of men. The changed heart will bring a clean life and there will be no more death.

(3) *Cursing forty-two children* (ii. 23-25). These children have been referred to by some as innocent babies, but the Bible does not say that. " Children " in the Scriptures ofttimes refers to adults, see Acts xxi. 5; Gal. iv. 19; 1 John ii., etc. These " children " were youths or grown men. Elijah, the hairy man, had been translated. The young prophet, who evidently was not hairy, had taken his place and had come to the city. These lads began to jeer at him, saying: " Go up, thou bald-head " — or, Elijah has gone, you go too. We do not want you, your God, nor your religion; away with you! The prophet cursed these men, and two she-bears (possibly mothers who can be dangerous in protecting their young) came from the woods and *tare* (it does not say devoured or killed) forty-two of them. The picture is one of God dealing with God-rejectors according to their own sin, certainly not for some other person's sin.

(4) *Filling the country with water* (Ch. iii.). Jehoram, the wicked king of Israel, and Jehoshaphat, the weak king of Judah, entered into a covenant of war against Edom. When things went wrong Jehoram, like all wicked people, blamed God, even though

God had never been consulted. The whole idea had been that of
Jehoram. Jehoshaphat, however, persuaded him to accept the
advice and help of the Lord's prophet, which he did. Elisha
scorned Jehoram, advising him to seek his own gods, and telling
him that he would not even look at him. He was only going to
intervene because he had regard for Jehoshaphat. The complaint
of the king was that his armies were in the desert and that they
had no water. Elisha's reply was : " Thus saith the Lord, Make
this valley full of ditches ". That was hot, hard work for thirsty
men, but that was the command. The promise was that if they
would dig, the Lord would fill. So it was, and even more, for the
water that saved the men caught a sun reflection, or else the freshly
dug red earth of Palestine coloured the water, so that the enemy
saw in the distance what they thought to be blood. Thinking that
Israel and Judah had rebelled and slain each other, they moved
forward to their own destruction.

Israel's victory came through digging in obedience to God.
We are called upon to dig, dig, dig, to open up the fallow ground.
Says Hosea : " Sow to yourselves in righteousness, reap in mercy ;
break up your fallow ground ; for it is time to seek the Lord, till
He come and rain righteousness upon you " (x. 12).

What ditches have you opened ?

Open your heart in love.

Open your Bible in faith.

Open your mouth in testimony.

Open your purse in tithes and offerings and see the Lord
open heaven and pour you out such a blessing that
will scatter your enemies and bring you glorious
victory.

(5) *Widow's oil multiplies* (iv. 1-7). This widow is thought
to have been the wife of Obadiah, the prophet who hid four
hundred of God's servants from Ahab. In the story she was without
a means of livelihood, was in debt, and could not meet her
liabilities. The creditor was about to take her two sons from her
in lieu of the debt. This was real impoverishment and is truly a
picture of the Christian Church as we find it today. We are debtors
to God. We are not fulfilling our commission to preach the Gospel
to every creature. We are not meeting our liabilities toward those
around us. We have lost so much love, power, and testimony, that
God seems about to take away from us the privilege of raising
two sons, for we have a responsibility toward the Jew and the
Gentile. We have won neither, and now the Mission Field is slowly
closing upon us. China, India, Africa, will accept our medical

men and our educators, but they are saying no to the missionary who has neither of these qualifications. It is a tragic picture.

In her desperation the widow appealed to Elisha, who enquired as to what she did possess. Only " a pot of oil ", but that was enough to save her if she were willing. Little is better than nothing; weakness is better than death. Elisha told her to borrow every vessel she could, borrow not a few, then shut the door and pour. She did so, and the oil flowed until there was not a vessel left empty. Sell the oil, pay your debt, and live on the rest, said the prophet, and thus the woman and her child were saved.

Impoverished Christian, what have you ? Church of Christ, what is there left ? Just a little strength, just a little love, just a few weak prayers, just a little of His Holy Spirit ? Then bring into the secret place of prayer all the *empty* vessels you can find, shut to the door, wait upon Him, confess your sin, and He Who seeth in secret will reward you openly. What are the empty vessels? Your will and affections, heart, mind, soul, your hands and feet, eyes and ears, thoughts and wishes, everything you have and are. These passions have been empty a long time. Those hands and feet have been lazy, eyes and ears indifferent, those thoughts and wishes selfish. Bring them all to Him. Allow Him to fill every part of your being with the oil of His Holy Spirit until you are Spirit-possessed. Then go forth to discharge your debt to God, meet your responsibilities to your fellow-man, minister to others and glorify God.

(6) *Raising the Shunamite's son* (iv. 8-37) From an impoverished woman our thoughts are turned to a wealthy lady, one who was given to hospitality, caring for the servant of the Lord and seeking no reward. Hospitality is commended ministry for which the Lord has promised His reward. Many a family has been enriched spiritually and morally through entertaining the visiting preacher.

Although she sought no reward, the Lord is no man's debtor. It was learned that she desired a son, and that son was given to her. However, her generosity did not immunise her from tragedy. God has never promised immunity from trouble to anyone. He has promised grace sufficient for every time of need. So it was in the process of time that her child died. The woman immediately went to the prophet. Upon hearing the news Elisha bade his servant take his staff and lay it on the child, evidently with the intent that the child would live, but it did not happen. We cannot relegate our spiritual responsibilities to others. Souls are not saved by the wave of a wand. Revivals do not come through organised meetings, or posters. Elisha must go in and shut the door, upon himself and death, and know the presence of the One Who is Master of both.

(7) *Death in the pot* (iv. 38-41)   In the two previous records the needs have belonged to individuals. Now it was a community. There was a dearth in the land. Elisha bade his servants gather herbs for the pot, but someone, not knowing the difference between a good vine and a bad one, gathered a poisonous gourd and shred it into the pot. When the meal was served it was bitter. Men today have gathered from the vine of the earth poisonous doctrines and cast them into the Church with the True Vine, until the world cries out because of the evil conditions. Elisha told them to bring meal and cast it in, and the death was removed. The meal of God's Word, the Manna from heaven, will right all the theories of men, and bring wholesome food to mankind.

(8) *Naaman's leprosy* (Ch. v.)   This incident is very well known. Naaman was great in many respects BUT he was a leper. Man is great and ingenious in many ways BUT he is a sinner and needs cleansing in the Blood of Jesus Christ. Men today make the same mistakes as Naaman did. Naaman went to the wrong place and to the wrong person, with a wrong plan, and went away in a wrong passion, having wanted to pay the wrong price, all because he did not listen to what the " little maid " said, nor do what the prophet said. Instead it was " I thought ". Forgiveness comes through obedience to God's Word, not through our thinking.

Gehazi's avarice is another warning note.

(9) *The borrowed axe* (vi. 1-7)   This links us with the Trespass Offering of Leviticus (Ch. vi.), where we are admonished to return borrowed goods. The man's concern was : " Alas master, it was borrowed ". The miracle of causing the iron to swim was not because of loss, nor because of a shortage of axes, nor because of any emergency — but it was borrowed. Christians should be more careful in their obligations to other people and other people's property.

(10) *The Assyrian army* (vi. 8 - vii. 20)   The king of Syria was at war against Israel, but every plan he made was counter-planned by the enemy until he decided that there was a traitor in the midst. It was revealed to the king that Elisha was the responsible man, and that God was making known to him the king's secrets. Therefore he sent an army to capture one prisoner, Elisha. This host frightened the servant of the prophet until Elisha prayed: " Lord . . . open his eyes, that he may see ", and God caused the servant to see what the prophet already knew, that they were

surrounded with the armies of heaven. Remember, they that are for us are more than all that are against.

In this incident the king of Syria failed to take into account the God of Elisha when he planned his campaign, as men to-day fail to reckon with God in their national and international affairs, and then wonder as to the reason why the failures and frustrations they constantly encounter.

In the global problems of to-day man looks on and says : " Alas, what shall we do ? ", whilst the child of God rests quietly in his God for deliverance. God's method of effecting that promised deliverance is often unexpected.

Noah must build an ark.

Sarah must have a son in her old age.

Gideon must reduce his army.

Here in the second attack that Benhadad made when he was reducing Samaria by famine it was a " sound " that caused the enemy to flee and leave everything for the hungry Israelites, as Elisha had declared.

The rations mentioned in Chapter vi. 24 show the highest prices for the poorest food. " The cab of dove's dung " should be explained. Whilst there are differences of opinion the general acceptance is " that it was a kind of chick-pea, lentil, or tare, which has very much the appearance of dove's dung, whence it might be named . . . a kind of pulse which was the fare of the poorer class of people ". A fourth part of a cab would be about three-quarters of a pint, which would cost 12-6d., or nearly $2.00-.

(11) *The Unforgotten Shunamite* (viii. 1- 6) The woman who had given hospitality to the servant of God had left the country because of the famine, and now returned anxious to regain lost possessions. She went to the king at the moment he was listening to a citation from Gehazi of Elisha's accomplishments. As the story of the raising from the dead was told, mother and lad appeared, and the king, so thrilled, granted her request. God is never debtor to those who minister in His Name.

(12) *Benhadad and Hazael* (viii. 7-15) In the opening verses of chapter eight there is a *sick king* who had refused God. Now he was enquiring of the prophet as to whether he would recover. Strange how Godless men will seek God when they think they are going to die ! He sent a gift (a bribe) by the hand of Hazael, his servant, who was a *sinful courtier* (for he longed for one thing — the throne) and this sick king was all that was between him and it. Elisha knew this, and said, with a penetrating look : " Go, say unto him, thou mayest certainly recover, howbeit the Lord

has shewn me that thou shalt surely die ". Hazael understood
perfectly. We then see a *sad prophet* as Elisha broke into tears,
but it was Hazael who needed to weep. Instead, with a stubbornness, he enquired the reason for Elisha's tears. " Because of what
thou art going to do to my people ". Hazael carried back the first
half of the message, which became a lie. The next day he
murdered the king and took the throne.

(13). *A deathbed council of war* (xiii. 14-19) Joash, or
Jehoash, king of Israel, knowing that the life of Elisha was ebbing
away, came to seek the counsel of the man whom he had despised
in his life. He wanted the privilege now it was almost gone.
Syria had been in constant aggression against Israel, so the king
wanted advice for future action. Elisha bade the king open the
window toward the east, the land of the enemy ; he then commanded him to put his hand to the bow and bring it to action.
The prophet placed his hand over the hand of the king, suggesting
supreme control. Now shoot — and he shot ! This would not
be shooting at a venture, but shooting with determination. It was
a sign of declaration of war.

Have you taken up the bow of service ?

Where have you shot the arrow of prayer to-day ?

Where have you shot the arrow of God's Word ?

Where have you shot the arrow of God's Love ?

Was His guiding Hand controlling your conduct ?

Elisha now bade the king to take the arrows and strike the
ground. This he did three times and then stopped. The prophet
reproved the king for not continuing to strike the ground. A
persistence in striking the ground would have revealed a persistence
in the heart of the king which would have brought him a complete
victory over his enemy, but he showed evidence of a half-heartedness which was going to mean only partial victory. How true of
so many of us when it comes to the work of the Lord or to our
resistance of the enemy ! How quickly we are ready to yield to
the way of least resistance. May the Lord challenge us to more
determined action.

2. THE KINGS

This is a story of tragic and steady decline. The kings were
but representative of the whole nation. G. Campbell Morgan
points out the fact of two thrones that were in opposition. On the
one side was the Throne of God, steadfast and immovable,
represented by the prophets of God who ministered throughout the
whole of this period. On the other side was the throne of the

nation, trembling and falling, becoming more and more corrupt as history moved along. Campbell Morgan also states that even the good kings, as Joash, Amaziah and Jotham, were not up to the standards of David. It could not be said of them " that they walked in the ways of David their father ". There was some measure of compromise in each life. Hezekiah and Josiah were the bright spots along the way.

An idea of the decline of the nation can be realised by listing the kings, stating which were evil and which were good : —

JUDAH			ISRAEL			
King	Reign (years)	Character	King		Reign (years)	Character
Jehoshaphat	25	Good	Ahaziah		2	Evil
Joram	8	Evil	Jehoram		12	Evil
Jehoahaz	1	Evil	Jehu		28	Zealous
Athaliah	6	Evil	Jehoahaz		17	Evil
Joash	40	Good	Joash		16	Evil
Amaziah	29	Good	Jeroboam	(II)	41	Evil
Uzziah	52	Good	Zachariah		6 months	Evil
Jotham	16	Good				
Ahaz	16	Evil	Shallum		1 month	Evil
Hezekiah	29	Good				
Manasseh	55	Evil	Menahem		10	Evil
Amon	2	Evil	Pekahiah		2 months	Evil
Josiah	31	Good				
Jehoahaz	3 months	Evil	Pekah		20	Evil
			Hoshea		9	Evil
Jehoiakim	11	Evil				
Jehoiachin	3 months	Evil				
Zedekiah	11	Evil				

More than half the kings of Judah were evil, and all the kings of Israel, the only exception being Jehu, and one would rather call him zealous than good. He walked in the ways of sin. Of all the kings mentioned in this book seven were good, twenty-one were evil, and one was zealous.

> 222 years of good reign.
> 266 years of evil reign.

As there is a repetition of the information concerning the kings of Judah in the book of Chronicles we will refer to them there and limit ourselves to the kings of Israel only. These were :

AHAZIAH (Ch. i.) the son of Ahab, who followed his father
on the throne and in his sins. He forsook Jehovah God for Baal-
zebub and died in his sin. He, having no son, was succeeded to
the throne by his brother

JEHORAM (JORAM) (Ch. iii.) He did not continue in the
sins of his father and brother as far as Baal worship was concerned ;
nonetheless he reigned in sin for twelve years following the ways of
Jeroboam. In his battles against Moab he sought and gained an
affiliation with Jehoshaphat and, later, with Ahaziah, kings of
Judah. He was slain by Jehu, and cast into the vineyard of Naboth
according to the Word of God to Jehu. " And thou shalt smite
the house of Ahab thy master, that I may avenge the blood of My
servants the prophets, and the blood of all the servants of the
Lord at the hand of Jezebel ". Upon the death of Jehoram the
throne was occupied by

JEHU (Chs. ix-x.) who reigned for twenty-eight years. This
man not only drove furiously but lived likewise. In a cruel and
ruthless manner he destroyed all the worshippers of Baal. Some
have wondered why God allowed such a cruel man to reign, but
it must be remembered that Baal worship was both cruel and vile,
and also very immoral. Such practices often know no other voice
than that of severity. Mercy is not in their vocabulary. A Jehu
is ofttimes needed to decide in a hard issue.

Unfortunately, whilst he was severe with one form of idolatry,
he overlooked another ; in fact, he engaged in the sins of Jeroboam
and worshipped the calves he set up. In destroying all the house
of Ahab he failed in that he let Athaliah escape. She married the
king of Judah and usurped a sinful authority, as did her mother,
Jezebel, before her in Israel. She was responsible for slaying all
the seed royal save Joash, who was hidden from her murderous
hand.

God promised that the seed of Jehu should sit on the throne
until the fourth generation, so Jehu was succeeded by his son

JEHOAHAZ (Ch. xiii.) Because of his wickedness and, of
course, with him the nation, he delivered them into the hand of the
Syrians and two of their kings, Hazael and Benhadad. Israel was
greatly reduced at that time. Previously Jehoahaz besought the
Lord and He, in the abundance of His mercy, gave His people
deliverance, yet they never repented, but continued in their sin.
He died after reigning seventeen years, and his son reigned in his
stead. This was

JOASH (JEHOASH) (Chs. xiii-xiv.) an evil king, yet he fought victoriously against the king of Syria and recaptured all that his father had lost. Although this man had no time for God or God's servant, Elisha, yet, when he realised that Elisha was at the end of life's journey, he sought his counsel. We have already noted that Elisha bade him strike the ground with his arrows and he did so three times, and that Elisha said : " Thou shouldest have smitten five or six times . . . whereas now thou shalt smite Syria but thrice". The last sentence of chapter thirteen is : " Three times did Joash beat him, and recovered the cities of Israel ". God is ever true to His Word, even when He is dealing with the disobedient.

For sixteen years Joash reigned and was succeeded by his son

JEROBOAM (Ch. xiv.) He followed in his father's footsteps, both in his sin and in establishing the nation of Israel. He reigned longer than any other king over Israel — forty-one years. Long and important as this reign was, yet only seven verses are given to this man. The writer has more to say about his contemporaries in Judah, Amaziah and Azariah. He does tell us that the prophet Jonah ministered at that time.

This long reign was followed by five shorter reigns :

ZACHARIAH (Ch. xv.) He was the son of Jeroboam and completed the four generations of Jehu whom God said would occupy the throne. It was a period of bloodshed. These kings did not live out their lives, but were slain, and the throne was changing from one family to another. This explains why the reigns were so short. When men persistently refuse God, the day will come when other men will refuse them. It is in the godless countries that kings and rulers are constantly moving in fear of an overthrow or the loss of their lives.

Zachariah reigned for six months and was slain by

SHALLUM (Ch. xv.) who wanted the throne but only had it for one month. He who obtained the throne through murder lost the throne by murder. Does not the truth reveal itself constantly : What a man sows that shall he also reap.

MENAHEM (Ch. xv.) For ten years this man reigned and robbed, for by taxation he sought to buy off the enemy and strengthen his somewhat insecure position on the throne. However, he was able to pass the throne on to his son at death, so that

PEKAHIAH (Ch. xv.) succeeded, but only for two years of sinful reign. Then he was assassinated by one of his captains,

PEKAH (Ch. xv.) who reigned for twenty evil years. By this time Israel had become sorely oppressed, and in this reign began again to lose her territory to Assyria. Another conspiracy, another murder, and the throne was occupied by the last king of Israel,

HOSHEA (Ch. xvii.) He reigned over an impoverished kingdom for nine years, during which time he made secret alliance with the king of Egypt, was besieged for two years by the kings of Assyria, and finally fell victim to Assyria, whilst Israel was carried away into captivity after little more than two hundred years of history as a kingdom.

The remaining chapters deal with

THE DECLINE OF JUDAH (Chs. xviii-xxiv.) Israel had already fallen, but Judah was following hard on her heels, not learning the lessons that her sister had taught her.

The kings who reigned in Judah, after Israel had gone away into Assyria, were Ahaz, Hezekiah, Manasseh, Amon, Josiah, Jehoahaz, Jehoiakim, Jehoiachin (or Jeconiah), and Zedekiah. Zedekiah was the last king. Gedaliah ruled as a governor after him. These are to be considered in the second book of Chronicles.

The book closes with an account of the Babylonian Captivity when Jerusalem was twice beseiged by Nebuchadnezzar, who destroyed the City and the Temple, carrying away the treasures and the people.

This captivity had been foretold for more than a century.

Isaiah and Micah had declared that it would be Babylon who would destroy them.

Jeremiah had warned them again and again. He ceased not to cry out to the people night and day with tears. He had told them it would be for seventy years — and yet the people heeded not.

As we read the story and see the steady decline, as we listen to the voice of the prophets, it all looks so clear that we stand wondering why Israel and then Judah could not see it. We wonder why they never repented of their sin. And yet, why do we wonder about it ? For with all of these lessons, pictures, and warnings, we live in a world and serve a Church where the very same th'ngs are being re-enacted before our eyes. Leaders and false prophets are leading the nations further into sin and farther away from God, whilst the true servants of Christ are preaching the Gospel. They are telling of the Coming again of Christ Jesus the Lord. They are making known that there is an impending day of judgment not far distant, and in the light of it all are telling men to repent and believe the Gospel, but their voice is like a voice in the wilderness. Nonetheless, in an hour such as we think not, the Son of Man will come. Some people are saying : " Where is the promise of His coming ? All things continue as they were from the beginning ".

It took Nebuchadnezzar twenty years to destroy Jerusalem, c.f. 2 Chron. xxxvi. 3-8 ; Daniel i. 3 ; 2 Kings xxiv. 14-16 ; Jer. lii. 28-29 ; 2 Kings xxv. 3-12 ; and Jer. lii. 30.

But it surely came to pass !

I CHRONICLES

THE SOVEREIGNTY OF GOD

"Thine, O Lord, is the greatness, and the power, and the glory, and the victory, and the majesty : for all that is in the heaven and in the earth is Thine ; Thine is the kingdom, O Lord, and Thou art exalted as Head above all. Both riches and honour come of Thee, and Thou reignest over all ; and in Thine hand is power and might ; and in Thine hand it is to make great, and to give strength unto all. Now therefore, our God, we thank Thee, and praise Thy glorious Name."

(1 CHRONICLES xxix. 11-13)

INTRODUCTION

The two books of Chronicles retell the history already written in the previous four books, firstly concerning the reigns of David and Solomon and then those things which took place after the division of the kingdom. They deal primarily with the kings of Judah and the Northern Kingdom. Israel is only occasionally referred to when there is an important connection that cannot be by-passed. II Chronicles deals more especially with Israel.

Jewish tradition maintains that Ezra was the author of these books and there is internal evidence that substantiates this. Ezra was a scribe. He wrote the book that has his name appended and also the book of Nehemiah. G. Campbell Morgan says : " There can be little doubt that the story in Chronicles was written at the return from the captivity, in order to encourage the people to build the House of God, for its central subject is the Temple of God ".

The suggestion is made that the scribe of the Most High God wrote the books of Ezra and Nehemiah firstly, and then linked his record of restoration with past failure by rewriting their history in these Chronicles. The author quotes from many sources, so that we have here a confirmation of things already recorded.

Believing the Bible to be the Word of God, we could call this " A Divine checking of Divine Inspiration ".

The book would then divide itself into three major sections :

(1) Generations of Man   —   " Love the brotherhood "

(2) Development of the Monarchy --   " Honour the king ".

(3) Establishment of worship   —   " Fear God ".

Thus we link them with a threefold requirement of 1 Peter ii. 17.

(1)   GENERATIONS OF MAN (Chs. i-ix.)

Nine long uninteresting chapters which are possibly unread by most people! But this is history, and few people like history in any case!! History is a record of facts, not the theories of men, nor the hypothesis of scientists. If we read the facts of history in the Bible and find them to be correct, ought it not to help us to accept the doctrines of the Word of God. Doctrines have to be proved by experience. If one wants cautiously or unbelievingly to hold back from a "risk" of the "experimental" then these things should become one's confirmation and so an impetus to one's faith in the New Testament.

Not all of the names are mentioned from Adam, or that would require the whole book. On the other hand the names are not taken in any haphazard fashion. There is purpose, continuity, and selection. The principal characters are complete that make for the continuance of history. Heredity or the family is always established as one of the great principles in the economy of God. He established the family in the beginning of time in man — He continues it in eternity in Christ Jesus. "For this cause I bow my knees unto the Father of our Lord Jesus Christ, of Whom the whole family in heaven and earth is named" (Eph. iii. 14-15).

> God established the family in our first parents, Adam and Eve.
> The Priesthood remained in the family of Aaron.
> Kingship was intended to be hereditary in the Royal Family.
> We are in the family of God by New Birth, and are called the sons of God and the children of God.
> When the land of Palestine was originally allocated it was given to tribes and sub-divided into families.
> The year of Jubilee was established that a family might regain lost inheritance.
> Stories like that of Ruth and Boaz declare the same principle. It is the great story of continuance.
> Levi was divided into families, each family having its own particular responsibility.

Whilst the Lord God recognises families and whilst all who are born again are registered in the Lamb's Book of Life, yet there is a matter of selection. In the first verse of the book Cain and Abel are by-passed for Seth. So throughout Scripture Seth is chosen from the family of Adam. Shem is selected from the family of Noah, Isaac from the family of Abram, Jacob from Esau, and so

down the line. Many are called, few are chosen. Out of the many
who are saved few stand out in service.

The callings and elections are of God.

Many people suggest that a list of names is a meaningless
thing and it could readily be left out of the Bible. Let us agree
with them. Then why do the same people become annoyed and
outspoken when they attend some public function or engage in
some activity of the Church and find that their name was not put
in the local newspaper or in the Church magazine or bulletin?
There is an increasing tendency to-day to mention all names. The
newspaper will do it to increase sales. Why does one need to
know the name of every guest at someone's wedding or the name of
every mourner at a funeral? But they are listed. How often
people criticise the Bible for doing the very things they do.

Names remove the idea of the mass or the crowd and give
personality and individuality. Might it not be recognised, therefore,
that God does not look on mankind as a crowd of humans which
populate a world. He sees us each as individuals. He knows us
in particular, deals with us as though there was no other person.
He knows us each by name and that name is written in the Lamb's
Book of Life, or it is not. Names must be known for reward. Cain
and Abel are missing from this record, but Seth finds a place there.
Cain had sinned and become a murderer, hence the blessing of
heredity passed to Seth, who came into the line of the " seed of
the woman ". Abel's name is missing because he had no genealogy, and these are chapters of genealogy. Your name, maybe,
is in the Lamb's Book of Life because of New Birth, but is it in
the " other books " that are going to be opened in the last day?
How many children have you against your name? Spiritual
children, those who have been born into the family of God through
your testimony and your Christian service. Names may be uninteresting to you but they are very important.

We are bidden to " Love the brotherhood ", meaning all mankind, but most people love themselves.

(2)   DEVELOPMENT OF THE MONARCHY (Chs. x-xxvii.)

Not only have we a relationship that is personal by reason of
birth, marriage or inheritance, but we have a much wider field of
responsibility and privileges in that, as members of the human
race and of society, we have a relationship with all men, so creating
a nation. Abram started with a family. God's promise to him
was : " I will make of thee a great nation " (Gen. xii. 2). A

nation is a great organisation. The first book of Chronicles tells
of its development, commencing with

THE DEATH OF SAUL (Ch. x.)   The tragedy of Mount
Gilboa brought to an end the reign of Israel's first king. He was
the man of muscle rather than a man of morals, one of outward
physique more than inward faith, the king of Israel's choice, but
not the king of God's ordaining. What is not of God usually ends
tragically. These first forty years were a time of probation. Saul
was followed by the man of God's choice — David.

THE ACCESSION OF DAVID (Ch. xi.) As a man he had
already proved himself a warrior. The lad who could put his
sheep before himself would be a man who would consider the
nation before his own desires. God ever seeks men of humility
and loyalty.

His first act was to secure a capital city, strong and independent
of any of the twelve tribes, and one that would have some central
position. Therefore he chose a city that was still in the hand of
the enemy. So

JEBUS WAS CAPTURED (Ch. xi.)   The Jebusites were
subdued, the city established, and its name changed to Jerusalem.
As a result of David capturing and enlarging the city, it became
known as the City of David. Joab had a great part both in the
capture and repair of the city. Whilst the Church on earth was
established by the Lord and belongs to Him, yet His servants have
a responsibility toward its maintenance and enlargement.

Concerning this city they could sing : " Great is the Lord,
and greatly to be praised in the city of our God, in the mountain
of His holiness. Beautiful for situation, the joy of the whole earth,
is Mount Zion, on the sides of the north, the city of the great king "
(Psalm xlviii. 1-2).

However, the strength of a city is not in its position or its
fortifications. This is found in the loyalty of its citizens. Cities
and nations are made up of people, of individuals ; so is the Church
of Jesus Christ. Therefore we have a record of

DAVID'S MIGHTY MEN (Ch. xi.) men who risked everything, men who counted not the cost, men who did exploits. God
is wanting men of this calibre to-day. Men who are true to their
trust and faithful to their God. " For righteousness exalteth a
nation but sin is a reproach to any people " (Prov. xiv. 34). David
knew the truth of this proverb for, having established his capital,
he immediately considered that this should be the dwelling place
of God. He sought, therefore, to bring up

THE ARK OF THE COVENANT TO JERUSALEM (Ch. xiii-xvi.)

This was a right thing to do, but it was done in the wrong way (see notes of 2 Sam. vi.).

The Philistines, objecting to David coming to the throne, showed their displeasure by warring against him. Twice they engaged in battle, twice David sought the Lord in prayer, and twice David had the victory (see notes on 2 Sam. v. 17-25).

David then did the right thing in the right way, for he prepared the priests to bring up the Ark of the Covenant to Jerusalem.

The Ark had been seven months in the hand of the enemy, three months in the house of Obed-edom, and twenty years with Abinadab, twenty-one years without an official resting place. It had gone from Shiloh. Now it comes to Jerusalem. God was in His rightful place as the Head of the nation, as King of kings. When God is in the midst of His people, praise is in their hearts. What a beautiful Psalm broke forth from the heart of David : " Give unto the Lord the glory due unto His Name : bring an offering, and come before Him : worship the Lord in the beauty of holiness " (xvi. 29).

Although the Ark was surrounded by praise and was ministered before with all the songs of the sons of Asaph, with the service of the porters, and the sacrifices of Zadok the priest with his brethren, yet it was resting in the humble abode of a tent (xvi. 1). It was in these circumstances that David, dwelling in his palace, conceived the idea that he would like to build a house for God to dwell in the midst of His people. So

A TEMPLE WAS PROPOSED (Ch. xvii.)

David saw himself in a beautiful palace whilst his God, Whom he worshipped, only dwelt in a tent. The gods of the heathen nations had their ornate temples — why should Jehovah have less ? David revealed his desire to Nathan, the prophet, who gave it full approval, but God met Nathan that night and told him that the project did not receive Divine approval. God did not condemn the idea, neither did He reprove David for suggesting it. God had three objections — (1) He had not requested it. Through the years He had been content to be a Pilgrim in the midst of a pilgrim people. Heaven being His throne and earth His footstool, He had never been limited to an isolated or local place as had the false gods. (2) The time was not opportune. David's suggestion was not cancelled, only postponed. The people were not ready. The conditions were not conducive. War was on every hand. Their environment was still fluid. Peace was not yet fully established. (3) David was not the man for the task. He was a man of war. "Thou shalt not build a house unto My Name, because thou hast shed much blood upon the earth in My sight " (xxii. 8). God promised, however, that his son, Solomon, should build Him a house. The truth has ever remained that one sows and another reaps. Nonetheless we are workers together with God. There can be no reaper unless there has been a sower. So often men resent God's disapproval, or God's appointment of a co-worker. They want to do it all. They want all the glory, it was their project. It was not so with David. He submitted happily to the Lord's Will. If he could not build, he could prepare. God grant us such submission.

The preparation for the future building of the Temple was manifested in the next move in the development of the Monarchy.

ENEMIES ARE ALL SUBDUED (Chs. xviii-xx.)   David was now engaged in a series of wars in which he subdued his enemies one by one.

The Philistines, who had been a constant source of irritation, were now overcome. (xviii. 1).

The Moabites, who had once sought to hinder Israel from entering the Land, were now servants to David. (xviii. 2).

Hadarezer, king of Zobah, was defeated by David even as he sought to establish himself at the Euphrates. (xviii. 3-4).

The Syrians came to help Hadarezer against David and instead fell with him before David. (xviii. 5-8).

The Edomites. Eighteen thousand died in the Valley of Salt under the hand of Abishai. (xviii. 12-13).

The Ammonites. David had desired to show kindness to the new king because of past kindness received from his father, but David's generosity was misinterpreted as the Ammonites abused David's men. This resulted in war and the defeat of the Ammonites and the Syrians who, for the second time, helped David's enemies to their own hurt. (xix).

This section ends with another uprising of the Philistines and a further subduing of them, at which time the sons of Goliath, all of them giants, were slain.

And yet there was an enemy over which David did not obtain a victory. "And Satan stood up against Israel, and provoked David to number Israel " (xxi. 1). David fell to this temptation, and without excuse. Apart from the fact that it was directly against God's command, he was reminded of it by Joab, who warned him not to do it. David became rebellious at this point and therefore wilful in his sin.

David, having chosen to commit this sin against the warnings of Joab, now had to choose the punishment that God would inflict upon him. This brought home to David in dread reality the consequences of his sin. Sin is something that is not only against God, not only against ourselves, but it has its repercussions on the lives of multitudes of innocent people. This is true of your sin and mine.

Although David was facing the judgment of God yet, in wisdom, he threw himself upon the mercy of God, as he said : " I am in a strait : let me fall now into the hand of the Lord ; for very great are His mercies : but let me not fall into the hand of man " (xxi. 13). Seventy thousand men became the victims of one man's sin.

David was also a man ready to confess his sin and failing, and he humbly sought God's forgiveness. This was a characteristic more marked in David than any other man. He desired to purchase property where the plague had stopped and to build an altar to the Lord. Ornan, the owner of the land, was willing to give it to him, probably thankful himself that he had escaped the plague. But David was not making a second mistake by accepting another man's offering. He would not offer to God that which had not cost him something. Neither is God willing to accept from us things which do not cost. That is the very reason why He asks for firstfruits.

THE KINGDOM ESTABLISHED (Ch. xviii. 14)   The statement is made at the end of chapter eighteen which lists the enemies that had been subdued, although other enemies were dealt with later. " So David reigned over all Israel and executed judgment and justice among all his people ". After the years of being hounded from place to place, constantly being pursued by one or another, spending months in caves and strongholds, roaming the wilderness, even dwelling with the Philistines, it must have been a consolation to David to find some years of rest.

In this same chapter he

APPOINTS HIS OFFICERS (Ch. xviii. 15-17)   These were :

Joab	.....	The General.
Jehoshaphat	.....	The Recorder (or Secretary).
Zadok	.....	The Priest.
Abimeleck	.....	The Priest.
Shavsha	.....	The Scribe.
Benaiah	.....	The Captain.

PREPARING FOR THE TEMPLE (Ch. xxii.)   With the enemies subdued and with the kingdom established, David now had time for other considerations. His heart went back to a previous desire. He had requested that he might build a house for God, but God had already refused him this privilege. It had not been a refusal of objection but one of policy, as was evidenced in the fact that God was permitting Solomon, the king's son, to build this Temple because he would be a man of peace. God was not condemning David for his wars. These had to be if the enemies were to be subdued and the kingdom established. It was a matter that God had appointed different men for different tasks. We cannot do the other man's work, only our own, and, if we do that, we shall learn that we are all workers together with Him.

Whilst David was not permitted to build, it did not mean that he could not *Prepare*. As a father he felt that he had an obligation toward his son. Then again, would his son do what he longed to see done ? One of the assurances that he could have was to prepare the material, make the task easier, and make the objective unavoidable.

Could not we in our day help our young people in their spiritual accomplishments, not by telling them what they should do and should not do, but by setting them noble examples and giving them the prepared material that they cannot go wrong ? Example is always better than precept. If we have a concern for the next generation we will not go on hoping that they will not be liberal in their outlook and materialistic in their service. We will be active in giving them such a stock-pile of well prepared fundamental material that they will not be able to build anything that is otherwise.

So David set the men to work to prepare iron, brass, cedar trees, gold, silver, stones. When one remembers that all of these materials have what we call typological values and meanings, that they represent such things as strength, judgment, humanity, Divinity, redemption, etc., then David was preparing for his son the fundamentals of the Christian Church, the things of which Christian Faith is built.

Moreover, he had workmen in abundance, men who could shape those stones, carve that timber, fashion those metals to perfect fitting and graceful design. Should not this generation help the next generation by preparing Ministers, Teachers, Instructors, men who know how to fashion the things of God so that they fit right into our lives and into the future Church of God with a grace and a perfection that will in themselves establish an acceptance ?

With the preparation of the material came a preparation of his son as David gave Solomon a charge. He reminded him that it was his desire, but God had made it Solomon's privilege.

Parents to-day are delinquent toward their children, saying that they must make their own decisions, they must find their own feet, they must worship how and where they think best. How very dangerous for the young ! How irresponsible of the parent ! ! David said : " Solomon my son is young and tender ; and the house that is to be builded for the Lord must be exceeding magnifical " (xxii. 5). So he called Solomon and said to him : " Now, my son, the Lord be with thee ; and prosper thou, and build the house of the Lord thy God, as He hath said of thee. Only the Lord give thee wisdom and understanding, and give thee charge concerning Israel, that thou mayest keep the law of the Lord thy God. Then shalt thou prosper, if thou takest heed to fulfil the statutes and judgments which the Lord charged Moses with concerning Israel : be strong, and of good courage ; dread not, nor be dismayed " (xxii. 11-13).

After these words of wisdom to his son, he turned to the leaders of the land, requesting them to give their moral and material help to his son (the next generation), saying : " Now set your heart and your soul to seek the Lord your God ; arise, therefore, and build the sanctuary of the Lord God, to bring the Ark of the Covenant of the Lord, and the holy vessels of God, into the house that is to be built to the Name of the Lord " (xxii. 19).

SOLOMON SUCCEEDS (Ch. xxiii.)   A long and noble life of service was drawing to its close but, whilst God removes His workers, the work goes on, and the throne was established in David's son, Solomon. Only the statement of succession is made here to complete the picture of

The establishment of the Monarchy and so close the second section of this book of Chronicles.

The Royal Line had now been set on its course to continue to move as an hereditary thing. It was permanently established to pass from father to son, which it did except where war or rebellion caused it to pass from one family to another. Behind and beyond all the fortunes and misfortunes of the earthly throne God has ever remained the true King of Israel. His Throne has been represented by an earthly throne. Sometimes, as at the present, there has been no throne in Israel due to their sin and rebellion, but the heavenly Throne continues. " Thy Throne, O God, is for ever and ever ; the sceptre of Thy kingdom is a right

sceptre " (Psalm xlv. 6). Because the throne and the monarchy
have been ordained of God there is the New Testament instruction
" Honour the king ".

(3) ESTABLISHMENT OF WORSHIP (Chs. xxii-xxx.)

To some degree there is an overlap because the monarch was
the one who desired to build the Temple and the one who prepared
the material.

Whilst some may not endorse a State Church and whilst God
never intended that the State and the Church should be related,
because the one is carnal and the other is spiritual, so that we are
told to come out and be separate, yet the fact remains that the one
is dependent on the other, that fact being that the nation should
not be controlling the Church but the Church should be leading the
nation. " Except the Lord build the house they labour in vain
that build it ; except the Lord keep the city, the watchman waketh
but in vain " (Psalm cxxvii. 1), or " Righteousness exalteth a nation,
but sin is a reproach to any people " (Prov. xiv. 34).

GIFTS MADE. Whilst worship is a spiritual thing and is a
communion between the worshipper and his God, and this worship
is best realised in the secret place, yet there is also a public worship
where men are instructed and where the Lord's praises are sung
and His Word and Will made known. This is the side of worship
which influences the world.

Whilst the Church is primarily an organism, it being the
Body of Christ, we, as believers, being members of that Body and
also members one of another, must know some organisation. This
is where the Temple of the Old Testament came in, and where
Church ministry operates to-day, that ministry which begins at
Jerusalem, or home, and reaches out to the uttermost parts of the
earth in missionary activity. In this realm God can only work
according to that which is given to Him.

David and the people gave iron, brass, cedar trees, stones,
gold, silver, etc. They also gave themselves in service.

MATERIAL PREPARED. It is one thing to present raw
material, but that in itself will not build an edifice to the glory of
God. That can only remain a stock-yard or a storage dump. Men
with skill and ability carved the stones, fashioned the metals, pro-
cessed the material, according to a master plan. Only thus could
the material become a holy Temple for the Lord.

Giving our money and our material possessions is not enough
for the establishment of the worship of God in this our day. That
can be an easy way out for some. Our gifts must be fashioned

by our prayers. Our service takes shape according to the motive with which we render that service. Our character, personality, and passions, our love for the Lord and for sinners, our loyalty and faithfulness to our tasks, these are the things that prepare the material, the gold, silver and precious stones of Christian life.

The building of a temple is one thing. The ministry of that temple is quite another thing. The narrative moves, therefore, to the

APPOINTMENT OF OFFICERS. Again we meet long lists of names, but they are not merely names. It was the allocation of the various duties and responsibilities of the Temple worship to different individuals, families, and organisations.

Firstly there was the appointment of the families of Levi.

24,000 had to oversee the work (xxiii. 4).

6,000 were officers and judges (xxiii. 4).

4,000 were porters (xxiii. 5).

4,000 were musicians and singers (xxiii. 5).

These were divided into courses so that men knew when they were on duty and when off duty.

As they entered into these responsibilities so old ones ceased. No longer would they have to carry the tabernacle as heretofore (vs. 26). All of this might be referred to as outward ministry — serving the tables of stone.

The second division was that of the sons of Aaron (Ch. xxiv.). These executed the priests' office, and engaged in that which was more spiritual.

Thirdly came the singers, the sons of Asaph, Heman, and Jeduthun. These had their respective tasks. Some used the harp, some the horn, others used cymbals and psalteries. There were two hundred and eighty eight of them.

Group four took in the porters, who kept the gates, again each man in his place. Others were responsible for the care of the treasures or the treasury (margin).

Fifthly there were officers who were responsible for the outward business of Israel.

The overall picture is that of organisation as we have it to-day. This could be applied as :

First division — the deacons who handle the business affairs of the Church.

Second division — the Pastor and his spiritual associates, sometimes called elders.

Third division	—	the choir and the music.
Fourth division	—	the ushers and sidesmen.
Fifth division	—	the Officers, as Secretary and Treasurer, the Church visitors, the Sunday School and the Missionary activity, and all other Departmental work.

This embraces a great number of people, thus giving opportunities of service so that we might be workers together with Him. The same distribution of work is recorded by Nehemiah. In the New Testament we are reminded that in the worship of the Church " He gave some, apostles ; and some, prophets ; and some, evangelists ; and some, pastors and teachers ; for the perfecting of the saints, for the work of the ministry, for the edifying of the body of Christ " (Ephes. iv. 11-12).

We are to learn that as there are celestial bodies and terrestrial bodies and each have their own glory, and as there is one glory of the sun, another glory of the moon, and a different glory for each star (1 Cor. xv. 40-41), and as the body is made up of different members, each having its own function and none able to take the place of the other (1 Cor. xii. 14-27), so every Christian has his place and his ministry in the Church. Only as we serve in *that* place and in *that* ministry are we effectively living in the Will of the Lord, and only thus shall the worship of the Church be established.

All this sets forth the title which has been given to this book —

THE SOVEREIGNTY OF GOD

COMMISSION OF SOLOMON. " And thou, Solomon my son, know thou the God of thy father, and serve Him with a perfect heart and with a willing mind : for the Lord searcheth all hearts, and understandeth all the imaginations of the thoughts ; if thou seek Him, He will be found of thee : but if thou forsake Him, He will cast thee off for ever. Take heed now ; for the Lord hath chosen thee to build an house for the sanctuary : be strong, and do it " (xxviii. 9-10).

May we learn that God is a God of order, that He calls specific men for specific tasks. His callings and elections are sure, and they are without repentance. Therefore it is only as we submit to His Will and obey His commands that His work will prosper, whether in the family, in the nation, or in the Church.

This third section, and at the same time the whole book, concludes with a wonderful demonstration of that true worship which God seeks. We use the word " seeks " in its full meaning for Jesus declared that, " The hour cometh, and now is, when the true worshippers shall worship the Father in spirit and in truth : for the Father *seeketh* such to worship Him " (John iv. 23).

Seeking suggests a difficulty in finding. There is little true worship to-day. Worship is not service, not ritual, not singing, not praying, nor is it preaching. These can be found in abundance. Very few of our hymns have a note of worship in them. Worship is that attitude of the soul when it reaches out toward God, with a deep sense of unworthiness, to praise Him and adore Him for what He is and Who He is. Thus David, who wrote so much of that book of worship, the Psalms, reached out to God in this last scene, with " Blessed be Thou, Lord God of Israel our Father, for ever and ever. Thine, O Lord, is the greatness, and the power, and the glory, and the victory and the majesty : for all that is in the heaven and in the earth is Thine ; Thine is the kingdom, O Lord, and Thou art exalted as Head above all. Both riches and honour come of Thee, and Thou reignest over all : and in Thine hand is power and might ; and in Thine hand it is to make great, and to give strength unto all. Now therefore, our God, we thank Thee, and praise Thy glorious Name " (xxix 10-13).

Thus he led the whole congregation in worship as they bowed before God and then offered their sacrifices. So David concluded his reign, and Solomon his son reigned in his stead.

God is high over all — therefore " Fear God ".

II CHRONICLES

THE HISTORY OF JUDAH

*" And this is the blessing of Judah : and he said, Hear, Lord,
the voice of Judah, and bring him unto his people : let his
hands be sufficient for him ; and be thou an help to him from
his enemies."* (DEUTERONOMY xxxiii. 7)

INTRODUCTION

This book is one that contains a great deal of repetition of
things already considered in II Samuel, I Kings and II Kings. In
fact there are some forty parallel passages, so that one must refer
readers back to these books for some of their information.

The second book of Chronicles is occupied with the reign,
words, and life of Solomon the king, and of the kings who
succeeded him so far as Judah was concerned. Israel is left entirely
out of the picture except where some connection with Judah
demands comment.

Commencing with Solomon it ends with the proclamation of
Cyrus permitting the people to return from their captivity and
authorising them to rebuild the Temple. The book may be divided
thus :

Solomon and his reign — Chapters i-ix.
The History of the kings of Judah — Chapters x-xxxvi.

SOLOMON AND HIS REIGN (Chs. i-ix.)

SOLOMON. We find the book opens with a note of confidence
and jubilant anticipation. " And Solomon the son of David was
strengthened in his kingdom, and the Lord his God was with him,
and magnified him exceedingly " (vs. 1).

If ever a life had a good beginning, this was the life. The fact
that he was " the son of David ", the beloved king, was in his
favour. The fact that he " was strengthened in his kingdom " was
not his doing. That was because the nation as such had accepted
him. The fact that " the Lord his God was with him " was a
certainty of success and blessing. The fact that God " magnified
him exceedingly " meant that Divine favours were resting upon
him. Yet none of these things in itself was a guarantee that things
must end perfectly. " Let him that thinketh he standeth take heed

lest he fall (1 Cor. x. 12). Not only does this apply to the individual, as with Solomon ; it also applies to a nation, as here it does to Judah.

These blessings were more than hereditary. There were personal qualities in this young sovereign. These were exhibited when, firstly, he acknowledged publicly God as the Giver of these gifts, and in return went up to Gibeon and offered a thousand burnt offerings — secondly, when God asked as to what He should give to Solomon, the reply came : " Give me now wisdom and knowledge " (i. 10). These things were granted and much more with them. The chapter concludes with a record of his fabulous possessions.

However, two weaknesses are to be seen in this chapter. W. Clarkson, in the *Pulpit Commentary,* points out that, contrary to the requirements of God, the Ark and the Altar had become separated. They should have been together in the Tabernacle. Instead the Ark was at Jerusalem, in a separate tent, whilst the Altar, with the rest of the Tabernacle, was in Gibeon. The Ark, containing the two tables of stone bearing the Law, would speak to us of obedience, whilst the altar is the place of sacrifice. These should never be separated. Saul did so and was reminded by Samuel that " to obey is better than sacrifice ". " What God hath joined together, let not man put asunder ". It is true that these were brought together again when the Temple was built.

The other weakness was that Solomon sought for wisdom and knowledge in order that he might go out and come in before this people. He was seeking wisdom and knowledge, which was good and God granted them, but it was a material wisdom, a secular knowledge. He wanted to act wisely before the people and to the people. He wanted knowledge to understand the people. How much better if he had sought the wisdom of God and spiritual discernment. so that he could go in and out before God ! Spiritual wisdom would have saved him from spiritual tragedy.

THE TEMPLE. Six chapters are devoted to this project. It has already been dealt with in 1 Kings so does not require space here, other than to summarise :

Preparation	.....	.....	Chapter ii.
Construction	.....	.....	Chapter iii.
Equipment	.....	.....	Chapter iv.
Dedication	.....	.....	Chapter v.
Supplication	.....	.....	Chapter vi.
Acceptation	.....	.....	Chapter vii.

Everything was of the very best. Might these things be applied to our lives seeing that we are the temples of the Holy Ghost and of God (1 Cor. iii. 16 ; 2 Cor. vi. 16) ?

Prepared	.....	by the convicting of the Spirit.
Constructed	.....	by the Blood of the Cross.
Equipped	.....	with love, devotion, prayer, etc.
Dedication	.....	by full surrender of life.
Supplication	.....	as we become workers together with Him.
Acceptation	.....	accepted in the Beloved to be for ever with the Lord.

OTHER BUILDINGS (Ch. viii.)   Like most kings of his day Solomon was a great builder. He spent the first twenty years of his reign building ; firstly the House of God, and then his own house. He also repaired old cities and built new ones. He constructed fortifications and established store cities. All this helped to strengthen his kingdom.

The children of the old inhabitants he made to become servants and subjected them to tribute. Only the men of Israel did he allow in the army. That, of course, was good policy, for these people could become " security risks ". In any case, according to God's command through Moses, they would be a " security risk " morally if not politically. We do not move far in the chapter before such a condition is confirmed.

Solomon had married a woman of one of the surrounding nations when he married the daughter of Pharaoh of Egypt. Some will suggest that she was a proselyte to the Jewish faith, but that cannot be proved. If she were, then her servants were not. If she had accepted the Jewish faith and had acknowledged Jehovah as the only true God, why was it necessary for Solomon to build a separate house for her, saying : " My wife shall not dwell in the house of David, king of Israel, because the places are holy, whereunto the Ark of the Lord hath come " (viii. 11) ? Is not that an admission that she was not holy ? She may have made a profession as a matter of diplomacy. Solomon seemingly was not sure. Maybe he had married her as a diplomatic move to gain the friendship of Egypt, but any motive other than real love is dangerous in marriage.

A political alliance can often be a spiritual jeopardy. In fact, an alliance or agreement that puts spiritual things in a second place is a grave danger to a family. Elimeleck and Naomi made that mistake when they took their children to Moab. Abram made that mistake when he took Lot with him.

If you put that business proposition before your children's spiritual life, if you choose that new home because it appeals and you like the area, but never pause to find whether there is a sure spiritual home for your children in the locality, you are running grave " security risks ".

If there were any question in the mind of Solomon as to whether the daughter of Pharaoh could dwell in the house of David then there should be a big question as to whether she was fit to share the life of Solomon, or be brought into a place where she might influence the life of a nation — and that is exactly what happened. She became the first of many other wives of other nations referred to as strange women in 1 Kings xi. 1-2. " But king Solomon loved many strange women, together with the daughter of Pharaoh, women of the Moabites, Ammonites Edomites, Zidonians, and Hittites : Of the nations concerning which the Lord said unto the children of Israel, Ye shall not go to them, neither shall they come in unto you ; for surely they will turn away your heart after their gods. Solomon clave unto these in love ".

SOLOMON'S WEALTH AND WISDOM (Ch. ix.)   This last chapter concerning Solomon records the coming of the Queen of Sheba who, whilst wealthy and wise in her own rights, apparently had many problems, maybe of life itself. So, hearing of one who was greater than herself, she called on him to discover whether what she had heard was true and, if so, to prove Solomon with hard questions. Could these be proverbs and puns as some have suggested, a game of wit against wit, or were her hard questions problem questions ? Who of us have not problems, difficulties, the mysteries of the ways of life, and questions concerning the life to come ? Is it not a consolation to know that a greater than Solomon is here, wise in understanding ! Yea, He is Wisdom, great in power and abundant in supply. We come with an open and enquiring mind, He sends us away with understanding. We come puzzled, He sends us on with peace. We bring Him our gifts, He causes us to depart with His treasures, so that we are constrained to testify that the half has never yet been told.

We hear much of the Queen of Sheba who called on Solomon for his wisdom, but vs. 23 says : " And all the kings of the earth sought the presence of Solomon, to hear his wisdom, that God had put in his heart ".

The chapter concludes with the death of Solomon. Neither wealth nor wisdom can deliver a man from death so far as this world is concerned, but the riches of His grace and the wisdom of His love can give us victory in death and bring us into the riches of those things which eye hath not seen nor ear heard, nor the heart conceived, but which await those who love Him.

THE HISTORY OF THE KINGS OF JUDAH (Chs. x-xxxvi.)

Immediately after the death of Solomon the nation was split into two. Ten tribes, reigned over by Jeroboam, became known as the House of Israel. The two remaining tribes, Judah and Benjamin, became the House of Judah and had Rehoboam as its first king.

These twenty-seven chapters deal exclusively with the House or Kingdom of Judah, from its formation at the death of Solomon through to its last king, then being carried away into the Babylonian Capitivity, and on to the decree of Cyrus permitting these people to return to their own land.

The period covered by these chapters would be about four hundred years, during which twenty kings reigned. The kingship was very much hereditary. It did not change families and create dynasties as did Israel. It was God's purpose that the Royal Line should be a hereditary thing.

Here is a list of the kings, the length of their reigns, and the quality of their leadership :

King	Reign	Quality	Chapters
Rehoboam	17 years	Evil	Chapters x-xii.
Abijah	3 years	Evil	Chapter xiii.
Asa	41 years	Good	Chapters xiv-xvi.
Jehoshaphat	25 years	Good	Chapters xvii-xx.
Jehoram	8 years	Evil	Chapter xxi.
Ahaziah	1 year	Evil	Chapter xxii.
Athaliah	6 years	Evil	Chapter xxii.
Joash	40 years	Good	Chapter xxiv.
Amaziah	29 years	Good	Chapter xxv.
Uzziah	52 years	Good	Chapter xxvi.
Jotham	16 years	Good	Chapter xxvii.
Ahaz	16 years	Evil	Chapter xxviii.
Hezekiah	29 years	Good	Chapters xxix-xxxii.
Manasseh	55 years	Evil	Chapter xxxiii.
Amon	2 years	Evil	Chapter xxxiii.
Josiah	31 years	Good	Chapters xxxiv-xxxv.
Jehoahaz	3 months	Evil	Chapter xxxvi.
Jehoiakim	11 years	Evil	Chapter xxxvi.
Jehoiachin	3 months	Evil	Chapter xxxvi.
Zedekiah	11 years	Evil	Chapter xxxvi.

Although the genealogy remained in the family it did not remain strictly lineal as God required, which meant father to son. Four times there was a deviation, always caused through sin. There was Athaliah, who murdered and reigned as a usurper for six years. She was the mother of Ahaziah. Then there was Joash, who was a grandson instead of a son. Jehoiakim was a brother, not a son, and, lastly, Zedekiah, who was an uncle of his predecessor.

FIRST PERIOD — REHOBOAM TO JEHOSHAPHAT

REHOBOAM (Chs. x-xii.) The nation was not divided because of the foolishness of Rehoboam nor yet because of the intrigue of Jeroboam. They were only the instruments God used to bring into being what had already been decided. In I Kings ix. where God appeared to Solomon the second time He said : " But if ye at all turn from following Me, ye or your children . . . and serve other gods and worship them : Then will I cut off Israel out of the land " (read I Kings ix. 6-9). Against this statement I Kings xi. 4 says : " For it came to pass, when Solomon was old, that his wives turned away his heart after other gods ". Here then was the root cause of the division. God caused the ten tribes of Israel to revolt and go their own way, leaving only the two tribes, and that for David's sake.

It is a sad story of how Rehoboam, the son of Solomon, sought the advice of the older men of experience and then despised it because it did not suit his own ego. What he lost in foolishness he wanted to restore through fighting, but God would not permit him to fight his own brethren, assuring Rehoboam that this had been God's own doing.

Jeroboam was the next one to display foolishness. Having gained the ten tribes he then forsook God and, in doing so, he cast out the priests of God and the Levites, and ordained his own priests for his own idolatrous worship. These servants of God, therefore, left Israel and joined themselves to Judah and Jerusalem and thereby strengthened Rehoboam.

But alas ! As Rehoboam became stronger he, too, forsook the law of God (xii. 1). Some people can only seek God and worship Him when they are in trouble. God permitted Egypt to attack Jerusalem, to reveal to Rehoboam that his selfish strength was no strength at all. Rehoboam repented. What a fickle man he was ! His was a life of good and evil, but he made his people to become just as fickle. After seventeen years of continuous wars and more evil than good he died, to be succeeded by his son.

ABIJAH REIGNS AND WARS (Ch. xiii.) Although the account in Chronicles does not tell us so, Abijah continued in the evil ways of Rehoboam. This fact is recorded in I Kings xv. 3. His reign was short. For only three years did he occupy the throne, during which time Jeroboam continued his wars against Judah. One battle is recorded ; in fact, it is about all that we know of this man's reign. The battle was unique in many respects. Reading the account as it is here it would lead one to believe that Abijah was a good king, but that was the deception of the man.

Abijah arrayed his army against that of Israel already gathered, but instead of opening a barrage of cannon fire he stood forth like a preacher and opened up a volume of words. His logic was good and his statements were true, but they brought no results because his character was not in harmony with his counsels. This is the failure of many preachers.

He reminded Jeroboam and Israel that God had given the whole nation to David for all time by a covenant of salt, which meant a binding covenant, that they had rebelled against the Lord, and that they had rejected the priests of God and established false priests to worship idol gods, but God, and all that God had ordained, was with them. All of this was true in principle. Therefore he urged the people to leave Jeroboam and come over on his side.

But whilst Abijah was making his charges against Jeroboam, Jeroboam was making troop charges against Abijah ; for he brought up an ambushment behind Judah. When Judah saw their plight they cried unto the Lord, then gave a shout of victory, and God fought against Israel so that there was a great slaughter. Verse 20 says that Jeroboam never recovered from that defeat, but it also seems that Abijah never recovered from that victory. Few men can take success. From this battle he turned to a life of selfish indulgence as is suggested by verse 21, with his fourteen wives and thirty-eight children.

ASA'S GOOD REIGN (Chs. xiv-xvi.) At last we meet a noble life, a leader who set an example to his subjects. For forty-one years he reigned and, during the first ten years, the land had peace and quiet, which seems to have been the exception rather than the rule. This may be expected when a God-fearing king like Asa is at the helm. Not only did he put away idolatry in every form but he also turned the hearts of the people to the Lord by his own example and encouragement.

With God on his side he fortified cities and strengthened the nation materially as well as spiritually. Walking with God does not mean immunity from trouble. This Asa learned when Zerah, the Ethiopian, declared war, with a host of one million men and three hundred chariots, whereas he only had five hundred and eighty thousand men and apparently no chariots. The odds were two to one against Asa militarily but, knowing that " if God be for us who can be against ? ", he did what many a General has done since. He prayed on the battlefield before entering into the attack. His prayer was : " Lord, it is nothing with Thee to help, whether with many, or with them that have no power : help us, O Lord our God ; for we rest on Thee, and in Thy Name we go against this multitude. O Lord, Thou art our God ; let not man prevail against Thee " (xiv. 11). This was a prayer of faith which received the reward of faith as God smote the Ethiopians. Such trust will bring such triumph in all the tests of life.

Lest Asa, like his predecessors, should become exalted by the victory, God sent Azariah, a prophet, to him to encourage him in his faithfulness. Asa responded to this and continued to remove idols. He even removed his own mother from being Queen because she had an idol. So for another twenty years or more the nation continued in peace.

Alas, this noble life did not end as it began, for chapter xvi. has to relate a sorrowful ending.

Baasha had come to the throne of Israel and, after reigning twelve years, he planned to attack Judah. His purpose seemed to have been a blockade of Jerusalem in order that none could go in or out, and so bring Judah to her knees in submission to Israel. Asa, instead of seeking the Lord as previously, used the treasures of the Lord's House to buy the support of Benhadad, king of Syria, against Israel, and thereby prevailed.

God sent Hanani to reprove the king because he turned from the power of God to the politics of the world. Instead of listening to the reproving voice of God, he took the Lord's servant and, with anger, cast him into prison. He also showed revenge on some of his people.

His life closed tragically in that he was diseased in his feet with a grievous disease from which he died. In his need he still did not turn to the Lord. One wonders what caused such a fall in what had been a noble life. One cannot consider such a life without being reminded of the injunction " Let him that thinketh he standeth take heed lest he fall ".

At his death he was succeeded by his son,

JEHCSHAPHAT (Chs. xvii-xx.)   He was a good king.   He walked in the ways of David and opposed himself to every form of idolatry.   He caused that the people should be instructed in the law of God by establishing a circuit of priests.   He also strengthened the nation during his reign of twenty-five years.

As a result of his godliness the fear of the Lord fell on the nations round about, so that they respected Jehoshaphat and, instead of warring with him, sent him gifts.   Thus the nation enjoyed peace and plenty whilst the king had riches and honour in abundance.

However, Jehoshaphat had one weakness.   He did not possess the courage to refuse other kings who sought affinity with him. As a result twice he found himself in difficulty.   The first was

His affinity with Ahab.   Ahab, king of Israel, was a wicked king, maybe as wicked as any.   He forsook God and worshipped Baal.   When he wanted to fight against Ramoth-gilead he sought the physical help of the king of Judah.   Jehoshaphat's reply was : "I am as thou art, and my people as thy people ; and we will be with thee in the war" (xviii. 3).   Nonetheless he did ask Ahab to enquire of God.   This seemed somewhat out of order.   Ahab had forsaken God. How could he ask Him, therefore, for guidance? Jehoshaphat should have made his own enquiry before he consented to Ahab.   Ahab sent for four hundred prophets to make his enquiry, but they were all "yes men" who found advantage in agreeing with their king.   Naturally they agreed with Ahab, and said "Go up".   Jehoshaphat asked as to whether there was not a further prophet.   Four hundred had been in unison in their reply. There was another prophet, a faithful servant of Jehovah, so faithful that Ahab hated him, but Jehoshaphat insisted that he should be consulted.

So Micaiah was brought before the two kings.   Knowing that Ahab was not wanting an honest revelation of God's Will but had a longing to go to war, sarcastically the prophet replied to the meaningless enquiry, for the Proverbs say : "Answer a fool according to his folly" (Prov. xxvi. 5).   Micaiah said to the king : "Go ye up, and prosper, and they shall be delivered into your hand" (xviii. 14).   Have your own way, for that is what you want ! Then prophetically he told him the consequences — Israel would be scattered upon the mountains as sheep that had no shepherd. (xviii. 16).

The battle took place, Jehoshaphat went with Ahab, but the battle was lost.   Ahab was slain and Israel was scattered without a shepherd.   Jehoshaphat, however, returned to his house in peace, but not to escape the reproof of God Who sent to him Jehu, the son of the same seer, Hanani, who had been thrust into prison for reproving his father, Asa. Jehoshaphat, being a better man than his father, accepted the reproof : " Shouldest thou help the ungodly, and love them that hate the Lord?" (xix. 2). He repented and continued to establish the people in the fear of the Lord.

An enemy now arose against Judah. It comprised the combined forces of Moab, Ammon, and Mount Seir. Jehoshaphat gathered Judah together and prayed to God. It was a wonderful prayer reminding God of His power and His faithfulness, and reminding Him, too, of the prayer that Solomon had offered in the Temple. God responded to the prayer and told him to line up his armies, but that they would not have to fight as God Himself would do the fighting. They were to stand still and see the salvation of the Lord.

So it was that the enemy destroyed each other whilst Judah gathered up the spoil in abundance.

Notice that Jehoshaphat did not wait until the battle was over before he gave thanks to God. He acted upon God's promise and appointed singers and set them before the army to say " Praise the Lord ; for His mercy endureth for ever ". Whilst they sang, God saved.

His affinity with Ahaziah. After God reproved him for his affinity with Ahab, and after he had proved God as the Almighty Deliverer, why did he fall into the same sin again and join himself with another wicked king of Israel — Ahaziah? That is a question we may never be able to answer. Nonetheless, it should remind us that the heart is deceitful above all things and desperately wicked.

So Jehoshaphat died and was buried with his fathers, after a long and faithful reign, apart from those two alliances.

SECOND PERIOD — JEHORAM TO HEZEKIAH

REIGN OF JEHORAM (Ch. xxi.) What a different story! This man was as evil as his father was good. He was one of many sons who shared in the wealth that their father had left. Apparently he was not the best in the family (see vs. 13), but he was the oldest and, therefore, was king by the law of lineage.

One of his first acts was to slay his own brethren and certain of the princes. Evidently he was seeking to secure his position, but that cannot be done when God is left out of the reckoning, for although he was thirty-two years of age when he came to the throne yet he only reigned for eight years. He had married the daughter of Ahab, the wicked king of Israel, Athaliah who, like her mother, was a murderess. He walked in the ways of his in-laws and not in the ways of his father.

Idolatry and fornication became the form of life for Judah which caused God to put His hand heavily upon both king and people.

The Edomites, who had been subdued by David, and had been servants of God's people, revolted, and, although Jehoram sought to check the revolt, they freed themselves. Then the men of Libnah did the same thing, so that the nation was losing its hold upon the satellite nations around.

Elijah, the prophet of Israel, was sent to tell how God's hand would be against the king personally, in that he would be stricken with a dread disease from which there would be no recovery. Thus it was. Enemies without and sickness within, his family taken from him and his people hating him, he died, a lonely and tragic figure, whilst his epitaph was written that he departed without being desired, and was buried in a common grave. Sin is really a disastrous thing.

AHAZIAH (Ch. xxii.) the youngest and only remaining son of Jehoram, succeeded his father not only to the throne, but also in his evil life. Influenced by his mother, he followed the ways of Ahab, but only for one year. Then God used Jehu to destroy him and his wicked family. As the result of this, Athaliah, in revenge, slew all the seed royal of Judah, or so she thought! She was not aware that one little baby had been saved by his sister.

ATHALIAH (Ch. xxiii) now occupied the throne as a usurper, and reigned for six years. During those same years Joash was kept hidden from the unscrupulous woman. In the seventh year of her domination Jehoiada, the priest, communed with the captains, the Levites and the people and, forming a body-guard, they brought the young king into the Temple and crowned him amidst the shouts of the people, " God save the king ". Athaliah, on hearing the shouts of the people, tried to save the situation, crying out " Treason, Treason ", but they laid hands on her, carried her outside the Temple, and slew her.

Jehoiada made a covenant between himself and the king and the people that they should serve the Lord. So the people rejoiced and the nation was saved as :

JOASH WAS MADE KING (Ch. xxiv.) Seven years old was Joash when he began to reign, and he reigned for forty years. So long as Jehoiada, the priest, lived, and influenced this young life, so long was it a noble reign. Joash repaired the house of the Lord, which Athaliah had desecrated. He subdued the worship of Baal, and he feared the Lord. We may thank God for those who influence our lives for good, but we must never rest on them. We must have our own personal convictions for, even though Jehoiada may live to one hundred and thirty years of age, yet the day must come when he is called away. It was not until then that we find the true Joash. It is when our props are taken away, sometimes in the form of parents, or teachers, or friends, that we find our true selves, and discover whether we are really loving and serving the Lord, or leaning upon and pleasing other people.

Tragically enough the Scripture declares : "Now after the death of Jehoiada came the princes of Judah, and made obeisance to the king. Then the king hearkened unto them. And they left the house of the Lord God of their fathers, and served groves and idols" (xxiv. 17-18).

God sought to display His grace by sending prophets to bring them back. The son of Jehoiada, the priest, reproved the king and the people but, instead of Joash remembering how much he owed to Jehoiada, who had brought him back to the throne as a child and had guided him throughout his life, he took that son and had him stoned to death.

One is not surprised, therefore, to hear that God raised up the Syrians against him, and that the king died at the hand of his own servants.

As one by one good men failed their God, we feel like crying out with those who said : "Who then can be saved ? "

AMAZIAH (Ch. xxv.) The same story is told again — "Ye did run well, who hath bewitched you ? ", for Amaziah was a good king until he had gained a victory over the Edomites. Then it was that he brought back their idols with him and began to worship the gods that had not been capable of delivering the Edomites out of his hand. Pride in his victory over Edom caused him to want to meet Israel. Although warned of the results, he insisted, and was defeated by Israel.

He ended his life in exile in Lachish, where he was slain. His body was brought back to Jerusalem for burial. He had reigned for twenty-nine years.

UZZIAH (Ch. xxvi.) This was a long reign and a righteous one until the end. Coming to the throne at the age of sixteen years, Uzziah remained as its occupant for fifty-two years. He has always been known as " good king Uzziah ".

During his reign he suppressed the enemy on every side, and did more than any king before him to restore the strength and prestige of Judah. He was a builder and a husbandman, a military leader, an inspiration to all. But alas! He was a man who could not take success. There are many like him. Maybe God withholds success from many of us because of this particular weakness of character. The turning point in this noble life is verse 16 : " But when he was strong, his heart was lifted up to his destruction : for he transgressed against the Lord his God ". Because he had been successful in every other walk of life, he thought he could do the same in the priestly order. Therefore he went into the Temple of the Lord to burn incense upon the altar of incense, but a good king will not make even a bad priest. This was not his prerogative. Wrong as this action was, it was made worse when Amaziah and eighty other priests went in to reprove the king for his conduct. They told him he had exceeded his duty and had trespassed. They commanded him to withdraw his feet from the sanctuary. Instead of humbling himself and obeying them, he was angered as though they were in the wrong and he was doing what was right. The priestly instrument — the censer — was still in the king's hand when God displayed His wrath and smote Uzziah in the forehead with leprosy. The forehead is the seat of the mind and the intellect. It is also the seat of pride and, as that pride swelled up in the king so that he could not be corrected, God touched it with a withering leprosy.

Leprosy in the forehead was one of the worst forms of the disease, which required complete isolation. This is declared in Lev. xiii. 43-46: " Then the priest shall look upon it : and, behold, if the rising of the sore be white reddish in his bald head, or in his bald forehead, as the leprosy appeareth in the skin of the flesh ; he is a leprous man, he is unclean : the priest shall pronounce him *utterly unclean ;* his plague is in his head. And the leper in whom the plague is, his clothes shall be rent, and his head bare, and he shall put a covering upon his upper lip, and shall cry, Unclean, unclean. All the days wherein the plague shall be in him he shall be defiled ; he is unclean ; he shall *dwell alone ;* without the camp shall his habitation be ".

What a tragedy ! This was the sin of presumption.

JOTHAM (Ch. xxvii) Little enough is said of this son of Uzziah, who reigned for sixteen years. His reign was a good one. He followed the Lord but it would appear that he never encouraged the people in the same following. We have to go to other books for his history.

AHAZ (Ch. xxviii.) He lived an evil life and for sixteen years led Judah deep into idolatry and all the abominations of the heathen. As a punishment God permitted the Syrians to carry a multitude of Judah into captivity as well as causing a great slaughter of their valiant men. Israel also warred against Judah and carried away a great host. However, Oded, a prophet of the Lord, persuaded Israel to return their captives, seeing they were brethren.

Edom, Philistia, Assyria in turn warred against Judah, but Ahaz sinned more and more, and worshipped the gods of his enemies, until the Lord brought Judah very low. So Ahaz died, not to be buried in the sepulchres of the kings.

HEZEKIAH (Chs. xxix-xxxii.) succeeded this evil man and did much to restore the damage that had been done. He repaired the Temple and reopened its doors. He spent a lot of time in cleansing and re-sanctifying the sanctuary. The offerings were restored and the Passover reinstated. In fact, it was a great religious revival that brought new heart to the nation.

Then Sennacherib, king of Assyria, sought to take Judah by guile, seeking to weaken the faith of the people in their God and in Hezekiah. However, Hezekiah encouraged the people in the Lord, whilst he and Isaiah, the prophet, spread the letter before God and cried to Him in prayer. So God dealt with Assyria and saved His people.

After this Hezekiah was sick unto death, but God restored him and prolonged his life. During that period he lost out with God in the matter of the ambassadors who came from Babylon. He did not consult God but, with a spirit of pride, showed them all that he possessed. That story is not told in this book. He died and was buried in honour, after twenty-nine years of noble leadership.

THIRD PERIOD — MANASSEH TO JOSIAH

MANASSEH (Ch. xxxiii.) lived a very different life. He reigned for fifty-five years, a great deal of which was in sin, undoing much of that which his father had done. He brought back every form of idolatry. Because of this God brought the king of Assyria against Judah once again, and they took Manasseh away into Babylon and bound him in fetters. There he repented of his sin and prayed to God. God heard his prayer, forgave his sin, and restored him to the throne. In those last days he sought to make good the evil he had done in earlier life. He slept with his fathers and

AMON (Ch. xxxiii.) his son, reigned in his stead. Two years of evil rule brought his life to an end at the age of twenty-four years, being slain in his own house by his servants. He was succeeded by his son,

JOSIAH (Ch. xxxiv.) Coming to the throne at the tender age of eight, he reigned for thirty-one years. It was a noble reign. At the age of sixteen he began his reforms. Ten years later he began to repair the Temple. During this time Hilkiah, the priest, found a book of the law of the Lord, given by Moses. This was read before the king, who rent his clothes and called the nation to hear the law and to repent of their evil ways. He caused that the Passover should be kept. There never was such a Passover since the days of Samuel.

After this Josiah went to battle against the king of Egypt and was wounded. Being brought back to Jerusalem, he died. He was buried amidst a great lamentation of the people that was led by Jeremiah.

FOURTH PERIOD — JEHOAHAZ TO THE CAPTIVITY

This is brief in its detail. The reigns were mostly short in duration. All is contained in the final chapter.

JEHOAHAZ, who was also known as Jehoaz and Shallum, reigned for only three months. He was removed by the king of Egypt, who put

JEHOIAKIM, previously known as Eliakim, in his place. He reigned for eleven years and did that which was evil. Nebuchadnezzar carried him into Babylon.

JEHOIACHIN, his son, reigned in his stead, but only for three months and ten days. He, too, was evil, and he also was taken into Babylon.

ZEDEKIAH, his brother, took the throne and became the last king of Judah. He reigned for eleven years. Another evil reign brought the chequered history of the kings to an end.

Although Jeremiah had been counselling the people to submit to Nebuchadnezzar for their own good, and God, in His compassion, had sought to win His people to Himself, yet they persistently rebelled until God permitted the king of the Chaldees to come and destroy the city and the Temple, and to carry the people and their king into captivity.

THE PROCLAMATION OF CYRUS

This proclamation means that the book does not close, nor the nation terminate, finally. Beyond the gloom and grief, the sorrow and the suffering, shines the ray of hope, the manifestation of the Grace of God, despite the fact of His judgment.

" Now in the first year of Cyrus, king of Persia, that the word of the Lord spoken by the mouth of Jeremiah might be accomplished, the Lord stirred up the spirit of Cyrus, king of Persia, that he made a proclamation throughout all his kingdom, and put it also in writing, saying, Thus saith Cyrus king of Persia : All the kingdoms of the earth hath the Lord God of heaven given me ; and He hath charged me to build Him a house in Jerusalem, which is in Judah. Who is there among you of all His people ? The Lord his God be with him, and let him go up " (xxxvi. 22-23).

EZRA

REVIVAL

*"For Ezra had prepared his heart to seek the law of the Lord,
and to do it, and to teach in Israel statutes and judgments."*
(EZRA vii. 10)

INTRODUCTION

The books of Kings and Chronicles relate the whole history
of the kings of Israel and Judah until the time that the Jews were
carried away into Captivity.

Ezra deals with the return of many of these people from the
Captivity, the re-building of the Temple and the City, and the re-
establishment of certain social and religious practices. Ezra is,
therefore, the first of the post-exilic books, which are six in number.
They are Ezra, Nehemiah, Esther, Haggai, Zechariah, and Malachi.
This means that these next three books belong to the period that
terminates Old Testament history, or these three historic books
run simultaneously with the last three prophetic books. All of
them cover a period of one hundred years.

The chronological order of the events of that century were :

B.C. 536 — 49,897 people returned from Babylon to
Jerusalem.

B.C. 536 — in the seventh month the altar was re-built
and the sacrifices began.

B.C. 535 — re-building of the Temple begun and
stopped.

B.C. 520 — work renewed by Haggai and Zechariah.

B.C. 516 — Temple completed.

B.C. 478 — Esther became Queen in Persia.

B.C. 457 — Ezra came to Jerusalem with a remnant.

B.C. 444 — Nehemiah re-built the walls.

B.C. 432 — Nehemiah returned again to Jerusalem.

This puts the named books all at the end of the Old Testament
in the following chronological order : Ezra, Haggai, Zechariah,
Esther, Nehemiah, Malachi.

The book of Ezra divides itself into two distinct parts. The first part covers a period of twenty years in which Zerubbabel, the Governor, and Joshua, the High Priest, were responsible for the rebuilding of the altar and the Temple. During this time Haggai and Zechariah prophesied. Then came an interval of fifty-seven years. It is to this interval that the story of Esther belongs. The second period of time in Ezra tells how Nehemiah, the Governor, and Ezra, the Priest, restored the city and brought about a great reformation. This covered a period of twenty-five years and extended into the book of Nehemiah.

ANALYSIS OF THE BOOK

The subject of the book as a whole is that of the return from the Captivity. The first return was led by Zerubbabel, who became " The man of the building ". Then a group came back with Ezra, who was " The man of the Book ". These make the main division.

The book can be divided again into five sections, and it is thus that it will be studied.

(1) Return by Royal Assent.
(2) Registration of People and Property.
(3) Rebuilding of Altar and Temple.
(4) Reinstatement of the Book of the Law.
(5) Reformation of the People.

(1) RETURN BY ROYAL ASSENT (Chs. i-ii and vii-viii)

This return was by no means wholehearted. In the two groups there were less than fifty thousand people of all classes who found their way back. This is very surprising when one realises the patriotism that has ever belonged to this people ; and also when one recalls the way they rebelled against Jeremiah when he foretold their captivity and advised them to yield to their enemy for their ultimate good. The return had been made easy and favourable because it was twice under royal assent.

The first royal proclamation was made soon after Daniel, who was a prophet of the exile, had prayed that they might return. This is recorded in the book of Daniel : " And I set my face unto the Lord God, to seek by prayer and supplication . . . yea, whiles I was speaking in prayer, even the man Gabriel, whom I had seen in the vision at the beginning . . . informed me, and talked with me " (ix. 3, 21, 22). Not only had Daniel prayed and received assurance that his prayer was heard and answered, but Isaiah had also given prophecy concerning this deliverance. " That saith of Cyrus, He is My Shepherd, and shall perform all My pleasure :

even saying to Jerusalem, Thou shalt be built ; and to the temple, Thy foundation shall be laid " (Isa. xliv. 28). This prophecy was made two hundred years before Cyrus was even born but, in the light of this prophetic utterance of Isaiah, listen to the proclamation of Cyrus : " Thus saith Cyrus king of Persia, The Lord God of heaven hath given me all the kingdoms of the earth ; and He hath charged me to build Him an house at Jerusalem, which is in Judah. Who is there among you of all His people ? His God be with him, and let him go up to Jerusalem, which is in Judah, and build the house of the Lord God of Israel, (He is the God) which is in Jerusalem. And whosoever remaineth in any place where he sojourneth, let the men of his place help him with silver, and with gold, and with goods, and with beasts, beside the freewill offering for the house of God that is in Jerusalem " (Ezra i. 2-4).

The second royal edict is in the second half of the book, at the time when Artaxerxes was reigning, and here is his decree : " Now this is the copy of the letter that the king Artaxerxes gave unto Ezra the priest, the scribe, even a scribe of the words of the commandments of the Lord, and of His statutes to Israel. Artaxerxes, king of kings, unto Ezra the priest, a scribe of the law of the God of heaven, perfect peace, and at such a time. I make a decree, that all they of the people of Israel, and of His priests and Levites, in my realm which are minded of their own free will to go up to Jerusalem, go with thee. Forasmuch as thou art sent of the king, and of his seven counsellors, to enquire concerning Judah and Jerusalem, according to the law of thy God which is in thine hand , " etc. (Ezra vii. 11-26).

We have made the remark of surprise that the return was not more wholehearted, but then has there ever been a national repentance ? A lot of people will sometimes follow the crowd, but that does not spell repentance. Such people are so fickle they will follow another crowd to-morrow. To-day they can cry : " Hosanna " ; to-morrow they will shout : " Away with Him, crucify Him ". God has ever had His faithful few, the remnant, and they have ever been the salt of the earth.

Should we look for national repentance or world-revival to-day we will be disappointed. The Lord has never promised it, neither has He given any indications. Instead, He has warned us of apostasy, of men being lovers of pleasure rather than lovers of God. The only mention of national revival is at the time when Israel will have returned to her land and the Lord will have come to the Mount of Olives to establish His Millennial Kingdom. Then a nation will be born in a day. That does not belong to the Day of Grace, but to the Dispensation of the Kingdom.

In the light of these things we should not give up in despair, but rather the reverse. We should not despair because we do not see mass revival, but seek faithfully to win one here and two there, which will help build the true Church of Jesus Christ.

This approach, of course, justifies the Word of God and encourages an otherwise discouraged worker, but it does not justify the sinner any more than it freed those who remained in exile from condemnation. Two reasons may be suggested as to why so many did not return — the first being that they had invested too much in Babylon. They had business ties, had purchased property, and had become involved in so many other interests. Babylon has always been used as a type of the world, and how true it is that worldly possessions and interests are the biggest hindrances for many people, who know they should be journeying heavenward, should be following the faith of their fathers, but they are not prepared to pay the price. They are holding tenaciously to their worldly possessions but, when death calls them from this scene, their worldly possessions will not hold on to them.

The other suggestion is that some refused, considering the journey too long, irksome, and dangerous. They had no choice in travel conditions when they were carried away by force. Many a person in the world to-day longs for heaven and the things of God, but is not prepared to live the Christian life of separation and sanctification. They consider the way of holiness hard and dangerous.

(2) REGISTRATION OF PEOPLE AND PROPERTY
(Chs. ii. and viii.)

Concerning *the people*, there appears to be a discrepancy in the numbers given in chapter two. The total as stated in verse 64 is 42,360, but if we total all the figures given we find the number is only 29,818. One of the reasons for this is that no figure is given for those who were the children of the priests, who were unable to prove their genealogy. Secondly, it is to be remembered that Israel went into the Assyrian Captivity, and Judah to Babylon. This means that these figures and families primarily concerned Judah, even though some of Israel were included. There would probably be a number of Israel coming from so many different families in such small numbers that it would not warrant listing the family.

When we meet chapters of this nature comprising numerous names and figures, we pass them by as we would a catalogue, the passenger list of a great boat, or the names that appear in the newspaper of some town in which we have no friends. Names do not mean anything until they are found in a list in which one's own name should appear, and then interest is very different. Beware if your name is not there! Names are important things, and records more important. The author remembers once visiting the National Library of Scotland and becoming very interested when he found his name listed, and his list of books. One title was missing, and it did not take long to find out why it was missing, and to take the necessary steps to ensure the omission was corrected!

God keeps a strict record. Our names are or are not in the Lamb's Book of Life. There are other Books recording all the acts we have performed. Our rewards are going to be according to those records. Records may be uninteresting, but they are very important. In this connection one is very interested in the appearance of the name of Antipas as a martyr in Rev. ii. 13. That name cannot be found in the annals of the martyrs written by men. Man overlooked that name, God did not.

Then there is Christian service. We are reminded that this, too, is not overlooked as we see listed priests, Levites, singers, porters, nethinims, servants.

Following the listings of the people comes a registration of *Property*. Included were :

Vessels :

  30 chargers of gold
 1,000 chargers of silver
  20 knives
  30 basons of gold
  410 basons of silver
 1,000 other vessels.

These vessels had been taken away by Nebuchadnezzar.

They had been kept in an idol temple by Merodoch.

They had been desecrated by Belshazzar.

They were given back by Cyrus.

They were dedicated things that belonged to the Temple and to God. Man had abused them and desecrated them, but they were numbered back to Jerusalem. We have spiritual gifts given to us by God to use in His service. If we abuse these gifts, if we allow the world to desecrate these Divine privileges, remember that the day is yet to be when we shall have to account before God for every holy gift.

Animals :
> 736 horses
> 245 mules
> 435 camels
> 6,720 asses.

These appear a small and insignificant matter for Holy Writ, but they have something to tell us. God is interested in everything because everything belongs to God. He has made a claim on man's possessions. He always will. He claims tithes, firstborn, firstfruits, etc.

The number of animals would suggest the poverty of the people at the time of their return :
> 1 horse to every 60 people
> 1 mule to every 175 people
> 1 camel to every 100 people
> 1 ass to every 6 people.

Bullion :
> 61,000 drams gold
> 5,000 pounds silver

Robes :
> 100 Priestly Garments.

These were the gifts of the chief of the fathers.

Added to these were :
> 100 talents of silver
> 100 measures of wheat
> 100 baths of wine
> 100 baths of oil
> Salt in unlimited supply.

These were granted to the people by Artaxerxes, the king, and brought up to Jerusalem by Ezra (Ch. vii.).

The latter things were the offerings of the people, something which the Lord is always anxious to receive.

(3) RESTORATION OF THE ALTAR AND TEMPLE (Ch. iii.)

If a nation is to be established or re-established then it must have solid foundations, and the foundations that are most important to a nation are those .which are moral and religious. The world has many great cities, some old, some new, some large, some small, but there is no city just like New York, with its towering structures and 100-storey buildings. New York can go upward because it is built on the solid rock of Manhattan. The world has many faiths, most of them national, limited to a country

or a race. There is but one Faith which has expanded to take
in all peoples of all races and all colour. It is the Christian Faith,
which is built upon the Rock of Ages.

Before the city was rebuilt the Temple was re-erected. Before
the Temple was rebuilt the Altar was re-established. This is the
right order. This is getting to the foundation of the Faith. " For
without the shedding of blood there is no remission for sin ". The
Church was built upon Christ, not Christ upon the Church.

In iii. 3 we read : " And they set the altar upon his bases ".
They removed the rubble and discovered the old foundation. It
was not a new altar. They were not establishing a new faith, but
moving back on to the foundations they had once forsaken. This
was what Elijah did when he contested the prophets of Baal on
Mount Carmel. " And Elijah said unto all the people, Come near
unto me. And all the people came near unto him. And he
repaired the altar of the Lord that was broken down " (I Kings
xviii. 30).

We ofttimes say that the way down is the way up, and it is
true. " Humble yourselves therefore under the mighty hand of
God, that He may exalt you in due time " (I Peter v. 6). So the
way back is often the way of advance. To go back does not
necessarily spell retreat. If we to-day are to accomplish anything
morally or spiritually we shall have to go back to the Faith of our
fathers.

This altar was built in the seventh month of their return,
and with it they established all that the altar represented — a full
worship of God.

In the following year Zerubbabel, and those associated with
him, turned their thoughts to the rebuilding of the Temple. When
Faith is laid as a foundation, Practice follows as the structure of
life. It was with great rejoicing that the foundations of the Temple
were laid. The instruments sounded, the people sang, the lost
was found, national life was returning for the exiles, but the joy
was mingled with sorrow, the songs were mellowed by sadness.
It was the new generation which was rejoicing in something it had
not before possessed (the captivity had been for seventy years,
so most of these people had been born in captivity). The older
people watered the triumphs with their tears. Killjoys ? Not at
all ! The older people had memories, sacred memories, which
must be respected. Were not these people returning to a former
faith ?

These foundations, which were new and wonderful to the
young, were small and insignificant by comparison with Solomon's

Temple which the older people once knew. To them this was good, but not good enough.

This is a great parable of Christian life. To go into the Gospel meeting, to enter the evangelistic campaign, to witness our young people singing the hymns, enjoying the choruses and listening to the message, responding to its truth, does one's soul good, and we rejoice with those who rejoice. But one has also been in the Bible Conference as some faithful servant of the Lord has expounded the depths and unfolded the riches of the Word, and there the old saint, the warrior of the way, has had his soul stirred, and with eyes moist has said : " Brother, that has done my soul good. That is the old-time exposition. That is something for which we long ". He is no killjoy. Just the man of experience who knows the good, the better, and the best. With Paul he covets the best gift.

Strange as it may seem, good work always finds its adversaries, but that is just how things operate in the economy of God. Resistance is the thing that makes for strength. The tree that meets the wind, the storm, and the drought, drives its roots down farther, and thus outlives the ravages of time. The summer flower that has never faced a winter wilts and fades as quickly as it comes. The Christian faith has faced opposition and unbelief, has met the wild beast in the arena, and the torture of its adversary. It has openly faced the scourge of the foe without, and has withstood the subtlety of the enemy within. That is why Peter says: " Beloved, think it not strange concerning the fiery trial which is to try you, as though some strange thing happened unto you " (I Peter iv. 12).

The opposition came firstly from the Samaritans. They had requested the privilege of helping Judah build the Temple, but had been refused. As a result they sought to hinder the building by weakening the hands of the people. This slowed down the work but did not stop it.

These Samaritans were not in opposition to God. They were not opposed to the religion that the Temple represented. In fact, they offered their co-operation. This is ofttimes true in life as we know it. If the world cannot share in the building they will not be able to share in the authority and control of the finished product. This would, in turn, deprive them of any possession. Men to-day are so selfish. They want to have their hand upon everything for whatever gain there might be, whether they gain authority to control the other man, or whether they gain wealth by robbing the other man. They mind not so long as they have gain. Men do not want

God or Faith to-day because that God and that Faith want *them*. It is a life that calls for sacrifices — they seek only self.

Men, therefore, do not attempt to overthrow the Church. That would be folly. Instead they seek to weaken the hands of the people by offering them counter-attractions.

In the days of Artaxerxes they tried another method. They suggested that these people were not patriotic, and that their practices were harmful to the king's realm and to those other people whose first interest was in their country. On this ground the enemy scored a temporary success, for the building programme was stopped.

This is the cry to-day. Take the Bible out of the schools, take Christianity out of politics. Faith is a personal matter. Let it remain there. If it is made a national foundation men are being robbed of their liberties. That is an unpatriotic position.

In chapter five the prophets Haggai and Zechariah come into the story. They encouraged Zerubbabel, and the work of building began again. A further interference came from the Governor, Tatnai, who sought their authority for building. They informed him that no one less than Cyrus, king of Babylon, issued the authority. This information was sent to Darius, king of Assyria, for confirmation. Not only were the facts proved, but the un-solicited support and blessing of Darius was given to the Jews so that the Temple was both finished and dedicated to the service of God. How often God turns the wrath of man to His praise, and makes His enemies to do His bidding.

This first section closes with the people keeping the Feast of the Passover, and with all of their enemies subdued.

After the fifty-seven year interval we come to the second section of the book and are introduced to the man whose name gives the title to the book — Ezra, Priest and Scribe.

(4) REINSTATEMENT OF THE LAW (Chs. vii-ix.)

The people were back in their land, the altar and Temple rebuilt, and their religion re-established. A further consolidation was required, so God raised up His next man. Zerubbabel had been the "man of the building", now came the "man of the Book". Ezra was a ready scribe in the law of Moses (vii. 6). He had made request to the king of Babylon that he might return to his country, and the request had been granted. He carried with him the decree of Artaxerxes and the offerings of the people. He also brought with him a small remnant of the people who were prepared to seek their own country. Something more Ezra brought

with him, and the most important thing — it was the determination
to establish the people of God in their moral conduct, so we read :
" For Ezra had prepared his heart to seek the law of the Lord,
and to do it, and to teach in Israel statutes and judgments " (vii.
10).

Notice the thoroughness of Ezra from the beginning. Having
gathered the group of emigrants, he collected them together by the
river and checked who they were. This took him three days (viii.
15). From this check he learned that there was no representation
of the tribe of Levi, the priestly tribe, exclusively. No Levites
meant no priests. This he corrected by commandment, he then
had two hundred and fifty eight Levites and Nethinims.

As the journey was difficult and the enemies many, and there
was a great quantity of gold and silver to carry it would have been
right to have claimed the protection of a band of soldiers, but
Ezra had learned that it is better to trust in the Lord than to put
confidence in the arm of flesh and in horses. He encouraged
the people to use the same faith by calling them to prayer and
fasting. Thus they made the journey without mishap.

Having arrived at Jerusalem, immediately he began to deal
with the moral issues. The principal sin was that of intermarriage
with the people of the nations round about. This had been forbidden in the law of God for two reasons. (1) God had called this
people out as a peculiar people. He had made them a people
distinct from all other peoples, and a nation through whom He
would bless the nations of the world. Intermarriage would quickly
rob them of this distinctive identity and make them to become one
of the nations, instead of one *among* the nations. (2) God had
become their God, and they were to worship no other god before
Him. Intermarriage would mean contamination with the heathen
gods and the establishment of idolatrous worship. Judaism is a
faith before it is a race. That was why Paul said : " He is not a
Jew, which is one outwardly ; neither is that circumcision, which
is outward in the flesh : But he is a Jew, which is one inwardly ;
and circumcision is that of the heart, in the spirit, and not in the
letter ; whose praise is not of men, but of God " (Rom. ii. 28-29).

Having heard of the sin of Israel (ix. 2), Ezra did not go to
preach at this people, neither did he chide nor rebuke, at least not
immediately. Of course, they would have to be told, and how
could they hear without a preacher. It must also be considered
" how can they preach unless they be sent ", and there is always
the danger of going to war against sin at our own charges. Therefore we should carefully observe the actions of this man of God.

He was in the Will of the Lord in coming to Jerusalem. That is accepted, but that is also in general. One needs to know one is in the Will of the Lord in each specific action.

The first thing Ezra did was to take this burden of sin to himself. He assumed personally a guilt and a sorrow. Of Jesus it was said : " He hath borne our griefs and carried our sorrows ". We have to learn to do the same. Secondly, with that sense of shame, he came before the Lord in prayer to intercede with God in their behalf. Thirdly, like Moses, Nehemiah, and other of the Old Testament saints, he identified himself with their guilt, praying " *our* iniquities ", " have *we* been in great trespass ", etc. Our method of praying is " *their* iniquities ", " *their* sins ". We keep ourselves so holily at a distance from the sinner that we can never win him, either in testimony or in intercession. Fourthly, the prayer was not a general confession, for such a prayer brings neither guilt nor forgiveness. The sin was named, unworthiness was confessed, blessings were recognised, the Lord's mercy was acknowledged, whilst the prayer closed with a complete yieldedness to the Lord for Him to do as He considered right. " O Lord God of Israel, Thou art righteous : for we remain yet escaped, as it is this day : behold, we are before Thee in our trespasses : for we cannot stand before Thee because of this " (ix. 15).

(5) REFORMATION OF THE PEOPLE (Ch. x.)

Revival has always followed prayer and confession. What have we done with this word " revival " to-day ? Preachers think they can carry revival around in a suitcase. Others can paste it on a billboard. One has witnessed men talking, pleading, conniving, making people stand up, making them sit down, pleading with them to testify, extracting from them confession — anything, everything, that will work up a revival. But revivals do not come up, they come down. Revival is not created by human effort. It is spontaneous, and wells from the soul.

When the revival broke out at Wheaton, Illinois, in 1952, no one was working for it. No plans had been made. The preacher had not even preached. It just came. That is exactly what happened here in Ezra's time. Ezra had not preached. He had not rebuked. In fact, he had not contacted the people. Chapter ten opens with the words : " Now when Ezra had prayed, and when he had confessed, weeping and casting himself down before the house of God, there assembled unto him out of Israel a very great congregation of men and women and children : for the people wept very sore " (x. 1).

Shechaniah, who acted as spokesman for the people, began in their behalf to make confession, and, not only so, but offered to make restitution. "Now therefore let us make a covenant with our God to put away all the wives, and such as are born of them" (x. 3). To make sure that this was no emotional stir, but a matter of real business, Ezra made them to swear (a serious business) that they intended to carry this thing out, and they did so.

What brought this conviction upon the people ? What caused them to weep and to tremble ? What was it that made them anxious to right their wrong ? Certainly not the emotions of man. Ezra had been before the Lord and the Lord had sent Holy Ghost conviction. That is the only kind of revival we desire to see. This was what happened in Wales at the turn of the century. Not men preaching revival and working for revival, but a soul pressed down with the sin of the community, praying and confessing before God.

Only after conviction had come to the people and they had expressed their longing to make full restitution did Ezra stand up to preach. This preaching was not to condemn them in their sin, but to control them in their repentance. National sin comes as a result of many individuals committing their own sins. National repentance and revival will come as each individual deals with his own individual sin, just as if he were the only sinner. The method with which they dealt with the situation was that time was given for each man to handle his own affairs and officially put away the woman with whom he was living illegally. The whole procedure took three months to complete.

Each man is named to make sure that there was personal acknowledgment of sin, personal confession of sin, and a personal dealing with sin.

This, and this alone, is revival.

NEHEMIAH

REBUILDING

" Except the Lord build the house, they labour in vain that build it : except the Lord keep the city, the watchman waketh but in vain" (PSALM cxxvii. 1)

INTRODUCTION

This book naturally is associated with Ezra and Esther. In fact, it is the sequence. There was a time when Ezra and Nehemiah were one book. The purpose of the book is to recount the rebuilding of the walls of Jerusalem and their dedication, and then to record the establishment of its citizenship.

The first two chapters give an autobiography of Nehemiah himself, the remainder of the chapters the work he accomplished, with two insertions. The first of these insertions is a list in chapter vii. of the families which returned from the Captivity, and the other insertion, in chapters xi and xii, six lists of names of the inhabitants of Jerusalem and the cities.

Nehemiah was a man of work and prayer. He was much more a man of action than a man of words. At times he was almost forceful in his manner, but a man of high integrity, with a zeal for God and a loyalty to his nation and city.

The chronological order places the book of Esther before that of Nehemiah, the order being Ezra, Esther, Nehemiah. His position as cup-bearer to the king was no doubt due to the influence of Esther. It has been pointed out that Artaxerxes was the son of Ahasuerus. This would make him to be the stepson of Esther. Esther, being a Jewess and probably still living, would, therefore, have used her influence to get Nehemiah, also a Jew, into such an honoured position. Apart from this the Jews might never have been saved. Thus can be seen the over-ruling hand of God.

The book may be divided into two main sections :

    (1)   Rebuilding the city walls. Chs. i - vi.
    (2)   Re-establishing the people. Chs. vii - xiii.

Zerubbabel had led back the first exiles ninety-four years earlier. Ezra had led a second contingent. Ezra had also been responsible for the rebuilding of the Temple and had led a revival of the people. This had been fifty-seven years later, but the walls of the city had never been rebuilt in all of those one hundred years. This need not mean an indifference on the part of Ezra. It could have been diplomacy. Walls meant fortifications, and such an act could have been interpreted in some quarters as preparation for aggression. As Ezra was their spiritual leader and not their political governor, he was possibly safer in leaving such a matter alone. On the other hand, one is conscious that there is no standing still. If a people do not advance then they deteriorate. The building of the wall must come, therefore, sooner or later.

(1) REBUILDING THE CITY WALLS (Chs. i - vi)

(a) *Preparation.* This introduces the man, Nehemiah. Although he was a Jew and, by his enquiry concerning Jerusalem, revealed his loyalty toward his city, he had probably never seen it. His ancestors could have been carried away several generations back.

That he was a cup-bearer to the king is surprising unless we accept the influence of Esther, as already stated, because it was not customary for a person of another country to handle the food of the king for fear of a plot against the king's life.

His position and his character suggest something of a noble birth. From Hanani he learned of the condition that was prevailing at Jerusalem, how that the walls were still heaps of ruins and the people impoverished. This brought to him great grief of heart so that he mourned, wept, fasted, and prayed certain days.

The rest of chapter one is the prayer that he offered to God. It is a prayer of confession, coming from a heart that was truly humbled before God. It was also a prayer that claimed the promises of God. It was a prayer with personal identification. So often we pray for the other man who is the sinner and we tell God what he has done, but when Nehemiah prayed he said : " Let Thine ear now be attentive, and Thine eyes open, that Thou mayest hear the prayer of Thy servant, which I pray before Thee now, day and night, for the children of Israel Thy servants, and confess the sins of the children of Israel, which WE have sinned against Thee : both I and MY father's house have sinned. WE have dealt very corruptly against Thee " (vs. 6 and 7).

Prayers of this kind are revolutionary. They bring definite answers. So many of our prayers are selfish and receive no answers — we pray amiss.

Moses prayed and the enemy was defeated.
Joshua prayed and the sun stood still.
Elijah prayed and the rain stayed.
Isaiah prayed and received his commission.
Daniel prayed and was delivered from danger.
Nehemiah prayed and the way to Jerusalem was opened.
Lord, teach me how to pray !

Another truth to be learned from Nehemiah and his praying is — Nehemiah prayed, then acted. Some of us pray but never act. Some of us act and never pray. Some of us act and then pray. Only Nehemiah was right. It is not : " Lord, I have done this ", but " Lord, what wilt Thou have me to do ? "

After four months of prayer, which could have taken place whilst the Royal Court was out of residence — a vacation period — Nehemiah was back at his duty of serving wine to His Royal Highness, but his heart was still heavy with the burden of Jerusalem. There was a changed attitude with this man, for he said : " I had not been beforetime sad in his presence " (ii. 1). In fact, sorrow was not permitted in the king's presence. That was why, when the king observed the sad countenance and made reference to it in verse 2, Nehemiah said : " Then I was very sore afraid ". It could have lost him his position.

Nehemiah was broken before God. The king saw that the outward countenance was a reflection of inward sorrow of heart and enquired the reason for it. When our heart is melted before God for others, God will melt the heart of others toward us and make the way plain.

Nehemiah made known to the king the cause of his grief. " The city the place of my tathers' sepulchres, lieth waste ". The appeal was right. That would move the heart of the king, for Eastern people always had a great respect for their dead. " For what dost thou make request ?", asked the king. The answer was quick and obvious. No ! Not at all ! ! This man was in communion with God. He had sought the Lord for mercy. Now he would seek Him for wisdom. Between the king's question and the cupbearer's answer, a prayer arose to God. " So I prayed to the God of heaven, *and* I said unto the king " (ii. 4-5).

Do we live in touch with the Lord so that without ceremony we can lift our hearts at any moment : " Lord, tell me what to say " ?

The request was made and granted. Nehemiah asked leave of absence that he might go to Jerusalem and rebuild its walls. He asked for more. He requested that authority for a sure and safe transit should be granted to him. He also asked for provision of the necessary materials. All of this and more was given him. He was in the Will of the Lord, and when the Lord gives He gives abundantly.

(b) *Inspection* Nehemiah took his journey to his beloved city attended by a Persian guard of soldiers and carrying his letters of authority. On his arrival quickly he learned that he had something he had not sought — enemies. Life is not a smooth-sailing thing. There can be storms and adversities even when Christ is in the boat. The Christian can look for unexpected storms, steep mountains to climb, barren deserts to cross, slippery places to encounter, but always the promise — His Grace is sufficient.

Strange as it may seem, anyone who will seek to do good and to help his neighbour will find enemies. Some people only prosper as they mount up the steps of the broken and the oppressed. Sanballats and Tobiahs are to be found everywhere, men who trade in the bodies and souls of others. (ii. 10).

As there were enemies without, there might be traitors within. Therefore Nehemiah kept his mission a secret between himself and his God, at least for the time being. The Lord has secrets which He holds with them that fear Him (Ps. xxv. 14 ; Prov. iii. 32). For three nights he surveyed the whole position and decided on his method of procedure. We can always afford to wait on the Lord before we begin any project. We should never give away Divine revelations or the movings of His Spirit within. We have a great enemy ever ready to creep in and frustrate.

When the time for action had come, then Nehemiah called together the rulers of the people and said : " Ye see the distress that we are in, how Jerusalem lieth waste, and the gates thereof are burned with fire : come, and let us build up the wall of Jerusalem, that we be no more a reproach. Then I told them of of the hand of my God which was good upon me ; as also the king's words that he had spoken unto me " (ii. 17-18). Quickly he gained the consent of the people : " And *they* said, Let us rise up and build. So *they* strengthened their hands for this good work " (vs. 18).

The opposition of the enemy was as immediate as the willingness of the people. It started with bitter feelings and false accusation, but it did not end there, it never does.

(c) *Building* Chapter iii gives some thoughtful detail concerning the building of the walls and the setting up of the gates. We live in a day when walls are broken down everywhere. The wall of love in the home that protected the family, the wall of

moral integrity that strengthened our nation, the wall of international friendship that maintained our peace, and the wall of
Divine Truth that was the bulwark of the Church, men have
pulled them down. The enemy is in our gates, whilst social, moral,
and religious ruin pile high.

These walls were rebuilt by the co-operation of all those who
had a love for, and a devotion to, their city. There were priests
and their people, rulers and their officers, merchants and their
men, fathers and their families, apothecaries and goldsmiths,
people from every walk of life. We are informed that some built
walls, some towers, others made gates, beams, bars, locks, doors,
etc. There was work for masons, carpenters, metal workers and
other artificers. Some gave money, some gave labour, others took
oversight, but there was work for all and a place for everybody.
We are workers together with God.

Some statements that can be underscored in this chapter are :

" *And next unto them* ". Each man had his place. God is a
God of order. Each worked in harmony with his neighbour to
his right and his left, otherwise there would have been a breach in
the wall for the enemy to enter.

"*He and his daughters*" (vs. 12) Women have their place
in the Church of God. It may not be in the pulpit, but God uses
them in departmental work. In fact, their contribution is no small
portion.

"*The Tekoites repaired another piece*" (vs. 27) No one
lays down his tools until the whole task is complete.

"*Everyone over against his house*" (vs. 28) Some of us find
ourselves travelling all over the nation, or across the world, yet we
had to begin at "Jerusalem". If you cannot do service on your
doorstep, if you cannot minister in the neighbourhood or community where you live and where you are known, then you cannot
serve anywhere.

"*But their nobles put not their necks to the work of the
Lord*" (vs. 5) This was said of the Tekoites. The chapter records, therefore, workers and shirkers. Which are you ?

It has been said that Jerusalem was once a beautiful city.
In Nehemiah's day it was in ruins and in need of repair.

Society was ordained of God. To-day it is sordid and in need
of cleansing.

The Church at Pentecost was a unit of power. To-day it is
the victim of paralysis and needs revival.

Man was made in the likeness of God. To-day he is the slave
of sin and needs salvation.

What are we doing in this work of rebuilding ?

(d) *Opposition* (Ch. iv.) This came from without and within. From *without* it was Sanballat and Tobiah. This started in chapter ii. with bitter feeling and developed into ridicule and angry words in chapter iv. By chapters vii. and viii. it became deadly action. To some, ridicule is the hardest thing to take. Said these men : " What do these feeble Jews ? " Will they build up a wall out of this rubbish ? If they do, it will be so weak that if a fox were to run over it it would fall down !

When these enemies learned that their ridicule had failed and the wall was continuing to go up, they became more angry and more active, for they then planned war (vs. 8).

The other enemy was from *within*. This came from weariness and discouragement of workers. " The strength of the bearers of burdens is decayed, and there is much rubbish ;" (vs. 10). One can appreciate how rubbish can discourage. The Church to-day is being hampered in its soul-saving ministry by the heaps of theological rubbish, the theories of men, the materialism of the unbeliever.

There was yet another problem coming from within. Verse 12 seems difficult to understand, but it is a picture of fear and selfishness. The verse is : " And it came to pass, when the Jews that dwelt by them came." They would be the families of those men who were building the wall, who lived in the villages round about, for it must be remembered that the wall was built in fifty-two days. The workmen never went home. They worked from the rising of the sun until the stars appeared. Then they slept on the spot against a night attack by the enemy (vs. 22). These families came up to the city ten times begging their men to return to their homes before the enemy came to destroy them. Obviously, then, it was fear of the enemy and a selfishness to have their men folk with them.

This all sums up to :

The open enemy said " We will stop it ".

The depressed worker said " We be not able ".

The half-hearted said " Success is impossible ".

Against this opposition Nehemiah pressed his cause and encouraged his workers. To half of them he gave trowels, to the other half spears, shields and bows, and to all swords. Then setting watchmen at intervals, equipped with trumpets for alarm, they worked with prayer and determination, and so the walls were built.

(e) *Usury* (Ch. v)   As soon as the enemy was subdued in one place he appeared somewhere else in some other form. There are always those who take advantage of times of emergency. The people had passed through hard and trying times since their return. The prophet, Haggai, gives an account of that poverty. Food was scarce and expensive, taxes were high, so that the people had been compelled to mortgage both land and houses. Others had borrowed money and some had sold their children as servants, and still they were oppressed. The rich people were showing them no mercy nor grace but were exacting from them heavy usury or interest. In their poverty they raised their voices in protest. When Nehemiah heard of it he was very angry. This was a righteous anger of which the New Testament says it is not sin. He rebuked severely the nobles telling them that he could have exacted money from the people, but he had not required of them anything in return for his services, thereby setting them an example. He required that not only should they cease in their unseemly practice, but that they should make restitution for the wrong they had already done. The rulers consented so to do, but Nehemiah wanted that this should be more than a meaningless promise. He called in the priests and desired an oath from those elders. Also he placed a judgment or curse against their failure to make restitution.

For twelve years Nehemiah and his servants governed the people without being a charge to them. He had " open house " for one hundred and fifty, and never took one advantage. May we never take advantage of weaker people in our living day by day.

(f) *Victory* (Ch. vi)   Whilst Nehemiah was handling the problem inside, Sanballat, Tobiah, and Geshem were active again outside. How tremendously active the enemy always is ! How constantly alert should we be ! ! Opposition does not necessarily spell God's disapproval. It does not in this story. Satan cannot afford to see the advancement of spiritual forces, hence his activity when we are active.

The new assault was entirely different from the previous one. It was much more cunning and subtle. From open rebellion it turned to crafty suggestion. As an enemy in combat these three men had failed. Now they posed as " friends " in consultation. The roaring lion tried to become an angel of light. They said : " Come, let us meet in some one of the villages in the plain of Ono " (vs. 2). Their scheme was to draw Nehemiah away from his work and his people. The world is ever trying to entangle the Christian so that he cannot be in the place of duty. But we have been warned ! " He that hateth dissembleth with his lips, and layeth up deceit within him : When he speaketh fair, believe him not ; for there are seven abominations in his heart " (Prov. xxvi. 24-25). The world is ever bidding us to be social, join this club, participate in this alliance, let us pull together, let us join forces, but God says : " Come out from among them and be ye separate ". Too many Christians are lacking time for Bible Study, the Prayer Meeting, etc. When the world invites, your answer should be that of Nehemiah : " I am doing a great work. I cannot come down ". There is no greater work in the world than the work of the Lord. Always give it first place.

The enemy never takes no for an answer. Four times they sent, four times Nehemiah refused. Then came an open letter of intimidation. It suggested disloyalty, rebellion, and traitorship. They offered to safeguard him, but the answer went back : " There are no such things done as thou sayest but thou feignest them out of thine own heart ". This has always been a scheme of the " father of lies ".

Moses was blamed for the trouble caused by Pharaoh.

Elijah was blamed for that for which Ahab was responsible.

Paul was charged with turning the world upside down.

The Christians were blamed for the destruction of Rome, committed by Nero.

It is still the same to-day.

Their third move was to get Nehemiah to hide in the Temple against would-be assassins, but, again, there was no yielding : " Should such a man as I flee ? "

The chapter ends with complete victory. " So the wall was finished in the twenty and fifth day of the month Elul, in fifty and two days. And it came to pass, that when all our enemies heard thereof, and all the heathen that were about us saw these things, they were much cast down in their own eyes : for they perceived that this work was wrought of our God " (vs. 15-16).

(2) RE-ESTABLISHMENT OF THE PEOPLE (Chs. vii. - xiii.)

FIRST REFORMATION. At last the walls were up, the doors and gates were in place, and the building was finished. This, however, did not mean retirement. It is not walls and buildings that make a strong city. It is the citizens, the people who live within the walls. It is not the buildings around us that we call Churches that make the True Church, THE Church comprises born again Believers irrespective of label.

The city must be protected. Officers were to be appointed. The first appointments were Hanani and Hananiah. The first man was Nehemiah's brother. The second was selected because " He was a faithful man, and feared God above many ". That is a great tribute to receive — " A faithful man ". How the Church is in need of such men to-day! There is a deal of difference between faith and faithfulness. In the first we have a confidence in God as the covenant-keeping God. In the second God reckons on us. He never fails, we too often do. This was the man Nehemiah chose to take care of the walls after they were built. He was responsible to see that the watch was always set, that the gates were opened and closed at their appointed hours.

How the Church should watch these things! We have been careless in seeing that the gates were closed at night so, under the cover of darkness, all kinds of things belonging to the flesh and the Devil have crept in. Then, too, we have been careless in the day about what went out. Evangelists and others with their campaigns and their testimonies have brought many people into the Church, but we have been slack in nurturing the young convert and building him up in his most holy faith, and so have permitted him to slip out again. Oh, for faithfulness in the Church!

This thought leads right into the second half of the chapter which concerns

Citizenship " Now the city was large and great : but the people were few therein, and the houses were not builded " (vs. 4). Again let it be stated, the strength of a city is in its citizens. Too many people were choosing to live outside in the suburbs. What use are the walls if the people are on the wrong side of them? God puts it into the heart of His servant to check the genealogy of those who came back from the Captivity under the hand of Ezra. The number was 42,360, plus 7,337 servants, and 245 singing men and women, an approximate 50,000. These had to be persuaded to move in, and so the city became established.

One may have a fine Church building, an excellent Board of Deacons, a good Constitution, and a worthy Statement of Faith, but these, in themselves, do not constitute a strong virile Church. That is found in a loyal, living, God-fearing, active membership, who are ever ready to serve the Lord, to minister to mankind, and to withstand the enemy. The Church is a God-ordained organism. Where would we be if the members of our bodies could become independent units, no longer subject to the control of the brain but, as detached members, could roam around and attach them-

selves to this and that without any obligation to anything ? Such a
state could not exist ; and God likens the Church to a body, with
all of its members subjected to the Head, and as the Church in
Christ so the local Church.

Chapter viii. is one of rejoicing as the city became established.
The struggles had been turned to jubilations as the sword and the
trowel were laid down, and the people began to gather around
the book. In this second half of the book of Nehemiah we are
turning from work and war to worship.

The people gathered with unity of purpose as they requested
that Ezra, the Scribe, should bring before them the book of the
Law. So large was the concourse of people that a pulpit had to
be erected to raise the Scribe in order that all might see and hear.
Then, solemnly and reverently, the book was carried to the pulpit.
This is still practised in many of the Presbyterian Churches in
Scotland. At the opening of the book all the people stood to their
feet as an act of worship. This is still practised in some of the
Evangelical Churches in America.

The Scribe opened the meeting in prayer, invoking the
blessing of the Lord, to which prayer the people responded with
a hearty Amen.

For six hours Ezra read and expounded the Word of the
Lord. The word " distinctly " in verse 8 means " with an
interpretation ". He " gave the sense and caused them to understand the reading ". If preachers were more clear in their
interpretation of the Scriptures to-day the people would be more
willing to listen. There is reason to believe that, secretly, people
have the same longing in their souls, but are disappointed because
they cannot satisfy it.

The reading of the Scriptures brought a deep humility to the
people as they sensed their unworthiness. " For by the law is the
knowledge of sin " (Rom. iii. 20). Again " For Godly sorrow
worketh repentance to salvation not to be repented of . . . "
(II Cor. vii. 10), and here were a repentant people. This sorrow
was not to continue because the Lord has said : " Blessed are they
that mourn for they shall be comforted " (Matt. v. 4). Thus the
people were encouraged to rejoice in the Lord, and with each other
" for the joy of the Lord is your strength ".

The next day the leaders and priests met together with Ezra
for further instruction in the Law of God and, whilst so doing,
discovered the command of God concerning the Feast of
Tabernacles. This Feast had to be celebrated in the seventh
month, and it was that very season when the Law was being

read (see Ch. vii. 73). The proclamation was made, and the
Feast observed, again with the daily reading of the Law. This
was revival !

In reading this portion and entering into the joy which was
that of the people it needs to be remembered that they had but
little of what we possess. They only had the Law, a section of
the Bible sadly neglected to-day, but it was their strength. To
this Law we have added as our inheritance
    All the Jewish history in the Promised Land.
    The consolation of the Psalms of David.
    The Wisdom that comes from the Poetical books.
    The Inspiration that is ours from the ministry of the
        Prophets.
    The Salvation that comes through the Gospel.
    The Doctrine revealed in the Epistles, and
    The Consummation which is declared in the Revelation.
Happy are those people whose God is the Lord !

The revival was still surging in the hearts of God's people as
the next two chapters tell of a

Sure Covenant Made   The introduction to this Covenant is
in the form of a doxology. It has been stated that this is one
of the most touching scenes in the lives of these people, that the
doxology is one of the grandest outpourings of praise ever
performed or recorded. It is a strange mixture of sorrow and
song, of repentance and rejoicing.

The people separated themselves from the strangers. Then,
in sackcloth and ashes, they made confession. The Word of
God was doing its own transforming work, as it always will if
we would but allow it. For the second time their repentance was
turned into rejoicing, as the Levites gave command " Stand up
and bless the Lord your God for ever and ever ". Then followed
the glorious song of praise. This could be called " Nehemiah's
Sonata in G ", consisting of three movements. The theme is
God — the movements :
    (1) God's Greatness
    (2) God's Guidance
    (3) God's Grace
MOVEMENT ONE — *God's Greatness*. This was a review of
the past. It starts at verse 6, and declared His Creative power
in heaven, earth, and sea.

    The glory of the heavens — " Thou, even Thou, art Lord
alone ; Thou hast made heaven, the heaven of heavens, with all
their host ".

The treasures of the earth — " The earth, and all things that are therein ".

The depths of the sea — " The seas, and all that is therein ".

This threefold power was not only to be seen in creation but also in the creature. So the song turns to Abram, the father of the faithful, who was

Chosen — " Thou art the Lord the God, Who didst choose Abram " (vs. 7).

Brought — " And broughtest him forth out of Ur of the Chaldees ".

Given — " And gavest him the name of Abraham ".

MOVEMENT TWO—*God's Guidance.* This was a reminder. God's power was not limited to the past. It also belonged to the present. The God Who brought them out of Egypt was the God Who led them in the wilderness, and also the God Who gave them the Land of Canaan.

The Lord Who saved us from sin is the Lord Who sanctifies us day by day, and Who will bring us into the Eternal Home.

From verse 12 to verse 19 are seen

His Providence guiding them —   The Pillar (vs. 12)
His Precepts enlightening them —   The Law (vs. 13-14)
His Provision supplying them   —   Manna and Water (vs. 15)
His Pity pardoning them   —   Forgiveness (vs. 16-17)
His Patience bearing with them —   Love (vs. 18-19)

MOVEMENT THREE — *God's Grace.* This is a record of His dealings with them in grace.

    (1)   He gave them His Spirit (vs. 20)

    (2)   He supplied their need (vs. 21)

    (3)   He fought their battles (vs. 22)

    (4)   He gave them an inheritance (vs. 24)

They continued to fail — He continued to be gracious.

Having declared the goodness of God and having confessed their own wickedness, in verse 33, they then moved toward making a covenant with God. It is declared in verse 38 " And because of all this we make a sure covenant, and write it : and our princes, Levites, and priests, seal unto it ". The list of those who put their seal thereto is given in chapter x. beginning with Nehemiah, the Governor, and followed by the Levites, the priests, the porters, the singers, the Nethinims, and then the whole of the congregation that had separated themselves unto the Lord, both men and women, old and young.

These were the people who had sinned together earlier. They had been into captivity together. They had builded together, fought together, prayed together. Now they had been standing together in confession, praise, and thanksgiving. These exercises of the last days were being established as together they entered into this Holy Covenant with the Lord their God.

The Covenant was a promise to walk in the Law of God and to do His commandments. The principles were

Prohibition in Marriage   They promised that, according to the command of God, they would not give their daughters in marriage to the people of the land, or take their sons; that marriage should be strictly among themselves. One of the tragedies of the modern Church is that it has been too free in allowing Christian people to marry the ungodly. We have no law to stop it, but the voice of instruction and warning should be used much more than it is. To marry an unsaved partner ofttimes means marrying the world and its pleasures, its sins, its systems, when the Lord has said : " Come out from among them and be ye separate ".

Observing the Sabbath   Said they : " And if the people of the land bring ware or any victuals on the Sabbath Day to sell, that we would not buy it of them on the Sabbath, or on the holy day " (x. 31). Here the Church has fallen very badly. Slackness in one thing on God's Day means slackness in many things. In this God is not well-pleased. He has given us six days to do all of our work and find our pleasure. He asks that one Day should be given to Him and that we should keep it holy.

Keeping the Sabbatic Year   This applied more to the land than to the people. It was to be rested.

The Temple Tax   This was a promise to take upon themselves the responsibility of the support of the House of God and its ministry, which still is the responsibility of the believer to-day. We have the added responsibility of maintaining the overseas work of missionary enterprise, although against that we have been relieved of much that belonged to the early Church in their care for the poor, as much of this has been taken over by governmental agencies in the form of pensions and social securities.

Firstfruits   God had ever required the firstfruits of man, beasts, and produce. He still looks for the firstfruits of all we possess, including our time and service.

Tithes   The allocated portion that is set aside for the Lord.

SECOND REFORMATION. It would appear that Nehemiah's purpose in getting the people to move into the city, in chapter vii.

had not been successful. At that time there were many murmurings and a lack of full surrender, but heart conditions had now been changed considerably, so another attempt was made. They were requesting that one in ten of the people should move inside the city walls and that they should cast lots to find out which should be the men. According to verse 2 of this chapter xi. it would seem that the men came forward on a voluntary basis and willingly offered themselves, which brought great rejoicing of heart and caused the people to bless those men. The Lord's work should always be done by those who are willing of heart.

The rest of the chapter, and much of the next, is given to the names of those families which moved in and of the work that became their responsibilities.

Now at last came the dedication of the walls several years after their erection.

This service was one of *purifying* (vs. 30), for God requires clean hands and pure hearts. It was a *processional* service. The Princes were brought to the walls. Then, dividing into two groups, one led by Nehemiah, the other by Ezra, they marched around the walls with the trumpeters. It was a service of *rejoicing*, as together the people sang and praised the Lord. It was a service of *worship*, as they offered great sacrifices to God. It was a service of *thanksgiving*, as they brought their firstfruits and their tithes and presented them to the Lord.

Once more the book of the Law of Moses was read to the people, and again they learned of failure on their part. The book of Nehemiah therefore closes with the rectifying of some wrong conduct and a reform in some abuses.

From this reading of the Law they learned that God had forbidden that the Ammonite and the Moabite should have a place with the people of God because they had refused to give the children of Israel passage through their lands, and had refused them bread and water when they were moving toward the Promised Land. Now these people were in their midst. A separation took place immediately. This could have been a sin of ignorance, if they were not aware that it was in the Law, but the next failure could never be considered ignorance. Tobiah was an Ammonite of the present generation and he was as defiant as his forefathers. He was the man who had opposed the building of the walls. He had insulted, ridiculed, and fought these people. He had used every source of cunning to deflect the purpose of Nehemiah. The priest, Eliashib, was now allied to this crafty enemy and had not only given him residence in the Temple of God but had moved out of the Temple some of the stores, which were the dedicated gifts of the people to their God, to make room for Tobiah's furniture. The enemy in his subtlety has done the same to-day. The Bible has been put out of man's philosophy. Worship has been replaced for his entertainment. Spiritual life has disappeared to be replaced by social life. Why does the Church allow such alliances with sworn enemies of the Cross ?

Nehemiah, who had possibly been absent for some time because he was still cupbearer to the king of Persia and would have to return from time to time, very quickly and thoroughly dealt with this situation. He put out the offender and cleansed the Temple. Oh, for such a cleansing to-day !

The next abuse to be handled by Nehemiah was a failure to meet the need of the Levites who had been driven to the fields, so that they became part-time workers. The Church may have part-time workers who give of their spare time to the Lord. That is good, but when a full-time servant, who has had a call from God for whole-time service as the Levites had, is driven to part-time work by the failure of the Church in their support, that Church has a trespass against God which must be corrected.

Finally, these people of God had already fallen down on the Covenant to which they had put their seal in chapter x. They were trading on the Sabbath Day. Nehemiah commanded the closing of the gates and the punishment of those who, whilst they could not sell, spent the day at the gates, waiting with greed in their hearts.

Mixed marriages was the other failure of their Covenant. This was also handled by their loyal, steadfast Governor, who never once turned to the right hand or to the left. He carried out to a finality all that God had put in his heart so that he could repeatedly say : " Remember me, O my God, for good ".

ESTHER

UNSEEN YET SEEN

*"Now unto the King eternal, immortal, invisible, the only
wise God, be honour and glory for ever and ever, Amen."*
(I TIMOTHY i. 17)

INTRODUCTION

There have been questionings from many quarters as to
whether this book should have a place in the Bible. Its canonicity
has been challenged and its Divine Authorship doubted because
the Name of God does not occur therein. This is a very weak
argument; in fact, it is one that tends to foolishness in the light
of the book itself. One might just as well declare that there is no
cream in the milk and, therefore, it should not be used, just because
the actual word " cream " is not printed on the bottle. The milk
is capable of revealing its own cream content, as this book declares
the over-ruling power of God at every turn in the story. The
Power that controls the world of nature in Genesis is the same
Power that controls the actions of men in Esther. God's Name
is not written on every tree that grows in the forest, nor upon
every cloud that crosses the sky, neither is it written in words upon
the stars of the Universe. Nonetheless God is in all of these things,
the Creator and Controller.

Scholars tell us that the Name of Jehovah does occur more
than once in the Hebrew Scriptures, but it appears in acrostic
form. Several suggestions are made for this. Maybe it is because
the secret of the Lord is with them that fear Him. He did it so
that His friends might know, but not his enemies, for at that time
His people were in the hand of their enemies. Many a soldier
going to war and pledged to secrecy of his whereabouts established
a secret code in his letters to his family, whereby they could know
where he was without telling the enemy.

Chronologically this book comes before the book of Nehemiah
by about thirty years. We have noted that in the book of Ezra
there was an interval of fifty-seven years between the two returns,
the one under Zerubbabel and the other under Ezra. It is in this
interval that the book of Esther belongs.

We have considered that Nehemiah probably gained his favoured position, as cup-bearer to the king of Persia, because of the influence of Esther. Esther had married the previous king of Persia and, although he had died, her influence continued to be felt in the next reign, which gave the Jews enough prestige to cause Nehemiah to become both a cup-bearer and a rebuilder of the walls of Jerusalem.

To sum this up would be — no Esther would mean no Nehemiah; no Nehemiah would mean no Jerusalem; no Esther would also mean no deliverance for the Jews at that time. Their extermination would have meant no Messiah, and no Messiah would have meant no Saviour for us, and no Saviour would have meant no Church and no New Testament. So, when a person says that the book of Esther has no place in the Canonical Scriptures, we discover that the removal of that little book removes almost the whole of the Bible. For that reason we must accept the Bible in its entirety. To wrest the Scriptures is to lose the Scriptures.

The key-phrase of the book is " For such a time as this ".

The first division of the book shows :

A GRAVE DANGER TO THE JEWS (Chs. i-iv.).
A GREAT DELIVERANCE OF THE JEWS (Chs. v-x.).

The second division would be at the three feasts :

THE FEAST OF AHASUERUS (Chs. i-ii.).
THE FEAST OF ESTHER (Chs. iii-vii.).
THE FEAST OF PURIM (Chs. viii-x.).

Esther's life is divided into three epochs :

ESTHER, THE ORPHAN.
ESTHER, THE QUEEN.
ESTHER, THE DELIVERER.

(1)   A GRAVE DANGER TO THE JEWS (Chs. i-iv.)

The Feast of Ahasuerus   The story opens with an introduction to the king of Persia, Ahasuerus. He is recognised as the Xerxes of history. If this is true, and we have much evidence of its veracity, then this was the famous king who led his armies against Greece. Persian inscriptions, which have been discovered in later years, reveal that the feast was held just prior to that campaign and in honour of it. So sure was the king of his victory that he celebrated it beforehand. Evidence also shows that this battle was fought in the period between the divorce of Vashti and the marriage of Esther.

The Palace of Shushan was a winter residence for these kings. An inscription found on the site in 1852 reads : "My ancestor, Darius, built this palace in former times. In the reign of my grandfather (Artaxerxes) it was burned. I have restored it ". From this we learn that Darius, who authorised the rebuilding of the Temple, Xerxes, who married Esther, and Artaxerxes, who gave Nehemiah permission to rebuild the walls of Jerusalem, all lived in this same palace.

That the king ruled over a great domain is evident from the first verse — one hundred and twenty-seven provinces.

There was nothing wrong with this feast when it began. That is, it was not a sensual feast, just commemorative. No hard rules were made. "The drinking was according to the law ; none did compel ". Much of it was a display of the king's riches and glory and his might. Maybe it was done to impress his lords of the strength of his dominion, to excite a confidence for victory and thereby create a good morale.

The thing that went wrong in the feast was that which spoils many a feast or celebration — too much drinking. Total abstinence is always the safe course.

The king was now being controlled by the effects of overdrinking rather than by his common-sense and decency. For " when the heart of the king was merry with wine, he commanded . . . to bring Vashti the queen before the king with the crown royal, to shew the people and the princes her beauty : for she was fair to look on ". It was against all the laws of etiquette, for men feasted by themselves and the women by themselves (compare vs. 3 with vs. 9). Moreover his intention was to expose her or exhibit her in some way which would have been humiliating for a woman and much more for a queen.

One can fully appreciate why she refused to obey the instructions of the chamberlains. As a woman she was within her rights. The king, however, became very angry and, in his anger, sought the advice of his wise men. They were quick to tell him that she should be deposed from the throne, their considerations being selfish ones, thinking of what the reactions of their wives might be, and what they might suffer as a result. Certainly there was no evidence of the love that the Lord teaches should exist between husband and wife.

The king seemed to be pleased with the suggestion and, without consideration, was always ready to put his signature to what would become an unalterable law with the Medes and Persians.

Here it was understandable because done under the influence of drink.

It would appear that next morning, when he was sober, he was very sorry when he remembered what he had done. Maybe he grieved over the fact that he had signed a decree that would not permit him to right the wrong he had established.

His servants were quick to act again, and suggested that he could rectify the loss of his queen by finding another. They would search the country for all the beautiful women. Then he could make his choice. To this he agreed.

The search was made, and many maidens were brought to the house of the women. Maybe women sought to be chosen. However only one requirement was in mind — that was beauty, but often that kind of beauty is only skin deep.

Young man, are you seeking a partner in life, one who will share your life, your joys and your sorrows, your successes and your failures ? Then look for a beauty that is deep, look for beauty of character, beauty of holiness, a beauty of soul that possesses calm and peace. The outward beauty will fade as the years go by — some of it will wash off at night ! You look for the beauty of the virtuous woman, the faithful woman. Her character will increase with the years, it matures and is a priceless treasure. The young man who finds such a wife finds a good thing, says the Proverbs.

In their search they found a girl who was beautiful, so much so that they made no other enquiry. Had they done so they would have discovered that she was an orphan being brought up by a relative. They would also have found that she was a Jewess, and either of these things would possibly have disqualified her. In fact, these two things were going to be used to bring a great upheaval into the nation. The name of the girl was Esther — the name of her guardian Mordecai, her cousin.

Some people think that if life is commenced with obstacles and privations, these mean a hindrance all through life. But environment, whilst it has its influence on life, is not the final factor. With these hindrances Esther became queen.

Up to this time " Esther had not showed her kindred nor her people ; as Mordecai had charged her, for Esther did the commandment of Mordecai, like as when she was brought up with him " (ii. 20). In this verse there is something good and something bad. The good thing was that, although Esther had risen in position, she had not lost her head, become proud, nor despised her old friends. As a girl she had been obedient, and always subjected to her cousin. Now that she was grown and had become a queen she still sought his advice and obeyed his counsel. What a contrast between Esther and Haman! Esther accepted promotion and remained humble. Haman was promoted and inherited the pride that goes before a fall.

The thing that was wrong in this verse was that Esther and Mordecai were in agreement not to tell who they were and what their nationality. God had forbidden that His people should intermarry with the people of other nations. Their secrecy might deceive the king, howbeit one cannot deceive God. They were in the wrong because they had deliberately disobeyed the command of God. It is true that God was using them to the overthrowing of their enemies, but that does not alter the fact that they were wrong. God could bring deliverance in His own way and without their help.

The Feast of Esther In honour of the marriage the king gave a great feast to all of his princes and servants, called *Esther's Feast*.

Mordecai had been promoted, evidently at the time of the marriage, for he now sat in the king's gate. This would make him a judge. Lot sat in the gate of the city as a judge, and Absalom did the same thing (II Sam. xv.).

We break from the story to get an incident, which at the moment was passing, but later was vital in the whole plot. Two of the king's chamberlains had sought to take the life of the king, and Mordecai, having discovered their scheme, had reported it to the palace. The fact had been established, the two men punished, and the incident was placed on record as a matter of history.

The story changes again at chapter three. The king, Ahasuerus, promoted one of his officers. He had evidently proved himself worthy, or it would not have come his way. He was lifted above all the other officers and made the king's prime minister. However, some people are faithful and trustworthy so long as their position is not over-important. Few people can stand promotion. They lose their head. They get so elated that everyone else is pushed down. Haman was such a man. The king had commanded that all of his servants should bow to Haman and do him honour. One man refused to obey this command. It was Mordecai. The reason for this was not because he held a grudge against Haman, not because he was jealous of him, not because he hated him. There was nothing personal in their relationship whatever. Mordecai was a Jew, and a good one at that. It is true that he had failed in allowing Esther to enter into this marriage, but that does not mean that he failed in everything else. God had given His laws and among them was one that said : " Thou shalt worship the Lord thy God, and Him only shalt thou serve ". Man was forbidden, therefore, to bow down before other men. On these religious principles Mordecai stood firm. His companions in office evidently knew this, and were opposed to him because he was a Jew. This is inferred in verse four : " . . . they told Haman, to see whether Mordecai's matters would stand : for he had told them that he was a Jew ". The answer is, of course, they would stand. Haman might disapprove, everyone might disapprove. There might be some opposition, but they would ultimately stand because, when a man honours God, God will honour him, and thus it was in this incident.

When it was brought to the notice of the proud Haman that Mordecai was not bowing, and the reason for his abstinence was given, he was filled with scorn and decided to take the man's life. That was rather a big punishment for a little omission !

On second thoughts he changed his mind, not for better but for worse. Undoubtedly, the Devil had laid hold of this man, making him to become his tool, for Haman decided that he would have the whole Jewish race, of which Mordecai was a member, completely annihilated. What had they done ? They were not even aware of Mordecai's conduct, so certainly they were not encouraging him in his behaviour. They were innocent, why should they die ? Of course, this was coming from Satan. He was a murderer from the beginning. From the time that God had said that the seed of the woman shall bruise his head, he had sought by many means to prevent that seed from coming and now, if he could use this infuriated man to destroy the whole Hebrew race, then the Christ could not come.

At this time it must be remembered that the Jews were still a suppressed race of people in an alien land, and would possibly be hated by men like Haman in any case.

Haman caused lots to be cast that would denote the most favourable day, the day when fortune would be on his side, for they were a superstitious people. The day was to be the thirteenth day of the twelfth month. Rather interesting, for thirteen in Scriptural numerics is the number of sin and Satan ! The devil is really having his way.

Haman approaches the carefree king, who seemed to take little in life seriously, a man who was always ready to give his signature without enquiring as to the rights and wrongs of the matters he signed. The prime minister came posing as a very loyal patriot of his master, and informed the king that he had within his kingdom some people who were a menace to the king and the nation, a people who were by no means law-abiding. So dangerous were they that Haman himself was prepared to pay a large sum of money to have them destroyed. Without question as to who these people were, or what damage they had already done, without enquiring as to the justice of such an extreme punishment, the king handed to Haman his ring which bore his signature. The king was not anxious to receive the money for, seemingly, he returned the offer, as he said to his premier : " The silver is given to thee, the people also, to do with them as it seemeth good to thee " (vs. 11).

This Satan-inspired man lost no time getting into his murderous business. He gathered the scribes, who also met on the *thirteenth* day, and they prepared letters to be sent to all the king's provinces requiring the death of all Jews. Eleven months would elapse between the issuing of the decree and the carrying out of it. This was due to the time it would take to get the command to provinces afar off and, of course, the fact that the casting of lots had determined the date. Haman thought that by casting lots and putting the decision to chance, or to the gods, he would gain their favour, but that may have proved to be one of the steps in his undoing. It allowed time for a counter-move on the part of the Jews, a move in which Esther could afford to take her time and thereby give Haman no clue. The information of this impending judgment reached the ears of the Jews in Shushan firstly ; so the chapter closes with : " And the king and Haman sat down to drink ; but the city of Shushan was perplexed ". The king and his premier could relax into their drinking habit without a concern for the grief that was now in the city and would soon darken the whole realm.

However, the people of God never took the matter lightly. With sackcloth and ashes they wept and fasted, and Mordecai led them. As he was not permitted to enter the king's gate in sackcloth he remained outside. These Jews were wiser than their brethren of to-day, and the Gentiles of to-day, for men have been told that the judgment of death has been passed upon them by God because of their sin, but they do nothing about it.

When Esther was told that her cousin, Mordecai, was in sackcloth, she sent him new raiment instead of finding out the cause of his grief. Many preachers do the same to-day. They seek to pacify the sinner with the garb of good works. These garments Mordecai refused ; such cannot alter nor remove condemnation.

Then it was that Esther enquired the reason for this sorrow, and learned the truth. Moreover Mordecai requested that she should appeal to the king for deliverance as she had access to the monarch. But this was not as easy as it sounded, for no person was permitted to come into the presence of his august majesty without permission, not even his wife, and she had received no invitation for thirty days.

As yet the nationality of Esther had not been revealed. It would not remain a secret much longer, for already Mordecai had had to declare that it was his Jewish faith that forbade him to bow to Haman. As Esther was known to be his cousin she, too, must be of the same nation — a Jewess. So it was that Mordecai sent a further message : " Think not with thyself that thou shalt escape in the king's house, more than all the Jews. For if thou altogether holdest thy peace at this time, then shall there enlargement and deliverance arise to the Jews from another place ; but thou and thy father's house shall be destroyed : and who knoweth whether thou art come to the kingdom for such a time as this ? " (iv. 13-14). This is the classic statement of the whole book and key to the whole situation.

Mordecai proved himself a man of tremendous faith in God as he told Esther that if she failed then God would bring deliverance from another source, but to him deliverance was already a fact. It was only the question of the medium through which it should come. Lord, give me such a faith !

Then, too, he saw that the strange turns that had altered life recently had not been the turns of fate, but that God was causing all things to work together for good to those who love Him, for he was now realising that the recent events which had brought Esther to the throne were the over-rulings of God. Therefore he challenged her to courage and faithfulness in the behalf of her people.

It was also this statement that awakened Esther to the reality of the danger they all shared and caused her to become a realist even to risking her life. There was no realism in the new raiment she had sent to Mordecai earlier.

Esther requested that the people should join her in three days of fasting, which would probably suggest three days of prayer and waiting on God. Then she would enter into the presence of the king and make known her request.

We should come into the presence of the Lord with prepared hearts and holy fear, for He is a Holy God. Of course, holy fear is different from the fear of losing one's life — which could have been the lot of Esther. Ours would be a filial fear, a reverential devotion.

GREAT DELIVERANCE OF THE JEWS (Chs. v. - x.)

The next chapter (v.) has always been a precious one for teaching the true attitude of worship. Esther had a great burden upon her heart and a serious emergency to meet. It was a matter of life or death for herself and all her people. Nonetheless there was a calmness that knew no hurry. She did not rush into the presence of the king, saying : " Oh, my lord, do something and do it quickly or we shall all be dead ! "

Firstly, she spent three days in preparation. Then she put on her royal apparel, for she was coming into the presence of His Royal Highness. She stood at a distance, just inside the door and, according to custom, it would be with arms folded and head bowed, or the attitude of worship which would say in effect : " As I stand here it is in humbleness. I acknowledge that thou art the king and that power belongeth unto thee. I know, too, that I have no right to be here without thy invitation, but I am looking to thee for thy mercy ". At the moment she was asking for nothing. She was giving adoration to the king. He, on seeing her thus standing, stretched out his sceptre. Quietly she walked forward and touched it. That meant that she was accepted. Obviously there was some reason that had brought her into the king's presence without invitation, so he asked : " What wilt thou, queen Esther ? And what is thy request ? It shall be even given thee to the half of the kingdom ".

What a perfect illustration this is. The Lord God sits upon the throne of His majesty. We, as the creatures of time, have no right into His presence, for He is holy and we are sinful. Even though we have been brought into His family by new birth, still we are unworthy creatures and have no claim by which we can come before Him other than that He has bid us to come.

Upon our hearts there may be burdens — yea, there should be ! Men around us are under the condemnation of death, for death has passed upon all men, for all have sinned. Those of us who have been redeemed must become intercessors for those who are still sinners. Why is it that our prayers are not always answered ? The reason may be seen in this story. We are always asking and never giving. If we could learn to come into the presence of the Lord on the Lord's Day morning and with humbleness and holy reverence worship Him, we would find Him stretching out the sceptre of His acceptance and saying : ' Beloved,

what is thy heart's desire ?　I am willing to grant it ' — to which
we may reply : ' Lord, my desire, and my request, is that I may
see souls saved in the evening meeting '.　God is seeking worshippers
and whilst we hold back that worship from Him He holds back
His blessing from us.

Esther could still afford to take her time and enjoy some
personal fellowship with the king, and at the same time keep the
enemy off his guard.　In fact she was doing more.　The enemy
was being made to display his own true nature of selfish pride.

The queen's request was that the king and his trusty friend
and servant would grant her their company at a feast which she
had prepared.　To this they readily consented.　At this feast the
king again sought from Esther the request which he realised had not
yet been made known.　Instead she invited them to a second feast
on the next day, when, if they would honour her, she would declare
the secret of her heart.

This invitation caught Haman right at his weak place.　He
went home highly elated and joyful in spirit to boast to his friends
of the great success that he had made in life, in that he himself
had won the confidence of the king, so that the king had promoted
him to the highest office in the realm and was being granted anything he requested, and now the queen had done him the same
honour.　For the second time she had prepared a feast for her
husband and on each occasion had invited the " worthy " Haman.

On his way out of the palace, amid the bows of the king's
servants, he passed that stubborn, rebellious Mordecai, who paid
him no respect whatever.　That was his " fly in the ointment ".
It spoiled everything and it must be almost a year before he could
mete out vengeance on him.　All this he told his friends, who
suggested, if he had such influence and was so close to the royal
pair, why not make a request for the death of Mordecai, set up
the gallows so that there should be no delay or time for an appeal,
and then obtain his death warrant next morning and enjoy the feast
at night.　This pleased the murderous Haman, and so the preparations were made.

" On that night the king could not sleep ".　What night ?
The night before the death of Mordecai.　What night ?　The night
before Esther made known to the king her request.　What night ?
The night before many of those provinces received the command of
the king demanding the death of all Jews.

No God in the book of Esther ?　Then why was it that the
king was so restless that night ?　Who took his sleep away from

him ? The Psalmist says : " He giveth His Beloved sleep " (Ps. cxxvii. 2). He can also take it away from His enemies.

If you could not sleep what would you do ? If a king could not sleep what would he do ? Take a sleeping draught ? Call in the Court Physician ? Send for the Court musician to play some soft music ? Read an interesting book ? To any of these things the king could have resorted but, instead, he commanded one of his servants to bring in the Chronicles of the kingdom, and to read the records of the realm. That should put anyone to sleep!

As the servant read laws, duties, functions, the diary of events from day to day, the king heard how that two of his servants had plotted to take his life, and that one, Mordecai, had revealed the plot and so the guilty men had been brought to justice. The servant read on — but wait, said the king. What was the reward given to the man who saved the king's life ? According to the records no reward had been given. With this the king was wider awake. No reward for a man who saved the king's life ? It is on record for men to read that the king of Persia was so ungrateful, so mean, that he failed to reward men for devotion ! This must be corrected without delay. Who was in the Court ?

At that particular moment Haman arrived, an early caller, for Mordecai must die before Haman could continue to enjoy life. The king, who ever consulted his officers before he acted, and himself not decided as to how he should pay this belated debt, asked his prime minister. " What shall be done unto the man whom the king desires to honour ? " As honours were falling on Haman, it seemed that here was coming another. Whom else would the king want to honour ? Selfish men only see themselves. Haman declared the things that would elevate him in the eyes of all the people of Shushan. To ask for more might have meant his own head, for he was going to get as near to that throne as he could, and get as much regal honour as was possible, without deposing the king. This was pride at its peak. The next utterance from the king was going to reveal the thing that Haman and all who associate themselves with such pride always forget. It was that " pride goes before a fall ". " . . . Do even so to Mordecai, the Jew, that sitteth at the king's gate : let nothing fail of all that thou hast spoken " (vi. 10).

How much of the surprise and disappointment that must have registered on that face did the king notice ? What a humiliation this must have been for the proud courtier, and what reverses and what surprises and what humiliation are coming to other of the enemies of the Lord and His people. Let us pray that we will not be among them.

This man had only just begun to fall. Sick with shame and covered with confusion, he hastened to his home to hide himself. Little was the encouragement that came from his wife and friends. " If Mordecai be of the seed of the Jews, before whom thou hast begun to fall, thou shalt not prevail against him, but shalt surely fall before him " (vs. 13). What caused this woman to make such an utterance ? Is it possible that she, or those wise men, were aware of the statement of Jehovah to Abraham : " I will bless them that bless thee and curse him that curseth thee " (Gen. xii. 3) ? This statement, of course, referred to the seed of Abraham, and therefore included Mordecai.

Whilst he was seeking consolation and refuge, the chamberlains came to take him to the feast that had only last night so elated him. Now he would give anything not to be present. He still did not know what was the purpose of Esther in inviting him. He had detected no danger there. But what did the king know ? How had he reacted to the incident of the morning ? That could have been a big question in his mind. Thus Haman came to the feast, heavy of heart instead of joyful in spirit.

Again the request was made by the king to Esther : " What is thy petition, queen Esther ? And it shall be granted thee ; and what is thy request ? And it shall be performed, even to the half of the kingdom ? " (vii. 2). Now came the big surprise for both king and courtier.

This beautiful woman began to make an appeal for her life and the lives of all her people, lives that had been signed away by the king himself. Who, asked the king, is responsible for such a state of affairs ? Then the accusing finger was directed at Haman. The infuriated king walked into his garden to cool his temper and make his decision as to his course of action, whilst Haman sought to appeal for his own life before Esther. The man who can slay a nation of innocent people is never prepared to die as a guilty person.

Upon the king's return to the palace it was told him of the gallows already erected for Mordecai. Then the king said : " Hang him thereon ". So the haughty courtier died a hated criminal. The story is a demonstration of the words of the Psalmist : " For without cause have they hid for me their net in a pit, which without cause they have digged for my soul. Let destruction come upon him at unawares : and let his net that he hath hid catch himself ; into that very destruction let him fall " (Ps. xxxv. 7-8).

These two verses have been paraphrased thus :
" He dug a pit,
He dug it deep,
He dug it for his brother.
And for his sin
He tumbled in
That pit dug for another ".

The king gave to Esther and to Mordecai the house of Haman and the power that had once been his, for now it was that Esther declared her identity with the Jewish nation and her relationship with Mordecai.

However, the Jewish nation still remained under the condemnation of death. The law had been established and the decree issued by the careless Monarch, and the law of the Medes and Persians could not be altered. Esther pleaded that he would do something whereby the letters of judgment could be reversed. She begged that he would do it for her sake, if he considered that she was pleasing to him. As he could not alter the edict he gave permission for letters to be written allowing the Jews to smite their enemies before the enemy could smite them.

In the judgment of God death has passed upon all men for all have sinned. This judgment cannot be reversed. So God, in His mercy toward mankind, sent His only begotten Son, Who became sin for us, and took its full penalty that we might be made the righteousness of God in Him.

The message was hastened to every part of the domain of king Ahasuerus, informing the Jews that the king had granted permission for them to lay hold of their enemies and destroy them. Not only were the Jews delivered from the Persian enemy, but another plan of Satan to destroy that race and to prevent the Christ from bruising his head was frustrated by God, Who ever giveth us the victory.

In honour of this victory when the thirteenth day of Adar was turned from destruction to deliverance, they established what was known as *The Feast of Purim.* For two days, the 13th and the 14th, they celebrated, feasted, and sent gifts one to another, and gave gifts to the poor. The city of Shushan had a third day of joy and thanksgiving.

After the feast Esther sent yet another letter to all the Provinces establishing the 14th and 15th days of this month as a permanent feast to be observed by Jews everywhere throughout all succeeding generations, and so to this day on the 3rd and 4th days of the month of March, the Jewish people meet in their synagogues for a service of thanksgiving in which the book of Esther is read and the name of Haman is cursed. Then they give themselves to fun and feasting.

The tragedy is that, in later years, their Messiah came and brought them a far greater deliverance, but they failed to recognise it. At Passover they keep a feast of remembrance for their deliverance from Egypt. At Purim they keep their feast and give their gifts because of the deliverance from Haman, but Christmas goes by for them. They celebrate the smaller deliverance, but are blind to the great deliverance from the tyranny of Satan, and to their Great Deliverer, their Messiah.

Neither have we Gentiles the right to point the finger at them in reproof, for we are no better than they. We keep Christmas as a feast of thanksgiving. We rejoice, we feast, we send gifts one to another, and we send gifts to the poor, even as they do. The tragedy is that man has become so pagan that he is more or less worshipping an old man called Santa Claus and has missed the little Babe lying in a manger, God's great Gift of a Deliverer, One Who came to save us from the condemnation of death.

JOB

THE PHILOSOPHY OF SUFFERING

*" There hath no temptation taken you but such as is common
to man : but God is faithful, Who will not suffer you to be
tempted above that ye are able ; but will with the temptation
also make a way of escape, that ye may be able to bear it."*
(I CORINTHIANS x. 13)

INTRODUCTION

Job is the first of five books known as the Poetical Books.
Thus we enter another section of the Bible. In these five books are
to be found philosophy, worship, and wisdom.

Job is an outstanding book in the realm of philosophy. Its
reasonings of life and man should be given due consideration,
for it enquires into many subjects that have perplexed the mind
of man throughout the centuries. It not only enquires but also
answers many of the problems, if only we would have ears to
hear.

Here are some of the problems with which the book deals :

Why are some men especially and exceptionally
prosperous ?

Why are other men crushed and overwhelmed with
tragedy ?

Is God really interested in mankind ?

Is there such a thing as disinterested love ?

What is the final outcome of this life ?

Is the grave the end or is there a beyond ?

Does God rule this world with justice ?

Can a man comprehend God ?

Can a man be just with God ?

Can we explain the mystery of suffering ?

It is this last question which is the basic subject of the book
of Job. The other questions are answered in pursuing this one.

As a starting point let it be said that we give the book the
title of " The Philosophy of Suffering " because there is no such
thing as the Mystery of Suffering.

267

The Bible speaks of the
> Mysteries of the Kingdom of Heaven (Matt. xiii. 11).
> Mystery of the Church (Eph. v. 32).
> Mystery of the Resurrection (I Cor. xv. 51).
> Mystery of Godliness (I Tim. iii. 16).
> Mystery of Iniquity (II Thess. ii. 7).
> Mystery of Babylon (Rev. xvii. 5).

but no mystery of suffering. Mystery is something that is hidden and not easily explained, but the Lord has been good enough to give us an explanation of suffering, and we must learn to accept the facts of life and profit thereby.

In the book of Job we see reasoning from two sides. On the one hand man is seeking to reason out the whole problem of pain and suffering, whether moral or physical, and in that reasoning man becomes the victim of Deism or Destiny. That is, man is the unwilling victim of a great Despot, a Dictator who allows no will, no choice. He is a victim of his circumstances, so what is to be will be. On the other hand God is showing that suffering has purpose. It is man *tested* and *triumphant*.

There are many approaches to the book, but a natural analysis seems to be :

> (1) An Introduction, which is a Prologue.
> (2) A Series of Discourses, which create a Drama.
> (3) A Conclusion, which is an Epilogue.

The same three sections can be called :

> (1) GENERATION (Chs. i-ii.).
> (2) DEGENERATION (Chs. iii-xlii. 6).
> (3) REGENERATION (Chs. xlii. 7-17).

These three things are fundamental to Old and New Testament alike. They belong to the world, to nations, to men.

> The world was generated or created in Genesis i. 1.
> The world degenerated because of sin. Genesis i. 2.
> The world was regenerated, which is the story of Genesis i. 3 onward.
> Man was generated — made in the likeness of God.
> Man then degenerated, or fell as a result of sin.
> Man is regenerated, or born again, when he accepts Christ as his personal Saviour and Lord.

This, too, is the story of Job.

(1) GENERATION (Chs. i-ii.)

Generation is the fact of existence. The world exists, man exists, Job existed. Some people would like to reason against the last sentence and say that Job never really lived, that he was just a fictitious character around whom the problems of life are reasoned. But this cannot be. The book opens with a very positive statement : "There was a man in the land of Uz whose name was Job ". In those few words are to be found the fact of place — Uz — and the fact of person — Job. If the character had been fictitious names would have been omitted, as they are in every parable of the Lord, where it is stated "A certain man ", "a certain king ", "Behold, a sower ". The only exception to this rule in the Lord's ministry is found in Luke xvi. : "And there was a certain beggar named Lazarus " (vs. 20). However, there is another exception in that account. It does not say that it was a parable.

Many facts can be established in the book of Job which would remove the idea of fiction. Uz was in the Eastern part of Arabia, near to Chaldea. This is somewhat verified in chapter one, for the Sabeans fell upon his plowmen, and the Chaldeans fell upon his camels. The Sabeans were natives of South Arabia and the Chaldeans of Chaldea. Both would have been adjoining territories and therefore neighbours.

It has often been asserted that this book is probably one of the oldest books in the Bible. A little evidence might prove helpful.

According to tradition the Jobab of Gen. xxxvi. 33 was the same person as the Job whom we here consider. This, of course, can be questioned, but Job had four friends who came to minister to him. *Eliphaz,* the Temanite, *Bildad,* the Shuhite, and *Zophar,* the Naamathite, are all mentioned in chapter two, verse 11. In the same chapter that the name Jobab appears, Eliphaz is also found. "These are the names of Esau's sons, Eliphaz " (Gen. xxxvi. 10). In verse 15 we read : "These were the dukes of the sons of Esau: the sons of Eliphaz the firstborn son of Esau ; duke Teman ". Thus the two names are identified as the same man. (See also I Chron. i. 45).

Bildad, the Shuhite, would be a descendant of Abram and Keturah according to Gen. xxv. 2. "And she bare him Zimram, and Jokshan, and Medan, and Midian, and Ishbak and *Shuah* ". Shuah was the father of the Shuhites.

Of Zophar we know nothing. His name means "chatterer " and chatterer he was !

The fourth friend makes his appearance in chapter xxxii. 2. Elihu, the Buzite. " Huz his firstborn, and Buz his brother " (Gen. xxii. 21). This would be the father of the Buzites and so a descendant of Nachor.

These Scriptures put all of these names into the same period of time in Genesis, surrounding the life of Abraham. This would cause one to believe that Job lived about that time and also in that area, for Uz would not be far from Ur of the Chaldees.

From the last chapter of Job it is learned that he lived another one hundred and forty years after the incidents recorded in the book. This brings Job into the life-span of that same era. Abraham died at one hundred and seventy-five years, Isaac at one hundred and eighty, Joseph at one hundred and ten, Terah at two hundred and five.

Prior to the Flood the age-span was in the nine hundreds. In the days of Moses it was one hundred and twenty years.

The book seems to have been written at a time when God was worshipped as Shaddai rather than Jehovah, and before idolatry became prevalent.

THE FIRST ASSAULT. Job firstly is introduced. He was a Patriarchal Chieftain, a man who was perfect and upright, one that feared God and hated evil, so far as his moral life was concerned ; a man of prosperity and posterity so far as his physical possessions.

The word " perfect " is not one that suggests sinless perfection, but it does make the man to become an example to all other men. The Lord suggested this when He said : " There is none like him in the earth ".

Then comes the introduction of the second character, Satan — " the accuser of the brethren . . . which accused them before our God day and night " (Rev. xii. 10). When he presented himself before God, the Lord asked of him : " Whence comest thou ? " to which Satan replied : " From going to and fro in the earth, and from walking up and down in it " (ii. 2), which should remind us that the Devil is not omnipresent, that he can only be in one place at a time.

In this particular instance it is to be noted that Satan did not come before God to accuse Job. It was God who introduced Job to Satan in the words : " Hast thou considered my servant Job ? " Could the Lord afford to introduce us to the great enemy of our souls ? Remembering that He will not tempt us above that which we are able to bear it shows that God had great confidence in this servant of His.

Had Satan considered him ? Of course. He leaves no faithful child of God alone. Satan's reply was : " Doth Job fear God for naught ? " This is the key to the whole book. Satan does not believe that there is such a thing as disinterested love. He believes a man only serves the Lord for what he can get out of it. He serves either for material gain and prosperity, or for eternal security. Man is more concerned in what he is saved from, or what he is saved to, than he is concerned for his Lord and Saviour, and the love of God. This he discloses in verses 10 and 11. Is the Devil right ? What is our motive in accepting Christ ? Do we want the gift or the Giver ? Is it salvation or the Saviour ? From the conduct of some Christians the answer is obvious. They ever speak of Christ's salvation but never speak of His Lordship — always what we can get from the Lord, never what we can give to Him.

Satan, therefore, was asking the Lord to test Job to find out his sincerity, because Satan believes in ulterior motive. There was nothing wrong in that. Peter's instruction is : " But sanctify the Lord God in your hearts : and be ready always to give an answer to every man that asketh you a reason of the hope that is in you with meekness and fear " (I Peter iii. 15). If man has the right to ask, then Satan certainly has the right. Our profession must be proved by our conduct and our testimony by our triumphs. What Satan said to God about Job then, he may be saying to God about us now !

James says : " Let no man say when he is tempted, I am tempted of God : for God cannot be tempted with evil, neither tempteth He any man : " (i. 13). Here is the difference between the Sovereign Will of God and His Permissive Will. God permits Satan to test His people is the obvious truth here. If one should have doubts as to this truth or the rightness of God in allowing it, then the answer can be found in the conduct of life.

Men build ships and aeroplanes. They make claims for their constructions, as to their ability and their safety, but man is not prepared to accept those claims. Says he, through the voice of the Law, " Prove them ". That is both reasonable and logical. So it is that the ship has to be handed over for its trials. If it comes up to the required standards it receives a certificate of seaworthiness — " A.1. at Lloyds ". The aeroplane is handed over to the test pilot, who manoeuvres the ship of the air until he is satisfied with its performance for safety. Then the plane is granted a certificate of airworthiness. The public may use it.

Even so, a man claims that he loves the Lord, that he has committed his life to Him, and can trust Him in all things. He stands up and sings : " I know Whom I have believed, and am persuaded that He is able to keep that which I have committed unto Him against that day ". The Devil hears that man's song, and goes to the Lord, as the accuser of the brethren, and says : " Lord, I just do not believe that man is speaking the truth. I want him tested ". That makes reason. So the Lord says : " There he is. I grant permission within certain limits. Do what you want up to those limits ". If we, as believers, prove ourselves faithful we defeat the enemy. We bring glory to God and He gives us a certificate of trustworthiness. Surely that is a sound philosophy and, if it is, then suffering is not a mystery. It has been defined and the reasons given.

Let it be re-emphasised that the Permissive Will is a Restricted Will, the Lord knowing that if Satan were allowed he would do his worst. God told him that he might touch Job's property, might touch his family, might touch his body, but he could not touch his life.

From what has been considered so far comes a very important truth, which is yet to be proved and established as we reach the end of the book, and that is that suffering does not always come as a punishment. It is not an evidence of Divine wrath but, often, the reverse. " For whom the Father loveth He chasteneth ".

The first assault was on Job's possessions, and in this he sinned not.

THE SECOND ASSAULT was on Job's person. " Skin for skin ", said the Devil. " Yea, all that a man hath will he give for his life ". That may be true in a selfish world, but not with a life that is fully surrendered to the Lord, for such a man is already dead to self. This is what the enemy does not believe and therefore must be taught.

But he had not finished yet. Many a man can bravely resist the physical tests of life, but will quickly fall on the moral. So then came the full weight of this second attack as his wife, the one who should have stood by in comfort and have offered him all of her moral support, said : " Dost thou still retain thine integrity ? Curse God, and die " (ii. 9). " In all this did not Job sin with his lips " (ii. 10). This was followed by the arrival of his three friends.

Now begins the drama of the book.

(2) DEGENERATION (Chs. iii-xlii. 6)

Already Job had been brought very low, in the losses that he had sustained in both wealth and health. He was now a sick man. His vitality was at a low ebb. How the Devil likes to kick a man when he is down! He has always been a coward. That is why we are told to resist the Devil and he will flee from us.

Let us bear in mind that these three men were Job's friends, and that they came to him with very good intentions. Their trouble was that they did not understand Job any more than does the world understand the Christian. The points of view are so different.

For seven days they sat in silence. That was a token of their deep sympathy. They were lost for words. Had they uttered any they would have been as mockery in this man's intense suffering.

Job was the first to speak. In amazing language, every statement of which is worthy of consideration, he cursed the day in which he was born, and wished that it had never been. He revealed that he had some wrong concepts of the grave and the future of the soul.

With this first utterance of Job begins the

DISCUSSIONS OF JOB'S FRIENDS. *Eliphaz* was the first to answer. He approached his subject kindly. He apologised to Job, then made comment on Job's past life, his integrity, the way he had strengthened others in their weakness and encouraged them in their problems, and now " it toucheth thee ". Job, you must have sinned to be suffering in this way. Who ever heard of a person suffering who was innocent? This man evidently knew little or nothing of the Devil, for the innocent are always his prey.

He related to Job a vision that he had from the Lord (iv. 13-21). Whilst the vision need not be doubted there is no proof that God had just given it to him to declare to Job. Eliphaz could have been using some old experience to try and confirm a point that he was making that Job had sinned.

So go on the reasonings of four men, three against one. It has been pointed out that the other two men, Bildad and Zophar, added nothing to what Eliphaz said. It was the same accusation but with more bitter words. Eliphaz suggested, the other men declared.

Someone has stated that the three men represented three approaches of man to human suffering :

Eliphaz — the approach of human experience.
Bildad — the approach of tradition.
Zophar — the approach of human merit.

The whole is an argument of philosophical reasoning as against sublime faith.

Job had a reply to each of these speeches. In answer to Eliphaz, who had charged him with sin, Job made reply that his grief and sorrow had not been appreciated by these men, that he himself could not express his grief. If it could be weighed it would be heavier than the sand, so he appealed to God to deliver him, that God would permit him to die. At night he longed for the day, and in the day his prayer was " My bed shall comfort me, my couch shall ease my complaint ". His cry was : " Lord, if I have sinned, why dost Thou not pardon my transgression, and take away mine iniquity ".

Bildad speaks in chapter eight. He was no comforter, no advocate. He was an accuser like the Devil. He started by saying: " Doth God pervert judgment ? . . . Behold, God will not cast away a perfect man, neither will He help the evildoers " (viii. 3-20). Job would agree with that. Eliphaz had suggested sin. This man did more, for he not only condemned Job for sin, but also declared that all of his children were sinners to the degree that God had cast them away for their transgressions (viii. 4). " For enquire, I pray thee, of the former age . . . " (vs. 8). This was the man of tradition. He was passing his verdict on the case according to the past and not according to its own merit. He was being general and not specific. Said he: " God will not cast away a perfect man " (vs. 20). That is true, but Job was not cast away. He was suffering but as yet had not discovered the reason. Although he could not understand the ways of God he still trusted Him. *Job* reasoned back in chapter nine, that it was true that God could not pervert judgment but, if his sufferings were due to sin or failure, then every man was doomed to the same suffering, for how can a man be just with God ? (ix. 2). It matters not what the approach might be, man would be guilty. Job proceeded to speak of the majesty of God as the great Creator and Sustainer of the Universe. Therefore, who was going to reason with Him the rights and wrongs of life ? He would prefer to make supplication to God rather than reason with God (ix. 15). Job reasoned on that, if goodness was that which delivered man from suffering, then it would be a condition that man could never reach. " If I justify myself, my own mouth shall condemn me " (vs. 10). " Though I were perfect . . . I would despise my life " (vs. 21). " If I wash myself with snow water, and make my hands never so clean ; yet shalt Thou plunge me in the ditch, and mine own clothes shall abhor me " (vs. 30-31).

At chapter ten Job changed his conversation. He turned from Bildad and expostulated with God.

Zophar was next to speak, and was the most uncharitable man of them all. He charged Job with foolish talk, empty talk and lies, just about the last thing this man should say, seeing his name means "chatterer"! The other men said that Job was being punished for some sin. This man said that he was only receiving a part of what he deserved and that God was holding back punishment (xi. 6). At verse 14 he suggested repentance.

Job sought to refute these false accusations by assuring Zophar that he did possess some wisdom and that he was not inferior to any of his friends who seemed to claim so much wisdom that it would die with them.

And thus the debate continued. Anger was kindled, sarcasm increased, accusations were multiplied, and in between wonderful utterances were made that leave us amazed at their knowledge of the laws of nature and the workings of God.

Job reached a place where he was feeling the pressure of the adversary. He cried out : " I am as one mocked of his neighbour " (xii. 4), but still the arguments continued until Job got his feet on to some very sure ground, so that in the midst of his sore trials, whilst his body was racked with pain, his friends and family were away from him and he was being pressed by these three accusers, he cried : " For I know that my Redeemer liveth, and that He shall stand at the latter day upon the earth : And though after my skin worms destroy this body, yet in my flesh shall I see God " (And after my skin hath been thus destroyed, yet without my flesh I shall see God) (margin) (xix. 25-26).

Throughout these reasonings Job maintained his innocence and held tenaciously to his God. The intensity of the accusations increased. They each, in turn, spoke of the sovereignty of God. Each told of the wonders of the Universe and the glories of God's handiwork as though each was trying to display the superiority of his knowledge, and to give the impression that he was speaking in the behalf of God, but none of them made any progress.

At the last the three men gave up. They claimed that they " Cease to answer Job because he was righteous in his own eyes " (xxxii. 1), but it was a stalemate. The three men had not convicted Job of his sin, and Job had not convinced them that he was innocent.

One might appreciate readily the reason that these men yielded to the argument saying that Job was righteous in his own eyes, for Job's last speech before them, or that part of it recorded in chapter xxxi., was a solemn protestation in which he used the word " IF " twenty times, and in so doing named twenty different kinds of sin which could have been committed, and then called for the judgment of God *if* he had failed on any count. This was a confidence in his innocence that ought to silence any accuser. The reasonings of men get nowhere in things that are spiritual, because they must be spiritually discerned.

A fourth man came into the scene of action,

Elihu, a comparatively young man who had listened silently to the whole debate. This youth has been condemned for his impertinent, boastful, self-conceited pride. He has been charged as the fool who runs in where angels fear to tread, but we must be careful about condemning when the Lord does not condemn. Ours has been a misjudgment upon this man. We have done to him what the other men did to Job. It is true that he came in with a great fanfare of trumpets. That is often due to lack of maturity, and for this reason youth has sometimes to be subdued. However, we must confess that wisdom is not the exclusive property of the old. Paul said to Timothy : " Let no man despise thy youth ".

On first reading these six chapters concerning Elihu, half of which seems to be introduction of himself, the subject certainly appears to be the essence of conceit but, on second reading, we learn that he was the only man who made a real contribution to the problem in question.

Much of the introduction is Oriental and will stand an amount of criticism, but this can be overlooked that we might benefit from the advice he gave and for his reasonings of the ways of God.

Firstly, he told Job that he was wrong to accuse God of injustice. " Then was kindled the wrath of Elihu . . . against Job . . . because he justified himself rather than God " (vs. 32). In chapter xxxiii. Elihu enlarged on the matter of injustice. Job had said : " I am clean without transgression : I am innocent ; neither is there iniquity in me " (vs. 9). That was Job's own justification. Then he made a charge against God : " Behold, He findeth occasion against me, He counteth me for His enemy, He putteth my feet in the stocks, He marketh all my paths " (vs. 10-11). Job was making himself more righteous than God.

Secondly, Elihu reproved the three men because they were wrong to accuse Job, inasmuch as they had no answer to his reasoning and yet they condemned him (vs. 3).

Thirdly, he assured them that he had listened to every thing that had been said, and that he was not going to use their arguments (vs. 14). These men had spoken of suffering only as a punishment inflicted by God for wrong-doing. Not so, said Elihu. It need not be penal. It could be preventive. Suffering could be for discipline, or for the development of character. Suffering could be a display of love and could purify the soul. These are the reasonings of verses 17-33. The phraseology is rather remote on first reading but, upon consideration, it is that to which we can all say Amen.

It was the first constructive statement that had fallen from man's lips that could bring consolation or comfort to a body and a mind as distracted as that of Job.

Those sentiments were also in harmony with the teaching of Scripture. " Whom the Father loveth He chasteneth ", and " The branch that beareth fruit He purgeth, that it may bring forth more fruit ".

If we accept these observations of Elihu, we can accept with a greater measure of grace and confidence those mysterious things of life which come to us within the Permissive Will of God, and if we do, can use them for the development of our Christian character.

Whilst Elihu made some definite contribution to the problem on hand, he also made some mistakes in his interpretation of Job's utterances.

To those who would charge this young man with presumption, pride, and folly — and many do — may it be pointed out that :

Against his forwardness there was a backwardness. He did speak last and not until the other men had become silent.

Against his pride, there was a humility. He acknowledged his seniors and confessed his silence because of his youth.

Against his approach there was a retreat on the part of the others, who had failed in their reasonings.

Against his opinion there was a claim of Divine Inspiration.

The discussions of these men being ended

GOD BEGAN TO SPEAK (Chs. xxxviii-xli.). It is late in the book before God's voice is heard. Need we ask the reason why ? But then, some people are slow in seeing the obvious thing. The reason why the Lord had not spoken before was because they never gave Him a chance ! God did not speak until they had finished. Is it not true of us to-day ? Whenever we meet a situation of any kind, we talk, reason, debate, argue, get other people's opinions, consult books, do anything, everything, except wait upon the Lord, and ask for His counsel.

> " Oh, what peace we often forfeit,
> Oh, what needless pain we bear ;
> All because we do not carry
> Everything to God in prayer."

Let us ever remember that God will always have the last word. If He cannot have it in time then He will have it in Eternity.

Before God vindicated Job in front of these false comforters, He vindicated His own position before Job. Job had charged God with a miscarriage of justice. In seeking to justify his own position he became a little unwise in some of his statements, so much so that Elihu had said that Job considered himself more righteous than God. Now God said : " Shall he that contendeth with the Almighty instruct Him ? He that reproveth God, let him answer ". Job had reproved God for not answering prayer, and for not coming to his aid. God was now letting Job know that He had both seen and heard everything. He had been the silent listener to every utterance. He had been a secret witness to everything that had transpired, as He is in the lives of all His creatures.

Job had been annoyed with his friends because they darkened counsel by words without knowledge, but Job had done the same thing himself, for he had questioned the moral government of God when he was not in a position to explain God's physical government. Thus the Lord asked Job to answer a few questions.

Explain the facts of creation ? Or the movements of the sea and how it is controlled ?

Tell what you know of the future life ?

Explain the secrets of light and darkness, of snow, hail, rain, dew, ice, and frost, those things upon which man depends but cannot control ?

Lift up your eyes to the heavens and tell how all the stars move in their own constellations and have their influence upon the earth ?

Consider the firmament above, the clouds, the rain and lightning. Can they obey your voice ?

Then there is the animal creation, both bird and beast. Watch them survive the ravages of nature. See the bird build its nest, and the wild animal bring forth its young without the help of man or science. Who is it that feeds that vast creation ? Who gave them instinct, the power of preservation, and the ability to continue their species ?

The animals that are all so different from each other in their habits and habitats and yet all the same so far as their own species are concerned. Who gave them this instinct?

It is the Creator asking the creature to explain His creative power. This is something that would humiliate any of us. To meditate these questions of the Eternal God causes man to realise how insignificant he is, and how Almighty the Lord is.

Job, who had said a great deal to his friends, had nothing to say to God. His only reply was : " Behold, I am vile (or, of small account) ; what shall I answer Thee ? (or, I am not prepared to answer Thee). I will lay mine hand upon my mouth. Once have I spoken ; but I will not answer (or, not again) ; yea, twice : but I will proceed no further " (xl. 4-5).

Whilst Job was not prepared to reason with the Lord concerning His creative power, neither was he prepared to confess to the Lord that, in seeking to justify his own position, he had failed to give the Lord the honour that was due to Him.

The Lord was going to pursue the fact of His power and authority a little further so, for the second time, He told Job to gird up his loins like a man and give the Lord some answers. God still considered that Job had failed Him in seeking his own defence.

Job, take My place, do My work, stretch out your arm and save the people, or speak and cause the earth to tremble, because you can speak with the voice of thunder. Array thyself with majesty, glory, and beauty, then take men and do with them what you will by abasing the proud, treading down the wicked, and hiding them in the dust. Job, when you have done these things " *Then* will I confess unto thee that thine own right hand can save thee " (ix. 14). It is a picture of God suggesting to Job that they change places with each other. This was an appalling arraignment.

Job had no answer yet, so God continued by bringing to his notice the two strongest creatures, Behemoth, or the hippopotamus, and Leviathan, or the crocodile. He asked him to consider their enormous power — one a land animal, mighty in strength, yet feeding on straw like the ox ; the other a reptile of the water-world. The crocodile is a reptile that fears nothing but everyone fears him. No man would choose such a creature as a pet or plaything. God was informing Job that these were just two of the many, many things which He had created. What could Job do with them, particularly the crocodile ? Could he cast a hook and catch such a creature ?

The controversy was over. Job was at the end of himself. His first confession was : " I know that Thou canst do everything ".

Job was acknowledging that there is no limit to the power of God, and no bounds to the wisdom of God, and this would mean no mistake in the justice of God. Job considered that his knowledge of God had only been hearsay, or second-hand information. Now it was experimental. He was seeing God as He really is and, in doing so, he was seeing himself as he really was. Such a revelation has always a humiliating effect upon the soul. So he cried out : " Wherefore I abhor myself and repent in dust and ashes ".

At the beginning of this trial he had rent his clothes and shaved his head, but this was more in self-pity. How long he had been like that we do not know, because we are never informed as to how long he endured this grief. Now he sat in sackcloth and ashes, an act of soul humiliation, whilst he confessed : " I uttered that I understood not ; things too wonderful for me, which I knew not " (xlii. 3). In his repentance he acknowledged his ignorance. Even so Leviticus tells us that ignorance can be sin and must, therefore, be confessed as soon as one is made aware of it.

God accepted Job's confession and granted him immediate pardon, as He always will because He is always more willing to forgive than we are to confess.

(3)   REGENERATION (Ch. xlii. 7-17)

This concerns Job's restoration.

Firstly, God spoke to Eliphaz and told him of His wrath against these three men whose judgment and attitude had been wrong. God addressed the three men through Eliphaz, who, probably, was the oldest. At any rate, he was the man who spoke first and so gave the others their lead. The Lord required that these men should take an offering to Job, and there offer it on their own behalf, and that Job would pray for them. How we should watch our conduct ! God has a wonderful way of humiliating the proud. The Psalmist said : " Though the Lord be high, yet hath He respect unto the lowly : but the proud He knoweth afar off " (Ps. cxxxviii. 6).

It is to be noted that the Lord had no reproof for Elihu, neither did He require from him either confession or offering. If God never reproved him, neither should we.

" And the Lord turned the captivity of Job, when he prayed for his friends ; also the Lord gave Job twice as much as he had before " (vs. 10).

The Lord doubled his property so far as the sheep, camels, oxen, and asses were concerned. These Job had lost in chapter one. This one can appreciate.

There are those who suggest that in the same way the Lord doubled his family, but here one could have some reservation. We are told that his brethren and sisters came to comfort him, as did also his acquaintances, but no mention is made of his wife. This lack of information does not mean that he had no wife, because we know he did. It does not mean that she had died, or another wife would have to be mentioned for the new family which is suggested, and it cannot be considered that they were divorced. A righteous man like Job would not do it. Moreover, it was not practised back in those earliest days. The fact remains that she is just not mentioned.

Could it be possible that Job's children never did die and that these were the same seven sons and three daughters ? There is a suggestion that all of this grief became the lot of Job because he had been caused to believe a rumour.

When the servant saw the house collapse under the pressure of the wind and, knowing that Job's family was there, he fled to tell Job what he saw, but did he stop to investigate as to whether the occupants of the house were dead ? One has two reasons for making the suggestion, the first being that God gave permission to Satan to touch Job's possessions, his body, but not Job himself. That meant his life. Would that statement grant the Devil power to touch the lives of his children who were also God-fearing ? Or has Satan the control of life ?

The second reason for the suggestion is that, when Satan has not permission to harm us, he has a wonderful way of robbing God's people of peace of mind, of trust in the Lord, and much more through his lies. He is the father of lies, and he so often sets a rumour going that can really bring distress, and is it not true that man is ever ready to believe a rumour, especially if it is a bad one ?

If such a condition did exist, then Job's family was restored to him, which would gladden his heart more than rearing another family.

So his latter days were days of richness and blessing. From the book we learn :

(1) That good men are subjected to testings.

(2) That such testings may bring a man low temporarily.

(3) That loss or suffering does not necessarily spell punishment.

(4) That Christian character can be maintained in adverse circumstances.

(5) That the end of all affliction is for ultimate good and is to the development of human character and for the glory of God.

PSALMS

WORSHIP AND EXPERIENCE

*"Praise waiteth for Thee, O God, in Sion : and unto Thee shall
the vow be performed"* (Psalm lxv. 1)

INTRODUCTION

Known as the great hymnbook of Israel, the Psalms is a book
of praise and, at the same time, one of human experience. One of
the things that makes the 23rd Psalm a beloved Psalm of everybody is that it is Divine in its origin and practical in its experience.
This can be truly said of so many of the Psalms.

Thinking of this book as a hymnbook, hymn singing is becoming as rare as worship, and soon the hymnbook will be an unknown
thing. More and more we find the preacher saying : " Take up
your song book and turn to song number — " He is nearer the
truth than most people realise. We have forfeited the hymnbook
for a song book as we are surrendering worship for work, and
devotion for duty. The author took one of the so-called hymnbooks
of the church and combed through its four hundred and more
songs to find only a score of hymns.

What is a hymn ? Augustine says : " A paean of praise to
the gods ". Another of the Fathers expresses it as " A spontaneous
outburst of praise to God ". The Apostle Paul speaks of hymns
and spiritual songs, so he evidently considered them different, and
so must we. An example of difference would be :

> *" All hail the power of Jesus' Name,*
> *Let angels prostrate fall.*
> *Bring forth the royal diadem*
> *And crown Him Lord of all."*

or

> *" Holy, holy, holy, Lord God Almighty,"*

which are hymns. They render praise to the Lord.

> " *Stand up, stand up for Jesus,*
> *Ye soldiers of the Cross* ".

or

> " *Lead, kindly light, amid the encircling gloom,*
> *Lead Thou me on* ".

are songs of challenge, or prayers. They are manward, not Godward. Many songs are sentimental, light, and appealing to our
senses. Some, especially choruses, have a tendency towards the
jazz.

Four of the greatest hymns of the world, abounding in praise
and deep in expression, are to be found in the first two chapters
of Luke. They are called " The Magnificat ", sung by Mary,
" My soul doth magnify the Lord " (Luke i. 46-55). " The
Benedictus ", sung by Zacharias, " Blessed be the Lord God of
Israel " (Luke i. 68-79). " Gloria in Excelsis ", sung by the angels,
" Glory to God in the Highest " (Luke ii. 14), and the " Nunc
Dimittis ", sung by Simeon, " Lord, now lettest Thou Thy servant
depart in peace " (Luke ii. 29-32).

Music is something that has ever been known to the Church.
In fact, it belongs to both time and eternity. " . . . Jubal, he was
the father of all such as handle the harp and organ " (Gen. iv. 21).
Moses sang after crossing the Red Sea (Exodus xv.). Deborah
sang at the triumph of Israel (Judges v.). David sang with his
harp. Christ's birth was heralded by the song of the angels. Paul
and Silas sang in prison. In heaven we are going to sing the song
of Moses and the Lamb.

In our own lives, mother sings her baby to sleep before she
teaches it anything. The Church sings its praises at all times.
Even in death we sing our odes of lamentation.

Before leaving the musical side of the book, there are a number of terms that have remained a difficulty, such as Selah, Maschil,
Michtam, and Sheggaion. Many scholars feel that these were
musical terms, and that they give evidence that many of the Psalms
were set to music and were sung in both public and private. The
word that occurs mostly is " Selah ", and is derived from a root
meaning " to raise ", and signifies " up ", which prompts the
suggestion that it was asking for a crescendo, an opening up in
the music.

This book has often been referred to as the Psalms of David.
It is true that he wrote more than any other person, but the evidence is that he wrote only about half of the book. The authorship
of the Psalms is divided thus :

73 are ascribed to David.
12 are ascribed to Asaph.
11 are ascribed to the sons of Korah.
2 are ascribed to Solomon.
1 is ascribed to Moses.
1 is ascribed to Ethan.

That only accounts for one hundred. The other third of the book remains anonymous, although the possibility is that David wrote some of them.

ANALYSIS

The nature of the book being different from the others means that it cannot be analysed as the others. Nonetheless there is one main division to be found that shows this book to be made up of five books, for there are five benedictions :

Book 1 ..... Psalms   1 - 41   Amen and Amen.
Book 2 ..... Psalms 42 - 72   The Prayers of David, the son
                               of Jesse, are ended.
Book 3 ..... Psalms 73 - 89   Amen and Amen.
Book 4 ..... Psalms 90 - 106 Amen, praise ye the Lord.
Book 5 ..... Psalms 107 - 150 Praise ye the Lord.

The Jews link these five books with the Pentateuch. One of the old Jewish Commentaries says : " Moses gave the Israelites the five books of the Law, and to correspond to these David gave them the book of Psalms containing five books ". There is to be seen a connection between them.

Book 1 ..... Psalms   1 - 41   ..... Genesis — Man.
Book 2 ..... Psalms 42 - 72   ..... Exodus — Redemption.
Book 3 ..... Psalms 73 - 89   ..... Leviticus—The Sanctuary.
Book 4 ..... Psalms 90 - 106 ..... Numbers — The Earth.
Book 5 ..... Psalms 107 - 150 ..... Deuteronomy—The Word.

Again, the classifications of the Psalms have put many of them into certain groups. As the Psalms cannot be considered separately in so condensed a work, the best way to survey the whole book in Digest form would be to consider the groups. These are :

(1)   The Songs of Degrees.
(2)   The Penitential Psalms.
(3)   The Alphabetic Psalms.
(4)   The Hallelujah Psalms.
(5)   The Imprecatory Psalms.
(6)   The Messianic Psalms.

(1)   THE SONGS OF DEGREES (Psalms cxx-cxxxiv.)

This group is to be found all together. They are also known as " The Ascents ". This is because it is generally recognised that they were songs which were to be sung by the people as they made their journeyings from time to time up to Jerusalem for the observance of their Feasts. Three times in the year all males had to present themselves at Jerusalem for the Passover, Pentecost, and Tabernacles. For this the people of the various cities would travel in companies. It made for companionship and also for safety. It was in such a company as this that Mary, Joseph, and Jesus travelled for the Passover, as is recorded in Luke ii. 41- 45. On the return journey it was discovered that Jesus was missing, " they supposing Him to have *been in the company* . . . and they sought Him amongst their kinsfolk and acquaintances ". As they travelled in such companies they would sing the songs of Zion. They sang as they travelled and they sang in their camps at night. These conventions were all of them seasons of gladness.

Jerusalem was built upon Mount Zion, Mount Acra, Mount Ophel, and Mount Moriah, " beautiful for situation, the joy of the whole earth ". The people would see the city a long way off and would be inspired by the sight of it, an inspiration which would bring outbursts of praise.

Again, being built upon the mountains, there would be a steady climb, hence the term " The Ascents ". With this background and environment the sentiments of these Psalms should take on new meaning :

" I will lift up mine eyes unto the hills, from whence cometh my help " (Psalm cxxi.).

" I was glad when they said unto me, Let us go up to the house of the Lord. Our feet shall stand within thy gates, O Jerusalem. Jerusalem is builded as a City that is compact together " (Psalm cxxii.).

" Unto Thee lift I up mine eyes, O Thou that dwellest in the heavens " (Psalm cxxiii.).

" They that trust in the Lord shall be as Mount Zion which cannot be removed, but abideth for ever. As the mountains are round about Jerusalem, so the Lord is round about His people from henceforth even for ever " (Psalm cxxv.).

" When the Lord turned again the captivity of Zion, we were like them that dream " (Psalm cxxvi.).

"Except the Lord build the house, they labour in vain that build it ; except the Lord keep the city, the watchman waketh but in vain " (Psalm cxxvii.).

"The Lord shall bless thee out of Zion ; and thou shalt see the good of Jerusalem all the days of thy life " (Psalm cxxviii.).

" Let them all be confounded and turned back that hate Zion " (Psalm cxxix.).

"For the Lord hath chosen Zion ; He hath desired it for His habitation. This is my rest for ever ; here will I dwell ; for I have desired it " (Psalm cxxxii.).

" As the dew of Hermon, and as the dew that descended upon the mountains of Zion " (Psalm cxxxiii.).

"The Lord that made heaven and earth bless thee out of Zion " (Psalm cxxxiv.).

They are but quotations from these Psalms, but they and the whole give a picture of loyalty, patriotism, and zeal toward their city and their God. There is no doubt that it was with bounding joy and enthusiasm that those people journeyed.

Let us learn something of this same devotion, this same love and passion, as we make our way into the sanctuary of the Lord's House, the church, and into His Presence.

We have lost a great deal along life's way. We have become a people of habit instead of a people of devotion. We are taking too much for granted and are losing the joys and privileges of the people of God. Let us come into His Presence with singing, let us enter His courts with praise, and go away with the peace of God ruling our hearts and our minds. We are on the upward way. Therefore we should be singing the songs of The Ascents.

(2) THE PENITENTIAL PSALMS

Scholars have put seven Psalms particularly into this group, although there are others that have similar characteristics. They are Psalms vi., xxxii., xxxviii., li., cii., cxxx., and cxliii. Five of these have the name of David attached to them.

David was a great warrior. With confidence he could meet his Goliath. The people could shout : " Saul hath slain his thousands and David his ten thousands ". He could mete out justice and judgment wherever they were required, but yet he was a man of a tender heart, sensitive to sin and failure. These Psalms are a revelation of those deep passions.

In Psalm vi. David seemed to be sick in body (2) and soul (3). He was depressed because of the constant pressure of the enemy on every hand. In his grief he poured out his soul in supplication to the Lord and he poured out his sorrow in tears, until he could bid his enemies depart because he had gained the assurance that his prayers were heard and answered.

It has been mentioned in the previous group of Psalms that we have lost the joy of song. Maybe it is because we have lost the sense of sorrow for sin.

In Psalm xxxii. most of us can repeat both the first and the last verses, " Blessed is he whose transgression is forgiven, whose sin is covered " (1), and " Be glad in the Lord, and rejoice, ye righteous ; and shout for joy all ye that are upright in heart " (11), but the secret of this blessedness is found in the intervening verses.

The first word of the Psalm is fuller than our Authorised Version gives it. In the Hebrew the word is a plural one and means " The blessednesses ". Multiplied are the blessings of the man whose transgression is forgiven, whose sin is covered. Something else is plural in the verse. " Transgression " is overstepping the mark, or going beyond. " Sin " is coming short of the standard. Going too far or coming too short, whichever way the failure, this man could rejoice in forgiveness, but the forgiveness had come to him through confession and repentance.

David was not expounding salvation in the sense that we understand it in our doctrines. It was not the sinner seeking salvation. It was the saint seeking sanctification. He was making confession of his failings as a saint, and was penitent because he had failed. This is made manifest in verse 6 : " For this shall every one that is *godly* pray unto Thee ".

Similar is the experience of Psalm xxxviii. David was in despair and he was crying to the Lord because of his failure and because, when his foot slipped (which is not persistent sin), his enemies were ready to rejoice. When the enemy can rejoice the Lord's cause is being defeated. David was sensitive to this and so said : " I will be sorry for my sin ".

Oh, that we were as sensitive to anything that would harm the Lord's Name and His cause ! Then, with penitent hearts, we would cry out : " Make haste to help me, O Lord, my salvation ".

Of all the Penitential Psalms the 51st is the best known. The expressions are sublime, and have become the prayer of many a discouraged saint throughout the ages.

One is greatly helped in understanding this Psalm and others which, like it, have a title. David uttered these words after Nathan, the prophet, had come to him from God to reprove him because of the sin he had committed with Bathsheba. The incident is recorded in 2 Samuel, chapters xi. and xii. David never seemed to realise the heinousness of his sin. It had not even occurred to him that it was sin even whilst he plotted the death of Uriah in order that he might obtain Bathsheba " legally " as his wife. When Nathan told his parable, David saw immediately the smaller sin in someone else and was ready to punish that sin. When the truth dawned upon his soul, he became a broken man and, in his brokenness, he sobbed these words of utter penitence : " Have mercy upon me, O God . . . Wash me throughly from mine iniquity, and cleanse me from my sin . . . Purge me with hyssop, and I shall be clean " etc. He confessed his sin, he sought the cleansing of the Lord, and asked for a return of joy. He then besought the Lord for deliverance from the crime of manslaughter (bloodguiltiness), and for a tongue that would show forth His praise. David had lost a great deal in that one sin. He lost almost everything except his salvation. When sin comes testimony goes. " Restore unto me the joy of Thy salvation . . . THEN will I teach transgressors Thy ways ; and sinners shall be converted unto Thee "

Thus it is with each of these Penitential Psalms.

(3) THE ALPHABETIC PSALMS

Most of us know the 119th Psalm as such. It is the perfect Psalm. However, there are eight Psalms that come under this category. The others are Psalms ix., xxv., xxxvii., cxi., cxii., and cxlv. A part of Psalm x. is alphabetic, but none of them is perfect. It has been suggested that this was done to help one to memorise, as to-day we use homiletics and alliterations as an aid to memory. Of course, the alphabetic arrangement cannot be found in our English Bibles. It appeared in the Hebrew form.

There are twenty-two characters in the Hebrew alphabet. Thus the 119th Psalm is divided into twenty-two portions, each of eight verses. Over each section our Bible shows the Hebrew letters, Aleph, Beth, Gimel, etc. In the prose of the Psalm every line of the first section begins with an Aleph; each line of the second section begins with a Beth; and so on throughout the whole Psalm.

The 119th Psalm comes into the fifth book of Psalms, which coincides with the fifth book of Moses — Deuteronomy — or the second giving of the Law, and concerns The Word. This Psalm is a fine example for there is a constant repetition of certain words which are all expressions of The Word.

Testimony 21 times, Precepts 21 times, Statutes 22 times, Commandments 22 times, Law 25 times, Judgments 20 times, Word 39 times, giving a total of one hundred and seventy references to the Word of God.

(4) THE HALLELUJAH PSALMS

There are ten of these Psalms, each beginning with the phrase: "Praise ye the Lord", and most of them ending with the same note of worship. They are Psalms cvi., cxi., cxii., cxiii., cxxxv., cxlvi., cxlvii., cxlviii., cxlix., and cl. Psalms cxi. and cxii. are the only two that do not end with the same phrase.

In these Psalms, none is attributed to David. All are anonymous. Everything is called upon to give praise to God for everything. Angels and humans, creation and creature, heaven and earth, voice and instrument, are all called upon to "Praise ye the Lord". The past, the present, and the future are brought into the great refrain and, lest anything should have been overlooked, then, "Let every thing that hath breath, Praise the Lord". This, truly, would be the greatest oratorio ever sung by the mightiest choir that could ever be assembled.

The cause of this praise? — Everything!

In Psalm cvi. Israel was caused to look to the past, the deliverance from Egypt, the provisions and the protections in the wilderness, and the mercies and blessings of Canaan, and all these despite their constant sinning. In Psalms cxi-cxiii. praise is to be rendered for the present things, all of which are in the realm of the moral and the spiritual. In the last of these Psalms, it is praise for the physical and material things such as are displayed in the realm of nature, all given for our good.

And the subject of praise? — The Lord Himself.

To-day His handiwork shews forth His praise. Everything around us tells us that God is good. But what of the redeemed? Those who have been blessed beyond measure and above deserving? Are we joining in the great Hallelujah Chorus — "Praise ye the Lord"?

(5) THE IMPRECATORY PSALMS

This is a subject that has long bothered man. The word "imprecatory" means "to evoke, as evil, by prayer, hence to curse".

These Psalms, three of which are outstanding (xxxv., lxix., cix.) find David calling down upon the heads of his enemies all the judgment and wrath of which he could think. They appear to be displays of hatred contrary to the teaching of Scripture in which the Lord says: "But I say unto you, Love your enemies, bless them that curse you, do good to them that hate you, and pray for

them which despitefully use you, and persecute you " (Matt. v.
44). Or again, the teaching of Paul : " Bless them that curse you,
bless and curse not " (Rom. xii. 14).

Firstly, it would be good to read again the three Psalms under
consideration. Here are some quotations :

Psalm xxxv. " Let them be confounded and put to shame . . .
Let them be as chaff before the wind . . . Let their way be dark
and slippery . . . Let the angel of the Lord persecute them . . .
Let destruction come upon him at unawares ".

Psalm lxix. " Let their table become a snare before them . . .
Let their habitation be desolate . . . Let none dwell in their tents
. . . Let them be blotted out of the book of the living ".

Psalm cix. " Let his prayer become sin . . . Let his days be
few . . . Let his children be fatherless and his wife a widow . . .
Let his children be continually vagabonds and beg . . . Let his
posterity be cut off . . . Let this be the reward of mine adversaries
from the Lord, and of them that speak evil against my soul ".
In this last Psalm, David extended the cursings from the man who
had wronged him to his family, and on to his future posterity.

After evoking the judgment of God upon his adversaries he
always moved on to invoke Divine blessing upon himself.

In answer to this problem we must give consideration to a
number of things and establish a correct relationship.

(1) Vengeance was the order of the day in Old Testament
times, and in many instances we see it practised in Old Testament
history. The life and reign of David are an example. It was
because of this practice in the Old Testament that Jesus taught
men to love their enemies, and to pray for those who despitefully
used them ; and Paul said " Bless and curse not ".

(2) It must be recognised that there was no personal
vindictiveness against an individual. It was always a wrath against
a group, or class, or community. There is no difference between
David saying : " Let mine adversaries be clothed with shame, and
let them cover themselves with their own confusion as with a
mantle " but " Help me, O Lord my God : O save me according
to Thy mercy ", than the prayer so many of us prayed during the
years of war : " Lord, bring to naught the power of the enemy
and cause them to suffer defeat. Lord, bless our cause, protect
our soldiers, prosper our armies, our air force, and give us victory ".
When we prayed thus we had no personal hatred against the

individual. It was the nation or the regime, the cause of our own suffering, that we asked the Lord to destroy.

If it should become necessary for a person to go to Court at any time, it should be in defence of the principles of justice, and never with a vindictiveness against an individual.

(3) The enemies of David were always the enemies of God, so that, again, the issue was not personal, but a display of righteous anger against some moral or spiritual wrong, which could be interpreted as a zeal for God.

(4) In no instance did David have the desire to inflict the punishment himself, to bring a sense of revenge or satisfaction. He ever asked God to mete out His own justice.

(5) Concerning the statements of Psalm cix. "Let his children be fatherless", or "Let his posterity be cut off", we must not interpret these as uncontrolled temper, but know that at that time, not only was a man identified with his sin, he was also identified with his family. They were one. Therefore that sin could become inherent and find continuance in the family. Thus it was with Achan, with Korah, and others. The whole family died. It was because of this that God taught Ezekiel : "The soul that sinneth, it shall die. The son shall not bear the iniquity of the father, neither shall the father bear the iniquity of the son" (Ezk. xviii. 20).

(6) In the days of the Old Testament man was his own avenger, hence the necessity of establishing Cities of Refuge against the avenger of blood. At one time, when David was wronged by the selfish, greedy Nabal, he gathered his men and moved forward to avenge himself on Nabal, but Abigail intervened and saved the situation. David had surely come a long way when he could hand this matter over to God and allow Him to mete out the punishments.

Upon such considerations it would appear that this word "Imprecatory" is what is at fault.

(6) THE MESSIANIC PSALMS

This is the largest group. There are more than a score and all of them speak of the coming of the Messiah. They foretell His suffering and His glory.

The book of Psalms is definitely a Prophetic book. The New Testament possibly quotes the Psalms more than any other portion of the Old Testament.

A. C. Gaebelein, in *The Annotated Bible,* gives a wonderful picture of Christ's relationship with the Psalms and the many times

He quoted from them. May we be permitted to give the following extract from that volume.

"*The Lord Jesus and the Psalms*. But there is another reason why believers love the Psalms. The Lord Jesus is not only revealed in this book as nowhere else, but He used the Psalms throughout His blessed life on earth, and even in glory. Here are His own prayers pre-written by the Spirit of God. The expression of sorrow, loneliness, rejection, and suffering describe what He passed through in His life of humiliation. The praise and worship, the trust and confidence in God, express likewise prophetically that life of obedience and trust. We believe when He spent nights in prayer to pour out His heart before His Father, on the mountain or in the desert, He must have done so by using the Psalms. He used the Psalms speaking to His disciples; with Psalm cx. He silenced His enemies. Gethsemane is mentioned in the Psalms; and in the suffering of the Cross He fulfilled all that the Psalms predict. In resurrection He used the 22nd Psalm : ' Go and tell My brethren '. He opened to His disciples the Scriptures ' that all things must be fulfilled, which were written in the Law of Moses, in the Prophets, and in the Psalms concerning Me ' (Luke xxiv. 44) as He had before told the two on the way to Emmaus ' Ought not Christ to have suffered these things, and to enter into His glory ? And beginning at Moses and all the Prophets, He expounded unto them in all the Scriptures the things concerning Himself '. When He ascended on high and took the seat at God's right hand, and God welcomed Him to sit down and to be the Priest after the order of Melchizedec, it was according to the Psalms. And in His messages from the throne in speaking to the Churches He uses the Psalms (Rev. xi. 27). And when He comes again, the Hallelujah chorus of the ending of this book will be sung by heaven and earth, and all the predicted glory, as given in the Psalms, will come to pass. This book then ought to be precious to us because it was precious to Him and makes Him known to our hearts. The Spirit of God also quotes the Psalms more frequently in the Epistles than any other Old Testament book ".

The above statement is a magnificent panoramic view of the Messianic Psalms

This same volume also points out another important fact. The Psalms contain more prophetic utterances concerning the Messiah than any other subject. Moreover, the statement has been made that the Psalms contain more prophetic declaration concerning the Messiah than does the prophecy of Isaiah, or any other prophetic book.

These Messianic prophecies can be divided into several classes, two of which are :

(1) *The suffering Messiah* — Psalms xxii., xxxv., xli., lv., lxix., cix.

(2) *The reigning Messiah* — Psalms ii., xviii., xx., xxi., xlv., lxi., lxxii., lxxxix., cx., cxxxii.

Concerning the *Suffering Messiah,* He Who became the Man of Sorrows, Psalm xxii. is not only the best known but probably the gem of them all.

This could be a key to many of the Psalms, as the Lord once said concerning the Parable of the Sower : " Know ye not this parable ? And how then will ye know all parables " (Mark iv. 13).

It is a psalm of experience which reveals that the author was speaking out of his own heart concerning things that had happened to him. But, at the same time, it can be seen how Divine Providence had permitted these things to happen in such a way and in such an order as to coincide with things that were to happen in the life of the Messiah. Again, the Holy Spirit controlled the utterances of the Psalmist that in words he predicted the sufferings of the Lord. David, not being aware of what would be the sufferings of Christ nor yet that He would utter the very same words, gave evidence that " the prophecy came not in old time by the will of man ; but holy men of God spake as they were moved by the Holy Ghost " (2 Pet. i. 21).

Many suggestions are made as to when and why David uttered these words, but to pinpoint the occasion is not necessary. David suffered a long period of testing as his life was sought by Saul, and as he faced the rebellion of Absalom, the treachery of his friends and the hatred of his enemies. For a long period everyone and everything seemed to be against him. In the midst of all these adversities one could hear him cry out : " My God, my God, Why hast Thou forsaken me ? Why art Thou so far from helping me, and from the words of my roaring ? " As one reads the Psalm, verse by verse, the application to David is perfect and its identity with Christ just as perfect. The ordinary reader may find some exceptions, as in verse 16, " They pierced my hands and my feet ". It is true that such did not happen to David, but the margin of the Bible points out the fact that " pierced " is in the Septuagint, Vulgate, and Syriac, but the other ancient versions use the word " bound ". The thought in the Hebrew is " Like a lion they tear or mangle my hands and feet ".

No doubt David was thinking of his enemies wanting to incapacitate him, and there was a method of doing this by cutting off the thumbs and great toes, as recorded in the first chapter of Judges, the opposite number to this being the anointing of these same members with blood in the dedication of the priests in Exodus xxix. 20. Therefore the word bound, torn, mangled, bitten, or pierced would do, but the Holy Spirit directed David to use the latter term.

The Psalm as a whole is the declaration of a need, a cry for help, and a rejoicing in deliverance granted.

In Psalm xxxv. David was lamenting again because of his persecutors, but this time it was because friends had become enemies, those whom he had blessed were cursing him. Those for whom he had interceded in their distress now mocked him in his distress. Read particularly verses 11-17. The sufferings of the Messiah included all of these, false witnesses, rewarding good with evil, exchanging His intercession with their rejection and mockery.

In Psalm xli. the particular verse is 9. "Yea, mine own familiar friend, in whom I trusted, which did eat of my bread, hath lifted up his heel against me". There is no doubt but that this refers to Ahithophel (2 Sam. xv. 12). In the sufferings of the Lord it would be Judas, but with Ahithophel there was also Absalom and many of the people who withdrew. With the Lord there was Peter who denied Him, whilst, of the rest, they all forsook Him and fled.

Psalm lv. is treated in the same way as Psalm xli. Here the verses are 12-14, and Ahithophel is the character in question.

David was deep in trouble again in Psalm lxix and was crying out because of those who hated him without a cause. From this Psalm come the words: " They gave me also gall for my meat ; and in my thirst they gave me vinegar to drink " (21).

Two great differences between the prophetic utterances of David and their fulfilment in Christ are (1) David was despised and rejected of men but never of God, whilst Jesus was not only forsaken of men but even His Father had to turn His back upon Him when He was made sin, and so *alone* He trod the winepress. (2) David, who was man, was ever seeking judgment and retribution for his enemies, using such words as, " Let them be blotted out of the book of the living, and not be written with the righteous " (Psalm lxix. 28) ; whilst Jesus cried : " Father, forgive them, for they know not what they do " (Luke xxiii. 34). What grace !

Much of Psalm cix. has reference to Judas so far as the prophetic side of the Psalm is concerned.

The second group of Messianic Psalms deals with a *Reigning Messiah*. The first of these is the second Psalm, sometimes known as " The Psalm of the Son ". It is a picture of the Lord Who, through the ages, has displayed His grace towards mankind, but has now come to the time when, as the Great Monarch, He sits upon the throne of judgment. It is that period often known as Armageddon, when the nations, being caused to imagine a vain thing by the god of this world, gather together against the Lord and His Christ. They have despised Him, now He despises them. He is going to reign Whose right it is. Because that day is fast coming, man is advised to serve the Lord and secure right relationship, for only those who put their trust in Him shall know deliverance.

In Psalm xviii. David was rejoicing in that every enemy, within and without, had been subdued. He was now reigning upon his throne, enjoying peace through victory. Verses 4 and 5 remind one of Calvary when the sorrows of death compassed Him. Then verses 7-9 would tell of the darkness over the earth whilst He hung on the Cross, and the trembling earth speaks of the earthquake that happened as He yielded up the ghost. In the latter part of the Psalm both are reigning supreme with all enemies under their feet.

Psalms xx. and xxi. tell of the King reigning in power. Psalm xlv. is glorious as the King takes His seat upon the eternal throne. He has left the throne of judgment of Psalm ii. to sit on the throne of righteousness and to be surrounded by those whom He has redeemed. " Thy throne, O God, is for ever and ever : the sceptre of Thy kingdom is a right sceptre. Thou lovest righteousness, and hatest wickedness ; therefore God, Thy God, hath anointed Thee with the oil of gladness above Thy fellows " (6-7).

Psalm lxxii. was written by Solomon, the son of David, when reigning in the prime of his life and in the prime of the kingdom, but the Psalm does not concern his kingdom as it does great David's Greater Son, for, in reading it, one learns that a greater than Solomon is here.

Likewise is the eternal throne established in Psalms cx. and cxxxii, and upon the throne reigns the King eternal, immortal, invisible, the only wise God, to Whom be honour for ever and ever.

CONCLUSION

And what can be said of the rest of the Psalms, those that do
not come into the classifications considered ? Each Psalm tempts
one to make comment, but space does not permit in such a
" Digest ".

A profitable suggestion is to read each Psalm, and then find a
title for it. A title must be short and suggestive — as an example:

Psalm i.   ....   Contrasted Characters.
Psalm ii.   ....   Messianic Monarchy.
Psalm iii.   ....   Divine Protection.

In doing this some Psalms can be put together in small groups
or comparisons, as, for example :

Psalm iv.   ....   An Evening Prayer.
Psalm v.   ....   A Morning Meditation.

or

Psalm xxii.   ....   The Cross   —   'Past.
Psalm xxiii.   ....   The Crown   —   Present.
Psalm xxiv.   ....   The Crook   —   Future.

or

Psalms civ., 1 - cv., 26   A summary of Genesis.
Psalms cv., 27 - cvi., 15   A summary of Exodus.
Psalms cvi., 16 - cviii., 13   A summary of Numbers.
Psalms cix.   A summary of Deuteronomy.

In the Psalms men are seen in all kinds of circumstances, in
battles, wanderings, dangers, escapes, deathbeds.

St. Basil said the Psalms were medicine for every disease.
They calm the soul and still the storm. They soften the angry
spirit and sober the intemperate. A Psalm can cement friendship
and reconcile those who are at enmity. A Psalm can put demons
to flight or summon angels to our aid. Quoting from St. Basil:
" The heroism of courage ; the integrity of justice ; the gravity of
temperance ; the perfection of prudence ; the manner of repentance ; the measure of patience ; in a word every good thing thou
canst mention. Therein is a complete theology; the prediction of
the advent of Christ in the flesh, the threatening of judgment, the
hope of resurrection, the fear of chastisement, promises of glory,
revelations of mysteries : all, as in some great public storehouse,
are treasured up in the book of Psalms ".

With St. Chrysostom, St. Augustine, Luther, and Calvin, and
other of the fathers, we would agree that there is no circumstance

in life, no mood of the soul, no fear, no ecstasy, no spiritual or physical condition, but what the Psalms cannot give expression and bring consolation.

Maybe the Established Church has an advantage here, in that they sing the Psalms which contain much more than many of the poor, sentimental songs we sing in churches to-day.

PROVERBS

THE BOOK OF WISDOM

" If any man lack wisdom, let him ask of God, that giveth to all men liberally, and upbraideth not ; and it shall be given him." (JAMES i. 5)

INTRODUCTION

If anyone should think that the Bible lacks morals, or that the Bible is not practical, or that the Bible is not logical (and many like to think that such things are true) then they should read the book of Proverbs. It is a book which should be given to every boy and girl in High School or College to-day. Here is the best counsel for young people just embarking on life. Here is warning for those who see no harm in anything. Here is instruction for the simple and admonition for the careless.

Bishop Lowth once said: " The Proverbs are so justly founded on the principles of human nature and so adapted to the interests of man, that they agree with the manners of every age and may be accepted as the rules for the directing of our conduct in every condition and rank of life ".

We are instructed how to walk in wisdom towards those who are without — to live in this evil world and not be contaminated by it.

Dr. Harry Ironside reminds us of the fact that the books of the Bible are not in chronological order. If they were, the book of Ecclesiastes would come before the book of Proverbs. This would give sequence of subject matter. Dr. Ironside also suggests that the closing verses of Ecclesiastes are the introduction to the book of Proverbs. It is, of course, the same author who writes both books. In Ecclesiastes Solomon sought to find wisdom, happiness, and satisfaction from the things that were under the sun, which is the human plane or the realm of man's philosophies, but everything proved to be a failure — just vanity. Instead of giving things up as a fruitless quest, he turned from that which was under the sun to the things which were from above. In this realm he succeeded because he sought after God and God revealed Himself, so that this book, like all the other books of the Bible, manifests itself to be God-inspired.

This causes us to understand that, although the book comprises a collection of proverbs, maxims, and admonitions, yet it is not the philosophical wisdom of man. It is not secular knowledge. It is distinctly religious.

The book, on its broadest basis, teaches " The fear of the Lord ", which is the key phrase of the Proverbs.

It teaches what God requires of men.
It teaches how God would have men behave.
It teaches piety — duty — justice.
Two Voices are to be heard throughout the book — the Voice of Wisdom and the Voice of Folly.
Two ways are open to the children of men — the Way of Godliness and the Way of Evil.

It is written to include :
The Creator and the Creature.
The King and his Subject.
The Husband and the Wife.
The Parent and the Child.
The Rich and the Poor.
The Learned and the Ignorant.

The book deals with such subjects as :
God and Man.
Marriage and the Home.
Youth and Old Age.
Wealth and Poverty.
Purity and Impurity.
Justice and Injustice.
Truth and Falsehood.
Pleasure and Misery.
Soberness and Drunkenness.
Diligence and Laziness.
Time and Eternity.

Referring back to the key phrase " The fear of the Lord ", there are two kinds of fear in the world.

Filial Fear, which shrinks from sin. This is godly fear or reverence.

Servile Fear, which shrinks only from punishment.

The great purpose of the book of Proverbs is to show that true wisdom is to follow Him Who is Wisdom, and, in so doing, to be numbered among the wise that shall shine as the brightness of the firmament (Daniel xii. 3).

ANALYSIS

Although this book differs from all the others, inasmuch as nearly every verse is a complete unit in itself, yet the book has something of a unity which allows for an analysis.
The main divisions are :

(1) WORDS OF WISDOM addressed to " My son " (Chs. i-ix.).
(2) VIRTUES AND VICES attributed to Solomon (Chs. x-xxiv.).
(3) MAXIMS AND OBSERVATIONS which were collected by Hezekiah, Agur, and Lemuel (Chs. xxv-xxxi.).

It has been suggested that the difference between the first two sections is that the first was *for* Solomon, and the second *by* Solomon. This would mean that God was the speaker, and " My son " would be Solomon the hearer.

(1) WORDS OF WISDOM — " My son " (Chs. i-ix.)

Would to God that every father would give such instruction to his son, and every mother to her daughter. The book opens with a great challenge to parental responsibility, *" My son "*. Young people are stepping out into a life they have not met previously. There are pitfalls, dangers, and temptations of which they are not aware. There are moral issues of which they are ignorant. Parents have been through these trials and are in a position, therefore, to guide young people.

" A *wise* man will hear " (vs. 5). Most young people "know" too much to hear anything. They are wanting to be teachers instead of learners, and thereby they become foolish because they are wise in their own counsels.

It is right and proper to seek and to obtain knowledge. Learning is an essential of life. Many people like to air their knowledge as a display of their superiority, but what is knowledge ? " THE FEAR OF THE LORD IS THE BEGINNING OF KNOWLEDGE " (vs. 7). Humbly to acknowledge the Lord as the Source of all things and the Master of everything is to begin the path of knowledge. It is the foundation of our learning, because He is the foundation. " All things were made by Him, and without Him was not any thing made that was made " (John i. 3).

Knowledge is followed by wisdom but, in between, there comes a note of warning to those who would walk the opposite way, who would prefer the companionship of the sinner, or who would take the way of least resistance. " My son, if sinners entice thee, consent thou not " (vs. 10). " If they say . . . We shall find all precious substance, we shall fill our houses with spoil : cast in thy lot among us ; let us all have one purse " (vs. 11-14). The warning is to watch your companions and watch your possessions, or the danger of trying to get something for nothing.

In vs. 20 we are introduced to WISDOM, not as an attribute or quality, but as a Person. " Wisdom crieth without ; she uttereth her voice in the streets ", or in the broad places, in the concourses where people gather themselves together. Wisdom is the Lord Himself.

Wisdom is not expressed in the language of men who seek to air their ideas as to what might have happened millions of years ago, and to explain to us the technicalities of an evolution of species or the theories of matter. So many of these theories explode within a little while.

Throughout this book Wisdom is confirmed as a Person, a Person Who
> is eternal (viii. 23) ;
> dwells with God (viii. 30) ;
> shared in creation (viii. 27-29) ;
> possesses all authority (viii. 15-16) ;
> is essentially Christ.

Philosophy seeks the unknown — gropes after God — tries to discover the secrets of life and the eternal ordering of things and, in so doing, remains in the dark. On the other hand Wisdom explains life and reveals the Divine economy. Hence the instruction " Get wisdom, get understanding ; forget it not ; neither decline from the words of my mouth. Forsake her not, and she shall preserve thee : love her, and she shall keep thee. Wisdom is the principal thing ; therefore get wisdom, and with all thy getting get understanding. Exalt her and she shall promote thee : she shall bring thee to honour, when thou dost embrace her. She shall give to thine head an ornament of grace : a crown of glory shall she deliver to thee. Hear, O my son, and receive my sayings ; and the years of thy life shall be many " (iv. 5-10).

Three great qualifications are required for obtaining true Wisdom. They are :

(1) *The acknowledgment of God.* " In all thy ways acknowledge Him and He shall direct thy paths " (iii. 6).

(2) *The recognition of parents.* " My son, hear the instruction of thy father, and forsake not the law of thy mother "

(i. 8). This is an oft-repeated principle of life found in both Old and New Testaments.

(3) *A separation from the world.* " My son, if sinners entice thee, consent thou not " (i. 10).

It may be put thus :

(1) Our relationship with God ....   The Divine.
(2) Our relationship with the family .....   The Human.
(3) Our relationship with the world .....   The Material.

Modern teaching is the reverse of this to-day. Its doctrines are that there is no room for God in thought or living — just one's own wisdom, but the wisdom of this world is foolishness and is to be confounded ; no room for the family relationship, instead it is free love, loose living, lax morals, self-indulgence, free expression. God has promised that if we honour our father and our mother our days shall be prolonged upon the earth. The Ephesian Epistle bids us to obey our parents in the Lord. The Word of God predicted a day when children would be disobedient to their parents and that such a day would be calamitous. That day has truly arrived. We are living right in it, with parents obeying their children, whilst parental honour has just gone to the wall. If ever the advice of the book of Proverbs was needed, it is now.

Young man, young woman, stepping out into life — where do you stand in this relationship ? If you are not honouring your parents and respecting your elders do not call yourself a Christian, for these things are characteristic of the apostasy of the last days.

Likewise parents, with all the God-given responsibility of parenthood, what is your relationship ? Are you displaying a love towards, and an understanding of, your young people ? Do you take them into your confidence and do you allow them to take you into their confidence, so that there is mutual respect each for the other ?

To these things must be added the third relationship. As Christians we should be in the world but not of it. We have to come out from worldly society. We must not consent to their methods, as we have already seen. They will ever lure with their rewards. Be careful of that raffle, that chance ticket, that something-for-nothing. It is a slippery path. Be careful of that " innocent " cigarette, that social drink, that occasional dance. You are identifying yourself with sinners, but Wisdom says " Consent thou not ".

One may smile at the narrow-minded preacher. One may laugh at the old-fashioned mother, but Wisdom says "I also will laugh at your calamity; I will mock when your fear cometh" (i. 26).

Repeatedly throughout these first seven chapters comes the same exhortation to acknowledge God and to seek that Wisdom which cometh from above. Its value is compared with all the things of the earth. It is ever found to be more precious than silver, gold, rubies, long life, or anything else that the soul may desire.

Just as frequently in these same chapters is the warning given to those who would despise the Lord and seek to make their own course through this world. Youth cannot find its own way. The snares and pitfalls are too many and too subtle. There is

The evil man (ii. 12), who rejoices in evil, loves the ways of darkness, eats the bread of wickedness, and drinks the wine of violence. His feet make haste to shed blood. He respects no one and nothing in his greed for gain. The simple are the prey of such men. Therefore "Enter not into the path of the wicked, and go not in the way of evil men. Avoid it, pass not by it, turn from it, and pass away" (iv. 14-15).

The strange woman (ii. 16). This term, in its first meaning, is not a stranger in the matter of relationship. It is a warning against fornication or adultery. She is a stranger to virtue, purity, and morality. She trades in the bodies and souls of men. Her tongue is smooth, her lips are like a honeycomb, her reasonings are subtle, her rewards are attractive, but her fruit is bitter and the results damning to the soul.

So dangerous is this woman that chapter seven outlines a description of her method and a declaration of her mischief.

Chapter nine brings into contrast again Wisdom and Folly. Each has built a house, and each invites mankind into its company. Both have prepared a feast which they desire to share with those who will accept their invitations.

The first house is built by Wisdom. It is strong, and is a place of security for the simple. It is hewn, which means that it would have been built out of natural rock. The seven pillars would speak of architectural beauty and completeness.

May it be suggested that seven pillars upon which Wisdom would stand secure to-day would be:

The other house is built on the highway with no portentous entrance. At the door sits the foolish woman, the woman who is void of sense or responsibility. Sometimes she sits at the gate of the city, but always with the same purpose, to lure away from the path of duty the young man who, in his simplicity, is not on his guard. She, too, has a feast, but it is stolen waters and bread that is eaten in the darkened places of moral delinquency. Her words are so subtle, her appeals so seemingly innocent, that he is not aware that his delinquency is a step to damnation, and that her previous guests have ceased to live, for the sinner is dead whilst he still liveth. Therefore, remember that " Except the Lord build the house, they labour in vain that build it " (Psalm cxxvii. 1).

This chapter ends the reasonings of Wisdom and Folly, and the advice that Wisdom gives to " My Son ".

(2) VIRTUES AND VICES OF SOLOMON (Chs. x-xxiv.)

This section commences with the words " The Proverbs of Solomon," and so begin the Proverbs proper.

The idea to be derived from the word Proverb, as it comes to us from the Hebrew, is " To set, or place side by side " or " by comparison ". This is readily seen as one reads the book. Right and wrong are placed side by side. Wisdom and folly are put together, virtues and vices are contrasted, allowing the one to expose the other.

It is not possible to give consideration to all the Proverbs because almost every verse stands alone without any relationship to the verse before or after ; and each verse is a mine of practical information and application to every-day moral living.

A few Proverbs have been chosen at random which would give a selection of some of the main issues that concern this moral life and that declare what is for man's good and what can be his downfall — truths that counsel young people as to the things which please God and things which displease Him.

There are some exceptions to the Proverbs, where a word of instruction is given instead. We will commence with one of these.

" . . . *He that winneth souls is wise* " (xi. 30). Solomon had said a great deal about wisdom in the first part of the book. This is the fruit of wisdom. A wise man makes safe investments. To win souls to the Lord is the greatest investment in this life because

(1) There is no greater joy or thrill for oneself.

(2) There is no greater benefit that one could bring to his fellowman.

(3) There is nothing that can bring more joy to the heart of the Lord.

(4) There is no better investment for eternity.

Said James : " Brethren, if any of you do err from the truth, and one convert him ; let him know that he which converteth the sinner from the error of his way, shall save a soul from death, and shall hide a multitude of sins " (James v. 19-20).

" *He that tilleth his land shall be satisfied with bread ; but he that followeth vain persons is void of understanding* " (xii. 11). Solomon used many words of warning concerning the sluggard, the man who is indifferent to his responsibilities, who ever tries to escape work, and who seeks any kind of means in order to obtain something for nothing. The warning certainly needs to be re-echoed to-day. We live in an age when there seems to be a general distaste for work, a desire for ease and pleasure, and an expectancy for governments to take the responsibility of old age. All of this is contrary to the teachings of the Scripture. Such people are void of understanding, and we are advised to have no dealings with them. It is for man to work with his hands, to enjoy the thrill and the satisfaction of accomplishment, to be not weary in well doing knowing that he will reap if he faints not.

" *Fools make a mock at sin ; but among the righteous there is favour* " (xiv. 9). The Hebrew word used for sin is " Asham " and means in this verse " Guilt or guilt offering ". Thirty-five times the same word is translated " trespass offering ". From this we learn that it is not so much the sin itself that is scorned, but the sin offering. The fact is that sinners usually enjoy their sin. They possess no sense of guilt. It must be admitted that there is pleasure in sin. Of Moses it is said that he chose " rather to suffer affliction with the people of God, than to enjoy the *pleasures* of sin for a season " (Heb. xi. 25).

What man mocks at is the *remedy* for sin, the escape from it, which is the trespass offering. The Lord Jesus Christ Himself is that Trespass Offering. " . . . he that believeth not is condemned already, because he hath not believed in the Name of the only begotten Son of God " (John iii. 18). It is not one's attitude towards sin that brings life or death. It is one's attitude toward the Saviour. It is a matter of relationship. " But among the righteous there is favour." The word "favour" means "acceptance". So the fool rejects Christ and the righteous accept Him.

"*The fear of the Lord is a fountain of life, to depart from the snares of death*" (xiv. 27). How strange it is that so many people are under the impression that to fear the Lord, which means to hold Him in holy reverence, to recognise His worthiness and our own unworthiness (which, of course, reacts in a life of submission and obedience), is a life of limitation and frustration — " I cannot do this " and " I must not go there ". To such this life of limitation is a life of stagnation ; but, said the wise man, it is " a fountain of life ", an ever-bubbling, unending display of exuberance and freshness. Who is not fascinated by a fountain ? The Christian finds the love of God new every morning, the joy of the Lord an unending thing. His is a life that is Life indeed. He is not limited, he is full to overflowing. The thing that binds, limits, and holds as a prisoner, is the snare or the booby-trap, that leads to the death from which the believing soul has already escaped.

"*The fruit of the righteous is a tree of life . . .*" (xi. 30). This is going back to the first verse considered in this section and has the same thought of abundance. If the godless man produces any fruit at all it is the sour grape, the crab apple, the bitter herb, the wild gourd. The tree left on its own quickly returns to a wild nature. Cultivation is necessary for wholesome fruit. The life cultivated by the Spirit of God brings forth fruit in its season, love in the time of hate, joy in the season of despair, peace in the midst of war, long-suffering when everyone else is impatient, and all the rest of the lovely fruit of the Spirit.

"*The eyes of. the Lord are in every place, beholding the evil and the good*" (xv. 3). This is to remind us all that, whilst we may deceive our neighbours and also deceive ourselves, we cannot deceive God. We may seek to excuse ourselves or our friends because of some act, suggesting that it was a slip, or that it was unintentional, or that we were not responsible, but we cannot bring any excuse to Him. He sees not only the act but the thought. He knows the inner reasonings and motives of man's heart, good or bad. His eyes are everywhere ; they slumber not, neither do they sleep : and it will be before Him that we shall stand and be judged.

"*The ear that heareth the reproof of life abideth among the wise*" (xv. 31). Life itself is the greatest school of learning. The world is the greatest University for training if only we had eyes to see and ears to hear. Job once said : " But ask now the beasts, and they shall teach thee ; and the fowls of the air, and they shall tell thee : Or speak to the earth, and it shall teach thee ; and the fishes of the sea shall declare unto thee " (Job xii. 7-8). The New Testament says something similar — " Doth not even nature itself teach you that, if a man hath long hair, it is a shame unto him " (1 Corinthians xi. 14).

All nature declares the glory of God. It also speaks of the judgment of God, and wise is the man who will heed the voice, whether in the book of His Word or in the book of nature.

"*Commit thy works unto the Lord, and thy thoughts shall be established*" (xvi. 3). The Psalmist bids us commit our *way* unto the Lord, and the Preacher our *works*. When we learn to do this our worries and anxieties will be gone for our thoughts will be established. No more will they wander here and there, but will rest in the Lord. When our outward work and walk are right our inward emotions will be right also.

It is the same thought as was expressed by David. " Cast thy burden upon the Lord, and He shall sustain thee ; He shall never suffer the righteous to be moved " (Psalm lv. 22). The word " burden " does not mean our cares and worries. The margin of the Bible notates it as " what He hath assigned thee ".

"*A just weight and balance are the Lord's : all the weights of the bag are His work*" (xvi. 11). The Lord requires from every man absolute honesty. The reason that Solomon said that " all the weights of the bag are His work " was because God had required these things from the beginning. When God gave His laws to Moses for governing His people He said : " Ye shall do no unrighteousness in judgment, in meteyard, in weight, or in measure. Just balances, just weights, a just ephah, and a just hin, shall ye have : I am the Lord your God . . . " (Leviticus xix. 35-36). These things were repeated also in Deuteronomy.

God has ever protected the poor. Any who wrong them will know God's judgment. He sent Amos to the rulers who were oppressing His people with this message : " Hear this, O ye that swallow up the needy, even to make the poor of the land to fail, saying, When will the new moon be gone, that we may sell corn ?

and the Sabbath, that we may set forth wheat, making the ephah small, and the shekel great, and falsifying the balances by deceit ? That we may buy the poor for silver, and the needy for a pair of shoes ; yea, and sell the refuse of the wheat ? The Lord hath sworn by the excellency of Jacob. Surely, I will never forget any of their works " (Amos viii. 4-7). The Lord is requiring the same honesty to-day, in all of our business affairs in life.

" *The hoary head is a crown of glory, if it be found in the way of righteousness* " (xvi. 31). Is it not of interest to see God's concern for those who are so often neglected by a busy, pleasure-loving, selfish world ? The Lord has an interest in the poor, the widow, and the aged.

Young man, that grey hair which you scorn, that elderly person for whom you have no time, his hair is his glory. It speaks of maturity, of experience. This is the man whom you should take into your confidence. He has the advantage of experience, which is of great value and the young could profit therefrom.

Young people, you are instructed many times in the Scriptures to respect old age.

Old warrior, do not become discouraged when your energy begins to wane. God has given you blessings such as you never possessed in the days of your youth.

One word more, and this is important to old and young. The verse continues with, " IF it be found in the way of righteousness ". The man who grows old in the ways of sin is an object of shame.

" *A wicked man taketh a gift out of the bosom to pervert the ways of judgment* " (xvii. 23). The purse was carried inside the clothing, tucked into the girdle, hence the expression " out of the bosom ". It concerns bribery, or buying of favours. There are many warnings against this practice throughout the Proverbs. Only the wicked engage in these things. As there is a great deal of bribery in the commercial and the political world to-day, this is timely admonition to all young people.

" *The words of a man's mouth are as deep waters, and the wellspring of wisdom as a flowing brook* " (xviii. 4). This verse is naturally referring to the wise man. From him there comes a constant supply of wisdom, words that come from clear and deep thinking. Deep waters are never impoverished by what they give. They come from an endless source, yielding a constant supply. Paul gave a wonderful picture of this as it related to the Lord. " O the depth of the riches both of the wisdom and knowledge of God ! how unsearchable are His judgments, and His ways past finding out ! " (Romans xi. 33).

This deep source of supply creates the flowing brook, from which many a weary and despondent traveller may find refreshment.

The Lord make me such a man !

" The Name of the Lord is a strong tower ; the righteous runneth into it, and is safe " (xviii. 10). This is a Name which is above every name. One is reminded of the Cities of Refuge established for the manslayer, but not for the murderer. The latter killed with intent, the former might slay by accident, and for him there was a place to which he could run and find refuge from the avenger of blood. Satan is the great avenger — Jesus is the greater Refuge.

" Whoso findeth a wife findeth a good thing, and obtaineth favour of the Lord " (xviii. 22). Many of the older versions translate the verse as " Whoso findeth a good wife findeth a good thing ". This seems to make better sense. Solomon is reminding us that marriage is of the Lord, and that God had said : " It is not good for man to be alone ". Where would society be to-day if man were to be deprived of companionship in the home ? No club nor fraternity can ever take the place of home life, its love, and its sense of security. Truly, then, the happily married man has obtained the favour of the Lord.

" Wine is a mocker, strong drink is raging : and whosoever is deceived thereby is not wise " (xx. 1). To-day this liquefied deception is dressed up in smart clothes and popularised on every hand and by every means, but let the brewer dress it as he will, it is still a deceiver and in the end will do its deadly damage. Foolish is the person who begins to meddle with it.

" There is gold, and a multitude of rubies : but the lips of knowledge are a precious jewel " (xx. 15). What a greed there is for gold ! Man will go to any length to make money. Women will barter their lives and risk their honour for costly clothes and precious jewels. Some people buy precious stones as a security against an evil day, but the Word of God assures us that the lips of knowledge are of greater value. To give a troubled heart good counsel that will set its feet on a right path, is worth more than all the rubies and the diamonds of any rich person's collection.

" Train up a child in the way he should go : and when he is old, he will not depart from it " (xxii. 6). The literal rendering

of this statement is : " Train up a child according to his way ".
This is a moral issue rather than the spiritual one so often given.
Man is counselled to train his child according to its bent in life.
If that boy has the ability to be an engineer, or has longings for
the mission field, if he should desire to be a doctor, or the girl
has a passion for nursing, encourage them and train them according
to their own ways and desires, because any other course will be
waste of time, talent and money, for, when they are old enough
to go their own ways, they will not depart from their natural
inclinations.

" *Remove not the ancient landmark, which thy fathers have
set* " (xxii. 28). These landmarks existed between the plots of
land and could be removed easily (see note on Deuteronomy xix).
God has set up landmarks of truth within His Word, indications
of what belongs to us and what does not, signposts that would
guide the pilgrim along the path that leads to God. Man is warned
not to move these. To do so will bring the curse of God upon
the one who thereby robs another of his rights.

" *A good name is rather to be chosen than great riches, and
loving favour rather than silver and gold* " (xxii. 1). The good
name refers to character or reputation. These things will hold
good when other things fail.

" *Buy the truth, and sell it not ; also wisdom, and instruction,
and understanding* " (xxiii. 23). Truth is one of the important
things we must have in this world of deception. Acquire it whatever it may cost. Buy it with study, patience, labour, research.
Then, having obtained it, by no means part with it. The world
is in desperate need of guidance and instruction.

" *My son, give Me thine heart, and let thine eyes observe My
ways* " (xxiii. 26). This would not be the language of Solomon,
but that of the Lord. Amidst the snares, pitfalls, and dangers that
are enumerated in this book, there is but one safe course. It is
to surrender the heart to the Lord at His invitation and to obey
Him.

" *Look not upon the wine when it is red, when it giveth his
colour in the cup, when it moveth itself aright. At the last it
biteth like a serpent, and stingeth like an adder* " (xxiii. 31-32).
This is a warning not to be deceived by the colour, the smell, or
the sparkle of wine as it is poured into the glass. Good as it may
look, the poison of the serpent is there and ultimately will reveal
its deadly power.

" *My son, eat thou honey, because it is good ; and the honey-comb, which is sweet to thy taste* " (xxiv. 13). Honey is a nutritious food at any time. It is especially so, and extra sweet, when in the comb. How often is the Word of God referred to as honey, and that Word is both good and sweet to those who know the relationship of sonship — " My son ".

" *Be not thou one of them that strike hands, or of them that are sureties for debts. If thou hast nothing to pay, why should he take away thy bed from under thee ?* " (xxii. 26-27). Striking the palms of the hands together has been substituted by a practice to-day of shaking hands as an act of agreement, or a pledge. We are not expected to stand as guarantors for other people's debts and commitments, especially if the other person is a stranger or a man of the world. If the guarantor has no assurance of the person's ability to carry out his own contract, nor yet any proof of his honour, he may stand to be the fool who will lose everything. " He that is surety for a stranger shall smart for it ; and he that hateth suretyship is sure." (xi. 15). In brief, have no partnership with the world.

" *Pride goeth before destruction, and an haughty spirit before a fall* " (xvi. 18). This has become a Proverb known to all. May we add to it — " God resisteth the proud, and giveth grace to the humble " (1 Peter v. 5), and again, " Though the Lord be high, yet hath He respect unto the lowly ; but the proud He knoweth afar off " (Psalm cxxxviii. 6).

" *A froward man soweth strife ; and a whisperer separateth chief friends* " (xvi. 28). A whisperer seldom has anything good to say ; that is why he whispers it. His information is often damaging to another person's character. Not infrequently is the whisperer's information second-hand and somewhat removed from fact. The act of whispering also creates suspicion which can dissolve close friendships ; therefore, avoid such a practice.

" *I went by the field of the slothful . . . and considered it well . . . sleep . . . slumber . . . sleep . . . so shall thy poverty come* " (Read xxiv. 30-34). These are verses that would lend to much enlargement. The application would be of the man who was blessed with a wonderful inheritance but by his lazy, indolent, and indifferent spirit, he allowed his field to deteriorate and to become an unprofitable field of weeds, with a broken-down wall that would permit the stranger and the wild beast to wander in and destroy. God has given to man a spiritual inheritance, a soul and a life to cultivate, that it might bring forth fruit to His glory, but

many have neglected this privilege. Indolence and indifference towards the Bible, and towards prayer-life, have permitted the weeds and tangles of this world's pleasures to flourish. The walls of conviction have tumbled until *anything* is allowed to come into such a man's life; remember, not because of open rebellion against God, but because of indifference, a lack of diligence, " a little sleep, a little slumber, a little folding of the hands to sleep ".
So end the Proverbs of Solomon.

(3)   MAXIMS AND OBSERVATIONS (Chs. xxv-xxxi.)

There were three sources from which these came — the men of Hezekiah, Agur, and Lemuel. The first five chapters are still the wisdom of Solomon, but they were sought out later by wise men who were instructed so to do by king Hezekiah.

" *He that tilleth his land shall have plenty of bread ; but he that followeth after vain persons shall have poverty enough* " (xxviii. 19). This verse can be used in connection with, and in contrast to, the slothful man considered in Proverbs xxiv.

" *As cold waters to a thirsty soul, so is good news from a far country* " (xxv. 25). The real value and refreshment of cold spring water is only known by those who have experienced the hot arid desert ; and only those who have loved ones in the far-off places of the earth, where they are physically out of reach, know the relief of mind which comes through correspondence. Likewise those who become most conscious of the barrenness of this world, its empty frivolity and its waywardness, are those who more fully enjoy the sense of God's presence and the beauty of His Word.

" *As he that bindeth a stone in a sling, so is he that giveth honour to a fool* " (xxvi. 8). A sling has but one use, and that is to propel a stone. If the stone be bound to the sling that it cannot come out, the purpose of the sling is destroyed Thus honour, prestige, wisdom, or any other worthy quality, is destroyed if given to a foolish man.

" *Boast not thyself of to-morrow ; for thou knowest not what a day may bring forth* " (xxvii. 1). This should remind us of a fact that we are always forgetting — our times are in His hands. We only possess the present moment of time ; therefore, we must spend it wisely and never leave until to-morrow that which can be done to-day.

" *A word fitly spoken is like apples of gold in pictures of silver* " (xxv. 11). It has been suggested that this verse may have

reference to some beautiful work of art, of some coloured fruit
built into a silver bowl of filigree work, but a better picture might
be seen from the fact that apples do not grow in Palestine, neither
are apples golden. The " apple " of the Bible refers to the orange.
Palestine is a citrus country and its oranges are well known. One
season's fruit still hangs on the trees when the blossom of the
following spring breaks forth. To see oranges hanging in the
midst of a surround of orange blossom is a sight to behold, as
well as a scent to enjoy. A word spoken at the right time is something just as beautiful.

" *Whoso keepeth the fig tree shall eat the fruit thereof ; so he
that waiteth on his master shall be honoured* " (xxvii. 18). The
thought is simple. In every walk of life the man who is faithful
in service is the man who will be truly rewarded.

" *The lambs are for clothing, and the goats are the price of the
field* " (xxvii. 26). God in His economy has made provision for
man's need in the wonderful world of nature which is all around
us.

THE WORDS OF AGUR (Ch. xxx.)

It is not known who Agur was, for there is no intimation
in the Scriptures. The style of the writing in this one chapter is
different from the rest of the book, which gives no confirmation
of the idea in the Talmud that it was but another name for Solomon.

In the opening verse he claimed his unworthiness. Then he
made an enquiry about God in vs. 4. He was stating that all
creation gives evidence that there is a God, but where is He ?
What is His Name ? What is His Son's Name ? These questions
are answered in the New Testament. There is a revelation of God
that the men of the Old Testament never knew.

Then he requested a normal life, not too much lest he lose
his faith in God, not too little lest he sin and take the Name of the
Lord in vain. Many of us would desire to pray such a prayer.

After a few more Proverbs we are brought to a section which
is so different. There is a series of quadruplets, each one demanding consideration.

(1) *Four detestable things* (vs. 11-14) They are called generations,
but the statement means classes or companies of people. They
are :

>   People who curse their parents.
>   People who are defiled.

People who are proud.
People who are greedy.

(2) *Four insatiable things* (vs. 15-16)   Things that are never satisfied :

The grave that ever receives and never gives.
The barren womb that cries " Give me children or I die ".
The earth, that receives the rain.
The fire, that saith not, " It is enough ".

(3) *Four inscrutable things* (vs. 18-20)   Things that never leave a footprint nor a mark behind them to evidence that they have ever passed that way :

An eagle in the air.
A serpent on the rock.
A ship in the sea.
A man with a maid.

The following lines give this suggestion :

" As a ship passing through the billowy water,
Whereof, when it is gone by, there is no trace to be found,
Neither pathway of its keel in the billows :
Or as when a bird flieth through the air,
No token of her passage is found.
But the light wind, lashed with the stroke of her pinions,
And rent asunder with the violent rush of the moving
         wings, is passed through,
And afterwards no sign of her coming is found therein."

(4) *Four intolerable things* (vs. 21-23)   These are unbearable because they are out of their right relationship or environment :

A servant when he reigneth.
A fool when he is filled (or prosperous).
An odious (hated) woman when she is married.
An handmaid that is heir to her mistress.

(5) *Four masterful things* (vs. 24-28)   Although they are little and weak, by their wisdom they overcome their limitations :

Ants that prepare their meat in the summer.
Conies that build their houses in the rocks.
Locusts that go about in bands.
Spiders that are in kings' palaces.

(6) *Four stately things* (vs. 29-31)   Majestic as they move forward in their goings :

> A lion, the king of beasts.
> A greyhound or war-horse in its harness.
> An he-goat which will lead a flock of sheep.
> A king to whom all men bow.

THE WORDS OF LEMUEL (Ch. xxxi.)

We are not told who Lemuel was. That he was a king is clearly stated, and as no king can be found of that name in the records of history, it is thought that the name may have belonged to Solomon. At any rate, the information which he gives comes to him from his mother, and what good advice for any mother to give to her children ! Avoid wine and women (evil women), and mete out justice to the poor and needy.

The book closes with that beautiful eulogy on the virtuous woman. What a contrast after all the warnings and admonitions concerning the strange woman with all of her evil ways !

" Whoso findeth a wife findeth a good thing, and obtaineth favour of the Lord " (xviii. 22). This is the description of that woman of virtue, industry and wisdom, the woman who is the faithful wife and the unfailing mother.

God help us all to follow her example, so that our children may rise up in the generations to come and call us blessed.

ECCLESIASTES

THE BOOK OF VANITY

*" Remember now thy Creator in the days of thy youth, while
the evil days come not, nor the years draw nigh, when thou
shalt say, I have no pleasure in them."* (ECCLESIASTES xii. 1)

INTRODUCTION

There is some difficulty in arriving at this word Ecclesiastes.
It has been thought to mean " The Preacher " because of the
opening words of the text, " The words of the Preacher ". This,
however, came from Martin Luther and the German translation.

In the Hebrew the word is " Qoheleth ", which comes from
the verb that means " to gather " or " to assemble ". In the
Greek there is a similar word which is known as " ecclesia " and
is recognisable with Ecclesiastes. It means a " called out people ",
hence the name of the Church, Ecclesia. From this scholars have
come to accept the word " debator ". The author, Solomon, the
son of David, is debating with the assembly the problem of life.

In chronological order this book should come before the book
of Proverbs. As has already been stated, the closing verses of
Ecclesiastes are an introduction to the book of Proverbs. To get
this order correctly is to understand better what is undoubtedly
a difficult book.

There are those who feel that the book is not entitled to a
place in the Holy Scriptures, that its teaching is not in harmony
with the rest of the Bible. On a casual reading, such a statement
might appear true, but on a careful reading, trying not to see the
book as a unit but rather as part of a unity, then its relationship
begins to make sense, and again one learns that " all Scripture is
given by inspiration of God, and is profitable ", including
Ecclesiastes.

The problem is that whilst the Bible is a book which is
quickening and life-giving, a book of hope and of anticipation,
Ecclesiastes is a book of despair and hopelessness. Life appears
to be a series of disillusionments and disappointments, nothing is
worthwhile.

Then, too, when it comes to the moral standards of life, this
book would seem to be contradictory. It says that man should

317

have a good time, enjoy all that this world offers, walk in the ways of his own heart, and in the sight of his own eyes. Let passions be the controlling factor of life. God is not in this picture !

If this were true, then, of course, it would not have a place in the Canon of the Bible. However, the fact is that such an interpretation is not true.

What, then, is the approach to this book, or what was

THE PURPOSE OF THE BOOK ?

The key phrase is " under the sun ", which is quoted twenty-nine times. Solomon, a man of time and means, set out in this book of Ecclesiastes to discover " What profit hath a man of all his labour which he taketh under the sun " ? The result of his search was vanity and vexation of spirit. " Under the sun " is on this earth and refers to earthly things and to the carnal nature. From human standards everything was failure. Having discovered this much, instead of giving up in despair, Solomon turned from the earthly sphere to that which is *above* the sun, the realm of the heavenly. The book of Proverbs is the " from-above-the-sun " point of view. By reading these two books in this order and from their respective viewpoints, and then making the comparison, most of the problems are gone, whilst Ecclesiastes reveals its own purpose as part of the inspired Word of God.

This word " vanity ", which is repeated thirty-six times throughout the book, is a word that means " nothingness ", or that which soon vanishes away. That was the name given by Eve to her second son — Abel, or Vanity. The second child had come to her in the same manner as the first, and these two children, with all who should succeed them, were here but for a short time and then would flee away. The other meaning of the name Abel is " meadow " and that takes our minds to the words of Moses in Psalm xc., who, when speaking of man, said : " . . . In the morning they are like grass which groweth up. In the morning it flourisheth and groweth up ; in the evening it is cut down, and withereth " (vs. 5 - 6) — vanity or nothingness.

In chapter one the Preacher made a threefold statement :
   " And I gave my heart to seek and search out " (vs. 13).
   " I communed with my own heart " (vs. 16).
   " And I gave my heart to know wisdom " (vs. 17).
He did not seek Divine revelation, or spiritual discernment. He studied human affairs as such, man in his pursuits, in his labours, in his pleasures ; ever reaching, never attaining ; ever seeking satisfaction, never finding it ; always looking for the new, ever

finding it old. He was occupied with earthly things, or man apart from God, everything that was material, and it all proved to be vanity and vexation of spirit.

You want to see man without God ? Just read this book. You want to understand this book ? Just look out into the world and there it is — VANITY.

It has been stated that the book of Ecclesiastes has no Divine authority because the Name of Jehovah does not appear therein, but there is reason for the omission. The Name Jehovah is associated with a " covenant relationship ", and that is a truth which is missing in this book. The writer was " under the sun ", where man was seeking to reason out the values of a life that was independent of God. Relationship was not being recognised. Therefore it is the name Elohim, which is the name of the Creative God, which appears every time.

The philosophical teachings of man to-day are to the effect that everyone becomes his own god. On the contrary Ecclesiastes, in giving a true picture of man, shows that, instead of man establishing his own salvation, actually he becomes a victim of his own circumstances.

What this book declares is known to be true from the practical life of the man of the world as he is seen to-day.

He seeks pleasure, but never seems to find it.

He longs for joy, but it never comes his way.

He looks for satisfaction, but it flees from him.

He reaches after the permanent, but it ever evades him.

So he continues to struggle after the illusive goal, but never reaches it because it is all vanity and vexation of spirit.

The question is asked therefore : Is there a moral issue to this book of Ecclesiastes ? And the answer is — yes ! Is there a spiritual application within its pages ? Again the answer is — yes !

This disappointing future of everything that is under the sun should cause a man to enquire as to whether there is anything above the sun that could meet his needs, satisfy his longings, and end this frustration.

Whether man likes to admit it or not, deep down in his thinkings and his emotions there is a knowledge and a longing for the things that are not of this world. His reason for pushing aside outwardly these thoughts is because he wants to get the best out of this world and, at the same time, he hopes inwardly for something better in the next world. In other words, man is wanting

the best out of both worlds and, in so doing, is losing the best
from either world — surely, this is vexation.

This thought is derived from a statement gleaned from the
Pocket Bible Handbook by H. H. Halley, from which the following
quotation is taken :

"*Eternity* (R.V.) iii. 11 (a more correct translation than A.V.
'world'), may suggest the key-thought of the book. The word
in Hebrew occurs seven times. i. 4, 10 ; ii. 16 ; iii. 11, 14 ; ix. 6 ;
xii. 5 variously translated 'forever', 'of old', 'long', 'everlasting'. God has set ETERNITY in the hearts of men. In the
inmost depths of his nature man has a longing for things eternal,
which nothing earthly can satisfy."

"Let us hear the conclusion of the whole matter : Fear God,
and keep His commandments : for this is the whole duty of man.
For God shall bring every work into judgment, with every secret
thing, whether it be good, or whether it be evil " (xii. 13-14).

THE THEME OF THE BOOK

This is threefold. It is DECLARED in chapter one,
DEVELOPED in chapters two to eleven, and DECIDED in chapter
twelve.

(1) DECLARED (Ch. i.)   " Vanity of vanities ; all is vanity "
was his first declaration, and this he said because everything around
him was the monotony of repetition.   In human nature it is one
generation after another, the child, the youth, the man, then old
age.   Unceasingly man has come and gone.   In the world of nature
the same principles are seen, spring, summer, autumn, and then
the winter of old age, and thus the years come and go.

With the sun, it rises every morning in the East and sets every
evening in the West, only to do the same thing again to-morrow.

Solomon considered the wind, to find that it moves in certain
circuits.   When he thought of the waters it is the same continuous,
unchanging circle.   The rain descends from heaven.   It waters
the earth, the waters find their way to the rivers, and the rivers
flow into the sea.   The process of evaporation draws the waters
back into the clouds to do the same thing all over again.

Our eyes see the same things day after day, and our ears hear
the same sounds, but we go on looking and hearing, yet are never
satisfied.   If we were, then maybe we would desire blindness or
deafness, but it is not so.

In relationship to the foregoing, Solomon said : " There is
no new thing under the sun."   This is a statement which is difficult

for most people to understand. Few enough were the inventions in Solomon's time, yet even in our own time there remains a great amount of truth in such an utterance. In the world of fashions there is a constant swing to and fro, whilst in what are called new inventions, a great deal is only placing old things in new relationships to give improved conditions. Solomon was thinking of the fundamental things of life, not just little gadgets, when he said : " Is there anything whereof it may be said, See, this is new ? It hath been already of old time, which was before us " (i. 10).

If an example may be used to illustrate the point, it would be the car. Solomon did not know such a thing, but here the principle is that of MOTION. He had a chariot, which was his form of transportation. Who invented the wheel, which is the fundamental thing to most forms of transportation ? Back in the book of Genesis Joseph sent the wagons to bring down his father into Egypt. So the wheel for transportation was known then, but man keeps on improving upon it.

The same applies to other scientific things such as radio, radar, atomic energy, etc. They are referred to as inventions. These things have ever been within the realms of nature. All that man has done is to discover their existence and then harness them for his use. A year or two ago they were called new. Now they are old.

In the last verse of chapter one Solomon made two statements that are as vivid to-day as can be. " For in much wisdom is much grief," which means that the more man discovers the less satisfied he becomes, and dissatisfaction is always a grief. Man to-day has discovered speed. Is he satisfied ? No ! He must have more speed, and more speed. He climbs into the atmosphere, then into the stratosphere, up into the ionosphere. Satisfied ? No ! He must have the moon.

Man has legs, he wants a bicycle. He has a bicycle, he wants a car. He has a car, he wants a larger one. He has a larger one, he wants an aeroplane. This is vanity and vexation.

He has a house, he wants a better one.
He has a home, he wants it modernised.
He has a camera, he wants colour.
He has colour, he wants movies.
He has movies, he wants sound.
He has a wife, he wants another man's wife.
He has a job, he wants a different one.
He has money, he wants more.

Can you find a man who is satisfied ? Never, whilst his neighbour has something better than he has. He is full of vexation of spirit. Was the Preacher right? A thousand times so; for, although man has moved a long way up the social scale since Solomon's day, he is still a very dissatisfied person. It must be confessed, therefore, " vanity of vanities; all is vanity."

(2) DEVELOPMENT (Chs. ii-xi.)

In developing this matter no one had more opportunity or greater ability than Solomon, for he was not only the wisest man and, therefore, able to discern, but he was also the wealthiest man and, therefore, he had the means whereby he could try everything and so speak from practical experience.

His wealth permitted him to build houses and plant vineyards, to gather servants and to make friends, to collect treasures and to enjoy pleasure, but, at the end, they all failed him, so that he found himself no better off than other men. Like them he must die and, after death, what would happen to all that he had collected, laboured for, or built, in his wisdom? The man who succeeded him might be a fool and destroy all that he had gained. This, too, is vanity.

How true to life as it is found in this generation! People have given money, and preachers have laboured and built strong Evangelical Churches in the past. They have instructed men in holy things and have established worthy causes, only to be followed by foolish men who have brought such work to ruin.

Businessmen have established great companies, statesmen have built up nations, men have built up assets — fools have destroyed in months that which took years of struggle and sacrifice.

In chapter three the Preacher turned from his own experiences to generalities, and here again man appears to be the victim of the circumstances of life over which he has no control. It is a monotony of doing and undoing that gets man nowhere. He is born to die. He labours to no end. He builds to pull down. He gets to lose. He weeps to-day, and laughs to-morrow. Now he loves, but he will soon be despising the very same thing.

God has set bounds beyond which man cannot pass.

God has set seasons that man cannot violate.

What can man do in this restless, ever-changing, never-satisfying, world? Just one thing — enjoy himself, eat and drink, and make the best of it. This is the reasoning of man to this very day, and it will always be the same.

THEN comes a statement from the lips of the " man under the sun ". " . . . God shall judge the righteous and the wicked "

(iii. 16-17). There has come to his mind a sense of justice on the part of God amidst all the injustices of the world, but, instead of pursuing this thought, like the man of the world he allowed it to flit away from him. Scared of any conviction, he fell back to the musings of his own heart. This would suggest a very important truth. Within the experience of every man there comes some revelation of God, some conviction of the Spirit, some opportunity for man to consider spiritual things. There are those who state that all men do not get an opportunity to be saved. Would it not be safer to say that all men do not get the *same* opportunity? If the Lord would have all men to be saved, then all men must at least have an opportunity. None of us knows the movings of the Spirit within the minds and consciences of men. The trouble is, as in this verse, the conviction is quickly brushed aside, man refusing to follow up his conviction even though he may have searched out every other avenue.

The carnal conclusion is that man and beast, everything that breathes, have the same end. All go to one place, all return to dust. Man's reasoning here is one of annihilation. This is strengthened by the next verse which is sceptical. It is not a statement of fact, it is a question of doubt as to who knows whether the spirit of man goes upward, or the spirit of the beast whether it goes downward to the earth. No one has seen that spirit move, so, with an uncertainty of the future, why not enjoy the things of the present!

One can appreciate to some degree such reasoning back in Solomon's time, prior to the death and resurrection of Christ and the revelations of the New Testament. The tragedy is, how can so many people think in such terms in these days of Divine revelation and grace?

The Preacher in chapter four pursued another line of reasoning. He had considered possessions. They made for vanity. He had reviewed life in general. That made man a victim of circumstances. He now considered the tragedies that make this world a valley of tears for some.

There were the weak people who were oppressed by the strong, the rich people who were envied by their neighbours because of their possessions, and the miser who lived alone and had neither friend nor relation yet went on getting for himself with no intention of helping another.

The popular young man, who to-day is surrounded by his hero-worshippers, is forgotten in the next generation.

The Preacher, still reasoning from a material level, tried to reason out from these things a balance between the prosperous with his possessions and the sluggard without a friend, and said : " Better is an handful with quietness, than both the hands full with travail and vexation of spirit " (iv. 5).

The fool is not only to be found in the business world and the world of society, but he is also to be found in the Church. He is the man who speaks before he thinks and then tries to withdraw from the situation in which he has become involved. It is because the fool acts that way that he is looked upon as the picture of instability and unreliability. These people may be found in the House of the Lord, but the Lord has ever made it clear that He will not tolerate such characters.

The fool, we have said, speaks first and thinks afterwards. That is why chapter five, verse 1 says : " Be more ready to hear than to give the sacrifice of fools " — the man who is rash with his mouth. This is dealing with the matter of vows, or promises, made under oath, either in the Name of God or in the name of something which cannot be performed (to use a common example, " I will eat my hat "). God binds men to vows, as Jacob, Jephthah, and others, when they said : " Lord, if You will do this, then I will do that." If one makes such a vow to God then it is offering the sacrifice of fools. If we would be wise we would weigh our words firstly, assuring ourselves of our ability to fulfil them, and then, probably, we would never make the promise. It is God's requirement in Old and New Testament alike. "When thou vowest a vow unto God, defer not to pay it ; for He hath no pleasure in fools : *pay that which thou hast vowed.* Better is it that thou shouldest not vow, than that thou shouldest vow and not pay " (v. 4-5). Compare this with Leviticus v. 4 : " . . . If a soul swear, pronouncing with his lips to do evil, or to do good, whatsoever it be that a man shall pronounce with an oath, and it be hid from him ; when he knoweth of it, then he shall be guilty in one of these."

The next verse states that one cannot be excused by saying that it was an error.

The latter part of this chapter deals with a number of things which need individual consideration, but such cannot be given in this Digest. One thing must be considered, however, and that is that, although we may see many injustices in the world, whilst we should be concerned about them in the interest of the wronged people, yet we must not be disturbed in our spiritual balance, remembering that God is not overlooking these things, for He,

Who is higher than all, is witnessing them now and will deal with all wrongs presently.

Some contradictions of life occupy chapter six. Solomon was not the only one to observe such injustices, for we still puzzle over what we call the irony of life when these conditions should be warning us not to lay up treasure here, not to count on this world. The disappointments of this world should only make us long the more for the world to come where perplexities will be unknown.

The contradictions, or the irony of life, were in such matters as the man who has wealth and not health. He has all for which his soul longs, but lacks that which his body demands. He lacks the power to eat, or knows not the sweetness of sleep. He has the things that money can buy and yet is deprived of the things that money can never buy.

Another complaint is that a man may have prosperity but not posterity, for, seemingly, he has no children, man's greatest inheritance, so that a stranger eateth of his prosperity.

The next man has a large family but he has no friends (vs. 3). It is not what one *has* but what one *is* that matters. A man may have largeness of family and length of days, such as may exceed all others, but, if his soul has been empty throughout his days, he will die with no one wanting him, no mourning hearts will follow him to his resting place, no one will remember him in the generations to come. So miserable is the end of that man that it had been better if he were never born.

In vs. 9 there is a man who loses the known in seeking the unknown, the man who has not learned that a bird in the hand is worth two in the bush, or of the dog who snapped at his reflection in the water but lost the bone that was in his mouth. As the Preacher expressed it here, it is better to have and enjoy what you see, than to have a desire that wanders after every imagination and so goes through life with no substance.

Life is only a shadow to all of these characters, dark and mysterious, and the reason is that, in seeking to live a life according to earthly standards and desires, man is turning his back upon light and upon the One Who said : " I am the Light of the world. He that followeth Me shall not walk in darkness but shall have the Light of Life " (John viii. 12).

The quest for satisfaction changes again at chapter seven. He had pursued the material life only to find that it was empty, worthless, monotonous, and vanity. Then he turned to the world of morals for satisfaction. He travelled a path that moralists and philosophers still traverse to-day. In brief it is — Be good, get a good name, avoid the house of feasting, consider the serious things of life. Get wisdom and avoid folly. Be a patriotic citizen, and a good social neighbour. These morals will make for a reasonable life. Do not be too good, nor too sinful, avoid excess, strike a happy medium, use your common sense. Is not this the natural man to-day ? Is not this the teaching of modern thought ?

Remember, these statements are not the revelation of God. These are the considerations of a man who is communing with his own heart, thinking his own thoughts and coming to his own conclusions. His verdict at the end of this chapter is that, whilst God has made man upright, many inventions (the introductions of the human mind) have altered the course of things.

In chapter eight he continued to follow the way of morality and wisdom. He sought to see the good that is in man but it did not bring him to any Utopia. Instead, he was in another blind alley. He still did not know that which shall be. Therefore he turned from wisdom to try mirth (vs. 15), but he had been there previously. This was not the first time he had said " . . . A man hath no better thing under the sun than to eat, and to drink, and to be merry ; . . . " or, in other words, make the most of this life because the ways of God are past finding out.

In the light, or should one say in the darkness, of investigations, as he had discovered life with all of its frustrations and vexations, Solomon sought to move from the past to the future and, in so doing, to assess the future by the past. His future, like his past, was remaining under the sun. The result was that he made some very big mistakes, but, again, we need to remind ourselves that man's carnal heart, with his human philosophy and his rejection of the spiritual, is reasoning in the same way to-day. It is that, irrespective of man's life, whether it be good or bad, there is but one common end for all — the grave.

Life has never been a respecter of persons. Sorrow and troubles overtake good and bad alike. Godly living brings no immunity from the tragedies of life, so the future will be the same — one common end. The righteous and the wicked, the clean and the unclean, the swearer and the refrainer, will lie together. This, of course, is true if he were referring to the body, the physical part of man, but he is not. He is referring to the moral and spiritual, and, in so doing, he is right in saying : " This is an evil among all things that are done under the sun, that there is one event unto all . . . they go to the dead " (ix. 3), which suggests that the greatest evil of all evils is death, but he is wrong in his verdict.

This reasoning acknowledges no future life. Death is the end of all. He considered that moral man was no better off than immoral beasts. He declared that " the dead know not anything, neither have they any more a reward ; for the memory of them is forgotten . . . " (ix. 5), " . . . there is no work, nor device, nor knowledge, nor wisdom, in the grave, whither thou goest " (ix. 10). This is what is referred to by some as soul sleep and by others as annihilation. To such, the grave is the end, but we know that there is a life which is beyond the grave and that, in that life, there is knowledge, there is reward, there is memory, and there the injustices of this life will be rectified. We know, too, that there is distinction between the righteous and the unrighteous, between the clean and the unclean, and between the swearer and the refrainer.

Fortunately this statement of despair is disproved at the end of the book, when the Preacher's eyes were lifted above the sun.

Because the searcher could only see what was in this life and had no conception of a life to come, and seeing that to him the grave was the consummation and there was no future loss or gain, there was but one logical conclusion — have a good time while you can. " Live joyfully with the wife whom thou lovest all the days of the life of thy vanity," (ix. 9), and whatever you want to do, do it with energy, delight, and self-satisfaction, because, if you do not enjoy life now, you cannot at any other time.

There is a lesson in this verse for those who know the truth, and who know the relationship of this life in time with that life which is in eternity. It is that this life is short, and its rewards are in eternity — therefore, " Whatsoever thy hand findeth to do, do it with thy might " (vs. 10).

Solomon's next reflection of life was its uncertainty. Man, with all of his power and importance, was not the controller of the affairs of life. Control was evidently somewhere else. Life is made up of times and seasons. If certain conditions coincide all is well. If they do not, so that the thing, although thoroughly done, is wrong in its timing or out of season, then there is failure. This made life to be a chance. It is like that to-day. One can make a perfect plan and do everything possible for its fulfilment, but if that plan coincides with a labour strike, a storm, a change in market values, a war, or a thousand other things that could happen, then there is unexpected gain, or hopeless loss. It was not the opportune time or season. This is what is meant by : " . . . the race is not to the swift, nor the battle to the strong, neither yet bread to the wise, nor yet riches to men of understanding, nor yet favour to men of skill ; but time and chance happeneth to them all " (ix. 11). Nothing is sure in this life. That is why we need to rise above the sun, and have a hope, " Which hope we have as an anchor of the soul, both sure and steadfast, and which entereth into that within the veil " (Hebrews vi. 19). Because nothing is sure here, therefore, " . . . brethren, give diligence to make your calling and election *sure :* for if ye do these things, ye shall never fall : " (2 Peter i. 10).

One further evil is considered in this self-righteous world, the sin of ingratitude. A poor man, in his wisdom, was able to out-manoeuvre a strong and powerful king, and thereby save a city. Yet no one remembered that same poor man.

Amidst the noise of war, the turmoil of the battlefields, the explosions of shell and bomb, and the shouts of victory, people forget the accomplishments of the council chamber where wisdom has done more than warheads. In this age of science, when newspapers ever report on the achievements of scientists, they never remember the miracles of the Book of Wisdom — the Bible, and the Gospel which has transformed men and nations.

Chapter ten is a list of comparisons between Wisdom and Folly which cannot be detailed here.

In chapter eleven the Preacher was beginning to reach a conclusion. Earlier he thought that life was made up of mere chance ; now he is speaking of purpose. The well-known verse : " Cast thy bread upon the waters : for thou shalt find it after many days " (xi. 1), refers to the casting of the rice seed upon the undulating land around the river Nile. In time the land dried, the crops grew, and the harvest therefrom became the mainstay of the life of the Egyptians. He then declared that what a man sows he reaps. The clouds gather and empty themselves without man's interference. The child is formed in the womb, but man cannot say how. In seed sowing we do not withhold our hand because we do not know which shall prosper, this or that.

He was confessing that there must be a Divine ordering somewhere, for so much is beyond man's thinking or control, and yet it is controlled.

When he began to recognise a Supreme Controller of the affairs of life, then the gloom began to disappear, and the tragedies began to lessen, so that in vs. 7 he was testifying : " Truly the light is sweet, and a pleasant thing it is for the eyes to behold the sun." At last he had the upward look !

The chapter concludes with two BUTS. In the light of all that has been considered, enjoy life here, BUT remember the days of darkness for they shall be many (vs. 8), or remember, death comes at the end. From this it is evident that he has accepted a life beyond the grave.

"Rejoice, O young man, in thy youth, and let thy heart cheer thee in the days of thy youth, and walk in the ways of thine heart, and in the sight of thine eyes : BUT know thou, that for all these things God will bring thee into judgment" (vs. 9).

The final chapter is the summing up. The theme has been declared and developed — now it is

DECIDED (Ch. xii.)

"Remember now thy Creator in the days of thy youth . . ." Seeing that everything under the sun is vanity, seeing that the increase of days brings an increase of sorrow, seeing that the end is the way of death — the decision is to get one's eyes off those things which are under the sun and focus them on to the Creator Who is above the sun, and to do it early, not in the days of old age when one's powers become latent and the joy of living has gone.

The concluding verses give a vivid picture of old age, when the body has worn out and the organs are failing in their respective functions. There are variations in some of the interpretations but in the main principle they remain the same.

We must yield our all to the Lord whilst we have our all, whilst the sunshine of joy and the radiance of living are ours. The day will come in the winter of life when we shall say : "I have no pleasure in them." It will be a day when :

"The keepers of the house shall tremble"	The arms, which are ever our defence.
"The strong men shall bow themselves"	The legs, which bend under the weight of years.
"The grinders cease because they are few"	The teeth, which decay and are removed.
"Those that look out of the windows be darkened"	The eyes, with their failing sight.
"The doors shall be shut in the streets"	The ears, that no longer pick up familiar sounds.
"He shall rise up at the voice of the bird"	Not because he can hear. It is sleeplessness.
"They shall be afraid of that which is high"	Fear, everything is out of reach and a trouble.
"The almond tree shall flourish"	Silver hair. Although the almond is pink it turns white when it falls.

" The grasshopper shall be a burden "	The least little thing becomes a burden.
" Desire shall fail " (" Desire " in the Vulgate and in the margin is caper-berry)	It was used as a stimulant to appetite, but the appetite has gone.
" Man goeth to his long home " or " To the house of his eternity "	This refers to the grave, the home of the body.
" The silver cord be loosed "	The spinal cord, or the cord of life.
" The golden bowl be broken "	Refers to the brain, the source of all action.
" The pitcher be broken at the fountain "	The heart, the fountain of life.
" The wheel broken at the cistern "	The circulatory system of the blood stream.

" Then shall the dust return to the earth as it was, and the spirit shall return unto God Who gave it."

There is a future life, there is a beyond, so " Let us hear the conclusion of the whole matter: Fear God, and keep His commandments : for this is the whole duty of man. For God shall bring every work into judgment, with every secret thing, whether it be good, or whether it be evil."

SONG OF SOLOMON

WOOED AND WON

" Behold, what manner of love the Father hath bestowed upon us, that we should be called the sons of God : therefore the world knoweth us not, because it knew Him not. Beloved, now are we the sons of God, and it doth not yet appear what we shall be ; but we know that, when He shall appear, we shall be like Him ; for we shall see Him as He is."

(1 JOHN iii. 1-2)

INTRODUCTION

This is a book which is little read because of its difficulties both in structure and language. As to the latter some people refuse to read it because they consider it to be vulgar and tending toward the immoral. This will be considered later.

Whilst from the analytical viewpoint it has to be admitted that it is one of the most difficult books to handle, yet from the devotional side it is one of the most delightful meditations.

The biggest problem is interpretation because there is a strong difference of opinion among the scholars as to how many characters there are in the story ; also there is disagreement as to whether it is a consecutive dialogue or a series of separate songs. Our best teachers are to be found in both schools of thought.

The problem is a serious one because, if there were in fact two characters, and it is suggested there were three, or if there were actually three characters and only two are seen, then words could be put into wrong lips, which means that the Word of God is not being rightly divided.

The school that suggests there were three characters points out a Shulamite girl who was espoused to a shepherd lover. Solomon, the king, fell in love with this girl and carried her away to Jerusalem and the shepherd followed. Whilst Solomon used every means within his power to win the girl's affection with flattering words and bountiful gifts and promises, she remained steadfast to her shepherd friend, so that eventually Solomon had to yield to defeat.

The other school of interpretation sees only the Shulamite girl and her royal lover who, at one time, disguised himself as a shepherd.

Each person has to make his own decision, but the interpretation given here will concern only two characters. The eternal triangle, with its sordid story, has broken up too many homes and has ruined too many families to be introduced into the Word of God.

Two most delightful books on this subject are :

Union and Communion, by Hudson Taylor.

Song of Solomon, by Dr. Harry Ironside.

Dr. H. Ironside, who was a master of Bible interpretation, paints a beautiful background to the whole book. This is how he tells THE STORY. Solomon had a great deal of property which had to be cared for by various agents. This property included some land and a vineyard right up in the north country in Ephraim, which he let out to vineyard keepers (viii. 11). The vineyard keeper could have been the brother of the Shulamite girl. This family comprised of at least a brother and two sisters, for there is reference to these. The question arises as to whether the brother and sister relationship was a perfect one, for the suggestion is made that she was only a half sister, inasmuch as the girl on one occasion said : " My mother's children (Hebrew — my mother's sons) were angry with me " (i. 6). She did not say : " My brothers," so they could have been the children of her mother but not of her father. Would this account for the hard life that seems to have been inflicted on this girl, for she is made to work very hard ?

It was her mother's children who were angry with her. They made her the keeper of the vineyards and, among other duties, she tended the vines and trapped the little foxes. Not only so but she had to take care of the sheep. The brother kept her so busy that she had no time for herself as is seen when one day, while she was out with the sheep, she became conscious that someone was nearby. Turning, she saw a stranger, a shepherd, who was looking at her. Immediately she bade him depart. Why should he stand thus staring at her ? Owing to her hard life she knew she was untidy and unkempt. She was aware, too, that her skin was dark and sunburnt due to being always out in the fields and the vineyards, so why should this man stand gazing on her ? She excused her appearance by the fact that so much of her time was occupied in her brother's vineyards that she had not had time to take care of her own vineyard, this referring to her own personal appearance.

As a result of this introduction, abrupt though it was, conversation developed. The stranger assured her that he had not noticed any untidy appearance. He had not even noticed the sun-tan as something detrimental. He had been admiring her beauty, her grace and charm. The conversation continued until he began to make overtures of love. He had fallen in love with her and was asking for a reciprocation. If she would love him, if she would pledge her loyalty and faithfulness, whilst he could not tarry longer just now, he would come back for her and they could be united in wedlock. The bond was established and a betrothal had begun.

With excitement, the despised, hard-working girl, who had never known previous attention, went home to tell the family that she had met a young man and they had fallen in love, but the family was not very encouraging. That was how men talked, it must not be taken seriously, she would never see him again. She left the family to go and tell her friends and neighbours, but their reactions were no more encouraging. She must not become excited. How could she know that he would ever come back. Men were like ships that pass in the night, they are here to-day but are gone to-morrow, and maybe by now he was saying the same things to some other girl somewhere else.

Despite all of the discouragement she still believed him. They had not met him. They did not know him. She had met him and talked with him — and believed him.

So much of the book, therefore, is the musing of a girl toward her absent lover. She thought about him during the day : " My beloved is like a roe or a young hart." She dreamed about him at night: " By night on my bed I sought him whom my soul loveth " (iii. 1). Sometimes her heart would beat with excitement at the thought of his return. Sometimes she wondered whether it were true — would he return or were her friends right ? So the passions of her heart rose and fell, as they do with all lovers.

After a long delay the day arrived when there was great excitement in the village. News came that a royal procession was moving through the countryside. The king's outriders had been seen, and the procession was moving toward this village. Excitement ran high, the flags were put out, everyone was breathless ! Then the king's advance guard entered the village and began to enquire as to where this damsel lived. Calling at the house they bade the girl prepare herself for an audience with the king. The natural response from the girl would have been : " No, no ! You have come to the wrong house. I am not the person you want. I am only a vinedresser and a shepherdess. It is a mistake." But the king's couriers would only have replied that they had their instructions and they must be obeyed. The king arrived, the chariot halted outside the house, and the maiden was led out for her presentation. As she moved forward and had her first glimpse of the king, she hesitated. She looked again, and with even more bewilderment she exclaimed : " But—but—you are that shepherd. You are the one who met me in the fields and told me that you loved me and that you would come back for me." She is filled with panic. Quietly and graciously the king replied : " Yes ! That is right, but I am the king. Then I was in disguise as a shepherd. Now I have come to fulfil my promise and to take you to myself." Then, to the amazement of the onlookers, the Shulamite was lifted into the chariot and they were gone.

Is not that a delightful story ? But let it be told again in application.

Jesus left heaven's glory and stepped down into this world of woe disguised as the Good Shepherd. He approached mankind in all his unworthiness and guilt, and began to make overtures of love. He demonstrated its reality at Calvary, and then asked for our love and loyalty. He told mankind that He must go away but that He would come back and receive us unto Himself. Having fallen in love with the Lover of our souls we told our kindred and our friends of His wondrous salvation. We told them He is coming back again, but they looked on, smiled, and sought to discourage us in our faith. Nonetheless, we believe and await the coming of our absent Lover. In this time of waiting sometimes our love and devotion are very real, sometimes we almost hear the footfall of His coming, and sometimes we are discouraged, disheartened, and our love lags. The day is coming, however — oh, glorious day ! — when the outriders shall be heard, the voice of the arch-angel and the trump of God, and He, Who came disguised as a Shepherd, will come in the fulness of His revelation, riding upon the chariot of the clouds. He will come King of kings and Lord of lords and, out of an astonished world, the despised Church shall be caught up to be united in wedlock, to be forever with the Lord.

Could a story be more beautiful ? Could an application be more perfect ?

In the light of this background re-read this wonderful Song of Solomon.

THE GENDERS

As to deciding whether there were two or three characters, one guiding factor can be the masculine and feminine genders. We will give these as they appear in the Hebrew. It is suggested that these be marked in the margin of your Bible. They will prove very helpful. Use the marks F., M., D. of J., and THE PEOPLE, as notated here.

The first verse is introduction.

Feminine	Masculine	The People	Daughters of
i. 2- 7	i. 8-11		Jerusalem
i. 12-13	i. 14-17		
ii. 1	ii. 2		
ii. 3- 6	ii. 7		
ii. 8-13	ii. 14		
ii. 15-iii. 4	iii. 5	iii. 6-11	
	iv. 1-15		
iv. 16B	v. 1		
v. 2- 8			
v. 10-16			v. 9
vi. 2- 3	vi. 4-vii. 7, 9		vi. 1
vii. 10-viii. 3	viii. 4		viii. 5A
viii. 5B-8	viii. 9		
viii. 10-12	viii. 13		
viii. 14			

There are two exceptions to be noted :—

(1) The first half of iv. 16 should be a query. Scholars are not sure as to who uttered those words.

(2) In ii. 7 ; iii. 5 ; and viii. 4, where the same words are repeated, in each instance it is the man who speaks, thus making it masculine, but the utterance is in the neuter gender, as is marked in the margin of your Bible, and so reads : " that ye stir not up nor awake love, till it please."

APPLICATION

Here is a story that can readily be applied to several different subjects. It may be taken

Literally.	The love of man and woman.
Dispensationally.	Jehovah God and Israel.
Doctrinally.	Christ and His Church.
Spiritually.	The Lord and the individual soul.

In all probability the Song was inspired with God and His relationship to Israel in mind, but for our personal profit and enlightenment the last two applications are combined.

ANTICIPATION (Ch. i. 1 - iii. 5)

Throughout the book it must be borne in mind that the Easterner is profuse in flowery language, so that what appears unnatural and even unbecoming to us would be perfectly natural to the Palestinian. Therefore, in reading remember " Unto the pure all things are pure ; but unto them that are defiled and unbelieving is nothing pure ; " (Titus i. 15).

The Shulamite spoke first and told how he was her

SOUL'S SATISFACTION. The figurative language of this book may be translated in this way : " For thy love is better than wine." According to man's judgment, wine is that which exhilarates, drives away cares, and gives him a " lift." Is this not true concerning the love of Jesus ? When life presses heavily meditate upon His great love, and it will lift us out of our cares, exhilarate our soul, and cause our troubles to become as " light afflictions."

In verse 3 : " Thy name is as ointment poured forth." As Mary's broken box of ointment filled the whole place with a beautiful fragrance that all could enjoy, so does the Name of Jesus.

> " How sweet the Name of Jesus sounds
> In a believer's ear ;
> It soothes his sorrows, heals his wounds,
> And drives away his fear."

> " Precious Name, O, how sweet ! "

In that time of her communion with the shepherd when they first met she asked him where he fed his flock, and where he caused them to rest in the heat of the day. His answer was not a direct one, but it was sufficient. He told her that, seeing she was a shepherdess and led flock, she ought to know. If not, all she had to do was to follow in the footsteps of the flock. Nathanael once said to Philip : " Can any good thing come out of Nazareth ? " ; to which he received the reply : " Come and see " (John i. 46). That would be an answer to many of our questions and problems to-day — just follow where He leads.

COMMUNION was enjoyed as they found themselves in each other's company. (i. 16-17). The lovers, in the place of meeting, with their hearts still aglow, would suggest that there was nothing in the world which attracted them. The city, with its dazzling sights and its tempting sounds, had no place for them. They were out in the midst of God's handiwork. Their green bed or couch referred to the grassy meadows in which they sat, whilst the cedar tree and the fir tree which spread their boughs above them, giving them shade from the hot sun, became their house. This explains Ch. i. 16-17 : " Behold, thou art fair, my beloved, yea, pleasant: also our bed is green. The beams of our house are cedar, and our rafters of fir." They were completely contented in their love for each other and their communion with each other. They were satisfied. Oh, that we might know such communion with the Lord that we could sing : " Take the world, but give me Jesus." Listening to their conversation, which expresses

HER DESIRES, one can see the importance of the genders, and placing the right words on to the lips of the right person. There are hymns and choruses that tell us that He is the Rose of Sharon and the Lily of the Valley, and from these sentiments preachers have found many sermons. But the statement of chapter ii. 1 : " I am the rose of Sharon and the lily of the valleys " is in the feminine gender, which means it was said by the Shulamite girl. Decidedly this changes the picture. No wonder Paul told Timothy to rightly divide the Word of Truth !

As the two continued to sit on their grassy couch and he poured upon her his affections and assured her that nothing else in the world was worth while, she began to feel her unworthiness of such affection, so, looking at the wild flowers growing around them, flowers which are profuse in Palestine, she picked out two of the common kind and said, in effect : " Do you see that rose of Sharon and those wild anemones ? They are so numerous and become so common that people trample them underfoot without a thought, and I am no more than those wild flowers. I am just common stock. No one before has ever interested himself in me. Yea, I am unworthy."

Our mind has ever gone to a beautiful little flower that grows in this country, called the lily of the valley ; but the Bible does not refer to such a flower. The statement is : " The lily of the valleys," the flower which grew all over the valleys which run between the mountains of Palestine, and, in all probability, the anemone, as common and as despised as the dandelion is with us. It is a picture of humiliation. It is the attitude that the child of God should take in the presence of the Lord, for we are so unworthy of His love.

In response to this humility he replied that she might be as a lily, but " as the lily among thorns, so is my love among the daughters," meaning to say that if she were no more than a wild flower, then there were many other things which grew wild that were not beautiful. The other people around were like the thorns. They were content with their sin and satisfied with themselves. There was neither grace nor love in their hearts.

Her humility of soul having been accepted by him, she spoke again and told him that he was as the apple tree among the trees

of the wood. This referred to the orange tree, for Palestine is a
citrus country. The girl then turned her thoughts from herself
to her lover, and from things beneath her to that which was around.
She looked upon the many trees, all of which could be ornamental,
but one of which was fruitful. To this tree she likened her lover.
He was different from all others in that he was fruit-bearing, one
could satisfy the soul with his refreshing fruit.

Is this not true concerning our Lord ? Cannot we sit quietly
under the shadow of His protecting grace, enjoy the fruit of His
love, and find ourselves in the banqueting chamber of His all-
sufficiency ?

The Shepherd spoke again in verse 14 : "O my dove, that
art in the clefts of the rock, in the secret places of the stairs ; let
me see thy countenance, let me hear thy voice ; for sweet is thy
voice, and thy countenance is lovely." These would be parting
words when they separated, as we would say in our day : " Let
me hear from you. Write me a letter." So he asked for some
communication. Jesus has gone, but He makes a request to His
loved ones that they find their way into the secret place of communion, into the stronghold of prayer. He desires to see their
countenance, reading His Word, and to hear their voice, talking
to Him in prayer. It is something in which He will find great
delight.

In reply she assured him that she did not want anything to
come and rob them of this new love, this intimacy which was
theirs. Then, thinking of her tasks in the vineyard to which she
must return until he came back for her, she remembered that one
of her responsibilities was to set traps in the springtime to catch
the little foxes which would take the blossom. The loss of blossom
would be the loss of fruit. These little foxes would speak of sin.
May we suggest the names of some of these little foxes, those that
would rob us of the fruit of the Spirit of Galatians v. 22-23 ? :

> Fear spoils Love.
> Hatred destroys Joy.
> War banishes Peace.
> Impatience ruins Longsuffering.
> Hardness removes Gentleness.
> Evil takes away Goodness.
> Doubt nips off Faith.
> Pride dispels Meekness.
> Passion kills Temperance.

In the last verse of the chapter she was longing for that day
to break when the shadows of espousal would give way to the

glories of holy wedlock, when they should be one. Her anticipation was for the day when he, who had temporarily gone, would be able to turn back upon the mountains and come for her. Ours is the longing soul waiting for the absent Lover as we cry : " O Lord Jesus, how long, how long ere we shout the glad song, Christ returneth ! "

As already noted in the early part of chapter three, she was dreaming about him. She had not only lost him but had a sense of loss that caused her to act until she found him. Only a dream, but dreams are sometimes caused by disturbed minds. A sense of distance in the heart of a believer will always bring a sense of darkness and night to the soul until the fellowship is renewed.

MANIFESTATION

In our opening story we told of the arrival of the king in his royal chariot. We meet this scene in the latter half of chapter three.

At verse 6 the procession was seen, and the people were enquiring as to why the king was coming in such pomp. Sixty valiant men surrounded the chariot as a great guard of honour. Each had a sword, so that they were also a body-guard. The chariot was magnificent, built of cedar and ornamented with silver and gold, with a canopy of purple. Fragrant were the perfumes which exuded from it. It is evident that this was more than a royal cavalcade. It was also bridal, hence the words in verse 10: " the midst thereof being paved with love ", but . . . where was the bride ? A wedding is always the bride's day. Everyone is interested in her, and seeks to add to the joys of her day. In the East she would be conveyed under a great canopy, but here it is the king who occupied the chariot. In fact, the bride is not mentioned in this chapter, although inferred.

In the heavenly marriage it is the Bridegroom Who is predominant. It is the Lord Who comes. It is the marriage of the Lamb, and the marriage supper of the Lamb. The church, the bride, is second on that glorious day.

The picture now changes as the lovers are seen

UNITED

As stated in the introduction, there is a question as to whether the book is a series of separate songs or a continuous dialogue. The book suggests lack of continuity, especially when we find a separation after marriage which cannot possibly belong to the spiritual. The wedding would be the consummation, after which there could be a reviewing of the past. Where these breaks come is the problem ! Whilst one could be here at chapter four, yet somehow there is continuity of thought.

Among the Syrians and others, after the marriage there comes the singing of the love-songs, when the bride becomes the centre of admiration and her qualities are praised. Could we not see this in chapter four ? She had become his wife and, therefore, he could sing her praises as he could not previously. The girl, who had once been full of blemish, dark-skinned, and hard-working, was now set forth by the bridegroom as one who was all fair. " There is no spot in thee." He detailed her beauty in a way that does not appeal to the Western mind but would be quite natural language to the people of the East.

What an unveiling of the Church of Jesus Christ as seen through the eyes of the Lord of that Church ! Here on earth it has been full of blemishes, failings, indifferences, coolness, lack of devotion, but now He is presenting it " to Himself a glorious church, not having spot, or wrinkle, or any such thing . . . holy and without blemish " (Ephesians v. 27).

This was God's eternal purpose. For this He created us and for this He died. Such a truth is declared in Ephesians i. 10-12. " That in the dispensation of the fulness of times He might gather together in one all things in Christ, both which are in heaven, and which are on earth ; even in Him : in Whom also we have obtained an inheritance, being predestinated according to the purpose of Him Who worketh all things after the counsel of His own will : That we should be to the praise of His glory, who first trusted in Christ." This is the Lord's greatest joy.

At chapter four, verse 8, we seem to come back from eternity to time, from the future to the present.

In the light of the glories that await the bride in that future home, it appears that there came a new call for separation from the life that is of this world. " Come with me from Lebanon, my spouse, with me from Lebanon : look from the top of Amana, from the top of Shenir, and Hermon." Come away from all of those high spots of the world, from all of those attractions and pleasures for, while they may be beautiful, they are also dangerous. In coming away from them, one is also coming away " from the lions' dens, from the mountains of the leopards." This is not your home, we seek one to come. His reason for calling her away from this world was because of his love for her.

The Lord is calling us away from this social world that we might find our fellowship with Him as surely as one day He will call us away from this physical world that we might enjoy His companionship, when we shall be with Him and like Him.

This is followed by a beautiful contrast as he likened his bride to a garden. Mountains are large and rugged. They are majestic in their grandeur and beautiful with their snowy peaks, for Mount Hermon is snow-capped the year round, but they lack friendliness and intimacy. These qualities belong to the garden, and more so to " the garden enclosed."

In the East, where the country is hot, dry, and dusty, gardens were enclosed, ofttimes by building the house on all four sides so that the garden became a central court. The eyes of the public never saw these beautiful gardens with their flowers, shrubs, and aromatic plants, nor the ponds that were usually in them. This was something that was precious and was for the owner's exclusive enjoyment.

Within such a garden there was often a spring. It was the spring which helped to make the garden. The walls or buildings might protect it from the cold winds and from the sand that blew, but still there cannot be a garden of fruits and flowers without water. Such a spring did not belong to the wayfaring man. He had no access to it. It was shut up *in* the garden and *for* the garden.

The Church is a garden of the Lord's planting. It is separate from the cold, bleak world outside. Man's soul is a garden. The man of the world grows the thorns of sin and the weeds of carelessness, selfishness, greed, hate, etc., but the soul of redeemed man is a garden, or should be, a place of rare delights. In it mature the exotic flowers and spices of the Lord's planting, an orchard of the fruit of the Spirit, the graces of Christian living, the virtues of soul devotion, peace, worship, humility, consecration, obedience, holiness — all of them watered by the Spirit of God.

This is what the Lord is seeking to develop in our lives, because this is what He is wanting to enjoy in the ages to come.

> " And every virtue we possess,
> And every victory won,
> And every thought of holiness
> Are His alone."

There has been an amount of reasoning as to who made the utterance in the first half of verse 16. " Awake, O north wind ; and come, thou south ; blow upon my garden, that the spices thereof may flow out." Some scholars think that it might be an invitation from one and some think it might have been a command of the other. She had a right to say MY garden. It was *her* soul. He had a right to say MY garden. It was *his* possession. Be that as it may, whilst the Church must come out from the world and be separate, whilst it is the peculiar treasure of the Lord, nonetheless the influences of the Church must flow out to refresh the souls of weary travellers. The radiance of our lives, the beauty of our characters, and the peace of God which rules our hearts, should influence the world for good. Sometimes the north wind of adversity and sometimes the south wind of responsibility are caused to blow, to bring these spices over the wall.

When she invited him into the garden (iv. 16) there was no delay in his response. " I am come into my garden, my sister, my spouse."

The One Who is more willing to forgive than we are to confess is also more willing to commune with us and to lead us than we are willing to allow.

SEPARATION, or should it be called Interrupted Communion ? How comforting are the words : " He knoweth our frame ; He remembereth that we are dust." (Psalm ciii. 14). In a devotion that was so intense and a love that was so loyal there came failure. Who of us has not come short in this respect ?

The bride is introduced in a sleepy condition, half asleep, half awake, neither hot nor cold. This is the insipid character of the Church in the last days. It is the thing which puts the Lord outside the Church, and it is the same thing that makes Him a stranger to the soul. He knocks for admission. Failure or faithlessness is never on the side of the Lord. She was too indifferent to rise, and began to make some feeble excuses. " I have put off my coat . . . I have washed my feet." Oh yes ! I love you but do not disturb me at this moment. I am resting ! !

Is this not the attitude of the child of God too often — " Lord, I want your love, I want your companionship. Yes, I want to serve Thee, but just at this moment I want my way. I am busy, or I am enjoying myself. Why must I talk about the things of the Lord at this moment ? "

My wife and I once stayed in a Christian Holiday Home in England. The suggestion was made that some of the guests might like to participate in the devotions at the breakfast table by reading the Scriptures. Out of the party of forty guests in a Christian Home, two had their Bibles with them on vacation. " Not just now, Lord. I am here for personal enjoyment." Is not that the tragic picture ?

The Lord does not retreat too quickly. He is One Who pleads, invites, encourages, so : "My Beloved put in his hand by the hole of the door." In the East the lock of the door is on the inside. Beside the lock is a hole large enough to put the hand through and reach for the key, but evidently no key was there. Therefore he had no access unless she arose to admit him, and this she failed to do. As a result he took his departure. It was then, when she saw her loss, that she arose to open, but it was too late, for he was gone.

How often do we find that through carelessness in our devotional life He withdraws Himself, and then, when we seek Him, we cannot find Him, and spiritual dearth comes into our experience. He hides His face from us until we seek Him with all our heart.

In her longing for Him she went out into the city. There the watchman and the keepers of the wall abused her. Our coldness toward the Lord is sure to bring misunderstanding from the world, and even persecution. The world does not like hypocrites.

Then she appealed to the daughters of Jerusalem, that they would help her to find him, but they had some questions to ask, for they were not able to interpret the passion that was now in her soul. Who is he? Why should he be different? Then she began to sing his praise and tell of his glory. This is always a healthy thing for the indifferent soul. It begins to generate a warmth of love that will drive out the coldness of indifference.

In chapter six verse 1 the daughters of Jerusalem spoke again : "If he were so wonderful,why did you let him go? How did you lose him? Where do you think he has gone?" Then she remembered the last words he spoke to her before this tragic night. He said : "I am come into my garden, my love, my spouse" (v. 1). That was where he was when she left him. She was seeking him without, when she should have been looking within — and immediately she found him.

RESTORED

So soon as they met he began to speak (vi. 4 - vii. 9), but, notice, there was no reproof, just love, as again he adored her beauty. The Lord is more willing to forgive than we are to confess. "Like as a father pitieth his children, so the Lord pitieth them that fear Him" (Psalm ciii. 13). His rejoicing in her continues right through to vii. 9. At verse 10 she was right back into her oneness and communion with him. "I am my beloved's and his desire is toward me."

There is a change here. In ii. 16 and vi. 3 it is " He is mine, I am his ", but now it is " I am my beloved's, and his desire is toward me." Everything is on his side now. She had lost confidence in herself. This is right relationship.

Her next remarks were :

" Let *us* go forth " (vi. 11).

" Let *us* lodge " (vi. 11).

" Let *us* get up early " (vi. 12).

" Let *us* see " (vi. 12).

She was going to remain very close to him in the future.

As they journeyed in each other's company, the daughters of Jerusalem saw their approach and asked : " Who is this that cometh up from the wilderness leaning upon her beloved ?" (viii. 5).

This is a question that should ever be on the lips of the world and on the lips of the carnal Christian :

" Who is this ? "	unknown. Christians should always be different from the world, different enough to cause questioning.
" That cometh up "	always an upward journey when we are in His company.
" From the wilderness " ...	This world is a barren place. Its desolation and death should always be behind us.
" Leaning "	a sense of her own inability. She leaned for strength and for guidance.
" Upon her beloved "	This is the rest of affection. This is a familiarity that brings content.

The bride was evidently not anxious to have that experience of separation again.   Therefore she said to him : " Set me as a seal upon thine heart, as a seal upon thine arm : for love is strong as death " (viii. 6).   She was asking for a signed contract that could not be broken.   We have the promise of the Lord : " Ye were sealed with the Holy Spirit of promise " (Ephesians i. 13).

As this delightful song draws to its conclusion, this girl, who had been so wonderfully privileged and throughout had ever been conscious of her unworthiness, allowed her mind to travel back to the old home, and she remembered her little sister. She made an appeal for her as she said : " We have a little sister, and she hath no breasts : what shall we do for our sister in the day when she shall be spoken for ? " (viii. 8).

In this verse we have one of those delicate subjects which has been beautifully handled by Dr. Ironside, who says : " No breasts " means " she is not grown up. As yet she is undeveloped." The inferences are that the girl had had privileges which had not been the lot of her little sister, and therefore she asked for his interest in her behalf. In the same figurative language of the book he replied in the affirmative, suggesting that if she would make known the need he would meet it.

Around the world on every hand can be seen undeveloped people, those who have not had the spiritual privileges which we are enjoying. We are no more worthy than they, but the Lord has seen fit to choose us and call us. Do we ever plead with Him in the behalf of others ?

The final utterance in the book came from the lips of the bride. " Make haste, my beloved, and be thou like to a roe or to a young hart upon the mountains of spices." May we turn this into New Testament language? " Come, Lord Jesus, come quickly." — the longing cry of the Church toward her absent Lord — the heart cry of every believer.

" Even so, come, Lord Jesus."

ISAIAH

THE SALVATION OF GOD

" Of which salvation the prophets have enquired and searched diligently, who prophesied of the grace that should come unto you : Searching what, or what manner of time the Spirit of Christ which was in them did signify, when it testified beforehand the sufferings of Christ, and the glory that should follow. Unto whom it was revealed, that not unto themselves, but unto us they did minister the things, which are now reported unto you by them that have preached the gospel unto you with the Holy Ghost sent down from heaven ; which things the angels desire to look into." (1 PETER i. 10-12)

INTRODUCTION

With this book we enter another section of the Scriptures — the Prophetical. Sixteen men ministered in the capacity of the Prophet. The term " Prophet " is wider in its scope than most people allow. It is usually considered that he is a man who foretells the future, but the term embraces to foretell and forthtell. More of their ministry belonged to the present and was *forthtelling,* than belonged to the future in *foretelling.* Whilst the other Prophets seemed to be limited to certain periods and events, Isaiah covered the whole future. His ministry was long — at least forty-one years, probably seventy years. He prophesied in the reigns of Uzziah, Jotham, Ahaz, and Hezekiah, according to his own testimony (i. 1), and in the reign of Manasseh according to tradition. Of these five kings, four were evil and only one good — hence the many denunciations.

All that is known about Isaiah's life is that he was the son of Amos (this was not the Prophet Amos). As to his death, tradition persists that he was sawn asunder by Manasseh. If this be true, then the reference in Hebrews xi. 37, concerning the heroes of faith, may be understood : " They were stoned, *sawn asunder,* were tempted, were slain with the sword."

Isaiah was devoted, earnest, and fearless throughout his ministry. He sought no court favour. He reproved kings, rebuked nobles, and chided the people for their rebellion. To one king he said : " . . . Is it a small thing for you to weary men, but will ye weary my God also ? " (vii. 13). To another he said : " . . . Set thine house in order: for thou shalt die, and not live " (xxxviii. 1). He charged the people with being " a sinful nation, ladened with iniquity," " evil doers," " a rebellious people," etc.

This does not mean that he and the other Prophets were hard, unemotional men ; it was usually quite the contrary. Some of the most outspoken men have been the most sensitive at heart. Their ministry has been very costly to themselves. It was true of Isaiah, of Jeremiah, and others ; with their sternness was sadness, with their severity, solace.

In introducing this book, the question is going to be asked — How many Isaiahs were there ? For two thousand five hundred years only one Isaiah was accepted. It was only about one hundred and seventy years ago that someone suggested that there might be a second author to the book. Critics followed the suggestion until they think they have found three ; and between one critic and another they have left Isaiah one quarter of the book which bears his name. Against all the theories of modern understanding, the first verse of the book itself says : " The vision of Isaiah the son of Amos . . . in the days of Uzziah, Jotham, Ahaz, and Hezekiah, kings of Judah," thereby recognising one Isaiah throughout. The New Testament quotes from this book twenty-one times and these quotations are taken from every section of the prophecy. Jesus quoted Isaiah without question. An example would be Matthew xii. 17-20 : " That it might be fulfilled which was spoken by Esaias the prophet, saying . . . A bruised reed shall He not break." This quotation is taken from chapter xlii., which is attributed to another author by the liberalists. Jesus said : " As spoken by Esaias *the* prophet."

Many are the appraisals of the literary qualities of this book. It has been commended for its beauty of poetry, grandeur of language, and mastery of expression, which make it rich in literary genius as well as forceful in Evangelical truth.

KEYWORD

This is " Salvation." The meaning of the name Isaiah is " The salvation of Jehovah." The message of salvation is through-out the book. Isaiah is full of prophecies concerning the coming of the Saviour, chapter liii. being the central gem of them all.

There are numerous symbols of salvation found in the book, such as :

THE MESSAGE

The main division of the book is twofold :

EVENTS PRIOR TO THE CAPTIVITY ..... Chapters i. - xxxix.

EVENTS BEYOND THE CAPTIVITY ..... Chapters xl. - lxvi.

The announcement of the Captivity is made in chapter xxxix. There is something very fascinating about the analysis of this book that has caused it to be referred to as the miniature Bible.

There are sixty-six chapters, equal to the sixty-six books of of the Bible. It has a twofold division of thirty-nine chapters and twenty-seven chapters, as mentioned above.

There are thirty-nine books in the Old Testament, and twenty-seven books in the New Testament.

The thirty-nine chapters are Prophetic, in harmony with the Old Testament.

The twenty-seven chapters are Messianic, balancing with the New Testament.

This parallel is true in broad outline. To what extent it can be developed in detail may be a question. It would certainly make an interesting study. However, some chapters can very definitely be harmonised.

The second book of the Bible is Exodus, with the account of Sinai and the giving of the Law.

The second chapter of Isaiah says : " . . . Come ye, and let us go up to the mountain of the Lord . . . for out of Zion shall go forth the law " (vs. 3).

The thirty-ninth book is Malachi and concerns the Captivity. Chapter thirty-nine of Isaiah deals with the Dispersion.

The fortieth book is Matthew, with the Gospel of Salvation for the Whosoever will. Chapter forty : " Comfort ye, comfort ye my people, saith your God . . . for her iniquities are pardoned." (vs. 1).

The sixty-sixth book is Revelation, with a new heaven and a new earth and a new Jerusalem (vs. 21 & 22).

In Isaiah, chapter sixty-six : " For as the new heavens and the new earth, which I will make, shall remain before Me" (vs. 22). " Rejoice ye with Jerusalem, and be glad with her, all ye that love her " (vs. 10).

A further analysis of the book would be thirty-five chapters Prophetic, five Historic (sometimes referred to as a parenthesis), and twenty-six Messianic.

To understand the book there must be an appreciation of the historical setting, much of which is to be found in the historical books of the Old Testament.

After the death of Solomon the nation had been split in twain, creating the kingdom of Israel (ten tribes), and the kingdom of Judah (two tribes). Israel had a series of evil kings, pulling the morals of the nation lower and lower. Idolatry had led them farther and farther away from God until His judgment had descended upon them and the kingdom of Israel was carried away by the Assyrians.

It was during this period of Israel's decline and fall that Isaiah was living and ministering to Judah at Jerusalem, beginning with the reign of good king Uzziah. Whilst this man was a good king he never ordered the removal of the sites of the idolatrous worship of past days. His son, Jotham, was more careless in this matter, so that idolatry crept back into the land whilst the king busied himself building cities and preparing for war in a time of peace ; but, when men turn away from God, He too prepares Himself for war. Thus it was that two heathen nations were competing for superiority, Assyria and Babylon. Babylon prevailed and was to become the menace to Judah. In the meantime Ahaz came to the throne. He was as wicked as any of the kings. As a punishment God sent the kings of Syria and Samaria against him. Instead of turning to God, Ahaz became politically involved with Assyria. The prophet reproved Ahaz for his move, but Ahaz would not accept the reproof or the sign that was offered to him, because he did not want to break the alliance he had made with Assyria.

In the days of Hezekiah, Sennacherib impoverished him and he, in turn, impoverished the Temple of God. The nation of Judah would have fallen then, and Jerusalem also, but for the intercession of Isaiah.

To quote from Halley's *Pocket Bible Handbook* : " For 150
years before the days of Isaiah the Assyrian Empire had been expanding, and absorbing neighbour nations. As early as 840 B.C.
Israel, under Jehu, had begun to pay tribute to Assyria. While
Isaiah was yet a young man, 734 B.C., Assyria carried away all
of north Israel. 13 years later (721), Samaria fell, and the rest of
Israel was carried away. Then, a few years later, the Assyrians
came on into Judah, destroyed 46 walled cities, and carried away
200,000 captives. Finally, 701 B.C., when Isaiah was an old man,
the Assyrians were stopped before the walls of Jerusalem, when
their army was routed by an angel of God. Thus, Isaiah's whole
life was spent under the shadow of the threatening Assyrian power,
and he himself witnessed the ruin of his entire nation at their hands,
except only Jerusalem."

EVENTS PRIOR TO THE CAPTIVITY (Chs. i-xxxix.)

PROPHETIC (Chs. i-xxxv.)

The Prophet was speaking to a people in pre-captivity circumstances. His message was one of reproof and warning. Following
one verse only of introduction, the Prophet, with a boldness inspired by love and a grandeur of language, moved straight into
his prophetic ministry, calling upon all creation to listen whilst
the Lord spoke.

God had a controversy with His people because of their ingratitude, which was less than that of the animal. " The ox
knoweth his owner, and the ass his master's crib : " (i. 3). An
animal knows a good master, and he knows from whence comes his
food and his shelter, but Israel did not know how to appreciate
their blessings. It was a nation as religious as it could be and yet
without a knowledge of God. Their sins had nullified their prayers
and offerings so that God loathed them. Whilst He hated their
practices, He loved the people as ever and appealed to them to
turn from their evil ways saying : " Come now, and let us reason
together . . . though your sins be as scarlet, they shall be as white
as snow " (i. 18).

Whilst in chapter one Isaiah pleaded, in chapter two he
prophesied, assuring them that, in the last days, God, according
to His grace and His promises, would establish the nation in peace,
causing swords to be turned into ploughshares and spears into
pruning hooks. There would come the day when people would
want to wend their way to Jerusalem because it would be established in peace. He contrasted the future glory with the present

gloom of sin and idolatry, and the pride and haughtiness of man which must be brought down.

The nation had fallen far from the glory it had enjoyed in the days of David and Solomon. The kingdom had been divided and it would fall even farther. During Isaiah's ministry, Israel was to become victim to the Assyrians and be carried away, and later, Judah too would suffer at their hands, and then in time they would be overwhelmed by the Babylonians who would carry them into exile. This would mean the termination of the throne. In spite of all these things, the prophet foretold a future day of blessing, when the Lord would wash away her filth and Jerusalem should be re-established (Ch. iv.). God would raise up a branch, or a sprout would come out of the stump of the family of David — a King to sit upon the throne of David. That King would be Jesus, great David's Greater Son, born in the city of David, hence He would be called " The Branch."

The next chapter is a parable. It concerns a vineyard for which the owner had done everything, sparing nothing, and yet the result had been tragic. It produced less than he had put into it. The question was asked as to what the owner should do. But what could he do more for the vineyard that he had not already done ? Nothing, except give it up, tear down the walls, and leave it a desolation.

The parable is followed with its interpretation. It was a picture of the nation's ingratitude. God had done for Israel and Judah everything it was possible to do, but, in return, they had rejected Him. Instead of producing fruit to His glory they were giving all they possessed to the enemy. Therefore God would have to deal with them accordingly.

The vision of chapter six has ever been a subject of interest. However, there are two schools of thought as to interpretation. The one believes this to be the initial call to the prophetic office ; the other that it was a renewed commission. In deciding the matter it must be noted that this vision was seen in the year that king Uzziah died, which would make the office immediately to follow that reign, but chapter one declares that his ministry was "*in* the days of Uzziah." There are five chapters of prophesying prior to this record.

Perhaps the key to the situation may be found in that it was in the year that a good king died after he had led a nation for fifty-two years. In these circumstances there would be a lot of anxious forebodings, but Isaiah was permitted to see another

King, One Who was not subjected to death, for he said : " Mine eyes have seen the King, the Lord of Hosts " (vs. 5). Until now the prophet had seen the nation. Hereafter he saw the King. The next chapter tells of that King's virgin birth. Chapter eight speaks " Of the increase of His government," and, as truth unfolds itself through the book, everything centres around the Messiah. the Anointed One.

At the sight of the glory of the Lord, Isaiah realised his own unworthiness and cried for cleansing. There was no hesitancy on the part of the Lord to meet that request. There never is ! With the cleansing there was no hesitancy on the part of Isaiah for service. There never should be ! It is one thing to know Jesus as Saviour, another to know Him as Lord.

We by-pass the sixteen years of the reign of Jotham to find Isaiah coming before Ahaz at the time when this wicked king, who was being attacked by Rezin and Pekah, was seeking an alliance with Assyria instead of seeking the aid of Jehovah. The Prophet assured the king that God was willing to intervene, and Jerusalem would not fall. God was offering to give Ahaz any sign he would like to ask as evidence, but the king refused the sign because he did not want to break his alliance with Assyria.

Lack of careful reading has led some men into wrong interpretation of this Scripture. God was giving a sign, and the sign concerned a virgin birth. The materialists seek to invalidate this sign by declaring that it could not refer to the birth of Jesus because Jesus was not born until seven hundred years later. This matter is dealt with under the heading of His incarnation on page 84.

Following this, and through to chapter twelve, is a picture that was not only immediate but one that was also prophetic. It concerned the attacks of Assyria which, at first, were successful against Israel, but finally failed through God's intervention. Assyria prophetically represents the enemies of God's people who, seemingly, succeed in their endeavours until the Messiah, He of Whose government and peace there shall be no end (ix. 7), comes forth to intervene, as a result of which a Kingdom of peace is established — the Millenial Kingdom of the last days as described in chapter eleven, when the wolf and the lamb shall lie down together, and a little child shall lead them. " In that day thou shalt say, O Lord, 1 will praise Thee ; though Thou wast angry with me, Thine anger is turned away, and Thou comfortedst me. Behold. God is my salvation " (xii. 1- 2).

THE BURDENS

Chapters xiii - xxiii. list ten of these " Burdens " or " oracles ". Up to this point, God, through His servant, had dealt with, firstly, Israel, and then Judah, revealing His justice and His mercy. Now He moved out to the Gentile nations around and dealt with them in judgment, Babylon, Philistia, Moab, Damascus, Egypt, the Desert of the Sea, Dumah, Arabia, the Valley of Vision, and Tyre. The only one that was not Gentile was the Valley of Vision, which referred to Jerusalem.

But Isaiah was not finished. From the surrounding nations he then moved out to the whole world (chapter xxiv.), as God would judge it because of sin, after which judgment He would bring Israel back into blessing, divine blessing in a millennial age because the time will have come when death has been destroyed. (xxv. 8).

In that day (xxvi. 1), which will be the Day of Jehovah, Israel will be singing a new song upon earth, whilst the saints will be singing a new song in heaven. Then she will be established a strong city, with walls, bulwarks, and gates, a city free from fear or war as the inhabitants sing : " Thou wilt keep him in perfect peace, whose mind is stayed on Thee: because he trusteth in Thee. Trust ye in the Lord for ever : for in the Lord JEHOVAH is everlasting strength " (xxvi. 3- 4).

Because of the ultimate blessing that is to be Israel's, there is an invitation in the latter part of the chapter (vs. 20) : " Come, my people, enter thou into thy chambers, and shut thy doors about thee : hide thyself as it were for a little moment, until the indignation be overpast," because the Lord is going to punish the earth. At a previous judgment of the earth God provided an Ark for Noah and his family and shut them within. Many scholars believe that God is going to use the ancient city of Petra in a similar way, and that such may be referred to here.

As for the Christian, he has the secret place of communion where he can shut himself away with the Lord in the hours of trial and trouble.

Isaiah, who had reached out to the uttermost parts of the earth and of time in declaring the Burdens, then came back home and pronounced five woes upon the nations of Israel and Judah in chapters xxviii-xxxiii.

(1) *Woe to the drunkards of Ephraim,* intoxicated with pride and self-esteem, which is only as a fading flower. It is here to-day.

To-morrow it is gone, and the place thereof is known no more. He compared their fading glory with His eternal glory.

(2) *Woe to Ariel,* meaning lion of God, and referring to Jerusalem, the place where David dwelt. Even though it may be a favoured city, the city of God's choosing, beautiful in situation and the joy of all the earth, yet, because of her sin, she must be punished. So he warned them of the great siege that was coming, and which is recorded in chapters xxxvi-xxxix. At verse 17 of chapter xxix he again showed that, in the midst of His anger, God would be merciful.

(3) *Woe to the rebellious.* In view of the warning of the previous chapter that Jerusalem would be besieged by the Assyrians, instead of repenting the people became more rebellious and turned to Egypt rather than to God for help. (The word " rebellious " is the same word as used in Deuteronomy xxi. 18 & 20 concerning the persistently disobedient son who had to be stoned to death). Isaiah then made known to them that the help which Egypt would give would be as a shadow, a useless thing, bringing them no help whatsoever.

Again, as in the previous woes, the chapter concludes with an offer of mercy if the people would repent.

(4) *Woe to them that go down to Egypt for help.* In chapter xxx. the rebuke is because they turned *from* God. In chapter xxxi. it is because they turned *to* Egypt. The nation is putting its trust in horses and in the arm of flesh. David had declared this to be futile. God revealed that flesh has no power whatever. Not only would the flesh of Egypt fail, but God would not use the flesh of Israel to destroy Egypt or Assyria but, " as birds flying, so will the Lord of hosts defend Jerusalem ; defending also He will deliver it ; and passing over He will preserve it " (vs. 5).

Some have interpreted this verse as aeroplanes flying over Jerusalem at the time of General Allenby's entry at the end of the first World War. That would be the arm of flesh again. The thought here is the same as the Lord used in the New Testament. It is the bird flying or hovering over its young to protect them from an enemy.

(5) *Woe to the spoiler.* The previous woes have concerned God's people. This one is against their enemy, Assyria. When the Assyrians have finished spoiling Judah, God is going to spoil them. So the Prophet cried to the Lord that He would be gracious.

In the next two chapters (xxxiv. & xxxv.), the Prophet was again carried away to the time of the end and was caused to see, not only Assyria and Egypt, but all the nations subdued by the Hand of the Lord, and the one-time suffering people of God becoming the people of blessing. The time had come when the desert would blossom as the rose, the mountains would display their glory, the weak would be strong, the suffering man would be delivered, the dry places would become places of refreshing, the way of holiness would be established, and nothing would exist to make man afraid — the Millennial Kingdom established.

With this the prophetic section of the book closes, and the next four chapters are

HISTORIC (Chs. xxxvi-xl.)

Again and again, throughout the reigns of Jothan and Ahaz, the Prophet had warned the people of coming judgment as a result of continued sin. Now there is the historical record of that siege of Jerusalem by Sennacherib in the days of Hezekiah. It is a repetition of the account given in 2 Kings xviii-xx. where it is related from Hezekiah's side, but now the historic side is put on record.

It is a grim story that need not be retold. The enemy sought to shake out of the people what little faith was left in Jehovah. Hezekiah sent to Isaiah and sought his intercession with God. God promised deliverance, not by the arm of flesh but by means of a rumour which would draw the enemy away from Jerusalem — and thus it was. The whole story of deliverance, and also of Hezekiah's restoration from the sickness that had brought him so near to death, is one that tells of the power of prayer.

There is now a complete change in the book. Thirty-nine chapters have been given to pre-captivity events, prophetical in nature and concerning Israel's arch-enemy, Assyria. The whole is in harmony with the Old Testament. The remaining twenty-seven chapters are

RELATIVE TO BEYOND THE CAPTIVITY (Chs. xl-lxvi.)
MESSIANIC (Chs. xli-lxvi.)

They relate to the great enemy, Babylon, and harmonise with the New Testament. After the Old Testament closes with the pronounced curses of Malachi, the New Testament opens with a message of salvation. So this section of Isaiah opens with "Comfort ye, comfort ye my people, saith your God. Speak ye comfortably to Jerusalem, and cry unto her, that her warfare is accomplished (all over), that her iniquity is pardoned (forgiven) : for she hath received of the Lord's hand double (" double " means *cancellation,* from an old custom of the East) for all her sins."

Chapter after chapter speaks of Christ, of redemption, and of salvation. The Messianic picture could possibly be summed up by understanding

ISAIAH'S VISION OF THE CHRIST

(1) THE EXALTED ONE. This would relate to the heavenly or the Divine side of the Messiah's life. Heaven is His throne and earth is His footstool.

Here He is as the One Who is supreme over all things. He is " the image of the invisible God, the firstborn of every creature: For by Him were all things created, that are in heaven, and that are in earth, visible and invisible, whether they be thrones, or dominions, or principalities, or powers : all things were created by Him, and for Him: And He is before all things, and by Him all things consist " (Colossians i. 15-17). To Him all angelic beings are subservient. Whilst cherubim and seraphim continually do cry " Holy, holy, holy," the creature on earth cries out " Woe is me, for I am a man of unclean lips."

When man has such an experience with God, when he can see the Lord's holiness and his own unworthiness, and humbly acknowledge it, then it is that man can be touched with a live coal and thus receive an enduement of power for an effective service.

How few of us know such an experience, and how few of us know such ministry !

This High and Lofty One Who filled heaven also occupied earth. He Who was the Son of God became the Son of Man, as He left His abode in the eternal, to minister in that sphere called Time.

(2) HIS INCARNATION

(a) *Birth* (vii. 14). " Behold, a virgin shall conceive, and bear a son, and shall call His Name Immanuel." This utterance was made seven hundred years before its fulfilment. Isaiah could not have made such a statement of himself. Man may reason as he will concerning the word " Almah," and whether or not it should be translated " virgin," if he wants to translate it " young woman " he can, but to what end ? The verse says : " Therefore the Lord Himself shall give you a sign." Seeing that young women conceive and bear children every day of the year, every hour of the day, and every minute of the hour, it is the natural course of life, so how could the common everyday affair become a sign to anyone ? To interpret one half of a sentence without any consideration of the other half of the sentence is surely foolishness, and produces error.

Some say that the sign was given to Ahaz and, therefore, had nothing to do with the birth of Jesus seven hundred years later. That is not true. The sign was not given to Ahaz. He had already refused to accept one. The sign was given to the nation in the words : " Hear ye now, O house of David . . . the Lord Himself shall give *you* a sign."

The prophecy states that Jesus should come, born of a virgin, and thus it was.

(b) *His Authority* (ix. 11-12). At a time when the nation was falling to Assyria and was walking in darkness, there would come a great light. " For unto us a child is born, unto us a son is given : and the government shall be upon His shoulder : and His Name shall be called Wonderful, Counsellor, the Mighty God, the Everlasting Father, the Prince of Peace. Of the increase of his government and peace there shall be no end, upon the throne of David, and upon His kingdom, to order it, and to establish it with judgment and with justice from henceforth even for ever. The zeal of the Lord of Hosts will perform this " (vs. 6-7). His Divine power is declared in His Names, His unending authority, His established throne and universal reign.

(c) *His Descent* (xi. 1). " And there shall come forth a rod out of the stem of Jesse, and a Branch shall grow out of his roots." This is linked with other prophecies possibly unknown to Isaiah. It lines up with facts as they are seen from other sources, that great David's Greater Son should be Messiah and Deliverer. Even though the direct line of ancestry might become obscure, or even an attempt to terminate it might be manifest, as in the destruction of all the seed royal (save one), or the ending of the throne as in the days of Zedekiah, followed by four hundred years of silence between the Old and New Testaments, yet " a Branch shall grow out of his roots." The tree might be cut down, but the old stock remains alive to sprout forth again.

(d) *His Enduement* (xi. 2-3). " And the Spirit of the Lord shall rest upon Him, the spirit of wisdom and understanding, the spirit of counsel and might, the spirit of knowledge and of the fear of the Lord ; and shall make Him of quick understanding in the fear of the Lord : and He shall not judge after the sight of His eyes, neither reprove after the hearing of His ears." Although He was the Son of God, yet He was endued with the Spirit of God and, when He commenced His public ministry, at the River Jordan He was anointed by the descent of the Holy Spirit.

Not only did Isaiah tell of the coming of the Messiah but he also revealed much concerning

(3) HIS MINISTRY

(a) *An Illuminator* (ix. 2) "The people that walk in darkness have seen a great light: they that dwell in the land of the shadow of death, upon them hath the light shined." This was declared by the prophet and fulfilled in Christ, Who said : " I am the Light of the world : he that followeth Me shall not walk in darkness, but shall have the light of life " (John viii. 12).

(b) *A Judge* (ii. 4) " And He shall judge among the nations, and shall rebuke many people : and they shall beat their swords into plowshares . . . " Under His righteous judgment peace will reign upon the earth.

Again in Ch. xi. 4 : " But with righteousness shall He judge the poor, and reprove with equity for the meek of the earth . . . " In Ch. xxxiii. 22 Isaiah says : " For the Lord is our Judge, the Lord is our lawgiver, the Lord is our King ; He will save us." As Judge He deals with the nations of the world, creating peace. He deals with the common people for their rights, and He governs the nations for their salvation.

(c) *A Reprover* (xi. 4) " And He shall smite the earth with the rod of His mouth, and with the breath of His lips shall He slay the wicked." The Psalmist also declares, " Thou shalt break them with a rod of iron " (Psalm ii. 9). It is not only man whom the Lord is going to punish, but also the Devil. " And then shall that Wicked be revealed whom the Lord shall consume with the spirit of His mouth, and shall destroy with the brightness of His coming " (2 Thessalonians ii. 8). His rod metes out justice for the righteous and judgment for the wicked.

(d) *An Intercessor* (liii. 12) " He made intercession for the transgressors." The chapter is dealing with the Cross, and it was there that the Lord fulfilled this statement as He said : " Father, forgive them ; for they know not what they do." That was in the most literal sense, but, more than that, the Blood that was shed upon that Cross has interceded for all sinners. Then, after the sinner becomes a saint, there comes His intercession at the Throne of Grace where, in the power of His resurrection life, He intercedes as the Great High Priest.

(e) *A Lawgiver* (xlii. 4) " He shall not fail nor be discouraged, till He have set judgment in the earth : and the isles shall wait for His law." " . . . He will magnify the law, and make it honourable " (vs. 21).

(f) *A Burden Bearer* (liii. 4) " Surely He hath borne our griefs, and carried our sorrows : " — not our sins only, but everything else. He bore our griefs that we might have relief. He bore our sorrows that we might have joy. He bore our stripes that we might be healed. He bore our chastisement that we might have peace. He bore it all — casting all our care upon Him !

> " *Bring Him thy sorrows, bring Him thy tears,*
> *Bring Him thy heartaches, bring Him thy fears.*
> *Go, tell Him plainly, just how you feel,*
> *Jesus will pardon, Jesus will heal.*"

He was more than a burden-bearer. Many people can help bear our burdens, but He was also

(g) *A Sin-bearer* (liii. 6) " . . . And the Lord hath laid on Him the iniquity of us all." " Whilst we were yet sinners Christ died for the ungodly." " Yet it pleased the Lord to bruise Him ; He hath put Him to grief : when Thou shalt make His soul an offering for sin " (vs. 10).

Remember, these are the prophetic declarations of Isaiah seven hundred years beforehand. The fulfilment is all found in the Gospel narrative of the New Testament.

(h) *A Liberator* (xlii. 7) " To open the blind eyes, to bring out the prisoners from the prison, and them that sit in darkness out of the prison house." We are rejoicing in that the Lord has done these very things for us. " Once I was blind, but now I can see, the Light of the world is Jesus. Once I was bound, but now I am free." " Stand fast, therefore, in the liberty wherewith Christ hath made us free, and be not entangled again with the yoke of bondage " (Galatians v. 1).

(4) HIS DEATH AND RESURRECTION

The Prophet is very detailed and very exact in his announcements concerning the sufferings of Christ, and yet he could not possibly have had any idea or appreciation of what it all meant. Here are great evidences that holy men wrote as they were moved by the Spirit of God, for Isaiah tells that He would be

(a) *Silent before His accusers* (liii. 7) " . . . as a sheep before
her shearers is dumb, so He openeth not His mouth." It could
be understood if someone were recording this *after* the incident,
but when we find it a prediction, how can man say that the Bible
is not a God-inspired Book ?

There was one moment when Jesus broke that silence. The
reason of this should be known. Many false accusations had been
made, to which Jesus had made no response. Caiaphas then challenged the Lord, but still no answer. When the High Priest could
get nowhere because of this silence, he remembered the Old Testament law which said : " And if a soul . . . hear the voice of swearing, and is a witness, whether he hath seen or known of it, if he do
not utter it, then he shall bear his iniquity " (Leviticus v. 1). This
swearing was that of an oath or adjuration (margin). Caiaphas
therefore took an oath as he said : " I *adjure* Thee by the Living
God, that Thou tell us whether Thou be the Christ, the Son of
God " (Matt. xxvi. 63). If at this juncture Jesus had remained
silent, according to the Levitical law He would have sinned. " Jesus
saith unto him, Thou hast said " and, in so saying, remained sinless.

(b) *Smitten and spit upon* (l. 6) " I gave my back to the
smiters, and my cheeks to them that plucked off the hair : I hid
not My face from shame and spitting." Compare this with Matt.
xxvii. 30 : " And when he had scourged Jesus (vs. 26) . . . they
spit upon Him . . . and smote Him on the head."

(c) *Bruised for our iniquities* (liii. 5) " He was wounded for
our transgressions, He was bruised for our iniquities . . . with His
stripes we are healed."

This was true in those sufferings immediately prior to His
being nailed to the Cross.

(d) *Died with the transgressors* (liii. 12) " And He was
numbered with the transgressors." Compare this prophetic statement with the historical record of Matthew xxvii. 38 : " Then
were there two thieves crucified with Him, one on the right hand,
and another on the left."

(e) *Buried with the rich* (liii. 9) " And He made His grave
with the wicked, and with the rich in His death : because He had
done no violence, neither was any deceit in His mouth." Matthew
records that " When the even was come, there came a rich man
of Arimathaea named Joseph, who also himself was Jesus' disciple:
He went to Pilate and begged the body of Jesus. Then Pilate commanded the body to be delivered. And when Joseph had taken
the body, he wrapped it in a clean linen cloth, and laid it in his

own new tomb, which he had hewn out in the rock . . . " (xxvii. 57-60).

It was customary for the bodies of criminals to be cast out into the valley. Isaiah therefore foretells the extraordinary thing — died with transgressors ; yet buried with the rich.

(f) *Resurrection* (xxv. 8) " He will swallow up death in victory ; and the Lord God will wipe away tears from off all faces." " He is not here for He is risen, as He said. Come, see the place where the Lord lay . . . And they departed quickly from the sepulchre with fear and great joy . . . " (Matt. xxviii. 6/8). The tears were wiped away !

(5) HIS FUTURE REIGN

Many are the references to that eternal dominion where He shall reign for ever and ever.

(xl. 22-23) " It is He that sitteth upon the circle of the earth, and the inhabitants thereof are as grasshoppers ; that stretcheth out the heavens as a curtain, and spreadeth them out as a tent to dwell in. That bringeth the princes to nothing ; He maketh the judges of the earth as vanity."

(lxv. 17) " For, behold, I create new heavens and a new earth : and the former shall not be remembered, nor come into mind."

(lxvi. 1) " Thus saith the Lord, The heaven is My Throne, and the earth is My footstool."

(lxvi. 22) " For as the new heavens and the new earth, which I will make, shall remain before Me, saith the Lord, so shall your seed and your name remain."

The book closes, as does the Bible, with a new heaven and a new earth and all flesh worshipping the Lord, whilst the rejector has been cast out into fire that shall never be quenched, and to an existence where his worm shall never die.

Then let us rejoice that " Behold, the Lord's hand is not shortened, that it cannot save ; neither His ear heavy, that it cannot hear " (lix. 1)

JEREMIAH

CERTAIN JUDGMENT *v.* ETERNAL LOVE

*" O house of Israel, cannot I do with you as this potter? saith
the Lord. Behold, as the clay is in the potter's hand, so are
ye in Mine hand, O house of Israel. At what instant I shall
speak concerning a nation, and concerning a kingdom, to
pluck up, and to pull down, and to destroy it : If that nation,
against whom I have pronounced turn from their evil, I will
repent of the evil that I thought to do unto them. And at
what instant I shall speak concerning a nation, and concerning
a kingdom, to build and to plant it ; if it do evil in My sight,
that it obey not My voice, then I will repent of the good,
wherewith I said I would benefit them."*

(JEREMIAH xviii. 6-10)

INTRODUCTION

Some years must have elapsed between the ministries of Isaiah
and Jeremiah, for Isaiah stated that his ministry was during the
reigns of Uzziah, Jotham, Ahaz, and Hezekiah, and Jeremiah made
known that he began " . . . in the days of Josiah the son of Amon
king of Judah, in the thirteenth year of his reign " (i. 2).

In between these mentioned reigns there were the evil reigns
of Manasseh for fifty-five years and Amon for two years. No
prophet seems to have ministered during those fifty-seven years
and the first thirteen years of Josiah. Josiah was only eight
years old when he came to the throne and so, at the beginning,
would have little influence for changing conditions even though he
himself was good. Therefore some seventy years of sin and backsliding intervened between these two major Prophets.

It was during the reign of good king Josiah that the nation
witnessed something of a revival, but, like so many revivals since,
seemingly it lacked depth and reality for, whilst there was a great
deal of outward profession, there was little inward change of heart,
for the people had continued in their idolatries.

After the death of Josiah there was a period of confusion.
The kings who followed were all of them weak. They struggled
against the strength of Egypt but with no avail ; then against
Babylon, until they finally succumbed and were carried away into
Babylonia. It was during these forty troublous years that Jeremiah
prophesied.

At that particular time in world history three nations were
seeking world supremacy — Assyria, Egypt, and Babylon. Assyria
had already subdued Israel but since then had weakened considerably. Whilst Babylon was proving herself stronger than Egypt,
it was obvious, even apart from any revelation from God to
Jeremiah, that Babylon had that passion for conquest which seems
to intoxicate so many nations. Judah also would fall victim to that
nation. As God's chosen people they need not, because He is
able to deliver, and ultimately He would deliver — that is *God's
Eternal Love.* Against this, however, Judah was a rebellious
people ,who had turned from God to idols — here *God's Certain
Judgment* operates.

This is the substance of the book of Jeremiah.

The fall of Jerusalem, as foretold by Jeremiah, proved to be
a very painful and wearisome thing for Judah, for not only were
they stubborn with God and with Jeremiah, who bade them yield
to Babylon, but they were also stubborn in their resistance.
Jerusalem was partly destroyed in 606 B.C. It was devastated
in 597 B.C., and finally overthrown and destroyed by fire in 586
B.C., after twenty long years of suffering.

Jeremiah's ministry was a long one. He saw seven kings on
the throne whilst his voice was lifted up against the people or,
rather, against their sin. He was *for* the people even though they
failed to recognise it. The kings who reigned were :

Manasseh	.....	697 - 642 B.C.
Amon	.....	641 - 640 B.C.
Josiah	.....	639 - 608 B.C.
Jehoahan	.....	608 B.C.
Jehoiakim	.....	608 - 597 B.C.
Jehoiachin	.....	597 B.C.
Zedekiah	.....	597 - 586 B.C.

His ministry was a constant cry against the persistent sin of
Judah, with a continual call to repentance. It was the warning
voice of God. It was the rejected voice by man. Sometimes it
has been referred to as the lone voice in the wilderness, although
this was not strictly so. Jeremiah had several contemporaries, for
whilst he preached in Jerusalem Ezekiel preached in Babylon to
those already in exile. Daniel and his companions maintained
their testimony in Babylon. At the same time Habakkuk was
prophesying in Jerusalem and Zephaniah was standing with
Jeremiah. Nahum was also predicting the fall of Nineveh and
Obadiah was telling of the impending doom of Edom.

KEYWORD

The keyword would be "repent." This is constantly re-echoed. Jeremiah's first message was that if they did not repent, then they would be carried away into captivity by the Babylonians. When Judah had gone too far in their stubborn refusal to obey God, so that there remained no hope of escape, then he changed his message and it became a strong plea to submit to Babylon. If they could not escape the captivity, they could at least be delivered from some of the disasters by yielding to the inevitable. Through all the gloom and the darkness there remained one gleam of hope, one shaft of light, which demonstrated God's grace even in the midst of His Judgment. It was always the promise that, ultimately, Judah would be restored and Babylon utterly destroyed — and thus it was.

THE PROPHET

It was these conditions of sin on the one hand and the know-ledge of an inevitable captivity on the other hand, plus the false accusations that Jeremiah was an unpatriotic man because of his message, that made him to be the sad and weeping Prophet he was. Nonetheless he remained the strong, faithful, and unflinching figure of his generation.

As to his personal life, he was of priestly descent and lived in Anathoth, one of the Levitical cities a little north-east of Jerusalem. He was not a married man, but he was a man of very tender affections and deeply emotional. This kind of ministry would be hard and unpalatable to such a character. These are the men whom the Lord calls, men who are fully aware of their inability because only such men would lean on His ability.

THE BOOK

It covers Jeremiah's ministry entirely — the first thirteen chapters concern the prophet's call and commission, and reveal the condition of the nation, and the remaining thirty-nine chapters deal with the prophet's ministry. The second section divides into:

(1) Prophecies before the fall of Jerusalem. Chapters xiv-xxxviii.

(2) Prophecies after the fall of Jerusalem. Chapters xl-xlv.

(3) Prophecies against the Gentile nations. Chapters xlvi-li.

The 51st chapter actually ends the book with the words "Thus far are the words of Jeremiah." The last chapter is an appendix added by another hand.

JEREMIAH'S CALL (Ch. i.)

Here is evidence of the eternal purposes of God. Like Cyrus and others, this man was elected for ministry before he was born. " Before I formed thee in the belly I knew thee ; and before thou camest forth out of the womb I sanctified thee, and I ordained thee a prophet unto the nations " (i. 5). The callings and elections were of God, so what had Jeremiah to say, or what have any of us to say ? All men who have the unction of the Holy One resting upon them have proved to be men of sincere humility. Jeremiah's reply was : " Ah, Lord God ! Behold, I cannot speak ; for I am a child." Man's inability is just where God displays His ability.

Jeremiah was about twenty years of age, not a child in years but one in experience. Moses spoke of his weakness to lead. Solomon referred to himself as a child. It is the child who depends upon his father. The youth wants to depend upon himself. Most of us are too grown up ! Jeremiah remained dependent upon his God to the end of his days.

Jeremiah's call, like others, was linked with a vision. His was twofold. Firstly he saw the rod of an almond tree. The almond has ever been a symbol of being " awakeful " or " watchful," because it is the first tree to awake after the long sleep of winter. Therefore it would tell Jeremiah of the alertness of God, that He was not asleep to all that had been happening in the nation and now He was about to move into action. The second thing the prophet saw in the vision was a cauldron and it was tipped away from (not toward) the north. It was ready to empty its contents and, when it did, these would come away from the direction of the north. Thus was God ready to pour out His wrath upon a sinful nation.

HIS COMMISSION (Chs. ii-xiii.)

Isaiah, by his warnings, had saved Jerusalem from overthrow by the Assyrians. Jeremiah was called upon to try and save the same people from the Babylonians, but this time the warnings were not going to be heeded. God made this known to Jeremiah, and the Prophet sought to persuade the people to yield to their enemy and thereby alleviate some of their sufferings. This was his persistent message. For twenty chapters Jeremiah appealed, advised, warned, and wooed, sometimes in strong denunciation, sometimes with all the tenderness of his heart, but always with no uncertainty. In chapter two he reminded Jerusalem of the happy days of the past when they walked with God. He also reminded them of the faithfulness of God as He brought their fathers through the wilderness into a land of plenty, and yet, at that time, they rebelled. The priests, the pastors, and the prophets all failed in their duties. They turned from God to Baal. He asked the question as to what other nation had ever changed their gods. Only Israel, and Israel was the only nation who had the true and the living God.

He charged them with idolatry and with the evil of spiritual adultery. In the next chapter (iii.) he revealed how God had punished them for this sin by withholding the rain. Because of her adultery God forsook Israel and gave her a bill of divorcement. Judah, instead of heeding the folly of Israel, followed in her footsteps and even did worse.

With pleadings which were tender and deep God begged His people to return and He would show them His mercy. If only they would acknowledge their sin there was forgiveness waiting for them. "I am married unto you." He wanted to forgive them. He wanted to bless them. He wanted Jerusalem to be a place of glory. "Return, ye backsliding children, and I will heal your backslidings" (iii. 22). What compassion! What love!! What tenderness!!! The forsaken husband pleading for his wayward wife.

There appeared to be no response on the part of His people so that His pleadings continued into chapter four. At verse 10 of that chapter it is Jeremiah who begins to speak in reply to all that the Lord has revealed. It is a lamentation as he realised the awful calamities that must befall the people whom God loved so much and whom he also loved. Very vivid and descriptive is his language as he told them of the coming of the armies from the north, of their great power, and of Judah's inability to withstand the advance. "Behold, he shall come up as clouds, and his chariots shall be as a whirlwind : his horses are swifter than eagles. Woe unto us! for we are spoiled" (iv. 13). The lament goes on with words as : "My bowels, my bowels! I am pained at my very heart ; my heart maketh a noise in me ; I cannot hold my peace, because thou hast heard, O my soul, the sound of the trumpet, the alarm of war," etc. (iv. 19).

As he continued in the next chapter he bade them find one righteous man, if they could, and the Lord would save them, but no! From the highest to the lowest, both king and people, prophet and priest, all have turned from God. "The prophets prophesy falsely, and the priests bear rule by their means ; and My people love to have it so . . . " (vs. 31).

Year after year he continued, night and day, his eyes running with tears, and, using descriptive language, he told the people of their inevitable sufferings and bade them flee from the wrath to come. Interspersed with these warnings of judgment are appeals for mercy, such as " If ye throughly amend your ways and your doings . . . then I will cause you to dwell in this place, in the land that I gave to your fathers, for ever and ever " (vii. 5-7).

The messages of chapters vii-x. were spoken in the gate of the Lord's House. Jeremiah continued to enumerate the awful crimes they had committed against the God of heaven. In their idolatry, father, mother, and child were participants (vii. 18), thus bringing confusion on their own heads.

Years of warning had accomplished nothing. The nation was deeper in sin than at the beginning. This was not due to failure or fault on the part of the prophet, but to a stubborn stupidity on the part of the people, who allowed themselves to be deceived with the idea that, because the Temple was in Jerusalem, God would protect the city and never allow it to be destroyed, and therefore they were safe despite what Jeremiah might say.

Is not such a condition typical of the modern day ? We are all right ! Britain and America are " Christian " countries. We have sent out missionaries. We have circulated the Bible. We have saved the world. We are the citadels of freedom. God will not punish us nor cause us to suffer ! So we compromise with our faith. We continue in our sins. We patronise God, but know nothing of love, devotion, and service. We are deceiving ourselves with a religious mask which is going to bring a tragic awakening some time. " Be not deceived ; God is not mocked " (Galatians vi. 7). The only one to be cheated is self.

Jeremiah is commonly known as the " Weeping Prophet," and the expression is usually used in a derogatory way. The *statement* is true. In his appeal he said : " Oh that my head were waters, and mine eyes a fountain of tears, that I might weep day and night for the slain of the daughter of my people ! " (ix. 1), but our *interpretation* is not always good. This attitude of pushing the prophet aside as a sentimentalist is wrong. He was strong, outspoken, courageous, and unyielding. He used every means he knew to try and reach those hearts which were as hard as flint, and those minds which were so corrupt.

He had been persistent in his warning of coming judgment. Now he changed his tense and spoke as though it had already happened, to see if that would jolt the people to their senses, for he said : " The harvest is past, the summer is ended (or, the

opportunities of gathering our blessings have gone), and we are
not saved . . . Is there no balm in Gilead ; is there no physician
there ? " (viii. 20-22). Has God made no provision for our sin ?
Has He no power to forgive and heal ?

Chapters nine and ten are a continual lamentation for this
people, for the city that was to become ruinous heaps, because
of their heathenish ways and their constant idolatry.

These first ten chapters reveal the condition of the nation, and
are followed by thirteen chapters of

WARNINGS AND REBUKES (Chs. xi-xxiii.)

The Lord reminded the people of the Covenant He had made
with their fathers back in the days when they came out of the land
of Egypt, a Covenant which they endorsed and one which required
complete obedience. He reminded them of the blessings that came
from obedience, and of the judgments that were pronounced against
disobedience.

As the people had disobeyed God in this request, He was no
longer obligated to bless them but, to the contrary, must keep
His part of the contract in bringing the foretold curses upon those
who turned from Him to other gods. They were now worshipping
Baal. Yea, they had as many gods as they had cities ! They had
set up as many altars in Jerusalem as there were streets.

Jeremiah's life had been threatened by the men of his own
city, Anathoth, as they had tried to silence the preacher. God
declared that it was the lives of these men which were at stake,
for He was going to destroy them.

God wanted the people to know clearly what their position
was so He bade Jeremiah demonstrate the truth before their eyes
as well as preach it in their ears. This was another evidence of
His mercy.

(1) *The Linen Girdle* (xiii.) The Prophet had to secure a new
girdle, such as men wore around their waists. It was not to be put
into water, that which usually softens new material, making it
more pliable. This he was to wear for a time before the people.
Later God instructed him to take this girdle and, journeying to
the river Euphrates, he was to hide it in a cleft in a rock, and
then return to his ministry. After a long period Jeremiah had to
go back and find the girdle. When he did, he found that it was
marred. The water and mud of the river had ruined the new
girdle. So corrupt was it that, seemingly, it could not be washed.
It was " good for nothing."

The girdle is usually a symbol of service. This God had desired from His people. He wanted them to serve Him to the praise of His Name. Instead they were serving other gods which would be to their destruction. Euphrates, where the corruption took place, was where Babylon stood, the nation which God was choosing to punish Judah.

(2) *The Drought* (xiv. & xv.) This next demonstration was not from Jeremiah but from God. It is a pathetic story. The drought was severe. Man and beast languished. The account is very descriptive. The heart of Jeremiah was broken as he pleaded with God, a pleading that almost became an argument between God and the Prophet, as Jeremiah reminded God of mercies and promises, as he made excuses for the people, seeking to put the responsibility upon false prophets; but God was as steadfast as the Prophet was persistent.

Then the Lord said : " Though Moses and Samuel (both inter-cessors) stood before Me, yet My mind could not be toward this people : cast them out of My sight, and let them go forth " (xv. 1). Every verse is worthy to be pondered. They are pregnant with truth, and searching in intensity. They leave the heart trembling before the Lord as one is made to contemplate the statement : " My Spirit shall not always strive with man " (Genesis vi. 3).

(3) *The Unmarried Prophet* (xvii.) Some prophets were told to marry. Jeremiah was forbidden marriage. The thought that was to be conveyed to the people was, Why should he marry and raise a family so that they should be given to the sword and the suffering that was determined upon this people ? God was seeking to make the truth real to these obstinate minds which refused to accept truth.

In the next chapter Jeremiah reminded them of the fact that the heart is deceitful above all things and desperately wicked. It will only believe what it wants to believe. He contrasted between the man who trusts himself and the one who trusts in the Lord and is, therefore, free from anxiety.

(4) *The Potter's Wheel* (xviii.), another picture of the Lord's grace. The Prophet was instructed to go to a potter's house and watch him at work on a piece of clay as it yielded to every touch of the master-hand whilst it spun on the potter's wheel. There was skill as the deft hands moved, but, whilst the Prophet watched, a calamity took place as the vessel became misshapen. No fault of the potter — there was a blemish in the clay, or a foreign body. The potter did not become angry because all that skill of his had

been wasted. Nonetheless, one may well imagine that he must
have been very disappointed. Removing the foreign body, if that
were the cause, he kneaded the lump together again and then began
to refashion it into another vessel. As Jeremiah stood, gazing
with admiration at the skill and grace of the potter, God spoke :
" O House of Israel, cannot I do with you as this potter . . . ? "
(vs. 6).

One could almost imagine the Prophet jumping for joy and
saying : " Lord, that is just what I am asking You to do." The
Lord would reply that that was just what He was willing to do,
and wanting to do, and able to do, if only they would be pliable
and yield to His Will. Jeremiah brought this truth to the people,
but, instead of yielding, they stubbornly said : " There is no hope "
(vs. 12). Instead of accepting the life God was offering, they sought
the life of Jeremiah to take it from him.

God then had another demonstration for the Prophet to
perform.

(5) *The Earthen Bottle* (xix.) He was to take an earthen
bottle and go to the Valley of the son of Hinnom and, after
addressing the people, break the vessel in their sight, and say :
" . . . Even so will I break this people and this city, as one breaketh
a potter's vessel, that cannot be made whole again . . . " (vs. 11).

These two pictures are relative. The clay in the hand of the
potter could be remade because clay is pliable, but when once the
clay vessel has gone into the oven and been baked, then the breaking is beyond repair. Judah was being told how hard their hearts
had become. Isaiah was declaring a similar truth when he said :
" And He shall break it as the breaking of the potters' vessel that
is broken in pieces ; He shall not spare : so that there shall not
be found in the bursting of it a sherd to take fire from the hearth,
or to take water withal out of the pit " (Isaiah xxx. 14).

The message Jeremiah preached in the Valley he also declared
at the Temple. For this he was put into the stocks, a painful
punishment. Although his feet and his hands were made fast, his
tongue was still free. Having passed judgment upon Pashur, the
false priest who had condemned him to the stocks, the meek and
gentle Prophet began to pour out an indignation against God and,
like others before him, cursed the day in which he was born. His
years of pleading and warning, his love and devotion toward his
God and His people, had ended in miserable failure, so, like Job,
Moses, and Elisha, he felt his life was not worth living. Who are
we to condemn him, for we all have these days of disappointment,

that sense of failure, when we want to put the blame on someone else ? Then it is that we want to try and find some failure on the part of God and His promises. At such times we may rejoice that He does not judge us according to our sins, nor reward us according to our iniquity but, instead, pities us as a father pitieth his children, remembering our frailty.

The time came (chapter xxi.) when, in the reign of Zedekiah, Babylon began to show its interest in the land of Judah, so that the king sent a message to the Prophet, asking him to enquire of the Lord concerning this matter. This was the first time that there had been any enquiry of God ! What must have seemed so strange to the people, and no doubt strange to Jeremiah, was that God told them to submit to the enemy and to allow the Chaldeans and the Babylonians to carry them away into captivity, and that, if they would go, and would show no resistance, then the Lord would spare their lives and bring them back again. If they remained in Jerusalem and resisted the enemy, if they would seek to defend Jerusalem, then they would suffer from a fearful siege and die by the edge of the sword.

This was what made Jeremiah look like an unpatriotic man, a traitor to his own country, but God had ordained it that way, and Jeremiah had to be faithful to God. Sometimes our faithfulness to God and to His Word makes us to appear unfaithful to our friends, but obedience to the Divine revelation of God must always come first, and we must not count the cost.

In chapter twenty-two God pronounced judgment upon three kings.

(1) Shallum   — king of Judah, who had been taken captive into Egypt. He should not return.

(2) Jehoiakim   — brother and successor to Shallum, because of his wickedness should be buried as an ass.

(3) Coniah   — son of Jehoiakim, because of his sin was to be written childless. He brought to an end the royal line as he and Zedekiah were carried into captivity.

His next judgment was upon the false pastors, prophets, and priests. As they had scattered the sheep, so would He scatter them, but the sheep He would regather to their land and would raise up a King of the line of David. His Name would be called Jehovah Tsidkenu — " The Lord our Righteousness " (xxiii. 6).

The Lord then gave to Jeremiah a vision of

Two Baskets of Figs, one basket of very good figs and the other of very bad figs. It was an emphasis upon a truth which He had already declared. He would be gracious to those who yielded to the captivity and would punish those who resisted it. Those who yielded would ultimately be delivered because, in yielding to their punishment, they would be acknowledging their sin and His justice. Those who did not yield would ultimately be destroyed because they were continuing to show a rebellious heart by suggesting they were not worthy of such punishment. God teach us to submit to our punishments as well as to receive our prizes !

For many years God had been sending His prophets, bidding His people to repent, but they had refused. Now for many years they must endure bondage. So came the declaration : " And this whole land shall be a desolation, and an astonishment ; and these nations shall serve the king of Babylon seventy years " (xxv. 11).

This was judgment but not a complete rejection, for in their exile God raised up other prophets who warned, comforted, and encouraged. The principal of these were Daniel and Ezekiel. Associated with the prophets were other examples, men such as Shadrach, Meshach, Abednego, and Mordecai, those who refused to bend their knees to the gods of that land, and leaders, such as Ezra and Nehemiah, who later led out those who had remained steadfast.

A further token of God's grace toward this stubborn people was that His announcement of seventy years' captivity in Babylon was followed with a promise of the destruction of their enemy, as in turn God would deal with Babylon and all of the other nations who had joined with Babylon in oppressing the people of God. At this point Jeremiah moved from the immediate to the ultimate in judgment, for the Prophet was making a similar utterance to the one made later by Peter, who said : " For the time is come that judgment must begin at the house of God : and if it first begin at us, what shall the end be of them that obey not the gospel of God ? " (1 Peter iv. 17).

Now note Jeremiah xxv. 15. God said to His servant : " Take the wine cup of this fury at My hand, and cause all the nations, to whom I send thee, to drink it." " To wit, Jerusalem, and the cities of Judah." (vs. 18). That was beginning at the house of God. Then came a long list of the nations who were to drink, ending with " and the king of Sheshach shall drink *after* them." (vs. 26). The margin shows that Sheshach is another name for Babel or Babylon. Babylon is the last power to fall, according to Revelation

xviii. 2. Babylon is to be re-established and will be the seat of Antichrist in the last days. As the Antichrist shall reign there, he is obviously the last king of Babylon. Hence the prophet Jeremiah was carried beyond the seventy years' captivity and the destruction of Nebuchadnezzar, to the time beyond Israel's long dispersion when God shall deal with her final enemies and restore her to her land of eternal blessing.

Chapter twenty-six puts on record a contest between the priests, prophets, and people, on the one side, and the princes and the people on the other side, for the life of Jeremiah. The people were on both sides. They may have been divided, or they may have changed about in their fickleness. One day they cried : "Hosanna to the Lord," and the next day "Away with Him." In our day we find people on the side of the evangelist and ready to make a profession of Christ, but they have forgotten it all within a few days of his departure. Nonetheless there are always the faithful ones who are able to prevail against the crowd because God is on their side. So Jeremiah's life was saved.

Jeremiah was not intimidated by this threat on his life. He submitted to it, if they could prove his guilt, and warned them of their guilt if they should shed innocent blood. Immediately upon his release God instructed him to demonstrate His Word again by making some bonds and yokes, symbols of service and slavery, and to wear these things before the people, after which he was to send them to kings round about, with a message from God. God, Who had created all things, had the right to give these things to whom He would. He has the power to lift up whom He will and to abase whom He chooses, and God had chosen Nebuchadnezzar, king of Babylon, to be His *servant* (xxvii. 6). Nebuchadnezzar required that all nations, including Israel, should be subservient. This tremendous authority of Nebuchadnezzar, declared by God through Jeremiah prior to the captivity, was confirmed by God through Daniel during the captivity. "Thou, O king, art a king of kings : for the God of heaven hath given thee a kingdom, power, and strength, and glory. And wheresoever the children of men dwell, the beasts of the field and the fowls of the heaven hath He given into thine hand, and hath made thee ruler over them all. Thou art this head of gold " (Daniel ii. 37-38). Nebuchadnezzar was subjected to none save God Himself. All nations were commanded to obey him and he was to rule them.

Moreover, this power was not his alone. It was to be a hereditary power. "And all nations shall serve him, and his son, and his son's son, until the very time of his land come (or his appointed end): and then many nations and great kings shall serve themselves of him (or shall enslave him) " (Jeremiah xxvii. 7). All of this is summed up in the expression " The times of the Gentiles." Of course, behind all this is a deeper and fuller significance which causes the picture before us to become a parable, even though it was factual in its own time.

(1) When God created all things in the beginning (Genesis i. 1), He gave the oversight of the earth to Lucifer. " Thou art the anointed cherub that covereth ; and I have set thee so ; thou wast upon the holy mountain of God " (Ezekiel xxviii. 14). As a result of pride, Lucifer lost his privilege and was cast out of the heavens.

(2) God then vouchsafed this power to the nation of Israel, in the call of Abram (Genesis xii. 3). " . . . in thee shall all families of the earth be blessed." With Israel as the head of the nations, blessings should have abounded, but she failed, turning from her God to serve idols. God had to remove her authority and for a time it has been transferred to the Gentiles.

(3) Nebuchadnezzar was now the servant of God, holding full earthly sway, but, instead of subjecting himself to God, he became presumptuous, abused his privileges, oppressed mankind ; the ill results will be found in the book of Daniel.

(4) The seventy years of exile for Judah in Babylon were an introduction to the seventy prophetic weeks of years of Daniel ix., between which there would come " the times of the Gentiles." This period began with Nebuchadnezzar as king of Babylon. It ends with another king of Babylon holding universal sway — Antichrist. He, too, will be destroyed when God's purposes are fulfilled.

(5) Then shall come to reign the One Whose right it is, for " He is before all things, and by Him all things consist . . . that in all things He might have the pre-eminence. For it pleased the Father that in Him should all fulness dwell ; " (Colossians i. 17-19).

Hananiah, the false prophet, sought to substitute the message of judgment with a false message of peace, even as the false prophets of liberalism do to-day. Hananiah received his own personal judgment from God, as will all false prophets.

PROMISES

The theme changes for the next nine chapters. Up to this moment Jeremiah had been preaching and demonstrating the Word of God. The next two chapters contain verbal instructions. They concern not only the time of Jacob's trouble but also the deliverance which would follow. In chapter thirty Jeremiah is instructed to " Write thee all the words I have spoken unto thee in a book." He would not go into exile with them, but this book could, to bring them hope in their deep despair. Then their sorrow would be turned to song. Then would God give them a new covenant. Then would their iniquity be forgiven, their sin would be remembered no more, and their city would be re-built.

Zedekiah cast Jeremiah into prison. Whilst there Jeremiah was instructed by God to buy a field in Anathoth and to seal the evidences for many days. Even so, Israel would come out of her prison in Babylon after many days and would again inherit her land and be able to buy fields and houses. This was a promise of the restoration of their land.

In the next chapter the prophet, still confined to the prison (as they would be) told of the restoration of the people. Read especially xxxiii. 19-26.

In chapter thirty-five God used the incident of the Rechabites to show that men are more willing to obey their fellow-men than some are to obey God.

Man's attitude toward the Word of God is shown as it was written by Baruch, and cut to pieces by the king — the representative of the people. To-day the liberalist will use his penknife of criticism and his fire of unbelief, but he cannot destroy the Word of God. The book was rewritten. The only thing such men do is to destroy themselves, for, of this king, Jeremiah said : " They shall not lament for him . . . He shall be buried with the burial of an ass, drawn and cast forth beyond the gates of Jerusalem " (xxii. 18-19).

Zedekiah showed a great deal of compromise. He refused God and His Word, but, in his difficulties, desired the prayers of Jeremiah, and secret information. The king might compromise, but never the Prophet. The Prophet might sink in the mire but the king sank in shame and moral corruption. The coloured man, the Ethiopian, had more courage than the king and gained permission to deliver Jeremiah from what would have been a slow and torturous death. The old clothes and rags that Ebed-melech found eased the sufferings of the steadfast Prophet. God rewarded this man for his charity and saved his life from the hand of the Babylonians (xxxix. 15-18).

So came the day when, according to the word of Jeremiah, the armies of Nebuchadnezzar besieged the city and it fell. The people were carried away into captivity. Zedekiah, after witnessing the death of his sons, had his own eyes put out and was then carried away in chains to Babylon.

The king, who meted out judgment upon the compromising Zedekiah, displayed his mercy upon the uncompromising Jeremiah. He was to be cared for and permitted to do as he wished. He could go to Babylon and be looked after, or remain with the remnant of his people. In any case, he was a free man. Jeremiah decided to stay in Judah and chose to live at Mizpah. Here the old man (near ninety), worn out with the strife and struggle that had been his through the long years, might have spent his last days, but alas, it was not to be. The people wanted to escape to Egypt but God, through the prophet, protested. Nonetheless they fled to Egypt and, amidst the protestations of Jeremiah, took him with them.

In Egypt he continued to protest against their idolatry and their worship and their offerings to the queen of the heaven.

Tradition has it that the people were so enraged against Jeremiah's rebukes that they stoned him to death in Egypt.

AFTER THE FALL OF JERUSALEM

Six chapters are given to God's warnings through Jeremiah to the nations round about — Egypt, Philistia, Moab, Ammon, Edom, Damascus, Kedar, Hazor, Elam and Babylon.

The last words of chapter fifty-one are : "Thus far are the words of Jeremiah." The end of this noble life of service and sacrifice is not recorded for us.

The last chapter gives a description of the siege, the fall and the destruction of the city and temple, also the carrying away of the spoil.

Learn that man may be stubborn, he may resist all the warnings of God, he may reject and despise the servant of God, nonetheless the Word of God remains to be fulfilled.

Disobedience must bring judgment.

LAMENTATIONS

" IS IT NOTHING TO YOU ALL YE THAT PASS BY "

" O Jerusalem, Jerusalem, which killest the prophets, and
stonest them that are sent unto thee ; how often would I have
gathered thy children together, as a hen doth gather her brood
under her wings, and ye would not !   Behold, your house is
left unto you desolate . . . "   (LUKE xiii. 34-35)

INTRODUCTION

In the original Scripture, this book is part of the prophecy
of Jeremiah. In our Bible it has been separated and is somewhat
in the form of an appendix.

It will be noticed that chapters one, two, four, and five have
each of them twenty-two verses, whilst chapter three has sixty-six
verses. There are twenty-two letters in the Hebrew alphabet. Each
of these chapters is a poem and each verse begins with a letter of
the alphabet in order, whilst in the third chapter there are three
verses to each letter and each verse begins with that letter. It is
constructed on the same principle as the 119th Psalm, which is the
alphabetical Psalm of twenty-two sections, each verse of each
section beginning with that particular letter. This construction
is entirely lost in the translation of the verses into the English
language.

Jeremiah, writing under Divine Inspiration, and being in the
Spirit as he wrote, found himself as a type or a representative of
the Lord Jesus Christ, Who in turn wept over the sins of the people
and over the city of Jerusalem.

The strain of the book is both tender and pathetic. The long
foretold fall of Jerusalem had become a reality. Warnings were
now of little avail, so Jeremiah sat and wept and uttered grievous
lamentations for the desolation of both city and its citizens, and
also for the glorious Temple, which was a shameful heap of ruins.

As he pondered the situation, he thought of the miseries caused
by the famine, of the termination of public worship, of the numerous tragedies the exiles would endure, and of how the whole
horrible nightmare was self-imposed. Things could have been very
different if only the people had repented of their evil ways and
turned back to God. How long-suffering the Lord had been, and
how faithful Jeremiah had been, but all with no result.

In this book of pathos he sought to encourage them even now to " despise not thou the chastening of the Lord, nor faint when thou art rebuked of Him " (Hebrews xii. 5). They still had the opportunity to repent of their evil ways.

This book is claimed to be the richest expression of patriotic feeling. It is beautiful in its structure and unique in its depth of sorrow.

In the Septuagint translation the following words precede the first verse of the Authorised Version : " And it came to pass after Israel had been carried away captive and Jerusalem was become desolate, that Jeremiah sat weeping : and he lamented with this lamentation over Jerusalem ; and he said . . . " This same verse, slightly altered in the wording but the same in principle, is found in The Vulgate, in Coverdale's translation (1535), in Mathew's Bible (1549), and several others of that century.

THE BOOK

As previously stated the book is made up of five poems, each chapter being one poem.

POEM 1. THE CONDITION OF ZION — A SOLITARY CITY
" How doth the city sit solitary " (i. 1)

HER DESOLATION. A while ago this city was full of people, a centre of activity. It was known as the City of David, built by Israel's most illustrious king. He had taken it from the Jebusites, when it was known as impregnable, and, building towers and fortresses, had made a strong city stronger. Many were the songs of triumph and glory that were sung concerning this city which was " beautiful for situation, the joy of all the earth."

Here are some quotations :

" Our feet shall stand within thy gates, O Jerusalem, Jerusalem is builded as a city that is compact together . . . Pray for the peace of Jerusalem ; they shall prosper that love thee. Peace be within thy walls, and prosperity within thy palaces " (Psalm cxxii. 2-7). " They that trust in the Lord shall be as Mount Zion which cannot be moved, but abideth for ever " (Psalm cxxv. 1). " Glorious things are spoken of thee, O city of God " (Psalm lxxxvii. 3).

Now this same city was a scene of desolation, ruin and shame, a dwelling place of the dragon and the owl, the cormorant, and the wild beast of the desert. What was the cause of this sudden change ? How could such a thing happen ? Was it a sense of security, that this city could not be destroyed, which caused the people to be so rebellious and stubborn toward the message of Jeremiah ? False security is a very dangerous thing. To-day men are so confident in their scientific discoveries, so satisfied with their increased learning, that God is no longer in their thoughts. One needs to remember that all that God has declared concerning the last days will be as certain in fulfilment as were the declarations of Jeremiah — all shall come to pass.

The Prophet asked : " How is she become as a widow ? She that was great among the nations . . . " (i. 1). She had lost her king, and her children had been taken away from her. Widowhood then was a pathetic thing. If the husband died, the widow was looked upon as though she were responsible for his death. The Jewish widow was considered as abject and as wretched as anyone could be. Her hair had to be cut short and a tight veil put around the head so that no trace of hair could be seen. The woman's hair was her glory, so Paul tells us in 1 Corinthians xi. 15. As a widow she was stripped of all glory. She had to put away all her ornaments, eat coarse food, and be considered almost an outcast from society. Such was the story of Naomi, who said " Call me not Naomi (pleasant), call me Mara (bitter) ".

Jerusalem was as one who had thus lost her husband. " Thy Maker is thine husband " (Isaiah liv. 5), but they had forsaken Him. She had also robbed herself of her own political sovereignty and had now to pay taxes and tribute to the nation who had suppressed her.

SHE COMPLAINED IN HER GRIEF because there was none to comfort her. She was friendless and forsaken. " The ways of Zion do mourn, because none come to the solemn feasts " (i. 4). This was a reflection of those better days when three times in the year the assembly went up to Jerusalem for the annual feasts. Then every road would be alive with people whose hearts were full of praise, the echo of their voices would be heard everywhere as they sang their " songs of degrees " or " the Ascents ", being Psalms cxx-cxxxiv. Now these " ways of Zion " were desolate.

" Her filthiness is in her skirts " (i. 9), refers to her idolatrous worship. This can be gleaned from many Scriptures, as Ezra vi. 21 : " And the children of Israel, which were come again out of captivity, and all such as had separated themselves unto them from the *filthiness* of the heathen of the land, to seek the Lord God of Israel . . . "

In verse 11 everything had gone. The few trinkets and sentimental treasures which they had managed to bring away with them, they have had to sell to their adversaries for bread, so that every pleasant thing had gone.

SHE APPEALED FOR SYMPATHY. The cry was: "Is it nothing to you, all ye that pass by? Behold, and see if there be any sorrow like unto my sorrow, which is done unto me . . ." (i. 12). It was a tragic appeal which was being made to all and sundry. Was there no one who would stop and consider? Yes! We will pause a moment and weigh up the evidence. Was there any city, or people, who suffered more? Perhaps not. But was there any city, or people, who were pleaded with so constantly and frequently as these, and was there ever any equal in the stubbornness and the rebelliousness of this people against all the persistent pleadings, warnings, and coaxings of the Prophet?

An answer must be given to Jerusalem, as the world will have to receive its answer by and by in its day of judgment. It is that the Lord is not unmerciful. Punishment is meted out according to the measure of persistent sin.

Jerusalem might appeal to man; she might appeal to God; she might spread forth her hands; but there was none to comfort. It would be the old cry : " Too late — too late."

The appeal which was made concerning this city in its great suffering has become a Messianic pointer, in that the words were used concerning the Lord and His suffering upon the Cross. " Is it nothing to you?" Does not Calvary demand some consideration? Does it not make its own appeal? Find some comparison if you can! But the answer remains ever the same. Ponder the immensity of the sin that brought the judgment, but with this one stupendous difference — Jerusalem was taking the burden of its own wilful sin, but Jesus was carrying the full load of the sin of the world, suffering " the Just for the unjust that He might bring us to God," and so the appeal would go to the ends of the earth : " Is it nothing to you, all ye that pass by? Behold, and see, if there be any sorrow like unto My sorrow."

SHE CONFESSED GOD'S RIGHTEOUSNESS. Here was the first confession. "The Lord is righteous; for I have rebelled against His commandments . . . " (i. 18). True repentance always vindicates God and condemns self. God makes no mistakes. His punishments are always just. The complaint was that there was no sympathy from the enemy, the agent that God was using. On the contrary " . . . they are glad that Thou hast done it . . . " (i. 21). In the last verse, the prayer is that these same afflictions would fall on the heads of their enemies — the Chaldeans. The evidence is that they did.

As this first lamentation is read, with all of its pathos pouring from the broken heart of Jeremiah, let this overall lesson be learned. Man may deserve what has come to him, he may have asked for it, but that does not mean that sympathy cannot be shown toward him and prayers offered for him. Always remember that if judgment has been escaped, it is not because of any worthiness on man's part.

POEM 2. CAUSE OF SORROW — JEHOVAH'S WRATH

"How hath the Lord covered the daughter of Zion with a cloud in His anger, and cast down from heaven unto the earth the beauty of Israel, and remembered not His footstool in the day of His anger " (ii. 1).

It is true that the Lord is slow to anger and plenteous in mercy. He is ever displaying that fact, but, against it, there is also another great fact, which is that His Spirit will not always strive with man (Genesis vi. 3), and that He is a jealous God (Exodus xx. 5). There comes a time when God has to mete out His judgment, much as it may grieve Him, otherwise He could lose His own authority, as parents are losing their authority to-day to just the extent that they fail to reprove and punish their children.

What seemed to concern the prophet in the early part of this chapter was that God in His wrath had overthrown and destroyed His own Temple, the centre of His own worship, and yet it was a Divine and a controlled anger, not the display of a lost temper. It was true that men had corrupted the worship of that Temple by their idolatrous acts but, again, this was a prophetic finger pointing to the destruction of another Temple — Christ's Body, a Temple free from sin or blemish. Man's sin had been responsible for the destruction of both temples, for God cannot let sin go unpunished. Consider the chapter with this background in mind.

THE SANCTUARY DESTROYED — " and cast down from heaven unto the earth the beauty of Israel." This referred to the destruction of the Temple. His footstool might, as has been suggested by some, refer to the Ark of the Covenant. God had intended it to be the place wherein His Glory dwelt but, as with Herod's Temple, they had made it a den of thieves. They were not exchanging money dishonestly nor bargaining for the biggest price they could get for the animal which was to become a sacrifice for sin, as were those in the Temple of the New Testament. There they robbed their fellow-men, but here they were robbing God of His worship, His honour, and all else that was His. God will not share His glory with another. God and Mammon cannot dwell together.

THE ALTAR BROKEN. " The Lord hath cast off His altar . . ." (ii. 7). The altar was the centre of all worship, for without the shedding of blood there is no remission for sin. The next verse states: " . . . He hath not withdrawn His hand from destroying . . ." Jeremiah was asking with astonishment how the Lord had done this ! God was recognising these things no more. They were gone, so completely gone that it was as if they had never existed. This was wrath indeed, but the day came when the people repented, a return took place, and the Temple was rebuilt. The Temple of Christ's Body was destroyed at Calvary, but was renewed on the third day. As one remembers his wrath, as Jeremiah witnessed it in his day, what will it be when " the great day of His wrath is come," a day from which there will be no return.

From the wrath as meted out upon the Temple, the Prophet's mind turned to that which was poured upon

THE PEOPLE. Jerusalem's misery was so abject and her condition so pitiful and appalling, because of the famine, that the daughters swooned, fainted, and died in the streets from hunger. The mother gathered the child to her breast and it died in her bosom. She gathered her children to her feet in vain. Women ate their offspring as soon as they were born, whilst the men, old and young, lay in the streets, slain by the sword. The picture was lamentable.

THE PRINCES AND THE PROPHETS had no message for the people. They were false and could only offer the people vain and foolish things. They were slain with the men of the city.

Added to all of this trouble was

A REJOICING ENEMY. " All that pass by clap their hands at thee ; they hiss and wag their head at the daughter of Jerusalem, saying, Is this the city that men call The prefection of beauty, The joy of the whole earth ? " (ii. 15). Such was adding insult to injury. The nation sought sympathy and only found abuse.

No wonder they cried " . . . let tears run down like a river day and night : give thyself no rest : let not the apple of thine eye cease. Arise, cry out in the night : in the beginning of the watches pour out thine heart like water before the face of the Lord . . . Behold, O Lord, and consider to whom Thou hast done this . . . " (ii. 18-20).

POEM 3. CRY OF JEREMIAH — GRIEF AND TRUST

The grief expressed in this chapter appears to be threefold, and yet it is blended into a oneness. It is seen, firstly, in Jeremiah, for the utterances were made by him. It was his voice which was heard, and, throughout, he was speaking in the first person. He declared his life of suffering, loneliness, and imprisonment. He did not do this in any sense of self-pity, but, rather, that he might encourage his fellow-mourners in the midst of their grief.

Secondly, Israel as a nation is in the picture, for the Prophet was not being personal in his grief, much as it fitted him. He was identifying himself with the nation, and actually he was expressing their grief and, at the same time, encouraging them in their trust ; but a careful reading readily reveals the third identity as the Lord. Jeremiah, as spokesman, was in the middle, behind was Israel, and before was the Lord God. Discover for yourself how many of the statements of this chapter apply to our Lord in the hour of His suffering. Two of the prominent verses are : " My flesh and my skin hath he made old : he hath broken my bones " (iii. 4). " He giveth his cheek to him that smiteth him : he is filled full with reproach " (iii. 30).

HE BEWAILED CALAMITY. In the first twenty verses there comes the first outburst of grief because he and they had walked in darkness. They had been hemmed in by their enemies ; within were bitterness and turmoil.

HE SAW GOD'S MERCY. The storm is always enhanced by the rainbow. The desert is relieved by the oasis. The sky is never so dark that somewhere a ray of light will not pierce it. Light is an amazingly penetrating thing. So it was that, amidst all the gloom, the suffering, and the dismay which had been pressing heavily upon Jeremiah, there came a ray of light, a beam of mercy. " It is of the Lord's mercies that we are not consumed, because His compassions fail not. They are new every morning : great is Thy faithfulness " (iii. 22-23). Who are we to complain because of our punishments ? All we deserve is death, and anything short of death is a display of God's mercies.

The thoughts of Jeremiah are most adequately expressed and applied in T. O. Chisholm's beautiful hymn :

> " Great is Thy faithfulness, O God my Father,
> There is no shadow of turning with Thee ;
> Thou changest not, Thy compassions they fail not,
> As Thou hast been Thou for ever wilt be.

Pardon for sin and a peace that endureth,
Thy own dear Presence to cheer and to guide ;
Strength for to-day and bright hope for to-morrow,
Blessings all mine, with ten thousand beside.

Great is Thy faithfulness !
Great is Thy faithfulness !
Morning by morning new mercies I see ;
All I have needed Thy hand hath provided,
Great is Thy faithfulness, Lord, unto me.''

The fact that God had been faithful in the past carried the probability that He would be faithful in the future, so Jeremiah took another step, and said : " The Lord is my portion, saith my soul ; therefoʳ will I hope in Him " (iii. 24). His thoughts were moving from ι past, with all its passions, into the present, where he found the Lord was still the portion of the waiting soul, and then on to the future where the peace of God can become the provision of the child of God. " Therefore will I hope in Him." This is a hope that maketh not ashamed. It is something that is sure and steadfast, so, with the Psalmist, he bade the soul to wait quietly for it. This is the light that will dispel the darkness, the confidence that will banish fears.

It is only the believing heart which is able to see beyond the problems of to-day to the hope of to-morrow, and, knowing that all things work together for good to them that love Him, can say : " For the Lord will not cast off for ever : But, though He cause grief, yet will He have compassion, according to the multitude of His mercies. For He doth not afflict willingly nor grieve the children of men " (iii. 31-33).

HE CONFESSED THEIR SIN. Seeing the grief of the people and meditating the grace of the Lord brought the Prophet to the place where again he realised that confession was the only thing that would bring a oneness between an afflicted people and an offended Lord. Therefore he began to confess their sin : " Let us lift up our heart with our hands unto God in the heavens. We have transgressed and have rebelled . . . " (iii. 41-42). So many people lift up their hands in despair when things go wrong instead of lifting up their hearts with their hands in confession.

The chapter ends with the Prophet interceding with God as

HE PRAYED FOR THEIR DELIVERANCE, using himself and his own bondage as an example of their bondage. From the dungeon he cried, and the Lord brought him salvation. From the dungeon of Chaldean slavery he sought the Lord's deliverance for Judah and the Lord's judgment upon the enemy.

POEM 4. CONTRAST OF DAYS — GLORY AND MISERY

This fourth lamentation is one of contrast. Jeremiah gazed upon the ruins of the temple and of the city. He thought of the suffering of the people who once were the inhabitants of this city and were now no more. They had either died in the great siege or were exiles in a far-off land. As he did so he drew some vivid comparisons.

Fine Gold and Dim Gold. Gold is not easily dimmed. It is not like silver, which tarnishes, or brass that corrodes, or iron that rusts. Gold maintains its beauty. The city of Jerusalem had been the joy of all the earth. The temple, built by Solomon, had been a blaze of glory. Its walls and doors had all been overlaid with pure gold, and its furniture likewise. Now, what had not been carried away was a heap of rubble. The gold was gone, the art gone, the magnificence gone, the service gone, the massive, costly stones broken down, and everything was tarnished and blackened from the fires that had raged in the streets. What a contrast! All the devastation would be a constant reminder of what once had been.

This was not only true concerning that ancient city, and other cities upon which enemies have wreaked their vengeance, but it is true of anything that loses its former glory because of a demoralisation. It is indeed true of all the graces of God when they are corrupted by man's greed or selfishness.

How is the gold become dim ? By the act of man taking the beautiful and the wonderful things of the earth that God has graciously given him and, by his indifference and neglect, allowing them to become dimmed by the smoke of hell and then destroyed by the powers of Satan.

Golden Vessels and Earthen Vessels. Not only had the glory of the Temple gone by reason of its destruction, but the priests were gone, the Levites were gone, the worshippers were gone. They had all corrupted themselves. " The precious sons of Zion ", who were comparable to golden vessels because of their skill and ability as priests, rabbis and others with all of their reverence and scholarship, those leaders of thought and of men who had been in a place of honour, had now become as earthen pitchers, as they went into exile — slaves in Babylon engaged in hard labour, vessels of clay. What deep humiliation !

Man has turned the glories which God has given him into carnal things. This condition is fully detailed by the Apostle Paul in Romans i. 23-32.

God gave to man the golden vessel of nature. He has turned it into an earthen vessel by abuse. Man has turned beautiful flowers into deadly drugs. He has taken the luscious grape and turned it into wine which mocks man and makes him a danger to his fellow-man. He has taken the natural elements of the earth and converted them into a power which can destroy that same earth.

Man has taken the golden vessel of human life and abused it. He has turned love to lust, natural genius to worldly ambition, possession to greed, whilst money has been made a god. His success becomes his doom, his graces become his disgraces.

He has taken the golden vessel of youth and turned it into a vessel of clay as thoughtlessly as a young man may yield his strength to the passions of life, as he despises *advice* because he desires *vice*. The young man permits the harlot to rob him of his character, and the young woman sells her purity for a mere pittance.

The precious sons of God can forfeit their spirituality for carnality as they surrender their testimony, or make compromises with the world, or allow their love for the things of God to wane, or dishonour the Name of the Lord.

Surely Jeremiah was speaking to us in our day.

Affection and Cannibalism. The third group to come under scutiny was the women, those wonderful mothers with their love and devotion toward their offspring. These had lost their natural affection in the straitness of the famine and were despising their little ones until they were classified as worse than animals, for " Even the sea monsters draw out the breast, they give suck to their young ones : the daughter of my people is become cruel, like the ostriches in the wilderness " (iv. 3). The ostrich has been known as the bird that lacks sense and affection. This is what the Lord had to say about the ostrich when He was speaking to Job : " . . . the ostrich which leaveth her eggs in the earth, and warmeth them in dust, and forgetteth that the foot may crush them, or that the wild beast may break them. She is hardened against her young ones, as though they were not her's : her labour is in vain without fear ; because God hath deprived her of wisdom, neither hath He imparted to her understanding " (Job xxxix. 13-17).

Mothers, human or animal, usually will make every conceivable sacrifice both to provide for, and in defence of, their offspring, but not here ; and the fathers were no better. The mothers did not satisfy their children's thirst nor the fathers their hunger.

One might say that this was force of circumstances, but their troubles were self-imposed by their own rejection of God. A man must watch his conduct for, when he loses his love for God, he so often loses love.

The fact here was that they went further than neglect. " The hands of the pitiful women have sodden their own children ; they were their meat in the destruction of the daughter of my people " (iv. 10). These parents became selfish instead of self-sacrificing. Beloved, we need God and His Son, our Saviour. Without Him " the heart is deceitful above all things, and desperately wicked ; who can know it ? " (Jeremiah xvii. 9).

As Snow and Coal. The last group of people brought into contrast was the Nazarites. Of them he said " Her Nazarites were purer than snow, they were whiter than milk, they were more ruddy in body than rubies, their polishing was of sapphire : Their visage is blacker than a coal ; they are not known in the streets : their skin cleaveth to their bones ; it is withered, it is become like a stick " (iv. 7-8).

The Nazarites, who were a separated people and had a vow upon them as to what they ate and drank, and, therefore, were a healthy people and of fine appearance, and who probably wore special white vestments, had now lost all their distinguishing marks. The " blacker than a coal " has a Hebrew reference to " duskier than the dawn " — the in-between light that makes discernment difficult.

The conditions were such that Jeremiah seemed to stand alone. Everyone and everything had been contaminated until no one could trust anyone.

Like as the eagle that hovers overhead, then with a swiftness swoops down upon its prey so that there is no escape, so Israel fell victim to her enemies.

POEM 5. CALL FOR MERCY — APPEAL TO GOD

This last chapter differs considerably from the others in that it is a prayer to God throughout. It is

A Piteous Appeal. The prophet was again telling God of the sufferings of the people, but the approach was different. This time it was not in complaint because of their suffering, nor yet was it a rebuke because of what God was permitting. Instead there was a confession. They knew that they, and their fathers, had sinned and brought all of these things upon themselves. It was an appeal to God to take notice of their intense suffering, and not to turn His back on them any longer. To turn to men when in need is useless. They had looked to Egypt for help, they had turned to Assyria for support, but both had failed them.

"Remember, O Lord." Many have prayed this prayer. Nehemiah prayed thus. Job, David, and others, had cried out : "Remember, O Lord," but then the Lord never forgets! He remembers our sins and our iniquities, until they are blotted out to be remembered against us no more. He also remembers that we are dust.

Humiliating Subjection. Here the Prophet asked that the Lord would remember and consider all that had come upon them.

As to the land, God had given it to Abraham and to his seed for an everlasting inheritance. Now it was in the hands of strangers and aliens. As to the people, God called them out as a peculiar people and had set His love upon them. Now they were a nation of orphans and widows.

As to their condition, God had promised to bless them above all the nations of the earth. Now they were slaves to a heathen nation, buying their water for money and their few privileges for hard labour.

Insult was added to injury when Chaldean servants were given an authority and made to rule over these servants of God who had known better days (vs. 8).

Sorrow had taken the place of joy. In verse 15 Jeremiah said : "The joy of our heart is ceased ; our dance is turned into mourning", which reminds one that the enemy tried to get entertainment from these exiles, but they refused with the words "By the rivers of Babylon, there we sat down, yea, we wept, when we remembered Zion. We hanged our harps upon the willows in the midst thereof. For there they that carried us away captive required of us a song ; and they that wasted us required of us mirth, saying, Sing us one of the songs of Zion. How shall we sing the Lord's song in a strange land ? If I forget thee, O Jerusalem, let my right hand forget her cunning" (Psalm cxxxvii. 1-5).

Then came another note of confidence. It was :

The Call of Conquest. "Thou, O Lord, remainest for ever ; Thy throne from generation to generation" (v. 19), or, "Lord, these things which we endure are temporary but Thou art eternal. Above the darkness, beyond the immediate, Thy throne is established and will be when all the thrones of earth have ceased to be."

The cry, therefore, was that the Lord should come and reign over them instead of forsaking them. This is somewhat expressed in the 21st verse, which is a beautiful

Prayer for Restoration. " Turn Thou us unto Thee, O Lord, and we shall be turned ; renew our days as of old." This prayer would cover the pleading, the lamentations, yea, it is the soul of the whole book. It is a confession of the soul which has wandered so far from God that it is not capable of finding its own way back. It has kindled so much displeasure from a merciful God that it feels incapable of lifting its head again. So, in anguish of spirit and a full sense of helplessness, the soul throws itself upon the mercy of God and cries : " Lord, turn us unto Thyself. It is only Thy mercy that can melt Thy anger. If Thou doest the turning then we shall be turned." Here is where saving grace must operate.

So may we, in every realisation of waywardness and disobedience, even before we feel the rod of His correction, pray — " Turn Thou us unto Thee, O Lord, and we shall be turned."

EZEKIEL

THE GLORY OF THE LORD

"And to you who are troubled rest with us, when the Lord Jesus shall be revealed from heaven with His mighty angels, in flaming fire taking vengeance on them that know not God, and that obey not the gospel of our Lord Jesus Christ: Who shall be punished with everlasting destruction from the presence of the Lord, and from the glory of His power; when He shall come to be glorified in His saints, and to be admired in all them that believe ... in that day."

(2 THESSALONIANS i. 7/10)

THE PROPHET

Like Jeremiah, Ezekiel was a priest by descent and a prophet by call, for verse 3 informs us that he was " . . . the priest, the son of Buzi." Ezekiel was a contemporary with Jeremiah and Daniel, and learned much from Jeremiah. Jeremiah had foretold the coming disaster. Ezekiel was with the people in their exile. Whilst Ezekiel ministered to the people of God in a strange land, at the same time Daniel ministered on the behalf of God to those who dominated these people, the rulers and the princes of world dominions.

Ezekiel engaged in prophetic ministry for about twenty-two years, beginning at the age of thirty according to verse 1. This was the age at which the Lord Jesus began His ministry, and the age that was required by the law of God according to Numbers iv. 3.

Unlike Jeremiah, he was a married man, but his wife was taken from him in death that it might be a sign unto the house of Israel (Ezekiel xxiv. 15-18).

One hundred times the Prophet is addressed as " Son of man ".

His ministry was to be a watchman unto the house of Israel, to warn them of their conduct, good or bad.

THE BOOK

Throughout it is a revelation of the goodness and the severity of God. This statement as made by Paul could readily sum up the whole of the prophecy: " Behold, therefore, the goodness and severity of God : on them which fell, severity, but toward thee, goodness, if thou continue in His goodness, otherwise thou also shalt be cut off " (Romans xi. 22).

The book, which concerns the Glory of the Lord, can be divided into three main sections :

    (1)   The glory appears (Chapters i-iii.).
    (2)   The glory departs (Chapters iv-xxiv.).
    (3)   The glory returns (Chapters xxxiii-xlviii.).

The scope of the book is vast, as that section which is historical is combined with that which is prophetical. It commences with the children of Israel going into the Babylonian Captivity, which was around 592 B.C., and ends with God's people enjoying the fulness of the blessing of the Millennial land which is still in the future, when the Lord will make all things new.

(1)   THE GLORY APPEARS (Chs. i-iii.)

The Prophet's Preparation. It has been stated that Ezekiel was both Priest and Prophet. A priest is one who speaks with God for the people, whilst a prophet is he who speaks to the people for God.

The priestly office was possibly Ezekiel's before he went into captivity, for that was hereditary. The prophetic office was conferred upon him whilst in exile and came through the vision of chapter one.

It is not possible to enter into all the detail of these visions, neither is it necessary. Sufficient at the moment are the principles.

Because of his priestly position, and also because he knew that many of the conditions prevailing were through the stubbornness of the people, the suggestion has been made that Ezekiel may have spent much time away from the people. At any rate he was in solitary meditation by the river Chebar when he saw the approach of a cloud, accompanied by a whirlwind. As the cloud came nearer it became brighter. Fire came forth from the midst of it, which might refer to lightning. A halo of light surrounded it until it was something more than natural. The supernatural was quickly confirmed by the appearance of four living creatures coming from the midst of it.

This description causes one to reflect back to some words of the Psalmist concerning the Lord. " . . . O Lord my God, Thou art very great ; Thou art clothed with honour and majesty. Who coverest Thyself with light as with a garment ; Who stretchest out the heavens like a curtain : Who layeth the beams of His chambers in the waters ; Who maketh the clouds His chariot : Who walketh upon the wings of the wind. Who maketh His angels spirits ; and His ministers a flaming fire " (Psalm civ. 1-4). This was the approach of the glory of God.

The Living Creatures. The creatures who appeared from out of this cloud were human in their general form but had four wings and four faces. These faces are found on the living creatures mentioned in Revelation iv., and are symbolical. The face of the man represents intelligence ; the lion, strength ; the ox, humility and service ; and the eagle that which can rise above the things of the earth and look into the face of the sun. These are the qualities of service — intellect, strength, humility, and vision.

Added to these were wings of responsiveness to that service, and, being joined, would denote unity in service.

The Wheels within Wheels. This second vision is a re-emphasis of the first. The living creatures had wings — heavenly flight. The wheels knew rotation and forward movement by earth contact. The wheels within the wheels are understood to be intersecting at right-angles. This would allow them to move forward in any direction as the living creatures with their four faces looked in every direction. The eyes suggest that there was an alertness to the opportunities of service.

The living creatures and the wheels were side by side, and above was the throne and the One Who sat thereon. The upper part of the Sitter on the throne was as the colour of amber, the lower portion was the appearance of fire. Round about was a rainbow. All of this is in harmony with the vision of Revelation iv. The whole may be summed up thus — The Lord of Glory sat upon the throne. His appearance was as amber (topaz), which tells of holiness, and fire (sardius), the evidence of justice (viii. 2). Holiness and justice are inseparable characteristics of the Lord. The rainbow is a reminder that He is also a covenant-keeping God.

Emanating from the throne were heavenly and earthly agencies, the heavenly represented by living creatures and the earthly by wheels. Both were ever ready to do His bidding day and night.

Ezekiel's Commission. It was not long before Ezekiel was joining the throng of those who serve Him, for from that same throne there came the call, " Son of man, I send thee to the

children of Israel, to a rebellious nation, that hath rebelled against
Me, even unto this very day " (ii. 3).

How many of the prophets found their call associated with a
vision! To see God in His holiness is to see man in his sin and
in his need, and all who do can usually testify with Paul to the
fact that they were not disobedient to the heavenly vision.

God never promised to Ezekiel an easy path. He has never
promised it to anyone, so why look for it ?

Eat the Roll. A hand holding a roll presented it to the Prophet,
which was then opened revealing that the parchment had writing
upon both sides. Ezekiel was told to eat this roll and to masticate
it. In doing so he found that, although it was full of lamentations,
warnings and woe, yet in his mouth it was as sweet as honey.

Of course, this was vision, not fact. A man does not literally
eat a book. The instruction which he was receiving he was to eat,
or take to himself the message of God. As food through eating
becomes an actual part of man, so was the Word of the Lord to
become part of the Prophet. There are similar references, such
as " Thy words were found, and I did eat them : and Thy Word
was unto me the joy and rejoicing of my heart " (Jeremiah xv.
16).

Having received the Word, he must then impart it. The Word
of God is never given for storage but for usage. It was not the
Prophet's responsibility as to whether the people received or rejected the message, but it was his responsibility to deliver it, and
it is ours to do the same in this our own generation.

This revelation greatly humiliated Ezekiel, but the Spirit
lifted him up, and he went and sat where the people sat. Whilst
there he received a further revelation, as God declared him to be
a watchman unto the house of Israel. A watchman was one
whose duty was to stand on the city wall, or on the watch-tower,
to keep his eyes open for any approach of an enemy and to advise
the city immediately so that it might prepare itself for attack.
The Prophet was to do this, but there was no promise that the
people would respond.

From the place of public announcement he was commanded
to go into a place of isolation, and to cut himself off from fellowship with his people, for the Spirit said " Go, shut thyself within
thy house . . . thou shalt be dumb, and shalt not be to them a
reprover : for they are a rebellious house " (iii. 24-26) — a reminder that " My Spirit will not always strive with man."

(2) THE GLORY DEPARTS (Chs. iv-xxiv.)

Prophecies proclaimed before the siege of Jerusalem. In a series of symbols, demonstrations, and parables, the Prophet made known the judgment that was to be poured out upon Jerusalem. These would be obvious in the eyes of the people. The first group included

The Sign of a Tile (Ch. iv.), upon which he portrayed the city in a state of siege, with battering rams around it. Between it and himself was established a wall of iron. This was to represent the hard and impenetrable wall set up between God and the city because of their sin.

The Sign of the Prostrate Prophet (Ch. iv.). Ezekiel was to prostrate himself under a burden for a length of time on his left side, and then for another period on his right side. Each day was to represent a year of burden, firstly for Israel the nation to his right, or north, and then for Judah to the left, or south.

The Sign of Famine (Ch. iv.) followed, when food and water would be by measure, and even the fuel would be in short supply. Dried cow's dung was a fuel in those days, but it was never used for the preparation of food. The demonstrations would be forceful.

The Sign of the Barber's Razor (Ch. v.). The Prophet had to take a sharp knife, literally a sword, and use it as a razor. The chapter explains itself when it is remembered that the hair was always considered a symbol of glory. It was the glory of the woman (1 Corinthians xi. 15), and the beauty of the old man (Proverbs xvi. 31 and xx. 29).

God was using pestilence, the sword, and capitivity in order to take away the glory He had previously given to His people.

Chapters six and seven continue the story of woes and desolation that befell both the people and their land, whilst two further chapters tell of the causes of the desolations. These were their idolatries and abominations, which are very vividly described (Chs. viii. & ix.).

The Glory Departs (Chs. x-xi.). The vision of God's glorious administration, which embraced both angels and men, heaven and earth, and which Ezekiel saw firstly at the River Chebar, was now above the Lord's House and His glory filled it. The departure of this glory was slow, declaring the Lord's reluctance to depart from His people. It was on the right side (x. 3), then it was over the threshold (x. 4), then it was lifted up (x. 15). The glory then mounted up from the earth (x. 19). " And the glory of the Lord

. . . stood upon the mountain which is on the east side of the city " (xi. 23).

The princes withstood the information which Ezekiel gave the people. His message was the same as that of Jeremiah. God must destroy Jerusalem and cause His people to go into captivity as a punishment for their sin, but, if they would accept their punishment and yield to Babylon instead of resisting it, it would prove to be to their ultimate good. However, the princes resisted the Prophet, declaring that the city would never be destroyed.

It was because of this contest that God sought to make His truth unmistakable by these living demonstrations of the Prophet, each of which was a parable.

The Captivity of Zedekiah, and those who went with him into Babylon, was demonstrated by the Prophet assembling his chattels and personal belongings and carrying them from one place to another, as would a person removing to some other abode. The picture of digging through the wall (xii. 5-12) became true, inasmuch as the king and his people escaped by night through a breach in the wall (read 2 Kings xxv. 4).

The Prophet then had to eat and drink his food with trembling and with carefulness. This was to denote the severity of the conflict and the hardness of the conditions of the immediate days.

The Opposition of God. In chapters thirteen and fourteen God showed Himself opposed to three classes of people.

(1) *The False Prophets and Prophetesses* — men and women who posed to be prophets but had no Divine call or anointing. A prophet is as a wall of defence for the people, warning them of danger and resisting any opposing force. These men, in their false declarations, were a menace to the people. Their wall was so weak, being built of bad mortar, that when the rain came it would be washed away.

Likewise were there women who prophesied falsely and they used every kind of feminine attraction in their attire and their conduct that would allure men to themselves and then to the false idols. Thereby they hunted the souls of men.

(2) *Elders of Israel.* These idolatrous leaders came to the Prophet, evidently with the intent of persuading him to turn to their ways or approve their conduct, but the Lord said that He would answer these men and deal with them Himself (xiv. 7).

(3) *Trespassing Men.* Upon these, God would pour out His four sore judgments, which He so often had to use — the sword, famine, the wild beast, and pestilence. In His anger, not even the saintly men of the past, who knew their God and could commune with Him, men like Noah, Daniel, and Job, would be able to prevail in causing the Lord to alter His mind (xiv. 20).

PARABLES (Chs. xv-xix.)

There are five chapters of these parables which give an indication of the condition of the nation at that time.

(1) *The Vine.* This particular tree has one sole purpose in life — to bear fruit. It cannot give shade to man or beast, and its wood has no use whatsoever. It has no trunk, and its stock and branches are twisted, useless things, hence the Prophet said: "Shall wood be taken thereof to do any work ? Or will men take a pin of it to hang any vessel thereon ? " (xv. 3). If it does not bear fruit, then cut it down and cast in into the fire and let it become fuel. John xv. 6 declares this.

This was true of Israel. God had created the nation for one purpose only, that it might bring forth fruit to His glory. If the nation fails in this it has failed completely ; and Israel had failed, so God is going to cast her into a fire of affliction. Already she had been burned at both ends by neighbouring nations, and now Jerusalem was to fall victim of the next onslaught.

(2) *The Foundling.* This picture exposes the moral corruption into which the nation had fallen after a merciful deliverance had been granted to it by the Lord. He does not even count them as the children of Abraham. "Thy father was an Amorite and thy mother a Hittite." Born of corrupt parents, and unwanted by them, they had not received the medical care to which they were entitled at birth, but with no eye to pity they had been cast into the open field to die in infancy. It was thus that the Lord found them, took them in, washed them of their defilements, and said : "Live " (xvi. 6). Being saved in babyhood they grew up, developed and became a nation. Then came the time of love, courtship, and marriage. Again the Lord protected and provided. He clothed them in beautiful garments and made them as a bride adorned for her husband.

In return for all these favours, instead of loving the Lord they turned to a vile life of harlotry and fornication that displayed a lamentable ingratitude. Therefore, according to their seed-sowing so must come their reaping.

(3) *Mother and Daughter.* " As is the mother, so is her daughter " (xvi. 44) — as is the cause, so is the effect. Sin has an amazing way of passing itself on from one generation to another, and sin, with all of its reactions, never seems to be a warning to others. The younger sister can prove to be worse than the elder.

(4) *A Great Eagle.* The Prophet reminded the nation of how Nebuchadnezzar, the great eagle of Babylon, came down and overshadowed Judah, and took from her " the top of the cedar ", referring to her king who was taken into captivity, and a puppet king, Zedekiah, was set up by Nebuchadnezzar. Instead of submitting to Babylon, as Nebuchadnezzar had expected, Zedekiah turned to Egypt for help. Egypt was the second eagle in this parable, for no more help could come from Egypt than from the Chaldeans. Ezekiel was declaring the same fact that Jeremiah was teaching, which was that Judah's only deliverance was in submission. They had sinned ; they must take their punishment.

(5) *Sour Grapes.* This introduces one of the great moral laws of God. Said the people : " The fathers have eaten sour grapes, and the children's teeth are set on edge " (xviii. 2). This was a parable which meant that the fathers had sinned and the children must be made to take the punishment, but God disagreed saying " All souls are mine . . . the soul that sinneth IT shall die " (xviii. 4). However, God has a natural law which also operates within the moral realm, and that is — reaping can only be according to sowing. If you do not want your children to do the reaping, then you had better not do the sowing.

(6) *The Young Lion* — as with the people, so with the kings. Judah had one king after another in these final years before the captivity, but each one failed the nation, whilst the last one was carried away as a prisoner into Babylon (xix. 9).

(7) *The Broken Vine.* The first parable concerned the Vine. Once it had been fruitful, fulfilling its purpose in life, but now it was broken down, dried up by the east wind, burned up by the drought, a picture of desolation — thus was Israel.

The next four chapters continue enumerating the gross sins of the nation in the face of the Lord's faithfulness to their fathers and to themselves, and also informing them that the period of His grace had now run out. He had taken up the sword of His vengeance and had placed another into the hand of Nebuchad-nezzar, so that now, as they stood at the parting of the ways, it would matter not which way they turned, they were doomed to punishment. The Lord had searched "for a man among them that should make up the hedge, and stand in the gap before Me for the land, that I should not destroy it ; but I found none " (xxii. 30). The priests and the princes had desecrated everything that was holy and that was Godward, and had done despite to all the human relationships that were manward.

In the account of Aholah and Aholibah (chapter xxiii.), the first being Israel and the second Judah, the Lord declared the intensity of the guilt of Judah by the fact that her elder sister Israel had engaged in these sins and God had, in no unmistakable way, shown His disapproval and had meted out His judgment ; yet, in spite of this, Judah had chosen to travel the same road and even made herself more abased.

This section of the book closes with two further demonstrations of the awfulness of God's judgment. The first was a parable. It concerned

A Boiling Pot (Ch. xxiv. 1-14). A cauldron was to be set over a great fire which was to be constantly fed in order to keep the fat boiling. Into the pot was to be put the choicest of the flock. When the contents had been consumed, then the empty pot was to be put back on to the fire that the scum, which would be clinging to its sides, might be consumed. The pot represented the city of Jerusalem, once called the Holy City and now called the bloody city. The flesh, which was to be consumed therein, was Judah, once the choicest of the people, now the scum of the earth. The consuming fire was Nebuchadnezzar and the Chaldeans, who not only dealt with the people but utterly destroyed the city.

God had come to a time when He declared that He could show no mercy and would accept no repentance, and thus it was.

The second demonstration was more than a parable. It concerned

The Death of the Prophet's Wife (Ch. xxiv. 15-18). The Lord took the wife of Ezekiel by sudden death. Although the Prophet was very fond of his wife, for she was the desire of his eyes, yet he was not to mourn for her according to the custom of those days. This would prove to be a great surprise to the people and would cause them to enquire as to the reason of his conduct. It was that God was going to take from His people the desire of their eyes, their own sons and daughters and their own glorious city, and in the hardness of their hearts there would be no lamentation, no sense of guilt, and, therefore, no realisation of repentance.

Let us ever be sensitive to the movings of the Spirit of God, and to the convictions of the Holy Spirit, in relationship to our failings and shortcomings. If we lose that sensitiveness, we have lost everything.

DURING THE SIEGE (Chs. xxv-xxxii.)

Whilst God dealt with His own people because of their sin, He also dealt with the other nations who had not known Him, but whom He used as instruments of punishment for His own people. There is no purpose in expounding the details of these chapters immediately because we shall meet these nations and their doom in more detail in the Minor Prophets. Sufficient here to mention the nations :

Ammon (xxv. 1-7)	.....	because they laughed at Israel's calamity.
Moab (xxv. 8-12)	.....	because they looked upon Judah as a heathen nation.
Edom (xxv. 12-14)	.....	because they took vengeance against Judah.
Philistia (xxv. 15-17)	.....	because of their despiteful heart toward Judah.
Tyre (xxvi. 1 - xxviii. 19)	.....	because she found pleasure in what she thought was the loss of Jerusalem and the gain of Tyre.
Zidon (xxviii 20-26)	.....	because they were as " a pricking brier " unto the house of Israel.
Egypt (xxix 1 - xxxii. 32)	.....	because she had always been an enemy to Israel, and sided with Israel's enemies.

(3) THE GLORY RETURNS (Chs. xxxiii-xlviii.)

After the Restoration

This final portion begins with three chapters of

Warnings and Promises in which there is to be found some repetition of the earlier part of the book. It concerns the Prophet being a watchman to the house of Israel and declares the warning

that he had to give of coming judgment, and of the tremendous
responsibility resting upon him if he failed so to do.

The Watchman of the City (Ch. xxxiii.). Not only had God
given this warning in chapter three, but Ezekiel had already been
faithful in obeying God and had given abundant warning, yet it
was repeated these years later. Does it not teach that things must
not be taken for granted, nor yet must a thing lose its import
by reason of repeated use ? There is ever a grave danger of service
becoming mechanical and automatic, and thereby meaningless.

Shepherd of the Sheep (Ch. xxxiv.). This next chapter changes
from rigid army life to rural shepherd life, although the truth
remains much the same. The Lord was reproving the shepherds
(the word " pastor " means the same) because they had fed themselves instead of the sheep. They had enriched themselves with
the wealth of this world instead of enriching the sheep with the
riches of His grace. In seeking their own comfort they had
neglected the sick and the wayward sheep. It was because of this
neglect that the sheep had been scattered far and wide, wandering
on the mountain, many of them becoming prey to the wild animal.

God expressed His anger against these shepherds and reminded them that He would require His flock at their hands. Not
only was this true concerning the leaders of Israel, but it is all
too true concerning the leaders of the Christian Church to-day.
Few are concerned with the souls of men. They are allowed to
wander and become the victims of the wild animals of false creeds
and dogmas. Because the pastors are failing to feed the sheep in
the green pastures of God's Word, the sheep are devouring the
poisonous weeds of human philosophy. Yet these same leaders
eat the fat, and clothe themselves with the wool taken from these
sick sheep. " Behold, I am against the shepherds, saith the Lord."

Returning to Israel, the nation that had been scattered and
neglected, the Lord was now making some heart-warming promises.
" Behold, I, even I, will both search My sheep, and seek them
out . . . I will bring them out from the people . . . I will feed them
in a good pasture . . . I will feed My flock, and I will cause them
to lie down . . . I will seek that which is lost " (xxxiv. 11-16).

The Lord is to bring His people back to their own land. He
will separate the rams and the goats, the good from the bad, the
oppressed from the oppressor and, in place of the false shepherds,
He is going to set up one True Shepherd. " And the Lord will
be their God, and My servant David a prince among them ; I the
Lord have spoken it " (xxxiv. 24). This, of course, is referring

to great David's Greater Son, the Lord Jesus Christ, the Good Shepherd, Who gave His life for His sheep. At last Israel is coming into the fulness of the blessings of the Lord and of the land.

The chapter closes with these words of assurance " Thus shall they know that I the Lord their God am with them, and that they, even the house of Israel, are My people, saith the Lord God. And ye My flock, the flock of My pasture, are men, and I am your God, saith the Lord God " (xxxiv. 30-31).

Doom of Edom (Ch. xxxv.). In chapter twenty-five God pronounced His doom upon the land of Edom along with six other surrounding nations. In chapter thirty-five He enlarged upon that judgment. These were the men of Edom, or Mount Seir, those who had a blood-relationship with Israel because they were the descendants of Esau, the brother of Israel. This nation had ever been belligerent. They had refused to allow Israel to pass through their territory. They had determined to subdue this people, even though they knew that God was with them. They had rejoiced when Israel was made desolate. Now God said that He would do those same things to them, and that they should be desolate. What was true concerning Edom will be true of all the nations of the earth who have either oppressed, or glorified in the oppression of, or have failed to help, the chosen race of God.

Restoration of the Land (Ch. xxxvi.). This chapter is addressed to the mountains of Israel. It concerns the land, not the people. For hundreds of years the land had been rugged and barren, a place of desolation and poverty, but God was now calling upon the mountains and hills, the valleys and the rivers, the barren wastes and the cities, to break forth into new life. The rain is to return, the mountains are to be clothed with verdant forests, the desert places are to blossom as the rose, and the waste places are to become fruitful orchards and vineyards, and the cities are to be filled with men who will have been cleansed from their filthiness. " A new heart also will I give you, and a new spirit will I put within you : and I will take away the stony heart out of your flesh, and I will give you an heart of flesh. And I will put My Spirit within you, and cause you to walk in My statutes and ye shall keep My judgments, and do them. And ye shall dwell in the land that I gave to your fathers ; and ye shall be My people, and I will be your God " (xxxvi. 26-28). Having prepared the land for the people, He then prepared the people for the land.

The next chapter records the

Restoration of the People (Ch. xxxvii.). This is the most known chapter of the whole prophecy. It concerns the vision of the *Valley of Dry Bones*. These bones, which were " very many " and " very dry ", represented the whole nation of Israel that had been scattered among the nations of the world for so long, and who had suffered so much misery and death at the hands of the heathen that one would have thought that, as a people, they would have been utterly exterminated. So the question was asked : " Son of man, can these bones live ? " Was it possible that bones so bleached and dry could be revived ? Ezekiel seemed to be reluctant to answer such a question. In the natural realm the answer would be in the negative ; but in the spiritual, if the mercy of God could go that far, the answer would be in the affirmative.

The Prophet, therefore, wisely put the answer back to God. " O Lord God, Thou knowest." The Prophet was then bidden to prophesy, with the result that " . . . the bones came together, bone to his bone, and . . . lo, the sinews and the flesh came up upon them, and the skin covered them " (xxxvii. 7-8). The valley was now filled with dead corpses. The Prophet was commanded to prophesy for the second time, calling for the breath of life and, as he did, the corpses came alive and stood up " an exceeding great army."

The Lord declared how this related to the regathering of the people of Israel to their land. The two stages are in accord with other prophecies. Firstly, the bone coming to his bone but the result something that was lifeless, is a picture of the return of the house of Israel in unbelief — still spiritually dead. The second prophecy relates to the day when " they shall behold Him Whom they pierced, and say Blessed is He that cometh in the Name of the Lord." With this full recognition of their Messiah they shall live.

The two sticks, which became one, in the latter part of the chapter, declare that, at this same time, when Israel is entering into Millennial blessing, the nation that divided into two kingdoms after the death of Solomon, and has remained as Israel and Judah ever since, will again be united as one people with one King.

Gog and Magog. The regathering of Israel into the Promised Land, for what is known as the Millennial Reign, will, of course, take place after the rapture of the Church.

A problem seems to arise. The battle of Gog and Magog, recounted here, appears to take place before the Millennial Reign but, according to Revelation xx. 7-9, it is at the end of the thousand years. The answer may be in Ezekiel xxxviii. 8 : " After many days thou shalt be visited . . . "

Gog and Magog undoubtedly refer to Russia, the " Prince of Rosh " is in the Hebrew. A group of other nations, with Russia, forms a Northern Confederacy, which includes Persia, parts of North Africa as Ethiopia, Libya, and Gomer (Germany). These, seeing Israel at peace, dwelling in unwalled cities without fear of invasion, and enjoying the prosperities of a fertile land which God has given to them, decide to invade the country and take possession of its abundance. These godless nations fail to see that the security of this people is in their God. God will meet such nations on the way and will destroy five-sixths of these Russian hordes with rain, hailstones, fire, brimstone, and pestilence. So great will be the slaughter that it will take all the carrion birds of the heavens and an army of men seven months to clean the land and bury the dead, whilst the nations will look on at the slaughter of the one side and the protection of the other side, and will confess that it was the Lord's doing. At the same time Israel will be made to realise that God is truly with them, and that the sufferings they had endured in past generations were all their own fault because they had forsaken Him and, thereby, forfeited His goodness.

THE TEMPLE

Three chapters are given to the description of this Temple, its dimensions and its many chambers, and the allotment of the priests and their functions. Space does not permit any detail. More important is it to see that, when this wonderful edifice is complete, the glory of the Lord returns, the glory which was on the Ark in the Tabernacle when God was in their midst, the glory which filled Solomon's Temple, the glory which Ezekiel had seen by the river Chebar and then at Jerusalem. The glory which had lingered and then slowly had moved from that Temple to the mountain and then to heaven before the people had been scattered, now returns and fills this new Temple. God is again in the midst of His people.

The great altar is built and measured, and the sacrifices reestablished.

THE WORSHIP

The Priesthood, of the tribe of Levi, will again function, but the privileges will be for the descendants of Zadok rather than Aaron, because of a failure in that family.

THE LAND

The land is to be divided for the second time. Joshua had once allocated the land to the various tribes. In the restored land it is to be divided into horizontal strips as described in chapter forty-eight, with a special portion set apart for the Lord in the midst of the land. In this they are to measure a square of twenty-five thousand reeds, which, in turn, is to be sub-divided into three horizontal strips, two of them ten thousand reeds wide, and one five thousand reeds wide. The whole is to be called The Holy Oblation. The northern portion is to be given to the Levites (xlv. 5), the centre portion to the priests (xlv. 4), and the smaller portion is for the city (xlv. 6). The balance of this holy portion is for the princes.

In the midst of the twenty-five thousand reed square shall be the Sanctuary (xlviii. 8). The city is to be in the five thousand reed strip at the south. This will put the Temple and the city at a distance from each other, which would give evidence that the Temple of Ezekiel will not be built in Jerusalem and, therefore, not on the old Temple area which has been profaned by the Moslems. The new Temple will be situated near Shiloh.

Might not this difference of situation account for the words of Isaiah : "And an highway shall be there, and a way, and it shall be called The way of holiness ; the unclean shall not pass over it ; but it shall be for those : the wayfaring men, though fools, shall not err therein. No lion shall be there, nor any ravenous beast shall go up thereon, it shall not be found there ; but the redeemed shall walk there ; and the ransomed of the Lord shall return, and come to Zion with songs and everlasting joy upon their heads : they shall obtain joy and gladness, and sorrow and sighing shall flee away " (Isaiah xxxv. 8-10) ?

Out from under the threshold of the Temple there will emerge the water of life. Flowing eastward via the altar and then southward it will increase in volume until it becomes a river in which a person can swim. As such it will pour itself into the Dead Sea, healing the dead waters and causing the place of barrenness to become a centre of life where men can fish. Trees of shade and fruit and healing balm will line the banks of the river.

What a picture of the waters of salvation, flowing out from God, bringing life wherever they flow.

DANIEL

"THE MOST HIGH RULETH"

*"Who is the image of the invisible God, the firstborn of every
creature: For by Him were all things created, that are in
heaven, and that are in earth, visible and invisible, whether
they be thrones, or dominions, or principalities, or powers:
all things were created by Him, and for Him: and He is
before all things, and by Him all things consist. And He
is the head of the body, the Church: Who is the beginning,
the firstborn from the dead; that in all things He might have
the pre-eminence. For it pleased the Father that in Him
should all fulness dwell;"* (COLOSSIANS i. 15-19)

THE PROPHET

It is to be remembered that God has a way of taking the
poor and the insignificant to do His bidding — a shepherd, a
herdsman, a fisherman, etc. — but there are times when He works
otherwise. He may have a physician as well as a fisherman, a
pharisee as much as a tax-gatherer, a prince or a gatherer of
sycamore. Daniel was a member of the royal family of Judah,
who, with others of high rank as well as low, had been carried
away captive into the land of Babylon. He was but a youth when
he was deported and so had spent most of his life in exile. His
captivity took place in the reign of Jehoiakim. He was a contemporary with Ezekiel and with Jeremiah, although each
ministered in a different sphere.

Daniel was outstanding in his wisdom and in his understanding
of the times. God seemed to have given to him a precision of
detail such as the other prophets never received. Soon after his
captivity, Nebuchadnezzar decided that certain of the better class
of the captives, those who were from families of responsibility,
and also any who were descendants of the royal line, should be
granted special privileges. They were to have a three-year course
of training, so that they might be educated in the language and
customs of their new country; also they were to be taught in all
the sciences of the Chaldeans so that such men might be able to
serve in the royal court. It must not be considered that this was
an honour bestowed on these captives because of the generosity

of their captors. It was a common practice of those days, and had two ulterior motives.

(1) It was customary for kings to use foreigners in their court. It gave the king prestige and reminded others of his power of conquest.

(2) By thus instructing these captives of high rank, it might cause them to lose interest and loyalty in their own country and in their own religion. This would strengthen the king's realm, and remove dissatisfaction and possible uprisings.

Of the men chosen for this training, the names are recorded of four who were outstanding in their ability, men who were stalwarts, faithful to the God of their fathers, and therefore men who must be broken so that they would yield to their new surroundings. These men were Daniel, Hananiah, Mishael, and Azariah. Their parents must have been God-fearing people because each name is related to the God of Israel.

> Daniel means " God is my Judge "
> Hananiah means " The grace of the Lord "
> Mishael means " He who comes from God "
> Azariah means " The Lord is a help "

Obviously these names would not be pleasing to Babylon, so they must be changed to conform with the worship of Babylon. These were the new names and their meanings :

Daniel to Belteshazzar	.....	The Treasure of Bel.
Hananiah to Shadrach	.....	The inspiration of the sun.
Mishael to Meshach	.....	He who belongs to the goddess Sheshach.
Azariah to Abed-nego	.....	The servant of Nego.

Whilst the names of these youths were changed, the Chaldeans had to learn that they could not so easily change their characters. They were Jews trained according to the law of Moses, which forbade the eating of certain meats which had been pronounced unclean (see Leviticus xi.). The law also required that a man should not touch any meat which had been offered to idols (Acts xv. 29). One of the requirements of these " privileged " men was that they should be fed daily with the king's meat, and with the wine which he drank. There was a possibility that such meat would first have been offered to idols, and also it could have been the kind which they had been forbidden to eat. The men requested, therefore, that they be excused. A trial was granted for ten days, with the result that God so honoured these men that they were healthier in body and clearer in mind than any others.

God will always honour those who honour Him, so let it be learned that it is possible to serve the Lord and to remain true to principles in any circumstances of life. No man has an honest excuse for compromise. To excuse oneself is to limit God either in His ability or in His willingness to stand by His people.

Here the Lord rewarded His faithful servants by endowing them with special gifts and abilities, particularly Daniel, who no doubt led the other three in their decisions and encouraged them in their faith.

THE BOOK

From beginning to end this book declares the sovereignty of God and reveals that He, as the Most High, ruleth over the affairs of men and of nations ; all power and might are His so that He can exalt, and He can cast down ; He it is Who openeth and no man shutteth, Who shutteth and no man openeth ; before Whom nations rise and fall as they submit to or reject His supreme Will : " Righteousness exalteth a nation, but sin is a reproach to any people " (Proverbs xiv. 34). The affairs of the world are known to Him with Whom we have to do, from the beginning of time to the very end.

This book of twelve chapters divides equally into two parts. Six chapters are *historical* and deal with the dreams of Nebuchadnezzar — six chapters are *prophetical* and are occupied with the visions of Daniel. The dreams and the visions are identical ; that is, both concern the rise and fall of the great empires of the world, but with this unique difference. A dream is earth-born and relates to the thoughts and the desires of men ; visions are a Divine revelation and belong to the rulings of God. When the two are put together, two aspects of the same thing are seen. The subject is world domination and politics. In the eyes of men these are as precious metals, seen in the Colossus of Nebuchadnezzar's dream. The same are seen as ferocious beasts in the Mind of God.

In these two parts, and in this light, the book is now studied.

HISTORICAL — DREAMS OF NEBUCHADNEZZAR
(Chs. i-vi.)

In chapter two Nebuchadnezzar dreamed a dream which, by the morning, he had forgotten as to detail, but the reaction of the dream left him with a troubled mind. In his unreasonableness he required that his wise men should make known to him both the dream and the interpretation. This they were unable to do, where-

upon the king commanded that all the wise men of his realm
should be slain. Men who are eaten up with selfish pride are
ever unjust in their demands upon others. Nebuchadnezzar committed more than one injustice here. Firstly, it was beyond all
reason that another should know his dream ; secondly, he did
not enquire of all his wise men, for Daniel and his companions
had been excluded ; and thirdly, he condemned them all to death,
including even those who had not been consulted, so Daniel and
his friends were under this condemnation. Daniel raised his voice
against this injustice as he appealed to Arioch, the Captain of
the guard, to tell him the reason for this hasty death-penalty.
When he learned the cause he asked for permission to see the
king. He told Nebuchadnezzar that, if he would give him time,
he would make known to him the dream and the interpretation.
Note the confidence Daniel had in his God. He did not suggest
that he would do his best. His answer to the king was very
positive. God gave to Daniel both the dream and the interpretation,
and he in turn brought them to Nebuchadnezzar.

Two things must not be overlooked at this point. Firstly,
Daniel was careful to thank God for the revelation when he had
received it, and, secondly, he was careful to give God the glory
as he witnessed before the king.

The First Dream — The Great Image (Ch. ii.). " Thou, O
king, sawest, and behold a great image " (vs. 31).

The head of gold represented Babylon (vs. 38).
The breast and arms of silver were an inferior kingdom
(vs. 39).
The belly of brass another inferior kingdom (vs. 39).
The legs of iron, a kingdom still more inferior (vs. 40).
The toes, part iron, part clay, a divided kingdom (vs. 41).
The stone cut out of the mountain, a universal kingdom
(vs. 34).

At this point it must be seen that Daniel only told Nebuchadnezzar as much interpretation as concerned himself. " Thou art
this head of gold " (read vs. 37-38). The rest represented inferior
nations, and the stone " what shall come to pass hereafter " (vs.
45).

It is known from later history that Babylon was followed by
several declining powers — Medo-Persia, Greece, and Rome —
but these were yet to be declared.

Several principles are to be seen in this Colossus.

(1) There was a steady fall in the value of the metals from gold to mixed iron and clay.

(2) The structure was top-heavy. It had a decline in the weight of gravity, for gold is heavier than silver, silver heavier than brass, and brass than iron.

(3) There was a degeneration in the power of the various empires, as also in the governmental authority, as they moved from absolute monarchy to an autocratic democracy and the decline of man.

Whilst Daniel did not tell Nebuchadnezzar what the other empires were, he did give us the information, for he declared them in other parts of his prophecy.

Daniel ii. 38 ..... " Thou art this head of gold " BABYLON

Daniel v. 30-31 ..... " In that night was Belshazzar the king of the Chaldeans slain. And Darius the *Median* took the kingdom . . . " ....MEDO-PERSIA

Daniel viii. 20-21..... " The ram which thou sawest having two horns are the kings of Media and Persia. And the rough goat is the king of Grecia." ....GRECIAN

Daniel ix. 26 ..... " . . . the people of the prince that shall come shall destroy the city and the sanctuary . . . " ....ROMAN

This Roman empire split and split and became a ten-kingdom confederacy.

The chapter concludes with Daniel and his companions being promoted to high offices, which seemingly did not please the other wise men of the realm !

The Golden Image — The Fiery Furnace (Ch. iii.). These servants of God, who had proved themselves faithful to their own God in a land of strange gods, were about to be tested again. They had been faithful in little things — their food. Now it was to be learned whether they would be faithful in big things — their worship.

No doubt Daniel, the leading man, had encouraged his friends in the matter of food. In this next test Shadrach, Meshach, and

Abed-nego were tested alone, and Daniel met the same test later and alone.

Nebuchadnezzar, in all his pride and glory, caused that a great image of gold should be set up on the plain of Dura, sixty cubits high, six cubits wide, and six musical instruments summoned all men to fall down and worship this image. Notice the sixes — 6 is the number of man. 666 is the number of the superman of the last day. This was man-worship, idolatry. How could the worshippers of Jehovah bend to such a god ? They could not. It meant positive resistance to the king, but to obey the king would be positive resistance to God. These men knew what the result would be, for a burning fiery furnace was the doom appointed by the king. Divine protection is the promise of God. " . . . when thou walkest through the fire, thou shalt not be burned, neither shall the flame kindle upon thee " (Isaiah xliii. 2). Who was going to win ? These men were prepared to trust God. They soon learned that the world was at enmity with them. They were not only opposing the pride of a king but resisting the jealousy of the world. This was the opportunity of the wise men who had been angered by the promotion of these men. Quickly they reported failure on the part of the three Jewish men to obey the king's command. The monarch gave these men an opportunity to repent and to worship his god. However, they were adamant (note their magnificent " but if not " — vs. 18), and were thrown into a seven-times heated fire. According to His promise, God was with them, so that the fire did not burn them. These three men have been referred to as " the men who would not bend, budge, nor burn."

But what was the result of the faithfulness of these men to their God and His worship ? Firstly, the king turned from his idolatry and recognised the True God of heaven, bidding all men to worship God, and, secondly, the men who sought to destroy them were used for their further promotion.

Learn that it never pays to serve the devil, and it always brings blessing when we trust the Lord.

The Second Dream — The Felled Tree (Ch. iv.). This dream, unlike the first, was remembered by Nebuchadnezzar. Nonetheless, the magicians and the wise men were still unable to interpret. God gave to Daniel the interpretation, who was greatly disturbed as a result.

The dream concerned a tree which grew and flourished in every way. It was great in size, beautiful in appearance, abundant in fruit, protective to both beast and bird, and provided food for many. Everything was well until some heavenly visitant cried out against it. The tree was to be cut down, but not totally destroyed, for the stump was to remain in the earth and to be protected.

The next verse (vs. 16) is somewhat deeper because, whilst speaking of a tree, the narrative suddenly changes from the impersonal to the personal. " Let his heart be changed from man's, and let a beast's heart be given unto him."

The interpretation given by Daniel is enlightening. The whole dream related to the king, who was being warned that although God had blessed him beyond measure so that his kingdom had prospered, instead of recognising the goodness of the Lord, the day was not far distant when, boastingly, he would take to himself the glory of all he possessed. In that day God would cut him down for his pride, take from him that proud mind, and cause him to be cast out from before men as an insane being. This condition would last for seven years, until he came to his senses and acknowledged that God was the Giver of every good and perfect gift. When he acknowledged God, God would acknowledge him once again, and restore him to his former place.

Twelve months later it all happened as revealed in the dream. (vs. 28-37).

May this teach us to walk humbly before our God, and recognise our nothingness and His almightiness, and that God ruleth in the affairs of men.

The Handwriting on the Wall (Ch. v.). This incident took place a few years later when the son of Nebuchadnezzar was reigning. His name was Belshazzar, who occupied the throne for seventeen years.

A little general history will be helpful to the background of this chapter.

Nimrod began to build the city of Babylon in the days of Genesis x. It was then called Babel. God stopped that building and the people were scattered, whilst their tongues were confused. Between 604 B.C. and 562 B.C., under the reign of Nebuchadnezzar, it became the finest city in the greatest empire of the world's history. The city was fifteen miles square, surrounded by sixty miles of wall eighty-seven feet thick, or wide enough to drive six chariots abreast. It was built with twenty-five streets running north to south, and the same number going east to west. The city was divided by the river Euphrates, which ran through its centre north to south. The river was walled on either side within the city, and at intervals there were gates of brass to give access to the water. Brazen gates were also at the ends of the principal streets which led out of the city. Beneath the city were subterranean passages, with wonderful chambers at various places made entirely of brass. These were banqueting halls. Over the river was a bridge, at either end of which was a beautiful palace. Close to one of these palaces stood the tower of Bel, or Babel as it was called when rebuilt in later years. This edifice consisted of eight towers, one above the other, with a temple on the top. Its total height was six hundred and sixty feet. The city also contained one of the seven wonders of the world, the Hanging Gardens.

Here Belshazzar was satisfied with a sense of security, for the city was considered impregnable. During all of his reign, Belshazzar had warred against Cyrus and the Medes and Persians. Cyrus had determined to capture that city. He made his plans and waited his time. The time had now come. One of the annual feasts to the heathen gods was in progress. This is the feast referred to in Daniel v.

The seventy years of Jewish exile were nearing an end and, maybe, it was in an act of defiance against God that Belshazzar sent for the holy vessels of Solomon's Temple, which Nebuchadnezzar had carried away years before, to use them in this riotous feast to his gods. This feast would have been held in one of those subterranean banqueting halls — when, over against the sacred seven-branched candlestick, he saw the fingers of a man's hand writing upon the wall. Once again the wise men of the realm were consulted, and once again they failed.

When the queen heard of the consternation of the king and his lords, and of the failure of the magicians to interpret, she told of Daniel, and of his abilities in the days of the king's father. Daniel was brought before the king and, having refused the royal reward that was offered, he gave to Belshazzar, the defiant king, the writing and the interpretation. " Thou art weighed in the balances, and art found wanting. Thy kingdom is divided, and given to the Medes and Persians " (v. 27-28).

The chapter closes with the words : " In that night was Belshazzar the king of the Chaldeans slain. And Darius the Median took the kingdom, being about three score and two years old " (v. 30-31) — not a young man to accomplish such a victory !

This would cause the question to be asked as to how such an impregnable city fell so easily. To quote from history and the Word of God, history tells us that the city was taken secretly by

Cyrus in 541 B.C. Cyrus drained the river out of the city and gained an entrance by the river bed. He entered through an unlocked gate of the river, found Belshazzar feasting, and slew him. So quietly was it done that some of the inhabitants did not know of it until three days afterwards.

Now hear the Word of the Lord. Cyrus and his victory and how he obtained it were told one hundred and twenty-five years before he was born. Read Isaiah xliv. 28 - xlv. 4 : " That saith of Cyrus, He is my shepherd, and shall perform all my pleasure ; even saying to Jerusalem, Thou shalt be built ; and to the temple, Thy foundation shall be laid. Thus saith the Lord to His anointed, to Cyrus, whose right hand I have holden, to subdue nations before him ; and I will loose the loins of kings, to open before him the two leaved gates ; and the gates shall not be shut ; I will go before thee, and make the crooked places straight : I will break in pieces the gates of brass, and cut in sunder the bars of iron. And I will give thee the treasures of darkness, and hidden riches of secret places, that thou mayest know that I, the Lord, which call thee by thy name, am the God of Israel. For Jacob my servant's sake, and Israel Mine elect, I have even called thee by thy name : I have surnamed thee, though thou hast not known Me."

The Den of Lions (Ch. vi.). Jealousy and selfishness are two of the greatest and most dangerous sins in the world. They are the root of a thousand other sins. In his selfishness man holds on to everything he has ; in his jealousy he hates the other man who may be better than he, and he will do anything to wreck the other man. This was what Daniel now faced. He had been promoted to first place in the realm on the ground of merit, to the displeasure of the other princes and presidents of the realm. Daniel, in his wisdom, gave no occasion to his enemies to bring any accusation against him. What the world cannot do honestly it will do dishonestly, so it was planned to catch Daniel in a trap, and this would have to be in connection with his faith in his God.

These enemies of Daniel persuaded the king to issue a decree which would require that for thirty days men should pray to none other than the king. This one act would impress the king's ego and put him on their side, and would destroy Daniel, whose loyalty could not be divided. If he were faithful to his God he would be disloyal to the king and lose his position. That was what they wanted. If he were faithful to the king he would lose out as a prophet, and that would please them.

The decree was made and duly signed and, according to the law of the Medes and Persians, there was no escape. They watched the conduct of Daniel. What these people forgot was that not only can a man be faithful to God, but that God is always faithful to His own. There was no yielding on the part of Daniel, not even a thought of secret worship. He prayed, as he did aforetime. The result was that he was cast into a den of lions. His enemies believed that they had won a decisive victory, but they had to learn that, when they opposed Daniel, they also opposed his God.

The enemy was happy and Daniel was content. The only troubled person was the king who, in his concern for Daniel, was unable to sleep. Hoping against hope, he went early in the morning to the den to find out whether Daniel's God was able to deliver. He learned that God was well able.

Daniel was promoted again, his enemies fell into the trap they had set for the servant of God, and the Name of God was set high in the kingdom of Darius and also in the reign of Cyrus, king of Persia.

Daniel's God is still on the throne !

PROPHETICAL — VISIONS OF DANIEL (Chs. vii-xii.)

The same empires of the world are seen from the Divine viewpoint, as the precious metals become ferocious beasts.

VISION 1 (Ch. vii.). Seventeen years back in history, in the first year of Belshazzar, Daniel said : " I saw in my vision by night, and, behold, the four winds of the heaven strove upon the great sea. And four great beasts came up from the sea, diverse one from another " (vii. 23). The first beast was like

A Lion with Eagle's Wings and a Man's Head. This was an emblem of authority, strength, and speed.

The Lion	.....	king of animals	.....	strength
The Eagle	.....	king of birds	.....	swiftness
Man	.....	head of creation	.....	authority

All of this referred to Nebuchadnezzar, king of Babylon, the head of gold. The plucking of the wings, followed by the lifting up from the earth, would possibly relate to his period of insanity followed by his restoration to power again.

The second beast which he saw was

A Bear with Three Ribs in its Mouth. This creature was told to devour much flesh. The bear is next in strength to the lion, but it is not majestic as the lion. Instead it is awkward and

ponderous. It does not gain by skill but by sheer brute force. This
was typical of the Medo-Persian empire, the two shoulders of the
image. The fact that "it raised up itself on one side" would
suggest that one part of the kingdom was stronger than the other.
This was true, as Persia was much stronger than Media. One
is reminded of the brute force, or the ponderous characteristic, as
the record of history shows how Xerxes went against Greece with
an army of five million men. He attacked by mass, not by skill.
An army of that size would "devour much flesh".

The three ribs were Lydia, Babylon, and Egypt, who formed
a triple alliance against Medo-Persia but were destroyed.

A Leopard with Four Wings of a Fowl and Four Heads. The
leopard is one of the most graceful of creatures. It is very agile,
and is swift in its movements. This speed was increased by the
wings of a fowl. (A fowl does not use its wings for ascent or
flight, only to increase its ground movement).

All this points to the Grecian empire. Under Alexander the
Great, the Greeks, with small but brave armies, overthrew Persia
and subdued most of the world in the span of about ten years.
"And dominion was given to it."

The empire was later divided into four kingdoms and given
to Alexander's four generals. These would be represented by the
four heads. The four kingdoms were Thrace, Macedonia, Syria,
and Egypt. This would correspond with the brass section of the
Colossus.

A Composite Creature — something Daniel had never seen
previously. It was dreadful, terrible, and exceeding strong. It had
great iron teeth, and destroyed everything around it.

This was the same creature which was seen by John, who
gave a further description. "And the beast which I saw was like
unto a leopard, and his feet were as the feet of a bear, and his
mouth as the mouth of a lion . . ." (Revelation xiii. 2). It will
be noticed that this composite creature embraced all of the
creatures which Daniel saw. Each kingdom had absorbed the
kingdom that was before, so that they were all in the last kingdom.
In both instances the creature had ten horns.

As Daniel mused on this sight he noticed the appearance of
another horn, springing up in the midst of the ten. Before this
one, three of the other horns were plucked up by the roots and
destroyed. He then saw that this new horn had the face and the
eyes of a man, and a mouth speaking great things.

There was no parallel to this in the image, so Daniel was troubled. In verse 15 he enquired of one standing by and received an answer. The ten horns were ten kings, and one was a king who should subdue three kings. Verse 21 declares that this horn would make war with the saints and prevail against them. Each of these kingdoms was subdued by the Ancient of Days, Who, with His followers, had final victory.

VISION 2 (Ch. viii.)

A Ram and an He Goat. The ram was the first animal to appear by the river bank. It had two horns, which grew in the vision. The one horn was higher than the other. This creature charged in three directions. It subdued everything that came near. Whilst the ram challenged all around him, a he-goat was seen coming with great speed from the west. This goat had an unusual horn protruding from between his eyes. He closed in with the ram, overcame it, broke its two horns, and stamped it to the ground. The he-goat then became stronger and stronger until its great horn was broken off and in its place there appeared four horns. Out of one of these horns there came a little horn which also waxed strong. It magnified itself and took upon itself dominion, resisting the powers which already existed, defaming the sanctuary, and causing the sacrifice to cease.

Gabriel gave the interpretation to Daniel. It belonged to the time of the end. That is not the end of time.

Much of the interpretation has already been given because it is a parallel of what has gone before, or a double emphasis.

The ram stood for Medo-Persia — vs. 20.

The horns, the two kings Darius and Cyrus — vs. 20.

The he-goat denoted the Grecian empire — vs. 21.

The Great Horn was the first king, Alexander the Great — vs. 21.

The Four Horns were the four kingdoms of Greece — vs. 22.

This reveals that the two horns of the ram, the two shoulders of the bear, and the two arms of the Image, were the same; so also the four horns and the four heads of the leopard were one.

The little horn was the prince of fierce countenance who is to withstand the Prince of princes (Christ) in the last days. That will be the Antichrist (vs. 23-25).

VISION 3 (Ch. ix.)

Daniel's Seventieth Week. Daniel was pouring out his heart in confession for his people who, as a result of their sin, were enduring their long captivity. He was also supplicating the Lord to show forth His mercy and forgive His people and to restore the sanctuary and the city which were now in ruinous desolation. The reason for this particular prayer was the fact that he had studied the prophecies of Jeremiah, and he knew that the judgment God had determined must almost be expiring. It is always a good thing to pray intelligently. As he ended his prayer Gabriel made his appearance bringing the answer to that prayer, and revealing to Daniel that, whilst the seventy years were expiring, there was still further judgment determined for further sin.

" Seventy weeks are determined upon thy people and upon thy holy city, to finish the transgression, and to make an end of sins, and to make reconciliation for iniquity, and to bring in everlasting righteousness, and to seal up the vision and prophecy, and to anoint the Most Holy. Know therefore and understand, that from the going forth of the commandment to restore and to build Jerusalem unto the Messiah the Prince shall be seven weeks, and three score and two weeks: The street shall be built again, and the wall, even in troublous times. And after three score and two weeks shall Messiah be cut off, but not for Himself ; and the people of the prince that shall come shall destroy the city and the sanctuary; and the end thereof shall be with a flood, and unto the end of the war desolations are determined. And he shall confirm the covenant with many for one week ; and in the midst of the week he shall cause the sacrifice and the oblation to cease, and for the overspreading of abominations he shall make it desolate, even until the consummation, and that determined shall be poured upon the desolate " (vs. 24-27).

To interpret these verses, one or two things need to be understood.

Whilst a calendar week is seven days, a prophetic week is seven years. Daniel's seventy weeks, therefore, is a period of 70 × 7 = 490 years. These seventy weeks were divided into three parts — 7 weeks, 62 weeks, and 1 week (vs. 25 & 27).

The Times of the Gentiles began in 606 B.C., when Jerusalem was first destroyed by Nebuchadnezzar and the Jewish people were taken away, and so Babylon, a Gentile nation, became the dominating nation. The Gentile nations have controlled world affairs ever since.

After seventy years of captivity an edict was issued for the rebuilding of the city. The record of this edict is found in Ezra vii. 12-13 : " Artaxerxes, king of kings, unto Ezra the priest, a scribe of the law of the God of heaven, perfect peace, and at such a time. I make a decree . . . " This was in the year 457 B.C.

The 69 weeks are made up of 7 weeks plus 62 weeks, equalling 69 weeks. This figure is multiplied by 7, for the prophetic week, thus making 483 years. The difference between 457 B.C. and 483 years is 26 years, so bringing one into the year 26 A.D. That was the year the Lord began His public ministry, and the Messiah had come. " After three score and two weeks shall Messiah be cut off, but not for Himself " (ix. 26).

That took place in A.D. 30, when Christ was crucified for the sins of the world. Then came the destruction of the city in A.D. 70, by the prince that should come (Titus). From that time the Jews were dispersed and ceased to be a nation until a confirmation of the covenant for one week. That is the week which stands on its own and is still future. It is known as Daniel's Seventieth Week, or the Tribulation.

VISION 4 (Ch. x.)

The Angelic Visitants. Daniel had spent three weeks in mourning and fasting. The reason for this fasting may be ascertained from a comparison of dates. According to the first chapter of Ezra, the edict of Cyrus for the return of the Jews to Jerusalem was made in the first year of his reign, and it is known that it was but a remnant of the people who returned with Ezra. This tenth chapter of Daniel was in the third year of the reign of Cyrus, or two years after the issuing of his proclamation. This suggests that Daniel was stricken with grief, and therefore interceded with God on behalf of an indifferent people who had lost their love for God. As a result God gave to Daniel a further revelation of their future.

As Daniel prayed he had a vision. So great was the sight that he was left paralysed with fear. He describes the One Whom he saw, Who must have been none other than the Lord Himself, for the description which he gives in verses 5 and 6 compares with the description of the Lord given in Revelation i. 13/16. Both Daniel and John fell down as dead, and both of them testified that a hand was placed upon them. In both instances the vision was not shared by another.

In fact, no vision from God, whatever its nature, is ever a shared experience. Abram was visited by God after Lot had gone his way. Jacob was *left alone;* and there wrestled a man with him. Moses was *alone* in the desert and *alone* on the mount. Daniel said : " And I *alone* saw the vision." Paul, on the way to Damascus, testified that the men with him heard the voice but saw nothing. John was an *exile* in Patmos. Spiritual experiences are always very personal and very sacred. Some are shared with people afterwards, many are not.

It would seem that the hand which touched the Prophet in verse 10 was not the hand of the One he had seen in the vision, for there could be a time element at verse 9, inasmuch as Daniel fell into a deep sleep. The hand must have been that of an angel. It was certainly not the Lord's, because he was sent, he was delayed, he needed the help of another, and he spoke in the third person.

The emphasis of the narrative at this juncture is the constant war which is taking place in the heavenlies. Let it be learned that prayer is heard by God as soon as it is offered, and that answers are sometimes delayed because of the activity of the god of this world. This is not because Satan is more powerful than, or even as powerful as, God. Michael, one of God's chief angels, combatted the " prince of Persia ", one of Satan's chief angels, and he won the battle and the answer came. This angelic being also had to fight his way back again. In the Epistle of Jude, Michael contended with the Devil concerning the body of Moses. In Revelation xii. Michael fights his last battle with Satan, who is cast out.

God gave the Devil his death-blow through Christ at the Cross. Since then the conflict has continued with the spiritual forces led by an angel, whilst Christ intercedes for us. It should be realised how real the spirit forces are around us, and how weak men are. We will rejoice that all the forces of heaven are on our side, and that the Angel of the Lord is round about them that fear Him.

VISION 5 (Ch. xi.)

The Kings of the North and South. The chapter is an enlargement of the history of the third great power — Greece. All that Daniel had made known was fulfilled in that empire more than two hundred years later. The kings of the north and the south were two of the divisions of that empire — Syria and Egypt.

Antiochus Epiphanes was the wilful king. Among other things
which he did, he slew eighty thousand Jews, captured forty
thousand, and sold forty thousand. He desecrated the Temple
by offering a pig upon the altar.

He was but a type of the Antichrist who is yet to come, so
that the Vision still holds an interpretation belonging to the last
days.

VISION 6 (Ch. xii.)

The Time of the End. The book closes with a reference
to the end of the age, a time of trouble for the world such as never
was. This is the Great Tribulation detailed in the last book of
the Bible, when Michael will be active in defending God's chosen
people.

Michael is the archangel. He is ever associated with resurrection. He had to deliver the body of Moses, as recorded in the
Epistle of Jude. It is at his voice that the dead will be raised
(1 Thessalonians iv. 16). Here in chapter xii some will be raised
to everlasting life and some to everlasting shame.

Daniel was instructed to close and seal the book till the time
of the end. That time comes when John, in Revelation, sees the
Lamb take that book, sealed with seven seals, out of the Hand
of Him Who sits upon the throne, the opening of which ushers in
the Tribulation and the final consummation of all things.

HOSEA

ESTRANGEMENT AND RESTORATION

" But ye go and learn what that meaneth, I will have mercy,
and not sacrifice ; for I am not come to call the righteous,
but sinners to repentance." (MATTHEW ix. 13)

INTRODUCTION

The narrative of this book is both sad and tragic. It is concerned particularly with the conduct of the Northern Kingdom, known as Israel. Their behaviour had been so disgraceful that God must expose it. Yet they had become so insensible to sin that they were not aware of it. God was about to establish an awareness in the heart of the nation and then, on an evidence of their repentance, He was prepared to forgive all that had been done and to restore all that had been lost. But in order to make these people sensitive to their sin, He had to demonstrate it in the life and conduct of His servant, Hosea.

THE PROPHET

Hosea meant " Deliverer and Saviour ", even as Joshua meant " Jesus and Saviour." One can see how the Lord over-ruled even in the naming of babies when they were born. What did a mother know about the future of her child when she called him Hosea or Isaiah or Joel or Nahum, or whatever name she did attach to him, and yet these and all the other prophets proved their names again and again.

Hosea was the first of what are known as the Minor Prophets, which are the shorter books of the Prophetic section. This man's ministry was decidedly longer than the book which bears his name, for his prophetic career was between sixty and seventy years, extending through the reigns of Uzziah, Jotham, Ahaz, and Hezekiah, as kings of Judah, and also that of Jeroboam II, king of Israel. He was contemporary with other of the prophets, as Jonah, Amos, Isaiah, and Micah, and probably with Joel.

Jeroboam II had brought to an end a dynasty of kings over Israel. Because of the sins of the people the period of twelve

421

years which followed the reign of Jeroboam was one of anarchy. Zachariah, Shallum, Menehim, Pekaliah, Pekah, and Hoshea, all took the throne in that short period, and each was slain.

Like Isaiah and Jeremiah, much of Hosea's ministry was demonstrated in signs, some of which would have been very unpleasant to the Prophet and most surprising to the people. The burden of his message was a coming judgment and a future blessing. Hosea was raised up to be a deliverer to God's people and their ultimate salvation, which was the meaning of his name.

THE BOOK

The book may be divided into two :

(1) Personal affliction — the dishonoured wife (Chs. i-iii.).

(2) National rejection — the sinful people (Chs. iv-xiv.).

(1) PERSONAL AFFLICTION—THE DISHONOURED WIFE (Chs. i-iii.)

The Lord was anxious for the nation to know how grievously they had sinned against Himself, and also to what extent His love and His mercy were reaching out toward them. Therefore He bade His servant, Hosea, to go and marry a woman, devoid of any moral principles — a harlot, a woman who had shared her life unlawfully with others, for their and her pleasure, a woman who had no honour, whose past had been such that she was not entitled to have bestowed upon her the right of honourable marriage or the privilege of wifehood. It could have been no easy assignment for a respectable Prophet, but he obeyed God, married the disreputable woman, and by her begat several children. By this he gave her the opportunity to become a respectable citizen in the community.

The Lord was seeking to make the picture obvious to the nation. Their great sin was that they had forsaken God and turned to serve other gods. This was contrary to every commandment. He had said : " Thou shalt have no other gods before Me . . . for I the Lord thy God am a jealous God, visiting the iniquity of the fathers upon the children unto the third and fourth generation of them that hate Me " (Exodus xx. 3-5).

God had called these people to Himself, had poured all His love upon them, had drawn them unto Himself, had caused that they should be to Him as a wife and He as a husband to them. In Isaiah liv. 5 it is stated : " For thy Maker is thine husband, the Lord of Hosts is His Name . . . " Therefore, to forsake God and turn to idols, to their many lovers, was equal to a woman leaving a true and faithful husband to go and live with other men.

The nation had played the harlot. She had lost her character, but God was willing to receive her back again, forgive her the past sin, and allow her to bring forth the fruit of righteousness to His honour and praise.

The Lord has done this for all mankind. Man was made in the image and likeness of God, created for Himself, but man turned every one to his own way. He went the way of the world and served the Devil but, whilst we were yet sinners, Christ died for us. He drew us back to Himself with the cords of love, lifted us from the miry clay, and in a life of holiness bids us bring forth fruit to His praise.

The amazing thing is that the Lord has done this without forfeiting His holiness — O, boundless, matchless love !

The Prophet's Family. With little in the way of introduction, the book opens with the Lord's most extraordinary instruction to the Prophet. " Go, take unto thee a wife of whoredoms and children of whoredom : for the land hath committed great whoredom, departing from the Lord " (i. 2).

The woman he married was Gomer, the daughter of Diblaim. There is a great deal of significance attached to names in the Bible and this book is certainly no exception. Gomer meant " confusion ", and she displayed it in all of her behaviour, as did the nation she was now representing. She was the daughter of Diblaim, a name that meant " two cakes ". Someone has pointed out that, if the " two cakes " could suggest plenty, the picture is a true one. It is when man has plenty and is self-satisfied that he turns his back on God to serve the gods of this world, and that to his undoing. Sin and confusion are so often the daughters of plenty.

This woman bore three children to Hosea. All three were named by the Lord, for He intended through His servant to cause Israel to understand some vital truths. When the first child was born " The Lord said unto him (Hosea), call his name

JEZREEL, for yet a little while, and I will avenge the blood of Jezreel upon the house of Jehu, and will cause to cease the kingdom of the house of Israel. And it shall come to pass at that day, that I will break the bow of Israel in the valley of Jezreel " (i. 4-5).

This statement should have caused some musings in the hearts of Israel. In fact, it should cause the mind of the Bible student to become quite active. What did this name Jezreel mean?

(1) It meant the valley of Jezreel, now called the Esdraelon Plain, also the valley of Magiddo. It has been the battlefield of the nation through the centuries and still will be. David fought Goliath there. Israel defeated the Canaanites there in the well-known story of Jael and Sisera (Judges vi.).

(2) Ahab's palace and the Temple of Baal were at this place (1 Kings xxi.).

(3) Elijah contested the prophets of Baal at the head of this valley (1 Kings xviii.).

(4) Naboth had a vineyard in Jezreel. Jezebel murdered him for the property. As a result Elijah said : " Thus saith the Lord, In the place where dogs licked the blood of Naboth shall dogs lick thy blood, even thine " (1 Kings xxi. 19). Again, " And of Jezebel also spake the Lord, saying, The dogs shall eat Jezebel by the wall of Jezreel " (1 Kings xxi. 23). This was literally fulfilled in 2 Kings ix. 30-57, when she was thrown from the window.

(5) In 1 Kings xxii. 37-38, when Ahab died in battle, the dogs licked up his blood as they washed the chariot. This was in Jezreel.

(6) Ahab was succeeded by Joram. He was wounded in Ramoth Gilead by the Syrians. He went down to Jezreel to be healed of his wounds but, instead, he was slain there by Jehu, and his body was thrown into Naboth's vineyard. It was through this slaughter that Jehu came to the throne. Jereboam II, who was reigning when Hosea was ministering, was a descendant of Jehu.

Thus God was speaking to both king and people when He told Hosea to name his son Jezreel.

God dealt with the nation which had turned away from Him so many times. God is going to do it again, for Armageddon is the same valley of Jezreel where He is going to deal with those who have shed the blood of His people, and with those who have trampled underfoot the Blood of the everlasting Covenant as though it were an unholy thing.

The second child to be born to Hosea was a girl, and God named her

LO RUHAMAH, which meant " Not having obtained mercy." Because they had rejected His mercy in the previous generation, there was none for them now. The nation had forsaken Him, now He was forsaking them.

The third child was another son, named again by God,

LO AMMI, meaning "Not My people." God not only withdrew His mercy, but He would even withdraw Himself. "For ye are not My people, and I will not be your God " (i. 9).

All this is understandable now because its fulfilment has been seen. God has given them up for the time being. He has scattered them over the face of the globe, and there they still are, forsaken although not forgotten. The Lord is long-suffering and merciful. Verse 10 is the ray of hope. It is a promise of God. "YET the number of the children of Israel shall be as the sand of the sea . . ."

These last two verses of chapter one are a promise of complete restoration. This hope of the future is continued in the opening verses of chapter two. The LO which is the negative, is dropped from the two names. Lo Ammi, "Not My people", became Ammi, "My people"; and the Lo Ruhamah became Ruhamah, "Loved" or "Having obtained mercy."

The chapter then returns from the blessings of the future to the tragedies of the present. Hosea was disowning Gomer as his wife. The reason for this was that he had picked her up out of harlotry and had brought her into a place of honour through legal marriage. He had loved her with a pure love, but she had failed to prove herself worthy for she fell back to her old ways. This made her position worse than it was at the beginning. Then she was a harlot, but now, because of a legal marriage and pledging herself to one lover, she had become an adulteress. She was still the mother of his children, but no longer the recognised wife of Hosea. Hence he said : "Plead with thy mother, plead ; for she is not my wife " (ii. 2).

This was true concerning Israel. Although God loved that nation, had taken her to Himself, had blessed her above all the nations of the earth, and had caused her to be fruitful in her increase, yet she forsook Him and fell back into idolatry. She took His gifts and blessings, and bestowed them upon her idols, until He had to withdraw her corn and wine, her wool and her flax, and so bring her down to nothingness and expose her before her lovers. Then, when she would learn her lesson, He would draw her into the wilderness (the solitary place) and speak in a friendly manner to her heart. In fact, right there in the valley of her trouble (Achor) He would open to her a door of hope and opportunity, so that she might return to her former relationship, into the place where she could call him "Ishi", which meant "My husband", instead of calling him "Baali", the meaning of which was "My lord". What amazing grace! Instead of forsaking her utterly He was prepared to bring her into an even closer fellowship. All this is so striking of the grace of our Lord Jesus Christ.

To forsake God has never been a profitable thing for anyone. The Lord sought to demonstrate this truth to the nation. Hosea had been good to this woman, Gomer, in receiving her as his wife in her days of loose love; now she had left him and was following other men, men who failed her as her husband had never done. So low had she fallen in her degradation that she became a slave who was put on to the open slave market to be bought by any man who might desire so to do. She had lost respect, honour, and freedom. God bade Hosea: "Go yet, love a woman beloved of her friend, yet an adulteress" (iii. 1), that was, one who had been beloved by a friend whom she had forsaken for others, thus making herself to become an adulteress. So the Prophet went to the slave market and there found the woman, his own wife who had left him. She left him for her freedom, he found her in shackles. In his love for this wretched character he purchased her for fifteen pieces of silver and one and a half homers of barley, so that again she became his wife. However, this time she was to prove herself, so he gave her a period of probation before she could enjoy the fellowship he desired and she needed.

All of this was so applicable to Israel. Sought out by God and blessed by Him, yet she wandered after other gods, but God did not forsake her. He sought her in her sin and shame. The nation is not with the Lord yet. She is on probation. She is passing through those "many days without a king, without a prince, and without a sacrifice, and without an image and without an ephod, and without teraphim" (iii. 4), but presently He is going to take to Himself this people whom He has chosen.

Likewise the Church, purchased in this world by His precious Blood, has been left here on probation. Presently He is coming to receive from the world His own, to enjoy an eternity of fellowship with Himself. We are His by creation, His by redemption — we are doubly His.

NATIONAL REJECTION — THE SINFUL PEOPLE
(Chs. iv-xiv.)

This is the second section of the book. It elaborates the sins of the nation in chapter four and those of the priests in chapter five.

God set up His court and brought in His prisoners. The nation was charged with having *no sense of honesty*. " There is no truth." In the last days, because the people receive not the truth, God is going to send a strong delusion that they shall believe a lie. These conditions in some measure were already existing. They had *lost all sense of morality*. Mercy had departed from their conduct with the poor. They were " swearing, and lying, and killing, and stealing, and committing adultery." It sounds as though they were breaking every commandment that God had made.

He charged them with *wilful ignorance*. If a man be ignorant, there is a measure of excuse and overlooking, but so much ignorance was wilful, " . . . because thou hast rejected knowledge, I will also reject thee . . . " (iv. 6). They were without excuse.

The next charge was *God-rejection*. " My people ask counsel at their stocks . . . " (iv. 12), that was, their idols who were on the top of every mountain and hill, and under every green tree.

Following His charge came His sentence. As to the land, it shall mourn (vs. 3). As to the people, " Ephraim is joined to idols: let him alone " (vs. 17). What a statement ! " Let him alone." God had done all He could to warn and to persuade. His patience had been exhausted. The period of the striving of His Spirit had come to an end — " Let him alone." If Ephraim would not learn by love and persuasion, then he must learn by hard, practical experience. It is a tragic thing when God has to do such things, and He never does it willingly.

God sometimes has to deliver a man over to Satan for the destruction of the flesh that the spirit might be saved (1 Cor. v. 5).

Chapter five is a continuation of God's judgment, but it is addressed more particularly to the priests and the princes, to the leaders of the nation, both spiritual and temporal, leaders who were no better than the led.

Ephraim is addressed a number of times in this chapter. There does not appear to be any reason for this other than it was the largest tribe of Israel, and so, like the priests and the princes, may have had some leadership.

God's dealings with them in the beginning were not violent. In verse 12 He said : " I will be unto Ephraim as a moth, and to the house of Judah as rottenness." Neither of these things makes a noise nor causes an alarm. One eats into the fabric of things, the other into the wood, but the work is devastating nonetheless. When Ephraim and Judah became aware of their condition, instead of turning to God for deliverance, they sought help from

the Assyrians who were unable to help. God then declared a change
in dealing with His people. He would be as a lion, and as a young
lion, which would tear in pieces and carry away. The process
would be faster and more alarming.

This should be pondered by all. As soon as things become
adverse in man's life, he ever wants to run to the world for help
instead of turning to the Lord in prayer and confession. As a
result, the conditions of life never improve. He goes on until the
Lord brings him very low. Even then repentance is often a
shallow thing. Man repents not because he is sorry for his sin
but because he wants to be rid of his punishment; not because
he is conscious that he has wronged the Lord, but because he is
concerned about self. This is the truth found in the next chapter.

A SHALLOW REPENTANCE (Ch. vi. 1-3)   The words are
good and the sentiments are fine. " Come, and let us return unto
the Lord . . . and He will heal us . . . He shall come unto us as
the rain, as the latter and former rain unto the earth." It tells
of the mercy of the Lord but there is no evidence of the sinfulness
of the people. That this was empty talk is evidenced by the Lord's
reply in verse 4 — and, remember, He knows the secret thoughts
of the heart. " O Ephraim, what shall I do unto thee ? O Judah,
what shall I do unto thee ? For your goodness is as a morning
cloud, and as the early dew it goeth away." Morning clouds whisk
across the sky but carry no water, and dew is refreshing but disappears just as quickly as the sun rises. The people had spoken
of Him Whose going forth is prepared as the morning and as the
rain (vi. 3). He used their same illustrations, but in reverse
meaning. God had to deal with them in judgment according to
their hearts and not according to their lips.

Even when the Lord wanted to be merciful and was ready
to forgive one iniquity, immediately another would spring into
being which could not be overlooked. In reproving them for their
manifold sins the Prophet used a number of figurative yet forceful
expressions, as

" An oven heated by the baker " (vii. 4). The Prophet likened
the nation to adulterers who were so eager in their sin of running
after other gods that they were like the heated oven which was
ready and waiting to receive the bread. The heat of the oven
would cause the leaven to begin to work until all became leavened.
The king (Jereboam II), as the baker, having put the bread into
the oven after kneading it, had gone to sleep and not awakened
until the whole was spoiled.

" *A cake not turned* " (vii. 8). The cake was like our pan-
cake. It was either put on to a heated plate of iron with a fire
underneath, or on the hearth with the hot ashes put on top. From
time to time the cake would be turned over until it was cooked
right through. A cake not turned, therefore, would be burnt on
one side but would remain uncooked on the other side. Either
way it could not be eaten, so, again, it was something totally
spoiled by carelessness.

Carelessness in spiritual or material things can make us useless
in the service of God, in our privilege of feeding others.

The next picture is not one of carelessness but one of self-
deception.

" *Gray hairs and he knoweth it not* " (vii. 9). The first signs of
old age appear. The nation was grown old in its sin. It was
losing its strength because it had given it away to strangers. The
grey hairs denoted that the prime of life was passing, and yet the
people refused to acknowledge it. It is always a tragedy when
a person refuses to face facts and realities, and tries to deceive
himself that he is not as old as he really is ; but more tragic is the
man or woman who, in advanced years, continues to make no preparation for the future life in their desire to hold on to the present
life. How earthbound so many people are ! Always running
to the doctor to help preserve this life, but never seeking the Great
Physician concerning the life to come.

" *A silly dove without heart* " (viii. 11). To quote from Adam
Clarke : " A bird that has little understanding ; that is easily
snared and taken ; that is careless about its own young, and seems
to live without any kind of thought. It has been made by those
who, like itself, are without heart, the symbol of conjugal affection.
Nothing worse could have been chosen, for the dove and its mate
are continually quarrelling."

In this foolishness of Israel they called upon Egypt and
Assyria for help, yet these two nations were rivals, one against
the other. Israel could not attach itself to the one without in-
curring the jealousy and displeasure of the other. Thus, like the
silly dove, constantly they were falling into snares, sometimes by
the Egyptians, at others by the Assyrians. By the former they
were betrayed ; by the latter ruined.

In chapters viii-x. there is further reproof because of the
idolatry which was abounding. Among his many flowery, yet
forceful, statements Hosea said : " For they have

sown the wind, and they shall reap the whirlwind" (viii. 7). The quotation is often made that what a man sows that he shall also reap. This is true inasmuch as, if a man sows wheat, he will reap wheat, and if a man sows tares, he will reap tares. But another thought comes to mind by this statement of the Prophet. It is that a man does more than reap what he sows. He harvests what he sows. In other words, he expects to gather very much more than that which he puts into the ground. If it be wheat that he sows, he expects a return of thirty, sixty, or a hundredfold, and the bigger the return the better he likes it.

Thus it must be expected in the world of morals. If the seed of unrighteousness be sown, a harvest of the judgment of God can be expected. On the other hand, if the seeds of submission and obedience to the Will of God are sown, then with confidence one may look for the multiplied blessings of the Lord.

Israel had here sown the seed of idolatry as they had accepted the gods of the other nations. In return they would reap the dominion of those other nations and the futility of their false gods.

In chapter nine they were acknowledging the false gods as being responsible for providing them with corn and wine, so the Lord threatened them with famine and exile, both in Assyria and Egypt, the nations in which they had been putting their trust.

He reminded them that He had looked in favour upon their fathers. They had been like grapes in the wilderness which bring refreshment to the traveller. God had found Abraham, Isaac, Jacob, and others, acceptable to Himself. They were the first-fruits, but these, their descendants, were very different. They had corrupted themselves through their lusts. Their glory, therefore, would take its flight, so that the thing for which they longed mostly should no longer be theirs — that was, posterity. They should not bear children and, even if they did, they would not be able to rear them. So the Prophet used another metaphor and said :

" *Israel is an empty vine* " (x. 1), with the next statement " He bringeth forth fruit unto Himself." It sounds contradictory, but the rendering elsewhere is " A vine emptying the fruit which it giveth," which means, the vine that casteth off her fruit before it develops and matures. Instead of bearing fruit for the good of others, it is bearing and yet is non-productive.

That is what happens to the nation, or the individual soul, which forsakes God.

" As hemlock in the furrows of the field " (x. 4), the hurtful weed which grows in the uncultivated field and is injurious to animals. So, in their barren and neglected hearts, had sprung up an anarchy which was proving harmful to society, and was bringing the judgment of God — as in society, so in religion.

"The thorn and the thistle shall come up on their altars " (x. 8). Eventually the people would cry to the mountains to cover them, and to the hills to fall on them, which is the language of the last days recorded in Luke xxiii. 30 and Revelation vi. 16.

Notice how much of the language of the Prophet is attached to the fields. They were an agricultural people, living close to the soil, so he was speaking in their language. His illustrations were unmistakable, his lessons unavoidable. Seedtime and harvest, crops and weeds, the cultivated and the wild, the wind and the rain, ploughing, fallowing, sowing, harrowing, watering, reaping, threshing — all are here. From the consequences of the neglected field of the heart, which does not remain void but, like the field, if it does not produce good will produce evil, Hosea turned to challenge the people to a more profitable manner of living for

" It is time to seek the Lord " (x. 12). They had sown unrighteousness long enough, and had reaped judgment all along the way. Why not sow righteousness, and reap mercy ? Why not give up that shallow scratching of the earth and dig deep by breaking up the fallow ground ? This meant, why did the people not get away from shallow profession and take hold of a real possession of the Lord and His grace ?

If man will but seek the Lord, He is waiting to be found of him, and is ready to pour out the early and latter rain of blessing.

Following the call to repentance Hosea went back to the nation's sins and spoke to them about their ingratitude. His language in chapter eleven is both tender and affectionate. Again he changed his metaphors.

Leaving for the moment those pictures of nature as seen in the field, he used the symbols of nature as seen in the family. These are more intimate. Maybe he was turning his appeal from the men to the women.

" When Israel was a child then I loved him " (xi. 1). Something here strikes one as being very pathetic. The nation, like the child, had grown up and was feeling that it could stand upon its own feet, make its own decisions, enjoy its own independence. It had pushed aside the parental care and admonition. This is

always hurtful to the parents whose love for their offspring never changes. Their minds go back to those earlier days of trust when the child ever ran for protection and counsel to the parent, who always had these things waiting for him. God was reminding Israel of those early days of the nation, when He brought them out of Egypt and did everything for them. O, how He loved them!

When they could not walk He took them by the arms and taught them how to put one foot in front of the other. He held them up every time they stumbled. When the child has gained his balance and learned his first steps, then reins are used to give the child some support whilst he thinks he is walking by himself. These are " cords of a man, with bands of love " (xi. 4).

Everything the saint has he owes to the love of the Lord. Everything he can do he owes to the strength of the Lord. Without Him he can do nothing ; therefore, he ought to realise how God's heart must be grieved when he forsakes His counsel, when he does not seek the Lord in prayer but just moves on in his own strength and seeks counsel from the world.

Through the Prophet the Lord showed to the people something of His tenderness as He likened Himself to the ploughman who lifted the yoke from the neck of the hot bullock to cool it off, or released the bit in the horse's mouth for a few minutes, which brought a little ease before it took its next long pull (xi. 4).

Yet for all this the people were intent on going their own way and backsliding and, for it, God permitted an amount of punishment. He must, for the one who spares the rod spoils the child. He had no alternative, His love demanded it, " For whom the Lord loveth He chasteneth, and scourgeth every son whom He receiveth. If ye endure chastening, God dealeth with you as with sons ; for what son is he whom the father chasteneth not " (Hebrews xii. 6-7). " Now no chastening for the present seemeth to be joyous, but grievous ; nevertheless afterward . . . " (Hebrews xii. 11).

The remaining verses of this chapter eleven show that God will not cast off for ever. His cry was : " How shall I give thee up, Ephraim ? How shall I deliver thee, Israel ? . . . I will not return to destroy Ephraim : for I am God, and not man ; the Holy One in the midst of thee " (xi. 8-9).

Through His servant God reproved Ephraim, Judah, and Jacob, because of their lack of stability and, at the same time, reminded them of His goodness to their fathers. Hosea used some more of those pithy sayings of his to drive home the truth of this instability.

"*Ephraim feedeth on wind*" (xii. 1), which is ever changing, is unstable, is empty. "And followeth after the east wind" which is usually a destructive wind. It leaves a parched and wasted land in its trail.

"*The balances of deceit are in his hand*" (xii. 7). Ephraim cannot be trusted in business. The Proverbs ever reprove the man who uses the heavy weight when buying and a light weight when selling. "A false balance is abomination to the Lord : but a just weight is his delight" (Proverbs xi. 1).

"*As the morning cloud, and as the early dew that passeth away, as the chaff that is driven with the whirlwind out of the floor, and as the smoke out of the chimney*" (xiii. 3). Cloud, dew, chaff, smoke, are all things which are easily moved and dissipated so that they cannot be found.

Warning and wooing continue until the grief which was in the Lord's heart can almost be felt. It was hurting Him every time He punished, therefore His constant reminders of His goodness to their fathers in the past and His continuous promises of future blessing if they would but repent.

The last chapter is one which cheers the heart. It contains

BLESSING. There was an exhortation to repentance and an acknowledgment of guilt, "for thou hast fallen by thine iniquity." God then gave to His wayward people the words to pray. "Take away all iniquity, and receive us graciously." If the Lord be willing on His part to forgive and to receive, then we will be willing to surrender our lives and offer our praise. No longer will we put our trust in kings (Asshur), nor horses (Egypt), nor yet idols, for in the Lord alone is mercy.

The prayer of the people was followed by the answer of God.

"*I will heal their backsliding.*" Backsliding is both a moral and a mortal disease. It brings death in its train ; but the Great Physician is ready to heal the disease. The Great God and Saviour was ready to pardon the sin and to deliver them from death.

"*I will love them freely.*" The word "freely" means "after a liberal and princely manner," — not in any half-hearted fashion, not as a matter of duty, but as a sheer delight. If Israel would turn its back on sin, then the Lord's promise was that He would

turn His back on His anger and, instead of pouring out the storm
clouds of His fury

" *I will be as the dew unto Israel*," that gentle, soft, refreshing
dew which distils refreshment, and causes nature to grow and
become fruitful. For a long time past there had been barrenness,
now it would be fertility.

> " *Drop Thy still dews of quietness*
> *Till all our strivings cease :*
> *Take from our souls the strain and stress,*
> *And let our ordered lives confess*
> *The beauty of Thy peace.*"

It is the dew which makes the lily grow, causes the cedars
of Lebanon to send forth their roots, and the olive tree to become
fruitful. The corn will grow again, and the vineyards will become
the scene of joy.

RESTORATION is the closing picture. The nation was back in
blessing, so that Ephraim now said : " What have I to do any
more with idols ? " He wondered why he had ever trusted in
them, why he ever forsook the Lord. That is a question we often
have to ask ourselves. Why did we ever allow ourselves to get
out of the way of the Lord ? It is always a question which has
no reasonable answer.

We, with Ephraim, must confess that the ways of the Lord
are right.

JOEL

THE DAY OF THE LORD

" But of the times and the seasons, brethren, ye have no need that I write unto you. For yourselves know perfectly that the day of the Lord so cometh as a thief in the night. For when they shall say, Peace and safety; then sudden destruction cometh upon them, as travail upon a woman with child ; and they shall not escape." (1 THESSALONIANS v. 1-3)

THE PROPHET

Nothing is known of Joel other than that he was the son of Pethuel, as is recorded in chapter i. 1. His name meant "Jehovah is God ", a fitting name for the man who had to declare this fact to a God-rejecting people. He was one of the earlier prophets and probably ministered in the reigns of Joash or Uzziah.

THE BOOK

The message of this short book concerns " The day of the Lord." It was in the light of the fact that such a day must come that Joel made a call for national repentance.

The book divides into two equal parts of one and a half chapters each. The first portion is HISTORICAL and deals with DIVINE JUDGMENTS. The second half is PROPHETICAL and speaks of the PROMISE OF DIVINE FAVOUR. It becomes a call for national repentance.

(1) HISTORICAL — DIVINE JUDGMENTS

Retrospect and prospect. The Prophet immediately called for the ears of all men. His proclamation was of national importance. It was also a challenge which none was able to accept. He called to the old men, those who had come through life and knew all that life had presented in joy and sorrow, in success and defeat, and could speak from experience. These, too, would be the men who would have heard the stories told by their fathers and grandfathers and would know much of what had happened in past generations. He wanted to know from them if they had ever

435

heard of such conditions as God was meting out on them in punishment.

After calling for a testimony from the past, he then asked for the establishment of a testimony for the future. " Tell ye your children of it, and let your children tell their children, and their children another generation " (i. 3). This must be kept on record as a warning to all succeeding generations.

May it be said that this is the most effective way to keep alive the testimony of the grace of God, to look back and to see the goodness of the Lord as witnessed by our forbears and to encourage our children to testify of the Lord's grace and mercy as they have known it. Such living testimony is always a death-blow to the theories of the liberal mind.

The Plague of Locusts. There has been a deal of reasoning amongst men as to whether this plague really happened or whether it was something that was symbolical and figurative, and referred to armies which would march at some future time, more particularly so because of the description in chapter two which can so readily be applied to armies of men. The answer is that, possibly, both are right. So many of the prophetic utterances had an immediate and a future fulfilment. A prophet is one who forthtells as well as foretells.

The nation had endured, or was enduring, the greatest plague of locusts ever experienced. It is agreed by most scholars that the four animals or plagues, to which reference is made, were all related. They were locusts in four different stages of growth. What the one stage missed the next stage secured.

Another question raised, and one which may not be easily answered, is — did all of these attacks take place in one season, or did they affect four years of harvest ? The judgments of God are sometimes short and sharp, and sometimes prolonged. There are times when He has to make His punishments long because it takes His people so long to come to their senses and repent of their sin. Sometimes prolonged punishment is ultimate mercy. The children of Israel had to remain wandering in the desert for forty years so that God could destroy a generation of people without annihilating a race. David had to choose between long suffering or a short, sharp punishment, after he numbered the children of Israel, in 2 Samuel xxiv.

Here is the definition of the locust in its four stages of growth:

THE PALMERWORM is the locust just emerged from its egg in the springtime. It is a wingless creature, often called the *gnawing locust.*

THE LOCUST is the same creature in late spring, still in its first skin. At this juncture it puts forth little ones, and so is called the *swarming locust.*

THE CANKERWORM is the third stage when it develops small wings which enable it to leap better, but not to fly. At this stage it does a great deal of devouring and is sometimes called the *licking locust.*

THE CATERPILLAR is the matured creature with its full wings, about three inches long with two antennae an inch long. It has six legs, the two back being longer thus enabling it to leap. This is the *consuming locust.*

This appalling plague of locusts left the nation in dreadful desolation, not a green shoot remained, not a vestige of vegetation anywhere.

The condition was worsened by the fact that there was also a drought in the land, which would prevent the trees from putting forth new shoots or the root in the ground from continuing to grow. This is expressed in the words " . . . the fire hath devoured the pastures of the wilderness, and the flame hath burned all the trees of the field " (i. 19). " The beasts of the field cry also unto Thee ; for the rivers of waters are dried up, and the fire hath devoured the pastures of the wilderness " (i. 20).

The Prophet was seeking to arouse the people to a sense of responsibility by telling them that this was not something that was uncontrollable, but rather that God had permitted the famine to happen because of their sin. They were fully responsible for the prevailing conditions. Moreover, greater calamities than these would be their lot if they persisted in these sins.

The problem facing the world to-day is how to awaken people to their sense of responsibility. What so often happens is that, instead of seeing their sin and realising that their trouble is self-imposed, people become full of self-pity and want to put the blame on to the weather, upon conditions, upon the government, upon God, upon any one or anything save themselves.

The Prophet was calling upon all men to awaken themselves and face the facts. He called the old men to review the past. He called the young to take heed for the future. He called the drunkard to awaken from his sense of fleshly satisfaction and know that it was his no longer. Yea, he called for a

National Mourning, even as a young virgin mourned for her husband. In a land where womanhood was so much despised, if a young married woman lost her husband and she had borne no children, she would be stricken with grief and would put on sackcloth. It was considered a shame for a woman not to be a mother. That was why Hannah, Rachael, and others, pleaded for children, and that was the reason for such rejoicing when a son was born. Joel was instructing the nation to be as stricken with grief because of its sin as such a young widowed woman would be.

Likewise he called upon the husbandmen because there would be no joy of harvest, no firstfruits to offer to the Lord.

He included the priests, who must put on sackcloth and ashes to come before the altar of the Lord with lamentation, for they would not be able to come with offerings and sacrifices. There would be none.

In chapter two two trumpets were to be sounded. (1) The trumpet of alarm, and (2) The trumpet of command. These trumpets had to do with the

DAY OF THE LORD. To-day is the day of salvation. It is also the Day of the Holy Spirit. Again, it is the day of sin. These are the predominant things in this present dispensation. The Day of the Lord is future.

> " *Our Lord is now rejected, and by the world disowned,*
> *By the many still neglected and by the few enthroned.*
> *But soon He'll come in glory, the hour is drawing nigh,*
> *For the crowning day is coming by and by."*

In that Day — the Day of the Lord — He will reign supreme. It will be a day of judgment upon the nations and will bring to an end the time of the Gentiles and their domination. It will restore the nation of Israel to a place of honour after a season of punishment.

Obviously this record did not belong to the generation of Joel's time. It was a warning for the future. The Day of the Lord is the period of time in prophecy known as The Tribulation and The Millennium.

Associated with this Day of the Lord there was the sounding of two trumpets, one in chapter two, verse 1, and the other in verse 15. These trumpets were introduced in the book of Numbers. They had to do with the Feast of Trumpets. In Ezekiel xxxvii. there were two alarms for the twofold return of Israel, found in the word "prophesy" in verses 4 and 9. The first blowing, or prophesying, took the nation back in unbelief. The second brought about an acceptance of their Messiah. Here are the same two trumpets.

(1) *The Trumpet of Alarm.* "Blow ye the trumpet in Zion, and sound an alarm in My holy mountain."

Using the great plague of locusts from which the people were enduring much suffering, the Prophet spoke in vivid language concerning the awful calamity which was to befall them in the last days when, instead of bands of locusts, there would be hordes of soldiers marching, against whom they would be as helpless as they were against the locusts. " . . . A great people and a strong ; there hath not been ever the like, neither shall be any more after it, even to the years of many generations " (ii. 2).

As already stated, this period refers to that of the Tribulation, when the king of the North will come down and cause such desolation in the land. There will be no yielding on the part of the enemy. " . . . They shall march every one on his ways, and they shall not break their ranks " (ii. 7).

This will be the Lord's doing. "And the Lord shall utter His voice before His army ; for His camp is very great ; for He is strong that executeth His Word : for the day of the Lord is great and very terrible ; and who can abide it ? " (ii. 11).

Whilst this completes the picture of the cursing which was to descend upon the nation because of its iniquity, the second half of the book cannot be entered until an introduction has been made to the secret of the great change, the pivotal point of all such change, which was

PRAYER. This is found in verses 12-17. The Lord spoke to the people when He pleaded with them " . . . Turn ye even to Me with all your heart, and with fasting, and with weeping, and with mourning. And rend your heart, and not your garments, and turn unto the Lord your God " (ii. 12-13). The admonition was to move away from all the outward form and pretence of sorrow, the false repentance, the shallow prayers, that could deceive men but would never deceive God. With a broken and a contrite spirit man must come and pour out his soul in deep humility and with confession before the Lord, and thereby learn that He is not an austere God Who delights in meting out punishment, but that He is a gracious and merciful God Who is slow to anger and is of great kindness, One Who is more anxious to turn away from meting out judgment than man is anxious to escape from receiving it.

In this call to prayer and repentance belongs the blowing of the second trumpet.

(2) *The Trumpet of Command.* " Blow the trumpet of Zion, sanctify a fast, call a solemn assembly " (ii. 15). This was the call to repentance, to fasting, to sanctification on the part of the nation, and to weeping and intercession on the part of the priests. Prayer is the pivot upon which everything swings. It is the thing which can turn the whole course of events, the dividing factor between cursing and blessing, between darkness and light, between failure and success, between victory and defeat. This applies to a nation, a church, or an individual. It is the vital point in all life and ministry, the great truth which has been put into the small capsule — " Prayer changes things."

Here is the prayer they were told to pray ; and, remember, this does not mean that one has to learn the words and recite them in formal fashion as so many people do " The Lord's Prayer." Formality is lifeless. It is not the words which are uttered, but the principles desired and breathed. " . . . Let them say, Spare Thy people, O Lord, and give not Thine heritage to reproach, that the heathen should rule over them : wherefore should they say among the people, Where is their God ? " (ii. 17).

2. PROPHETICAL — DIVINE FAVOUR PROMISED

What a change takes place at this 18th verse, from trouble to triumph. " THEN will the Lord be jealous for His land, and pity His people." See how ready the Lord was to succour and to deliver His people. How He waited to be gracious ! As soon as they humbled themselves under His Hand, and prayed and sought His Face, immediately He turned to bestow upon them His favours. Again His blessings extended as far as His judgments. Everything which had been touched in the past with His anger would be smiled upon with His grace. There was the promise of restoration for

(1) *The Land.* At the time the land was barren from the plague of locusts and bleached by the drought but, upon the people turning back to the Lord, He said " . . . I will send you corn, and wine, and oil, and ye shall be satisfied therewith : and I will no more make you a reproach among the heathen." Instead He declared that the enemy would become the people who would be barren and desolate (vs. 19-20).

(2) *The Beasts.* " Be not afraid, ye beasts of the field, for the pastures of the wilderness do spring, for the tree beareth her

fruit, the fig tree and the vine do yield their strength " (vs. 22). This was against the statement of i. 20 : " The beasts of the field cry also unto Thee ; " and in verse 18 of the same chapter : " How do the beasts groan ! The herds of cattle are perplexed, because they have no pasture ; yea, the flocks of sheep are made desolate."

(3) *Man.* " Be glad then, ye children of Zion, and rejoice in the Lord your God " (vs. 23). In the past they had been worshipping their idols and giving to them the honour that was due to His Holy Name. Now the Lord was to have His rightful place in worship.

(4) *Supplies.* " The floors shall be full of wheat, and the fats shall overflow with wine and oil. And I will restore to you the years that the locust hath eaten, the cankerworm, and the caterpiller, and the palmerworm, My great army which I sent among you. And ye shall eat in plenty, and be satisfied, and praise the Name of the Lord your God, that hath dealt wondrously with you ; and My people shall never be ashamed " (vs. 24-26).

These verses have never been fulfilled in the fulness of their significance and promise. It is true that God's people came into a measure of blessing when they returned to their God, but the fulness will not be until they enter into their Millennial rest. There has ever been a gnawing of the locusts here and there as God's ancient people have been hounded from nation to nation, suffering at the hand of all other nations. Our own generation has seen an enormous amount of suffering endured by this people, as millions of them have died in concentration camps, mangled, mutilated, and murdered. They have not eaten in plenty, nor been un- ashamed, but that day is coming when they shall be the head and not the tail, when they shall settle down in peace, every man under his own fig tree and vine, and God will be in the midst of them.

In this can be seen a spiritual application which relates to the Church. It has been passing through a period of need, and still is. The locusts of unbelief, scepticism, and materialism have been eating into the life of the Church, leaving it spiritually im- poverished. It has lost the art of worship in the abundance of programmes and organisation. More is heard of Sunday School contests than of Soul Consecration ; more of feasting in the Church basement with this supper and that than feeding on the Word of God in the Church at the mid-week Bible Study. This has pulled down the moral fibre of the nation, but God has promised to restore these years of famine if the Church will return to Him in prayer and repentance.

(5) *Worship.* " And ye shall know that I am in the midst
of Israel, and that I am the Lord your God, and none else : and
My people shall never be ashamed " (ii. 27).

In the Millennial reign the nation of God's people will worship
Him. In the eternal glory of heaven the saints will worship Him
day and night — but what of worship here and now ?

This leads into what may be one of the best known quotations
of this prophecy. It concerns the

OUTPOURING OF THE HOLY SPIRIT. People are very
concerned about the daily supply of their material needs and are
greatly exercised should there be any failure in these things. Joel
had just been dealing with such matters but now there was a move
on his part toward the things of the Spirit. Unfortunately most
people are not over-concerned with this supply, and yet it is the
more important matter, and somehow the two are inter-related,
for when the spiritual is neglected God ofttimes withholds the
material. That was exactly what had happened with both Israel
and Judah.

In that day of Millennial blessing, when the earth will be
bringing forth abundantly of its fruits, the Lord is going to pour
out abundantly of His Holy Spirit, so that " . . . Your sons and
your daughters shall prophesy, your old men shall dream dreams,
your young men shall see visions : And also upon the servants
and upon the handmaids in those days will I pour out My Spirit.
And I will shew wonders in the heavens and in the earth, blood,
and fire, and pillars of smoke. The sun shall be turned into darkness, and the moon into blood, before the great and the terrible
day of the Lord come. And it shall come to pass that whosoever
shall call on the Name of the Lord shall be delivered : for in
Mount Zion and in Jerusalem shall be deliverance, as the Lord
hath said, and in the remnant whom the Lord shall call " (ii.
28-32).

Some explanation is needed here because, in the second chapter
of The Acts, when the Holy Spirit was poured out upon the
disciples who were gathered together in the Upper Room, Peter
said : " This is that which was spoken by the Prophet Joel." Upon
consideration, it will be seen that all that Joel said did not come to
pass, only the first part, for the sun was not darkened, the moon
was not turned into blood, and the great and terrible day of the
Lord did not come.

Joel's prophecy is very wide in its scope. It concerns the
last days, and it is generally considered that these are the last

days, for it is the Church period, or the last dispensation in which the gospel is offered. This can be gleaned from such Scriptures as " God, Who at sundry times and in divers manners, spake in time past unto the fathers by the prophets, hath in these *last days* spoken unto us by His Son . . . " (Hebrews i. 1-2) ; or, " This know also, that in the *last days* perilous times shall come " (2 Timothy iii. 1). This period began on the Day of Pentecost, when the Holy Spirit was outpoured and the Church was brought into being, and continues until the Church is complete.

Returning to Joel, he spoke about the early and latter rain. " Be glad then, ye children of Zion, and rejoice in the Lord your God : for He hath given you the former rain moderately, and He will cause to come down for you the rain, the former rain, and the latter rain in the first month " (ii. 23). It must be understood that Palestine only knew two major rainfalls each year, one in October, known as the early rain, and the other at the end of April, called the latter rain. When Peter said : " This is that which was spoken by the prophet Joel ", he was referring to that early rain. The latter rain would come after the Church period. Then would be the time when He would shew wonders in the heavens and in the earth. Then would come the great and the terrible Day of the Lord.

The last chapter is a description of that dreadful Day of the Lord and the outpouring of the latter rain of Millennial blessing, and must be read thus. Some misinterpretation is abroad because people have taken some of these verses out of their context. The first two verses read : " For, behold, in *those* days (note the future tense), and in *that* time (still future), when I shall bring again the captivity of Judah and Jerusalem, I will also gather all nations, and will bring them down into the valley of Jehoshaphat, and will plead with them there for My people and for My heritage Israel, whom they have scattered among the nations, and parted My land " (iii. 1-2).

Deliverance of God's people. Firstly God is seen delivering His own elect people. That is what is meant by " bring again the captivity ". It is bringing them back out of the captivity.

Although the end of the seventy years of captivity was envisaged, yet the Prophet was looking through it and beyond it to a final deliverance. To-day God's people are scattered over the face of the earth but, when the Lord returns, He is going to have His people back in their own land. Then comes the

Destruction of God's enemies. " I will also gather all nations and will bring them down into the valley of Jehoshaphat " (iii. 2).

There was no such place as the valley of Jehoshaphat in Palestine in the days of Joel's prophecy. One has to look deeper and farther for the truth. The name Jehoshaphat belonged to one of the kings of Israel, and meant " The judgment of Jehovah." In his day God gave him a great victory over his enemies, the Moabites and the Ammonites, and thereby judged those nations. This is recorded in 2 Chronicles xx. That particular battle was fought in the valley of the Kedron which separated Jerusalem from the Mount of Olives. About the fourth century *after* Christ this same valley became designated the Valley of Jehoshaphat, no doubt in honour of the king's victory.

With this in mind, Joel could not have been thinking of any particular location on earth but, rather, of a valley in which God would gather together the nations of the earth that He might mete out His judgment upon them. This Valley of Jehoshaphat, therefore, must refer to the same conflict which is to be fought in the valley of Megiddo, or the battle of Armageddon, recorded in the latter half of Revelation xix, where all the kings of the earth gather together their armies against the Lord and His Christ.

In this same verse (Joel iii. 2) is another word which must be defined. It is the word " plead." " I will also gather all nations, and will bring them down into the valley of Jehoshaphat, and will *plead* with them there." This was not pleading for mercy, as one might think, but, rather, pleading for judgment to be meted out upon the nations. The thought can be more readily seen where the same word is used in the same sense in Isaiah lxvi. 16 : " For by fire and by His sword will the Lord *plead* with all flesh ; and the slain of the Lord shall be many."

The rest of the verse shows that these nations are to be judged because they have been responsible for scattering the Lord's people and for " parting My land." The land of Israel has been claimed by the Lord as His property, not only here but also in Leviticus xxv. 23. Even to-day Palestine is a divided land, part of it having been allocated to the Arabs by the British Government. So long as such conditions prevail, the responsible nations will not know the blessing of the Lord and must anticipate judgment to come.

Britain may take land from Israel and give it to the Arabs, but notice that the Lord is taking nations away from the British Empire, and instead giving her great problems with other nations such as Egypt, Cyprus, etc.

Not only have the various nations divided the land, but some
of them have done despite to the people of the land, reducing
God's people to wretched circumstances, using them as slaves,
and making prostitutes of them. They have bartered these people
like chattels and as though they possessed no soul. They have
sold and resold these Israelites, moving them so far away from
their own land as to make it impossible for them to return, but
God will bring them back from the uttermost corners of the earth,
and He will punish these nations in the same fashion — an eye
for an eye, and a tooth for a tooth.

To be the recipients of the goodness of the Lord is a blessing
indeed, but to fall into the hands of a righteous God Who has
said : " Vengeance is Mine, I will repay " is calamity of the first
order. When God begins to fight who can withstand ?

Let the nations prepare for war, let them augment their armies
by calling every man to arms, let the farmer turn his agricultural
implements into weapons of war, let the peasant take up arms and
say to himself " I am strong ", the Great Husbandman is going to
put in His sickle, and the enemy will be cut down as the grain in
the day of harvest. He will trample down the Christ-rejectors as
the grape-gatherer treadeth out the grapes.

" *Mine eyes have seen the glory of the coming of the Lord ;*
He is trampling out the vintage where the grapes of wrath are
stored ;
He hath loosed the fateful lightning of His terrible swift sword ;
His truth is marching on.

He has sounded forth the trumpet that shall never call retreat ;
He is sifting out the hearts of men before His judgment seat.
O be swift, my soul, to answer Him ! Be jubilant, my feet !
Our God is marching on."

Let us not be so indiscreet as to take a text out of its context
in order to preach what may seem convenient to ourselves, and
thereby do despite to the Word of God. Many have been the
preachers who have used the Scripture : " Multitudes, multitudes
in the valley of decision " as a basis for a so-called revival
message. God cannot bless a distorted message which is so far
removed from the truth. He has never declared that souls would
be saved in multitudes, neither has He promised world-revival. To
the contrary, He has declared a falling away from the Faith, and
an apostasy as last-day conditions.

The summarisation of this chapter is that, into the valley
of the judgment of Jehovah shall come all nations which have

wronged Israel, desecrating the things of God, and carrying away
the people of God. Upon these nations God will mete out the
things they desired to inflict upon Israel. Therefore, the proclamation was made for an all-out war, turning ploughshares into
swords and pruning hooks into spears. They will gather together
until there are multitudes in the valley of the judgment of Jehovah,
then called the valley of decision, not because, as is commonly
taught, men are deciding for Christ bringing spiritual revival. This
will be the Day of the Lord. The Church, already complete, will
have gone to be with the Lord. It is the valley of judgment, not
the valley of blessing. It is God Who is making the decision, not
man. It is war, not peace. God is putting in the sickle " . . . for
the harvest is ripe . . . the press is full, the fats overflow ; for
their wickedness is great " (iii. 13). This is the same detail as is
to be found in the Book of the Revelation. It is Armageddon,
when God decides the doom of the wicked and metes it out
accordingly.

JUDAH AND JERUSALEM SHALL FLOURISH. " So shall
ye know that I am the Lord your God dwelling in Zion, My holy
mountain ; then shall Jerusalem be holy, and there shall be no
strangers pass through her any more " (iii. 17). Immediately
following that great time of tribulation there will be ushered in
the reign of peace, known as

The Millennium. " And it shall come to pass in that day,
that the mountains shall drop down new wine, and the hills shall
flow with milk, and all the rivers of Judah shall flow with waters,
and a fountain shall come forth of the house of the Lord, and
shall water the valley of Shittim " (iii. 18). All of this speaks of
fruitfulness, fertility, and abundance from the earth, and the same
from the Lord in spiritual blessing, as the fountain of truth, the
waters of salvation, flow out from the house of the Lord, the
temple of that day.

The prophecy ends in the same manner as the prophecy of
Ezekiel — Jehovah Shammah, The Lord is there.

Thus Joel becomes another testimony and another witness to
the righteous acts of God, to His dealings with the God-rejector,
and to His abundant grace to all who will acknowledge His
lordship.

AMOS

PUNISHMENT AND PARDON

*" For ye see your calling, brethren, how that not many wise
men after the flesh, not many mighty, not many noble, are
called : But God hath chosen the foolish things of the world
to confound the wise ; and God hath chosen the weak things
of the world to confound the things which are mighty,
And base things of the world, and things which are despised,
hath God chosen, yea, and things which are not, to bring
to naught things that are : That no flesh should glory in His
presence."* (1 CORINTHIANS i. 26-29)

The book of Amos divides itself into four sections.

(1) *Introduction,* firstly of the Prophet, and then to the
surrounding nations.

(2) *Addresses,* the first of these being a series of parables
in chapter three. The second address is a call for preparation to
meet God in chapter four, and the third address embraces chapters
five and six.

(3) *Visions.* These were five in number.

(4) *Prophecy,* which was a final declaration of restoration
in the last days.

(1) INTRODUCTION (Chs. i-ii.)

(a) *The Prophet.* Amos, whose name meant " Burden ",
was one of those many people whom the Lord has seen fit to take
out from obscurity rather than out from the school of the prophets.
The Lord has a wonderful way of taking the things that are not
for the fulfilment of His purposes. He found Moses in the
backside of the desert, David in the green pastures, Elisha behind
the plough. He found Esther, the orphan, in her cousin's home,
Matthew at the receipt of customs, James and John mending nets
by the seashore, William Carey mending shoes at the cobbler's
bench, and David Livingstone at the weaver's loom in Blantyre,
Scotland. Here He found a herdman caring for sheep and gathering the wild fig of the desert, a man who possibly had no thought
of ever doing anything else all his life-time.

447

Amos seemed to testify to this fact that he was seeking no social advancement or any self-glory, as he said to the priest of Bethel : " . . . I was no prophet, neither was I a prophet's son ; but I was an herdman, and a gatherer of sycomore fruit : And the Lord took me as I followed the flock, and the Lord said unto me, Go, prophesy unto My people Israel " (vii. 14-15).

Amos came from a town called Tekoa which is mentioned a number of times in Scripture. Joab sought a wise woman from Tekoa to help him in a scheme to save an individual, Absalom (2 Samuel xiv.). God sought a God-fearing man from Tekoa to help Him in the salvation of a nation, Amos.

The Tekoites are mentioned as helping to rebuild the walls of Jerusalem in the days of Nehemiah (Nehemiah iii. 5). This Tekoite was called upon to help rebuild the moral structure of Israel.

Tekoa was in the south, about twelve miles south east of Jerusalem ; but, whilst the Prophet was of Judah, his prophetic ministry was to the House of Israel.

Amos ministered during the reigns of Jeroboam II, who reigned for forty-one years over Israel, and Uzziah, who ruled Judah for fifty-two years. These two reigns had brought a great amount of stability to the nation. They had peace from their enemies and a great deal of material prosperity and moral security. However, these things are not always conducive to spiritual well-being. When all goes well with man there is always the tendency for him to forget his God. This was exactly what had happened at that particular time. The true Prophet had been pushed to one side, whilst the false prophet and the deceitful prophet were being entertained, the result of which was the introduction of idolatrous worship and the gross sins that usually accompany it.

It is in the light of this background that the prophecy must be considered, but, before so doing, a link-up of the time element might be useful. This is given in verse 1. If this prophecy were " . . . in the days of Uzziah king of Judah, and in the days of Jeroboam the son of Joash king of Israel, two years before the earthquake ", then Amos possibly would have met Jonah. As Amos would be nearing the end of his ministry, Isaiah and Micah would have begun their ministry. Hosea, too, would have been in the field of service. So the same conditions which prevailed in the lives of these other prophets would form the background of the book.

It was to this nation, apparently secure and certainly self-satisfied, that this unexpected voice of warning as to coming judgment was lifted.

(b) *The Nations.* Before condemning the nation of Israel, Amos sounded the voice of judgment against the surrounding Gentile nations. This, of course, would have pleased the Jewish people and, as a result, Amos would have gained their ear. Then it was that he turned his voice to their sins and their judgment, ending with their restoration if they would repent.

In the first two chapters he tells of the judgment that was to fall on six Gentile nations, saying in each instance : "For three transgressions of — and for four." This is an expression or form of speech such as is used to-day when it is said : "Three or four times", or "Half-a-dozen times", which means an indefinite number of times. It is to be understood that God was not reproving these nations because accidentally they had failed Him once or twice or even three times, but because they were failing Him constantly. It was for deliberate opposition and rebellion.

The nations named were Damascus, Gaza, Tyrus, Edom, Ammon, Moab, after which came Judah and Israel. The Lord gave a reason for His judgment upon these nations, although many more could be found.

Damascus, because of their cruelty to Gilead (see 2 Kings xiii. 7).

Gaza. This was one of the principal cities of the Philistines, who constantly made inroads against Israel.

Tyrus. Many were the judgments pronounced against the city which had forgotten its brotherly covenant made between Solomon and Hiram.

Edom. The Edomites had ever been a bitter enemy of Israel They refused them passage through their land when they journeyed to Canaan, as did also

Ammon. The reason for their judgment given in these verses is not recorded in Scripture.

Moab, because he burned the bones of the king of Edom. 2 Kings iii. 26-27 records this.

Judah, for despising the law of God. This was a continual failure of the people.

Israel, for their continual neglect of the poor in their own selfish desires.

Were the words of Amos the Words of God ? Or were they the musings of an eccentric man who thought he had a message ? This can readily be decided, for a very casual glance at history will reveal that Gaza, Tyre, Edom, Ammon, and Moab are no more. They are only names to be found on old maps and in historical records. The pomp and glory of these nations have been forgotten. Desolate land marks an area where these places once stood. Damascus still exists, but occupied by Moslems. The former masters are no more. What of Judah and Israel ? One is familiar with the history of these people, their dispersion, suffering and shame ; but God is going to revive His own people again after their punishment because of His promise to Abram, Isaac, and Jacob, and also to David.

(2)   FIRST ADDRESS (Ch. iii.)

Parables. Having enumerated the crimes of the people in two chapters, Amos then spoke of their ingratitude. The surrounding nations were being punished for their sin, but they had never had the privileges which belonged to Israel. Therefore Israel's sins were the greater. It is what God declared as He said: " You only have I known of all the families of the earth " (iii. 2). This nation had been separated from all nations. God had called them His people. His law had been given to them. His promises were vested in them. He had fought their battles for them, bringing them victory. In His promises He had made many covenants with them which were conditional and necessitated that they should walk with Him in obedience and in fellowship. The nation had failed to keep its part of the contract, which would mean that the Lord would be relieved of His part for " Can two walk together except they be agreed ? " (iii. 3).

This is a question of all time. It did not only belong to Israel in her relationship with God. It belongs to the Church in its relationship with Christ, Who is the Head. How can there be union with the Lord and the enjoyment of His blessing unless that Church is walking in harmony with the revealed Will of the Lord, and is in agreement with all that the Lord has declared in His Word. Furthermore, it belongs to the believer and his relationship with his Saviour. It applies as much to-day as to yesterday. God has made great and precious promises to us. The Bible is full of them but they can be meaningless if one seeks to accept His Saviourhood without acknowledging His Lordship. Submission

to His Will is agreement with His Authority. Let it be learned
that to walk with God is not an occasional act, but a habit of life
to be enjoyed. Both of the parties must be willing if they are to
walk together in an atmosphere of harmony.

To walk with God is not an accident. It is pre-arranged and
pre-decided — " They be agreed ".

The outlook and the desires must be the same if fellowship
is to be experienced.

So the question remains, " Can two walk together, except
they be agreed ? "

It was obvious at this time that Israel was not in agreement
with God, therefore not walking with Him. Instead they were
going in the opposite direction. As a result, God was pronouncing
His judgments, and God is not a God of words but of action. The
Prophet gave some illustrations of this to encourage repentance.
These are the parables :

(a) *The Unequal Yoke* (iii. 3). Whilst this has been dealt
with above, the picture which would be in the minds of the
Prophet and the people needs to be recorded. In the East many
a poor man might be the owner of a single ox or bullock but,
with one animal, it was not possible to plough. What could be
done would be for two such men to share their animals and thereby
help each other but, instead of so doing, such a man might put
his bullock on one side of the yoke and some other beast on the
other side, such as an ass, a camel — or even his wife ! The
picture is obvious. Two diverse creatures have two different gaits,
the bullock has one stride and the donkey another. The result
would be that the yoke would roll from side to side giving both
animals a sore neck. These could not pull together because their
step did not agree. Hence the Lord gave the command: " Thou
shalt not plough with an ox and an ass together " (Deuteronomy
xxii. 10).

(b) *The Roaring Lion* (iii. 4). " Will a lion roar in the
forest, when he hath no prey ? Will a young lion cry out of his
den, if he have taken nothing ? " A lion does not roar when it
is contented and satisfied. Usually it roars before it springs. It
does this as soon as it sees its prey, and thereby strikes terror into
its victim which becomes paralysed with fear, making it an easy
prey. There are many references to the Lord roaring as a lion.
It is always a preparation to His meting out His judgment upon
those who have become His enemies.

(c) *The Bird and the Snare* (iii. 5). " Can a bird fall in a snare upon the earth where no gin is for him ? Shall one take up a snare from the earth, and have taken nothing at all ? " This is a picture of certain judgment. A bird cannot be caught in a snare that does not exist, and neither could Israel. If there were a snare or a calamity into which Israel could fall then God had put it there with purpose.

In the second statement the word " one " is not in the original, hence the italics in our Bible. The thought is not that of a man taking up the snare, but the snare itself, springing up from the ground, caused by an animal which has touched something that releases the spring. Thus a snare cannot spring up without having its prey. Even so God has set His judgments, and man will not be able to escape.

(d) *The Trumpet* (iii. 6). " Shall a trumpet be blown in the city, and the people not be afraid ? " The trumpet is the alarm, warning of war or invasion that would bring distress to any people. So the Lord was warning His people before of that which was about to take place.

(3) SECOND ADDRESS (Ch. iv.)

This chapter is addressed to the women of the land whom Amos called the kine of Bashan. They were living lives of luxury and indulgence, squeezing everything they could out of the poor and encouraging their masters to do the same. In their self-indulgence they were becoming like fatted beasts prepared for the slaughter. It has been often stated that the moral standards of a nation are never higher than the moral standards of its women. Man may have the power of leadership, but it is the woman who has the power of influence, and the hand that rocks the cradle rules the world ! It was Eve who influenced Adam to eat of the fruit of the tree. It was Delilah who influenced Samson to yield the secret of his strength. It was a maid who caused Peter to deny his Lord. It was Jezebel whose influence controlled the actions of Ahab, ruled the nation of Israel, and caused Elijah to seek a place of hiding ; and Jezebel was the woman who, calling herself a prophetess, was responsible for teaching and seducing the servants of God to commit fornication and to eat meat sacrificed to idols in Revelation ii. 20. It was Lois and Eunice who influenced the life of Timothy so that from a child he knew the Holy Scriptures. Whether it be for good or for ill, women have influence, and Amos was charging them because they were using their influence for ill.

As they had deprived the poor of the essentials of life, God was robbing them of their essentials, for He was withholding the rain and sending famine, drought and pestilence. Yet they repented not of their sin. Five times in this one chapter the statement is made : " Yet have ye not returned unto Me, saith the Lord " (vs. 6, 8, 9, 10, and 11).

So came the challenge " Prepare to meet thy God " (vs. 12). This text is ofttimes used for a gospel message and becomes a challenge to men to leave their sin and to prepare themselves to meet the Lord in His grace and mercy, and rightly so. But that is not the strain in which the Prophet spoke. He was saying that because they had not turned from their sin and returned unto the Lord, therefore they must prepare themselves to meet Him in judgment. The fact is that every man will have to stand before his Creator one day, so he had better prepare himself to meet the Lord in mercy, or be prepared to meet Him in anger for, when all is said and done, He is God and we are but men. He is the Creator and we are only the creature.

(4)   THIRD ADDRESS (Chs. v. & vi.)

His third appeal took the form of a lamentation. The Psalmist said : " God is our refuge and strength ". To forsake God is to forsake both of these attributes. Here were a people without a refuge and without strength ; in fact, they were continually losing what little strength they had. The thousand became a hundred, and the hundred became ten, so, if these people were to survive, something would have to be done and done quickly. The message from God was : " Seek ye Me, and ye shall live " (v. 4). They had sought the idols of Bethel, Gilgal, and Beersheba, but all to no avail and, if God should inflict further punishment, their condition would be more than pathetic.

A comparison was drawn up which should more readily bring about a decision. On the one side was God's almightiness. He created the stars and put them all in place in their various constellations. He turned darkness into light and light into darkness, and controlled all the forces of nature. He was also ever ready to defend the oppressed and to come to the help of the man who was wronged.

Against His almightiness came their corruption. They were " treading upon the poor ", " taking away their burdens of wheat ", " afflicting the just ", " taking bribes ", " turning aside the poor from their right ". All of these things were abominations to the Lord.

If they would repent and turn from these evils the Lord would forgive. If not, then they would not live in the houses they had built for themselves, nor would they gather the grapes of their vineyards, nor drink the wine thereof.

To flee from the judgment of God would be foolishness, for it would be " As if a man did flee from a lion and a bear met him ; or went into the house, and leaned his hand on the wall, and a serpent bit him " (v. 19). Not even going to church and being religious and offering peace-offerings would avail. If there is no change of heart, such things are cloaks through which God can see. They are as useless as Adam's fig-leaves !

Again Amos denounced the rich for their indolence, superstition, luxury, and self-indulgence. Because they considered themselves so secure, they would be the first to go into captivity.

(5) VISIONS (Chs. vii.-ix.)

Five visions were given to Amos which he declared to the people.

(1) *Locusts.* The text says " grasshoppers ", but to us the word would be insignificant because the creature known by that name can do no harm. In the East the grasshoppers were locusts in their early stage.

The first mowing of grass, according to some scholars, became the king's property. It was a firstfruits and was used as a method of taxation on the fields. Thereafter the reapings belonged to the people. It would appear that only the people suffered loss from these grasshoppers, and the king would escape, but a question might arise as to whether the king was worthy of such immunity. Another interpretation is that, if the locusts took the first shoots that appear, there could be recovery in the second, in which case the plague would not be too hurtful to the nation, so God in His timeliness sent the locusts when they could perform the greatest damage. Both interpretations could have a measure of correctness. One great truth is that man cannot dictate to God. He is the God of all nature, and man is always wiser to submit to His Will than to resist His ways.

These records were not a record of facts. They were visions of the future which God was making known to His servant. At the end of the first the Prophet prayed for the forgiveness of God for these people. The nation was small, said Amos, and they would not be able to recover. God heard and answered the prayer.

(2) *Fire.* This term ofttimes refers to a drought, when the constant sun and the lack of rain leave everything burnt, whilst the pools and the water supplies are dried up. The Prophet repeated his prayer except that he did not use the word " forgive " but the word " cease ", and again God responded to the prayer, for He is " slow to anger, and plenteous in mercy " (Psalm ciii. 8).

(3) *The Plumbline.* A plumbline is used to ascertain that a wall is absolutely upright. It is used constantly in building because, should one layer of stones be out of line, all that follow will be farther and farther out of line, and the wall will topple. God had built this nation according to predetermined laws and principles, but in this vision the Lord was not building. The wall was already there. He was checking the wall and revealing the fact that that which was once upright now had a tilt in it. It had become out of line. What had caused this ? Usually it is because foundations have given way. The lesson is, therefore, that a nation, when it has moved from its moral foundation, must be pulled down. So long as it stood thus there could be a collapse which might injure others. Said the Lord : " I will not again pass by them any more " (vii. 8). Twice the Prophet had pleaded for mercy ; twice the Lord had responded, but He would not allow him to ask again. The nation had gone too far in its sin. There is a limit even to God's mercy.

If they would not accept the gift of His grace when it was offered, then they would have to take the steel of His sword as it was wielded.

There was nothing broad or distant in this vision ; it belonged to that time. Neither was it limited ; it touched " the high places of Isaac ", i.e. their idols scattered all over the land, " the sanctuaries of Israel ", the temples which they had built, and " the house of Jeroboam ", the palace and its occupants.

Amaziah withstood Amos. Amaziah, who was one of the idol priests of Bethel, reported the matter to the king, declaring that Amos was conspiring to overthrow the king and country. The priest, who felt that the Prophet was usurping an authority that did not belong to him, did the very same thing himself, instead of awaiting the king's answer. Amaziah began to issue his own commands. He had no authority to banish anyone from the country. The utterance was both bitter and sarcastic. He called him a seer but, if he had believed that, he would have listened to him. He told him to go to Judah and prophesy and eat his bread, suggesting that Amos was paid for his task, and that he had better ply his trade elsewhere. He also pretended that he was giving the Prophet the opportunity to escape with his life. This reasoning was both old and new. It is the language of all the materialists and the false teachers of to-day. They seek to use an authority which they do not possess to intimidate the faithful servant of the Lord. They seek to deprive him of his Divine Call by suggesting that there is lack of training, understanding, etc., and he is merely making a living out of the people. They would love to silence the evangelical voice or relegate it to some other land.

Amos was not to be intimidated. Instead, he faced the priest with a bold and revealing truth. Without any pretence, he gave his testimony : " I was no prophet, neither was I a prophet's son ; but I was an herdman, and a gatherer of sycomore fruit ; And the Lord took me as I followed the flock, and the Lord said unto me, Go, prophesy unto My people Israel " (vii. 14-15). In these words he told Amaziah that he had never taken up the prophet's role as a profession, neither as a means of livelihood. No school of the prophets had ever trained him. God had spoken to him so unmistakably and given him this commission so clearly that it would be impossible for him to take the advice of the priest and run away or even desist from his prophesying. Would to God there were more ministers to-day who were as assured of their calling as was Amos, and as taught of the Lord as he was.

What the Prophet had declared previously had been to the nation. Instead of silencing the Prophet, Amaziah had a very rude awakening when Amos made a further prophetic utterance to the priest concerning the awful doom that awaited his own family, when he would learn that the false gods whom he was serving would bring him no help, but that the God of Israel, Whom he had rejected, would mete out His vengeance upon this God-rejector.

The nation would certainly fall by the sword, as Amos had already predicted and, when it did, the wife of the priest would become a harlot — not that she would play the harlot but the enemy would use her against her will. Women were usually carried away as prisoners, but his daughters, with his sons, would die by the sword. He himself would be carried away by the enemy into their country, and there, in a polluted land, he would die. To die and be buried in a foreign land and to leave behind no posterity to perpetuate a family name was indeed a humiliating thought for an Israelite.

Having dealt with the interfering priest, who seemingly retired from the scene, whilst the king evidently decided to do nothing in the matter, the Prophet returned to his visions.

(4) *The Basket of Summer Fruit.* Summer fruit is different from the autumn fruit, inasmuch as the latter has a keeping quality and, therefore, can be stored. But not so the summer fruit; that has to be used immediately because it is perishable. The vision is, therefore, one of immediate judgment. The nation was ripe and ready for it. Summer fruit is very beautiful in appearance. Outwardly it is attractive, but it has no inward ability to continue. That this was the picture is declared in the second verse by the Lord : "The end is come upon my people of Israel" (viii. 2).

The fruit had matured and ripened over the weeks of summer. It had been hand-picked, to be found in a basket, and yet it remained perishable within itself. Israel had matured over the years in which God had cared for her. She had been hand-picked, in that God had taken her from among all the other nations round about, yet she failed Him because, as a people, they preferred to go their own selfish, sinful way instead of submitting to the Lord.

As quickly as the attractive basket of fresh summer fruit could become a heap of corruption upon the garbage dump, just so quickly would the songs of the Temple turn into the howlings of a smitten people. The sword in that day would cause so many dead that they would not be given proper burial. The bodies would be cast aside, probably into large communal graves, with a dread silence that speaks of awe and fear.

At verse 4 Amos returned to the subject of earlier chapters, the appalling avarice of the people which was causing them to lose every vestige of decency. In their greed for money and luxury they were illtreating the poor, until they were helpless in their poverty. The people fretted concerning religious holidays and sabbath days because they were not permitted to trade on such days. Instead of those being periods of rest, they were seasons of agitation, because they would not pass quickly enough. One fears that God will hold this age responsible for its Sunday trading and other things that desecrate the Lord's Day in the greed for making money. Dishonesty was also named. "Making the ephah small, and the shekel great". The Proverbs have a great deal to say concerning that crime which is an abomination to the Lord.

These greedy "kine of Bashan" so impoverished the poor that the poverty-stricken people were compelled to sell themselves for the debts they already owed, or that they might secure for themselves a pair of shoes — meaning the bare necessities of life. The food that was given them in return for their slave labour was the poorest of the poor. These are things that God will never overlook, for He hears the cry of the poor and the oppressed, and presently will come down to deliver them.

When God does begin to deliver then the tables are turned. As God dealt with the Egyptians for the bondage and oppression of Israel, as God reversed the edict of Ahasuerus in the day of Esther, so He would turn the feasts of these gluttonous people into fasts, and their songs into sorrow.

The punishment which was to be inflicted on His people at that time was different. They had not only robbed the poor materially, but also morally and spiritually, and for this the Lord was going to punish them. Their treatment of the poor was in every degree contrary to His law. Therefore, because they had despised the law of God, He would take it away from them. One of God's sore punishments has always been famine. Now He was going to inflict upon them a famine of His Word. "They shall wander from sea to sea, and from the north even to the east, they shall run to and fro to seek the Word of the Lord, and shall not find it" (viii. 12).

How true this has been concerning the nation of Israel to whom the declaration was made! God withdrew from them the knowledge of Himself. When their Messiah came, as prophesied within that Word, they failed to recognise Him and, therefore, crucified Him. Paul states that "Their minds were blinded : for until this day remaineth the same vail untaken away in the reading of the Old Testament : which vail is done away in Christ. But even unto this day, when Moses is read, the vail is upon their heart" (2 Corinthians iii. 14-15).

It is necessary to know that, if men will continue to refuse the Word of God and act contrary to its precepts, if Liberalists will continue to deny the statements of God's Word, seek to materialise the things which are spiritual, and spiritualise the things that are practical, the same famine will come upon them. It is already becoming more and more difficult to find churches which are true to the Word — the famine is coming. Presently the Lord will come into the air, the true child of God will be caught up to meet Him at His coming, and then the world of unbelievers and the church of sceptical religionists will be left to run here and there, but will find none who can explain the Word of God.

(5) *The Lord at the Altar.* This is the last of the visions which Amos had. The subject has changed somewhat because the others showed the judgment of God, but here the Judge Himself is met. The Lord is abundant in mercy. New every morning

is His love and at eventide His mercies fail not. The Christian is ever conscious of the Lord's goodness but, although He is slow to anger, when His anger is poured out it is as abundant as His grace. It is a fearful thing to fall into the hands of an angry God.

There is a difference of opinion as to whether the Lord stood by the altar at Jerusalem, or by the idolatrous altar at Bethel. As God was dealing with the rejector he would not be found at the altar of Jehovah, and as God was destroying the Temple it must be presumed that it was the idolatrous Temple. " Smite the lintel of the door, that the posts may shake." As no particular door is mentioned and as He was standing at the altar, and the altar would be in the Temple, one concludes that the picture is that of the Lord destroying the idol worship which had done such devastating work in the midst of His people.

The next verses are very dramatic. They are showing that there is no possible escape for the sinner from the judgment of God. Many people live in hope that God will be so merciful that there will be an escape from judgment in the next life. Such is true for those who accept His mercy in the present, but man must not think he can spurn God's mercy to-day and then be able to enjoy an eternity at his own convenience. The chapter is very emphatic in its denial of this.

In chapter ix. 9 the picture is very unusual. " For, lo, I will command, and I will sift the house of Israel among all the nations, like as corn is sifted in a sieve, yet shall not the least grain fall upon the earth." The word " grain " in the Hebrew is TSEROR and means " pebble ". The Septuagint uses the definition " fragment ". In threshing the wheat, the grain was laid on a cobble-stone area, and a threshing instrument was pulled over it. This threshing instrument was a heavy sled, the under part of which was full of square holes. Pieces of broken and jagged flint were hammered into these holes, thus creating sharp teeth. This implement is referred to in Isaiah xli. 15. " Behold, I will make thee a new sharp threshing instrument having teeth : thou shalt thresh the mountains, and beat them small, and shalt make the hills as chaff."

As the sled was dragged over the corn, the straw was torn to pieces and the grain knocked out. After that, the grain was winnowed — separated from the chaff. This was done by the wind. Thus it can be seen that the sieve was not used for separating the chaff. That had already been done. In the process of threshing it can be appreciated that little chips of flint would break away from those teeth and become mixed with the wheat. The sieve was used for this purpose, the grain slipping through ; the hard foreign bodies of flint, which became entangled in the mesh, being picked out, not a " fragment " would fall to the ground ! It is a further illustration of what has gone before — there is no escape for the ungodly.

The book closes with a

(6) PROPHECY (Ch. ix. 11-15)

" In that day will I raise up the tabernacle of David that is fallen, and close up the breaches thereof ; and I will raise up his ruins, and I will build it as in the days of old." When God has dealt with sin and idolatry, then will be established the true tabernacle and the true worship. The Prophet Amos, like the other prophets, was looking away to the future Millennial blessing of the nation.

It is interesting to notice that Amos, the herdman and sycomore gatherer, used so many illustrations that were agricultural. He conveys the reader away into the promised land of milk and honey — a land which has become so fruitful after its years of barrenness, owing to lack of rain, that " the plowman shall overtake the reaper, and the treader of grapes him that soweth seed." The harvests are going to be so abundant that the ploughman will be ready to plough before the gathering of the remainder of the last crops has finished. God had promised this in His laws in Leviticus xxvi. 5-6.

The people, who for years have been scattered over the face of the earth, will be back in their land, their cities rebuilt, and God in the midst, for the final promise is " And I will plant them upon their land, and they shall no more be pulled up out of their land which I have given them, saith the Lord thy God."

He is faithful Who hath promised.

OBADIAH

THE RETRIBUTION OF EDOM

" And Esau said to Jacob, Feed me, I pray thee, with that same
red pottage ; for I am faint : therefore was his name called
Edom."   (GENESIS xxv. 30)

INTRODUCTION

Nothing whatever is known of the Prophet Obadiah. Some
scholars have tried to identify him. There is certainly no evidence
that he was in any way associated with the man of his name who
protected a hundred prophets of the Lord from the hand of Ahab
as recorded in 1 Kings xviii.

Maybe the Lord withheld the identity of the man, whose name
means " the servant of the Lord ", because He desired that His
people should be concerned with the message and not the
messenger.

THE BOOK

The book is the shortest in the Old Testament, containing
only twenty-one verses, but its message is twofold :

(1) THE DESTRUCTION OF EDOM (Verses 1 - 16).

(2) THE RESTORATION OF ISRAEL (Verses 17 - 21).

This division becomes very interesting when it is remembered
that these two people were the descendants of two brothers —
Jacob, whose name was changed to Israel, and Esau who, because
of the colour of his hair, which was red, and the sale of his birthright for a pot of red herbs, was called Edom, which means " red ".

Before dealing with these two men as individuals, a consideration of them in their association with each other might establish
a background upon which to work.

Jacob and Esau were brothers, but God chose one against
the other before they were born. This is found in the words of
Genesis xxv. 21-26. " And Isaac intreated the Lord for his wife,

461

because she was barren : and the Lord was intreated of him, and Rebekah his wife conceived. And the children struggled together within her ; and she said, If it be so, why am I thus ? And she went to enquire of the Lord. And the Lord said unto her, Two nations are in thy womb, and two manner of people shall be separated from thy bowels ; and the one people shall be stronger than the other people ; and the elder shall serve the younger. And when her days to be delivered were fulfilled, behold, there were twins in her womb. And the first came out red, all over like an hairy garment, and they called his name Esau. And after that came his brother out, and his hand took hold on Esau's heel ; and his name was called Jacob : and Isaac was three score years old when she bare them."

This becomes a problem to many. Some see the picture of pre-destination, or election, a condition over which man has no control. This is strengthened by the statement of Malachi through whom the Lord said : " Yet I loved Jacob, and I hated Esau " (i. 2-3).

Whilst there appears to be an act of favouritism, on further consideration it is obvious that there is not. To the contrary there is a display of eternal grace. Morally, Esau was the better man, but what he had in moral character he lacked in spiritual perception. Outwardly there was nothing attractive in Jacob. He was ever ready to drive a hard bargain, yet somewhere behind that scheming nature of his there must have been a longing after the spiritual, for he was seeking to obtain spiritual blessings which already his brother possessed. Decidedly he used wrong methods, but God saw and Grace looks beyond the unworthiness of man to the need of man and finds delight in meeting it.

As to loving one and hating the other, this is what is known as a relative idiom. It was not a literal hatred, but a love that was poor by comparison with another love. God IS love, therefore He cannot hate. The Christian is exhorted to love the brethren, to love his enemies, to love and obey parents, and yet, in what appears to be a contradiction, the Lord said : " If any man come to Me, and hate not his father, and mother, and wife, and children, and brethren, and sisters, yea, and his own life also, he cannot be My disciple " (Luke xiv. 26).

All this means that one has to love his people, but love for the Lord comes first. It must be the greater love and, if the circumstances arise when a decision has to be made between the two, that decision must always be for the Lord, even though it may appear an unnatural rebellion against those who are ours by family ties.

It must be understood that the word " hated " did not relegate the man to a lost eternity or anything like it. This same fact applies to the subject of pre-destination. No man is pre-destined to be an unregenerate sinner for all time and a victim of punishment for all eternity, otherwise freewill and grace both take wings and vanish.

Esau was the father of the Edomites, and this book deals with the judgment of that nation, not of the individual.

Jacob and Esau, like Isaac and Ishmael, are a parable of the life of the spirit versus the life of the flesh. Esau was the possessor of spiritual blessings, blessings which, in the flesh, he inherited and yet did not appreciate their worth, and so was prepared to sell them for fleshly desires and appetites. On the other hand, Jacob, who was largely dominated by the flesh and the things of this world, had a desire for that spiritual blessing which was not his by inheritance, and so was transformed by the power of the Spirit.

Edom was ever an enemy of Israel, as the flesh has ever warred, and ever will war, against the spirit.

(1) THE DESTRUCTION OF EDOM (Verses 1 - 16)

The Doom pronounced. To understand some of the expressions used by Obadiah, it will be necessary to know the geographical position of this land called Edom, Seir, and Idumaea. Prophecies concerning Bozrah also belong to this same picture, Bozrah probably being the capital city. The country occupied by these descendants of Esau was really rugged country, its terrain terrible. The region was south of the Dead Sea.

Many are acquainted with the discovery of the famed city of Petra, made more than a century ago, that hidden city of temples and tombs as well as dwelling places, all hewn out of the walls of the canyons. Petra is the word " rock " from whence came the name of Peter, which the Lord gave to Simon.

The following is a description of this city : " It is located in the mountain like as a crater of a volcano. It has but one entrance and that is through a narrow winding defile or canyon from twelve to forty feet wide, the sides of which are precipitous, and at times so close together as to almost shut out the blue sky above and make you think you are passing through a subterranean passageway. The height of the sides varies from two hundred to a thousand feet and the length of the canyon is about two miles.

No other city in the world has such a wonderful gateway. The sides of the canyon are lined with wonderful monuments, and temples, carved out of the rocky sandstone of the sides. Once inside the rocky enclosure of the city we find the ruins of magnificent buildings, tombs and monuments. The cliffs that surround the city are carved and honeycombed with excavations to a height of three hundred feet above the floor of the valley and the excavations cut as they are out of the different coloured strata of the rock, such as red, purple, blue, black, white, and yellow, lend a beauty to their appearance that is indescribable and overpowering to the beholder."

Within this natural stronghold the people would feel very secure and confident. So the Prophet spoke : " The pride of thine heart hath deceived thee, thou that dwellest in the clefts of the rock, whose habitation is high ; that saith in his heart, Who shall bring me down to the ground ? " (vs. 3) But God had already sent His ambassadors out among the nations that were around. Already they had heard the call to war. God was looking upon the defeat of this exalted nation as an accomplished fact as He said : " Behold, I have made thee small among the heathen (nations) : thou art greatly despised " (vs. 2).

What Obadiah said to this people, God had said many times. " The pride of thine heart hath deceived thee." It is always thus " Pride goeth before a fall." The word " deceived " carries the idea of " elated pride ". This proud self-confidence elated Pharaoh, Nebuchadnezzar, Belshazzar, and many another, and all of them saw the hand-writing on the wall and fell before the God Whom they opposed.

Edom, in his elation, thought he could build his nest like the eagle, high enough to be out of the reach of the fowler. He thought that, like the eagle, he could soar high into the heavens, up among the stars, beyond the reach of the arrow of the enemy. He had to learn that he could not get beyond the reach of God, nor yet the judgment of God if that were what he deserved.

These things are written as truths for both men and nations to learn, but Oh ! How dull we are in understanding ! ! How slow to learn the lessons so plainly written.

Verse 5 gives an indication of the completeness of God's judgment. " If thieves came to thee, if robbers by night, (how art thou cut off !) would they not have stolen till they had enough ? If the grapegatherers came to thee, would they not leave some grapes ? "

A thief takes what he wants, whether from the home or from the vineyard. The rest he leaves. When God dealt with Edom not a vestige would be left behind, not a gleaning in the vineyard. God punished Israel but left the remnant from which there could come future blessing. But Edom is no more ; the last known descendants of Esau appear to be the Herods in the opening chapters of the New Testament. Herod the Great, Herod Antipas, and Herod Agrippa I were Edomites, and they were as cruel to the Israelites as all their ancestors had been. The empty dead city of Petra is all that remains, an evidence of a " once upon a time " great people.

The nation was then threatened with one of the inexorable laws of God, " whatsoever a man soweth, that shall he also reap." Edom had been very uncharitable to his brother ; in fact, had opposed him. As he had treated his brother so he was to be treated by his own friends. " All the men of thy confederacy (those in whom he had put his trust, those upon whom he called to help him against his brother, those to whom he now looked for moral support) have brought thee even to the border " (vs. 7). The suggestion is that the ambassadors had been sent out to the nations around to solicit their help, but none of them was prepared to become allied to Edom and the ambassadors had come back to the borders of their own country empty-handed.

Forsaken by her friends, Edom was being left to fight her battle alone. No wonder the Psalmist declares that it is better to trust in the Lord than to put confidence in princes. Men are not trustworthy. They will take all the help they need but are never prepared to give it when help is expected of them. With no aid coming from outside, the nation was compelled to look inside. They would have to win this battle by their own wisdom and might, but both of these qualities were going to be taken away from them, for God had committed them to a complete end.

The cause declared. Most of the nations were judged by God because of their idolatry. It was the most common sin. Here, however, it was different. It is bad when a nation wars against another nation. It is worse when man wars against his own nation, in what is called Civil War. It is wrong for one man to resist another by fighting, but it is worse when brother fights brother. This was the cause of God's judgment at that time. " For thy violence against thy brother Jacob shame shall cover thee, and thou shalt be cut off for ever " (vs. 10). Neither was it a temporary flare-up because of a difference of opinion or a misunderstanding. It was an established hatred which had existed for years and in which there was a cherished delight whenever there was an opportunity for one to hurt the other.

The brothers, Jacob and Esau, had known a re-union after years of separation, not so much because they willed it as it was that God required it. " And the Lord said unto Jacob, Return unto the land of thy fathers, and to thy kindred ; and I will be with thee " (Genesis xxxi. 3). An angry uncle helped to drive him in that direction. However, they met happily, and a reconciliation was made, and together they buried their father.

At heart Edom never forgave himself, and neither did he forgive Jacob concerning the day when Jacob secured his birthright from him in exchange for a pot of red herbs. Esau would have given anything to undo what he had done. He was filled with remorse, but it was too late.

(1) *Edom's Malice toward Israel.* As the years went by and both of these men grew into nations, they also grew farther and farther apart, and Edom eyed Israel with jealousy as he witnessed God's blessing upon that nation. Toward the end of the forty years of wandering in the wilderness, as Israel approached the promised land, it became necessary for them to pass through the territory of their brother, Edom. Moses sent to the king of Edom for that permission. The request was gracious and brotherly (read Numbers xx. 14-17), but it was refused. Moses appealed again, and his request was as reasonable as it could be, and would have been granted by a stranger. His request was " We will go by the high way : and if I and my cattle drink of thy water, then I will pay for it : I will only, without doing anything else, go through on my feet " (Numbers xx. 19). Edom not only refused but prepared to resist. This was the first crime, and to refuse the people of God is to refuse God.

(2) *Helping Israel's enemies.* When strangers, or other nations fought against Israel, Edom, instead of coming to the aid of his brother, stood and looked on with an indifference that made him as guilty as if he had been one of the enemy. In verse 12 the Lord reminded him that in some other conflict he was not merely indifferent but highly elated, for He charged him that he had " rejoiced over the children of Judah in the day of their destruction " and that he had " spoken proudly in the day of distress ".

(3) *Plundering Jerusalem.* The next charge is one against Edom for making gain out of his brother as he " laid hands on their

substance " (vs. 13). And yet more, for in verse 14 he moved into active participation with the enemy against Israel, as he cut off the way of escape for the fleeing fugitives and even returned some into the hand of the enemy. These were grievous things for brother to do against brother, and it was for such things that God was about to annihilate this people. Note the progression of evil — (1) Indifference, (2) Elation and pleasure, (3) Personal gain, (4) Participation.

Would we consider that Edom had made himself a victim of God's judgment ? If so, then we have a sense of right and wrong; yet too many of us act similarly toward our brethren in Christ because they do not belong to the same church or the same denomination, or jealousy arises because they are having more blessing. So, because we do not see eye to eye, we are indifferent to them and their work, or walk past with a smile at their pro- gramme or their way of doing things. Before long we are laying hands on their substance, trying to " steal their show ! ", or take their members, and before we realise it there is open opposition to them. Yet all the time they are our brethren, washed in the same precious Blood, serving the same Lord, and presently will be sharing the same heaven. Beware, lest the Lord has to deal in judgment with us because our hearts are not right with Him. Let us take heed, lest we fall into the same condemnation.

Sowing and Reaping (verses 15-16). It has already been stated that what a man sows that shall he also reap. Obadiah was declaring it in the words " As thou hast done, it shall be done unto thee : thy reward shall return upon thine own head ". God is a God of justice, and this was justice rather than retribution. The New Testament expresses the same principles — " With what measure ye mete, it shall be measured to you again " (Matthew vii. 2).

Dr. Pusey declares it from the history of that time, as he explains the words of verse 16. " ' For as ye have drunk upon My holy mountain, so shall all the heathen drink continually . . . '. Edom drank the cup at the hand of Babylon ; Babylon drank it at the hand of the Medes ; the Medes and the Persians drank it at the hand of the Macedonians ; the Macedonians drank it at the hand of the Romans ; the Romans, in their turn, drank it at the hands of the Barbarians."

Many are the illustrations in the Scriptures of those who were caused to drink their own medicine. Jacob, who cheated others, found himself cheated. Haman, who built the gallows, hung thereon himself. Adoni-Bezek, who cut off the thumbs and toes of others, found his own amputated.

Edom is no more. God's punishment was complete. These same judgments on Edom were declared by other prophets, as Isaiah (xliii. 5 ; lxiii. 1), Jeremiah (xlix. 7-22), Ezekiel (xxv. 12), Daniel (xi. 41), and Amos (i. 11).

(2) THE RESTORATION OF ISRAEL (Verses 17 - 21)

Whilst God dealt with the one in judgment because of sins, He dealt with the other in mercy because of His promises. " But upon mount Zion shall be deliverance . . . " God had chosen Zion as the place of the throne. David reigned there. Although there had been much sin and desecration, yet the Lord would restore that which had been lost.

> " Glorious things of thee are spoken,
> Zion, city of our God.
> He, Whose Word cannot be broken,
> Formed thee for His own abode."

As the Lord dealt with the enemy of Israel in punishment and then restored Israel to blessing, even so will the Lord deal with all the enemies of His Church upon earth, and then receive that Church into the glories of the eternal land. The writer to the Hebrews seems to take this very matter of Obadiah and to apply it to the Church when he says : " Lest there be any fornicator, or profane person, as Esau, who for one morsel of meat sold his birthright. For ye know how that afterward, when he would have inherited the blessing, he was rejected : for he found no place of repentance, though he sought it carefully with tears. For ye are not come unto the mount that might be touched, and that burned with fire, nor unto blackness, and darkness, and tempest, and the sound of a trumpet, and the voice of words ; which voice they that heard intreated that the word should not be spoken to them any more : (For they could not endure that which was commanded, And if so much as a beast touch the mountain, it shall be stoned, or thrust through with a dart : And so terrible was the sight, that Moses said, I exceedingly fear and quake :) But ye are come unto mount Sion, and unto the city of the living God, the heavenly Jerusalem, and to an innumerable company of angels. To the general assembly and church of the firstborn, which are written in heaven, and to God the Judge of all, and to the spirits of just men made perfect, And to Jesus the

Mediator of the new covenant, and to the blood of sprinkling, that speaketh better things than that of Abel " (Hebrews xii. 16-24).

" And there shall be holiness ", not only a restored land but a restored state. Much had been lost in sin, but now sin was going to be lost to holiness, for Christ is reigning, and the nation will be possessing her possessions. How many are the promises of God to usward, and how few of them are ours to-day because we do not know how to possess them ! Doubt, fear, and sin, rob us of so much, but there is coming a day of restitution and restoration.

As the book closes it seems that the land, which was once divided and allocated by Joshua, and has since been parted by the nations of the world in their quest for a solution to the Arab-Israel problem, is going to be divided again to rightful owners, and " THE KINGDOM SHALL BE THE LORD'S ". This has been the promise made by the Lord and maintained by all of His servants, the prophets. God's people, the Jews, will return to their land, the land shall prosper, and He will reign Whose right it is.

JONAH

THE RELUCTANT MISSIONARY

> "*An evil and adulterous generation seeketh after a sign; and there shall no sign be given to it, but the sign of the prophet Jonas: For as Jonas was three days and three nights in the whale's belly; so shall the Son of man be three days and three nights in the heart of the earth. The men of Nineveh shall rise in judgment with this generation, and shall condemn it: because they repented at the preaching of Jonas; and, behold, a greater than Jonas is here.*" (MATTHEW xii. 39-41)

INTRODUCTION

The authenticity of this book has long been disputed by scholars, and it has been challenged as to its integrity because of one statement, whilst a score of other historical facts have been ignored. There are historical data, geographical features, quotations from the history of the Old Testament, and references made in the New Testament, none of which can be denied, and yet men would have the whole book removed because of a single "problem" in their mind, which is "How can a whale swallow a man?" If these scholars were really wise, and if they were genuinely honest, they would know that this is no problem. They are creating dishonestly a difficulty because, if what the Bible says historically is true, then what it says doctrinally and morally is true. Because they do not want to believe the latter, as it touches their personal life, they seek to falsify the former and thereby seek their conscience.

The actual statement never mentions a whale. It says: "Now the Lord (He is omnipotent and the Creator) had *prepared* (that means a special miracle for the special occasion) a great fish . . ." (not a whale, or any other common species). This asks for no argument, no reasoning, no logic, no science. It is a Divine statement that must be accepted in the realm of the Divine. If one cannot believe this, then God is not God, the Bible is not the Word of God, and man is the innocent victim of every whim and fancy that may exist.

As to the historical background of the book, the law of God demanded that everything must be done in the mouth of two or three witnesses. This is declared in Deuteronomy xix. 15. The two witnesses to this book were (1) The Old Testament, " He restored the coast of Israel from the entering of Hamath unto the sea of the plain, according to the word of the Lord God of Israel, which He spake by the hand of His servant, Jonah, the son of Amittai, the prophet, which was of Gath-hepher " (2 Kings xiv. 25). (2) The New Testament and the words of Jesus Himself. " For as Jonah was three days and three nights in the whale's belly ; so shall the Son of man be three days and three nights in the heart of the earth " (Matthew xii. 40).

It is important that a true interpretation of this book is obtained. Jonah has been referred to as a runaway prophet ; he has also been set up as an example of race prejudice, but the truth lies much deeper than either of these suggestions.

Nineveh, the city to which Jonah was to preach, was the capital of the Assyrian Empire which, at that time, dominated the world. It had oppressed many peoples, the Jews being one of those peoples. The question is — How would a person react to-day if he were instructed to go into an alien country, to a people who had oppressed and cruelly treated his own people, and were still his enemy, and preach to them the mercy of God ? His refusal would be considered by his friends as reasonable and patriotic and no one would blame him. It would seem that Jonah was being asked to prolong the life of the nation which was seeking to exterminate his own nation.

From this it must be seen that God was asking Jonah to do something that was both hard and unpalatable. One does not seek to justify Jonah. Obedience to God is a first essential of a servant of God. Facts must be faced so that it might be known how to interpret intelligently the book.

In the light of the foregoing would it not be more honest to call Jonah a reluctant missionary rather than a runaway prophet ?

God sometimes asks His children to do hard things concerning which they find themselves asking a lot of questions, and of which they are not always fully convinced, nor to which they are completely obedient. We must be slow at condemning other persons, but quick to learn the lessons that come from their failure lest we be carried away also in the same error.

The prophecy, and, remember, it is a prophecy, has a tendency to lose its prophetic teaching in the details of the historical facts. The prophecy concerns the nation of Israel whose ministry was to make known the grace of God to all peoples. God had intended that these, His people, should be the missionary people of the world but, because of a national pride and a dislike of the Gentile nations, they failed in their commission. The result was that they encountered many storms, they have been entombed in the nations of the world but never destroyed. They have burned but never been consumed, and presently they will be returned to their land, to become the proclaimers of God's truth.

Added to this was a prophetic picture of the Lord's death and resurrection.

THE BOOK

This divides itself readily according to the four chapters.

(1) A Divine Command evaded (Chapter i.).

(2) A Penitent's cry answered (Chapter ii.).

(3) A Second Commission obeyed (Chapter iii.).

(4) A Prophet's complaint rebuked (Chapter iv.).

(1) A DIVINE COMMAND EVADED — or THE MISSION OF JONAH (Chapter i.)

Jonah, who belonged to Gath-hepher, a town near Nazareth, was a prophet. One day he heard the voice of God calling him to a particular sphere of service. How the Lord spoke to Jonah, or to any of the prophets, is not told. The question is ofttimes asked to-day — How can I know when the Lord speaks to me ? The answer must ever be a negative one. I do not know how the Lord speaks to you. I can only know how and when the Lord speaks to me. The Lord does nothing in a stereotyped fashion. Sometimes He speaks in the night watches, sometimes it can be by voice or vision. It can be by the still small voice, or it can be heard through the voice of a sermon or through the admonition of a friend. It can be through a circumstance or series of circumstances. God has a thousand ways of speaking. That is why the question cannot be answered for another. Each individual must know by conviction, by a blending of spirits, by a definite " something " surely known though undefined.

Jonah was fully aware of his call. He had no doubt in his mind that he was to go to Nineveh. His trouble was that he had no willingness in his heart to obey. This was a positive disobedience to a Divine revelation ; in fact, it could be said that it was open rebellion when he determined to go the opposite way. It is surprising how far man can go in disobedience and how far the mercy of God will extend to reach him !

Would it not be wise to examine our spiritual life so that one may be assured that " lack of understanding " is neither a mis-interpretation nor a lack of willingness ?

Any journey which is away from God is a downward one, and to go down is both easy and hard ; easy because no self-effort is required, but hard because of the consequences. Going down can often increase in momentum until it becomes difficult to stop, and control becomes a lost thing. Jonah went down to Joppa, he went down into the ship (vs. 3), down into the sides of the ship (vs. 5), down into the sea (vs. 15), down into the belly of the fish (vs. 17), down to the bottoms of the mountains (ii. 6), and it would have been down into death had it not been for the mercy of God.

Another tragic statement in these opening verses is " so he paid the fare " (vs. 3). It may be considered that this was right and honest, but some are more concerned with being honest with their neighbour than with God. They make sure that all of their commitments with men are discharged, but they are ever debtors to God. They rob Him of time, worship, service, and a score of other things. When He offers salvation as a free gift they are not willing to accept it. Man so often makes this same mistake to-day. He wants to pay his way to heaven and this he seeks to do by works.

Another mistake of Jonah was that he thought he could flee from the presence of the Lord, so he planned for another country afar off. He had not learned that many other men, from Adam onward, had tried to do the same thing and failed ; neither had he learned the truth that David had comprehended when he said : " Whither shall I go from Thy spirit ? Or whither shall I flee from Thy presence ? If I ascend up into heaven, Thou art there : If I make my bed in hell, behold, Thou art there. If I take the wings of the morning, and dwell in the uttermost parts of the sea ; Even there shall Thy hand lead me, and Thy right hand shall hold me. If I say, Surely the darkness shall cover me ; even the night shall be light about me. Yea, the darkness hideth not from Thee ; but the night shineth as the day : the darkness and the light are both alike to Thee " (Psalm cxxxix. 7-12).

Man cannot flee from God nor from his responsibilities so easily as he sometimes thinks. The only thing a man gains from his flight from God is trouble, and more trouble, and this trouble is not the anger of a hard God but, rather, the dealings of a merci-ful God Who is not willing that any should perish.

Joppa, the coastal town from which Jonah sought to make his escape because he would not preach *to another nation,* is the same Joppa to which eight hundred years later men came *from another nation* asking Peter to go and preach to them (Acts x.).

Jonah did not seem to be troubled by his conscience for, having boarded the vessel, he went down below and slept soundly. Even when a storm arose that was severe enough to cause experienced mariners to become panic-stricken, Jonah slept on oblivious of the dangers.

Both Israel, in her day, and the Church in this day, have not been fully aware of the dangers of their age, the needs of man and the responsibilities that are his as he is related to the emergencies of life.

The world, being godless, is therefore superstitious, and so the shipmaster believed that some person was responsible for the storm, and lots were cast; but the storm was God's doing, so He permitted the lot to fall upon the guilty man for whom the Lord had, nevertheless, a great concern. He was still a prophet of God even though at the moment he was rebellious.

Jonah was subjected to a catechism from the men of the vessel, as a result of which he made a full confession, telling them that he was a servant of the Living God and that he was seeking to escape from a responsibility. He also intimated that he was responsible for the storm. It must be noted that, whilst he confessed his transgression to man, he did not confess to God, and neither did he repent of his sin. In fact, he was prepared to meet death before he would meet God. Is not that like stubborn man, forgetting that after death he will have to meet God? It is better to meet God in mercy this side of death than meet Him in judgment the other side of death where there is no mercy.

As the shedding of innocent blood could start a blood-feud, the sailors were not too anxious to cast the Prophet of God overboard, and so used might and main to bring the ship to land, but what can man do when God is on the other side! So at last Jonah was cast overboard, the sailors beseeching the Lord to deliver them from the responsibility of taking his life. This request was certainly granted because the life was never taken!

The extent of God's mercy and grace toward a disobedient servant is revealed in the next statement, "Now the Lord had prepared a great fish to swallow up Jonah." There is no need to worry about the size of its throat, or the action of the gastric juices, or the possibility of suffocation. When the Bible says "Now the Lord had *prepared*", the Lord knew every one of those problems and how to solve them, so He is asking no man to reason it out for Him. It need not be thought that the abode was a comfortable one. No prison ever is, and Jonah was not entitled to any kind of reward. When Israel disobeyed God's instruction concerning themselves, so that they had to be scattered in the nations of the earth, they in their disobedience have not found their conditions to be very comfortable. Yea, we all of us have to say that it is of the Lord's good mercies that we are not consumed.

This chapter closes with the man who, trying to master God, found that God was his Master, and in his extremity he yielded, and so

(2) A PENITENT'S CRY ANSWERED, or PRAYER AND DELIVERANCE (Chapter ii.)

Jonah, however, did not yield too willingly. He spent three days and three nights as a prisoner before he prayed. When he did pray he confessed to the distress he was in, not to the sin he had committed, for he said : " I cried by reason of mine affliction unto the Lord ". It may be assumed that Jonah did all that was humanly possible to discover some way of escape from the interior of that water monster, but his strugglings were of no avail. Not until Jonah learned that there was no possible way of escape from either his conditions or his God did he yield, and declare himself willing to fulfil the vow that he had made to God when he became a prophet. With that willingness came the return of faith as he prayed : " But I will sacrifice unto Thee with the voice of thanksgiving ; I will pay that that I have vowed, Salvation is of the Lord " (ii. 9). The cry of faith came as he was yet in the fish, he was still a helpless victim. He did not say that Salvation *could* come to him. It was not " perhaps ", or " hope so ", but " Salvation IS of the Lord ". He claimed it as an accomplished thing, and an accomplished thing it was, for " the Lord spake unto the fish, and it vomited out Jonah upon the dry land ".

Thus it will be with Israel after all their years of bondage and affliction. They will at last awaken to the fact that all their trouble has been self-imposed. Then will come the day when in faith and triumph they will cry, " Blessed is He that cometh in the Name of the Lord ", and a nation shall be born again in a day. Israel will be back in their land to enjoy the blessing of the Lord.

Complete submission to God brings complete deliverance from God.

(3) A SECOND COMMISSION OBEYED, or PREACHING AT NINEVEH (Chapter iii.)

A comparison between the first three verses of chapter one and the first three verses of chapter three give an interesting approach to this third chapter.

" The word of the Lord came unto Jonah " (i. 1)
" The word of the Lord came unto Jonah the second time " (iii. 1).

The Word of God remains steadfastly the same. It never changes to suit the convenience of man. Man must learn to adjust his life to its precepts.

" Arise, go to Nineveh, that great city " (i. 2).
" Arise, go unto Nineveh, that great city " (iii. 2).

God's objectives remain the same — His interest in mankind. But whilst principles remain the same, there are some fascinating little differences.

" Cry against it " (i. 2).
" Preach against it " (iii. 2).

That sounds like the difference between judgment and mercy. His anger saw the wickedness that came up before Him. His love sees the helpless sinner and reaches out towards him. If Jonah did not want to cry against it lest they repent, how much more might he want to refrain from preaching.

" But Jonah rose up to flee " (i. 3).
" So Jonah rose and went " (iii. 3).

It is always best to move in the right direction at the first, but, if a mistake is made, repentance is always the answer.

" Unto Tarshish " (i. 3).
" Unto Nineveh " (iii. 3).

Tarshish, the place of man's choosing, was never reached. Nineveh, the place of God's election, was where he preached.

" From the presence of the Lord " (i. 3).
" According to the word of the Lord " (iii. 3).

Jonah's right to choose will ever be man's right. May we always choose rightly.

" Now Nineveh was an exceeding great city of three days' journey " (iii. 3). This statement has puzzled many people. Suffice it here to state the size of the city. The city itself was only three miles by one and a half miles. (When one says " only ", it needs to be borne in mind that the City of London is only one mile square, which would make Nineveh considerable). It is the Metropolitan area of London that covers nine hundred square miles. The suburbs of Nineveh likewise stretched thirty miles in one direction and ten miles in the other, three hundred square miles, approximately the size of the city of Chicago. It would take three days to walk round such a city proclaiming its doom.

This queen city of the earth was built by Nimrod, the mighty hunter before the Lord, who went into Assyria and built Nineveh (Genesis x. 8-11). It had massive bulwarks, being surrounded by five protecting walls and three moats. The city was mighty in power, mighty in wealth, and mighty in sin, but, when God binds the strong man, he is weak ; when God convicts of sin nothing else matters. "Yet forty days, and Nineveh shall be overthrown" (iii. 4).

Forty is the number of probation, the period of testing, the days of grace. Moses was in the mount forty days ; Israel wandered for forty years ; Saul, David, and Solomon, each reigned for forty years ; Jesus was tempted of the Devil forty days ; His resurrection was proved by forty days of infallible proofs. Thus is was with Nineveh.

The people of the city, from the king downwards, were soon in sackcloth and ashes — repenting of their sin. What was it that brought the conviction and that weakened a strong city ? Not battering rams, not advancing armies, but the simple preaching of the Word of God. Said God to Jonah : "Go and preach". Said Jesus to His disciples, "Go, and preach". Says the Lord to His Church, "Go ye into all the world and preach the gospel". Let us put aside our church programmes, our singing parties that are doing so much entertaining, our films and singspirations, and the rest, and preach the gospel. These other things may have their place but God has not promised to bless them. It is by the preaching of the Word that men are saved. The promise is that His Word shall not return unto Him void. Some may seek to justify these other things, but let it be observed that our Christianity in practical living to-day is just as shallow as the method used. Sound preaching produces sound Christians, sentimental ministry means sentimental Christians. The Church to-day lacks the great preachers of yesterday and, if persecution came, it would be found that the Church of to-day would also lack the martyrs of yesterday.

One evidence of the change is the singing. The hymns of worship and adoration, containing beautiful expressions of theology and profound truths, have been substituted in many instances by jazzy tunes and senseless words. When young people have to bob up and down in their seats when they sing, and chorus singing takes more the form of entertainment, men will never be seen sitting in sackcloth and ashes, the sign of repentance, neither will the mighty days of Pentecost be witnessed. Let us preach the Word, in season and out of season.

It is often said that the place is hard where one lives and serves. But something has to be done to reach the people. Nothing could be harder than a wicked Nineveh, but preaching humbled that city.

Your city is not harder than was Ephesus where Paul fought with beasts but, by preaching and praying, there was established the Church of the Ephesians.

(4) A PROPHET'S COMPLAINT REBUKED, or DISPLEASURE AND CORRECTION (Chapter iv.)

" But it displeased Jonah exceedingly, and he was very angry. And he prayed unto the Lord, and said, I pray Thee, O Lord, was not this my saying, when I was yet in my country ? Therefore I fled before unto Tarshish, for I knew that Thou art a gracious God, and merciful, slow to anger, and of great kindness, and repentest Thee of the evil. Therefore now, O Lord, take, I beseech Thee, my life from me ; for it is better for me to die than to live " (iv. 1-3).

This statement is very revealing. It manifested what was deep in the heart. Jonah had claimed repentance. He had shouted " Salvation is of the Lord " when his own life was at stake, but he had no concern for the salvation of others. The Church is full of similarly selfish people to-day. They are in those meetings which give pleasure to themselves, but they will not be found in the prayer meeting. If God should do some mighty work in the Church and send the Holy Spirit upon it in sanctifying, cleansing power that would sweep out of the Church some of the things which have been mentioned, if a deep work of grace brought a great transformation, many would be displeased exceedingly, and very angry. Jonah was no mere individualist. He was one of a great company. Could a prayer be more tragic or pathetic ? What a mercy that God does not answer every prayer according to our praying, but always according to His Will.

Jonah certainly did not preach because he wanted to but because he had to do so. Contrast this selfish prayer with the self-sacrificing prayer of Moses toward a people who had sinned. " And Moses returned unto the Lord, and said, Oh, this people have sinned a great sin, and have made them gods of gold. Yet now, if Thou wilt forgive their sin — ; and if not, blot me, I pray Thee, out of Thy book which Thou hast written " (Exodus xxxii. 31-32).

God had been merciful to Jonah and saved him, yet he laid an indictment against God because He had been merciful to this city and saved it.

This anger of Jonah did not abate, for the more the Lord displayed His mercy so much the more did Jonah declare his anger. When in verse 4 God asked His servant, " Doest thou well to be angry ? ", Jonah made no reply but walked out of the city. The second time the Lord asked him the same question, in verse 9, Jonah said, " I do well to be angry, even unto death ".

" So Jonah went out of the city, and sat on the east side of the city, and there made him a booth, and sat under it in the shadow, till he might see what would become of the city " (iv. 5). His innermost longing was that it might be destroyed. How different was the attitude of this man from that of another who had prayed for a city and then watched for the results. " And Abram gat up early in the morning to the place where he stood before the Lord : and he looked toward Sodom and Gomorrah, and toward all the land of the plain, and beheld, and, lo, the smoke of the country went up as the smoke of a furnace " (Genesis xix. 27-28).

God is very persistent with rebellious man. In His long-suffering He does not give up quickly. God was showing His mercy to a merciless man. " And God prepared a gourd." Note this word *prepared* — " God prepared a gourd ", " God prepared a worm ", " God prepared a vehement east wind ". It is the same word " Now the Lord had prepared a great fish ". Four things God prepared in this account, each one to do a particular piece of work and then to pass on. God can use ordinary things, or extraordinary things, to do His bidding.

> The fish was for salvation.
> The gourd was for protection.
> The worm was for destruction.
> The wind and sun were for exhaustion.

Jonah appreciated the growth of the gourd and was very glad for the protection it afforded him, but his selfishness still never caused him to wonder why it should have grown so quickly, or why in such a place, or why he should be entitled to it, seeing the frame of mind he was in and the reason why he had placed himself in such an exposed position. We are all guilty of taking too much for granted and thereby fail to count and enjoy most of our blessings.

Does it occur to us that the God Who gives us health, strength, food, friends, homes, and a thousand other blessings, for which we never say "Thank you", but even think that we are fully entitled to them, is the same God Who can take them away from such ungrateful creatures! He prepared a worm in this instance. Sometimes it is a war, a storm, an accident, a pestilence. Then, when man finds himself exposed to the rugged world, he seeks to blame God, and even dares to ask the question — What have I done to deserve this ?

God was asking Jonah, and He has asked man ever since, a very pertinent question. If he has a right to expect the goodness and the provision of God, then surely other people have the same right ? If he thinks that Nineveh, because of its sin, had no right to God's salvation, then neither did he have a right to it, because there was a time when he, like them, was under the same condemnation.

Now comes a further indictment that calls for a close self-examination.

There has been a great amount of speculation as to the meaning of this last verse. "And should not I spare Nineveh, that great city, wherein are more than sixscore thousand persons that cannot discern between their right hand and their left hand ; and also much cattle." Scholars have suggested that this would be the number of children in the city. Maybe, but most children know right from left. Such an interpretation might have to be qualified with young children or infants, and the interpretation could still be correct. It probably is that both infants and cattle are innocent creatures, and the Lord was appealing for the city because of the innocent who were in it. This was so when Abraham appealed for a city. It was because of the righteous who were in it.

Might one venture to qualify this interpretation. The expression is still current, "He does not know his right hand from his left", which means that he does not know the difference between right and wrong. Was that the condition of Nineveh ? It is the condition of much of the world to-day. They have never read the Ten Commandments, they have never heard the gospel, they do not know the meaning of salvation. They are not innocent, but they are ignorant. Jonah was not ignorant ; he was aware of the goodness of God but wanted selfishly to keep it to himself.

Israel, as a nation, failed God in this respect. The Church has failed the world in holding back the message of salvation.

Are we going to be charged by God that we, as Christians, with our knowledge, our privileges, and all the blessings of salvation, have been so selfish that we have contented ourselves with our church activities, our social functions, our Christian fellowship, and have never lifted a finger to rescue the perishing or to care for the dying ?

It was learned at the beginning the reason for Jonah's displeasure — a patriotic spirit toward his own people, rather than a devoted spirit toward the souls of lost men. This could readily be a missionary book, for so many are more concerned with their own political advantages and disadvantages than they are with the dying souls of humanity.

Lord, send us revival !

MICAH

CONTROVERSY AND ARRAIGNMENT

*" Now learn a parable of the fig tree ; When his branch is yet
tender, and putteth forth leaves, ye know that summer is
nigh : So likewise ye, when ye shall see all these things, know
that it is near, even at the doors. Verily I say unto you, This
generation shall not pass till all these things be fulfilled.
Heaven and earth shall pass away, but My Words shall not
pass away."* (MATTHEW xxiv. 32-35)

INTRODUCTION

Nothing is known of Micah other than the fact that he
belonged to the southern kingdom of Judah for it is declared that
he came forth from Moresheth-gath.

The name Micah means " Who is like unto Jehovah ", which
is in harmony with the very last declaration of the Prophet, which
was : " Who is a God like unto Thee . . . " (vii. 18).

His ministry, which covered a period of about forty years,
was exercised during the reigns of Jotham, Ahaz, and Hezekiah,
all kings of Judah, yet that same ministry concerned the northern
kingdom of Israel as well as Judah being addressed to Samaria
and Jerusalem. Micah was also a contemporary of Isaiah.

He witnessed some great changes in the nation, for the first
and the last kings were evil, whilst the reign of Ahaz was good.

To understand the prophecy it must be realised that its background concerned the Assyrian invasion, out of which the Prophet
developed some of the results of a greater invasion that would
take place in the last days, when the Lord would grant His people
a glorious deliverance, but not before they had taken their own
punishment.

THE BOOK

It divides into three sections, each beginning with the call
to " Hear ". Each section moves into a wider field. The divisions
are :

    (1) HEAR, ALL YE PEOPLE (Chapters i-ii.).

    (2) HEAR, O HEADS OF JACOB (Chapters iii-v.).

    (3) HEAR YE, O MOUNTAINS (Chapters vi-vii.).

and concern certain warnings of judgment, followed by Messianic hopes and concluding with promises of the future.

(1) HEAR, ALL YE PEOPLE — WARNINGS (Chapters i & ii.)

Judgment declared (i. 7). Without delay Micah moved right into his subject by declaring the indignation of God toward His people because of their sin. The language of the Prophet is very descriptive. He describes the Lord of glory stepping down from heaven to earth, leaving His holy temple that He might become a witness of their unholy conduct. The people were called upon to recognise His mighty power, by the picture of the mountains melting under His feet, and the valleys turning into wax and fleeing before Him as waters rush in torrents down the face of the cliffs. The cause of this melting was the fury of God against the sins of the people.

It was Samaria, or the Northern Kingdom, to which he first directed his attention. They had forsaken Jehovah, the One and only God, for their many gods. Graven images were set up everywhere, in niches, on the walls, and in the homes. Larger idols were established upon the mountains of Israel surrounded by trees, hence they were called both " high places " and " groves ". The people bent the knee and bowed in worship to these ; to such they offered their prayers and expected answers. All of this was so contrary to the laws of God given them through Moses, such as " Thou shalt not make unto thee any graven image ", " Thou shalt not bow down thyself to them ", " Thou shalt fear the Lord thy God and serve Him ". Had God not told them that He was a jealous God, that He would not share devotion or worship with anyone ? Idolatry to Him was as debasing as adultery. Both meant sharing love and loyalty with others, and such things the Lord abominates.

Micah was declaring that these were the things with which God would have to deal, destroying both the system and those responsible for establishing it.

Like a canker this disease was spreading and affecting Judah and had reached Jerusalem. So ashamed was the Prophet that he cried : " Declare ye it not in Gath ". Gath was one of the principal cities of Philistia, and the Philistines were ever the enemies of God's people. They loved to rejoice in the calamities of Israel. When Saul was slain in battle, David in his lamentation said : " Tell it not in Gath, publish it not in the streets of Askelon ; lest the daughters of the Philistines rejoice, lest the daughters of the

uncircumcised triumph " (2 Samuel i. 20). Micah was anxious
that the enemy should not know the sin of Israel, just as David
was anxious that they should not know their defeats.

Chapter one, verse 6, was as literally fulfilled as it is stated,
so that one does not have to guess at the meaning. Samaria, with
all its palaces, was built on a hill. When it was destroyed, the
stones of those buildings went rolling down into the valley below.
Since then the sides of the hill, which were once occupied with
buildings, are now terraced and are the places of vineyards. Men
ought to read all of these prophecies and then study the history
of the nations, cities, and people who were addressed, noting the
literalness and the detailed exactness of the fulfilment of all that
was declared. If they did, they might be much more concerned
with the things God has declared which concern the future, for thus
will it be because the mouth of the Lord hath spoken it.

Micah mourned for Judah (i. 8-9). Like the mourner of the
East who puts off his apparel for the garments of mourning and
howls in professional style, beating his hands upon his breast
(called wailing) as a symbol of his grief because of the death of
some member of the family, so Micah was displaying his grief for
the sins of Judah, sins which must bring death in their train unless
there were repentance. How little sorrow for sin is seen to-day!
Not the sorrow of the sinner, for many of them are not even
conscious of sin, but sorrow or grief in the heart of the Christian
for SIN. Maybe if the Church showed more grief because of sin,
the sinner might have more sense of the guilt of his sin. There
is a cure for sin. It is in the Saviour's Blood but, if men will refuse
the remedy and will persist in their sin, then they can sink to a
position where there is no remedy.

In the closing verses of chapter one, Micah brought to their
memory a number of cities upon which God already had meted
out judgment, reminding them that thus God would deal with them
also.

Sins of the Rich (ii. 1-3). Idolatry was the fundamental
crime but, alas! it brought other sins in its train. The man who
forsakes God is also the man who forsakes moral integrity for,
apart from God, the heart is deceitful above all things and desperately wicked. Thus it was that in chapter two the Prophet made
known that, added to their first sin, were covetousness, violence
and oppression. These iniquities they devised upon their beds
during the night watches and then put them into practice by day.

The soul of the wicked knows no rest because it knows no peace or satisfaction.

The nation was charged with the same sins as were laid against it by Amos — the oppression of the poor. In verse 3 the Lord promised to inflict upon them the same things. They had practised evil, now God would put a yoke of evil upon their necks from which they would not be able to free themselves, and which would bow them down in humiliation.

Lamentation (ii. 4-6). As a result of God's dealings, Israel was to be brought low and they would engage in a lamentation in which they declared that they were " miserably miserable " because God had changed the glory of the nation into desolation. They did not declare that they had previously changed the goodness of God into corruption. The parable referred to appears to be a taunt. The enemy used the same words of Israel's lament and threw them back at the people in a song of mockery. Maybe the Lord was telling His people that their own lament was no deeper than that, for it was sorrow without repentance. This lack of repentance was realised as in the next verse the false prophets and the leaders of the people bade Micah to withhold his prophesying. They objected because the message was always against them, making them to feel ashamed.

Men have never wanted the truth, even when they know that it is the truth, because they desire to continue in their sin.

Reproof for injustice (ii. 7-9). The Prophet answered those who wished to silence him. The Spirit of the Lord was not straitened by these words. The Lord had not lost His patience but was still long-suffering. They must know that, if the Lord failed to reprove men when they sinned, then man might readily question the faithfulness of God Himself. He spoke these words because, on the one hand, His justice required it, and, on the other hand, the people needed it. Let man, therefore, not seek to silence the voice of the Lord through His prophets or through His Word, but interpret it in its true meaning and profit thereby.

Promise of restoration (ii. 10-13). Why continue in those ways of sin ? Why cling to the things of this world ? They are all polluted and corrupt, so arise and depart. God has a glorious future for His people. Even though the people may go into exile the Lord would bring them through.

The last verses of this chapter look away to the Millennial blessing, to the day when Messiah shall reign and they will be as

a great flock of sheep in the rich pasture land to which He has
led them, all of them bleating with the sense of contentment. The
picture is a very refreshing one. " The breaker is come . . . "
(vs. 13) — the Emancipator, the Messiah Who has come to break
the bondage of the past and set the captive free. " . . . And the
Lord (would be) on the head of them."

(2) HEAR, O HEADS OF JACOB — MESSIANIC HOPES
   (Chapters iii-v.)

The Prophet having spoken to the people then reached out
to the princes, those who were more responsible for the conditions
that were prevailing. " Hear, I pray you, O heads of Jacob, and
ye princes of the house of Israel ; is it not for you to know judgment ? " (iii. 1). These heads included the princes and judges,
the prophets and the priests. They had turned the minds of the
people away from the truth. They had set themselves up as the
lords of God's heritage but were not discharging their duties. Firstly
Micah dealt with the

Princes. These were descendants of the royal line and should
have known how to rule and to execute judgment. There was no
justice left in these men. They hated the good and loved the evil.
They were cruel in their practices toward the people, dealing with
them as though they were no more than animals, so cruel to them
as though they only existed that the princes might feed on them,
satisfying their carnal desires and worldly ambitions. The day
would come when these princes should cry for mercy, but the
Lord would have a deaf ear in that day. They would be dealt
with as they had dealt with others.

Secondly, he turned to the

Prophets. There were many who came out of the school of
the prophets to engage in this particular ministry who had never
been called or endued by the Lord. There are many of them to-day
who pass through theological seminaries and come out to take up
Christian ministry as a profession, who know nothing of the
anointing of the Holy One. These are referred to as false prophets.
It must be recognised that false prophets need not necessarily refer
to worshippers of idols ; these were called the prophets of Baal,
or of Ashteroth, or of some other deity. The false prophets
prophesied in the name of God even though He had not sent them.
The Lord declared this on a number of occasions, e.g. " Then the
Lord said unto me, The prophets prophesy lies in My Name : I

sent them not, neither have I commanded them, neither spake
unto them ; they prophesy unto you a false vision and divination,
and a thing of naught, and the deceit of their heart " (Jeremiah
xiv. 14). As a result of this " they make My people err " when
they should be directing their feet in the ways of righteousness,
guiding their thoughts in the ways of holiness, and leading their
hearts into the light of understanding. Therefore when they shall
come to seek the true light of prophecy, they will discover themselves groping in darkness and possessing no vision.

Against all this deception Micah claimed that he was the true
Prophet of the Lord, seeking not his own but seeking the things
of the Lord and the good of God's people. Thus he said : " But
truly I am full of power by the Spirit of the Lord, and of judgment,
and of might, to declare unto Jacob his transgression, and to Israel
his sin " (iii. 8).

Micah summed up the situation as to the ruling class, every
one of them had been corrupted. They had all lost the vision
and the privilege of their respective callings. They had become
mercenary and materialistic. The princes judged for reward, the
priests taught for hire, the prophets divined for money. They were
all being bribed, and at the same time claimed to have the authority
of the Lord.

What was true of Micah's day concerning Israel is true to-day
concerning the Church, and the world at large. Statesmen have
become politicians seeking graft. The ministry has become a
profession seeking self. The evangelist has become a competitor
seeking crowds. How desperately in need is the Church of men
like Micah who can say : " I am full of power by the Spirit of
the Lord ".

The destruction of Zion (iii. 12). How often man destroys the
very thing he seeks to build up ! With his money and his hands
he builds up, but with his motives and his heart he tears down.
The enemy is blamed, or the climate, or the economy, for the
trouble he is in, and he fails to recognise that those things are the
agencies of God for punishment, and never the *cause* of the disaster.
That is always *his* sin.

How literally was this last verse of the chapter fulfilled.
" Therefore shall Zion for your sake be plowed as a field, and
Jerusalem shall become heaps, and the mountain of the house as
the high places of the forest." The destruction of the city by the
Chaldeans is well known, and many have testified to its being
ploughed as a field. Thomson in *The Land and the Book* states

"The whole of the hill here is under cultivation and presents a most literal fulfilment of Micah's prophecy".

The author has, on a number of occasions, lectured with a plough which is the property of the Rev. L. T. Pearson, whose father-in-law, the late Rev. Samuel Schor, saw a farmer using this very plough on Mount Sion. So thrilled was he to see a "prophetic plough" at work that he purchased it from the farmer that he might place it in an exhibition which has for years declared the authority of the Word of God.

As Micah closed the first section with an anticipation of Millennial blessing, even so did he close the second portion of his prophecy.

Future Glory foretold (Ch. iv.). From the ploughed fields and the ruinous heaps of the present, Micah lifted his eyes and looked out on to a glorious horizon of the promises of God. His mind moved from the calamities of the immediate to the blessings of the ultimate. Whenever the Christian becomes depressed by the sights of this present evil world, through which the Devil would whisper his suggestions of defeat and failure, then he should look up and look out! He does not belong to this world, neither is this the end. He moves toward a city whose Builder and Maker is God. As we are surrounded with wars and rumours of wars, look up and look out for He, the Prince of Peace, is going to reign, Whose right it is. Micah did this concerning Israel. The true Church of Jesus Christ must do the same.

As the former temple had stood upon Mount Moriah giving it an exalted position in the old Jerusalem, so the temple of God in the Millennial land will be exalted high. This need not refer to any physical elevation, but it is spiritual attainment, when the worship of the Lord will come before everything else and His Name shall be exalted in the midst of the people. Many nations will desire to share in the blessings of that day. To-day the Jew is despised, Israel is scattered. Then they shall be the head and not the tail. "In those days it shall come to pass, that ten men shall take hold out of all languages of the nations, even shall take hold of the skirt of him that is a Jew, saying, We will go with you : for we have heard that God is with you" (Zechariah viii. 23).

In the beginning of this era the gospel emanated from Jerusalem, where Jesus lived and died, and where the Church found its birth on the Day of Pentecost, and found its way throughout the earth as it was preached to all nations. Then all nations will find their way toward that centre of worship, for God will be in their midst. The kingdoms of this world will become the kingdoms of the Lord. No United Nations Organisation will be needed then, for He shall judge or arbitrate among the nations, and war will be no more. Instead, they will learn the art of *Peace*. Swords and spears will become the implements of peaceful pursuits, for man will engage in agricultural activities, and then enjoy the results of his labours as he sits under his own vine or fig tree — relaxed ; for none shall make him afraid. What an experience that will be for God's chosen people, because now they must scarcely know the meaning of that word, relaxed. Tension, fear, hate, and being hounded from place to place, have been their portions ever since the day their forbears said : " His Blood be on us and on our children " (Matthew xxvii. 25).

Revival after captivity. From this soul-stirring vision of the future, Micah came back to the present. Before that day comes there is to be a time of sorrow because of their sin. He used the picture of a woman in travail — her sorrow soon forgotten in the joy of a son who had been born. The pains of childbirth were the result of sin. Said God to Eve : " I will greatly multiply thy sorrow and thy conception ; in sorrow thou shalt bring forth children " (Genesis iii. 16). So now the nation must endure its sorrow because of its sin, but beyond its grief and its captivity it could look for a glorious emancipation.

Rescued by God. In the last three verses of chapter four, God reminded them that their deliverance would not be because of what they were, or what they would do, but because of what He would do.

That is true concerning ourselves and our future glory.

Chapter five, verse 1, was a reminder that the nation would constantly have to be vigilant because the enemy would be ever around her. The Chaldean army was yet to come up against the city when Micah uttered the words of this first verse, and the Romans were in conquest at the time when the second verse was fulfilled.

This fifth chapter is noteworthy because in it is the only prophecy in all of the Old Testament Scriptures that told where Christ, the Messiah, was to be born, and this utterance was made by Micah seven hundred years before it was fulfilled. " But thou, Bethlehem Ephratah, though thou be little among the thousands of Judah, yet out of thee shall He come forth unto Me that is to be ruler in Israel : Whose goings forth have been from of old, from everlasting " (v. 2).

The question has been asked about six verses back : " Is there no king in thee ? Is thy counsellor perished ? " (iv. 9). Yes ! Micah prophesied through the reigns of Jotham, Ahaz, and Hezekiah, and was a contemporary of Isaiah, but there was to be a King Who would be King of kings.

Bethlehem means " house of bread ", *Ephratah* signifies " fruitfulness ", the little insignificant place of Judah ; insignificant, that is, so far as the world assesses things. But can a " house of bread " be so insignificant ? Can the place of fruitfulness be so despised ? Can the little community that gave to the nation its noble king, David, be so forgotten ? Is it not true that many of the greatest blessings of life are despised because they are so common ? Man speaks of his power-plants, his electricity, his factories, and his armaments, but where would any of these things be without that precious commodity so often wasted — water ? And Bethlehem, the tiny city of Judæa, gave to the world the Bread of Life.

The Prophet not only told of the obscure birthplace of great David's Greater Son, but also of the majesty of the place from whence He came. " Whose goings forth have been from of old, from everlasting " (v. 2). It was an announcement of His pre-existence in eternity and His co-existence with God. This was the One Who would bring His people into the glories of that future kingdom of peace and righteousness for He was " to be ruler in Israel ".

Micah not only prophesied the birth of the Messiah, which is an established historical event, but he also gave some indication of the life and ministry of the Lord, and, again it must be remembered, this was seven hundred years before Christ's birth. Micah had reminded the false prophets that he was a true Prophet of the Lord and here is some of the evidence of that statement. He spoke of the Lord as

A Shepherd. " He shall stand and feed in the strength of the Lord . . . " (v. 4) reminding one of the words of Isaiah, " He shall feed His flock like a shepherd ". Micah who, as has been pointed out, was a contemporary of Isaiah, used quite a number of similar phrases and illustrations. David, the shepherd of Israel, had come out of Bethlehem and was afterward exalted to the position of a king. Jesus, Who was a King, humbled Himself and became a shepherd and found His way into Bethlehem that he might stand in the midst of His people, both to feed them and to lead them.

The Prince of Peace. At the time when the Assyrians should come against the land, the Lord would deal with the enemy and subdue them. There is such an account in 2 Kings xix., in the days of Hezekiah. There is a future day when all enemies shall be put under His feet and He shall reign Whose right it is. In that day it will not only be the enemies without but also the enemies within that will be subdued — witchcraft, soothsaying, graven images, and all else that is foreign to the true God.

This fifth chapter begins with the introduction of Christ as the Babe of Bethlehem. It ends with the same Christ as the Lord of the earth. " And I will execute vengeance in anger and fury upon the heathen, such as they have not heard " (The word " heathen " means " nations ").

(3) HEAR YE, O MOUNTAINS—PROMISES (Chapters vi.-vii.)

The Prophet in this closing section comes back into the present. The call to the mountains and hills was, of course, figurative language. Sometimes mountains referred to the larger cities, and hills to the smaller villages. Micah was calling upon the nation as a whole, small and great, to hear the message he had for them. It could be a call to the whole world to listen.

This was his farthest outreach. God had a controversy with His people in which He reminded them of further sins. Chapter six declares *God's fourfold controversy.* In it He complained of their *ingratitude, ignorance, injustice, and idolatry.* How pathetic was the appeal he made, and how reasonable did the response of the people appear to be, until it is examined. This chapter is worthy of all the meditation that the child of God can give it. The conditions are as prevalent to-day as they were at any time, and the self-deception as real now as it was in Micah's day.

Observe firstly, God's complaint (vi. 3-5). " O My people, What have I done unto thee ? And wherein have I wearied thee ? Testify against Me " (vs. 3). The Lord spoke in a similar strain through Malachi many years later. He is speaking to us right now, in the midst of our half-heartedness and our liberal attitude toward His Word. He asks why we should be so cool and half-hearted, why we should forsake His Word and turn to the wisdom of this world ! He is asking the unsaved why they should refuse Him and go their own sinful way. " Testify against Me." To this challenge we must all stand silent with our heads bowed in shame. What accusation can we bring against the Lord of Glory ?

When Israel had no answer, the Lord reminded them of His own faithfulness, of just a few things He had done for them. He had brought them out of Egypt, He had redeemed them from slavery, He had given them leaders as Moses, Aaron, and Miriam, He had delivered them from men like Balak who would have cursed them — all these things and a multitude more. Why then had they forsaken Him ? Here were blessings enough that should demand a life of devoted service in return. But what of the Christian to-day ? The Lord would say to him that He had called him out of the world, had redeemed him from sin, had given him spiritual leaders in the Church, had given him a Bible to guide him, had given him the Holy Spirit to teach him, had given him pardon, peace, and sonship — what more could He give ? We must confess that He has been faithful and we have been faithless.

Secondly, consider man's reply (vi. 6-9). In it he is acknowledging his failure by a willingness to do something that will correct the situation. Man's enquiry is " Wherewith shall I come before the Lord, and bow myself before the high God ? " (vi. 6).

(1) Shall I come before Him with burnt offerings ? (law).

(2) Shall I bring calves of a year old ? (quality).

(3) Shall I please Him with thousands of rams ? (quantity).

(4) Shall I bring ten thousands of rivers of oil ? (impossible).

(5) Shall I give my firstborn, the fruit of my body, for the sin of my soul ? (sinful).

To all of these suggestions the Lord took a negative attitude. " They have a zeal of God, but not according to knowledge. For they being ignorant of God's righteousness, and going about to establish their own righteousness, have not submitted themselves unto the righteousness of God " (Romans x. 2-3).

Seemingly these people were ready to pay a high price for their iniquity. They were prepared to pay it according to the law ; for the law required some of the things which they suggested. Their mistake was they were not prepared to discontinue their sins. That is evidenced from verse 10 onwards, where it is declared that the treasures of wickedness were still in their houses. They wanted to continue with their wicked balances and deceitful weights. The rich still wanted to wrong the poor. These things had already been named against them earlier in the prophecy. Hence the

Prophet's answer to their enquiry was : " He hath showed thee, O man, what is good : and what doth the Lord require of thee, but to do justly and to love mercy, and to walk humbly with thy God ? " (vi. 8).

It is the same truth that was voiced by Samuel : " Hath the Lord as great delight in burnt offerings and sacrifices, as in obeying the voice of the Lord ? Behold, to obey is better than sacrifice, and to hearken than the fat of rams " (1 Samuel xv. 22). God required but one thing from them and He requires the same thing from His Church — it is *obedience*. Obedience is a display of loyalty and a recognition of the Lordship of the One Who is obeyed.

This was the one thing Israel was not prepared to do, for from the last verse it is evident that they preferred to keep the statutes of Omri and to walk in the ways of Ahab — both of them evil kings.

The voice of the Lord had appealed but the ears of the people were deaf. They were prepared for any form of religion, whatever it cost their pockets, but were not prepared for a life of complete surrender which interfered too much with the standards of morals they had set for themselves. This was assessed as too costly.

The Prophet mourned. His ministry had accomplished nothing. A real valuation of the life that now is with that which was to come was so far removed from the people that Micah cried out in his distress : " Woe is me ! for I am as when they have gathered the summer fruits, as the grapegleanings of the vintage ; there is no cluster to eat ; my soul desired the firstripe fruit " (vii. 1). The harvest had been picked, the gleaners had followed until all that was left on the tree was one solitary fruit here or there which had escaped the eye. Micah felt as lonely as that. All the good men had been taken away and he had become as a lone voice in the wilderness. With Elijah he might be crying out : " And I, even I only, am left ". With their desire for blood and their delight in evil, the message fell only on deaf ears.

The love of sin robbed man completely of security. Man could no longer trust his wife, children rose up against their parents, so that a man's enemies were those of his own household. How much of this was seen in Europe during the second world war ! It is the doctrine of Communism which is pervading all nations to-day. If a man cannot trust God, he just cannot trust. If God cannot direct, there is no direction. If what God has said can be disproved, then there is no foundation. In other words, when

God goes everything has gone, and that is the direction toward which the world is hastening to-day. The more man refuses God the more man loses of life. Thus the Prophet declared that

Confidence is only in God. "Therefore I will look unto the Lord ; I will wait for the God of my salvation : my God will hear me " (vii. 7).

If men be in opposition to God, then they must learn that God is opposed to them. He will smite them with the rod of His mouth and they shall not be. Yet the Lord has always had the faithful remnant, the seven thousand who have not bowed the knee to Baal. These God will always protect. They may fall at times but never wilfully ; therefore He will restore them. Micah told the enemy this : " Rejoice not against me, O mine enemy : when I fall, I shall arise ; when I sit in darkness, the Lord shall be a light unto me. I will bear the indignation of the Lord, because I have sinned against Him, until He plead my cause, and execute judgment for me : He will bring me forth to the light, and I shall behold His righteousness " (vii. 8-9).

God's goodness to Israel. This brought forth the triumphant cry of the Prophet with which he terminated his message. "*Who is a God like unto Thee?*" He exists without equal. He has no equal in his love, for He loved us when we were unlovely. He has no equal in His pardon ; He is the only One who can forgive, and remember our iniquities no more. He has no equal in His mercy ; " He retaineth not His anger for ever, because He delight-eth in mercy " (vii. 18). He has no equal in His compassion ; " He remembereth our frame." He remembers that we are dust and so is moved with compassion toward us. He has no equal in His grace for He casts all of our sins into the depths of the sea. He has no equal in His rewards, for He has given unto us eternal life and we shall never perish.

" Who is a God like unto Thee ? "

Whilst the prophecy is somewhat disjointed, the principles to be learned are :

(1) That sin is a reproach to any people, that it must bring its reward.

(2) That only obedience will satisfy a Holy God.

(3) That repentance is always possible.

(4) That God's grace is always greater than His judgment.

NAHUM

THE BURDEN OF NINEVEH

*"To Me belongeth vengeance, and recompence ; their foot shall
slide in due time : for the day of their calamity is at hand,
and the things that shall come upon them make haste."*
(DEUTERONOMY xxxii. 35)

THE PROPHET

Very little is known of this Prophet of the Lord, as is true
also concerning most of the Minor Prophets. His name is understood to mean "Consolation" and he certainly brought that to
the oppressed people of Judah, even though the same message
would have brought no consolation whatever to the enemy. He
is called in verse 1 "Nahum the Elkoshite". It is not certain
where Elkosh, his birthplace, was, but there is some evidence that
it was near Capernaum. As Capernaum means "The City of
Nahum" or "The City of Consolation", there is the possibility
that he established the city which became so well known during
the ministry of the Lord.

What is known is that Nahum was born in Galilee, and so
was Jonah who also preached against the sins of the people of
Nineveh. Later, another arose out of Galilee Who preached
against the sins of the world. The Pharisees, when questioning
the authority of Jesus, made quite a big mistake when they said
to Nicodemus : "Art thou also of Galilee ? Search, and look :
for out of Galilee ariseth no prophet" (John vii. 52). He was
the third prophet to have come out of Galilee, and He, the third,
had been foretold.

Seeing that the Scripture gives no more than one verse concerning the Prophet himself, and there is so often the tendency to
get the eye focused on a man — on the preacher instead of the
preaching — the lesson must be centred around the prophecy and
not the Prophet. The message concerns the city of Nineveh.
Therefore, in order to appreciate the message, it will be necessary
to know something of

THE CITY

The whole prophecy concerns the doom of a great city, Nineveh, which city was the capital of the great Assyrian Empire. This empire came out of Babylon being founded by colonists from Babylon. For centuries Assyria was either subject to or in conflict with Babylon. Assyria had been responsible for the destruction of Israel, as Babylon was for the captivity of Judah. Both the cities of Babylon and Nineveh were founded by Nimrod (Genesis x.). For years Assyria had expanded by absorbing her neighbour nations, then deporting the people in the hope that they would lose their patriotism. They were exceedingly cruel to their captives. Some Biblical evidence of the oppression she inflicted upon Israel can be ascertained by the facts that in

B.C. 840 — Israel paid tribute to Assyria in the days of Jehu.

B.C. 747 — Thirteen years later the rest of Israel fell and also Samaria (2 Kings xvii. 6).

B.C. 734 — In the early days of Isaiah Assyria carried away all Northern Israel (1 Chronicles v. 26).

B.C. 715 — Later they attacked Judah and carried away two hundred thousand captives (2 Chronicles xxxii.).

B.C. 701 — The Assyrians were routed before Jerusalem when God intervened (Isaiah xxxvii.).

At the time of Nahum's prophecy, Nineveh was known as the "Queen of the earth". It was built on the loot of the nations, by slaves who suffered terrible brutalities. Nahum likened it to a den of ferocious lions. The city was thirty miles long and ten miles wide. It was surrounded with five walls and three moats. The inner city had walls one hundred feet high, and wide enough for four chariots abreast. This was the city against which Nahum pronounced doom.

THE MESSAGE

This prophecy was made one hundred years before it was fulfilled, but all came to pass exactly as the Prophet had declared it should.

The book divides according to its three chapters.

(1) Judgment declared (Chapter i.).

(2) Judgment delivered (Chapter ii.).

(3) Judgment deserved (Chapter iii.).

(1) JUDGMENT DECLARED (Chapter i.)

Title. In the introductory verse there is an indication that this vision was written in a book. This is not stated in the other prophecies. The possibility is that Nahum made his declaration against the city, as did Jonah one hundred and fifty years earlier, but that it was also written so that when it came to pass one hundred years later men might see that it was according to prediction, which would also declare that these people were without excuse and that vengeance was with justice. May it be said that thus it will be at the end of this age. The written Word of God, in the day of reckoning which is yet to be, will become a testimony against all who have refused it.

A Jealous God. God has declared this from time to time. He made known the fact when He gave to man the Ten Commandments at Sinai : " . . . For I the Lord thy God am a jealous God, visiting the iniquity of the fathers upon the children unto the third and fourth generations of them that hate Me " (Exodus xx. 5). God is jealous of all that is right, therefore He must punish all that is wrong. God is also jealous of His Name, and has declared it for our information. " Thou shalt not take the Name of the Lord thy God in vain ; for the Lord will not hold him guiltless that taketh His Name in vain " (Exodus xx. 7).

The first half of that statement tells of His jealousy, the second half of His vengeance. Assyria had been guilty of these sins in no uncertain way. Their crimes had mounted up to heaven. A glaring example of their guilt is recorded in 2 Kings, chapters xviii. and xix. It was during the reign of Hezekiah when Assyria made its attack upon Judah. Ten years earlier Israel had fallen to Shalmaneser, king of Assyria. Now Sennacherib was laying siege against Judah and Jerusalem. Sending Rabshakeh as his mouthpiece he tried to break the morale of the people by declaring the greatness of the power of the king of Assyria and the weakness of the God in Whom they trusted. He said some very daring things about the God of Israel. " Thus saith the king (Sennacherib), Let not Hezekiah deceive you : for he shall not be able to deliver you out of his hand. Neither let Hezekiah make you trust in the Lord, saying, The Lord will surely deliver us, and this city shall not be delivered into the hand of the king of Assyria " (2 Kings xviii. 29-30). " Who are they among all the gods of the countries, that have delivered their country out of mine hand, that the Lord should deliver Jerusalem out of mine hand ? " (2 Kings

xviii. 35). This is blasphemy that the Lord will not permit. God must vindicate His Name, His Honour, and His people.

One may well tremble to-day for those who deny the Saviour's Virgin Birth, the efficacy of His Blood, and the authority of His Word. Let it be known that the Lord will take vengeance on His adversaries.

A Mighty God. Assyria would line up Jehovah with all the helpless gods of the nations and then boast of her own strength, but God said to Isaiah : " . . . Be not afraid of the words which thou hast heard, with which the servants of the king of Assyria have blasphemed Me. Behold, I will send a blast upon him, and he shall hear a rumour, and shall return to his own land : and I will cause him to fall by the sword in his own land " (2 Kings xix. 6-7).

God said much more through Nahum to this city that could boast of its strength, and speak of the insignificance of Jehovah. He declared a great contrast of His character. " Slow to anger . . . and will not at all acquit the wicked " (vs. 3). What comfort is to be found in this verse for the believer ! The slowness of the Lord's anger was demonstrated with the city when it is remembered that this was the second voice in Nineveh. One hundred and fifty years earlier Jonah had been sent there to preach repentance. He re-corded that it was a great city and a wicked city. It was because of their cruelties that Jonah did not want to preach to them for he did not desire their life prolonged. God dealt with Jonah on this matter when He caused the gourd to grow and then to wither, for He said : " Thou hast had pity on the gourd, for which thou hast not laboured, . . . should not I spare Nineveh, that great city, wherein are more than six score thousand persons that cannot discern between their right hand and their left hand ; . . . " (Jonah iv. 10-11). The message of Jonah was ultimately one of mercy. The message of Nahum was one of doom.

In the days of Jonah the people of Nineveh had repented and found forgiveness, but they had since fallen back into sin. Nahum prophesied one hundred years before the judgment was meted out. That gave the city two hundred and fifty years of grace — surely God was slow to anger and plenteous in mercy ! This is a fulfil-ment of the words of the Lord to Jeremiah : " At what instant I shall speak concerning a nation, and concerning a kingdom, to pluck up, and to pull down, and to destroy it; If that nation, against whom I have pronounced, turn from their evil, I will repent of the evil that I thought to do unto them. And at what instant I shall speak concerning a nation, and concerning a kingdom, to build and to plant it; If it do evil in My sight, that it obey not My voice, then I will repent of the good, wherewith I said I would benefit them " (Jeremiah xviii. 7-10).

Nineveh, the once repentant city, now boasted of its strength and power, its impregnable position, with its mighty bulwarks and its powerful armies. Its king had insulted the God of heaven as though He were insignificant and helpless against this monarch, so He replied : " . . . Great in power . . . The Lord hath His way in the whirlwind and in the storm, and the clouds are the dust of His feet. He rebuketh the sea . . . and drieth up all the rivers ; . . . The mountains quake at Him, and the hills melt ; . . . Who can stand before His indignation ? His fury is poured out like fire, and the rocks are thrown down by Him " (i. 3-6).

Neither Sennacherib, the proud king, nor Rabshakeh, the haughty general, nor Nineveh, the mighty stronghold, could stand before the Creative God, how much less before the indignation of a Holy God ? This is the God Who is to be met not only by the proud Assyrians but by all nations of men who reject Him. It is a fearful thing to fall into the hands of the living God. Little did these proud leaders realise that Jerusalem would continue centuries after Nineveh had been forgotten.

Hezekiah, the king of Judah, and Isaiah, the Prophet, as well as many of the Lord's saints since that day, have learned the truth declared by Nahum : " The Lord is good, a stronghold in the day of trouble, and He knoweth them that trust in Him " (i. 7).

The latter part of the chapter gives some indication of the judgment of the nation in the days of Sennacherib, which was, of course, different from the doom of Nineveh, even though in some sense it might have been part of it. The statement in verse 11 would obviously refer to Rabshakeh. For many years Assyria was a source of trouble to both Israel and Judah. It must have been a great day when Judah was finally delivered, and so the cry of ecstacy : " Behold upon the mountains the feet of Him that bringeth good tidings, that publisheth peace " (i. 15). This was an echo of the same song of triumph of Isaiah lii., where in verse 4 it is learned that the emancipation was from the hand of the Assyrians who oppressed them without cause.

Evidently the invasions and sieges had brought to an end some of the feasts which should have been observed. Judah, therefore, was instructed to keep those solemn feasts.

(2) JUDGMENT DELIVERED (Chapter ii.)

God uses one nation to punish another, and then in turn punishes it. This is seen again and again in history, and it was definitely stated by God to Habakkuk in answer to his great problem.

Assyria had been used by God to punish the children of God. He had used them to fulfil His purpose, a purpose in which God found no delight, for He does not punish men willingly any more than does a loving parent. He wills not the death of any sinner. Isaiah said concerning Him : " In all their affliction He was afflicted, and the angel of His presence saved them : in His love and in His pity He redeemed them ; and He bare them, and carried them all the days of old " (Isaiah lxiii. 9).

Whilst God found no pleasure in punishing, the Assyrians found sheer delight in so doing. God now was using Babylon to punish Assyria, and so it went down the line.

The opening verses of this chapter are most descriptive. Nahum declared to Nineveh that the enemy had come and that, although they thought that they were strong, they had better watch their fortifications and keep their eyes on every move the enemy made. Although they strengthened themselves and gathered their armies, yet they were to know that nothing could save them.

Assyria had emptied the land of Israel. Its peoples they had carried away into captivity, so that the land was one of spoilation. Now God was permitting this great army of the Chaldeans to do the same thing to them.

One must be very careful in Bible interpretation. Here are two verses to which men have done despite. Why is it that so many people want to see everything in the form of prophecy fulfilled in their own lifetime, as though God had His mind only on one generation ? It would be better if Christians would be as concerned that all Divine revelation as to sin, salvation, sanctification and holiness, which do belong to each successive generation and therefore to *this* generation, were fulfilled in their own personal lives.

The two verses mentioned are 3 and 4, in which has been seen a picture of the modern motor-car, speeding down the highways, colliding at times, and carrying their headlights as torches. Surely God was not interested in industrial progress and, if He were, why only in our generation ? Fifty years ago the " jostling " motor car was not known, and in fifty years time it may be a thing of the past. Radar-control could remove the collisions and do away with the headlights. Man might motor on a beam, as does the aeroplane. Many things could happen to make the car obsolete.

Again, why should the Prophet leave his subject — the doom of Nineveh — to interject a twentieth century condition, and then leave it again as something irrelevant ?

All that has to be done is to read history in the light of prophecy, and prophecy is as clear as the light of day. These verses are obviously referring to armies and chariots entering a city at the same time as the gates of the river were opened into the same city.

Quoting from a historical record, which would be the best commentary of the verses under consideration, Diodorus Seculus described it thus : " There was a prophecy that Nineveh should not be taken till the river became an enemy to the city. And in the third year of the siege, the river, being swollen with continuous rains, overflowed every part of the city, and broke down the wall for twenty furlongs ; then the king, thinking that the oracle was fulfilled, and the river had become an enemy to the city, built a large funeral pyre in the palace and, collecting together all his wealth and his concubines and eunuchs, burnt himself and the palace with them all — and the enemy entered at the breach that the waters had made and took the city."

This is exactly as it was described by Nahum. " The gates of the rivers shall be opened, and the palace shall be dissolved " (ii. 6), and again : " But with an overrunning flood He will make an utter end of the place thereof " (i. 8).

With such access the enemy entered so fast that the chariots raged in the streets and jostled one against another. The princes were so drunken from their feasting to their gods that they were helpless in their defence, and they fulfilled vs. 5 " He shall recount his worthies ; they shall stumble in their walk ; they shall make haste to the wall thereof, and the defence shall be prepared."

As the historical records referred to the death of the king and his concubines who perished in the fire, and said nothing concerning the queen, it is thought by some that verse 7 probably referred to her in her escape : " And Huzzab shall be led away captive, she shall be brought up, and her maids shall lead her as with the voice of doves, tabering upon their breasts ". Of course, it could refer to the city, as such, being led away. The picture is one of mourning.

From the beginning when Asshur built this great city, at the time when Nimrod built Babylon, it had been as a " pool of water", a place to which men turned for protection as a man would turn to the water for quiet and refreshment, a place of certainty, but they would turn to the city no more. Instead it was just the reverse. They would now flee from it, and not even take one look back. Man's confidence goes when God begins to act.

All the loot which Nineveh had taken from the oppressed nations, the silver and the gold and the furniture, would now be taken from her. " She is empty, and void, and waste : . . . " (ii. 10). This is the picture of Nineveh to-day, a place of desolation. Men may ask the question — where is Nineveh ? " Where is the dwelling of the lions, and the feedingplace of the young lions; where the lion, even the old lion, walked, and the lion's whelp, and none made them afraid ? The lion did tear in pieces enough for his whelps, and strangled for his lionesses, and filled his holes with prey, and his dens with ravin " (ii. 11-12). All of this means — where is the place where the victorious generals consumed the wealth they brought back from the overrun and suppressed nations ? They enriched their sons (whelps), they shared with the old lions (the princes), they stripped the women of those countries of their jewels and their ornaments that they might adorn their own women (the lionesses), they filled their treasure-houses (holes), and palaces (dens), and none made them afraid. But where are they now ? The city was so completely destroyed that old history books and commentaries record that " the site of Nineveh is a mere matter of conjecture ". It was only in the last century that two British archaeologists, Layard and Rawlinson, unearthed the ruins of Nineveh.

Does not this scene of such complete a devastation of so strong and proud a city when God's anger is outpoured remind one of another scene which is still future ? " And the kings of the earth and the great men, and the rich men, and the chief captains, and the mighty men, and every bondman, and every free man, hid themselves in the dens and in the rocks of the mountains ; And said to the mountains and rocks, Fall on us, and hide us from the face of Him that sitteth on the throne, and from the wrath of the Lamb : For the great day of His wrath is come ; and who shall be able to stand ? " (Revelation vi. 15-17).

Again, " And the great city was divided into three parts, and the cities of the nations fell : and great Babylon came in remembrance before God, to give unto her the cup of the wine of the fierceness of His wrath. And every island fled away, and the mountains were not found. And there fell upon men a great hail out of heaven, every stone about the weight of a talent : and men blasphemed God because of the plague of the hail : for the plague thereof was exceeding great " (Revelation xvi. 19-21).

As surely as the fall of Nineveh was fulfilled in detail, and God's anger against that city is now past history, so surely will God visit mankind again in His anger. Know, therefore, that it is an awful thing to fall into the hand of an angry God.

Sinner, why not flee into the only place of refuge, which is the riven side of the One Who took the curse of sin upon Himself, the Son of God, Who died at Calvary enduring the curse of sin that we might escape it ?

The chapter could be summed up in the verse from the Proverbs : " Righteousness exalteth a nation ; but sin is a reproach to any people " (Proverbs xiv. 34).

(3) JUDGMENT DESERVED (Chapter iii.)

The first three verses continue to tell of the doom that fell upon Nineveh, a city of blood, a city of deception, where none could trust his neighbour. The enemy continued to press hard and unrelenting. There was no yielding even though the city was filled with her dead until they could not move without falling over the bodies.

The cause ? This must be declared because God is just and it must be known that He does not inflict upon men more than they deserve.

Her crimes were named. They must stand as witnesses. They were — idolatries, sorceries, luxury, intemperance, and licentiousness. These she had practised against herself. Then there were warfares, plunderings, robberies, and cruelties, which she had inflicted upon the other nations that were round about her. She had never regarded the rights and privileges of other people, but had brought them all into subjection to herself. She had exposed other peoples in their weakness. God was now going to expose her in her filth and sin.

One cannot help looking around the world to-day as one reads these things, noting that history repeats itself, and that God also will repeat Himself. He is still just and holy and will still deal with the sinner according to his sin. As God used other nations and then punished them, so surely God is going to use Russia for meting out some of His judgments, after which He will deal with that evil nation.

Other cities had fallen. Lest Nineveh should seek to justify herself, lest she should try and pull a veil over the eyes of her people that defeat was an impossible thing, lest she should seek

to build up the morale of the people around the supposed impregnable strength of her great city, Nahum reminded her of God's
dealings with other cities. " Art thou better than populous No
(No Amon) ? " (iii. 8). Certainly Nineveh was no better in position.
It stood on the River Nile and was surrounded by waters that
became her ramparts and fortifications. Neither was she better
with friends, for that city knew the support of Egypt and Ethiopia,
Put and Lubim. (Put refers to the wandering nomads of Africa).
Nineveh could not boast of being better than any other nation
morally, yet that city fell a complete victim of the judgment of
God.

These are solmen words which should be read with a great
deal of introspection. " Art thou better than populous No ? "
The peoples of Britain and America have an air of confidence as
though they were better than any other people. From some of
man's standards this may be true, but how do we stand in the
eyes of God ? If, in making assessments, moral standards are
considered, it must be remembered that in the eyes of God the
Western nations have had greater privilege than most other nations,
and responsibility must be measured by privilege. If religion is
the standard, it will be discovered that its power is being denied
whilst man works for a one universal Church. The growth of
spiritism and kindred faiths, the loss of parental control, the increase
of drug addicts, the doctrine of free-love and self-expression, and
the open divorce court, is not a very different list of crimes from
those laid against Nineveh. All nations and empires in turn have
fallen, and every one because of God-rejection — Israel, God's
chosen people, included, but the nation of Israel is the only one
to which God has promised restoration. Ought man not, therefore,
to take heed ? When Queen Victoria could say that the Bible
was the secret of Britain's greatness, Britain was a world power
with a far-flung empire. She is no longer the first power in the
world, but is losing her empire, her prestige, her honour, just as
fast as her peoples are forsaking God. Prosperity seems to rise
and fall with the acceptance or rejection of the Bible. The acceptance or rejection are thermometers of spiritual life. Art thou
better than populous No ? Art thou better than mighty Babylon ?
Art thou better than Nineveh, queen of the earth ? These have
already gone. What nation will fall next ? Lord, send us revival !

None can save her. In the awful, drunken condition in which
Nineveh found herself, she became an easy prey to the enemy.
She was not necessarily drunken because of excess wine. To be

drunken in pride, ease, self-complacency, or any other vice over which one has lost self-control, is dangerous and can be fatal. Here Nahum likened the city to a fig tree whose fruit was so ripe that the least shaking of the tree would cause the fruit to fall, whilst below were the wide-opened mouths of the enemy ready to devour. So far as that nation was concerned it was now too late. She was doomed by God and none could save her.

Verses 16-18 are poetical, but their interpretation reveals that the strength of Assyria became its own weakness. The statement : " Thou hast multiplied thy merchants above the stars of heaven : " (iii. 16), means that they had gathered so many hired soldiers that they were without number. " Thy crowned are as the locusts, and thy captains as the great grasshoppers, which camp in the hedges in the cold day, but when the sun ariseth they flee away, and their place is not known where they are " (iii. 17). There were so many armed forces that they, like locusts, were consuming everything the nation had, and so robbing it of its wealth.

These troops, again like locusts, encamped in the cold day, or in the day of their need, if they could find a supply and a protection, but, when the sun arose and they felt its warmth, they were gone. A nation that hires mercenaries, never hires loyalty or patriotism. Such a soldier is likely to become a deserter and to flee when the battle is hot.

Nineveh knew yet another weakness. Whilst genuine devotion might be a missing quality in a soldier hired from a foreign country, such should not be amongst one's own rulers, but the next verse states : " Thy shepherds (or rulers) slumber ". They had become indifferent to the needs of their country, and the people were scattered never to return.

" There is no healing for thy bruise : thy wound is grievous " (iii. 19). Neither was there to be found any sympathy, for the book closes with the nations that had moaned under her sin and cruelty now clapping their hands and rejoicing over her end.

Many are the lessons to be learned from the fate of this great empire and this mighty fortress.

(1) God is gracious and longsuffering.

(2) God's Spirit will not always strive with man.

(3) God is just, rewarding the good and punishing the evil.

(4) What God declares He will perform to the full.

(5) What God did with Nineveh He will do to all sinners, and the place of the wicked shall be known no more.

(6) Nahum is declaring that the Eternal God still rules over the affairs of men. His Divine Sovereignty says — So far, and no farther.

(7) When God's time comes, man with all his pomp, power, and pride, may know that his time has ended, and not without retribution.

(8) No man or nation can build selfishly and save his soul.

(9) No man or nation of greed will ever have gain.

God has decreed : " Vengeance is Mine, I will repay."
God can be depended upon to judge the godless.
God can be trusted to reward the faithful.

> " God of our fathers, known of old
> Lord of our far-flung battle line,
> Beneath Whose awful hand we hold
> Dominion over palm and pine —
> Lord, God of Hosts, be with us yet,
> Lest we forget — lest we forget ! "

> " The tumult and the shouting dies,
> The captains and the kings depart ;
> Still stands Thine ancient sacrifice,
> A humble and a contrite heart,
> Lord God of Hosts, be with us yet,
> Lest we forget — lest we forget ! "

> " Far called, our navies melt away,
> On dune and headland sinks the fire ;
> Lo, all our pomp of yesterday
> Is one with Nineveh and Tyre !
> Judge of the nations, spare us yet,
> Lest we forget — lest we forget ! "

> " If, drunk with sight of power, we loose
> Wild tongues that have not Thee in awe ;
> Such boasting as the Gentiles use,
> Or lesser breeds without the Law —
> Lord God of Hosts, be with us yet,
> Lest we forget — lest we forget ! "

" For heathen heart that puts her trust
In reeking tube and iron shard,
All valiant dust that builds on dust,
And guarding, calls not Thee to guard,
For frantic boast and foolish word —
Thy mercy on Thy people, Lord ! "

(RUDYARD KIPLING)

HABAKKUK

WATCH AND PRAY

" And they say, How doth God know ? and is there knowledge in the most High ? Behold, these are the ungodly, who prosper in the world ; they increase in riches. Verily I have cleansed my heart in vain, and washed my hands in innocency. For all the day long have I been plagued, and chastened every morning. If I say I will speak thus ; behold, I should offend against the generation of Thy children. When I thought to know this, it was too painful for me : Until I went into the sanctuary of God ; then understood I their end. Surely Thou didst set them in slippery places : Thou castedst them down into destruction." (PSALM lxxiii. 11-18)

INTRODUCTION

This little prophecy is somewhat different from all the others. Firstly, nothing whatsoever is said concerning the Prophet Habakkuk, who he was, where he belonged, and so on. The only other prophet who was divorced from any personal association was Malachi.

The second thing that is noteworthy is the fact that all the other prophets spoke to men on the behalf of God and were His mouthpieces. Habakkuk spoke to God on the behalf of men. His ministry was more of the priestly order than the prophetical, prayer not prophecy, yet the Scripture speaks of him as a prophet. His writings come in the section of the prophets, and he is quoted in the New Testament as a prophet, for Acts xiii. 41 is a quotation of Habakkuk i. 5.

The authority of this book has never been questioned.

As to the period of time, Habakkuk was no doubt a contemporary of Jeremiah and prophesied during the reign of Josiah. There is evidence that he ministered after the fall of Nineveh and the destruction of the Assyrians, inasmuch as Assyria is not mentioned by him. On the other hand his ministry was before the two tribes were carried away into Babylon, because he foretold the destruction of the Chaldeans as Nahum had prophesied the doom of the Assyrians.

The message concerns that which he was caused to see of the future (i. 1). This is what makes it to be a prophecy. The big difference with Habakkuk was that others, having seen the future, warned men of impending judgment, whereas he interceded with God for the removal of judgment.

The background of the book will help in interpreting its message. The Prophet had witnessed the reformation under the hand of Josiah, the last good king in Judah. He watched the fading glow of the setting sun of Assyria. A great world-kingdom was dying before his eyes. Egypt and Babylon were struggling with each other for supremacy, that they might take the place of the vanishing empire. Josiah had died in this struggle. The Chaldeans became the nation which obtained the mastery.

Habakkuk knew the terrible consequences that would come out of this struggle he had witnessed. He knew that his people would fall victims to this power, for each successive world-empire had oppressed the people of God. This was the Prophet's great heart-ache. This was the reason for his intercession and, out of it all, he had to learn that *The Just shall live by faith.*

Whilst admitting that Judah had sinned and deserved punishment, Habakkuk could not understand why a nation more wicked than Judah should be the instrument used when they were deserving of the greater punishment. This was not the exclusive problem of Habakkuk. It has been the big question-mark in the minds of God's people in every generation. As God made known to His servant the whole truth in such a way as to turn the doubts of the Prophet into an assurance of faith, and converted his complaining into a confidence which called forth praise, considerable profit will be gained from a meditation of this book.

THE BOOK

It divides into three main sections according to its three chapters.

        (1)   Vengeance of God meted out by the Chaldeans (Chapter i.).

        (2)   Judgment of God on the Chaldeans (Chapter ii.).

        (3)   Prayer to God by Habakkuk (Chapter iii.).

The whole is a series of prayers and their answers.

(1) VENGEANCE OF GOD METED OUT BY THE CHALDEANS (Chapter i.)

A Complaint. One may gather from this opening statement :
" O Lord, how long shall I cry, and Thou wilt not hear ! " that

the Prophet had been witnessing the sins of the people and had been pleading for a long time with, seemingly, no reply, for there was desperation in this cry : " O Lord, how long . . . even cry out unto Thee of violence, and Thou wilt not save ! " Why is it, Lord, that I have to live in such a wicked generation and witness such evil ? Violence and strife and contention abound. The law is pushed aside, the righteous are oppressed, the evil man reigns triumphant and I am helpless to stop it.

Beloved, do we ever become so burdened because of sin ? Are we jealous for truth and for that Holy Name which is blasphemed every day ? Are we concerned about dispensing the righteous laws of God ? Are we ever in anguish of soul because our prayers for others (not our selfish prayers) are seemingly not answered ? If so, let us pause here a little. God is going to give an answer to the apparent neglect, but it must ever be borne in mind that there are many answers to the question. With Daniel it was an adversary who sought to hinder the answer from coming. In the case of the Syrophenician woman, her prayer was misdirected. Ofttimes our prayers are very selfish and the answer we hope for would ruin our spiritual lives.

There are other prayers which remain unanswered because they are not sincere, believing prayers. They are merely words. Then there are the prayers that are out of the Will of the Lord. When prayers are unanswered one had better look into every other direction than to God for the reason. He is faithful Who has promised. So here is a complaint that was unfounded. " And Thou wilt not hear ! "

The Prophet was admitting a cause for the lack of an answer, even though he was not aware of it, for he had confessed to iniquity, violence, strife, contention, and a complete failure to keep the law. He had testified to the fact that wickedness was prevailing, the righteous were oppressed, wrong judgment was practised. Does not all of this demand punishment ? Has not God the right to deal summarily with such people ? " When judgment does not proceed from the seat of judgment upon earth, it will infallibly go forth from the throne of judgment in heaven."

God's answer. At verse 5 God answered the Prophet's first prayer. It was not the answer which Habakkuk sought. He had asked that the Lord would stop the sin that was abounding, but God cannot stop sin. He bids man to do that. Repent, confess, turn, come — these are the words of the Lord to sinners. He warns, He invites, He encourages. As soon as men are willing to turn from their sin, the Lord is willing to impart the strength so to do. If they repent, He will heal ; if they confess, He will forgive; if they turn, He will receive, but, if there is no willingness to forsake sin, then punishment is the only thing open to Him.

Habakkuk looked for mercy but, instead, found that there was only judgment awaiting his people. The Lord told him to look around among the nations of the world and take notice, " for I will work a work in your days which ye will not believe, though it be told you " (i. 5).

A Chaldean invasion. The Lord then revealed to His servant the severe punishment He was about to bring upon His people for these very sins. It would come from this new power which had arisen — the Chaldeans, a bitter and a hasty nation that would march mercilessly through the whole land and would overrun it so fast that their horses would be swifter than the leopard, and their behaviour would be as fierce and as untameable as the wolf of the evening. They would descend like the eagle upon its prey, and would leave nothing behind, as does the east wind that carries everything before it, stripping the land and leaving a trail of barrenness.

This must have been a heavy burden on the heart of the Prophet as he went to tell the people. Nonetheless the unrepenting people never listened to the warning of God. They hoped against hope that God would be merciful and that judgment would not fall and, if it did, it would be in some future generation ; but it did happen, and within thirty years — within the lifetime of those to whom Habakkuk made the declaration. Thus was fulfilled the Word of God : " For I will work a work IN YOUR DAYS which YE WILL NOT BELIEVE though it be told you " (i. 5).

Prayer. In his first appeal the Prophet complained that God was indifferent to man in his sin. Now he sought to coerce God by appealing to His holiness. Lord, Thou art eternal, holy, pure, and just. Thou canst not destroy Thy people even though it is necessary to punish them ; Lord, how can those pure eyes of Thine look upon the treachery of this godless Chaldean nation ? How canst Thou remain silent, when this nation is more wicked than the people they are seeking to annihilate ? When they have gathered Thy people into their net like the fishes of the sea, they, in their idolatry, will sacrifice unto their nets and praise their gods for the victory. In their elation they will empty their nets and then pursue other nations. Lord, art Thou going to allow the wicked to prosper and the godless to rejoice ?

This has been the problem of every generation. This is what constitutes " the mystery of suffering ". Why do evil men prosper? Why do godless nations succeed? Why are they permitted to oppress the righteous? Every righteous man is conscious of his failings and he knows that correction is a necessary thing, but why at the hands of the wicked?

Many people bemoan this fact. They express themselves freely, they chafe under such circumstances and murmur against what they call the injustice of God. These things so often narrow the vision and warp the understanding. One fails to see the glory of the future because of the gloom of the present, and forgets that storms are passing things, not permanent. Men grope in the fog and think there is no way out, forgetting that fogs only last for a few hours and will soon dissipate themselves.

(2)   JUDGMENT OF GOD ON THE CHALDEANS (Chapter ii.)

Here must be learned one of the greatest lessons of this book, for, when Habakkuk received no answer, he sought to climb above the mists and the clouds of doubt and scepticism into the pure air of faith, as he said : " I will stand upon my watch, and set me upon the tower, and will watch to see what He will say unto me, and what I shall answer when I am reproved " (ii. 1).

One of the hardest things to do is to wait, especially when one has a burden in prayer and the answer is delayed.

The best place to do the waiting is the place where one can do the watching. If man can climb the tower of faith he will rise above the polluted atmosphere of the world, for mists and fogs are earth-born, and so is doubt. The tower is the place of expanded vision. It is above the discouraging voices of the world. Said the Psalmist : " He maketh my feet like hinds' feet, and setteth me upon my high places " (Psalm xviii. 33), and Habakkuk closed his prophecy with the same words. The hind is the sure-footed creature, agile in its movements, which can climb to the highest crag of the mountain range and drink in the pure air of the upper regions.

> " Lord, lift me up and let me stand
> By faith on heaven's tableland ;
> A higher plane than I have found,
> Lord, plant my feet on higher ground."

Men are told to watch and pray. That can also mean pray and watch. Abraham did that when he had interceded with God for the deliverance of Sodom. His was the same cry : " Wilt Thou also destroy the righteous with the wicked ? Peradventure there be fifty . . . forty-five . . . forty . . . thirty . . . twenty . . . ten righteous . . . " (Genesis xviii.). God promised, and Abraham returned to his place. " And Abraham gat up early in the morning to the place where he stood before the Lord. And he looked . . ." (Genesis xix. 27-28), or " he looked out " for the answer. Abraham not only prayed but returned to his watch-tower to look for the answer. God could not save the city ; He *did* save the righteous who were in it.

The person who can wait for the answer will always receive it. Moreover he will be in that heart condition that will permit him to accept the answer, whether it be positive or negative, pleasing or displeasing.

God's answer. God made known that, whilst He was going to use the Chaldeans as an instrument of judgment, He was also going to judge the Chaldeans. They were lifting themselves up against the nations. God would presently lift up other nations against them, which nations proved to be the Medo-Persians.

The personal pronoun " he " is used instead of " they " because the Lord intended this to be a parable. It had an immediate prophetical interpretation as well as a long-distant one. What is true concerning nations is also true concerning individuals.

The Prophet was told to write the visions upon tablets, in large, plain, readable letters which could be read quickly, so that the reader is not delayed in seeking an interpretation.

Two pictures are to be found in this one. Firstly, it was customary to put public notices in public places where people could read them clearly and then pass the information on by word of mouth. This was the local means of communication.

The second was to write the message on a tablet and for the runner to carry it to another who would take it over the next stage as in a relay race. And what of the message ? " THE JUST SHALL LIVE BY HIS FAITH " (ii. 4). The margin says " in his faithfulness ".

Habakkuk had complained that the righteous were being oppressed and that injustice was on the throne. The answer was that, seemingly, that was the case. It was only the just who should live, and that not by his circumstances but by his faith. There might be some delay before the fruit of faith was seen. Evil might not be removed immediately ; but wait, for deliverance will surely come.

This message must move across the nation — " The just shall live by his faith ". Man cannot live in his sin. He will surely die. Judah cannot live by resisting the enemy. They will surely die. The Chaldeans will not live by their victories. They shall surely die. BUT the just shall live, and that by his faith.

We, too, who have received the message and have appropriated the truth that the just shall live by his faith, must run with the news. It must not only be carried across our own nation, but it must be heralded across the world. It belongs not only to the days of the prophets, but it must be conveyed through all the corridors of time, and the message must be kept plain and understandable. Thus it has been, and thus it must remain.

It was declared by Habakkuk in the face of a Chaldean invasion, " The just shall live by his faith ". It was relayed by Paul " . . . to all that be in Rome, beloved of God . . . The just shall live by faith " (Romans i. 7 & 17). It was relayed again in Hebrews x. 38 : " Now the just shall live by faith . . . ", followed by that roll of honour of the men and women who lived, accomplished, and died in faith, ending with the words " And these all, having obtained a good report through faith, received not the promise : God having provided some better thing for us, that they without us should not be made perfect " (Hebrews xi. 39-40).

The same message was relayed to Europe early in the sixteenth century by Martin Luther as he cried out, " The just shall live by faith ", thus lighting the torch of freedom — The Reformation.

And the message is still being relayed in every part of the world, in this twentieth century — " The just shall live by faith ". " Not of works, lest any man should boast " (Ephesians ii. 9).

May the message never be confused by modern thought, ideologies, programmes, or anything else, remembering that every man is doomed to death, and will die without hope unless the message of faith is carried to him.

Then followed a series of five woes. These were to be taken up as a taunting parable, which means they had a future message of condemnation. Not only were these woes to fall upon the Chaldeans, but also upon the followers of Satan in the last days.

Woe to the dishonest (ii. 6-8). " Woe to him that increaseth that which is not his ! . . . " This nation, which had enriched itself by plundering other nations, would find that men would rise in revenge and spoil her of all her booty. In our day Russia has done this very thing. Presently she shall drink the cup of her own crimes — God is just.

Woe to the covetous (ii. 9-11). " Woe to him that coveteth an evil covetousness to his house . . . " This was the act of tearing down other people's homes to build their palaces, other people's plants to build their industries, other people's rights and freedoms to build their civilisation. Be it known that all that they build will topple down around them, as their structures will witness against them, as stone, joist, and beam fall asunder.

Woe to the iniquitous (ii. 12-14). " Woe to him that buildeth a town with blood, and stablisheth a city by iniquity ! . . . " Again this was establishing a nation by crime, murder, war, taking from man the peace, the home, and the family, to which he was entitled. The Lord is going to establish His Kingdom by and by, as stated in Isaiah xi. 9, and, when this comes to pass, then " They shall not hurt nor destroy in all My holy mountain : for the earth shall be full of the knowledge of the Lord, as the waters cover the sea." Habakkuk quoted this, meaning that when His kingdom is established these other kingdoms will fall.

Woe to the debased (ii. 15-17). " Woe unto him that giveth his neighbour drink . . . " It is demoralising to allow oneself to come under the stupor of drink so that man ceases to be accountable for his conduct, but greater is the sin of the man who compels his neighbour to drink with the intent of doing him moral harm. God will surely judge such a man.

Woe to the idolatrous (ii. 18-19). " Woe unto him that saith to the wood, Awake ; to the dumb stone, Arise, it shall teach ! . . ." This condemnation was to fall on those who had created their own helpless gods. If God will punish those who wrong His creatures, how much more when men despise Him, and, contrary to His Word, make to themselves graven images, and worship them, whether they be to demons, nature, or " saints ".

None of these things is overlooked or forgotten by God for " The Lord is in His Holy Temple : let all the earth keep silence before Him " (ii. 20).

God has spoken from the throne of His power and authority.

Ye worshippers of dumb idols of stone, keep silence.

Ye worshippers of powerless and ineffectual " saints ", keep silence.

Ye worshippers of film stars and playwrights, keep silence.

Ye worshippers of the mammon of this world, keep silence.

He is speaking from heaven His temple, He is speaking with His Divine authority. " Thou shalt worship the Lord thy God and Him only shalt thou serve " (Matthew iv. 10).

(3) PRAYER TO GOD BY HABAKKUK (Chapter iii.)

" Let all the earth keep silence before Him." This included Habakkuk. He had no more questions, no more reasonings. He had learned that God was on His throne and that He is just and holy. So, in complete submission, he opened his lips in adoration and praise. If there were any request at all, it was for God's mercy.

Prayer. " O Lord, I have heard Thy speech." He had come to realise that it was necessary for Judah to be punished, and that she must go into captivity. When he learned that he could not pray for deliverance *from* it, then he prayed that God would give them grace sufficient *in* it. If God would not withdraw the punishment, then Habakkuk's prayer was that the Lord would not withdraw Himself. " O Lord, revive Thy work in the midst of the years . . . " (that was, in the midst of those years of captivity). Lord, melt their hearts, revive Thy Word in those hearts, and make Thy people ready against the day of Thy deliverance. In the midst of those years, when Thy wrath is being displayed, remember Thy mercy. What a prayer ! What a heart of compassion ! ! What an understanding of God ! ! ! The Prophet who, at the beginning, thought he saw injustice in God could now only see abounding mercy, even though God was still angry with His people.

Should we not pray in similar fashion ? God has the right to be angry with the wicked every day, for godlessness abounds everywhere ; but, Lord, revive Thy work in the midst of these the closing days of time ! Thy Church to-day is lukewarm ; it is neither cold nor hot ; and, Lord, Thou hast the right to spew it out of Thy mouth but, in the midst of these apostate days, remember mercy. Revive Thy work in the midst of these years so that there may be some preparation in the hearts of Thy people for Thy coming again.

The heart of the Prophet warmed, and his faith began to mount up on wings of ecstacy. He broke forth into majestic language concerning the Lord's faithfulness and power as it had been demonstrated in the past on the behalf of a faltering and failing people. " God came from Teman, and the Holy One from mount Paran. Selah. His glory covered the heavens, and the earth was full of His praise " (iii. 3). Thus he continued through to verse 16.

Seemingly he began at Sinai, when God displayed some portion of His power as the mount was on fire with His glory and shook with that power. The pestilence and burning coals, or burning disease, related to the plagues poured out upon the Egyptians, whilst the nations around were in fear of Him (iii. 7). The opening up of the Red Sea brought salvation, and the parting of the Jordan their deliverance (iii. 8). The Lord then uncovered His bow and brought it into action — subduing the nations which occupied Canaan, thus giving it to the tribes of Israel, and even causing the sun and the moon to stand still so that He might complete His victories (iii. 9-12). Habakkuk returns to the triumphs over the Egyptians, in verses 13-15.

If God wrought so wondrously in bringing His people out of Egypt, could He not do it again to bring them out of the bondage of Babylon ? There is no limitation to His power, and His mercy is past finding out.

Habakkuk had climbed in faith and trust, and yet had not reached the pinnacle. That is in verse 17. It is the triumph of

Confidence. To enter into the full significance of the verse it will be necessary to enter into the emotions of verse 16. It is easy to say " I will trust in the Lord " when everything is in our favour. It is natural to say " I will rejoice in the Lord, I will joy in the God of my salvation " when the battle is over and the victory has been secured. Such was not the Prophet's standing. The conflict was still ahead, the battle had yet to be fought, the outcome was desperately uncertain so far as the arm of flesh was concerned. In fact, as Habakkuk contemplated the disasters which must fall, and had just learned that there was no escape, he said that his whole being had given way. He trembled within, his lips quivered, his resistance melted. He longed that he might be at rest in his grave in that day so that he would not have to see that invading army.

All that was the natural man ; but then all the vitality of the spiritual man surged through his soul as he reached the mountain-top of faith and cried that, although everything was against him and against the people whom he loved, let the fig tree fail to blossom in the spring, let the vines be barren, let the olive shake off her berries before they are ripe, let the harvest field languish and wither, let the sheep die and the cattle perish, let everything that is physical and material fail — the spiritual cannot. In the face of every disaster Habakkuk could say " *YET* I will rejoice in the Lord, I will joy in the God of my salvation " (iii. 18). Although circumstances were as dark as could be, and although everything was taken away from him that it was possible to take, he still believed that God was able, God was all-sufficient.

That was the same faith which enabled Abraham to lift the knife to slay his son, after he had said to his servants " I and the lad will go yonder and worship, and come again to you " (Genesis xxii. 5).

From whence did Habakkuk find such faith, such confidence in the unfailingness of his God ? He declares it in the last verse: " The Lord God is my strength ", but that was the source of his faith — the Lord God. Where did he find it ? Away up on the mountain-top, on the watch-tower of prayer and communion.

> " *Oh, for a faith that will not shrink,*
> *Though pressed by many a foe,*
> *That will not tremble on the brink*
> *Of poverty or woe.*
>
> *A faith that shines more bright and clear*
> *When tempests rage without ;*
> *That when in danger knows no fear,*
> *In darkness feels no doubt.*
>
> *Lord, give us such a faith as this,*
> *And then whate'er may come,*
> *We'll taste, e'en here, the hallowed bliss*
> *Of an eternal home.*"

ZEPHANIAH

THE GREAT DAY OF THE LORD

*"When the Lord turned again the captivity of Zion, we were
like them that dream. Then was our mouth filled with
laughter, and our tongue with singing: then said they among
the heathen, The Lord hath done great things for them. The
Lord hath done great things for us; whereof we are glad.
Turn again our captivity, O Lord, as the streams in the south.
They that sow in tears shall reap in joy. He that goeth forth
and weepeth, bearing precious seed, shall doubtless come
again with rejoicing, bringing his sheaves with him."*

(PSALM CXXVI.)

INTRODUCTION

Nothing is known of the author of this book other than that
which he relates himself in the title verse (vs. 1). From this verse
two things are learned.

(1) *His ancestry.* Most men name their father in their
identity. This was the only Prophet who recounted four generations.
He went back as far as Hezekiah, who is acknowledged by most
scholars as the famous Hezekiah, king of Judah, who, in his day,
led a reformation.

This introduction may have been made by Zephaniah to give
himself some prestige in that he came from a godly family and
belonged to the royal line. It would probably help to give him a
hearing with the people, although he never used his position as
his authority. That came to him from the Lord, so the opening
words are : " The Word of the Lord which came unto Zephaniah."

(2) *The time of his ministry.* " In the days of Josiah the
son of Amon, king of Judah." As Josiah reigned for thirty-one
years there is some questioning as to when Zephaniah's voice was
heard, but most scholars concur in placing his activity in the
earlier part of that reign, before and maybe during the revival of
Josiah's time.

The reformation in the days of Hezekiah had proved to be
a very shallow thing. There had been a profession, with little
evidence of any deep work of grace, or of a real possession. It
was a form of godliness without the power thereof. A great deal
of weeding had been done but the roots were left, so that sin and
idolatry had sprung up again everywhere. Thus it was that, when
Josiah came to the throne, he faced the same conditions that had
been known by Hezekiah. In Josiah's work for reformation the
ministry of Zephaniah must have played its part.

The prophecy of this book differs from most of the others,
inasmuch as the other prophets were all concerned with, and
prophesied to, Judah and Israel. The exceptions were Obadiah,
who prophesied concerning Edom only, and Nahum, who dealt
with the burden of Nineveh. Zephaniah was called upon to deal
with the surrounding nations — Philistia, Ammon, Moab,
Ethiopia, Assyria, and Nineveh, and show how these fitted into
the programme of God.

The theme of the book is The Way of Salvation through
chastisement.

THE MESSAGE

This was threefold :

(1)   A declaration of retribution (Chapter i.).

(2)   An exhortation to repentance (Chapters ii - iii. 8).

(3)   A promise of redemption (Chapter iii. 9-20).

(1)   A DECLARATION OF RETRIBUTION (Chapter i.)

" I will utterly consume all things from off the land, saith
the Lord " (i. 2). It was to be a destruction of the land, of Judah
and Jerusalem, of idolators and God-rejectors, of princes and
merchants.

Whilst this message is somewhat a continuance of the one
given by Habakkuk, and it is generally recognised that the Prophet
is referring to the Chaldean invasion, yet it is to be noted that no
specific mention is made of the Chaldeans. The reason for this
could readily be that Zephaniah, speaking as he was moved by
the Spirit of God, left out the identity of the enemy because God
wanted man to know that not only was He about to punish these
nations for their sins, but that presently He would punish the
whole world for its sin in that final day of retribution.

The evidence has a stronger bearing on the last days than
upon the immediate days so far as the opening verses are concerned. There will be an utter consumption of all things, which

will include the fish of the sea, when the earth shall be burned up in fervent heat, according to 2 Peter iii. The statement of verse 7, " . . . for the Lord hath prepared a sacrifice, He hath bid His guests " is a reminder of the invitation which the Great God extends in Revelation xix. 17-18 : " . . . Come and gather yourselves together unto the supper of the great God : That ye may eat the flesh of kings, and the flesh of captains, and the flesh of mighty men, and the flesh of horses, and of them that sit on them, and the flesh of all men, both free and bond, both small and great ".

It would seem that the conditions, as they prevailed in Israel, were used as a parable because the same conditions would be prevalent in the last days, and the punishments which God would mete out upon Israel would be as a parable and picture of the final doom He would inflict upon a God-rejecting world, when the Day of the Lord had come.

In verses 4-13 the Prophet, in descriptive language, dealt with God's judgment upon Judah and Jerusalem, in particular because of their idolatry in worshipping Baal and Chemarim and the hosts of heaven — the star-gazers. The fall of Jerusalem is described in verse 10. There would be a break through at the Fish Gate when the battering rams would cause the walls to begin to yield, and then at the next gate there would come a crashing down of the great fortifications, causing a great cry to rise from the inhabitants of the city. There would be no escape, no hiding place from the enemy, for the city would be searched with candles. All the dark and secret places would be brought to light.

At verse 14 the Prophet stretched his vision to the final overthrow of Jerusalem in the Day of the Lord. Then the trumpet shall sound and the judgment of God which has been described by so many of the prophets will fall.

All the silver and gold that the nation may have accumulated to itself will not be able to bring the least deliverance, for this was not merely the envy of nations that was being displayed, but the wrath of God which was being poured out.

This is the declaration of God's retribution in the last day. It has not been poured out as yet, neither had the judgment of the Chaldean invasion fallen upon them when Zephaniah was uttering these warnings. Therefore there was still time to turn back to God, so chapter two is

(2) AN EXHORTATION TO REPENTANCE (Chapters ii-iii. 8)

It was a call to repentance on the part of Judah, but of judgment on the part of the surrounding nations. They are referred to as a people or nation " not desired ", which means a nation that had no sense of shame, no sense of guilt. If they had, they might have attempted to flee from such judgment, not that they could. Instead the Lord bade the people gather themselves together. In His mercy He was going to make a final appeal to their better judgment. The decree had been issued and it would be carried out with a speed that was swift and final. They would move into judgment like the chaff into the wind that is carried away and gone, for none could prevent it. The Lord had declared the judgment, but, at the moment, had not implemented it. Therefore they could yet seek the Lord ; there was the opportunity for those who were meek enough to seek Him, and thereby enjoy His protection in the day of His anger.

From Jerusalem and Judah the Prophet moved out to God's judgments upon the surrounding nations, all of which at some time had oppressed Israel. God was showing that He respects no persons. Sin is sin wherever it is and in whomsoever it is, and it must be punished. It matters not whether it is in Israel or in the heathen nations, whether it is in the church or in the world, whether it is in the sinner or in the saint. Sin is sin, and God is just.

The Philistines came first, as they were the nearest neighbours. They were an influential people, often at war against the children of Israel. They had built five major cities, four of which are mentioned here — Gaza, Ashkelon, Ashdod, and Ekron, and also possessed the sea coast. All of these were to come under the judgment of God. Gaza was to be forsaken, Ashkelon was to become a desolation, Ashdod was to be driven out, Ekron was to be rooted up, whilst the sea coast was to become a place for shepherds, instead of the land of merchants and a place of harbours and ships. Philistia was territory promised to Abram but never possessed by Israel. The battles were many and the possession long delayed, but God here declared that He would leave no inhabitant so far as Philistia was concerned.

Thus it was, for all has been literally fulfilled. Travellers to-day tell of the desolate wastes and the ruinous sites which mark where these cities once used to be. What, at one time, were great and fenced cities, is now open pastureland where sheep graze contentedly. The Gaza which now exists is not even on the same site. Archaeologists bear united testimony to this almost complete obliteration.

Moab and Ammon. Both of these men were the illegitimate sons of Lot, and both were a thorn in the flesh to Israel. They were charged with the same sins — reproaching and reviling the people of God and rejoicing in their calamities. God had heard all that these nations had said against His people, as He hears all the insults and accusations that are made against His people to-day. What is said against the followers of the Lord is said against Him, and He deals with such things so that the child of God need have no fear. He is going to deal with present enemies as He was then dealing with Israel's enemies.

He declared that Moab and Ammon would be as desolate as Sodom and Gomorrah, and this surely came to pass. The territory is still as bleak and barren as can be. Owing to the brimstone and the salt nothing can grow, not even a blade of grass.

Ethiopia. Little is said about the Ethiopians either in this chapter or anywhere in the Bible. It is known that they helped the Egyptians against Israel in the days of Rehoboam (2 Chronicles xii. 3), and that they fought against Asa, king of Judah (2 Chronicles xiv. 9). Although they were a people who were far off from Israel, God did not forget them in the day of His judgment.

Assyria was that great empire with its fabulous capital city of Nineveh, at one time the pride of men. Both Jonah and Nahum had preached against this city. In the days of Jonah they repented, but Nahum had predicted the doom of the city because their repentance did not last. The book of Nahum relates much, and now a further description of the judgment is given. What was once a mighty fortress was to become an arid waste. What were once broad streets, where people and soldiers moved, were now to become a resting place for cattle, " flocks shall lie down in the midst of her " (ii. 14). Pelicans would make their homes where princes once abode ; wild animals would seek refuge amidst the ruins ; the lintels of the one-time stately doors of palaces would become perches for the birds, and the windows that once let out the strains of music of the song and the dance would then echo with the song of the birds which would nest therein.

Man may build his cities or his empires, his business or his houses, in defiance of God, but God can pull down the defiant man with all of his pride and his possessions until there is nothing left. Nineveh boasted " I am, and there is none beside me ". Now she is not, but the Eternal One Whom she defied remaineth and will remain, and so will all those who put their trust in Him.

The first eight verses of chapter three are a continuation of the second chapter. The Prophet returned to Judah and Jerusalem, where he started, and now reproved the people for not receiving the correction which the Lord had brought to them. He reproved four classes of people who were somewhat responsible for the prevailing situation.

Her Princes were cruel. They were likened to roaring lions tearing and devouring their prey, for they had devoured the poor who had come to them for help, showing them no mercy.

Her Judges were corrupt. They were as evening wolves that prowl hungrily around. Thinking only of themselves and their own satisfaction, they failed to mete out justice but devoured the innocent in their greediness for gain.

Her Prophets were unfaithful. They were frivolous and light. They had no message from the Lord. They could only speak of things that suited them but which brought neither guidance nor revelation.

Her Priests were polluted. They desecrated the temple, distorted the law, and demoralised everything.

The Lord, Who is just in all His ways, appealed yet again. He reminded them that He had cut off all the nations round about. He had caused nothing but desolation to remain of the cities, and not an inhabitant of any kind. In the light of this the Lord had expected some response on the part of His own people. Surely they would believe Him and receive instruction so that they might not suffer the same doom, but, alas, it was not so. Instead they had corrupted themselves.

(3)   A PROMISE OF REDEMPTION (Chapter iii. 8-20)

" Therefore wait ye upon Me ", or " wait ye for Me ". The statement was made in the good sense and was given to those Jews who had remained steadfast in their faith. Men had rebelled against God. In justice He must deal with them but, in the fury of His indignation, the faithful must not give up in despair, but must be patient " . . . for My determination is to gather the nations, that I may assemble the kingdoms, to pour upon them Mine indignation, even all My fierce anger : for all the earth shall be devoured with the fire of My jealousy " (iii. 8). This devouring was not a complete annihilation, but punishment until there would come a measure of understanding and repentance. Because He is a jealous God — jealous of His Name — He will not share His glory with another. These people had worshipped other gods. They must learn that Jehovah is God and beside Him there is no other.

Heathen to be restored. When God will have finished His work of judgment then He will cause the nations of the earth to recognise Him so that many of those who had blasphemed His Name, and had rendered their worship to the gods of man's making, the idols and the groves, etc., will become a people of a pure tongue (or lip). They will be worshippers of God — calling upon the Name of the Lord, and they will " serve Him with one consent " (iii. 1). The word " consent " is the word " shoulder " in the literal rendering ; it also means " of one accord ". The picture is that of many shoulders coming under a heavy load, each taking an equal weight and all moving in unison as though it were only one shoulder. In this statement many people are to be seen, all engaged in one work and all having one purpose — to carry the gospel throughout the world.

Whilst there was a local setting to the prophecy, yet Zephaniah was reaching out into a realm of which, possibly, he never dreamed — beyond the days of the Tribulation, beyond the judgments of the great Day of the Lord, to the Millennial Rest, when in peace and quietness Israel shall dwell in the land and all nations shall flow to it. Isaiah expressed it thus : " And it shall come to pass in the last days, that the mountain of the Lord's house shall be established in the top of the mountains, and shall be exalted above the hills ; and all nations shall flow unto it. And many people shall go and say, Come, ye, and let us go up to the mountain of the Lord, to the house of the God of Jacob ; and He will teach us of His ways, and we will walk in His paths : for out of Zion shall go forth the law, and the Word of the Lord from Jerusalem " (Isaiah ii. 2-3).

As the nation of Israel had been scattered to the uttermost parts of the earth, now they were to be brought back again to the land — that is, the faithful ones, referred to as " My suppliants ", and they are coming back to worship the Lord and to bring to Him an offering.

The closing scene is one of

Israel restored, comforted, and exalted. This will be when Israel is the head and not the tail, for the times of the Gentiles will have ended. The past of Israel's sins will be forgotten because forgiven. Instead of pride, which was so often their downfall, there will be humility. The poor people of verse 12 are the " poor in spirit " to whom God had promised the kingdom of heaven (Matthew v. 3). This restless people, who have travelled the earth either in search of business and money or because they have been hounded by their enemies, will then be at rest " . . . for they shall feed and lie down, and none shall make them afraid " (iii. 13).

In verse 14 the nation is called upon to sing. " Sing, O daughter of Zion ; shout, O Israel ; be glad and rejoice with all the heart, O daughter of Jerusalem ". Once before these people had been asked to sing but they could not respond. It was the enemy who then made the request. " By the rivers of Babylon, there we sat down, yea, we wept, when we remembered Zion. We hanged our harps upon the willows in the midst thereof. For there they that carried us away captive required of us a song ; and they that wasted us required of us mirth saying, Sing us one of the songs of Zion. How shall we sing the Lord's song in a strange land ? " (Psalm cxxxvii. 1-4). Now they were to be back in their own land ; sorrow has been endured for the long night of exile, but now they joy in the joy of the morning.

It is a glorious picture of an exalted people who have stepped out of grief into gladness, out of bondage into liberty, out of exile into home, out of rejection into acceptance, with the Lord in the midst of them. The Lord is as delighted in having His people back as they are to be back. Notice the exuberance of the Lord in verse 17. " The Lord thy God in the midst of thee is mighty ; He will save, He will rejoice over thee with joy ; He will rest in His love, He will joy over thee with singing."

Then there are His promises in the " I will's " of the concluding verse :

" I will gather them that are sorrowful."

" I will undo all that afflict thee."

" I will save her that halteth."

" I will get them praise and fame."

" I will make you a name and a praise."

All of this concerned God's elected people — Israel — but the Church is God's chosen people in Christ. As such we are pilgrims and strangers here. We are in a foreign land. This is not our home. We seek one to come. We have been told that in the world we should have tribulation, but to be of good cheer because He has overcome the world. Therefore we look for a city whose Builder and Maker is God, and the day is not far distant when the clarion call of the last trumpet shall summon us into our eternal rest. When He shall be in the midst of His people, and around the throne of God in heaven we shall join with that great host of blood-bought ones who sing His praises day and night — we shall praise Him for ever and ever, for great is our God and greatly to be praised.

HAGGAI

CONSIDER THY WAYS

*" Therefore the ungodly shall not stand in the judgment, nor
sinners in the congregation of the righteous. For the Lord
knoweth the way of the righteous ; but the way of the ungodly
shall perish."* (PSALM i. 5-6)

INTRODUCTION

Zephaniah and Haggai stand next to each other in the Bible,
and it is easy to finish reading the one and move on into the other,
but, in history, these two books stand some hundreds of years
apart. The first prophet spoke of retribution, the other of return.
In between these books there had come the voices of Jeremiah,
Ezekiel, and Daniel, as well as others. Tremendous things had
transpired. Israel had been carried away and Judah had wept by
the waters of Babylon for seventy years, during which time they
had been learning their lessons the hard way.

Chronologically the books of Ezra, Nehemiah, and Esther,
fit into this ministry. In other words, these three books contain
the history of the children of Judah after their return from the
captivity, whilst Haggai, Zechariah, and Malachi prophesied to
these returning people, hence they are known as the post-exilic
prophets.

The time had come for the emancipation of these people, so
God, Who controls the affairs of men, raising up one here and
putting down another there, Who has His hand upon the unbeliever
as well as the believer and Who causes even the wrath of men to
praise Him, put it into the heart of Cyrus to become the agent
for His people's deliverance. Cyrus was not a godly man. It
has been considered that he was, but archaeology, which has
brought so much to light through its discoveries, has revealed that
Cyrus was a worshipper of Bel-Merodach, a Babylonian god. It
was a custom at that time, when a king conquered another people,
to allow them to continue in their worship in the hope of appeasing
their god, and also to win the support of the oppressed people.
It was for this reason that Daniel and his companions were
promoted.

Thus it was that Cyrus issued an edict for rebuilding the Temple of the God of the Jews.

Under this edict the people began to raise money and also prepared themselves for the return to their land. Two men were chosen to lead this exodus — Zerubbabel and Joshua. It was a small remnant who made the first return. Ezra recorded the numbers.

On their arrival back into their land they began to rebuild out of the great heap of rubble which was then the site of Jerusalem. They rebuilt the altar, then began to lay the foundations of the Temple, but much opposition was encountered, firstly, by the Samaritans, who were then occupying the land, having been placed there by the Assyrians. These wanted to be friendly and offered their help in building the Temple. This offer was declined by Zerubbabel because they were an idolatrous people and would thereby profane God's holy house. Whilst Zerubbabel was right in his decision, the Samaritans thought otherwise and, therefore, became bitter opponents. They succeeded in stopping the erection of the building so that no more was done in the lifetime of Cyrus, nor yet in the reigns of his two successors.

Secondly, during this same period, the people, who had returned with an enthusiasm, lost heart. They had anticipated prosperity and happiness. They had expected peace and plenty. They thought that because they had repented they would walk back into the earlier days of the blessing of God without any problem. Instead, they faced ruins, not buildings ; they worked a barren land which was slow to respond to their labours ; there was a shortage of the essentials of life, and they were surrounded by a hostile people. In the face of this their zeal waned, and their patriotism for their land and the worship of their God became a matter of indifference.

All that interested them then was building houses and getting food for themselves, whilst the reinstatement of their worship in their Temple and their own citizenship could wait. They had become self-centred. They would be satisfied with their own house, their own garden, their own pleasure, and everything else became of no consequence.

In the meantime some radical changes had taken place which had altered the circumstances. Darius had taken the throne. The obstacles which had stood in the way had been removed. The original decree for rebuilding the Temple had been discovered. Every assistance was being offered. There was but one thing missing — the *will* on the part of the people. All this can be found in the books of Ezra and Nehemiah, and much of the spirit and attitude can be readily appreciated. The thing that was obviously needed at this moment was a challenge. That is exactly what this book of Haggai is. God has His man for every need, and Haggai was God's man of the hour for Israel.

Some scholars have complained of a lack of character in the book, that the message is tame, it contains too much repetition, and that it does not display the work of a genius. Some of this may be true if the book is judged merely on its literary value. What must be seen is that the message of the Prophet was most effective in its challenge, and that it fully accomplished its purpose. Many lectures, addresses, discourses, and challenges are listened to and approved. No one would argue the truth presented or the reality of the need revealed. The preacher was excellent; the lecturer was fluent; the speaker was convincing; and yet nothing is accomplished because all is allowed to remain theory and not practice. Such men do not achieve their objective — Haggai did.

As to the Prophet himself, nothing is known. The name Haggai means " Festive ". Some wonder whether he was given that name because he was born on a feast day, others query whether it referred to this time of rejoicing when the Temple was rebuilt, but all such things are conjecture. Therefore the message must be studied rather than the messenger, which is what the Lord always desires.

THE BOOK

It has only two chapters. Its keyword is " Consider ", which is repeated five times in the thirty-eight verses. The expression " The Word of the Lord " is also found five times, whilst the statement " Saith the Lord " is quoted twenty times. This makes the book to be one of authority.

The message of the book concerns the Temple and the Land, the condition of the one being dependent entirely upon the condition of the other.

The two chapters divide into five sections dealing with Ruin, Rebuilding, Restoration, Reflection, and Rest.

(1) RUIN (Chapter i. 1-11)

In the light of the introduction it is to be seen that the prophecy makes known what God had to say about the situation for, so far, only man's point of view has been described. God, never wanting a man, had chosen Haggai to make known to this returned remnant what His thoughts were concerning existing conditions.

It must not be overlooked that the return had taken place sixteen years earlier, and that, during that period of time, the hopes of the people had risen and then had been shattered ; also that throughout those sixteen years the people had not heard the voice of a prophet. Ezra, who had led the people back and directed them, was a scribe. The last prophetic voice these people had heard was probably that of Daniel whilst they were still in captivity.

It was after the work of rebuilding had stopped that the name of Haggai appeared in the book of Ezra. " . . . So it ceased unto the second year of the reign of Darius king of Persia. Then the prophets, Haggai, the prophet, and Zechariah the son of Iddo, prophesied unto the Jews that were in Judah and Jerusalem " (Ezra iv. 24 - v. 1).

God then spoke through His appointed servant. " Thus speaketh the Lord of hosts, saying, This people say, The time is not come, the time that the Lord's house should be built . . . Is it time for you, O ye, to dwell in your cieled houses, and this house lie waste ? " (i. 2-4).

This statement must not be allowed to pass unnoticed for it belongs too much to us. It is the story of procrastination. These people were not refusing the Lord, they were not denying Him and, probably, they were not aware of their own slackness. " The time is not yet come." They had only just returned to the land ; there were generations of time ahead.

Are we not all guilty of such reactions ? Business must be dealt with immediately or it might be lost ; the family must be considered first, we owe it to them. Man is only young once, education, recreation, and admiration have foremost place with youth. The time has not come yet to consider these serious things of the Spirit. Lots of things could be suggested by the people of Haggai's time as to why it was not opportune — the opposition of the people around, their own poverty, the losses they had sus- tained from bad harvests, the extra time they had to put in the fields — but there were also a number of things which could be stated to show that it was the time to build the Lord's house. The fact that they were back in the land called for the re-establishment of their heritage. The fact that the Temple was in ruins demanded rebuilding. The remembrance that Isaiah had declared that in the days of Cyrus the foundations of the Temple should be laid

(Isaiah xliv. 28) and they were now in those days, and also the realisation that the holy vessels of the Temple, which had been carried away by Nebuchadnezzar, had been restored to them by Cyrus. They had the furniture but not the building.

Then why put it off? There was but one answer, which remains the answer to all the procrastination in spiritual things to-day. Men are lovers of themselves more than lovers of God. They prefer the material things of this life to the spiritual things of the life to come.

In the light of this, Haggai said to his people, and the Spirit of the Lord says to the people of to-day, " Consider your ways ". Has your conduct brought you blessing? Has your selfishness brought you supply? How can you enjoy the comfort of your own house whilst the house of God remains a heap of ruins or in disrepair? If you will consider your ways and weigh up all the conditions which prevail you will learn that you are robbing yourselves of blessing every day.

Why is it that ye sow your fields and yet reap a bad harvest?

Why is it that ye are eating and drinking yet are never satisfied?

Why is it that ye clothe yourselves with garments not capable of keeping you warm? (This may have reference to unusually cold weather).

Why is it that your wages are not meeting your needs?

Why is it that ye look for much and get so little?

Why is it that when you store your food it perishes?

Man has blamed the weather, the seed, nature, etc., when all the time God has withheld His favour. He has shut up the heavens that it rain not, thus causing the drought. He has withheld the dew, and so caused the fruit to become impoverished. He has caused the cattle to be barren, so that there are no calves in the stall. He has caused all their labour to be failure. The reason? Because the house of God has been left desolate, whilst men have said that it is not the time to build the Lord's house, but it has been the time to build their own houses.

Are not these words " Consider your ways " searching? Surely the world is upside down to-day, everything is going wrong and fear is possessing the hearts of many because of the distressing conditions. Why are all of these things happening?

What is it that is wrong with the world? There is no peace, so politics and leaders are blamed for the international situation.

Farmers are ruined on every hand, here because of prolonged droughts and there because of flooding conditions, so men are blamed for having denuded the land of her forests or the local authorities for lack of flood control. Weather conditions seem to be changing and for these the atomic blasts are held responsible. Labour unions are considered to be responsible for the instability of economy, and rising taxes for shortage of money. Parents are charged with child delinquency. We blame everybody for everything but never blame ourselves. God is saying to all mankind, " Consider your ways ".

More money is spent on liquor than on education ; more on pleasure than on food. Money is poured into foreign aid and social reform, whilst missionary activity has to be curtailed for lack of funds. The amount of money spent on pleasure, clothes, cars, boats, television, vacations, cosmetics, and other luxuries, is stupendous, whilst almost every Christian society and organisation is asking for money or labourers. Men will give a pound for some trivial thing and put a penny in the offertory at the service. They will pay a dollar admission to almost anything whilst they put a dime into the offering at church.

" Consider your ways." God is permitting the international crisis, the weather conditions, and the moral collapse, because the will and the desire to appropriate and appreciate spiritual things have been lost. Man goes to church only when it is convenient, and it takes very little to make it inconvenient. Anything will keep people away from the house of God — too hot, too cold, too wet, friends who come or friends who must be visited, an outing, a vacation, too tired, not feeling well, a dislike of the visiting preacher. Not one of these things would hinder from attending social functions. Then one wonders why children are indifferent to the things of God. It is so easy to blame the age in which one lives when all the time it is the example that is set.

What about family devotions ? Is it not time the family altar was built ? If the family altar were built to-day there would not be the risk of a broken home to-morrow. Let us stop blaming other people, cease to divorce social life from spiritual life, and — consider *our* ways.

The challenge is followed by a commission, for ruin can be rectified by reconstruction, sin can be removed by salvation. " Go up to the mountain, and bring wood, and build the house ; and I will take pleasure in it, and I will be glorified, saith the Lord " (i. 8).

(2) REBUILDING (Chapter i. 12-15)

The call of the Prophet must have been very effective for there was an immediate response on the part of the people. It was on the first day of the sixth month that the Prophet addressed the people (i. 1), and on the twenty-fourth day of the same month they were engaged in the rebuilding — only a matter of three weeks for words to become actions.

The response was whole-hearted. From the Governor, Zerubbabel, and the high priest, Joshua, down to the last person " . . . *all* the remnant of the people, obeyed the voice of the Lord their God, and the words of Haggai the prophet, . . . " (i. 12). The term " remnant " does not imply a remaining few of the people so far as this particular incident was concerned. It was true of the nation as a whole, but it was the remnant who had returned and, therefore, it was only the remnant who were addressed by Haggai, and all of them responded.

Their action was not a half-hearted one, neither was it only a matter of duty. It was a full realisation of guilt on their part, for verse 12 records that " the people did fear before the Lord ". As soon as the spirit of conviction moved the people to fear and to action, so soon did there come the consolations and the assurances from the Lord, Who is ever slow to anger and plenteous in mercy ; for " Then spake Haggai the Lord's messenger in the Lord's message unto the people, saying, I am with you, saith the Lord " (i. 13).

Oh, for a season of Holy Ghost conviction in the lives of God's own people in our day, which would summon men to action in building up " the faith which was once delivered " and to a life of full surrender and obedience, that we may hear Him say " I am with you ".

The second chapter introduces the subject of

(3) RESTORATION (Chapter ii. 1-9)

" In the seventh month, in the one and twentieth day of the month " the Prophet addressed the people for the third time. The significance of what he said will be more fully appreciated if the date on which he spoke is noticed — the twenty-first day of the seventh month. From Leviticus xxiii. 34 it is learned that the Feast of Tabernacles was observed on the fifteenth day of the seventh month, and for seven days, which meant that that Feast terminated on the twenty-first day, which was the greatest day of the Feast. Jesus kept this Feast of Tabernacles (John vii., note vs. 2), and it was "In the last day, that great day of the feast, Jesus stood and cried, saying, If any man thirst, let him come unto Me, and drink " (John vii. 37).

This was the day in which Haggai spoke, and he spoke to thirsty souls. They had been building now for a month. Probably they had not done very much more than clear away the rubble. Then they halted to observe this most festive of all their feasts, at which both corn and wine were normally carried into the Temple. But there was no Temple at that moment, and they had no corn nor wine because they had had such appalling harvests. Present conditions would cause despondency instead of rejoicing. So the Prophet asked "Who is left among you that saw this house in her first glory ? " (ii. 3). There would not be many, for the exile had been seventy years in duration, so only those who had passed the four-score years would have remembered. There were some, as is evident from Ezra iii. 12, " but many of the priests and Levites and chief of the fathers, who were *ancient* men and had seen the first house, when the foundations of this new house were laid before their eyes, wept with a loud voice."

The Prophet then asked " Is it not in your eyes in comparison of it as nothing ? " (ii. 3). The present was discouraging by contrast with the past, so he told them to get their eyes off that which was behind, not to discourage the people of the present generation by what *had* been, but encourage them as much as they knew how, for " I am with you, saith the Lord of hosts " (ii. 4). All the promises which God made when they came out of Egypt would yet be fulfilled, and His Spirit Whom He gave to them at that time was still with them.

God was still the possessor of all the silver and the gold that was in the world, so that, although the people were impoverished at the moment, and although that Temple was mean in comparison with that which was past, yet God would do mighty things in the future, so that the first Temple, which Solomon built, would become insignificant in the great day of their Millennial glory. They were encouraged to do their utmost in the present because only the present belonged to them. The past belonged to their fathers, the future to their children. The only thing to do in fulfilling the eternal purposes of God is to yield to Him a life of full surrender and obedience NOW.

As to that future, the " Desire of all nations " (ii. 7) refers to a Person, the Lord Jesus Christ. Firstly, He will come for His people and they shall be caught up to meet Him in the air as their Coming Lord, and shall enter the temple not made with hands eternal in the heavens. There they will revel in the glories of their great God and Saviour, Jesus Christ.

After that the Lord comes back to this earth and the Jewish nation, to whom Haggai was ministering, shall recognise their Messiah. He will establish His Millennial kingdom. Jerusalem will become the place of peace and Christ will reign in their midst. The lion and the bear shall lie down together in that age of peace. Then the greater than Solomon shall reign and we shall reign with Him.

Ezekiel had much to say concerning that day, that temple, and that reign, when the departed Shekinah glory returns to the land and its people.

(4)   REFLECTION (Chapter ii. 10-19)

It was two months later when the Prophet spoke again, on the twenty-fourth day of the ninth month. Once more it was a comparison of past and present. The date, too, is an important factor. That is the reason why it is there. The ninth month was the month of ploughing and seed sowing. The people were concerned about it. For a number of years they had been without, and the reason had been their neglect of the Temple. This they had remedied, having turned back to God and having rebuilt the house of God, but harvests cannot be hurried. The harvest comes months after seed-sowing and, in the meantime, the people had to live. The question was — how ? Or would God work a miracle for them ?

Therefore the Prophet took them back to the law, and to the power of communication. He asked two questions which were the same in principle, but one was negative and the other positive. If a man were carrying in his garment the flesh of an animal that had been set apart for a sacrifice and was, therefore, classified as holy, would anything else touching that holy thing become holy by communication ? The answer was a negative one. The holy flesh or garment had no power to impart holiness.

The reverse then followed. If someone, who was unclean, touched that holy thing, would it then become unclean, and the answer was yes. Uncleanness had power to contaminate more than cleanness had to make holy. Disease is communicative, health is not. Sin can mar holiness, holiness cannot cleanse sin.

Therefore the good works of the people could not eradicate the sins of the past. Past crop failure would not fill the barns for this season. Their sin had caused the ground to become barren, but their holiness could not be communicated to the soil to make it fruitful. They would have to endure their hardness a little longer, for what a man sows he reaps. However, the promise was " . . . from the day that the foundation of the Lord's temple was laid (from that day) I will bless you " (ii. 18-19). The seed was still in the barn, and there was not a bud on the vine, fig tree or olive. The sap had not yet begun to flow so there was no indication as to whether the next harvest would be good or bad.

But right then the Lord was giving them the promise of an abundant harvest, for He had already commenced to bless them. The blessing back-dated to the time when they laid the foundations of the Temple. They could eat everything they had and empty their scantily stocked barns to the last grain without a worry as to the future. That was already secure. What a glorious promise! If men were only faithful and obedient they might know that the promises of God are yea and amen in Christ Jesus the Lord.

(5) REST (Chapter ii. 20-25)

The closing verses seem to suggest a moving out to the end of the age. God had promised them immediate temporal and material blessing. Now He was promising them greater blessings for the future. There is no evidence of any overwhelming happenings in Zerubbabel's time which would answer to a shaking of the heavens and the earth, but, in the last days, God is going to deal with the kingdoms of the earth. He is going to overthrow all who have risen up against Him and against His people. He will subdue powers and cause men to slay each man his brother in the confusion of Tribulation days, during which time He has promised to protect His own until the indignation be overpast. Then, when He brings His people into the blessing of rest, He is going to bless Zerubbabel in a special way. One wonders whether God is using the name of Zerubbabel, who was governor of the people, as the representative of all His people and, therefore, this blessing will be national. The promise was " I will make thee as a signet; for I have chosen thee " (ii. 23). The signet ring was a precious token. It was worn by the Eastern princes upon their right hand, and was prized greatly. One recalls that Pharaoh took the ring from his hand and put it upon Joseph's hand, arrayed him in vestures of fine linen, and put a golden chain about his neck. (Genesis xli. 42). God is going to honour His people in the day to come.

Some think that the recognition of Zerubbabel and the giving of the ring refers to God honouring His Son in the last days, but

He is already a Prince. He is the Prince of Peace and God hath already highly exalted Him and given Him a Name which is above every name.

When man honours God, God honours him.

ZECHARIAH

ISRAEL'S RESTORATION — CHRIST'S RETURN

" Now learn a parable of the fig tree : When his branch is yet
tender, and putteth forth leaves, ye know that summer is
nigh : So likewise ye, when ye shall see all these things,
know that it is near, even at the doors. Verily I say unto
you, This generation shall not pass, till all these things be
fulfilled. Heaven and earth shall pass away, but My Words
shall not pass away." (MATTHEW xxiv. 32-35)

INTRODUCTION

Zechariah was the son of Iddo. He was a man of influence
and one of many visions. He was contemporary with Haggai,
continuing and supplementing that which was given by Haggai.
He was of the priestly family.

The book is the second of the three post-exilic books which
conclude the Old Testament. The message is far-reaching because
it not only deals with an immediate deliverance and blessing but
also declares the final blessings of God's people.

The book divides into three parts :

    (1)   Prophetic utterances and visions (Chapters i-viii.).

    (2)   Judgment of the nations (Chapters ix-xi.).

    (3)   Israel's future (Chapters xii-xiv.).

(1) PROPHETIC UTTERANCES AND VISIONS
(Chapters i-viii.)

The opening verses, which are a call to repentance, are a
confirmation and a support of what Haggai had told the people.
God reminded them that not only was He aware of all the failures
and sins of their fathers (which meant all the past generations),
but He was sore displeased, and that it was this Divine displeasure
which had brought all the suffering and shame. As the people
sought to correct their folly and as they turned to the Lord in
repentance, even so would He bless them in the years to come
Then came the Lord's promises for that future.

Firstly, the Prophet saw *eight visions,* all in one night, in which there was a continuance of thought and history.

(a) *The horses among the myrtle trees* (i. 8-17). Remembering that Zechariah prophesied at the same time as Haggai and from him it was learned that God had been punishing the returned remnant for not rebuilding the house of the Lord, but now His people had repented and the Temple was in the course of reconstruction, the vision becomes somewhat clearer, even though some difficulties remain.

The red horse rider is recognised by most scholars as representing the Lord. He had been riding forth in war, hence the colour of His horse. At this moment He was standing among the myrtle trees which were in the bottom ; i.e., in the valley where the myrtle tree usually grew. It was not a tall, shady tree, but a sweet-smelling shrub which grew in low and shady places. Thus they were a picture of Israel who, having returned from seventy years of captivity and now suffering because of lack of harvests, were very much humiliated, and were confessing their failure. The horses of varied colour, which were behind the Chieftain and who had been walking through the earth, could have represented the various nations that had been at war with God's people — Babylon, Assyria, Greece, etc. These testified that the earth was still and at rest. The Lord was displeased with this fact (i. 15). The suggestion is that, whilst God used these nations to punish Jerusalem, they had overstepped their prerogative, had enjoyed their duty, and exceeded it in using much cruelty. In overrunning the nation they had enriched themselves and were now sitting at ease enjoying the spoils of conflict.

The question was asked as to how long the indignation of the Lord was going to remain against Jerusalem, seeing that the seventy years of captivity were already expired. The Lord's reply was that His anger had already ceased because His people had begun to rebuild His house, and His blessings, which were now beginning, would continue to multiply.

The last verse of this section (vs. 17) possibly refers to the Millennial blessing yet to come. This is suggested because these prophecies were twofold. A prophet is one who forthtells and foretells. Zechariah declared the rebuilding of Jerusalem in his own time, which, of course, was in the days of Nehemiah, and he foretold the final regathering of the whole house of Israel in the last days when the Times of the Gentiles shall have come to an end.

(b) *Four horns and four carpenters* (i. 18-21). Horns are usually symbols of power. These four horns were representative of the powers which had been responsible for subduing and scattering both Israel and Judah. Several suggestions are made as to why there were four horns. They could readily remind one of the four great empires which had inflicted so much on God's people, and had certainly scattered them — Babylon, Medo-Persia, Greece, and Rome. These were the four which Daniel saw in his visions. They could represent God's four sore judgments — war, famine, pestilence, and death. These were often mentioned and were to be used again as seen in the breaking of the first four seals which produced four horse-riders in Revelation vi.

Secondly, they could suggest pressure coming from the four corners of the earth, but however one interprets, the principle is the same. These four horns were responsible for scattering the people of the Lord because of their sins.

The carpenter is the man who makes or repairs, so there is introduced the power of destruction and the power of recovery, and the one is equal to the other. Four horns may have pushed the people to the ends of the earth, but God is going to restore them and with equal strength is going to punish those nations. The fact that the horns are then referred to as the Gentiles strengthens the belief that the great Gentile empires were in question.

To get the local sequence, as the enemies of Judah had been punished, and those who had been responsible for the destruction of God's house and who had from time to time hindered its re-establishment, had also been punished, then there was nothing to prevent the rebuilding. This was indeed the time.

(c) *The Man with a measuring line* (ii. 1-13). God had promised a re-establishment of His people and a rebuilding of the city. It is known already that Ezra built the temple, followed by Nehemiah who rebuilt the city. The surveyors had already gone forth with the measuring line, but God was declaring to the remnant that the day would come when the line would not be required because Jerusalem would expand beyond all the walls of limitation so that the people would dwell in an unwalled city. That would have been considered a danger for so important a city because of possible enemy attack, but the Lord assured them that there would be no danger. He would be their protection, for He would be as a wall of fire, such as an enemy could not penetrate. God would be in the midst of her so that she should not be moved.

In fact, He would be so sensitive that as surely as the eyelid automatically shuts to protect the pupil of the eye at the slightest approach of any foreign body, so surely would He rise to the protection of His people. It is a picture of a spontaneous reaction against anything which is alien.

(d) *Joshua, the High Priest* (iii. 1-10). Note the progression — the enemy repelled, the people restored, the city rebuilt, and the temple re-established. Then came the revival of the priesthood. Joshua was a descendant of the Aaronic family, but the priesthood had fallen into disuse for a long time. It had become corrupt in the days of Eli and had not existed during the years of captivity, but now, with the return to the land, Joshua, the son of Josedech, had been established as the representative of the people before God. Zechariah saw this same Joshua in his fourth vision. He stood before " the angel of the Lord ", who is usually recognised as representing the Lord. Beside the High Priest stood Satan as an adversary. The unusual thing was that Joshua was clothed in filthy garments, which was so contrary to the garments of glory and beauty which belonged to this office. However, these were taken from him in the vision, and he was cleansed and worthily reclothed.

Is this not a reminder that both the priesthood of old and the people it represented had become dreadfully contaminated with sin and corruption ? It was the work of the High Priest to intercede before the Lord for His people, but it was also the purpose of Satan to resist such appeals and to be the accuser of the brethren. In the past failure of the people, who in their sin had gone into captivity, it would appear that Satan had prevailed in the conflict, but this vision showed otherwise. Satan was being rebuked, and the people, because they were God's people, were being snatched as brands from the burning, Jerusalem was being restored, the defiled priesthood was being cleansed and renewed, the former glory was being restored and the mitre was being replaced upon the priest's head. The reason for this was that " The BRANCH ", or the Messiah, is coming and He is coming to reign.

The stone which was before Joshua could represent the nation, as the stone cut out without hands in Daniel's vision represented the establishment of a kingdom which will subdue all others, being the Millennial kingdom. This was probably the same kingdom, because the eye of the Lord has always been upon it.

Still referring to the stone, God is going to remove the iniquity of the land in one day and, in that same day, every man will sit with his neighbour under his own vine and under his own fig tree, and that is certainly a Millennial promise as declared in the fourth chapter of Micah. Great David's greater Son, the Great High Priest, has come to reign and to minister.

(e) *The Golden Candlestick* (iv. 1-14). The seven-branched candlestick had stood in the Tabernacle of old giving light to those who served in the holy place. Ten such candlesticks had furnished Solomon's Temple. Here it was one again, but with some marked differences. The previous candelabra had to be fed at regular intervals with oil, each lamp separately. This candlestick had a bowl, or a reservoir, of oil on the top which could feed automatically the lamps by means of seven connecting pipes. The bowl was fed in turn from two pipes which connected two olive trees that stood to the right and left of the candlestick.

Zechariah enquired as to the meaning of it all and was informed that the light of the Tabernacle had been sustained because man had carried in the oil, but the days were now coming when the old must give way to the new, when law must yield to grace, when man must submit to God. Zerubbabel, as governor and as the responsible man for rebuilding the Temple, must know that the future glory of the Temple was not going to be dependent upon what he or anyone else might do in the flesh. All the renewals which were now coming to Israel, and will come, would not be because of man for, through the Prophet, God was saying " Not by might, nor by power, but by My Spirit, saith the Lord of Hosts " (iv. 6). The candlestick had given light to the Tabernacle. Soon the nation of Israel would become the light-bearer to the world. God had appointed them to be the missionary nation. In the past they had failed, but the life of God would flow into the nation as the life of the olive trees was flowing into this candlestick. " Arise, shine ; for thy light is come, and the glory of the Lord is risen upon thee. For, behold, the darkness shall cover the earth, and gross darkness the people ; but the Lord shall arise upon thee, and His glory shall be seen upon thee. And the Gentiles shall come to thy light, and kings to the brightness of thy rising (Isaiah lx. 1-3).

Zerubbabel was informed that he would meet difficulties but, whilst they would rise up like mountains, the Lord would smooth them out like plains, so that not only would he lay the foundation of this Temple but he would also have the joy of completing it

amidst the shouts of the people, "Grace, grace unto it" (iv. 7).
In the eternal purposes of God, Christ, Who is the foundation
of the Church, will also be the Head.

The two olive trees were referred to as God's two anointed
ones. In this instance they were Zerubbabel and Joshua, governor
and priest, the two Divine offices of king and priest, the temporal
and the spiritual. Elsewhere these anointed ones may be seen
in Moses and Elijah on the Mount of Transfiguration, or as typi-
fying the saints who pass through death or are raptured. In
Revelation they are the two witnesses who lay down their lives.

(f) *A Flying Roll* (v. 1-11). This roll of judgment seems
to have been unrolled at the time when it was measured at twenty
cubits by ten cubits. It has been pointed out that the writing was
on both sides. This could readily refer to the two tables of Law,
and thereby mean that the next move in God's dealings with His
people would be to put the law in its place and to mete out judgment to those who disobeyed. The law was written on two tables.
and on both sides (Exodus xxxii. 15). The scroll was written on
both sides. Judgment on the one side of the scroll was for theft.
and on the other side for swearing (oath). This would be the
same division of the Commandments — the first four are Godward
(swearing) and the remaining six are manward (theft).

On the return from captivity, as recorded in the book of
Nehemiah, Ezra read to the people from the book of the Law.
There they learned of their sins and of God's wrath, and there
they repented.

The vision, therefore, is one of the re-establishment of the
Law, and the judgment of God upon the evil-doer.

(g) *The Ephah of Wickedness* (v. 5-11). Whilst it is not
easy to interpret all of these visions, and there are many and varied
interpretations given, it would appear that up to this point most of
them have related to the period of restoration immediately following
the Babylonian Captivity but, from this point on, the Prophet's
vision expanded and reached out to the time of the end and to the
fuller blessing of God's people.

In this vision he saw an Ephah, with wickedness inside, being
carried to a base in the land of Shinar. An Ephah was the largest
dry measure of Palestine. This could readily be to the people a
symbol of commerce and trade. Within the Ephah was a woman,
called Wickedness — speaking of the corruption of the commercial
world. A weight of lead kept this corruption inside. Two women,
with the wings of a stork, carried the Ephah through the heavens

toward a particular destination. The stork is an unclean bird —
still speaking of evil. It is also a migratory bird. The women were
aided by the wind, which was in their favour. This could represent
the fair winds of trade which assisted them in their purpose. The
destination was the land of Shinar, and the objective was to build
a house " upon her own base " (v. 11). This meant a return to
some former occupation. Babylon is the land of Shinar.

Might not all of this refer to the rebuilding of Babylon, the
trade of the world moving in that direction until it becomes a
great city of commerce ? Does not the book of Revelation declare
this fact in chapter xviii. ? Its merchandise (vs. 12 & 13) begins
with gold (which may cause the rush back to that part of the
world), and ends with slaves and with the souls of men, showing
the corruption of this commerce. It is from such a point that
Antichrist may rule this world.

(h) *The Four Chariots* (vi. 1-8). These depicted God's
government and authority in all the earth, as they moved in every
direction, north and south, and to and fro. In His supremacy
He is not limited in the performance of His Will but is a God
of diversity, as declared in the various colours of the horses which
moved each into his particular realm.

The mountains of brass, over which none of the chariots
moved but passed between, have been recognised by many scholars
as a picture of the steadfast, unchanging, immutability of God ;
the God, Who, by Divine decree created all things, and by Divine
power has sustained everything, will in the time to come bring all
things into subjection to His Divine Will.

The Crowning of Joshua (vi. 9-15). Certain leading men of
those who had returned from the captivity were called upon to
become representative men who were to take silver and gold and
make therefrom crowns. (The plural word would suggest " a
noble crown " or " a combined crown ", as of intertwining wreaths.)
These were to be placed upon the head of Joshua, the high priest.
Then came the cry " Behold the man whose name is The
BRANCH " (vi. 12). This announcement did not concern Joshua
any more than it did in chapter iii. 8. It called attention to the
shoot and offspring of David, to the rod out of the stem of Jesse
— great David's greater Son, the Lord Jesus Christ.

Zerubbabel was building the Temple and Joshua was ministering therein as the High Priest. Jesus Himself was the One Who
was to be seen building a spiritual Temple. In it He would sit
and rule upon His throne and should be a Priest. But priests did

not sit on thrones and reign. They stood as ministers and served. The whole picture is symbolical. The combination of the two great offices is to be seen in the one Person, Jesus, Who is both Priest and King, and Who, as such, will reign for ever and ever in the Temple not made with hands.

This first section closes with an enquiry concerning

Fasting (vii. 1 - viii. 23). For a number of years the people had kept various fasts. The Rev. George L. Robinson, in his book *The Twelve Minor Prophets*, names four of these annual fasts. (1) When Nebuchadnezzar took Jerusalem in the fourth month (Jeremiah lii. 6). (2) When the Temple was burned in the fifth month (Jeremiah lii. 12). (3) When Gedaliah, the governor, was murdered in the seventh month (Jeremiah xli. 1-2). (4) When the seige of Jerusalem was begun in the tenth month (2 Kings xxv. 1).

The time had come when the Temple was being rebuilt, so the people were enquiring as to whether they should continue the fast of the fifth month, which was in memory of the destruction of the Temple.

The Lord's answer was that their fasting had been a worthless thing for years past. Fasting was a sign of repentance. For seventy years they had fasted but never repented. Therefore, it held no merit. It was merely a dead formality with them. His question was " Did ye at all fast unto Me, even to Me ? " (vii. 5). In fact, many of their fasts had become feasts and they were not aware of it, just as to-day many of the remembrances of the church, as Easter and Christmas, have been paganised. The Lord's Supper has lost its worship to formality. The solemnity of the marriage vows is lost in the processional — the dress parade.

The Lord bade them give up their empty ceremony and become sincere in their practice, by caring for the widow and the fatherless, the stranger and the poor. Better if they found the shoulder which would lift burdens, ears that would find out the need, and hearts that would melt in sympathy. To sum it up " . . . To obey is better than sacrifice, and to hearken than the fat of rams " (1 Samuel xv. 22).

Developing the theme of chapter seven further, in chapter eight God reminded them of the intensity of His jealousy for that city which He had chosen and loved, a jealousy which caused Him to pour out His fury upon the nations who had been the instruments of His judgment. It had been necessary for Him to turn His back upon Zion so that it had become a byword amongst the nations, but now He had returned to Zion and His love would be as intense as His fury had been. He would dwell in the midst of her and what had been a city of lies and deception would be known as a " city of truth ". Death, which was a punishment for sin, would be delayed as sin was reduced, so that the streets would be filled with aged people who would be able to enjoy their old age without fear, whilst children should fill the streets. Children, which are a heritage, were ever tokens of the Lord's goodness and favour.

Everything else over which they had sighed and lamented would be turned to blessing, labour would be restored (viii. 10), the fruit of the field would be abundant (viii. 12), and prosperity would be on every hand. As God would do His part in blessing them, so must they in blessing each other. They must be truthful, just, and peaceable (viii. 16).

In the light of all this, not only one fast but all their fasts must be abolished and, instead, they would celebrate the Lord's goodness in feasts of joy and gladness. So great will be the blessings of the Lord in that day, which will be the Millennial day, that all nations will covet their privileges and long to identify themselves with God's people.

(2) JUDGMENT OF THE NATIONS (Chapters ix-xi.)

The Coming King. In preparation for those days of blessing, which the Lord had promised should be, He was going to deal with the nations round about so that they would not be a source of danger to the peace that He desired to establish. Hadrach, Damascus. Tyrus, Zidon, and the cities of the Philistines had long since suffered their doom. Then would come the Prince of Peace to establish His kingdom. This verse was wonderfully fulfilled. " Rejoice greatly, O daughter of Zion ; shout, O daughter of Jerusalem ; behold, thy King cometh unto thee ; He is just, and having salvation ; lowly, and riding upon an ass, and upon a colt the foal of an ass " (ix. 9). The prophecy, and its fulfilment in Matthew xxi., has been seen as a picture of both poverty and humility. Whilst one does not want to remove these attributes, which were true of Christ, such would not have been the first reactions of the people who saw Him ; neither were they the truths that He wanted them to appreciate first and foremost. To the eastern mind the picture would be one of peace rather than poverty. The horse was the symbol of war. The Lord's description of a horse, as He gave it to Job, was : " Hast thou given the horse strength ? Hast thou clothed his neck with thunder ? Canst thou make him afraid as a grasshopper ? The glory of his nostrils is terrible. He paweth in the valley, and rejoiceth in his strength ; he goeth on to meet the armed men. He mocketh at fear, and is not affrighted ; neither turneth he back from the sword. The quiver rattleth against him, the glittering spear and the shield. He swalloweth the ground with fierceness and rage ; neither believeth he that it is the sound of the trumpet. He saith among the trumpets Ha, ha ; and he smelleth the battle afar off, the thunder of the captains, and the shouting " (Job xxxix. 19-25).

In contrast to this mighty war-charger the easterner recognises the ass as the emblem of peace. Does not the text record this as one reads on into the next verse. " And I will cut off the chariot from Ephraim, and the horse from Jerusalem, and the battle bow shall be cut off ; and He shall speak peace unto the heathen . . . " (Zechariah ix. 10).

He, the Prince of Peace, was setting up His kingdom that He might reign in righteousness. What greater news could come to a war-weary, war-stricken people ?

As to that nation, so to the individual to-day, to the heart which is torn asunder by the voices of the world, all so conflicting, none satisfying the sin-sick soul. The Lord is here to give the peace of God that passeth all understanding, to bestow the peace that was made through the Blood of the Cross.

In this coming time of peace men shall cease to enquire of their idols which have deceived them throughout the years. When men ask of God, He gives. That idols could never do. As a result of their idolatry the people found themselves without a shepherd. That was the time when the enemy came and scattered the flock. The Prophet had come back from the future and was reminding them that the path to that glorious future was not going to be easy. God would provide for them a Good Shepherd to lead them and feed them, and with Him He would also provide under-shepherds in the form of prophets, pastors, and teachers.

However, they would spurn the voice of the under-shepherds and totally reject the Good Shepherd. In fact, they would sell Him for the price of the common slave.

Thus the Prophet gave utterance again to the coming of the Messiah and their treatment of Him, words which were so literally fulfilled : " And I said unto them, If ye think good, give me my price ; and if not, forbear. So they weighed for my price thirty pieces of silver. And the Lord said unto me, Cast it unto the potter ; a goodly price that I was prised at of them. And I took the thirty pieces of silver, and cast them to the potter in the house of the Lord " (xi. 12-13).

Shepherds. God had caused the Prophet to act as a shepherd and to feed the flock of people with His Word but they had not responded. They listened more to the voice of the hirelings who were leading them as sheep to the slaughter. As a shepherd, Zechariah had two staves, which might be equivalent to the rod and the staff of the shepherd. With the one he protected, with the other he guided and provided. In their rejection of him as a shepherd he asked for his wages. Making no demands he left them to pay that to which they considered he was entitled. The amount was thirty pieces of silver, the price of a slave. What insult ! What rejection ! !

Little did the Prophet appreciate that, in a similar way and for the same price, they would sell their Messiah — the Good Shepherd.

Because the people refused the Good Shepherd, the Lord said He would raise up a false shepherd who would not visit, heal, feed, nor help the flock in any way. Instead, he would feed *on* them (xi. 16-17).

This is true of many under-shepherds to-day who take the name of pastor or preacher. They become the head of a church but they starve the flock. The text here is pointing to the Antichrist who will dominate the world and mankind before the millennial blessing descends upon the land.

(3)   ISRAEL'S FUTURE (Chapters xii-xiv.)

Jerusalem restored. The great and eternal God, Who stretcheth forth the heavens, layeth the foundations of the earth, and formeth the spirit of man, the great Creator was speaking. He was declaring what He was going to do for Jerusalem and with her enemies. His strong protection of that city would make her " a cup of trembling " in the hand of all other nations (xii. 2), a burdensome stone (something too heavy to move) for all people (xii. 3), a source of panic for all the cavalry which approach her (xii. 4), and an unquenchable fire, as in a ripened cornfield, to all the enemies (xii. 6), so that the weakest in the city would be strong, yea, stronger than the strong, for God was about to destroy all the nations that opposed Jerusalem.

Man should be very careful of his attitude toward God's people, and governments should be careful of their decisions concerning the land of Israel in these days of international unrest and uprisings. There is a tendency to support the nations which oppose Israel and, in so doing, such are opposing themselves and also the decisions God has already made concerning that country. It must not be forgotten that God will rise up on the behalf of His people.

The chapter closes with a deep sense of penitence on the part of these restored people as they shall look upon Him Whom they pierced. It is not easy to ascertain when this will be, as there does not appear to be any other record of such grief at the time of His coming but, rather, the contrary, for when they see Him they will cry out " Blessed is He that cometh in the Name of the Lord " (Matthew xxiii. 39). When the scripture was fulfilled according to John xix. 37, there was no record of sorrow.

In that day of penitence God is going to open a fountain to the house of David and to the inhabitants of Jerusalem. Sin and uncleanness will be removed. It is the fountain of His grace. The fountain of Blood is already open. That fountain is for the " whosoever will ". Millions out of every tongue and nation have been supplied. This fountain is " opened to the house of David ".

No more will be heard the voice of the false prophet. If a man should dare to prophesy in the Lord's Name without the Lord's anointing (xiii. 3), then he must be dealt with according to the law of Moses. " If there arise among you a prophet, or a dreamer of dreams, and giveth thee a sign or wonder, and the sign or the wonder come to pass, whereof he spake unto thee, saying, Let us go after other gods, which thou hast not known, and let us serve them . . . that prophet, or that dreamer of dreams, shall be put to death . . . " (Deuteronomy xiii. 1-5). Later in this same chapter it is recorded that a man's own family, as witnesses, must be those who will take his life.

By this means false prophets will be subdued. They will confess their real identity.

Chapter xiii. 6 has ofttimes been applied to the Lord, but in the text it applied to the false prophet who, having some marks upon his body, was caused to confess that they were received in the house of his friends, the suggestion being that they might have been self-inflicted in the house of his gods, or they could have been imposed in punishment by his family. It is obvious that it does not relate to the wounding of the Lord.

The last chapter introduces the glorious consummation. It is

The coming of Christ to reign, also known as the Day of the Lord. It must be remembered that this prophecy was made to God's people, the nation of Israel, and not to the Church. Therefore the subject of this chapter is not the Rapture, when the Lord comes into the air to take His Church, but the Revelation, when the Lord literally comes back to this earth to reign, and in that day the Church, or the glorified saints, will come with Him, and we shall reign with Him.

This Revelation of Christ is preceded by the period known as the Tribulation, mentioned in chapter xiv. 2-3. The Tribulation takes place in a period of time between the Rapture of the Church and its return with Him.

In that first phase of His coming, He comes into *the air* and the Church goes up. In this second phase He comes to *the earth* " And His feet shall stand in that day upon the Mount of Olives, which is before Jerusalem on the east, and the Mount of Olives shall cleave in the midst thereof toward the east and toward the west, and there shall be a very great valley ; and half of the mountain shall remove toward the north, and half of it toward the south " (xiv. 4).

Other physical changes also will take place. The waters that shall issue out from the Temple, as described by Ezekiel (xlvii), shall begin to flow. Moving east, then south, they will divide, half going into the Great Sea (Mediterranean) and half emptying into the Dead Sea, so that this inland body of dead water shall come alive. It will be linked with the Great Sea and shall be the habitation of fish. The atmosphere will be clarified, which means that much of sin's contamination and curse will be lifted, and Jesus shall reign. The wilderness shall become a place of fruitfulness.

Although the opposing nations will have been destroyed (that is, their power), there will be a remnant of people left who will annually find their way to Jerusalem and worship the Lord of Hosts, and keep the Feast of Tabernacles. Any who refuse will know the punishment of the Lord.

In that glorious day when He shall reign, when sin shall have been suppressed, when Satan shall have been cast into the bottomless pit, it will be " HOLINESS UNTO THE LORD ". The common things will become uncommon. Everything will be sanctified, from the bells on the horses with their message of peace, seeing that wars have ceased, to the pots and the pans.

" Holiness unto the Lord, is our watchword and song,
Holiness unto the Lord, as we're marching along.
Sing it!   Shout it !!   All day long,
Holiness unto the Lord, now and for ever."

MALACHI

THE LAST VOICE

*" I know thy works, that thou art neither cold nor hot. I would
thou wert cold or hot. So then because thou art lukewarm,
and neither cold nor hot, I will spue thee out of My mouth.
Because thou sayest, I am rich, and increased with goods, and
have need of nothing; and knowest not that thou art
wretched, and miserable, and poor, and blind, and naked:
I counsel thee to buy of Me gold tried in the fire, that thou
mayest be rich; and white raiment, that thou mayest be
clothed, and that the shame of thy nakedness do not
appear; and anoint thine eyes with eyesalve, that thou
mayest see. As many as I love, I rebuke and chasten; be
zealous therefore, and repent."* (REVELATION iii. 15-19)

INTRODUCTION

Nothing is known of Malachi other than that the name means
" My messenger ". As a post-exilic prophet, he was not only
" My messenger " but he was also the Lord's last messenger to be
heard for four hundred years. The next voice to be lifted in
Israel was that of John the Baptist, who was the forerunner and
the herald of the coming Messiah.

Malachi's message was one of condemnation. He was opposed
to a cold formality and a dead religion. The above verses from
the book of Revelation are a summary of the whole of Malachi's
prophecy.

The period of Malachi's ministry seems to have been a few
years after the time when Nehemiah rebuilt Jerusalem in the year
445 B.C. The two men ministered in their respective capacities
after the return of the people from exile. The conditions prevailing were the same in both books. Therefore it may be considered that the reformation, which took place during the time
of Nehemiah, was only temporary and, when Nehemiah left them
to return to Persia, the people fell back again into idolatry. As
a result of their rebellion God allowed them to meet a series of
conflicts which brought the nation into a serious economic crisis.
Everything was against them. Crops were poor, fruit was failing,

the priests were corrupt, and the people were sceptical. They murmured against God, they failed in giving their tithes, they intermarried with the heathen, and they practised divorce freely. It was a land of apostasy, and Malachi was God's man for the hour.

It is to be observed that the Old Testament closed with an apostasy but yet with a faithful few, and the New Testament closes in exactly the same circumstances.

The book seems to take the form of a dialogue between Jehovah and His people. This is recognised by the repetition of certain phrases as "Ye say", and "Wherein have we", and "Thus saith the Lord of Hosts". The Lord reminded them of His concern for them, of His love, constancy, provision, and protection, and of their faithlessness and indifference on each count. The people had become so insensitive to their sin that they challenged the statements of the Lord with these words :

" Wherein hast Thou loved us ? " (i. 2).
" Wherein have we despised Thy Name ? " (i. 6).
" Wherein have we polluted Thee ? " (i. 7).
" What a weariness is it ! " (i. 13).
" Wherefore (will the Lord punish) ? " (ii. 14).
" Wherein have we wearied Him ? " (ii. 17).
" Wherein shall we return ? " (iii. 7).
" Wherein have we robbed Thee ? " (iii. 8).
" What have we spoken so much against Thee ? " (iii. 13).

This line of argument will be followed as the book is studied, for men are reasoning in the very same way to-day

THE BOOK

As stated, it is one of apostasy for which the Lord voiced His disapproval of the priests and people alike. Their declension was not only religious but also social and moral. This must always be so because faith in God is the foundation of everything, and, when foundations give way, the whole structure of human society must fall.

RELIGIOUS DECLENSION OF THE PRIESTS (Chapters i. 1 - ii. 9)

(1) *Concerning love.* It is in the light of the book as a whole that the detail is sought to be interpreted. If the nation were so insensible to sin, it was a wonder that God had any patience with the people or made any appeal to them ; but He did,

and this for the last time so far as the Old Testament Scriptures were concerned. It must be remembered that this was after the seventy years of captivity, after their return to their own land, and after God had displayed both judgment and mercy, yet from neither of these had they learned any permanent lessons.

Although it was the last appeal in the Old Testament, it was not the final appeal during time. After a silence of four hundred years God made His biggest, costliest, and most practical appeal in sending His only begotten Son to be their Redeemer and Messiah.

" I have loved you, saith the Lord " (i. 2) to a disobedient, gainsaying people, a people who were considering sin to be righteousness, who were satisfying the lusts of the flesh by putting away their rightful wives and marrying heathen women, and who offered God their blemished animals and their worthless possessions. What grace ! What love ! ! Who can fathom it ?

God was displaying His love for the unlovely. He was appealing to a sinful and a perverse generation, telling them of His love for them, and the only reply he received was " Wherein hast Thou loved us . . . ? " (i. 2). Does it not make one shudder to think of the impudence of man toward his Maker — of the sinner toward his Redeemer ?

But what has man to say to-day, after another two thousand years of mercy and grace, during which time God has given His Son to be the Saviour of the world ? He is asking where the love of God is. He claims that things are his by hard work, or by his ability. He is healthy because he takes care of himself. He is entitled to all of these things. They are his and he wants no interference. The moment some affliction does come the cry is, " What have I done to deserve this ? " Man to-day is very self-important, very self-satisfied, and yet he lives a life which does not stand moral examination. Oh, how merciful the Lord is !

The Lord's reply to insolent man was, " Was not Esau Jacob's brother ? . . . yet I loved Jacob, and I hated Esau . . . " (i. 2-3). Here is a statement that has proved problematic to so many minds, causing the question to be asked — How can a God of love hate ? The answer is that He cannot.

The statement must be read in its context. The subject of these first five verses is the Lord's love toward His people. The word " hate " is a relative idiom. It is not an actual hate. It is a comparative hate as against the intense love which is on the opposite side.

Another thing to bear in mind, when reading these verses, is that the Lord was speaking neither to nor of Jacob and Esau as persons. From these two men there sprang up two nations, Israel and Edom, and of these nations the older should serve the younger. Both of the nations revolted and both of them were dealt with by God, Who in justice meted out His judgment upon them. Malachi told of God's judgment upon Edom in verses 3 and 4, how the land should be laid waste and desolate and, however they might seek to rebuild, the Lord would destroy. God's indignation should be for ever. The prophecy of Obadiah was concerned with this judgment. As God said, thus it was.

With Israel things were different. Whilst she was deserving of punishment, yet it was only temporary. They had been restored from their captivity, they would be restored yet again ; a future blessing was awaiting them. This was the Lord's answer to a people who said " Wherein hast Thou loved us ? "

May a reminder be given that, not only has God shown His love in giving His Son, but He has made some wonderful promises in the Name of that Son, which will yet be the blessings of those who will accept His love.

(2) *Concerning the Temple.* This concerned the Lordship of the Lord and His right to honour as a *Master.* His complaint was threefold :

(a) *Polluted offerings.* He told them of the respect that they had for each other. A son would honour his father and a servant respect his master. Honour was given where honour was due. The Lord was both a Father and a Master, and yet the priests, who were His children and His servants, had utterly despised Him, but again their sin-seared souls were oblivious of such behaviour, so that they asked " Wherein have we despised Thee ? " It was in offering polluted bread and sacrificing blind, lame, and sick animals. God had asked for unleavened bread, and the first-fruits of the land, which included the choicest of the flocks. They, in their greed for gain and in the mere motions of worship, had brought the worthless. Therefore He asked them if they would offer such things to the Governor. Would man to-day give his left-overs to a king or a queen ? Would he offer the cheapest of gifts to a president ? Indeed not. Better offer no gift at all than give that which is inferior, better to forget than to pretend, because such is an insult. (Read Deuteronomy xvii. 1).

One must read carefully and prayerfully, for all scripture is given by inspiration of God and is for instruction or for correction, and there are many who need to be corrected on this point to-day. If you say " Wherein ? ", it is applicable to the man who can buy his new house, his modern car, pay his subscription to this club and that society, who will take his friends out and treat them well, but when it comes to God, with reluctance he contributes the smallest amount he can. He boasts that he sent his old stuff to the church jumble sale or the sale of work. He gave his discarded clothes to the missionary, the broken furniture and the threadbare carpet to the mission. Away with that rubbish! Why insult God, and His servants who have given everything for the mission field ? God is saying to that man, " I have no pleasure in you " (i. 10). God is asking from man a tithe of all he possesses. He is asking for first-fruits, not leavings. Be careful lest He say, " Thou fool, this night thy soul shall be required of thee ; then whose shall those things be which thou hast provided ? So is he that layeth up treasure for himself, and is not rich toward God " (Luke xii. 20-21).

(b) *Pagan service.* At verse 10 the Lord was saying, according to marginal notes and according to the old translation, " O that there were one among you that would shut the doors that we might not kindle (fire) on mine altar in vain ". Everything that the priest did was for reward. They would do no work except for pay, even for the smallest service they required some remuneration. The sacrifices and the sacred things of the altar had been commercialised and, therefore, corrupted, so that God could no longer accept them. The table of the Lord had been made a contemptible thing.

As a result the Lord declared that, as they had forsaken Him, so He would forsake them. The day was coming when, from sunrise to sunset, the Name of the Lord should be praised among the Gentiles, and *they* would offer a *pure* offering. At this time the Gentile nations were referred to as heathen. This was the last voice of the Old Testament. The next time God spoke it was in the Person of His Son Who, through the Gospel, brought salvation to the " whosoever will ", so that to-day it is the redeemed of the Gentiles who are praising the Lord and serving Him. The old priesthood has gone, and Israel is not the missionary nation that it should be.

(c) *Paltry worship.* Not only were they bringing the torn, the lame, and the sick animals for their offerings, but they were pretending that it was all they possessed, that they had nothing better. Therefore the Lord said : " . . . Cursed be the deceiver, which hath in his flock a male, and voweth, and sacrificeth unto

the Lord a corrupt thing " (i. 14). God cannot be deceived.   He
knows what is in the stalls, in the purse, and in the bank.   Man
may cheat his neighbour but he cannot cheat God.

(3) *Concerning ministry.*   Owing to the fact that the priests
had corrupted the holy ministry which had been entrusted to them,
God would now corrupt their own seed.   He would reprove their
posterity and take from them the priestly privilege.   God had
made a covenant with the family of Levi, recorded in chapter ii.
5-9, a rendering of which reads thus : " To reward the piety and
zeal of their ancestors, I chose them and their posterity, by a
lasting covenant, to be My ministers ; and they, according to
the Law of their office, served Me with sincerity and diligence ;
and by their example and instructions, turned many from their
wicked courses.   (This incident is recorded in Numbers xxv.,
concerning a deliverance from the curse of Baal-peor.   Read
particularly verses 10-13.) But ye, instead of instructing the people
from My Word, led them aside by your doctrine and example and
made them to abhor My service, and thus violate the terms on
which ye hold your office.   I will therefore punish your impiety
and partiality in your decisions by rendering you openly contemptible."

SOCIAL DECLENSION OF THE PRIESTS AND PEOPLE
(Chapters ii. 11 - iii. 18)

Illegal marriage and divorce.   The Prophet reasoned that
they all had one father inasmuch as they were the descendants
of Abraham, and they were all created by the same God.   Therefore they were all brethren and, as such, they should maintain
the integrity cf the family.   Instead, contrary to the law of God,
they had intermarried with the nations round about and had taken
to themselves the daughters of the heathen.

Added to this, those who were already married were committing a double sin.   Firstly, they were divorcing their rightful wives,
a thing God has ever frowned upon.   This was to give them
freedom to commit their second sin — to marry illegal wives.

Marriage is made in the Lord.   Therefore it is something of
great sanctity.   It holds the blessing of the Lord and, because
the Lord is jealous of His Name and His Honour, He will not
permit men to break vows and contracts made in His Name.   He
hates all loose marriage conduct.

Scepticism.   In the last verse of this chapter they tried to
excuse themselves.   The other nations prospered in their sin,

therefore they followed, saying : " Every one that doeth evil is good in the sight of the Lord, and He delighteth in them ; or, Where is the God of judgment ? " (ii. 17).

This was an awful indictment to lay against God. When evil people prosper and God's children often suffer, injustice is the only interpretation the world can see. We too often judge from the immediate instead of from the ultimate, and forget that God judges from the ultimate and not from the immediate. If man can find one injustice in the character of God then he has divested Him of His holiness, and if that is done then He ceases to be God, and we become just the helpless victims of some unknown fate.

The Coming of the Lord. The opening verses of chapter three are in the light of what has been revealed in chapter two. The chapter commences with an interesting play on words. The name of the Prophet who was addressing the people was Malachi, which means " My messenger ". Said the Lord, through him, " Behold, I will send My messenger " (iii. 1). Here was a messenger of the Lord giving them the last warning under law. The next one would be John the Baptist, making the first announcement of the advent of the Messiah Who will be the last Messenger. He will be the very Word of God — made flesh and dwelling with His people. In effect Malachi was saying to them — " You who have refused My messenger (Malachi) who is now with you, think that you will receive that messenger (the Messiah) with open arms, and then your troubles will be over ! I stand in doubt of you. You think that you are daily waiting for His coming and that you will find great delight in Him. Be not mistaken. Because of your attitude towards Jehovah to-day you will find that you will not be ready for Him in that day. He shall come suddenly to the Temple that you have despised. He shall come as the Messenger of the Covenant you have failed to keep, and you will not be able to abide the day of His coming. If you are so insensible to sin when His earthly messengers warn you, if you cannot see your failures when man points them out to you, how do you think you will be able to stand in the presence of His holiness ? "

Instead of mercy it would be judgment for most of them because He would come as

The Purifier. As the refiner of silver sat over the crucible of molten metal simmering upon the fire, and from time to time removed the dross that rose to the top until he obtained a perfect reflection of his face in the silver, which was the evidence that the metal was then pure, so the Lord was going to deal with the sons

of Levi until all of these sins and abominations were removed, and
they, in holiness, would begin to reflect the glory of Him Who had
chosen them.

The Christian sometimes finds himself in the furnace of
affliction and chafes because of the unpleasantness of his circumstances. He complains that he does not deserve such treatment,
which is true; he is only worthy of death! But the Lord is
seeking to remove those blemishes and weaknesses which rob him
of Christlikeness, which is His greatest desire. Paul said : " For
whom He did foreknow, He also did predestinate to be conformed
to the image of His Son that he might be the firstborn among many
brethren " (Romans viii. 29).

Whilst the Lord would be gracious to those who would respond to His dealings with them, to the rejector He would be swift
in meting out His judgment, dealing with sorcerers, adulterers,
deceivers, oppressors, and rejectors. Lest sinners should consider
that His judgment was severe, He reminded them, and us, that
it is only because of the unchanging qualities of His character as
the One Who is longsuffering and compassionate that we have not
already been consumed, " For " said He, " I am the Lord, I
change not : " (iii. 6).

In the light of these facts, He called them away from

Backsliding. " Return unto Me, and I will return unto
you . . . " (iii. 7), but again came the cry of injured innocence,
" Wherein shall we return ? " When a man is not sensitive to the
realisation that he is not in closest communion with the Lord, when
he raises a question as to any weakness in His holiness, one may
have some misgivings as to whether he knows anything of holiness
at all ; but, when a man is in deliberate sin and then seeks to
justify his relationship with the Lord, one may have doubts as
to whether such a person has ever known the Lord.

The people enquired as to where they had gone that would
necessitate a return. What had they done wrong that needed to
be rectified ? What had they taken from God that needed to be
restored ? The Lord's reply was that the whole nation was under
a curse because they had robbed Him of tithes and offerings.

Let us be very honest in our interpretation of this verse and
the next. In view of the charge of robbery the Lord made an
appeal to the nation in the words, " Bring ye all the tithes into
the storehouse, that there may be meat in Mine House, and prove
Me now herewith, saith the Lord of hosts, if I will not open you

the windows of heaven, and pour you out a blessing, that there shall not be room enough to receive it " (iii. 10).

This verse has been badly abused, has been cited with selfish intent, has been spiritualised beyond the reasoning of the context, until some of the people who use this verse are almost as guilty as the people against whom the Lord had laid the charge.

One of the larger denominations in America abuses this verse by suggesting, yea, insisting, that the Church is the storehouse. They require that church members must put all of their giving into the local church. The local church will put it into the denomination under what is known as a " collective programme " It would seem that, from then on, it is no longer the people's concern as to how their money is spent. This is certainly not the meaning of the verse.

Another interpretation of tithes and offerings is that one tenth of one's income be given to the Lord, which is tithe, and everything above the tenth is offering. This has become so legalistic that the gifts may be made to any charity, whether it is God-honouring or not. With some individuals the motive does not rise above the level of income-tax relief !

Tithing in the Old Testament meant very much more. " Thou shalt truly tithe all the increase of thy seed, that the field bringeth forth year by year. And thou shalt eat before the Lord thy God, in the place which He shall choose to place His Name there, the tithe of thy corn, of thy wine, of thine oil, and the firstlings of thy herds and of thy flocks ; " (Deuteronomy xiv. 22-23). " And all the tithe of the land, whether the seed of the land, or of the fruit of the tree, is the Lord's : it is holy unto the Lord. And if a man will at all redeem ought of his tithes, he shall add thereto the fifth part thereof. And concerning the tithe of the herd, or of the flock, even of whatsoever passeth under the rod, the tenth shall be holy unto the Lord " (Leviticus xxvii. 30-32).

Abram gave to Melchizedec tithes of all (Genesis xiv. 20). Jacob vowed to give to God, " . . . and of all that thou shalt give me I will surely give the tenth unto Thee " (Genesis xxviii. 22).

From these and other scriptures it is learned, firstly, that money or income is not mentioned ; secondly, that in the early days it related to the increase of the field and the flock ; and thirdly, that with both Abram and Jacob, they volunteered the tenth of *all*.

The principle of the tithing was not money but possessions. Money would come into the *all* as a possession. Man to-day is limiting his tithing to money, which is only part of his possession.

God is desirous of having the first-fruits of our lives, our love, our service, our strength, our families, as well as our material gains.

Tithing only seems to be mentioned once in the New Testament and then it is a reference to Abram and Melchizedec, with no application to the Christian. The Lord does not demand, for this is the dispensation of Grace. The Lord does not ask a tithe. He asks for all, a consecration of everything we have and are. If tithing is not in the New Testament how can the Church possibly be "the storehouse"? Is it not a fact that Divine principles can be lost through narrow-minded, ofttimes selfish details?

One is not seeking to excuse the Church or to move from it the responsibility of liberality. On the contrary, the Christian is exhorted to lay up according to the way God has prospered him. 2 Corinthians ix. is a great chapter on Christian giving, but it does not concern tithing. It is liberality, not grudgingly, and not of necessity.

Whilst the ministry must be maintained and the man who lives in the Gospel must live by the Gospel, yet giving is not to the church but to the Lord. Love, devotion, worship, energy, service, time, all of these things must be given to the Lord. This makes the storehouse to be His great heart of love. The Christian is told to lay up treasure in heaven, that is, with Him.

To come back to the verse in question and its meaning, Old Testament tithing came from the fields and flocks. By that means the sons of Levi, who had no inheritance on earth, were maintained.

Malachi prophesied at the same time as Haggai, and both ministered in the days of Ezra and Nehemiah. By reading those books it is learned that, when the children of God returned from their captivity to Jerusalem, they built themselves houses, but failed to build the house of God, claiming that it was not the time.

Haggai told of a great dearth in the land, for which the people blamed the seed, the weather, and the land. They blamed everything save themselves. Then it was that the Prophet Haggai told them that the drought, the famine, and the loss of their flocks and herd, were due to the fact that they were leaving God out of their lives. Therefore He was leaving them out of His blessing. He called for the rebuilding of the Temple as a cure for all their troubles.

Malachi was doing exactly the same thing. Now read the whole statement in the light of these things. "Bring ye all the tithes into the storehouse, that there may be *meat* in Mine house, and prove Me now herewith, saith the Lord of hosts, if I will not open you the windows of heaven (rain), and pour you out a blessing, that there shall not be room enough to receive it (harvest). And I will rebuke the devourer (locusts) for your sakes, and he shall not destroy the *fruits of your ground ;* neither shall your *vine cast her fruit* before the time in *the field,* saith the Lord of hosts. And all nations shall call you blessed : for ye shall be a delightsome land, saith the Lord of hosts " (iii. 10-12).

The language is plain and must not be turned into something else. What has to be learned from it is that the principle remains true for to-day and for the Christian. If we will acknowledge God and His claims on us, if we will give to Him the portion of our love and life to which He is entitled, then in turn He will pour out upon us all of those promises of blessing that are yea and amen in Christ Jesus.

Let the question be asked seriously — Am I robbing God and, in so doing, am I robbing myself ? God is a rewarder of them that diligently seek Him.

One more challenge was levelled against this people by the Holy One. " Your words have been stout against Me " (iii. 13). Again they pleaded ignorance, so that He had to elaborate. Their complaint was that there was no gain or profit in serving the Lord. They claimed to have deprived themselves of much but had gained nothing. The wicked were those who prospered ; they were the happiest people. Yea, they went so far as to suggest that they were the people who knew the delivering power of the Lord. This was not the first time that man had thus complained, and by no means the last time for such an accusation. Man seems to be only capable of measuring success by what he possesses at the particular moment. He seems to lack the power to evaluate the material as against the spiritual, or the future against the present. He has fallen constantly by his own short-sightedness.

Therefore the Lord drew a contrast by declaring the true position of the believer, or

" *They that feared the Lord . . .*" Firstly, they " spake often one to another " (iii. 16). The backsliding people spoke of walking mournfully, but the saint is the one who fellowships joyfully. Secondly, their conversation was around one central topic of interest. It was their Lord, and that Name which is above every name. The righteous still love to talk of the things of the Lord. It brings joy, hope, and inspiration. It increases faith and knowledge, and establishes faith. These are some of the earthly gains.

Then it is learned that, whilst they remember Him, He remembers them. It so delights His heart that He writes it all in a book of remembrance. These things are evidently going to add to the pleasures of eternity. He will remember our conversations and reasonings over the portions of Scripture which were not easily understood and there unfold them in all the fulness of their glory so that the Christian will find himself continually feasting upon hidden manna.

A further privilege of the saint is ownership. " And they shall be Mine " (iii. 17). To have no fellowship is truly a loss, but to have no ownership is a tragedy known only to those who are in such a condition — no friend, no relative, no one to whom one can go in need ! God has made a claim of ownership and, because of it, we are able to make a similar claim. " I am His, and He is mine, for ever and for ever "

This ownership will be neither casual nor careless for He makes His claim on us at a time when He will be making up His jewels, or, as the margin renders it, " . . . in the day that I do make (even) a peculiar treasure ".

The Lord has many precious things — the precious Blood, precious promises, precious faith, etc. His own people, Israel, He often called a peculiar people, and here the word " jewels " is the same, " a peculiar treasure ". In the New Testament His saints also are referred to as peculiar people (Titus ii. 14 and 1 Peter ii. 9). The word " peculiar " comes from a latin word " Peculliam ", which was a priceless treasure carried as a locket around the neck of a Roman soldier, as a person might carry a photograph or some hair of someone very dear to them in a locket to-day. When God separates the sheep from the goats, the wheat from the chaff, the gold, silver, and precious stones from the wood, hay, and stubble — in that day the righteous are going to be separated unto Himself as the precious, whilst He deals in judgment with that which is vile.

The last verse of the chapter is very searching. If one cannot see the difference between serving the Lord and not serving Him, if one thinks it a miserable life with no gain, if one thinks the wicked are just as well off — then wait until that day when it will be learned, too late, which is the real life. " Then shall ye return and discern between the righteous and the wicked, between him that serveth God and him that serveth Him not " (iii. 18).

THE DAY OF THE LORD

Man may think that he is having his own way, that he is master of most situations, but, whilst this may be his day, the time is not far distant when he will learn Who is really the Master. God is going to deal with that rebellious heart and with that proud mind, and then man will learn that pride goes before a fall, as he will be consumed as the stubble (which is usually so dry that it makes ready fuel for the fire) ; whilst the righteous, who have been oppressed and despised by the haughty sinner, will flourish. He, the Sun of Righteousness, is going to shine upon them with His glory, whilst the healing balm of His Presence will cause them to forget all the privations of the past, and heal all the aches of disappointments and all the wounds of falls and failings.

As the Old Testament closed, this last voice said, " Remember ! " — remember the law, the statutes, the judgments, as given by God to Moses at the beginning. Remember them, because by them man was expected to live and, by them, presently he shall be judged. This can be repeated to all those who belong to the New Testament age, to the day of His Grace. Remember ye the Word of the Lord ! That Word is the power of God unto salvation. By it we should live, for it contains the precepts of life, and, by it, we shall be judged. It is the Word that liveth and abideth for ever.

The closing words of the New Testament are, " For I testify unto every man that heareth *the words of the prophecy of this book,* if any man shall add unto these things, God shall add unto him the plagues that are written in this book. And if any man shall take away from *the words of the book of this prophecy,* God shall take away his part out of the book of life . . . " (Revelation xxii. 18-19). " Behold, I will send you Elijah the prophet before the coming of the great and dreadful day of the Lord " (Malachi iv. 5). Significantly, the names of Moses and Elijah are linked together as the Old Testament closes. The two men were found together early in the New dispensation, for they were on the Mount of Transfiguration as witnesses of His glory, and they are found together again at the close of the present age, as recorded in Revelation xi.

The law of God required that everything should be established in the mouth of two or three witnesses. Some of us have reason to believe that the two men in white apparel who were at the tomb on the resurrection morning, and the two who stood by at the ascension of the Lord, were the same men.

Moses was the man who passed through death, was buried, and raised by God. Elijah was the man who was translated. These witnesses therefore would represent all saints who will meet the Lord in the last day, whether through death or by translation at His coming.

The last two words of the book of Malachi, the last two words of the Old Testament, the last two words of the law, were " a curse ". That was all the law could offer, and so closes a wonderful Book and an amazing dispensation, to be followed by four hundred years of silence — no voice from heaven or from the mercy seat.

The next voice was the voice of the Son. " God . . . hath in these last days spoken unto us by His Son . . . " (Hebrews i. 1-2), Who came to deliver us from the curse of the law and of sin, and to clothe us in the abundance of His grace.

ST. MATTHEW

"BEHOLD YOUR KING"

"Rejoice greatly, O daughter of Zion; shout, O daughter of Jerusalem: behold, thy King cometh unto thee: He is just, and having salvation; lowly, and riding upon an ass, and upon a colt the foal of an ass" (ZECHARIAH ix. 9)

INTRODUCTION

The Books of Matthew, Mark, Luke, and John are often referred to as the four gospels. Strictly they are not. There *are* four gospels. They are the Gospel of the Kingdom, the Gospel of the Grace of God, the Glorious Gospel, and the Everlasting Gospel. An examination of these will reveal that they are preached at different times, by different people, to different people, each having a different message, with different results. Therefore they cannot all be the same.

These first four books of the New Testament are but one of these four Gospels, namely, the Gospel of the Grace of God.

It is not the Gospel *of* Matthew, but the Gospel *according to* Matthew. This is obvious by opening the Bible to the second book of the New Testament, the title of which is "The Gospel *according to* St. Mark". The subject of the book is in the opening verse: "The beginning of the gospel OF Jesus Christ, the Son of God". Thus it is with all four writers.

Another common fallacy is that these four writers are referred to as four apostles. Only two were apostles, Matthew and John.

The four narratives are four independent accounts of one life, thereby giving a full-length portrait of that character — Jesus. Many are the descriptions that have been given. Augustine spoke of them as four trumpets gathering the Church from East, West, North and South, into a holy unity of the faith. Calvin referred to them as four steeds drawing Christ's chariot. Bengal likened them to four parts of music which could be sung separately but which sounded best when blended into a harmony. Others have likened them to the four creatures of Revelation, or to the Blue, Purple, Scarlet, and White of the Tabernacle. Jerome compared them to the four rivers which broke out from the river of Eden.

However one likens them, and whatever the metaphor used, all four are characteristically different and yet all four make perfect harmony. Although holy men wrote as they were moved by the

567

Spirit of God, yet those men were never robbed of their personality nor of their individuality. Rather, they were used by the Holy Spirit. Each book, therefore, is coloured by the personal viewpoint of the writer but, at the same time, controlled by the Holy Spirit.

Thus Matthew wrote with the eyes and the mind of a publican ; Mark of a servant ; Luke of a physician ; John of a fisherman. These will be noted as each book is studied.

Matthew, or Levi, was a publican, or tax-collector, before he was called to apostleship. This he was pleased to record himself : " A man, named Matthew, sitting at the receipt of custom " (ix. 9). In the call of the twelve he stated again, " Matthew the publican " (x. 3). None of the others was designated by trade.

Matthew tells that Jesus sat at meat in his house. In his humility he does not state that he " made him a great feast in his own house ". Luke gives that information. It has been pointed out that Matthew never exalted himself, neither did he write a single word against publicans ; on the contrary, he continued to identify himself with that profession long after he had left the business. When he prepared this feast for the Lord he invited the publicans. He quoted the Lord as saying that publicans could enter the kingdom of God. Some professions take a bad name, not because they are wrong, but because of wrong-doers within that profession.

Mark and Luke tell how the Lord asked for a penny to enquire whose superscription was thereon. Matthew, the publican, was more precise. "Show me the tribute money," and "Render therefore unto Caesar the things which are Caesar's" (xxii. 19/21). He appeared always to be a very patriotic man. He had collected taxes for his country and revealed a loyalty for that country and for those who were in authority. That was the nature of the man, and he was the man whom the Holy Spirit chose to write about the One Who was the King of the Jews. Throughout his writing he recognized Jesus as a King, and saw everything through those eyes.

THE BOOK

The King and the Kingdom are naturally associated, and thus the book divides itself : —

    (1)   The King's Advent.
    (2)   The Laws of the Kingdom.
    (3)   The King's Life and Service.
    (4)   The King's last days.

(1) THE KING'S ADVENT (Chapters i. - iii.)

(a) *Birth.* Kingship being hereditary, everyone is interested in the birth and genealogy of a royal child. Usually the child is born a prince or a princess, to become a king or queen in due course. Only once or twice in the world's history has a child been born a king, due to the fact that the father died before the child was born. Here is One Who was born a King, hence the narrative begins immediately with His genealogy, to prove His right to the throne.

The interest in this particular genealogy is the manner in which it differs from that which was set forth by Luke. The physician, who was writing concerning the Man Christ Jesus, travelled back in his record to the first man, Adam. Matthew began with Abraham, but the introduction to the pedigree is " Jesus Christ, the Son of David," David, the king ; and, as one follows through the line, the descent of the Royal line is obvious all the way.

The reason for starting with Abraham was because God had promised to Abraham that his seed should become a nation. That nation, in turn, became a kingdom when the people demanded a king in the days of Samuel.

The first announcement of His Kingship was made as the Wise Men came to pay their homage and enquired : " Where is He that is born King of the Jews ? " (ii. 2). The birth of one King disturbed the temper of another king, so Herod sought the destruction of the Babe.

It would be timely to make reference here to the

Virgin Birth, as the Prophet Isaiah is quoted at chapter i. 23. The scholars may be right when they state that the word "Almah" could mean "young woman," but what purpose is served if such a general expression be used instead of the specific? The statement is: "Therefore the Lord Himself shall give you a sign; Behold, a virgin shall conceive, and bear a son, and shall call His Name Immanuel" (Isaiah vii. 14). If the word "Almah" be translated "young woman" then it ceases to be a sign, seeing that young women bear sons every hour of the day, and one supposes every minute of the hour! As the text stands in the A.V. it is more acceptable to the believer than it can possibly be in the other translation to the materialistic mind.

The second consideration of the Virgin Birth is to understand that it has both a moral and a legal basis. Most people recognise the moral that if Jesus had been born according to ordinary human generation then He would have been born a sinner, for man is born in sin and " shapen in iniquity." The legal side of the story is that the Royal Line had been terminated as a result of a sin committed by Jechonias, or Coniah. This was recorded by Jeremiah (read Jeremiah xxii. 24-30). The last verse of this scripture says : " Thus saith the Lord, Write ye this man childless, a man that shall not prosper in his days : for no man of his seed shall prosper, sitting upon the throne of David, and ruling any more in Judah."

Coniah had seed before this curse was pronounced, hence the statement " *write* this man childless." From the genealogy in Matthew, chapter i., it is learned that Joseph was of the seed of Jechonias. For this reason neither Joseph nor any descendant of his could sit upon the throne. Thus it can be seen that the Devil had made a move to prevent Christ from reigning as the King of Israel.

Mary had no claim to the throne at all. She descended from David through Nathan. Joseph had descended from David through Solomon. Therefore, according to human generation, Christ could never have a legal claim to the throne.

However, there was a law which gave to an adopted child the full right of inheritance. If the parents had children of their own after legal adoption they had to take their own place. The adopted child would count as firstborn. The fact that Joseph and Mary married between the conception and the birth of Jesus meant that, when Jesus was born, Joseph, now the husband of Mary, must adopt the child as firstborn. Thus Jesus became heir to what belonged to Joseph — the throne — and could sit upon it because He was not Joseph's seed and, therefore, not the seed of Jechonias. So Virgin Birth by-passed a legal blockage, and God destroyed the work of the enemy in order that Jesus might be a King.

(b) *Infancy*. Like His birth, it was beset by many dangers. There were those who sought to worship Him, and there were those who sought to have Him destroyed.

When considering the Wise Men, do not think the number to be three, because the Bible does not say so, and do not speak of three gifts. There were four. The three gifts could have been sent, but not the fourth. These men, having come on a long tedious journey, came not to a baby but to a young Child. Before Him they fell down and worshipped, thus presenting the greatest gift — themselves. Then they opened their treasures (ii. 11).

God still desires man and his worship before anything else — the giver first, then his gifts.

Because of the anger of Herod and his determination to destroy the Child, Joseph and Mary fled with Him into Egypt. Thus was another scripture fulfilled : " Out of Egypt have I called My Son " (ii. 15). Some sixty Old Testament scriptures were quoted by Matthew as being fulfilled.

After the death of Herod the family returned and settled in the city of Nazareth. So the curtain falls upon the early life of Jesus. The next time He is introduced He is thirty years of age.

(c) *Ordained.* Chapter three introduces the first prophetic voice, after four hundred years of silence which followed the ministry of Malachi.

John, as a great herald and forerunner, came onto the scene to proclaim the coming of the King. "Repent ye," said he: "for the kingdom of heaven is at hand" (iii. 2). The only reason the Kingdom was at hand was because the King had come. With the introduction of the subject of the Kingdom of Heaven, that over which there is a diversity of opinion is met. Clarence Larkin gives a well-balanced definition of these New Testament expressions:-

(1) *The Kingdom of God* is an all-embracive term for the whole of God's economy — Heaven, Earth, and Hell, Angels, Men, and Demons. Everything that exists in time and eternity.

(2) *The Kingdom of Heaven* is within the Kingdom of God and is the Messianic earth-rule of Christ, which means that it relates to the Jews, for He is their Messiah, and it comes to this earth. It was *from* above, never *up* above.

(3) *The Universal Church* embraces the whole of what is called Christendom, and includes all creeds and faiths the world over. It is covered by the word " religion ".

(4) *The True Church.* This is made up of all those who are truly born again by the Spirit of God and through the efficacy of Christ's Blood, independent of any denominational label or affiliation.

With John's proclamation there came the anointing, or the ordination, as " Jesus, when He was baptised, went up straightway out of the water : and, lo, the heavens were opened unto Him, and He saw the Spirit of God descending like a dove, and lighting upon Him : And lo a voice from heaven, saying, This is My beloved Son, in Whom I am well pleased " (iii. 16-17).

Jesus was anointed with the Holy Spirit at the commencement of His earthly ministry.

The disciples were anointed with the Holy Spirit on the Day of Pentecost for the ministry of the Word.

To-day Christians need the same anointing, remembering that the promise is " Ye shall receive power, after that the Holy Ghost is come upon you : and ye shall be witnesses unto Me . . . " (Acts i. 8).

Following the anointing came the Temptation, which is so often the case. When God begins to work in a life, Satan is very active in that same life. Through this temptation Jesus was tempted in all points as we are — through the lust of the flesh, the lust of the eye, and the pride of life. He defeated the Devil at every round of the battle with "It is written," and that same sharp two-edged Sword has been given to every believer. It is because of the effectiveness of the Sword of God's Word that men are abusing it in such measure to-day, so that, if they cannot blunt its edge, they will get the soldier to lose his confidence in it and lay it aside.

(2) THE LAWS OF THE KINGDOM (Chapters iv. - vii.)

The Lord had now entered into His public ministry, the first part of which was confined to Galilee. He called to Himself the first of His disciples, or followers. They were Peter and Andrew, James and John, all of them fishermen, not brilliant minds but loyal hearts. The Lord has always used ordinary people in His service, not because He despises the extraordinary but because the man who is conscious of his own inability more willingly yields to the authority of another.

Teaching. The fame of the Lord quickly spread abroad as He both taught the people and healed the sick. Owing to the gathering of the multitudes, He withdrew Himself and His disciples to a mountain and gave to them a set of laws, known as the Laws of the Kingdom, or The Sermon on the Mount. Those laws would govern any kingdom or nation to-day, and observing them would bring a true and lasting peace to this poor war-torn world.

The discourse began with the Beatitudes. Daniel Webster, one of America's most outstanding lawyers, said : " The greatest legal digest was the Sermon on the Mount." Coleridge picked out the Beatitudes from this Sermon and referred to them as " the richest passage in literature."

In the discourse which followed the Lord told of the influence of the Christian in the world. He should be as salt, that which has a purifying effect and which acts as a check to corruption; also as light, which is an all-pervading thing. It dispels darkness wherever its presence is. The world is both dark and corrupt as a result of sin and, unless our influence is felt sufficiently to remedy this spiritual darkness, we are not fulfilling our life's work. Should this not make us examine ourselves before a Holy God?

God's Word is going to accomplish its purpose, and if it is not through us then we are going to be the losers, for there is to be a day of reward.

Spiritual standards were then established in a relationship between God and man. Murder, adultery, swearing, revenge and hatred, motives, laying up treasure, judgment, prayer, the Golden Rule, the Narrow Way, fruitage, false teachers, and false foundations, were all considered, so that man is left without excuse as to his manner of conduct.

(3) THE KING'S LIFE OF SERVICE (Chapters viii. - xx.)

Teaching is one thing, service is quite another. The Lord's life was full of both. Two chapters deal with some of that service to man as He demonstrated *His power over nature.* Ten miracles are recorded in the two chapters viii. and ix.

Seven declare His power over disease as He healed

The leper	....	viii. 2-4
The Centurion's servant		viii. 5 13
Peter's wife's mother	.....	viii. 14-15
The sick of the palsy	.....	ix. 1-8
The issue of blood	.....	ix. 20-22
Two blind men	.....	ix. 27-31
A dumb man	....	ix. 32-35

In these miracles Jesus never used the same method twice. Some came to Him exercising their own faith, others were healed through the faith of someone else, whilst in the case of Peter's wife's mother, no one appealed to Jesus. He saw the need and met it. We just tell Him the need, not how to meet it!

One miracle showed His power over nature.
He stilled the storm ..... viii. 23-27
One miracle revealed His authority over the spirit world.
He cast out demons ..... viii. 28-34
One miracle declared His dominion over death.
He raised Jairus'
daughter ..... ix. 18-26
In this last instance there was a delay, and a reason for the delay.

More teaching. Chapters x., xi., and xii. are of ministry, interspersed with healings which were more of a general nature.

Firstly, the twelve disciples are introduced, also called apostles. In x. 1 they were called " disciples," which meant they were followers. In verse 2 they became " apostles " or " sent ones," for He gave to them a commission and sent them forth to do the same things which He Himself was doing, preaching, healing, and trusting, for theirs was to be a life of faith, they to minister to the spiritual and physical needs of the people, and the people to minister to their material needs.

It is difficult to find where this order of things changed. The Church has switched from faith to salaries and, in the forfeiture of faith for material things, it has lost faith in spiritual things, which may be the answer to our not being able in His Name to heal the sick, raise the dead, cast out devils. The Lord did say something about when the salt has lost its savour it is good for nothing! How much good are we to-day? Apart from the above, are we even seeing souls saved?

Again, it must be noted that the Lord never promised these " sent ones " immunity from the trials of life, nor freedom from enemies; but, rather, the reverse. They were alerted against deceivers — wolves in sheep's clothing. Life has never changed so far as the moral world is concerned. Therefore serious heed should be taken to this admonition for this pack of wolves is ever increasing in size, thus increasing the dangers of the true sheep.

The Lord assured them, and us, that whilst persecutions must be, His grace and strength would be equal to every emergency. He Who cares for sparrows and knows the number of the hairs of our head, is able to keep the trusting soul. If we are prepared to lose in this life then we shall be making great gains in the life to come. Service here means reward there — sacrifice here means a crown of life hereafter.

Matthew then returns to the King's forerunner who, at Herod's pleasure, was in prison. John was not completely cut off from the world, for news had been reaching him concerning the Lord's ministry. He who had announced the King had become hesitant. Was this really the King, or only a forerunner? Maybe his own imprisonment had discouraged him. The Lord sent words of comfort to His suffering saint and then told the multitude of the greatness of John's character. He was the greatest prophet on earth, but the humblest saint in heaven would be greater than he. Heaven, with its rewards, starts on a higher level than man's highest attainment on earth.

The Lord gave an intimation of His own rejection, pronouncing woes upon the unbelieving cities. These were fulfilled. Chorazin, Bethsaida, Capernaum, are no more. As His judgment is always mingled with mercy, so those words of woe were followed with the sweetest invitation : " Come unto Me, all ye that labour and are heavy laden, and I will give you rest " (xi. 28).

Chapter twelve is one that would teach man not to be legalistic and make the laws of God to become irksome burdens, because His yoke is easy and His burden is light. It also teaches that man cannot please himself by using his liberty as a cloak of maliciousness. He has a duty toward the Lord, and toward the Lord's Day, which it is very important to observe. This comes first, but we also have a duty toward our neighbour which is not to be neglected. The problem to-day is that we have lost our concern Godward and manward. Most of the things men do on the Lord's Day are selfward and that is where they are wrong. When they shop on Sunday or engage in pleasure they neither honour God nor help their neighbour. They just please themselves. What of the foolish notice the tradesmen display: "Open on Sunday for your convenience." That is a lie. They are open for business and profit. If the employer opens his shop for your convenience you should be as "honest" and stay away for the employee's convenience.

This teaching upset the legalistic Pharisees so that they sought means whereby they could destroy the Lord. He withdrew Himself from these enemies but not from His ministry. The crowd followed, the needs of men revealed themselves, and He met them. This increased the anger of the Pharisees who, because He healed a man who was possessed with an evil spirit, accused Him of being possessed of evil spirits Himself and empowered by them. So blasphemous was this accusation that the Lord gave a special warning to prevent other people from committing such a sin. It is in chapter xii. 31-32 : "Wherefore I say unto you, All manner of sin and blasphemy shall be forgiven unto men ; but the blasphemy against the Holy Ghost shall not be forgiven unto men. And whosoever speaketh a word against the Son of man, it shall be forgiven him : but whosoever speaketh against the Holy Ghost, it shall not be forgiven him, neither in this world, neither in the world to come." Jesus said that He cast out devils by the Spirit of God. The unpardonable sin, therefore, is attributing to the Devil the work of the Holy Spirit.

When the people sought a sign as an evidence of His authority the Lord refused to give one because man must not live by signs but by faith and, if the evidences already given in the miracles which He had performed were not sufficient, no sign would ever satisfy such unbelieving hearts.

The Parables of the Kingdom (Chapter xiii.). These parables relate to the Kingdom and are important because they hold a key which, in the hand of the believer, can reveal what are otherwise the mysteries of the Kingdom.

The definition of the theme of the Kingdom is somewhat elusive because of the many applications of the term in the Bible. Some, like Herod, thought it to be a political kingdom and that Jesus was to be a political king who might endanger Herod's position. The Lord destroyed that idea. Said He: "My kingdom is not of this world (of this world order) : if My kingdom were of this world, then would My servants fight, that I should not be delivered to the Jews: but now is My kingdom not from hence" (John xviii. 36). His Kingdom was from above. Its constitutions were formed up there, and were to be lived out down here. Fundamentally, as already stated, it was the Messianic earth-rule of Christ and, therefore, can be limited to the Jewish nation.

This Kingdom was declared to Abram by prophetic utterance. It was announced as at hand when the King came to this earth. It was preached by Jesus, the Twelve, the Seventy, and John the Baptist. It was rejected by the Jews in their rejection of the King, as they cried " Away with Him, crucify Him " (John xix. 15), and " we will not have this Man to reign over us " (Luke xix. 14). In the rejection of the King the establishment of the Kingdom was postponed. During that period the Church has been in existence. When the Church is complete and taken out of this world at His coming, then will the Kingdom be re-established for a thousand years.

Spiritually all of this can apply to the reign of Christ in the hearts of believing men and women, but it must be borne in mind that such truth is application and, therefore, not the first principles of the narrative.

The Kingdom must not be confused with the Church, which had not been established and which is a spiritual body rather than an earthly people.

The Parables that relate to this Kingdom are : —
> The Sower and the Soil.
> The Wheat and the Tares.
> The Mustard Seed.
> The Leaven hid in the Meal.
> The Treasure hid in the Field.
> The Pearl.
> The Drag-net.

All these are in chapter thirteen, and in each instance there was the introduction of something that was foreign. As an example, the Lord used the Parable of the Sower and the Soil, saying : " Know ye not this parable ? and how then will ye know all parables ? " (Mark iv. 13).

The Sower and the seed remained the same throughout. It was the soil which differed in the power of its receptivity. Palestine is a citrus country. It grows fruit, oranges, grapes, olives, figs. Some of these are used as symbols of the nation. Said the Lord: " Now learn a parable of the fig tree ; When his branch is yet tender and putteth forth leaves, ye know that summer is nigh " (xxiv. 32). Some trees, if not cultivated, grow wild because they are natural to that country. Hence, in the wars mentioned in the book of The Revelation, it is recorded : " . . . see thou hurt not the oil and the wine " (Revelation vi. 6).

Christ, knowing that His own people were going to reject Him, took upon Himself the position of a husbandman who went forth into the field of the world and cast into it something new — wheat, or seed of His Word, or the Gospel. From that seed would come a new harvest — the Church.

This new message had a very varied reception but, according to the measure in which it was received, so it brought forth fruit.

The next parable shows that when Christ began the work of the Gospel the enemy began sowing the tares of dissension.

Further Kingdom parables are related in chapters xviii., xx., xxii. and xxv., and are : —

The unmerciful servant.
The vineyard labourers.
The marriage feast.
The ten virgins.
The talents.

From this list comment must be restricted to one parable, and the most important one is The Ten Virgins. Again, here is a matter of acceptance or rejection, but instead of seed it is oil. The illustration is entirely Jewish. The oil is *not* a type of the Holy Spirit because the parable does not concern the Church. The narrative was given prior to the formation of the Church, and prior to the pouring out of the Holy Spirit. The Holy Spirit had not as yet been given because Christ had not been glorified.

Three questions were asked in chapter xxiv. — (1) " When shall these things be ? " (2) " What shall be the sign of Thy coming ? " (3) " And of the end of the world ? "

Questions 1 and 2 are answered in chapter xxiv., telling of the coming of the Lord for His Church.

THEN, when Christ has come and the Church has gone, "THEN shall the Kingdom of Heaven be likened unto ten virgins " (xxv. 1). Many people have referred to these virgins as bridesmaids. This they were not, for they were all men. (The dictionary and Revelation xiv. 4 declare that a virgin can be a man.) These virgins were outside the house at night. Their responsibility was to announce to the bride and her friends, who were inside the house, the arrival of the bridegroom. Women would never be allowed outside after dark in the East. The Bridegroom was not seeking His Bride. He was calling His friends.

After the Church is caught up into the air, the Lord is going to invite His friends to be present at the Marriage to act as witnesses and to share in the joy of the occasion, but not to be married to Him. That is the exclusive privilege of the Bride. These friends, who will be invited, are those referred to as the Tribulation Saints. They are not in the Church. They are in the Kingdom, as was John the Baptist. He lived prior to the Church as they live after it. John the Baptist said that he was only a friend of the Bridegroom.

Concerning these virgins, or friends, some had oil and some had not. The oil was the oil of endurance. " But he that shall endure unto the end, the same shall be saved " (xxiv. 13). Our salvation is not dependent upon endurance. It rests in His grace.

Chapter fourteen is followed by seven chapters which are overshadowed with a sense of

The Approaching End. The Lord's ministry expanded at that time to Galilee, Phoenicia, Decapolis and Perea. The first shadow to cast itself was the beheading of John the Baptist. The forerunner of His ministry was the forerunner of His death. Herod shed the first blood in his resentment of truth and yet not the first, for Herod the Great had. He had ordered the death of all male children, but that was in fear of his position. Now it was opposition to truth. "At that time Herod the tetrarch heard of the fame of Jesus" (xiv. 1). This fame created a fear in the heart of Herod, especially so because Christ's authority was established by a series of miracles which followed. These miracles included

> Feeding five thousand.
> Walking on the sea.
> Healing a Syrophenician's daughter.
> Healing a multitude of divers diseases.
> Feeding four thousand.

Between these miracles there was also His teaching, as He reproved the Scribes and Pharisees for their unbelief. On the subject of unbelief He enquired as to the opinions of men concerning His identity. He found that they were very diverse. "But Whom say ye that I am ? " Peter answered : "Thou art the Christ, the Son of the living God" (xvi. 15-16). There was no hesitancy in his testimony. God had made it known to Peter, and only that which is revealed by the Father is true.

Upon such a solid rock of assurance as to Deity was Christ to build His Church, and to all who accept the revelation of the Father, concerning the Son as the Divine One, will be given the key of the Gospel which will unlock dark and doubting souls and set men free, for the Gospel " . . . is the power of God unto salvation to every one that believeth " (Romans i. 16). To withhold that Gospel is to keep men bound in sin.

The shadows continued to fall as the Lord began to make known to His disciples " . . . how that He must go unto Jerusalem, and suffer many things of the elders and chief priests and scribes, and be killed, and be raised again the third day" (xvi. 21). Satan was quick to react, through a disciple, to such a statement. He was anxious to destroy the Christ, but the way the Lord was going would not fit into his plans. Neither would a resurrection. Satan was out to do everything that would cause the Lord to trip somewhere and to die *like* a sinner, not *for* the sinner.

As an encouragement to the disciples in the testing hours which were to come, they were privileged to witness the Transfiguration which would associate a glory with the shame of His death.

Further teachings and miracles make known His requirements from mankind, which must be considered as they are found recorded by the other narrators.

(4) THE KING'S LAST DAYS (Chapters xxi. - xxviii.)

These last weeks were spent in and around Judæa. They outline

The King's greatest work. He, Who had set His face to go up to Jerusalem, knowing that He would fall into wicked hands and be crucified, never once flinched in what became to Him the path of duty. For this purpose He had come into the world.

Triumphantly He rode into His capital city on an ass, which animal, as was learned in Zechariah's prophecy, had a fuller significance than humility. The horse suggested war, the ass told the people He was coming in peace. He was the Prince of Peace on His way to Calvary that He might make peace through the Blood of the Cross.

Upon arrival at the Temple, He found no symbols of peace. What should have been a house of prayer was a centre of dishonest trading, a den of thieves. The place of consecration had been turned into a scene of desecration. He displayed an authority which drew the praises of the common people.

That night He returned to Bethany. Next day He *returned to the city,* when His authority for yesterday's behaviour was questioned by the leading religionists. The Lord disarmed His would-be accusers with a question which left them embarrassed before the people. Having silenced those who had come to silence Him, He spent the rest of that day ministering in the Temple. That would have been in the outer court. His teaching included

The parable of the two sons (xxi.)
The wicked husbandman (xxi.)
The rejected corner-stone (xxi.)
The wedding invitation (xxii.)
The tribute money (xxii.)
Marriage and the Resurrection (xxii.)
The greatest Commandment (xxii.)

and a whole series of woes in chapter xxiii., pronounced against the Scribes and Pharisees because of their pride and hypocrisy, ending with that great lament " O Jerusalem, Jerusalem, thou that killest the prophets, and stonest them which are sent unto thee, how often would I have gathered thy children together, even as a hen gathereth her chickens under her wings, and ye would not! Behold, your house is left unto you desolate. For I say unto you, Ye shall not see Me henceforth, till ye shall say, Blessed is He that cometh in the Name of the Lord " (xxiii. 37-39).

From the Temple He went to the Mount of Olives. There He sat down and taught His disciples things concerning the end (chapters xxiv. - xxv.). This was referred to earlier in the chapter, and is known as the Olivet Discourse.

Whilst the Lord and His disciples were conversing together on the Mount concerning the destruction of Jerusalem's Temple, the desolations of the last days, and the coming again of Messiah, the chief priests, scribes, and elders were also assembled together in the palace of the High Priest. Their subject was the destruction of that Temple which the Lord would rebuild in three days — His body. Their decisions were the very things that would bring about the desolations the Lord foretold. These men would die in their crimes. He, Whom they sought to destroy, would live and reign for ever.

That night and the next day Jesus spent in Bethany in the house of Simon, the leper. There Mary anointed Him against the day of His burial, though she wist it not. She was expressing her love in the fullest way she knew, sacrificial worship. To many, such giving is waste ; to Him, it is worship.

The Betrayal. Judas was neither asked, pressed, nor threatened. Voluntarily he offered to betray his Lord for whatever reward he might obtain from the enemy. How true is the Scripture which declares the heart to be deceitful above all things and desperately wicked ! How we need ever to be on guard, lest voluntarily we betray our Saviour's love for some passing and regrettable satisfaction.

Judas thought he would deceive the Lord with a kiss. Jesus would think he was a friend, whilst he planned as an enemy, but Jesus was aware of the heart of Judas even whilst he sat at the Passover table.

Our Hallelujahs, our activity in the Church, our presence at the Lord's table, might deceive man but not the Lord. Secret sins cannot be hidden behind the motions of life. The Lord will be saying : " . . . One of you shall betray Me," and to reply, " Lord, is it I ? " is to add insult to injury.

Jesus was back in Jerusalem when He kept the Passover and established the Lord's Supper. From there

He went out to Gethsemane. Forsaken by His disciples, He prayed alone, until the betrayer's kiss that took Him to the Cross was planted on that holy brow.

As this great story of the greatest sacrifice is told by all the writers of the Gospel, detail will be enlarged upon in the next chapter of this book. However, Matthew, writing concerning the King, states that over the Cross were written the words : " THIS IS JESUS THE KING OF THE JEWS " (xxvii. 37). No protest of His enemies could bring an alteration to those words, for the statement was truth.

So He died, not defeated but triumphant, as was manifested in the wonder of His resurrection.

He, Who was born King of the Jews, was proclaimed a King and anointed as such in the day of His rejection, was crowned with a crown of thorns, and a reed became His sceptre, but no sword was given to Him for His Kingdom is not of this world.

The book closes with a Royal Commission, " Go ye therefore, and teach all nations, baptising them in the name of the Father, and of the Son, and of the Holy Ghost : Teaching them to observe all things whatsoever I have commanded you ; and, lo, I am with you alway, even unto the end of the world, Amen " (xxviii. 19-20).

ST. MARK

" BEHOLD MY SERVANT "

*" Behold My Servant, Whom I uphold; Mine elect, in whom
My soul delighteth; I have put My Spirit upon Him: He
shall bring forth judgment to the Gentiles. He shall not cry,
nor lift up, nor cause His voice to be heard in the street. A
bruised reed shall He not break, and the smoking flax shall
He not quench: He shall bring forth judgment unto truth.
He shall not fail nor be discouraged, till He have set judgment
in the earth: and the isles shall wait for His law"*

(ISAIAH xlii. 1-4)

INTRODUCTION

As Matthew saw in Jesus a King, and wrote accordingly, so
Mark recognised Him as a Servant, and furnished such information.
Although these two characteristics are as far removed from each
other as can be, yet they harmonised in this wonderful Person —
Jesus. Matthew gave a great deal to the matter of Christ's ministry
of teaching, more than he did to the miracles which the Lord
performed.

Mark, who saw the Servant, saw in the Lord One Who was
ever active, and so recorded more of what Jesus did than what
He said. The keyword of the book is " straightway," which occurs
nineteen times. The word " immediately " (which has a similar
meaning) is found seventeen times.

Because Mark recognised the Lord as a Servant there is no
introduction to the book. The writer moved right into his subject.
Some scholars think that Mark wrote later than the other narrators
of the Gospel. That might be possible, but not very much later.
He would not be more than one generation removed from the
Lord's ministry. The point is made here owing to the fact that
these same men state that Mark makes no reference to the Virgin
Birth because, writing later, he had time to realise that it was
only a false rumour which had been spread abroad. This is as
weak an argument as it is possible for anyone to raise.

Mark does not refer to the birth of Jesus at all. He gives
no genealogy. He makes no reference to early life. Mark begins
to write at the place where Jesus began His ministry. The reason
for this is quite natural. He is writing about a servant, and who
is interested in the birth of a servant? No one! If a child should

583

be born into the Royal Family almost every newspaper of the
world would carry the news as headlines. Everyone would be
interested in the details — but it was never put into the newspaper
when I was born, not even on the back page of the local paper!
Why? I was only a servant, born of humble parents. No one
was interested, except the immediate relatives and friends of my
parents. It was not until I began a ministry in word and with
pen that some people began to find out that I was even here.

Thus it is with this second book of the New Testament. It
begins with the Lord's public ministry : " The beginning of the
Gospel of Jesus Christ, the Son of God " (i. 1).

Before considering the message of the Book, a word should
be said concerning

Mark, the writer. Mark was not an apostle. There is no
evidence that he ever followed Jesus. In fact, there is no evidence
that he ever saw Jesus. He was a companion of the apostles. His
story comes at a later date and is in the Acts of the Apostles. He
was the man who accompanied Saul and Barnabas to Antioch
(Acts xii. 25). That was about A.D. 44. He started with them
on their first missionary journey, but turned back.

Later, about A.D. 50, he wanted to accompany them on a
second journey, but Paul refused. This was the cause of the
division between Paul and Barnabas so that they parted, Paul
taking Silas with him and Barnabas taking Mark (Acts xv. 37/41).

Twelve years later (A.D. 62) Mark was in Rome with Paul
(Colossians iv. 10). Later, Paul was asking for Mark. He sought
his company in the closing days of his life (2 Timothy iv. 11).
This information establishes the fact that Mark's ministry was
later than that of the Lord.

There is also evidence that Mark was a companion of Peter
(1 Peter v. 13). Peter never wrote concerning Christ's ministry,
as did Matthew and John, but, in his later years, he did tell Mark
all the things which were still vivid in his memory, and it would
appear that Mark wrote them. This is ascertained by the fact
that, although Mark was never with Jesus, the language is of one
who was, and who must have been, an eye-witness. For example,
he tells how Jesus " looked and deeply sighed." In the healing
of the deaf man at Decapolis, the record says : " He took him
aside from the multitude." When He gave sight to the blind man
at Bethsaida, it says : " He took him by the hand and led him
out of the town." With the demoniac child it is recorded : " took
him by the hand and lifted him up, and he arose." This minute

detail is the proof of the eye-witness and, therefore, suggests that all the information came from one such as Peter.

As Matthew wrote with the Jew in mind, so Mark wrote thinking of the Gentiles. Matthew quoted more than sixty times from the Old Testament, from the law and the prophets, which were Jewish. Mark makes scarcely any reference to the Old Testament.

THE BOOK

The Book may be divided thus : —

(1)	The Servant announced	.....	Chapter i.	1 - 8
(2)	The Servant equipped	.....	Chapter i.	9 - 13
(3)	The Servant at work	.....	Chapter i.	14 - xiii. 37
(4)	The Servant suffering	.....	Chapter xiv. - xv.	
(5)	A new day	.....	..... Chapter xvi.	

THE SERVANT ANNOUNCED (Chapter i. 1-8)

Mark tells of the proclamation as it had been declared long before by Isaiah. John the Baptist was about the same age as Jesus, but had commenced his public ministry a little earlier as he was to be the forerunner of the Messiah. His ministry had been very successful, for all Jerusalem and Judæa had followed him. They were being saved through his ministry, and baptised. He was referred to as " the prophet of the Highest " at the time of his birth. Jesus declared that of all who were born of women there had not risen a greater than John the Baptist. But now John was announcing the coming of the One Who was greater than he ; greater in Himself, for John was not worthy to stoop down and unloose His shoes, and greater in power, for " I indeed have baptised you with water : but He shall baptise you with the Holy Ghost " (i. 7-8).

With this announcement Jesus stepped out of obscurity into publicity as He came from Nazareth to Jordan to be baptised of John.

THE SERVANT EQUIPPED (Chapter i. 9-13)

Having submitted Himself to the baptism of John, as He *came up* out of the water, the Spirit *came down* and rested upon Him, whilst another proclamation was made, this one from heaven. " Thou art my beloved Son, in Whom I am well pleased " (i. 11). What a testimony to come from the Father ! If Jesus needed the outpouring and indwelling of the third person of the Trinity —

the Holy Spirit — how much more do believers need Him before
they can perform any effective service for the Master.

As surely as the Lord God gives, so surely does the Devil
want to take. The temptations of the Devil in the wilderness were
no evidence or proof that the Lord had failed or would fail. As
we surrender fully to the Lord we, too, will find an active adversary.
That was why Peter said : " Beloved, think it not strange concerning the fiery trial which is to try you, as though some strange
thing happened unto you : But rejoice, inasmuch as ye are partakers of Christ's sufferings ; that, when His glory shall be revealed,
ye may be glad also with exceeding joy " (1 Peter iv. 12-13). It
is all part of the equipping.

THE SERVANT AT WORK (Chapters i. 14 - xiii.)

In Eastern Galilee. Capernaum became the centre of the
Lord's earlier ministry. He went there after John had been put
into prison, and He continued to preach the message which John
could no longer preach. It was " The time is fulfilled, and the
kingdom of God is at hand : repent ye, and believe the gospel "
(i. 15).

He called to Himself the first four of His disciples who, when
they were called to become fishers of men, straightway left their old
occupation.

Notice the three " straightways " in that one single account
— verses 18, 20, 21. He might only be a Servant, coming not to
be ministered unto but to minister and to give His life a ransom
for many, but the people recognised in this ministry an authority
which did not belong to the Scribes. People to-day recognise the
authority of the message which comes from a Spirit-filled man
as against all the talk of the unbelieving heart.

Healing. The Lord gave Himself, without reserve, in service
to mankind. He cast out an unclean spirit and healed Peter's
wife's mother. After dark He healed many diverse diseases, cast
out many devils, and yet was alone with His Father in prayer
long before the light of the new day appeared. The next day
He began moving around the villages, teaching in the synagogues
and healing men wherever He moved.

Returning to Capernaum. The news of His arrival brought
people in their multitudes, all seeking His kindly help and none
being turned away empty.

Sick of the Palsy. Faith and determination began to grow in the hearts of men who, for so long, had been pressed with the weight of this world. This was demonstrated by four of them bringing a friend for healing. When they discovered that there was no approach to the Lord by ordinary means, they used extraordinary ones as they tore aside the temporary roofing used for sun protection over the inner courts of houses, and so let down the sick of the palsy to the feet of Jesus. At the exercise of their faith Jesus did something which was different from His other miracles. The man was brought for physical healing but, instead, the Lord did the greater thing. He gave him spiritual healing in the words "Son, thy sins be forgiven thee" (ii. 5). Of course, there was purpose in doing it this way. Physical healing could be proved because it would be seen, but spiritual healing belongs to the realm of faith. Such a pronouncement would raise the indignation of the religious sects, so that they charged Him with blasphemy. The Lord was then ready to deal with those unbelievers by demonstrating His power in the realm of the seen in order to prove His power in the realm of the unseen. Therefore He remonstrated with the rulers, and then bade the palsied man to arise and carry home the bed which once carried him.

Call of Levi. Another disciple was added to His small company, another who was unworthy in himself. He was Levi, the despised and hated publican, despised by men but loved by the Lord. Levi was so grateful to the Lord for his deliverance that he lost no time in bringing others, who were in like condition, to the Lord. Oh, that we had the same zeal!

Fasting. Grace was so foreign to these legalistic minds that they found fault with everything Jesus did or allowed. They raised a question on fasting, but the Lord showed that fasting was like weeping. It was something which might endure for a night, but joy cometh in the morning, and a new day had certainly come for those who had recognised the voice of the Bridegroom and who were rejoicing in His presence.

The Sabbath (iii. 1-6). Their next question concerned the Sabbath. They were positive slaves to it according to the letter of the law. The spirit was long since dead. The Son of man is Lord of the Sabbath and we must be also, controlling it for our good. It was made for us and for our blessing.

The traditions of the fathers were making of non-effect the Word of God. These rulers were making men become the victims of a creed. Jesus had come to make them victors through the Cross.

As the Lord's ministry of healing increased, so His need of being alone increased. If only Christians would follow His example how much more effective their ministry would be! There is quantity in all of our organisational set-ups and in our personal rush of life, but what is being accomplished?

In chapter iii. 13 He went up into the mountain, took with Him His disciples, and in that quiet retreat He not only called them to the ministry but it was there that He gave them the power to do the same things which He Himself had been doing — to preach, to heal the sick, and to cast out devils. When did the Lord withdraw that power? Never! Why are we not using it? With all of our medical and scientific advances, our need to-day is infinitely greater. Every hospital is full and new ones are ever being built; mental institutions are overcrowded. The world is *not* getting better, and what of the Church? If He has not withdrawn the power to heal the sick and to cast out devils, then the only answer is that we have lost it; lost it in the rush of life, and it will be found again when we can learn the lesson He taught — retreating from the demanding world to be alone with God and then to come out and meet the demands of the world.

> " *Then, fresh from converse with your Lord, return*
> *And work till daylight softens into even.*
> *The brief hours are not lost in which we learn*
> *More of our Saviour and His rest in heaven.*"

To do the will of God is man's greatest blessing, for in that obedience he is drawn closer to his Lord than by any other means. This He taught when He dissociated Himself from earthly relationships and indicated who were His mother and His brethren.

In the light of what has just been stated, the word "obedience" must not be interpreted " service," for worship is included. We obey Him when He says " Go — witness." We also obey Him when He says " Come — worship." " Come ye yourselves apart ... and rest a while."

The Parable of the Sower and the Soil is in chapter four. The principle of the parable was dealt with in Matthew. Let it be added here that three-fourths of the soil was faulty — the wayside, the stony, and the thorns, as against the one-fourth which was good ground; but the wayside could be ploughed, the rocks could be blasted and removed, and thorns could be uprooted. God wills not the death of any sinner. Prayer can prepare any kind of soil for the reception of the Word of God.

God never made things bad in the beginning. Sin has been responsible for so much, but sin can be destroyed. Why not seek the good and rebuke the evil ? After all, men do not light a candle to put it under a bed or a bushel where it will be smothered and go out. Instead, they set it high on a candlestick, which, in the East, is a three-legged tripod about fifteen inches high, so that it might do the work for which it was created.

Stilling the Storm (iv. 36-41). At the end of that day they took a boat and went to the other side. Again they were moving from the multitude to solitude, and that is something the Devil does not appreciate, so a storm struck the boat. The Master was asleep after the hard day of work. The disciples, when they saw the waves lashing into the boat, lost faith. No storm can destroy the Son of God, and they were in His company and, therefore, were safe, but fear laid hold of them and they cried out : " Master, carest Thou not that we perish ? " but He rebuked the sea, as He will rebuke all the forces which rise up against His people, and immediately there was a calm.

Upon reaching the other side, the enemy was still seeking to rob them of their quietness for, immediately upon arrival, they were met by

A Demoniac (v. 1-21). This soul was being torn day and night by evil spirits. Now they cried out against the presence of the Lord, but again He rebuked the enemy, and He, Who had brought calm to a troubled sea, now spoke peace to a troubled soul. The healed man wanted to remain with the Lord. But no ! he must go his way and tell what great things the Lord had done for him. Jesus Himself must retire to be with His Father.

Is it not strange how men are ever sending the Lord, the source of all blessing, out of their lives? They prayed Him to depart out of their coasts. The little boat recrossed the lake. Then came two more miracles of healing, the one so different from the other.

Jairus' daughter (v. 22-43). A wealthy man, pleading for another, witnessed a delay that would take the last ray of hope as news was brought that his daughter had died. The Lord performed the greater miracle and raised the child from death. The other was a woman with

An issue of blood (v. 22-43). Poor because she had spent all, she came with her own need, exercising tremendous faith. She was the cause of the delay in the other man's urgency, and received an immediate deliverance, teaching that the Lord deals with every person as an individual. He alone knows what is best for us and what will bring the greatest glory to Himself.

How sad is that which follows! The Lord decided to go unto His own and minister, and so He journeyed

To Nazareth. There He was not able to do the mighty things He had done elsewhere because of the unbelief of the people. Instead, He declared a truth which, tragically, has always remained true, that " A prophet is not without honour, but in his own country, and among his own kin, and in his own house " (vi. 4). When men said " Is not this the carpenter's son ? " God made it clear that " This is My beloved Son, in Whom I am well pleased " (Matthew iii. 17).

Feeding Five Thousand. The statement in this well-known story is one which is repeated in other places. Jesus " was moved with compassion " and, whenever He was, something happened. It has been stated that in the Greek the expression means " burning upheaval " or " stomach upheaval ", a condition experienced at times when we meet someone in extreme poverty or physical weakness, and feel so helpless. The stomach seems to be affected, and we say " I felt so sick for them." This is the meaning of " moved with compassion," and also of the term " bowels of mercy."

The Lord was ofttimes moved for man's physical need as well as his spiritual need. In this instance, as the multitude had hastened around the seashore, whilst He crossed the lake, so that they "outwent" the boat and were there first, when He saw them His pity welled up within and He was moved with compassion because they were as sheep without a shepherd. The Rabbis should have been feeding their souls. Instead, the people were neglected and spiritually starved. So He began to teach them many things, and they appeared to be willing listeners.

Out of the primary came the incidental. The day closed with the people so hungry for His teaching that they had become stranded for the material things of life, and so the Lord provided for them. His teaching was " Seek ye first the kingdom of God . . . and all these things shall be added unto you " (Matthew vi. 33). He was putting His teaching into practice.

Many lives, and churches, are impoverished because they provide for the material and the social at the expense of the spiritual. When we become moved and burdened for man's spiritual condition, and concerned with feeding his soul with the Word of God, THEN shall we see God again working miracles on our behalf.

Having sent the people away satisfied, He made another attempt to go to a quiet place. The people had robbed Him of this quietude before by following. Previously He would have taken His disciples; now He went alone for He had sent the disciples by boat to Bethsaida. The tired disciples were having a hard time, rowing but making no progress because the wind was against them. He was not with them this time, but He saw them and their need. He always does. "Jesus knows all about our struggles," and He came to them walking on the sea, calming their fears with " Be of good cheer ; it is I, be not afraid " (vi. 50).

It would appear that the Lord had difficulties and hindrances whenever He sought the place of solitude. This should help us to understand why we do not find it easy to get alone with the Lord. Most of these hindrances are created by the enemy, but such should cause us to realise its importance.

Traditions. More than half of chapter vii. is given to those soul-deadening traditions which were making life so unbearable for the people that everything was a burden to them. Christ came to lift burdens, to remove sadness, and to bring joy and freedom.

The Lord's ministry then moved into

Northern Galilee as, firstly, He travelled to Phoenicia, as far as the borders of Tyre and Sidon. This was a long journey in order to meet one woman, especially a Gentile, but she was a woman with a need and a faith, and that was all that mattered. He then returned to Decapolis and healed a man who was both

Deaf and Dumb. Sometimes He but spake the Word, which was sufficient. Here He chose to use means.

Feeding Four Thousand. These people had been longer without food than the five thousand. The need was greater, but in a similar way He met the need. He is still the Servant and is still ministering to others.

Crossing the lake again He came to Bethsaida and

Healed a blind man, the man who, in his first vision, saw men as trees walking. Some have suggested that men carrying great loads of brush could look like trees, but that is not the answer, for the Lord touched him a second time which corrected the impaired vision. Was it partial faith to which the Lord gave a partial sight in order to stimulate a complete faith ?

Confession of Peter. He boldly declared the Divinity of Christ, which, undoubtedly, came to him by revelation, and yet later he was the one who denied his Lord. Thomas doubted, the others were intimidated, Peter denied. Lord, guard Thou the words of my lips !

Profit and Loss is the language of the world, but this, the most important transaction of life, is neglected by most. " What shall it profit a man, if he shall gain the whole world, and lose his own soul ? Or what shall a man give in exchange for his soul ? " (viii. 36-37).

The Mount of Transfiguration (ix. 1-10) was one of the few occasions when Mark turned his eyes from the Servant to see the Lord. He saw Him in that glory which was not reflected, but which radiated from His Own Being as His whole figure changed and He had communion with the world beyond. So wonderful was the scene that Peter, James, and John would tarry long there but, inspiring though it was, they were reminded that the Mount was but a place of renewal, not residence.

We may abide when our task is finished, but as yet there is need below and we are here to minister to that need. Whilst those disciples were enjoying the blessings of the mountain top, the other disciples were enduring the struggles of the valley. They were embarrassed because they were not able to exercise the power which had been given to them. "Why could not we cast him (the dumb spirit) out?" There must be a spirit of co-operation. We are not workers *for* God, we are workers *with* God. "This kind can come forth by nothing, but by prayer and fasting" (ix. 28/29).

True greatness is taught in the latter part of the chapter as some of the disciples reasoned among themselves as to who would be greatest. The Lord showed that it was he who could be smallest, as He set a child in the midst and taught them humility.

From Galilee Jesus moved into

Perea for the ministry recorded in chapter 10. The first subject for discussion concerned that of

Marriage and Divorce, and it is defined so clearly by the Lord that there should be no disputes about it to-day. " What therefore God hath joined together, let not man put asunder " (x. 9).

Why do people go to Church and ask the servant of God to unite them in the bonds of holy matrimony and then, in a few years, go to the law court and ask the judge to break the bond? If the Church has the responsibility to create the bond, then it alone should have the responsibility to dissolve it. If this were so, then probably the breach could be healed, the problem solved, an understanding established, and the marriage saved.

Suffer little children (x. 13-16). The disciples would have sent them away, but with the Lord there is no barrier, neither age, colour, race, nor social standing. Never turn away anyone who desires to find the Lord.

The rich young ruler (x. 17-27). No one said nay to him when he came. How we are given to partiality! No wonder James reproves us. In the case of this young man he was his own barrier. He wanted to follow the Lord but he was not prepared to pay the price. A child may come — he has no preconceived ideas ; he is ready to accept with childlike faith. This rich man must do the same. The Lord did not intend him to become poor in order to find salvation. He wanted him to lose the love he had for his riches ; then he would be rich indeed.

The matter of the camel going through the eye of a needle has been used as a proverb of the impossible. The Lord never said that it was impossible. He said it was easier. Men have associated the statement with a sewing needle, but the small gate, through which people passed when once the large city gates were closed, was called the needle's eye. It was made for people, not for transport. However, if a camel were brought to its knees and released of all the merchandise which it carried on its back, then with an effort the camel would go through the gate. It is easier to get a camel released of the bales and bundles which would prevent it from passing through that gate, than it is to get rich people to yield the things which prevent them from entering the narrow gate that leads to heaven.

James and John (x. 35-45) asked for privileges which cannot be given. They must be earned. Our position in heaven will depend upon the material we supply whilst on earth — that is, spiritual material.

Blind Bartimaeus (x. 46-52). Jesus was leaving Perea for Jerusalem, and passed through Jericho, when a blind man cried for help. The crowd sought to silence him but he was persistent and cried the more : " Thou Son of David, have mercy on me." Jesus stood, asked the man what his request was, and granted it to him. So far as Mark's narrative is concerned that was Christ's last miracle of healing. Jesus was never at Jericho again. If Bartimaeus had remained quiet when the people told him, he would have lived and died a blind man. Instead, he laid hold of his opportunity, and thereby received his sight. Jesus may not pass your way again. Life is an uncertain thing. Have you claimed His salvation, His sanctification, His blessings? Do not delay in seeking that which you need.

THE SERVANT'S LAST DAYS (Chapters xi. - xiv.)

Entry into Jerusalem. "Though He were a Son, yet learned He *obedience* by the things which He suffered " (Hebrews v. 8). " . . . became *obedient* unto death, even the death of the Cross " (Philippians ii. 8).

Oh, the fickleness of men! To-day they are shouting "Hosanna" — to-morrow it will be "Away with Him!!"

The Barren Fig Tree has been a problem to many people. The three verses 12-14 need to be read carefully. The complaint was that " the time of figs was not yet " so why expect them, and why curse a tree for something for which it was not responsible ? It seems that the Lord lost His temper when He cursed it. The Lord ever had full control of His passions, and to accuse Him of losing His temper is to charge Him with sin. To curse a tree for not bearing fruit in the out-of-season period would be an injustice, which also would be a sin. Such a false charge would be our sin, so the incident must be considered again. Do see that the Lord *never* came looking for figs. The record states : " He came, if haply He might find *any thing* thereon."

A fig tree yields two crops in a season. The first is a berry which forms in the spring. It is the harbinger of the fig — no berry in the spring, no fig in the summer. This berry is edible but not marketable. Owing to the fact that it has no market value any traveller is permitted to pick and eat such berries. They are referred to as the " untimely figs." " And the stars of heaven fell unto the earth, even as a fig tree casteth her *untimely figs,* when she is shaken of a mighty wind " (Revelation vi. 13). Jesus came looking for those berries and, when He found none, He knew that there would be no fruit later in the year, so He cursed the tree and it withered so that it could not be a disappointment to other men.

If we do not produce the berries of service here, there will be no fruit of reward in heaven. We may not be cursed or withered, but we shall be saved though as by fire.

Cleansing the Temple. The same applies here. Casting out the money changers was not an act of violence but of righteous indignation. The Temple had been abused and, therefore, must be cleansed. What was established to be a house of prayer must not be permitted to become a den of thieves. Many of our churches to-day are needing the same severe cleansing. If we do not do it in time, the Lord will do some casting out in eternity, when it will be too late for repentance.

Parable of the Husbandmen (xii. 1/2). This parable was too forthright for the Pharisees and the Elders to misunderstand, knowing the intent of their own hearts. They had already done despite to some of the prophets, and were already seeking occasion when they might find it convenient to end His ministry. It was only their fear of the people that held their hands. They must cause Him to look guilty in the eyes of the populace.

Tribute Money (xii. 13-17), or taxation, was a touchy subject as to the matter of loyalty. A declared disloyalty one way or the other could divide popular opinion. In such matters we are to be as wise as serpents and as harmless as doves, as was the Lord when He said " Render to Caesar the things that are Caesar's, and to God the things that are God's."

The Sadducees (xii. 18-27) challenged Him concerning marriage and the resurrection. They did not believe in the resurrection. (Someone has said that was why they were sad-u-see!) The Lord met their challenge. Then came

The Scribes (xii. 28-34) asking for the greatest commandment. The questioner was given two commandments, which embraced all ten.

The signs of the times occupy the whole of chapter xiii.

SERVING UNTO DEATH (Chapters xiv. - xv.)

Chapter xiv. concerns the things which led up to the death of the Lord. In the house of Simon at Bethany He was

Anointed by Mary (xiv. 3-9), who brought a box of costly ointment and poured the perfume upon His head, to the indignation of the selfish people. She did it in worship — He accepted it against His burial.

Judas plots (xiv. 10/12) because of a lust for money, to betray One Who had ever been a friend to him.

The Passover (xiv. 13-25). It has often been said that someone had to betray the Lord, and it was not the fault of Judas but his misfortune to have been the chosen man. Such statements are far removed from truth. No one asked Judas to do it. He volunteered ; also the Lord gave him the opportunity to repent when He said : " It is one of the twelve, that dippeth with Me in the dish " (See note on John xiii. concerning the Sop).

From the fellowship of that table the Lord walked to the loneliness of a garden.

Gethsemane (xiv. 26-42). Alone — resisting the powers of darkness which would seek to persuade Him to allow this cup to pass, but He cried " . . . Not what I will, but what Thou wilt." Whilst He struggled with such agony as to extract a perspiration even to blood, the disciples slept. Although we are ashamed of them, we make no comment. We cannot. We are, most of us, no better than they. We are only what we are by His grace.

The Betrayal (xiv. 43-45). The traitor disciple, who pretended to be a trusted friend, betrayed Him with a kiss. How wicked can the human heart be !

Falsely accused (xiv. 46/55). " . . . As a sheep before her shearers is dumb, so He openeth not His mouth" (Isaiah liii. 7). Not only was He accused, but He was likewise abused. Only one word from Him and every persecutor would have been a dead man. Yea, they deserved to be! "But He was wounded for *our* transgressions. He was bruised for *our* iniquities, the chastisement of *our* peace was upon Him; and with His stripes *we* are healed" (Isaiah liii. 5). This is additional to His death by which we are saved. Death can be instantaneous. It can come without suffering. Jesus did more than die. He suffered, bled, and died alone. Believer, contemplate these things. Is it not possible that He suffered to deliver us from suffering, as He died to deliver us from death? Too many are denying Him and His power in the matter of Divine Healing. It should provoke much thought.

Peter's Denial (xiv. 66/72). This denial was during those sufferings.

THE SERVANT'S LAST HOURS (Chapter xv.)

Before Pilate (xv. 1-14). Pilate was conscious of the innocence of his prisoner but had not the courage of his convictions and, therefore, allowed Him to suffer. He thought he could wash his hands of blood, but that could only be if he could wash his conscience of guilt. Jesus stands to-day before some preachers, who know that He is the Son of God, and that He is truth. They know that their colleges have been false witnesses, but, afraid of their companions and of the crowd, they have not the courage of their conviction to pass an honest verdict, and thereby they allow Him to suffer at the hands of men, trampling underfoot the Blood of the Covenant as an unholy thing. Friend, with Pilate you may try to wash your hands, but your feet are stained, and one day you will have to *stand* before Him.

In the praetorium (xv. 15-20). The things done to the Lord in mockery, the insults, the buffetings of the common soldiers, would never have happened if Pilate had been true to his trust. Neither would the blasphemy, God-rejection, and crime exist as it does in the world to-day if the Church had been true to its trust. So it was that the Lord was

Crucified (xv. 21-41) amidst further abuse. He was numbered with the transgressors, and bore the sins of many ; whilst the few, as the Centurion, the malefactor, the women, the disciples, recognised Him as the Lord and Saviour. He was

Buried (xv. 42-47) in a borrowed tomb. Why not borrow it ? He only wanted it for three days. It would not be worth buying even if, like Abram and others, He could have afforded it. The conclusion was

A NEW DAY (Chapter xvi.)

Resurrection (xvi. 1-8). He Who lived and died to be the Servant of man, rose again as Master, Lord of death, and Destroyer of the powers of darkness. Man must now bow at His feet.

After His resurrection He appeared to

> Mary in the garden,
> two disciples journeying to Emmaus,
> the eleven as they sat at meat.

To them He gave the great commission " Go ye." Then He *ascended* to the right hand of the Father.

To-day we continue to fulfil that great commission, until from the clouds of glory He will cry " Come up higher."

ST. LUKE

"BEHOLD THE MAN"

"For there is one God, and one Mediator between God and men, the Man Christ Jesus; Who gave Himself a ransom for all, to be testified in due time" (1 TIMOTHY ii. 5-6)

INTRODUCTION

The distinctive personality of these Gospel writers has ever proved to be interesting, each giving his own particular approach to the subject.

Luke is known to be the author of two books — this one which bears his name, and also the Acts of the Apostles. This is brought to our knowledge principally by the fact that, in introduction, both books are addressed to the same unknown Theophilus, and that the one is a continuation of the other. "The former treatise have I made, O Theophilus" (Acts i. 1).

Luke was not one of the apostles. He was a physician. Colossians iv. 4 says "Luke, the beloved physician." As such he would be a man of learning and culture, and would have some ability for writing. He seemed to desire to use this ability to the profit of all.

With the tremendous happenings at that particular time, because of the ministry of Jesus and because of the opposition of some of the powerful classes, it can be readily realised that there would be a great deal of confusion, caused by lengthy reports and long discourses, as well as fragments of information coming from here and there. Some things would be recorded facts, some would be rumour, some would just be people's opinions, and some distorted truth from enemies, which would mean that truth and error would be abounding. Therefore it would be very difficult to know what to believe. Such circumstances prevail to-day, in a time of war, in political arguments, or in a national tragedy.

It was in these circumstances that the scholarly Luke stepped in to create order out of chaos. This was his declaration and introduction : "Forasmuch as many have taken in hand to set forth in order a declaration of those things which are most surely believed among us. Even as they delivered them unto us, which from the beginning were eyewitnesses, and ministers of the word ;

It seemed good to me also, having had perfect understanding of all things from the very first, to write unto thee in order, most excellent Theophilus, that thou mightest know the certainty of those things, wherein thou hast been instructed " (i. 1-4).

This precision, this continuity of thought and matter, is to be seen throughout the book.

Luke was different again in that he was a Gentile, which had an influence on what was written, and would have had his appeal to the Greeks as Matthew had to the Jews.

The difference of expression, the emphasis, and the detail reveal the tender touch and the understanding heart of a doctor.

He tells how the twelve and the seventy were sent out " to preach the Kingdom of God *and to heal the sick."* He is the only one who quotes the Lord as saying *" Physician, heal thyself."* He tells of the leper who was *" full of leprosy "* ; the Centurion's servant *" Who was sick and ready to die,"* ; Peter's wife's mother who was *" ill of a great fever "* ; the deformed woman who was *" bowed together so that she could in no wise lift herself "* ; and the woman with an issue who *" had spent all her living on physicians, neither could be healed of any."*

Then, too, from the human side, the tenderness of the writer is seen in his attitude toward the weaker folk. Concerning children he states that the daughter of Jairus was an " only daughter " : that the demoniac boy was an " only child " ; that they were infants who were brought to Jesus. Concerning *women,* much of our knowledge of the Virgin Mary comes from the pen of this man, and all that is known concerning her cousin, Elizabeth. He tells about Mary Magdalene, Joanna and Susanna, about Martha's anxiety and busyness, and Mary's quiet meditation. He had a sympathy for *widows,* and mentions Anna, the widow in the temple, at eighty-four years of age ; he records the parable of the importunate widow, and tells of the widow of Nain following the bier of her *only* son.

When it came to man, Luke so often used the term " a certain man." The identity of man did not seem to count too much with Luke. He was concerned with THE MAN Christ Jesus. A *certain man* went down from Jerusalem to Jericho — the ground of a *certain man* brought forth plentifully — a *certain man* made a great supper — a *certain man* had two sons — a *certain man* had a fig tree — there was a *certain rich man* who was clothed in purple.

The lost sheep, the lost coin, and the lost son, were recorded only by Luke.

Prayer is also a prominent subject of the book : —

Jesus was praying when the Holy Ghost descended upon
Him.
Jesus retired to the wilderness for prayer.
Jesus went up into the mountain to pray.
Jesus prayed on the Mount of Transfiguration.
Jesus was praying when the disciples said " Teach us
to pray."
The man gained his three loaves by importunity.
" Ask, and it shall be given you."
" Men ought always to pray and not to faint."
" Two men went up to the temple to pray."

THE BOOK

Like the others, it is one of ministry. The first twenty-one
chapters cover the Lord's ministry through service, and the last
three His ministry in suffering.

MINISTRY THROUGH SERVICE (Chapters i. - xxi.)

Early Life. After the introduction, already dealt with, Luke
goes back farther than Matthew for his commencement.

Gabriel visits Zacharias (i. 5-25). Being a doctor he told
of the birth of John the Baptist as well as the account of the birth
of Christ. John had a miraculous birth. His life and ministry
were declared before he was born. He was given to Elizabeth
and Zacharias late in life, and in answer to prayer. Zacharias
temporarily lost his speech because of his lack of faith, and regained it when, in obedience to a God-given revelation, he wrote
" His name IS John " (i. 63).

The Annunciation (i. 26/45). What a delightful story is that
of the birth of Jesus, so beautifully told that the church has been
retelling it ever since, without the thought of intruding into realms
that do not belong to us.

What of the days of testing, fear and anxiety, for the young
couple so happily engaged to each other ! Firstly, there was the
announcement of the angel, then the wonder of Mary as she said:
" How shall this be, seeing I know not a man ? " (i. 34), followed
by the perfect submission of this innocent girl. " Behold the hand-

maid of the Lord ; be it unto me according to Thy word " (i. 38).
What miracles would the Lord continue to perform to-day if we,
His children, knew that same submission which could say " Thy
Will be done, whatever it may mean to me, Lord. I submit."

Luke does not refer to Joseph, but there is always an after-
math to faith and submission. There must be, because we have
an enemy who is ever active against all such demonstrations.

Mary could trust God, but would Joseph trust her ? What
of their friends ? How about gossiping neighbours, who are always
ready for a sensational story, can make so many things appear
sordid, and who have no respect for people's feelings or privacy ?
Such is the work of the enemy. Mary would leave Nazareth for
the hill country. Where should she go ? To her cousin, Elizabeth.
She would understand. One might imagine Mary being filled with
more fear as she neared her destination. Elizabeth might understand, but what of Zacharias ? He was the priest. What would
he have to say ? Upon arrival, she discovered that no explanation
was needed. The Lord had gone before and prepared the way,
as He always does. As all the fears and pent-up feelings yielded,
Mary broke forth into an outburst of praise known as

The Magnificat (i. 46-55). " My soul doth magnify the
Lord . . . " This is one of the great hymns of the Church. A
hymn, according to Augustine, is a spontaneous outburst of praise
to the gods. There are four great hymns in the first two chapters
of Luke. The Magnificat (i. 46-55) ; The Benedictus (i. 68-79) ;
The Gloria in Excelsis (ii. 14) ; The Nunc Dimittis (ii. 29-32).

Although the Roman Catholics are wrong in their adoration
of Mary, whom they consider to be the Queen of heaven, when
she was but the channel, or the medium, whom God honoured to
bring the Christ into the world, and who herself confessed that
she was a sinner when she said "And my spirit hath rejoiced in
God my Saviour," yet the Protestants, in their abhorrence of the
Catholic position, have come short in that they almost forget her
altogether, whereas the angel and Elizabeth both declared "Blessed
art thou among women."

Birth of John the Baptist (i. 57-66). John was sent to be the
forerunner of the Christ. As Mary's pent-up heart broke forth
into the Magnificat, so the tied tongue of Zacharias loosened
into a paeon of praise known as the Benedictus (i. 68-79). In it
he declared John to be " the prophet of the Highest ; for thou
shalt go before the face of the Lord to prepare His ways."

The Birth of Jesus (ii. 1-7). Born in Bethlehem, the city of David, wrapped in swaddling clothes and lying in a manger, from heaven's glory to earth's poverty, Jesus, King of kings, became Man to dwell among us.

The Shepherds (ii. 8-18). Whilst the world slept, ignorant of the fact that one of the world's greatest events was taking place, " as heaven comes down our souls to meet," the revelation was made known to humble, watchful shepherds who, like Simeon, were waiting for the " Consolation of Israel." Heaven announced to the world, through the shepherds : " Unto you is born this day in the city of David a Saviour, which is Christ the Lord." These shepherds were undoubtedly men of faith, for they said one to another : " Let us now go even unto Bethlehem, and see this thing which IS come to pass " (ii. 15).

The Nunc Dimittis (ii. 29-32). This was at the time of the Circumcision, when Simeon rejoiced in the fact that God had privileged him to see His salvation.

At Nazareth (ii. 39/40). Life became normal for the Child Jesus. He grew and was subject to His parents, as all children should be. For thirty years that life was hidden except for the one look at Him in

The Temple, at the age of twelve (ii. 42-52). This was the age when the Jewish boy was made a " son of the law." (It is thirteen in this country).

The picture is sufficient to allow us to know of His growth and His wisdom, and gives an assurance that, at that young age, He had an awareness of Who He was. " Wist ye not that I must be about My Father's business ? "

A lesson comes from his parents, who travelled a day's journey presuming that He was in the company. This was to their sorrow. Too many people take things for granted with regard to the Lord and to spiritual things and, like His parents, have no reason for so doing. Let us make sure that we are travelling together, that He is in our company and that He is our Saviour.

John the Baptist (iii. 1-20). John knew a successful ministry as he preached the Gospel of the Kingdom, baptised his followers and announced the Coming of the Messiah, Whose power would be infinite. He declared that He Who was to come would baptise with the Holy Ghost and with fire. John was hesitant when Jesus came and sought baptism at his hand, and must have been surprised when he saw Him come up out of the water, the One Who would baptise in the Holy Ghost, being baptised Himself as the Holy Ghost descended upon Him. Being thus equipped He was ready for public ministry, and we, too, must know that same equipment by the Spirit.

The Genealogy (iii. 24-38). Matthew's record was royal, Luke's legal. Matthew gave the lineage of Joseph, Luke gave it of Mary. Matthew started with Abram, to whom the first promise of a nation was made. Luke went back to Adam — Adam, the first man, for he was writing of the Second Man, the Lord from heaven.

Following Christ's baptism was

His Temptation (iv. 1-13). It was pointed out that, when Mary yielded to the Will of the Lord, doubts and fears followed. When Jesus was ready for service, Satan was ready for sifting, and we must not expect to escape these things.

The temptation was threefold — the lust of the flesh, hunger — the lust of the eye, " showed unto Him all the kingdoms of the world " — the pride of life, a display of his power ! All temptations come through one of these three channels. That is why it is recorded that He was tempted in all points as we are. His victory may be our victory. " It is written " — the sharp, two-edged sword of the Word of God is the weapon the Devil fears more than any other.

In verse 5 the Devil showed the Lord all the kingdoms of the world in a moment of time. Compare that with Ephesians ii. 7 : " That in the *ages to come* He might shew the exceeding riches of His grace . . . " He is rich — we are rich in Him.

MINISTRY IN GALILEE. This begins at chapter iv. 14. Luke introduced this so differently from the others. " He taught in their synagogues." At Nazareth He read from Isaiah's prophecy " The Spirit of the Lord is upon Me, because He hath anointed Me to preach the gospel to the poor ; He hath sent Me to heal the broken-hearted, to preach deliverance to the captives, and recovering of sight to the blind, to set at liberty them that are bruised, to preach the acceptable year of the Lord. And He closed the book " (iv. 18-20).

The Old was closed because the New was beginning. " Think
not that I am come to destroy the law, or the prophets ; I am not
come to destroy, but to fulfil " (Matthew v. 17), and He was
already fulfilling.

Here is a strange paradox which has never ceased. They
" wondered at the gracious words " (iv. 22). " When they heard
these things, (they) were filled with wrath " (iv. 28). This was at
Nazareth, His own city, and amongst His own people. They thrust
Him out, so that He moved to Capernaum and through all Galilee,
where He healed many who were sick.

Jesus Teaching (Chapter v.). Much of the teaching is in the
other narratives ; therefore matters already commented upon are
by-passed. The last four verses are new.

New bottles for new wine (v. 36-39) New cloth on an old
garment makes the rent worse. New wine in old bottles causes
a burst. (Bottles then were made of skin). The Scribes and
Pharisees, the rabbis and other religionists, were so obsessed with
their laws and their traditions that they were not capable of receiving this new doctrine. They only burst with anger, and became
cruel in seeking reprisal. This new wine of the gospel must go
into new bottles, the bottles of the common people who heard
Him gladly and received His Word.

Jesus and the Sabbath (vi. 1-12). Both in the matter of
plucking the corn and healing the withered hand, Jesus declared
that keeping the Sabbath was a matter of principle and not a matter
of ritual.

Beatitudes and teaching (vi. 20-49). Most of this section is
a summary of the Sermon on the Mount, detailed by Matthew.
In these verses the Lord teaches

How to love	.....	your enemies.
How to give	.....	without seeking return.
How to judge	.....	self first, then fruit.
How to build	.....	on rock foundation.

The Centurion's servant (vii. 1-10). Worthiness for this healing
was not claimed by the centurion. None of us is worthy of anything, save judgment. Praise came from the people. This would
possibly be a rare exception, to find people praising a centurion,
who were not usually kind men. This man was. He was con-

cerned for his servant. He was also very humble. He never said that his servant was not worthy, but " I am not worthy that Thou shouldest enter under my roof." The Lord honoured and rewarded him for his faith, not his worthiness.

The Widow of Nain's son (vii. 11-18).

Christ's teaching concerning John (vii. 19-35). (See Matthew xi. 2-19).

Anointed by Mary (vii. 36-39). (See Mark xiv. 3-9).

The Parable of the Debtors (vii. 40-50). Simon had complained of the conduct of Mary, when he was failing badly in his own behaviour. The Lord dealt with Simon in this parable. According to our realisation of forgiveness and our sense of appreciation, so is the measure of our love. Mary was fully conscious of her indebtedness, but Simon lacked even first principles of courtesy.

The Sower and the Soil (viii. 1-15). Reference has been made to this parable both in Matthew and Mark, but an additional thought here may be helpful. It concerns the seed which fell by the wayside. This wayside was not the suggested footpath made by some passers-by.

Two men, possessing land adjoining, would plough, but not to the limit of their boundaries. Each would stop at a point where he could cut two more furrows. The reason for stopping short was one of mistrust. The first man could have ploughed further, but would not lest the other man claimed it as his. The second man could have ploughed but refrained lest there should be a quarrel as to ownership at the time of harvest. The result of this was that a strip of unploughed land was seen alongside each field. When the seed was cast, some of it fell on that wayside, and the birds of the air were awaiting it. This was lost harvest because neither man would plough. Why not? There need be no argument because the law required that a certain amount should be left as gleanings for the poor and the stranger.

Too much spiritual harvest is lost to-day because too many Christians are shelving their responsibilities believing these belong to someone else.

The Lighted Candle (viii. 16-18). Candles are made for light. Candlesticks are made that candles may be placed to advantage, not for themselves but for all who are in the house, in order that they may see. This world has been darkened spiritually and morally by sin. Christ is the Light of the world and we are to be His light-bearers. Hiding behind excuses, or what are considered to be other people's responsibilities, will never help anyone. " Let your light so shine before men, that they may see your good works, and glorify your Father which is in heaven " (Matthew v. 11).

Comment has already been made upon the next subjects. They include

Stilling the storm (viii. 22-25). See Mark iv. 36-41.

Healing the Maniac of Gadara (viii. 26-40). See Mark v. 1-21.

The raising of Jairus' daughter (viii. 41-56). See Mark v. 22-43.

Healing the issue of blood (viii. 43-48). See Mark v. 25-34.

The Twelve commissioned (ix. 1-6). See Mark vi. 7-11.

Feeding Five Thousand (ix. 10-17). See Mark vi. 35-44.

True Discipleship (ix. 18-27). See Mark viii. 27-30.

The Transfiguration (ix. 28-36). See Mark ix. 1-10.

Casting out demons (ix. 37-42). See Mark ix. 14-29.

Teaching (ix. 43/62). In the general teaching of the Lord, in chapter ix., is the statement of the last verse, "No man, having put his hand to the plough, and looking back, is fit for the kingdom of God." The illustration, when understood, is forceful. The wooden ploughs of those days were very crude and fragile, and only scraped the top of the earth. They had but one handle, hence the accuracy of the statement "hand" (not "hands") "to the plough."

If, whilst ploughing with so crude an implement, the ploughman interested himself in what was happening around and beyond, instead of what was in front, it would be possible for him to miss seeing a partly buried rock. To hit such an obstacle would mean the collapse of the plough, necessitating certain repairs. Delay at such a time could mean losing the short rainy season, and thereby missing the whole harvest. Man is being taught that, when he is called to put his hand to the plough of Christian service, then he should give that service his undivided attention. One cannot look back to the world and, at the same time, be successful in serving the Lord.

GALILEE TO JERUSALEM was the next section of the Lord's service to man. This commenced with

The Seventy sent out (x. 1-24). These disciples were not promised open-arm reception or the plaudits of men. Success was not a word in their vocabulary. They would meet enemies, would know resistance, would be refused, and yet they were not to make provision for this rejection by carrying extras. The one thing which was required of them was faithfulness. They must preach the Word, whether accepted or rejected.

The preacher to-day should not be the popular man. He should be the persistent man, refusing to adjust his preaching to the whims of the people. God is going to punish the rejector, and the same God is going to reward His faithful servants.

The Good Samaritan (x. 25-37). This parable, which was given in answer to a question, " Who is my neighbour ? ", has an interpretation not very well known to-day. Your neighbour is not the friend down the street whom you invite to your home for a social time, expecting him to return the compliment and do a little better ; nor the man you patronise because you will want to use his influence a little later. Your neighbour is the other man, who-ever he may be, who is in need of your help. The last words of this classic story are " Go, and do thou likewise."

Martha and Mary (x. 38-42). Martha's trouble was that she was cumbered, or bothered, because of much serving. In real eastern style Martha was preparing a great feast for the Lord. She was going to receive Him as an honoured guest. Becoming frustrated by service and by the lack of her sister's help, she became impolite to the One she was planning to honour. She charged Him with being responsible for her sister's neglect, as she addressed Him, " Lord, dost Thou not care that my sister hath left me to serve alone ? " She did not mean to do this, she was just bothered by work.

The Lord's answer was challenging. He said, " Martha, Martha, thou art careful and troubled about many things." These were the many dishes which she was preparing for this feast. " But one thing is needful." The word " thing " is " dish " in the original. The Lord was implying, " Martha, you have become confused in preparing a great feast and making Me to be an honoured guest, but I would prefer you to prepare an ordinary meal, in the common family dish, and to receive Me as one of the family."

God is not pleased with those who prepare a special feast for
Easter Sunday or Christmas, or even a Sunday morning, and then
have no time for Him during the rest of the year. He wants a
place in our everyday life. The Christian should always be serving
Him, and ever learning from Him. This is the " good part,"
which shall not be taken away from us.

Prayer (xi. 1-13). This prayer is commonly known as The
Lord's Prayer, which is not correct. The Lord's prayer, or the
recorded prayer which the Lord prayed, is John xvii, but in this
eleventh chapter one of His disciples said : " Lord, teach *us* to
pray ", and He replied, " When *ye* pray . . . ". This makes it a
disciple's prayer. The prayer is Jewish in its entirety. It concerns
the Kingdom, not the Church. It asks for daily bread. Men
meaninglessly recite these words to-day, with their larder full and
a bank security, yet they pray, " Give us *this* day our daily bread "
(Matthew vi. 11). They ask that their sins be forgiven to the same
measure that they forgive others — and most of us are unfor-
giving! The deliverance from evil refers to the " evil one."
Much of the prayer is against the day when the evil one, or Antichrist, will be reigning, his will being done on earth, and without
his mark there will be neither buying nor selling, so God must
provide the daily bread.

Against the evils of such days the Lord brought assurance in
His illustration which followed. If a father knows how to give
good gifts to his children when they ask, how much more shall
the Heavenly Father know how to minister to the good of His
children.

The rest of the chapter deals with the traditions of the fathers,
recorded elsewhere.

The Rich Fool (xii. 16/21). In the previous verses the Lord
was seeking to teach true values and right relationships. He warned
the people of the hypocrisy of the Pharisees and of their covetousness. All that a man may get out of this world will never be his
sufficiency in real need. Real need is often spiritual or moral,
and of what use is all the material gain in such a crisis? The
Lord is the only One Who can meet us spiritually, morally, and
materially. He knows us. He has every hair numbered, which
means that He knows us better than we know ourselves. Even the
common sparrow, despised by the wealthy man, is not forsaken
by the Lord.

Then comes the parable of the man who, in his greed, piled
up all that he needed for years to come. His only interest was *self*.

His only concern *now*. He had no lack in material things, but no accumulation in the moral toward his neighbour, nor in spiritual toward his God. Then God met him face to face, and he discovered himself to be the greatest pauper living. May we be more concerned for that eternal soul than for the transient body, and seek the things which are to come, " for where your treasure is : there will your heart be also " (xii. 34).

The Christian should conduct himself in the light of the knowledge that the Lord, Who has gone away, may return at any time, and we will not want to be ashamed at His appearing.

The Barren Fig Tree (xiii. 6-10). This was not a wild tree of the field, but a tree which had been cultivated, fed, pruned, and given all the attention that was possible, but it had never responded. For three successive years it had remained barren. The owner would have cut the tree down, but the vinedresser asked for another year of grace in order that he might nurture it.

The people would appreciate that the Lord told this against themselves. God had been gracious to Israel throughout the years, despite their rebellion and their failure to bring forth the fruit of righteousness. Then, when they were worthy of death, He sent forth His Son, and with His Son a final opportunity for the people to repent of their sin and to bring forth the fruit of repentance.

The Woman with an infirmity (xiii. 11-13).

Teaching (xiii. 14-35), concerning the Sabbath, mustard seed, leaven, the strait gate, etc.

The Sabbath Day (xiv. 1-14). See Mark iii. 1-6.

The Great Supper (xiv. 15-35). The Lord had prepared great things for His people, those whom He had chosen to be a peculiar treasure unto Himself, but they had rejected His invitation, His peace and pardon. They made every conceivable excuse. They wanted a king, like the other nations in the days of Samuel. They wanted gods of their own making which they could see, from Moses' day and down. They chose of the gods of the nations around in the days of the kings, and now they were choosing the traditions of the fathers in preference to the Word of God. Presently they were going to ask for Barabbas instead of Jesus. Their reasons were so foolish, and so lacked any sound judgment that, in the parable, the Lord showed to them how stupid their reasoning was, in the excuses they made for not attending this supper. One had bought a piece of ground, and must go and see it. Another had bought five yoke of oxen, and must go and prove them. The third had married a wife. Who ever heard of men buying ground before seeing it, or purchasing oxen before proving them ? If the business had already been contracted, everything else could wait. If he had married, his wife could be included in the invitation. There was not a single reason — they were excuses. They did not want the supper so the lord sent for the socially unworthy. When His own people refused Him, when scribes and rulers, Pharisees and Sadducees, rejected Him, He turned to the outcasts, the Gentile nations, and offered to them His salvation. " He came unto His own, and His own received Him not. But as many as received Him, to them gave He power to become the sons of God . . . " (John i. 11-12).

To-day the truth remains. Whilst the rich and the learned so often despise Him, He continues to receive the humble and penitent hearts.

The Lost Silver, Sheep, and Son (xv. 1-32). This has ever remained the classic chapter of Luke's writing. The piece of silver was not part of the woman's dowry or her savings, as is sometimes suggested. A lost coin would not cause so much distress, or, finding it, result in such widespread jubilation. The ten pieces of silver constituted the wedding chain, and would hold the same sentimental value as a wedding ring to-day. Yea, more ! Such carelessness could be used by the husband for divorce, if he chose, and, among some classes, a man had only to say " I divorce you " three times, and a woman was divorced with no court of appeal and no redress. Her condition was a pitiful one. With such a possibility the concern in the story can be appreciated.

The threefold parable is telling in its development.

The lost silver was lifeless material.

The lost sheep was a wandering individual.

The lost son was a wayward personality.

Each brought rejoicing to the owner upon reunion.

The silver might speak of the world which has been cursed by sin and has become a " Paradise lost," but is to be a " Paradise regained." The sheep might be a reminder of the sinner, man who had wandered from God, and He, as the Good Shepherd, sought that wandering lamb. The son would represent the child of God who has backslidden, one who has left the Father's house

and His bountiful supply for " the husks that the swine did eat,"
and then returns in repentance. The father waited with a heart
of love, but the boy must come back.

Silver and sheep are irresponsible things, but not a son. He
has reason, he makes decisions, and so is a responsible creature.
Is it not a tragedy that we, as brethren, have not more concern
for our wayward fellow brethren ? We frown on their conduct
instead of seeking to retrieve them.

The Unjust Steward (xvi. 1-18). This story has been a problem to many minds. As to an injustice there is no doubt. He had
wasted his master's property, resulting in his dismissal. Then he
robbed his master to buy off a few friends ; yet, in the face of
this, he is commended for his conduct.

Firstly, the commendation did not come from the Lord but from
the master whom he had wronged. Secondly, he was not praised
for his misbehaviour, but for the clever way in which, selfishly,
he made provision for his future.

To understand the application of the parable, which has been
the greatest problem, it must be remembered that the chapter
division was never made by Luke, but by more recent scholars
who, although they had good intentions, have not helped. The
three parables which precede this were given to the Pharisees and
scribes who were murmuring against the Lord because He was
receiving publicans and sinners. Having shown them the hardness
of the world toward the needy, and the love of the Father for the
sinner, He then addressed His disciples in continuation, saying,
in effect, that the world sought the prodigal whilst he had money,
but he failed to make friends with the world and so became the
loser.

If a man wants the friendship of the world he must become
worldly with it, endorse its sins, approve its behaviour, and then
it will receive him into its habitation. If he is not prepared to go
all the way, better not go any of it. It is a warning against backsliding, not an approval of sin. " No servant can serve two
masters."

The Rich Man and Lazarus (xvi. 19-31). Sufficient to say
that this was not a parable. In a parable the scripture either states
the fact or says " A certain . . . " The character is never named
because the character is fictitious. Here the beggar is named as
Lazarus. It is the only picture which is given of the life beyond the
grave. It also declares, in no uncertain words, that, as a tree

falls, so it lies — no second chance, no passing from one realm to another. As we decide in this life, so shall we dwell in the life beyond.

But men would be persuaded if some miracle happened, if someone rose from the dead ! This brought a negative answer from the Lord — and negative it will remain, because Jesus rose from the dead, but man still remains an unbeliever.

Further instructions concerning behaviour and faith are given in chapter xvii., and also truth concerning the

Second Advent (xvii. 20-37). The signs of the times and the suddenness of His return are foretold.

The Unjust Judge (xviii. 1/14). Although he had no mercy he yielded to the widow because of her importunity. If an unjust judge would respond to intercession, how much more will not the Just Judge answer those who call on Him, providing they call for that which is right and according to His Will.

This is illustrated by the two men who went up to the Temple to pray. The man who asked for something received that for which he asked. The other man received nothing because he asked for nothing.

The Rich Ruler (xviii. 18-30). See Mark x. 17-27.

The Blind Man at Jericho (xviii. 35-43). See Mark x. 46-53.

Zacchaeus (xix. 1-10). Nothing will hinder the man who has made up his mind to see Jesus, and nothing will prevent Jesus from finding him. The man may be little of stature, but he can climb a tree, and sycomore leaves cannot hide him from the Lord. When the two met there was a full surrender of the one, and a complete forgiveness from the Other. How weak are the excuses of most people for their lack of knowledge of the Lord !

The Parable of the Pounds (xix. 12-27). Again it is the lesson of reward for faithfulness. In the previous verses it concerned salvation ; in these verses it is service. The Lord has gone away, but to each of us He has given one or more talents, or abilities for service, against which there is to be a day of reckoning when we stand before the Bema of Christ. Then it will be stones or stubble. May we not be ashamed at that day !

JERUSALEM. This was where the Son of Man concluded His earthly ministry for man.

His entry into Jerusalem (xix. 28-48), amidst the praises of the people, annoyed the Pharisees. When they objected He said that, if the people were silenced, the stones would cry out, and archaeologically they have.

In the Temple He taught the people many things, concerning

The Parable of the Vineyard Labourers (xx. 9-18). This was against the people for their rejection of the prophets, and it was also a prophecy as to how they would presently deal with the Lord. " This is the heir ; come, let us kill Him."

The Tribute Money (xx. 19-26). See Mark xii. 13-17.

The Sadducees (xx. 27-42), who endeavoured to catch the Lord on the subject of resurrection, but whenever men sought to entangle the Lord they became victims of their own arguments. Thus it is to-day with all who seek to twist the Word of God.

The scribes also tried to use their subtlety, but the Lord silenced them, warning His disciples of their pretence and hypocrisy.

The Widow's two mites (xxi. 1-4). This scripture teaches that God does not measure our giving by the amount but by the proportion. He does not look at the money but at the motive. This woman was the biggest giver — she gave all.

The Signs of the times and His Second Advent occupy most of chapter xxi, instructing us to keep the upward look for our " redemption draweth nigh."

MINISTRY IN SUFFERING (Chapters xxii. - xxiv.)

LAST DAYS. This part of His ministry, the great purpose for which He came into the world, is recorded by all four narrators.

The Last Supper (xxii. 1-38). Luke gives more detail to this feast than any other writer — how the room was found, its preparation, the feast, and the conversations. Peter was warned of an impending fall.

The Garden (xxii. 39-53), where the Lord prayed and was betrayed.

For the trials, the Crucifixion, the Lord's death, burial, and resurrection, see Matthew and Mark.

The Emmaus Walk (xxiv. 13-35), is an exclusive record by Luke. The resurrected Lord joined company with two sad and disappointed travellers, and made their heart burn within them with the glow of a new hope and an assurance of victory, as He expounded unto them the Scriptures and, later, made Himself known in breaking the bread. The same Jesus still lives, still walks with His children, still communes with willing hearts, is still revealing the Scriptures and making Himself known to the communing heart.

This book, which opened amidst the joy of Christ's Birth, and recorded those great hymns of praise, closes with the same note of joy. " And they worshipped Him, and returned to Jerusalem with great joy : and were continually in the Temple, praising and blessing God. Amen."

ST. JOHN

"THIS IS MY BELOVED SON"

"God, Who at sundry times and in divers manners spake in time past unto the fathers by the prophets, hath in these last days spoken unto us by His Son, Whom He hath appointed heir of all things, by Whom also He made the worlds"
(HEBREWS i. 1-2)

INTRODUCTION

This fourth writer of the Gospel message is different in every respect from the other three men. One is not surprised when it is remembered that the writer was John, the son of Zebedee, one of the inner circle of the Apostles, the one who leaned on Jesus' bosom in his intimacy with his beloved Lord, and who is referred to as "the disciple whom Jesus loved."

When Jesus was on the Cross He saw the anguish of His mother, and knew that she needed, as a companion, one who would understand her deep longings and the things which she "pondered in her heart." He chose John. John was deep, he was different, and all this manifested itself when, years later, he wrote this narrative, and also the three Epistles which bear his name, as well as the Book of the Revelation.

The emphasis of the whole of this book is the Deity of Christ. Whilst Matthew, Mark, and Luke recorded the actions of Jesus, especially Matthew and Luke, John was content with the Words of Jesus. It was what He said, rather than what He did.

Much of the narrative of this book can be woven into the movements or actions of the other books. If John had not shared in the writing of the Gospel a great deal of its beauty would have been lost, because we would have been without a John iii. 16, or v. 24. The "I am's" are nowhere else. We would have been deprived of John x., concerning the Good Shepherd, and lost the comfort of John xiv. which has brought peace to so many troubled hearts, and so much solace in the hour of bereavement. "Let not your heart be troubled . . . In My Father's house are many mansions . . ."

These are but a few of the glories of this book which are found nowhere else, and it is all narrative, and more than narrative.

There is something deep, something holy, something that belongs to Deity. John uses expressions which are different from the other writers. He speaks of the " logos," the " Paraclete," etc. Both here and in his Epistles he makes constant reference to The Life, The Light, The Truth, and The Spirit, and tells us that these things and Love, are the very essence of God.

THE BOOK

The Analysis is threefold : —

(1) *The Public Manifestation of His Deity* seen in His ministry and miracles (Chapters i. - xii.)

(2) *A Private Revelation of His Deity* in the Upper Room and in the Garden (Chapters xiii. - xvii.)

(3) *The Final Consummation of His earthly work* revealed during His final days on earth (Chapters xviii. - xxi.)

To these are added a prologue and an epilogue.

PROLOGUE (i. 1-5)

The Eternal Word (i. 1-3). Mark begins his narration with the commencement of Christ's earthly ministry.

Matthew goes back farther and begins with Abraham, to whom the Covenant promises were made.

Luke goes back to the beginning of time, to the first man, Adam, and then introduces the Second Man, the Lord from heaven.

John travels beyond them all, back to before time. He steps into a past eternity and announces the Lord as the Eternal, Pre-existent Christ — Deity. " In the beginning was the Word, and the Word was with God, and the Word was God. The same was in the beginning with God. All things were made by Him ; and without Him was not anything made that was made."

This is a statement of fact as to the eternal, pre-existent Christ — One with the Father. No bolder, clearer statement of His Deity is needed. He was " The Word." He was with God and He was God. Words are expressions. The only way man has of expressing himself is in words. Animals have no words, therefore they have no self-expression. When man uses words, he not only expresses but he expresses himself. The other person only learns what he thinks, and how he reacts, by those words. Expressions and self, therefore, are closely related. Jesus was and is God. He is also the expression of God. That Word became flesh and dwelt among us. This is the story of His Incarnation.

He came to manifest the Father, and to make known the Will of God. He said on one occasion, " He that hath seen Me hath seen the Father " (xiv. 9).

He is identified with the Creative God of Genesis i. 1 : " All things were made by Him: and without Him was not anything made that was made " (i. 3).

The Light of Life (i. 4-5). " In Him was life ; and the life was the light of men." John the Baptist declared it in i. 7. Jesus discoursed it in chapter ix. John the Apostle developed it in his Epistles. Life is dependent upon light. Without the one there cannot be the other. Light is life. Here life is light, the light of knowledge and understanding.

THE PUBLIC MANIFESTATION OF HIS DEITY (Chs. i. - xii)

HIS MINISTRY AND MIRACLES

The incarnation (i. 14). Matthew and Luke tell of the coming of the Messiah from the human side, His genealogy and His entrance into the world. John speaks from the Divine angle and sees His exit from the Eternal. " And the Word was made flesh, and dwelt among us."

John — The Forerunner (i. 15-38). Because the Jews had ever looked for Elijah to come as the forerunner of the Messiah, they enquired concerning John, as to who he was. He declared himself not to be Elias, but yet the forerunner. John had the privilege of introducing the Messiah to the Jews, and the Saviour to the world. That same privilege is ours.

Calling the disciples (i. 39-51), Andrew, Peter, and Philip. " Philip findeth Nathanael." When Jesus saw Nathanael He said : " Behold an Israelite indeed, in whom is no guile ! " That was a great statement from an all-knowing God. Few of us could be referred to as guileless. Nathanael was surprised that the Lord knew him, and enquired : " Whence knowest Thou me ? " The Lord's reply was : " When thou wast under the fig tree, I saw thee " — away in the quiet place of communion and meditation. No man ever goes there without the Lord knowing it.

Marriage in Cana (ii. 1-11). Jesus is interested in our physical and material life, as well as the spiritual. Marriage was established by God and is honourable, and He graced this one with His presence.

The subject of the wine will not be broached. Sufficient to say that the wine of the East and the alcohols of to-day are two different things, and also that the Lord never acted contrary to the teaching of Scripture. The Scripture states that " Wine is a mocker, strong drink is raging ; and whosoever is deceived thereby is not wise " (Proverbs xx. 1).

In the conversational part of the story Mary went to Jesus saying : " They have no wine." She evidently felt that He was able to help. His reply was : " Woman, what have I to do with thee ? " — more correctly, " What is that to do with Me ? " — " Mine hour is not yet come." This was no rude rebuff, as might be considered to-day according to our standards of conversation. Although His hour had not yet come, within a very short while He was doing the very thing He said He could not do. One has ofttimes wondered what happened between the request of Mary and the miracle of Jesus which brought Him unto the hour. The Lord has ever worked by schedule. He has a strict timetable.

He had a time to arrive. " But when the *fulness of the time* was come, God sent forth His Son, made of a woman . . . " (Galatians iv. 4).

He had a time to commence His ministry. " Mine *hour* is not yet come " (John ii. 4).

He had a time to die. " . . . And no man laid hands on Him ; for His *hour* was not yet come " (John viii. 20).

There was a time for the Holy Spirit. " And when the day of Pentecost was *fully* come " (Acts ii. 1).

There is a time for His return. " But of that day and that *hour* knoweth no man . . . but the Father " (Mark xiii. 32).

Many more could be listed.

The statement " This *beginning* of miracles did Jesus in Cana of Galilee " (ii. 11), explodes all the theories, traditions, and foolishness of the Apocrypha, and other such writings, concerning the miracles of His childhood. Those days of His childhood have been withheld from us by the Spirit of God.

Cleansing the Temple (ii. 13 - 22). It should be recognised that there were two cleansings of the Temple. In this instance it was at the beginning of the Lord's ministry. The other was three years later, during the week of His Passion.

This demonstration of His power, with its accompanying ministry, made deep impressions on some lives, among them a learned member of the Sanhedrin, named

Nicodemus (iii. 1-21). So impressed was he that he came to the Lord secretly by night, acknowledging Him to be a God-sent teacher, and enquiring of Him the way of salvation. Too much has been said about Nicodemus coming secretly to enquire of salvation, and not enough of the bold testimony of Nicodemus when, at personal risk, he sought to defend Jesus before the Council (vii. 50-52); and again, later, when he secured the Body of Jesus for proper burial. Better come at night than not come at all, or stand at a distance and criticise.

To this learned man the Lord taught clearly and plainly " Ye must be born again."

John's Testimony (iii. 22/36). Some division of opinion sent men to John concerning the ministry of Jesus and the followers who appeared to be switching from John to Jesus, which brought John's wonderful reply: "He must increase, but I must decrease." Oh, that we all might learn such a lesson!

> the other a woman.
> the other a sinner.
> the other unlearned.
> the other a Gentile.
> the other, He went to her.

The Woman of Samaria (iv. 1-42). From conversation with an intelligent and religious man, Jesus moved to converse with a common, sinful woman — a Samaritan. Note the points of contrast : —

One a man	.....	.....	the other a woman.
One religious	.....	.....	the other a sinner.
One learned	.....	.....	the other unlearned.
One a Jew	.....	.....	the other a Gentile.
One came to Him	.....	the other He went to her.

He went out of His way to offer this woman the Water of Life. " And He must needs go through Samaria." The woman never appreciated all that was implied when Jesus offered her Water which would ever satisfy her thirst. She thought of natural thirst — He was speaking of spiritual thirst. But her request was. " Sir, give me this water," and He did.

We do not have to understand theology before we can be saved. We accept salvation by faith, and enjoy revelation thereafter.

This story has been very simply summed up thus : —
  " The Saviour of the World
  Met at Sychar's Well,
  A Samaritan Woman,
  And gave her Salvation's Water
  And she became a Saved Woman
  And a Soul Winner."

In His conversation He also taught her, and us, a great deal about true worship. " But the hour cometh, and now is, when the true worshippers shall worship the Father in spirit and in truth ; for the Father seeketh such to worship Him. God is a Spirit ; and they that worship Him must worship Him in spirit and in truth."

Ministering in Galilee (v. 43-54). Following these conversations Jesus began His ministry of healing, and performing His miracles. All the miracles of the Lord, as recorded by all four writers, have been classified to set forth the demonstrations of His power, thus : —

(1) *Provision for Human Need*

(a)	Marriage of Cana	John ii. 1-11
(b)	Feeding of five thousand	John vi. 1-14
(c)	Draught of fishes	Luke v. 4-11

(2) *Power over elements*

(a)	Commanding the waves	Luke viii. 22-25
(b)	Walking on the sea	John vi. 17-21

(3) *Power over disease*

(a)	Healing the leper	Mark i. 40-45
(b)	Healing ten lepers	Luke xvii. 11-19
(c)	Sick of the Palsy	Matthew ix. 1-8
(d)	Withered hand	Luke vi. 6-12
(e)	Pool of Bethesda	John v. 1-16
(f)	Blind man	Mark viii. 22-26
(g)	Pool of Siloam	John ix. 1-41
(h)	Two blind men	Matthew xx. 30-34
(i)	Healing of deaf	Mark vii. 31-37
(j)	Casting out evil spirits	Mark ix. 14-29
(k)	Woman with infirmity	Luke xiii. 11-17
(l)	Issue of blood	Mark v. 25-34
(m)	Centurion's servant	Luke vii. 1-10
(n)	Syrophenician Woman	Mark vii. 24-30

(4) *Control over death*
   (a) Jairus' daughter   .....   Mark v. 22-43
   (b) Widow of Nain's son .....   Luke vii. 11-15
   (c) Raising of Lazarus   .....   John xi. 1-46

Bethesda's Pool (v. 1-47). In defence of the miracle on the man at Bethesda's Pool and the opposition of the Jews because it was performed on the Sabbath Day, the Lord reminded those who desired to bring Him into the limitations of the law that the same law required that everything should be done in the mouth of two or three witnesses. Therefore Jesus called upon those witnesses for His authority : —

   (1) John the Baptist   33-35
   (2) The Works themselves   36
   (3) The Father   37

Feeding Five Thousand (vi. 1-14). This has been recorded by all four narrators. John gives extra information. He tells how the loaves and fishes were procured. "There is a lad here." Some have suggested that he was a baker's boy who sold such things where crowds were gathered together. Two things are against such a suggestion. With five thousand hungry people around he would have been sold out ; and, secondly, Jesus would not have taken from a baker's boy his master's property. That would have been teaching the boy to steal. The quantity of food would have been the boy's personal lunch which evidently he had forgotten to eat in the excitement of the day. Then the Lord asked for it — a big request from a hungry boy ! It gives a picture of full, voluntary surrender, in which the boy lost nothing for he ate with the rest, as much as he wanted, but had the added thrill that his lunch had fed the five thousand. Our little can go a long way when it is in the hands of the Lord.

After feeding the five thousand, the multitude followed Jesus only for the loaves and fishes. He reproved them for their carnal desires, and taught them to seek the Giver rather than the gifts, telling them that He would feed and satisfy the hungry soul — and He is the same to-day.

Out of this miracle John leads into a discourse on the Bread of Life, but, before so doing, Jesus retired to the mountain for solitude. The disciples took a ship, with the intention of going to Capernaum but, instead, encountered a storm. Jesus came to them

Walking on the sea (vi. 15-21). The disciples never recognised Him until He spoke, saying : " It is I ; be not afraid." Then they received Him into the ship. The statement used by the Lord, " It is I ", is noteworthy. In the Greek it is " I am ", and would make it the first of the " I am's " recorded by John.

" I AM " is the great, unchanging, ever-present Name of Jehovah-God, and of His Son, Jesus Christ. Said God to Moses : " I AM that I AM," and again " I AM hath sent me unto you " (Exodus iii. 14). Said Jesus : —

I AM, be not afraid	John vi. 20
I AM the Bread of Life	John vi. 35
I AM the Light of the World	John viii. 12
If ye believe not that I AM He, ye shall die in your sins	John viii. 24
Before Abraham was, I AM	John viii. 58
I AM the door	John x. 9
I AM the Good Shepherd	John x. 11
I AM the Son of God	John x. 36
I AM the resurrection, and the life	John xi. 25
I AM the Way, the Truth, and the Life	John xiv. 6
I AM the True Vine	John xv. 1

Peter's Confession (vi. 66-71). Because of a withdrawal of many of the disciples, the Lord said to the twelve : " Will ye also go away ? " Peter's reply was : " Lord, to whom shall we go ? Thou hast the words of eternal life. And we believe, and are sure that Thou art Christ, the Son of the Living God." To this strong affirmation which Peter made on behalf of the twelve, Jesus had to tell them that " one of you is a devil ", and it is in the definite article — " One of you is *the* devil," referring to Judas.

The Feast of Tabernacles (vii. 1/39). This was a great annual festival which lasted for eight days, during which time the people dwelt in booths. A great deal of reasoning was going on as to whether the Lord would attend this Feast because the Jews were seeking His life. However, their reasonings were soon settled for, in the midst of the Feast, Jesus made His appearance in the Temple, and on the last day "That great day of the Feast, Jesus stood and cried saying, If any man thirst, let him come unto Me and drink." He was speaking of the Holy Spirit not yet given but Who, when He was given, would flow from them in an abundance of life and power.

Night on Olivet (viii. 1). Read the last verse of chapter vii. and the first verse of chapter viii. together, without the chapter division. " And every man went unto his own house. Jesus went unto the mount of Olives." No man invited Jesus to his home. How many nights did Jesus spend on the mountain ?

Woman in adultery (viii. 2-11). This was a shameful act on the part of the scribes and Pharisees, both toward the Holy Son of God and toward the sinful woman, but the Lord caused them to walk out in shame themselves, as He said : " He that is without sin among you, let him first cast a stone at her."

Jesus, the Light of the world (viii. 12-59). See comments on " light " in the Epistles of John.

The Lord left no doubt as to the personality of the Devil as He reasoned with these arguing Pharisees.

Healing the Blind Man (ix. 1-41). He Who had declared Himself to be the Light of the World now showed Himself to be the light of the blind, bringing this man out of physical darkness, and then out of spiritual darkness. The Pharisees did their utmost to disprove or disqualify the miracle, but all reasoning and every unkind act fell dead against the concrete living testimony : " One thing I know, that, whereas I was blind, now I see." Such a testimony to-day would be the biggest death blow to all liberalism.

The Good Shepherd (x. 1-18). This will ever be one of the choice chapters of the Bible. Three of the " I AM's " are in this chapter.

The story may be better interpreted if it is appreciated that there are two different sheepfolds. The shepherd roams the countryside during the period of May to October, and he would use the public sheepfolds. On his return the sheep would be in the fold belonging to the farm. During this time, while the shepherd is home, the porter would be responsible. However, as soon as the shepherd comes for the sheep, and they hear his voice, they are ready to follow.

Whilst the Good Shepherd has gone Home, He has left His sheep here under the care of the Porter, Who would be the Holy Spirit. We shall be led by the Spirit until the day arrives when we shall hear the voice of our coming Lord and we will be caught up to meet Him.

As to the sheepfolds out in the open country, these, being public property, had no doors, only a doorway. If one shepherd occupied the fold that night he would lie across the doorway. If several shepherds were present then they would take it in turns to stand in that doorway, but the shepherd did actually become the door. No wild animal could get in, no lamb could get out. Jesus said : "*I AM the door.*"

With regard to the shepherd, he gave himself to the care, provision and protection of the sheep. If circumstances required that a shepherd must temporarily leave his sheep, he would engage a hireling. Hirelings were men waiting to be hired, hence the name. These had but one interest — the money they would get for the task. Having no personal interest in the sheep, if any danger should arise, the hireling sought the safety of his own life first. Said Jesus : "*I AM the Good Shepherd :* the good shepherd giveth his life for the sheep " (x. 11).

Teaching on His Divinity and Eternal Life (x. 19 - 42)   In this discourse, which took place in Solomon's Porch, the Jews had said : " If Thou be the Christ, tell us plainly." He did. He said, amidst many things : " I and My Father are one," and, " I AM the Son of God." This was His own confirmation of a truth which had been declared by many.

John the Baptist called Jesus the Son of God							John i. 34
Mark	,,	,,	,,	,,	,,	,,	Mark i. 1
John	,,	,,	,,	,,	,,	,,	John xx. 31
Nathanael	,,	,,	,,	,,	,,	,,	John i. 49
Peter	,,	,,	,,	,,	,,	,,	Matthew xvi. 16
Martha	,,	,,	,,	,,	,,	,,	John xi. 27
The Disciples	,,	,,	,,	,,	,,	,,	Matthew xiv. 3
Gabriel	,,	,,	,,	,,	,,	,,	Luke i. 32
The Centurion	,,	,,	,,	,,	,,	,,	Matthew xxvii. 54
Evil spirits	,,	,,	,,	,,	,,	,,	Matthew viii. 29
God	,,	,,	,,	,,	,,	,,	Matthew iii. 17
Jesus here calls Himself		,,	,,	,,	,,	John x. 36

It is the language of the Devil to say " IF Thou be the Son of God."

Raising Lazarus (xi. 1 - 46).   Jesus had been notified concerning the sickness of Lazarus yet delayed His help for two days, during which time the helpless condition of Martha and Mary became a hopeless one. Lazarus was no longer sick, he was dead. Do we not often face this problem in life, the apparently unanswered prayer which puts upon our lips that word of doubt — " IF " ? " . . . If Thou hadst been here, my brother had not died." We do not always appreciate the ways of God. This delay was to bring temporary grief to the women, but greater glory to God.

Through that death came the revelation of another of those glorious " I AM's ", which has brought comfort to thousands upon thousands of sad hearts in the hour of bereavement and of hopelessness. " Jesus said unto her, *I AM the resurrection, and the life;* he that believeth in Me, though he were dead, yet shall he live : and whosoever liveth and believeth in Me shall never die " (xi. 25-26).

In demonstrating His power, the Lord never once did by the supernatural anything that man could do in the natural. This miracle gives a perfect example of it. " Jesus said, Take ye away the stone " and " Loose him, and let him go." Jesus could have done those things but He did not. He only did what man could not do — raise the dead. The Lord has never encouraged laziness, or indifference to our own responsibilities.

Plot on Christ's Life (xi. 47-57). Strange as it may seem, the rulers sought to destroy the One Who came to save. Men curse the Name of Him Who came to bring blessing to all men. Why is it that we do not allow Him to reign in our lives ? He is the only One Who is able to control all things.

Anointed by Mary (xii. 1-9). The Lord was back with his friends at Bethany. He had done a great deal for that family. He had restored Lazarus to his sisters, but there was much more. Jesus was everything to Mary. Her sins had been forgiven, she had sat at His feet and learned of Him, and now, as an expression of her love, she broke over His feet a box of precious ointment. Her hair, which was the glory of women and, because of it, they kept covered by a veil, she took and used upon those same blessed feet which had carried so much into their home and lives. This was a love which was giving all that it had. It revealed the depth of her character.

It also revealed another character. What was worship to the loving heart was waste to the greedy heart, and Judas began to show his nature. The Lord, Who has respect unto the humble but knoweth the proud afar off, said : " Let her alone ; against the day of My burying hath she kept this." She had been saving this ointment for anointing the dead, but had learned that it was better to give a bouquet to the living rather than to the dead. A word of praise and encouragement to-day is worth more than all of the eulogies to-morrow.

Entering Jerusalem (xii. 12/15). See note on Matthew xxi.

Foretelling His death (xii. 23/36). These words must have been heavy on the heart of the Lord, as not only did He intimate His death with such words as "Except a corn of wheat fall into the ground and die, it abideth alone; but if it die, it bringeth forth much fruit," but He also indicated the kind of death. "And I, if I be lifted up from the earth, will draw all men unto Me."

In His struggle with the thought of death, He gained a victory when He said : " Father, glorify Thy Name," to which there came the response : " I have both glorified it, and will glorify it again."

The section closes with a challenge to the people to believe Him and, in so doing, to believe the Father. If they would, they would honour the Father. As to the Pharisees, they only honoured themselves, for they preferred the praises of men.

PRIVATE REVELATION OF HIS DEITY (Chapters xiii. - xvii.)

IN THE UPPER ROOM

More is learned from John of the intimacy of the Lord and His disciples in those sacred hours than from any other writer, because it was he who, at that time, leaned on Jesus' bosom.

Washing their feet (xiii. 1-17). To understand " And supper being ended " in verse 2, when it appeared only to have begun, it must be borne in mind that here is a record of two feasts. When the Lord sat down with His disciples it was to keep the Feast of the Passover, an annual event. Before He arose from that table He had instituted the second feast, known as The Lord's Supper, or the Breaking of Bread, or The Communion.

As the first feast was beginning to come to an end, Jesus arose and washed His disciples' feet. This washing was perfomed always by servants at the beginning of a feast, but the disciples had no servants and, evidently, the Lord had none, when He should have had twelve. All would have ministered to the Lord, but none was willing to minister to the other. The Lord, therefore, had to teach them humility in service. Peter was not willing for the Lord to be humbled on his account, but neither was he willing to offer to change places. How like most of us !

The traitor revealed (xiii. 18-30). " Verily, verily, I say unto you, that one of you shall betray Me." This caused consternation and enquiry amongst the disciples. " Lord, is it I ? " Jesus answered : " He it is, to whom I shall give a sop, when I have dipped it."

An explanation of this would be helpful. Sometimes at feasts given by Easterners, there could be an offended guest at the table. It was customary to have guests sit in an order of priority. Thus the host would say to one : " Come up higher ", and to another : " Sit down there." If a guest should consider that he had been wrongly placed and was entitled to a higher position, such a person would sulk, refuse to eat, and make things generally unpleasant. The host could not change the seating arrangement because that might upset those who were already occupying the higher seats. Only one thing would remedy the tragedy. The host would seek the daintiest morsel from the dish upon the table (which could be a sheep's eye !) and, taking it from that dish with his own hand, place the morsel right into the mouth of the offended guest. Immediately everyone would be happy. This was called the " giving of the sop." It told the offended guest that the host held no grievance.

This is of great importance because many declare that Judas had no alternative. He had been elected to do this thing. Such is not true. Foreknowledge might know his decision, but it does not control. The Lord gave Judas an opportunity to repent when He offered to him the sop. "After the sop Satan entered into him." This declares that Judas was still a free agent. Not until he had determined to go ahead with his crime did Satan enter into him. Then he became Satan's tool. Matthew indicates that Judas left the table before the Lord instituted the new Supper. There is no room at the Lord's Table for a traitor; such who sit there eat and drink damnation to themselves.

After giving His disciples a new commandment, that they love one another, and having told Peter of the fall he was going to encounter, the Lord left the Upper Room, in the company of His disciples, for

THE GARDEN

The Comforter (xiv. 1-31). When the disciples moved away from the Upper Room into the darkness of the night, and accompanied their Master on His way to the Garden, they were very heavy of heart. Much had been revealed to them. There was the sense of losing their Lord. As they took that journey the Lord

sought to reassure them with those familiar words : " Let not
your heart be troubled : . . . I go to prepare a place for you. And
if I go . . . I will come again."

Chapters xiv. - xvi. are the Lord's conversation, which have
to be fitted into the actions which the other three writers record.

The Lord promised that the disciples' reward would be to be
with Him later. When Thomas questioned where and how, He
replied : " I AM the way, the truth, and the life ; no man cometh
unto the Father but by Me."

I am the way	.....	.....	.....	follow Me.
I am the truth	.....	.....	.....	believe Me.
I am the life	.....	.....	.....	rest in Me.

If we love Him and obey Him, His promise is that He will
not leave us comfortless, but will send another Comforter, even
the Spirit of Truth. His work would be not only to comfort but
to lead us into all truth. This He has been doing throughout this
present dispensation, which is the dispensation of the Holy Spirit.

The bequest of Peace (xiv. 27-31). " The peace of God,
which passeth all understanding." Peace was a common word to
the Easterner. The word " Salaam " was their everyday salutation.
" Peace be unto you," and the reply would be, " Unto you be
peace," but, like many of our expressions, it became meaningless
through repetition. A man might meet another with the intent of
doing him harm, and yet would say " Salaam." That was the
reason why Jesus said : " Peace I leave with you, My peace I
give unto you ; *not as the world giveth,* give I unto you." The
world might not mean what it says — Jesus certainly does.

I AM the Vine (xv. 1). Still journeying toward the Garden,
the possibility was that they passed a vine or a vineyard, and so
the Lord took up another line of thought suggested by what He
saw. " I AM the true vine, and my Father is the Husbandman."

A vine, so far as the main plant is concerned, does not bear
fruit. It is responsible for pulsating life through all of the branches
so that they become the fruitbearers. Even so, the Life of the
Lord is the life of the believer, and the believer is the producer
of the fruit of the Spirit so long as he abides. If the fruit is to
be of the best quality a great deal of pruning is necessary. The
pruners strip the vines of every branch, leaving only the stock.
In the spring the stock would reshoot, so that next year's fruit is
actually on new branches. Would this not suggest that we cannot
bear fruit upon past experience but only by constant abiding ?

A branch is not that which attaches itself. It is something which comes forth from the vine. This is emphasized in the Lord's illustration and application. "Ye have not chosen Me, but I have chosen you, and ordained you, that ye should go and bring forth fruit, and that your fruit should remain" (xv. 16). When we are producing fruit then we are imbibing joy.

This abiding will produce two things, the

Friendship of Christ (xv. 13-17), and the

Enmity of the world (xv. 18-27).

The Holy Spirit promised (xvi. 1-31). As they arrived at the Garden of Gethsemane, the Lord told them again of His departure, which was now at hand, and also its necessity. He told them that, upon His departure, there would come the Holy Spirit Who would be their source of supply. He would convict the world of sin, but would guide them into all truth.

Fifty days after His departure the promise was fulfilled. The Holy Spirit descended on the Day of Pentecost, and has remained in the world as the strength of the believer ever since.

The Lord concluded this long conversation with these words: "These things have I spoken unto you, that in Me ye might have peace. In the world ye shall have tribulation; but be of good cheer; I have overcome the world."

At this point He withdrew Himself from them, bidding them to watch and pray. Matthew says: "He went a little farther, and fell on His face, and prayed." John records

The Lord's Prayer (xvii. 1-26). This prayer was on the eve of His suffering. Although He knew it, yet He never mentioned it. He had already prayed "Nevertheless not as I will, but as Thou wilt" (Matthew xxvi. 39).

Two things made the subject of this prayer. The first was the glorification of the Father, and the other the care and protection of His children, not only the disciples but all believers. "Neither pray I for these alone, but for them also which shall believe on Me through their word; That they all may be one . . . Father, I will that they also, whom Thou hast given Me, be with Me where I am; that they may behold My glory, which Thou hast given Me." The Lord, Who prayed that prayer in the shadows of the Garden, has been praying it ever since in the glory of the Throne, and our joy and assurance are that the prayer is already an answered one.

CONSUMMATION (Chapters xviii. - xx.)

LAST DAYS. After His prayer alone in the Garden with His
Father, the Lord joined His disciples again, saying : " Rise, let
us be going : behold, he is at hand that doth betray Me "
(Matthew xxvi. 46). So they moved farther into the Garden
across the brook Cedron.

The Betrayal (xviii. 1/12). Judas, the traitor, was awaiting
Him, with a band of men. The Lord showed to these men His
power and their helplessness as He said to them: "Whom seek ye?"
and they all fell to the ground, again showing that His death was
not the result of treachery, nor because of the power of men —
they had none. It was because of sin, the sins of all men. He
was giving Himself an offering for sin.

Peter came to the Lord's defence with the use of a sword,
but that sword had to be sheathed. My kingdom is not of the
world order, Jesus once said, or my servants would fight. (v. 36)

Before Caiaphas (xviii. 13 - 24).

Peter's Denial (xviii. 25 - 27).

Before Pilate (xviii. 28 - 40).

Scourged (xix. 1 - 12).

Condemned (xix. 13 - 15).

Crucified (xix. 16 - 37).

These verses have been dealt with in the other narratives.
The reader is referred back to them.

John, the Beloved, does give an additional scene. It concerns
himself.

Jesus, on the Cross, did not think of Himself. He had prayed
for His enemies. He had made a promise to the dying thief. Now
He made provision for His mother who, it is presumed, was
a widow, as Joseph is never mentioned. As a mother she had
already witnessed too much, so the Lord looked down upon her
in her anguish and said: "Woman, behold thy son." Then,
looking toward John, He said: "Behold thy mother," and from
that hour John took her away and cared for her. But did not
Mary have other children who could care for her? Yes, and no
doubt they would have done so as a duty, but Mary was in need

of more than duty. She needed understanding and sympathy, which the brethren of Jesus could not give because they did not believe in Him.

Both Mary and John understood the Lord as no one else did. Therefore they could commune together concerning Him and comfort each other's heart.

If Jesus thought of others while suffering, how much more now that He is in glory ! If Jesus, whilst on the Cross, could make provision for a widow, will He not provide for widows now that He is on the Throne ?

The Resurrection (xx. 1-31). The women were the first messengers of the resurrection because they were first at the tomb, and that was because they were first in their love. If only the women of our land knew how much the Lord has done for them ! It is only in the countries where the gospel has been proclaimed that women are free.

The position of the grave clothes is carefully recorded as it is the evidence that the body was never stolen. The resurrected Christ breaks every fetter.

Mary Magdalene was the first to meet the Lord.

Appearances (xxi. & xxii.). He appeared

(1) To Mary Magdalene.
(2) To ten disciples (Thomas missing).
(3) To eleven disciples (including Thomas).
(4) At Tiberias where He gave His disciples a multitude of fish.

At Peter's suggestion the disciples had returned to their former occupation, but they were not successful. They toiled all night and caught nothing. The Lord had called them to be fishers of men, and still intended them to follow their new calling even though He was no longer with them in person. When those tired, hungry, wet and cold men reached shore, every need had been met in a fire and breakfast awaiting them, a provision that was independent of the draught of fishes the Lord had given them from the sea.

Then came the final conversation of this book of conversations. " Simon, son of Jonas, *lovest* thou Me ? " Lord, you know that I am *fond* of You. This was repeated, Peter using a different word from the one his Lord used. Peter had lost out. His first love had waned into a fondness. Jesus was seeking to restore Peter, not remind him of a threefold denial as some say. Jesus removes sin to be remembered against us no more. The third time Jesus came down to Peter's level. Peter, are you really *fond* of Me ? This grieved Peter and yet he could not rise to that first love, that Divine love.

The day came when Peter proved his *love* for his Master in no uncertain way.

EPILOGUE

Like the prologue, it makes this book different from the others, for John's last words are : " And there are also many other things which Jesus did, the which, if they should be written every one, I suppose that even the world itself could not contain the books that should be written. Amen."

Earthly kingdoms may end (Matthew).

The Servant's work may terminate (Mark).

The Lord's humanity may cease (Luke).

but His Deity knows no end. " And there are also many other things."

THE ACTS OF THE APOSTLES

BEGUN AND CONTINUED

*" And it shall come to pass afterward, that I will pour out
My Spirit upon all flesh ; and your sons and your daughters
shall prophesy, your old men shall dream dreams, your young
men shall see visions ; And also upon the servants and upon
the handmaids in those days will I pour out My Spirit . . .
And it shall come to pass, that whosoever shall call on the
Name of the Lord shall be delivered . . . "* (JOEL ii. 28-32)

INTRODUCTION

J. Sidlow Baxter has pointed out that this book holds the
same relationship with the New Testament as the book of Joshua
does with the Old Testament.

Joshua is not a part of the Law, yet it is a continuation of it.

Acts is not a part of the Gospel, yet it is a continuation of it.

Joshua is not one of the Historical books, yet it introduces
them.

Acts is not one of the Epistles, yet it introduces them.

Joshua is a liaison between Law and History.

Acts is a liaison between the Gospel and the Epistles.

This is appreciated from the two keywords " Begun " and
" Continued."

The title of the book is not the best. It was attached to the
book by translators at a much later date, possibly when they were
compiling the Bible. It is, of course, a companion volume to the
Gospel and, at the same time, a continuation volume. The weakness of the title is quickly seen when it is realised that the greater
part of the book concerns Peter and Paul. The eleven apostles
are only mentioned once, Judas and Matthias twice, and John five
times. Other prominent characters such as Stephen, Philip, Barnabas, Mark, Silas and Timothy were not apostles. It has been
suggested that the " Acts of the Holy Spirit " might have been a
more fitting title, or Luke might have called it " The Second
Treatise."

The Author of this book was the Holy Spirit. His penman
was Luke. This has never been questioned. Like the gospel
which bears his name, it was addressed to Theophilus.

As stated in the introduction to the Gospel according to Luke, it is natural that, when some unusual thing happens which catches the imagination of the world, many people want to express their views, but it cannot be assumed that all which is written is authoritative. This has always been so, and is true to-day. People become confused, and know not what they should believe.

As an instance, during World War II many newspaper editors and correspondents, some of them eye-witnesses in particular theatres, expressed their opinions about war, its rights and wrongs, its conduct, etc., but most of us would consider that the memoirs of Sir Winston Churchill were authoritative. He knew the secrets. He had the overall vision. So in the days of the Lord, amidst the calculations and miscalculations of men, the Spirit of God moved upon the systematic mind of Luke to write, as he declares in Luke i. 1-4. Now the same writer continues, reminding his addressee that the former things were only the beginning of the ministry of Jesus — what He said and did. The former concerned the Life that was limited to the flesh. The latter concerns the Glorified Lord operating in the fulness of His resurrection life. Did He not say to His disciples : " . . . He that believeth on Me, the works that I do shall he do also ; and greater works than these shall he do ; because I go unto the Father " (John xiv. 12).

THE BOOK

The theme of the book is the Supremacy of the Holy Spirit in the Church. It is the progress of the Gospel as it passes from its initial establishment into the development of the Church, as it moves from Jerusalem through Asia to Rome, and to the uttermost parts of the earth, as it expands from Jews to Gentiles.

On earth Christ completed His work in Redemption.

In heaven Christ continues His work in the Church.

The work of Redemption He did alone. His present work is accomplished through the ministry of His servants.

The book has two major divisions : —

HOME MISSIONS (Chapter i. - vii) — In Jerusalem.

OVERSEAS MISSIONS (Chapters viii. - xxviii) — In Samaria and to the uttermost parts of the earth.

HOME MISSIONS (Chapters i. - vii.) — In Jerusalem.

Luke's starting point is

The Ascending Lord, which is where the future ministry begins; but, firstly, he reminisces a little, thus creating a link with the past. He refers to the resurrection, and the disciples' return to Jerusalem; also the promise given by the two men in white apparel that this same Jesus would so come in like manner as they had seen Him go.

After their return from the Mount of Olives to the city, the disciples appointed a successor to Judas. He had to be an eyewitness of the life and death of the Lord. Every man who takes any office in the Church should be a witness to the things of God, a man who has met with God, and knows the power of God. Matthias was chosen and continued with the apostles.

IN JERUSALEM (Chapters i. - vii)

PENTECOST (ii) " And when the day of Pentecost was fully come . . . ". This was nothing new. It was one of the seven Feasts established by the Lord in Leviticus xxiii. It was observed annually, fifty days after the presentation of Firstfruits. The Jews still keep it in commemoration of the giving of the Law at Sinai.

The day was not new, but what happened on that particular day was new. Yea, it was the fulfilment of that which the Old Testament had anticipated, and which the Lord had promised. " If I go away I will send you another Comforter, even the Holy Spirit of Promise."

The Lord had bidden His disciples tarry at Jerusalem and wait for the promise of the Father. One hundred and twenty of His followers were doing this. They were of one accord in one place, when the Holy Spirit descended upon them and endued them with a power which previously they had not possessed. Thus a group of individual people was fused into one body. The timid were made brave. Here ordinary people became the founders of the greatest community of all time — the Church.

Whilst this work does not permit detail, two important truths must be declared because of the abundance of misinterpretation which surrounds this chapter : —

(a) *Tongues* (ii. 1-13). There is a difference between " speaking in tongues," as in the Acts of the Apostles, and " the gift of tongues," as mentioned in 1 Corinthians xii. In the former,

the act was one of worship, and was Godward. In the latter, it
was a ministry toward the Church and was manward. Therefore
it always required an interpreter for man to understand.

(b) *Peter's preaching.* It has been commonly asserted that
God gave this gift to enable the Apostles to preach to all and
sundry who were there from the surrounding nations, and that,
when men learned to speak languages other than their own through
Missionary Colleges, this gift was withdrawn. This is far from
truth.

The ministry of tongues was not given to Peter and the eleven
for preaching. It was given to the hundred and twenty in the
Upper Room for praising. There was no one in the Upper Room
to whom they could preach. The people outside, who could
overhear what was happening inside and could hear their own
tongue, testified that they were praising God.

When Peter stood up, supported by the eleven (there is no
indication that the eleven did any speaking) he began with the
words " Ye men of Judæa, and all ye that dwell at Jerusalem . . ."
Peter did not address the visitors from the other nations. Therefore he did not need to know their languages. He addressed the
people who dwelt in Judæa and Jerusalem. They were Jews and,
therefore, he spoke in the Jewish language. He charged them
with crucifying the Lord of Glory. That charge did not belong
to the nationals.

The promise of the Holy Spirit, and the accompanying power,
was not exclusive to that day and those people. " For," says the
Apostle, " the promise is unto you, and to your children, and to
all that are afar off, even as many as the Lord our God shall call "
(ii. 39). If we have been called of God then the promise belongs
to us.

Peter was the example of the change which had taken place,
and of the power which had been given. He was a new man.

The man of cowardice was now the man of courage.

The man of doubts was now the man of determination.

Peter's Sermon (ii. 14-40). This was the first of three sermons
preached by Peter, and recorded in chapters ii., iii., and iv.

Sermons have been delivered by tens of thousands all down
the ages, preached by

The Apostles	.....	as Peter and Paul.
The Early Fathers	.....	as Augustine and Ignatius.
The Monks	.....	as St. Bernard and St. Francis
The Reformers	.....	as Luther and Tyndale.
The Puritans	.....	as Knox and Baxter.
The Methodists	.....	as Wesley and Whitfield.
The Revivalists	.....	as Moody and Finney.

There are libraries of sermons, but here is the very first sermon of the Church, a sample for all sermons.

It was intensely personal, coming from Peter's own heart and bringing conviction to the hearts of the people.

It had one central theme — Christ, His life, death, resurrection, and ascension. He preached Christ and Him crucified.

It was impregnated with Scripture. He quoted the Old Testament, from the Psalms and the Prophets. He brought in many witnesses, but never himself. It was not what Peter thought but what God said. He caused his hearers to become witnesses themselves with such words as, " As ye yourselves know."

The result of such preaching was that people were added to the Church daily.

EARLY MINISTRIES

PETER AND JOHN (Chapters iii. - v.)

Healing of the lame man (iii. 1-11). This was the first miracle performed after the departure of the Lord and the inauguration of the Church. It was evidence to the world that, although the Lord had withdrawn Himself, His power was still present to heal. Nowhere in Scripture is there any indication that that power was ever withdrawn. If the Lord has not changed, then we have to confess that we have. Our unbelief, our lack of obedience, our worldliness, something on our side holds back that which the Lord not only promised but, in that early Church, performed.

As a result of this miracle the people gathered together in wonderment. This gave Peter the opportunity, which these early servants of God never missed, to preach the Word. The incident, therefore, gave occasion for

Peter's second sermon (iii. 12-26). This was as sound in its theology as the first. In it he charged the people with being responsible for the death of the Lord of Glory, Whom they crucified but Whom God raised from the dead. One of the important statements in this sermon was, " And now, brethren, I wot that through ignorance ye did it, as did also your rulers" (iii. 17). If they had done that thing wilfully (as it so appeared) then they would have been murderers, and there was no pardon for the murderer. He, too, must die. If they did it in ignorance, then the charge would be one of manslaughter. For such God had provided cities of refuge. Peter confirmed what the Lord had already said on the Cross : " Father, forgive them ; for they know not what they do " (Luke xxiii. 34). Oh, the boundless grace of God !

This preaching brought adherents and opponents, so that these preachers were brought

Before the Sanhedrin (iv. 1/37). It was an august assembly — rulers, elders, scribes, Annas the high priest, Caiaphas, John, Alexander, and as many as were of the kindred of the high priest — all of these to try two ordinary fishermen who had been filled with the Spirit of God ! Peter answered in no uncertain words, the Peter who had retreated from a servant girl when seeking to cover his identity with the Lord, of him it is now written: "Now when they saw the boldness of Peter and John and perceived that they were unlearned and ignorant men, they marvelled; and they took knowledge of them, that they had been with Jesus" (iv. 13). Moreover, neither threats nor imprisonments could silence these men. Instead, they prayed for more boldness. This was granted as again the Holy Spirit descended upon them.

Ananias and Sapphira (v. 1/11). There was nothing wrong in keeping back part of the price. There is nothing wrong in keeping the whole, except that one robs himself of blessing. The trouble was one of deception. They presented a part of the price with the pretence that they were giving the whole. The incident should have tremendous challenge to every heart that, although man may deceive his neighbours, he cannot deceive God. The Lord not only knows the heart but He knows the secret thoughts and intents of the heart. This sin was not the result of a sudden impulse, but the deliberate planning of a husband and wife.

This demonstration of God's power brought great fear upon the Church because, whilst many were added to it, it brought further opposition, so that the apostles were cast into prison. The contest between God and the world, between the Gospel and the powers of darkness, became very apparent. The high priest put the apostles into prison — God took them out. The rulers increased their threats against them — God increased their boldness. When the authorities killed Stephen, God produced a Paul, and so the Gospel spread until it touched the uttermost parts of the earth.

Stephen (chapters vi. - vii.). The call of Stephen should teach much. The Church had grown very rapidly, and with its growth came numerous problems. Christianity brought with it concern for the poor, the widow, and all who were oppressed. Christianity gave birth to hospitals, relief funds, education, and all the blessings of mankind, which are now handled by Governments and Municipal Authorities. The growth of this social side of the Christian life became more than the apostles could handle, so seven men of holy character were appointed to become deacons, of whom Stephen was one. These were to care for the administrative affairs of the Church, whilst the apostles would give themselves continually to prayer and to the study of the Word.

Two lessons are to be learned. Firstly, Stephen was not chosen to be an apostle, or a preacher, but a deacon to care for the material side of the Church, yet he and the others had to be men full of the Holy Ghost, and so should every man be who is elected to the diaconate to-day ; and, if deacons, how much more ministers !

Secondly, most ministers are so involved in committee work, visitation, and other responsibilities, that the pulpit has suffered considerably, and also the spiritual life of the Church.

The synagogue might suborn men to falsify Stephen's conduct, but they could not change his character. This caused alarm as they beheld his angelic appearance, and more so as, with holy boldness, he preached to them the whole of God's dealings with man through the Old Testament, truths they could not gainsay, concluding with a fearful charge against his hearers for having betrayed and killed the Son of God. In anger they cast him out of the city and stoned him to death — Stephen, the first martyr of the Christian Church.

With this martyrdom of Stephen the enemy seemed to have obtained the first taste of blood. Now the wolf came in to scatter the sheep. The leading man of this persecution was Saul of Tarsus, who had witnessed Stephen's noble death.

This death, instead of quenching the believers, became the medium for the dissemination of the Gospel. Thus the book moves into the field of

OVERSEAS MISSIONS (Chapters viii. - xxviii.)

IN SAMARIA (Chapters viii. - ix.)

When the adversary stopped Stephen from ministering to the Jews he opened the way for Philip to preach to the Samaritans. Philip was the man who could preach to the crowd in Samaria, enjoy great success, and yet leave it, at the Lord's bidding, to minister to one man in the desert and lead that individual, an Ethiopian, to Christ. Oh, that God's servants to-day could be so sensitive to the leading of God that they could gladly leave the city for the solitary place, the crowd for the few, and not interpret it as failure. Philip expounded the Word as faithfully to the one as to the many.

Paul. Chapter ix. introduces a character who will dominate much of the New Testament in his ministry for Christ. He is introduced as Saul, the bigoted Pharisee, the persecutor of the saints but, by the power of God, he became Paul, the devoted apostle, the preacher to the Gentiles.

Saul quickly learned that authority was the prerogative of the Lord, and yielded to that authority with : " Lord, what wilt Thou have me to do ? " Later he was heard saying : " I was not disobedient to the heavenly vision." This is the only way to a life of spiritual accomplishment.

It was with some timidity that Ananias visited Saul at God's instruction. With his misgivings, it is delightful to hear him say: "Brother Saul."

After Saul's conversion, for a time the Church had rest round about, during which rest the believers were edified and multiplied (ix. 31). To-day the Church is seeking rest through pacification and modification. These things do not make rest — they create death.

During this time Saul was reaping a little of what he had sown. He, who had been an enemy of the Church, was now surrounded by enemies. On the one hand the Jews, whom he had served, now sought to kill him ; and, on the other hand, the Christian Church, which he had joined, would not receive him because the believers feared him. However, God provided for him a faithful friend in Barnabas, who defended him before the Church.

Peter (Chapter ix.) Verse 32 records further ministry of Peter in the form of miracles of healing. He found a man who had been sick for eight years and, in the Name of Jesus, he bade the man arise. This was in Lydda. Whilst there, a message came to him from Joppa, six miles away, telling of the death of Dorcas. On his arrival at Joppa, instead of finding the death chamber filled with professional mourners, he found a group of lamenting widows, testifying to the charity of this woman who had spent her life making garments for the poor and needy. Peter raised Dorcas from the dead, causing rejoicing in many hearts. The name of this woman has been immortalised by the Dorcas Societies throughout the Church to-day.

TO THE UTTERMOST PARTS OF THE EARTH
(Chapters x. - xxviii.)

This section deals with

PAUL'S CHURCH-ESTABLISHING MINISTRY. The first three chapters deal with *preliminary events* which, whilst they lead into the ministry of Paul, are actually concerned with Peter.

The Gospel was about to move out to the Gentiles. The hand of God was upon two men at the same time, Cornelius over in Macedonia, and Peter, in Joppa, who was being prepared for his unwelcome task by a vision in which he saw a sheet descend from heaven containing all kinds of animals, clean and unclean. Peter, with all of his Jewish pride, would sooner go hungry than eat that which he considered unclean, but God was preparing him for ministry to men whom the apostle considered unclean because they were not Jews. In fact, the men were already on his doorstep, with the invitation from Cornelius. Peter was ready, and journeyed with those servants to Caesarea. There he learned that God is no respecter of persons, and that the Gospel is for "whosoever will," for, as Peter preached, the Holy Ghost fell upon those Gentiles as He had descended upon the Jews in Jerusalem, so that they were baptised in the Holy Spirit and then in water.

Accused and Vindicated (Chapter xi.). One would have thought that the Church at Jerusalem would have rejoiced in this news, but it was otherwise. They laid an indictment against Peter.

" . . . The circumcision contended with him, saying, Thou wentest in to men uncircumcised, and didst eat with them." They were more concerned with their ritual than they were in the salvation of others. However, Peter vindicated his own character by a full explanation of what had happened. At first the Church was silent — then they rejoiced. Lord, give us a passion for souls which will cause us to forget ourselves and our petty ideas !

Antioch. The last twelve verses of chapter xi. relate thirteen years of vital Church history, from the death of Stephen to the famine in Jerusalem. They were vital because they were the touchstone of Christian ministry, the liaison between East and West, between Jew and Gentile. The Acts of the Apostles declares the course of the Gospel from Jerusalem to Antioch, and from Antioch to Rome. It was the passing of the spiritual centre of the East to the world centre of the West. Antioch was the half-way place. Antioch was the break-away from the old and the inception of the new. It was the last of three great moves which had resulted from the persecution at Jerusalem.

(1) The foundation of the Church in Samaria through Philip.

(2) The growth of the Church in Judæa through Peter.

(3) The forming of the Church in Antioch through — not Peter, Barnabas, nor Paul — but a small group of unnamed, unknown men who, being scattered, preached the Word as they went. They formed the Church, and it was there that believers were first called Christians.

The Council at Jerusalem sent Barnabas to investigate the things that were happening. So delighted was he in what he found in that city that he sought a pastor for them. The man of his choice was the man he had defended eight years earlier, the man who had retired to his own city of Tarsus to witness for his Lord — Saul. For the next two years these men, Barnabas and Paul, laboured together. Did we say Barnabas and Paul ? That was not for long. It very quickly became Paul and Barnabas, and how graciously Barnabas, the senior man, slipped back in order that Paul might have the place of honour which God had made for him. Lord, make me as gracious as Barnabas, as well as giving me the courage of Paul !

Persecution. "Now about that time Herod the king stretched forth his hands to vex certain of the Church" (xii. 1). With those words comes the introduction to the Church's third persecution.

It was at this time that James was killed, and Peter was put into prison.

How strange are the ways of God! They are past finding out. James was permitted to die, and Peter was miraculously delivered from prison when guarded by sixteen soldiers, chains, and bolted doors. Yet it is not for us to question the actions of a Supreme Being Whom we know to be an all-wise unerring God. Against the deliverance of Peter was something more harmful than soldiers or chains — a praying people who did not expect their prayers to be answered. Unbelief has hindered the Lord from doing much.

Ordination. "Separate Me Barnabas and Saul for the work whereunto I have called them." This ordination of Barnabas, the Son of Consolation, who came from Cyprus, and Saul, the one-time persecutor from Tarsus, was the commencement of the great missionary enterprise which has never ceased. "They sent them away" (xiii. 3). "So they, being sent forth by the Holy Ghost, departed" (xiii. 4).

Thus from Antioch there began officially the great overseas missionary programme, across Asia, through Europe, and to the uttermost parts of the earth.

PAUL'S FIRST MISSIONARY JOURNEY
(Chapters xiii and xiv.)

Seleucia — Cyprus — Salamis — Paphos — Perga — Antioch in Pisidia — Iconium — Lystra — Derbe — Pisidia — Pamphilia — Attalia. Each name calls to mind events which took place therein.

This is the chapter which begins with Barnabas and Saul, and ends with Paul and Barnabas. It also records Paul's first sermon, scriptural throughout, and Christ-centred. It declares Christ's death for sin and His resurrection for our justification. The sermon was also personal — that was, to his hearers, not himself. This was typical of all Paul's preaching, and should be of our preaching. It was always effective. It was a savour of life unto life, many believed — or of death unto death, there was much opposition.

Paul always preached to the Jews first, even though it was the Gentiles who believed. Neither did the Apostle modify his message to the unbelieving Jew. He hoped that they would modify their persecution.

The difficulties of those early preachers were not limited to
one source. In Lystra, when they healed an impotent man, instead
of persecution it was exultation. The people acclaimed them as
gods and worshipped them. To some this is a more subtle temptation than rejection. When Paul and Barnabas established themselves as men, not gods, the fickle mob, who yesterday hailed
them as deities, to-day stoned them as demons. They dragged
Paul's body out of the city, believing him to be dead. Evidently
he was only unconscious. Fourteen years later, when writing to
the Corinthians, he referred to this incident when he said :
" Whether in the body . . . or whether out of the body, I cannot
tell " (2 Corinthians xii. 1- 4).

After this the apostles moved on, revisiting many of the
Churches, confirming the saints, exhorting them in the Word,
and ordaining elders.

On their return to Antioch they had a testimony meeting,
not to tell the people what they had done, but declaring " all that
God had done with them, and how He had opened the door of
faith to the Gentiles " (xiv. 27).

A difference of opinion concerning the Gentile converts, as to
whether or not they should be circumcised, called for

A Council Meeting (Chapter xv.) at Jerusalem. It was a
stormy meeting. The two factors seem to have been very strong.
The chapter is more like the minutes of a business meeting ! The
detail is left out, only the bare facts are declared. So important
was this meeting that Joseph Parker has referred to its outcome
as the

Magna Charta of the Christian Church. The issue was that
the Judaizers wanted the converts circumcised, and thereby bring
them under the ritual of the Jewish law. Paul and Barnabas had
withstood it. The Church Council must settle it. Peter was the
first to speak. He reminded them that they had all found this law
burdensome, but had to observe it because, as Jews, they were subject to the law of Moses, but the Gentiles had never been brought
under that law. As they were not bound, why bind them? Paul
and Barnabas were the next speakers. They just presented facts,
without opinions.

James was evidently the chairman, for he summed up. He
endorsed all that Peter had said. Although he was legalistic himself, he sensed that this was not some new thing to be opposed,
but some old thing they had failed to appreciate, for what Peter

declared was agreed upon by the prophets (xv. 15). Thereupon he passed sentence.

(1) It was not necessary for them to be circumcised.

(2) They must avoid eating meat offered to idols (idolatry).

(3) They must not commit fornication (common amongst the heathen).

(4) They must avoid eating things with blood in them.

(5) These Gentiles were to be instructed in the reasons for these abstentions.

This pleased both the Council and the Church, and a letter was sent to the Gentile Churches accordingly.

The sum and substance of the whole is that men who are under grace are free from the law, except in the things which obviously please God.

The Magna Charta is Grace and, therefore, does not need the addition of works.

So far as the Acts of the Apostles is concerned, Peter is not mentioned again after this meeting.

PAUL'S SECOND MISSIONARY JOURNEY
(Chapters xvi. - xviii)

What a pity that these two saints of God should have quarrelled! The Lord seems to have over-ruled it to the establishment of two tours instead of one ; Paul took Silas and went in one direction, Barnabas took Mark and went another way. One of Paul's important ministries was to return to Churches and establish saints, a ministry which is forgotten to-day in an enthusiasm for evangelism. If the saints were built up, which is the real work of the Church, they would become the soul-winners. God has never promised crowds. It is the one by one personal work which should count.

This second tour took Paul and Silas to

Lystra. Here Paul found Timothy, who became his companion and, later, a pastor.

Troas. Being forbidden by the Holy Ghost to preach in Asia, they came to Troas where they heard the call to Macedonia. In response they went to its principal city

Philippi, not to find the crowds awaiting, but to find a few faithful women, meeting for prayer at the river side. To these Paul ministered, and so came the first European convert — a woman, named Lydia.

Another woman was delivered from demonism. Again this did not bring a revival but a row, and the apostles, who had taken a sea voyage to Macedonia, were cast into prison. With bleeding backs, and feet secure in stocks, they had made a mistake, they had misunderstood the Lord's leading! Not at all. God moves in a mysterious way His wonders to perform. These men of God could sing in the midst of defeat and disappointment. They learned that this experience brought them into the lives of the jailor and his family, whom they were privileged to lead to the Lord.

Thessalonica — where the apostles " turned the world upside down."

Berea — where the people were commended as being noble because they searched the Scriptures for a verification of what they were being taught.

Athens — the city of learning where Socrates, Plato, Aristotle, and others, had taught their philosophies. Where art and idolatry were prominent, Paul came with his message of salvation. Notice how he addressed them — " Ye men of Athens." Usually he said, " Men and brethren," but there were no brethren here. In the religious outlook of this city they worshipped anything that men sought to deify and, lest they should fail some deity, they had set up an altar to such a one — the unknown god. Where their worship ended, Paul began. He introduced to them the God they did not know, showing His supremacy, His dignity, and His doctrine.

The result was a division of opinion — some mocked, some would hear more, some believed. Paul never returned to Athens. Those who procrastinated and said, " We will hear thee again " never had that opportunity. To-day is the day of salvation.

Corinth. Paul ministered for eighteen months. Here he met Aquila, Priscilla, Gallio, and others.

PAUL'S THIRD MISSIONARY JOURNEY (Chapters xix. - xxi.)

Ephesus. This was a wicked city ; the people prided themselves in their evil ways. It was the seat of the worship of Diana. Paul stayed three years in Ephesus, and for two of those years he reasoned in the school of Tyrannus. So hard was the place that at one time he said : " I fought with beasts at Ephesus." This did not mean that he fought with animals, but with men of bestial character. Once the city was in a great uproar because the people feared that Diana would be dethroned. Out of his many labours there was established a Church, to which the Epistle to the Ephesians was written, as well as the message of Revelation ii. 1-7.

Greece. This was a revisit, and was for three months. Again Paul met opposition.

Troas — for seven days. Here he preached all night, and raised to life Eutychus, who had fallen out of a window.

In xx. 7 is a statement often repeated : " Upon the first day of the week, when the disciples came together to break bread . . ." Paul was ever preaching in the synagogue on the Sabbath Day to the Jews, and breaking bread on the first day with the believers. This does not harmonise with the teaching of the Seventh Day Adventists, neither does it support their argument that the Catholics changed the day !

Miletus — Paul wanted to return to Ephesus. As the way was not opened, he sent for the elders of that Church to come to him at Miletus. He told them that he would be seeing them no more, because he was going to Jerusalem and was not sure what kind of reception he would receive. However, he was as ready to die for Christ as he had been to live for Him. He requested that the saints at Ephesus should be as faithful to the Lord as he had been to them. At the same time he warned them of trouble which they would meet. The wolves of false doctrine would come in and scatter the flock.

After a sad farewell he left them, as he sailed for Jerusalem, visiting many cities *en route*. It must have been a sad journey, for he was saying good-bye to many friends, and he was also being reminded that his experience in Jerusalem was going to be anything but pleasant. Yet, in the midst of these circumstances, he could say : " I go bound in the Spirit . . . but none of these things move me, neither count I my life dear unto myself, so that I might finish my course with joy . . . For I have not shunned to declare unto you all the counsel of God " (xx. 22-27).

PAUL IN JERUSALEM (Chapters xxi. - xxvi.)

After being received graciously by the brethren, Paul reported to James and the elders concerning the work the Lord had permitted him to do. The elders rejoiced with Paul, but reminded him that there were many who, because of their religious bigotry, were not rejoicing. Although they sought to take precautions against these enemies, the enemy was not always particular about truth. A rumour fanned them into a fury, in which Paul almost lost his life. He was rescued by soldiers. On the steps of the castle he made his defence, declaring his citizenship, and giving his testimony of salvation. All was well with his hearers until he mentioned the Gentiles (xxii. 21). Then their anger broke again. " Away with such a fellow . . . " This brought him before the Sanhedrin. Once more a true and faithful testimony was borne by the apostle, and that night the Lord came to him with a word of encouragement, saying : " Be of good cheer, Paul ; for as thou hast testified of Me in Jerusalem, so must thou bear witness also at Rome " (xxiii. 11).

He was sent, with a bodyguard, to Caesarea, which was the Roman capital of Judæa. There he faithfully declared his testimony of God's grace and power, and made known the Gospel before Felix the Governor, Festus the successor, and Agrippa the King. Of these three rulers — Felix trembled, Festus hesitated and then resisted, Agrippa was almost persuaded. All were convicted — none was converted.

During these trials, Paul, as a Roman, appealed to Caesar for justice. The appeal took

PAUL TO ROME (Chapters xxvii. - xxviii.). This was the beginning of the world programme that has reached to the uttermost parts, and has never ceased. Paul, the prisoner, is often seen as Paul, the pilot, not only directing souls through the moral shallows of life, but now of the ship that was to have taken him to Rome. Bad judgment on the part of the captain of the boat brought it into storms and, eventually, a shipwreck. Paul encouraged the men aboard by showing them his own trust in the Lord.

What a message we have for a storm-tossed world, sinking in sin, if only we would preach it and live it ! " Wherefore, sirs, be of good cheer ; for I believe God . . . "

What was a calamity to the occupants of the ship was a consolation to the inhabitants of the island of Malta. It brought to them salvation and the healing power of the Lord.

After three months on the island of Melita they sailed again, at last reaching Rome. Paul arrived as a prisoner but, through the courtesy of someone, he was not cast into prison but allowed his own house and a certain amount of political freedom, even though always under guard. He no longer travelled for the Lord, but he continued a wonderful ministry to all who came to him, and through the medium of his pen. From Rome he wrote what are known as the Prison Epistles — Ephesians, Colossians, Philemon, and Philippians.

The apostle was released for about four years, but was re-arrested by Nero who, having destroyed Rome by fire, sought to lay the responsibility of it upon the Christians. It was in those last days, whilst awaiting his death, that he wrote his second epistle to Timothy, telling him that the time of his departure had come. He exhorted Timothy to be as faithful in the Word as he himself had been. The workmen move on, but the work must continue.

Timothy, too, was faithful in all things, and so were others who followed him. Now it is our turn to continue telling the same message. May we be as faithful, may we be as steadfast.

The book does not end with Paul's death but with his ministry, a ministry which has never died and never will.

ROMANS

HIS RIGHTEOUSNESS — OUR JUSTIFICATION

*" Look unto Me, and be ye saved, all the ends of the earth :
For I am God, and there is none else. I have sworn by
Myself, the word is gone out of My mouth in righteousness,
and shall not return, That unto Me every knee shall bow,
every tongue shall swear. Surely, shall one say, in the
Lord have I righteousness and strength : even to Him shall
men come ; and all that are incensed against Him shall be
ashamed. In the Lord shall all the seed of Israel be justified,
and shall glory"* (ISAIAH xlv. 22-25)

INTRODUCTION TO THE EPISTLES

Before approaching the Epistle to the Romans, it would be profitable to consider the Epistles as a whole, for this section of the Bible, like the others, is complete in itself.

All of the Epistles, known as the Church Epistles, were written to the Church of Jesus Christ. They deal with Doctrine and Conduct. The study of them is important to the children of God, as they are those who make up that Church.

Although the Epistles are not in a chronological order, they certainly appear to be in a Divine order. Whilst the Epistle to the Romans is the sixth in chronological order, it is definitely first in Christian doctrine. It has been pointed out by Leon Tucker that until we know

The Righteousness of Romans
we cannot move on to

The Order of Corinthians,
The Liberty of Galatians,
The Calling of Ephesians,
The Joy of Philippians,
The Head of Colossians,
The Coming One of Thessalonians,
The Substance of Hebrews.

Wisely he points out that, in the Epistles, there is a movement from Jewish ground to heavenly places, from the Gospel of the Kingdom to the Gospel of the Grace of God.

In approaching an Epistle written by Paul to a Church it is necessary to have some knowledge of the city in which the Church was situated, and some information about the Church, for only as one knows the conditions which caused the letter to be written can one rightly interpret the contents of the letter.

ROME

This city, the capital of Italy, was the capital of the vast expanding Roman Empire. It was a world metropolis.

At the time in question large numbers of Jews were living in Rome. Most of them had been taken there in the first place as slaves. History records that these Jewish slaves were not easily subdued by those foreign powers, any more than they could be readily suppressed by the aggressors in their own country of Palestine. The Jew would never yield his forms of religion, and most rigidly he kept the Sabbath Day. The result of all this was that the Romans gave to these people their liberty. A town was built for them across the river Tiber but, whilst many had liberty, many more were punished.

In the city of Rome at this time a Church came into being. How, no one knows. Paul had never been there — he said so. Peter had never been there, even although the Catholics like to declare otherwise.

This Church was made up of Jews and Gentiles, each having their own interpretation of things, so that there was some friction.

To this Church Paul had longed to make a visit. He had planned one several times, but on each occasion he was hindered ; so, not sure whether he would ever get there, he wrote to them this Epistle.

The argument of the Epistle can now be discerned as Paul reasoned the matter of justification, as to whether the Jew with his law had any advantage over the Gentile Christian who was without the law.

The many names mentioned in the salutations of the last chapter indicate how many personal friends Paul had and knew in this city which he had never visited. They must have gone from him — now he longed to go to them.

INTRODUCTION TO ROMANS

This book has been praised by many for its immense value as a book of doctrine.

Luther said : "It is the chief book of the New Testament."

Godet said : "It is the Cathedral of the Christian Faith."

Griffith Thomas said : "It is a theological education in itself."

B. H. Carroll stated : "It is the most fundamental, vital, logical, profound, and systematic discussion of the whole plan of salvation in all the literature of the world. It touches all men ; it is universal in its application ; it roots, not only in man's creation and fall, but also in the timeless purposes and decrees of God before the world was, and fruits in the eternity after this world's purgation."

The Epistle was written by Paul from Corinth toward the end of his third missionary tour and addressed " To all that be in Rome, beloved of God, called to be saints " (i. 7). These saints would probably come from all parts of Asia. Rome was a great metropolis. The Romans were famed road-builders, making travel easy for those days. There were strangers from Rome in Jerusalem on the Day of Pentecost (Acts ii. 10). Many of those saints may have become Christians then when three thousand were added to the Church, and after that daily such as were being saved. Stephen, Aquila, Priscilla, as well as Peter, had all had their influence upon the moving populace in Jerusalem.

Of this we are assured, there was a group, or groups, of believers in Rome whom Paul had never seen, but he had a great desire both to see them and to minister unto them. However, he had misgivings about reaching Rome. He was preparing to leave Corinth for Jerusalem, but he had also received a number of warnings that a visit to Jerusalem might mean imprisonment or even death. (Read Acts xx. 22-23 ; xxi. 4 and 11).

With this uncertainty in mind he wrote the Epistle. Having his letter all but complete he found a woman who was taking the sea voyage from Corinth to Rome, and requested that she should convey this letter for him. In consenting to so small a request, she became honoured by becoming the bearer of one of the most valuable letters, not only to Rome, but to the Christian Church worldwide, and for all time. Her name was Phebe. This is mentioned in the footnote to the Epistle.

In these circumstances Paul brought his Epistle to a conclusion by sending salutations to a number of people. These are listed in the last chapter. In return for her kindness, he gave to Phebe an introduction to the saints, which is worthy of note. " I commend unto you Phebe our *sister*, which is a *servant* of the Church which is at Cenchrea. That ye receive her in the Lord, as becometh saints, and that ye assist her in whatsoever business she hath need of you ; for she hath been a *succourer* of many, and of myself also " (xvi. 1-2).

Three words stand out in this recommendation. —

Sister. This was a recognition of womanhood, which the Gospel has always maintained.

Servant comes from the same root as our word deaconess.

Succourer, suggests the nature of her ministry — helping others, serving the sick. Paul was sick at Cenchrea.

What a beautiful illustration of the Beatitude, "Blessed are the merciful for they shall obtain mercy."

THE BOOK

THE DIVISIONS OF THE BOOK. It divides naturally into three main sections : —

(1) DOCTRINAL (Chapters i. - viii). This includes
The sinner and his salvation (i. - v.).
The saint and his sanctification (vi. - viii).

(2) DISPENSATIONAL (Chapters ix. - xi.). This deals with Israel and His sovereignty.

(3) PRACTICAL (Chapters xii. - xvi. This tells of
The servant and his service.

THE MESSAGE OF THE BOOK

The whole could be summed up in one verse : " For I am not ashamed of the gospel of Christ ; for it is the power of God unto salvation to every one that believeth ; to the Jew first, and also to the Greek " (i. 16). This matter of salvation is expounded throughout the book.

The narrative opens in real Pauline style — seven verses without a full stop! So, in one lengthy sentence, he makes his introduction and salutation. In it he declares himself and his call, Christ's humanity and divinity, also His resurrection, and the source of grace and salvation. After this Paul makes known his desire to see the saints in Rome (i. 10).

(1) DOCTRINAL (Chapters i. - viii.)

(a) THE SINNER AND HIS SALVATION (Chapters i. - v.). Before entering into his reasoning and revelations, he declares the medium of this glorious salvation. It is

The Gospel, the only thing which is the power of God unto salvation. It can only be appropriated by faith. It is universal, and it is something of which he is not ashamed. This Gospel is the good news of deliverance. Because man needs such deliverance, the Apostle continues in his reasoning to reveal what man is by nature.

Man's Guilt. Man is guilty because, in that Gospel, God has declared both His righteousness and His wrath. Therefore man should be acquainted with the truth. These things are declared in the repetition of the words " of God." In the verses under consideration there is the power of God (16), the righteousness of God (17), the wrath of God (18), and the truth of God (25). There are five other possessive things of God in this first chapter, and one can continue to mark them off all through the Epistle.

This guilt of man is declared in that the heart is given to idolatry (23), to uncleanness (24), to sexuality (26-27), to moral corruption (29), to wilfulness (32). It is a dreadful indictment which leaves a man stripped of any vestige of goodness, any moral claims, or worthiness. The heart is deceitful above all things and desperately wicked.

In the next chapter the Apostle declares that

Sin is Universal. There is not one of us who can point his finger at another, and charge him with sin. In so doing, we condemn ourselves in that " all have sinned and come short of the glory of God." " There is none good, no, not one."

The Jews tried to excuse themselves because they were a privileged people, but the Apostle said that sin is sin, whether committed by the Gentile or by the Jew. God is no respecter of persons, but is just in His dealings with men, whoever they are and whatever they are. He knows no partiality, any more than sin does.

The fact would be that, if preference were made, could it be granted to the Jew as a favoured people, or should it be given to the Gentile who had never been brought under the law ?

Paul points out that there is no escape for the Gentiles because, although they had no law, nature itself taught men what was right and what was wrong and, therefore, they would be a law unto themselves (ii. 14) ; whilst the Jews, having been given the law and having been brought up under it, by their knowledge had the greater responsibility. The man who claims the right to teach, claims the right to understand. After all, their Judaism was a faith before it was a race. It was a creed rather than a credential. Hence the statement : " For he is not a Jew which is one outwardly . . . but he is a Jew which is one inwardly . . . in the spirit, and not in the letter ; whose praise is not of men, but of God " (ii. 28 - 29).

This caused the Jews to ask the questions with which chapter iii. opens : " What advantage then hath the Jew ? Or what profit is there of circumcision ? " They were seeking to hide themselves behind a national pride and to use the same as a smoke-screen for indifference or a cloak for maliciousness. The Apostle's reply was : " Much every way . . . ", or their advantages were many because there had been committed unto them the

Oracles of God. As a result, they should be better informed than any other people BUT, if they acted contrary to their knowledge and privileges, then they must come under the same condemnation as other people. Otherwise the position would be " Let us do evil, that good may come " (iii. 8), but such would be an impossible situation. Therefore it must be concluded that, so far as the matter of sin is concerned, the Jew is no better than the Gentile.

Their position was made worse as Paul sought to declare the true *purpose of the law.* By it the Jews were seeking some measure of justification but, said the Apostle, " by the deeds of the law there shall no flesh be justified in His sight : for by the law is the knowledge of sin " (iii. 20). Law does not cover sin, it reveals it, for where there is no law there is no sin, for sin is the transgression of the law.

How many people say, " I am good, I do this, I do that, I am honest and I keep the law, therefore God cannot punish me." Such are acting contrary to this as well as to other Scriptures. When man has done all the things of which he desires to boast, the Word of God comes to him and says : " By the deeds of the law, there shall no flesh be justified in His sight " (iii. 20). Such a person has only justified himself in his own sight, and that will be of no use when he stands before a Holy God. Says James : " For whosoever shall keep the whole law, and yet offend in one point, he is guilty of all " (James ii. 10), or, just as guilty as if he had committed all.

Justification. If the Epistle to the Romans went on in this fashion it would be a dark and gloomy book of despair and hopelessness. However, a great change takes place at verse 21 of this

third chapter. With those two transforming words of "BUT
NOW" an introduction is made to the *Righteousness of God* which
comes by faith. "But now the righteousness of God without the
law is manifested, being witnessed by the law and the prophets;
Even the righteousness of God which is by faith of Jesus Christ
unto all and upon all them that believe . . . "

The subject is now the RIGHTEOUSNESS OF GOD as
against the SINFULNESS OF MAN.

The law revealed sin	.....	NOW God is taking it away.
The law revealed guilt	.....	NOW God is giving grace.
The law stripped a man	.....	NOW God is clothing him.
The law gave the wages of death	....	NOW God is bringing the gift of eternal life.

This RIGHTEOUSNESS OF GOD, if accepted
                             brings JUSTIFICATION.

This JUSTIFICATION OF GOD, if accepted
                             brings REDEMPTION.

This REDEMPTION OF GOD, if accepted
                             brings PEACE.

These things come, not by the law, but by faith. "Therefore
we conclude that a man is justified by faith without the deeds of
the law" (iii. 28).

Two examples of this truth are given in chapter iv.

(1) *Abraham*. He is called the father of the faithful. By
faith he stepped out for an unknown land, by faith he remained in
that land, by faith he looked for a city whose Builder and Maker
is God, by faith he and Sarah received their child, and by faith
he offered up Isaac. In all of these things Abraham believed God,
and it was counted unto him for righteousness. "He staggered
not at the promise of God through unbelief; but was strong in
faith, giving glory to God . . . therefore it was imputed to him
for righteousness" (iv. 20-22).

Not a thing in that life could be attributed to works or to
law. Not a thing that he did was because the law demanded it.
"The law came by Moses", and Abraham lived long before
Moses and the law. Obviously, therefore, he was justified by faith
without the deeds of the law.

(2) *David.* " Even as David also describeth the blessedness of the man, unto whom God imputeth righteousness without works, saying, Blessed are they whose iniquities are forgiven, and whose sins are covered. Blessed is the man to whom the Lord will not impute sin " (iv. 6-8). David had sinned — he had broken the law, he had committed murder, he had committed adultery. In his wretchedness he had cried to the Lord for mercy, and the Lord had heard his cry, forgiven him and restored to him the joy of His salvation. God instantly imputed to him His righteousness — by the deeds of the law? Decidedly not, but by faith. What God did for Abraham and David, and others, He can do for all.

The chapter closes with the information that, whoever we may be, Jew or Gentile, bond or free, justification through faith may be our enjoyment. "Now it was not written for his sake alone, that it was imputed to him ; but for us also, to whom it shall be imputed, if we believe on Him that raised up Jesus our Lord from the dead ; Who was delivered for our offences and was raised again for our justification " (iv. 23-25).

Faith is the root of Justification. The Apostle follows it with a consideration of *its fruit.* This fruit is progressive in its development. " Therefore being justified by faith, we have PEACE with God through our Lord Jesus Christ " (v. 1). " Therefore " means " because of." With the realisation that sins are forgiven, that we are justified — counted as though we had never sinned — naturally the peace of God is going to rule our hearts.

This is the first development. Some people seek to make their peace with God. Such a thing cannot be done. He has established peace, man accepts His justification and then finds the Blood of Jesus whispers peace within. This peace enables one to GLORY — firstly, to glory in the Lord, and then to glory in tribulation. It is the glory that excelleth. It rises above tribulation, trial, distress, finding them to be as light afflictions that work a far more exceeding and eternal weight of glory. TRIBULATION is not sent for harm but for good, not for punishment but for production. The snow and the frost, the biting winds and the cold of winter, never ruin the earth. They sweeten and purify it, destroying pests and other things, so that the soil becomes productive in the next season.

So with the believer, tribulation worketh PATIENCE. It develops the soil of the soul. It sweetens character. It destroys the pests of selfishness, ease, and pleasure, until we look not at the immediate but at the ultimate. Thus, like the husbandman who waits patiently for the harvest, we must be patient and wait for the coming of the Lord.

James writes : " Ye have heard of the patience of Job, and have seen the end of the Lord ; that the Lord is very pitiful, and of tender mercy " (v. 11). This is the patience that worketh EXPERIENCE so that we can say, " We speak that we do know and testify that we have seen " (John iii. 11). Experience is that which consolidates and stabilises. When the blind man had experienced healing, men could reason all they would, his testimony could never be altered, " . . . One thing I know, that, whereas I was blind, now I see " (John ix. 25). This in turn brings HOPE, not the kind of hope which belongs to the world, which savours doubt. This hope is a confidence, a hope that never disappoints. The man who has this hope is never made ashamed. Paul sees this hope as an anchor which will hold on to the unseen yet firm rock that lies at the bed of the sea, steadfast in spite of all the billows which toss the vessel on the restless sea above, for he says: " Which hope we have as an anchor of the soul, both sure and stedfast, and which entereth into that within the veil " (Hebrews vi. 19). That anchor of hope is held by the cable of LOVE ; not the loose, sentimental love of the world, which is as fickle as the tossing waves, but the LOVE OF GOD. Was there ever such a love ? Could it ever be challenged ? The faith, which brought justification in verse 1, has carried us through into the fulness of the love of God that has been shed abroad in our hearts by the Holy Ghost which is given unto us (v. 5).

Paul, who was ever masterful in his ability to expound his theme, declares the greatness of this love by a comparison. Man's love for man seldom travels so far as death. In some extreme circumstance he might give his life for a very dear friend, or for a noble cause. BUT Christ died for us whilst we were yet sinners, alienated from Him by evil works, disobedient toward Him in His divine will. Through this love on His side alone, alienation has been changed to reconciliation.

The rest of the chapter contrasts between two men in the use of the expression : — '

"By one man." It is the comparison of the carnal man and the spiritual man.

The First Man	The Second Man
Adam.	Christ.
The Old Man.	The New Man.
Of the earth.	From heaven.
In him all men are sinners.	In Him we become saints.
Walks after the flesh.	Walks after the Spirit.
Brought condemnation.	Brings justification.
Was disobedient unto death.	Was obedient unto death.
In Adam all die.	In Christ we are made alive.

Five times in these same verses do the words " much more " occur, referring to the abundance of His grace which excels and exceeds the measure of our sin and, therefore, brings to believing man his salvation.

Having led the sinner out of his sin into the glorious salvation which is in Christ, the Apostle moves on ; the sinner has become a saint, and salvation must expand into sanctification, so the second point in this section is

(b) THE SAINT AND HIS SANCTIFICATION (Chapters vi. - viii.). Paul sets up a reasoning which takes place between the natural man and the spiritual man. The spiritual man has accepted by faith Christ's finished work on his behalf. He has yielded to the fact that salvation is not of works, but is all of grace. Immediately, the natural man, who is full of pride and self-conceit, resists such a position. He desires that his own merit should have some claim somewhere, so he argues that, if grace be such a wonderful thing, why not continue sinning in order to give grace an opportunity to display its full ability ? However, the answer comes back — No ! The sinner cannot sin any more because he is no longer a sinner. He has died to himself, and a dead person cannot sin. The ordinance of baptism was established to that end, for baptism by immersion is an outward testimony of such a death and burial.

When a person dies, all his relationships die with him. He is then known as the deceased. He no longer has a wife — she becomes a widow. He no longer has debts — they are annulled. He no longer has engagements — they are cancelled — he is dead. This should be the relationship of the saint with his old life. Dead to sin, therefore freed from sin (vi. 7). But, having died to the old life, he is raised again in newness of life, the life which is set apart unto God, and lived to the glory of God. This is sanctification.

The man who continues in sin cannot embrace grace. To the contrary, he spurns it. The only thing such a person can receive is wages, or reward for the things he does — and that is, death. The man who has died to sin receives from God a gift, and that gift is eternal life.

In chapter vii. the illustration is changed, although the theme remains. In this instance it is the relationship of a married woman. Her first husband is law. To him she is bound so long as he lives. The only thing that can break that relationship is death. If death takes place she is free to marry again and, in so doing, does not become an adulteress.

If Christ died in our room and stead, when He died we died with Him, thus freeing us from the bondage of the old life and making it legally possible for us to marry again. This new union is with the risen Lord, thereby bringing us into the life of the Spirit.

This does not bring one into a condition whereby sinless perfection can be claimed, for Paul now speaks of a conflict within, a battle between the spiritual and the carnal.

Notice the language of verses 10 - 25. The predominant word is "I". It is mentioned thirty-two times in this section, also " me " and " my " fifteen times. This was a losing battle. Paul did not know the matter of a surrendered life. His was a struggling life, with evil getting the victory again and again until, in misery and despair, he cried out, " Who shall deliver me from the body of this death ? " (vii. 24). Then he learned that " In me (that is, in my flesh) dwelleth no good thing." What I cannot do, Christ can. Then came the surrender. " Not I but Christ," which immediately brought the victory of Romans viii. 1. " There is therefore now no condemnation to them which are in Christ Jesus, who walk not after the flesh, but after the Spirit."

The flesh life is the carnal life.

The Spirit life is the Christ life.

They that are in the flesh cannot please God.

Although the law was good and just, although it was God-given, and the Psalmist could say that the law of the Lord was perfect, yet it had a weakness. It was that weakness which necessitated a new covenant and brought Jesus into the world. " For what the law could not do, in that it was weak through the flesh . . . " (viii. 3). What was it that it could not do ? Justify. " For by the work of the law shall no flesh be justified " (Galatians ii. 16). Why could it not justify ? Because it was made weak through the flesh. What flesh ? Not sinful flesh, but sinless flesh. The law required the sacrifice of a lamb or a bullock, but how could such a creature take man's place and justify his sin, seeing it had never known sin, never been tempted, and never known victory or defeat ? It could not. The only thing that such a sacrifice could do was to cover the sin, not remove it.

> " Not all the blood of beasts
> On Jewish altars slain,
> Could give the guilty conscience peace.
> Or wash away the stain."

For this reason " God sending His own Son in the likeness of sinful flesh, and for sin, condemned sin in the flesh " (viii. 3).

> " But Christ the heavenly Lamb
> Takes all our sin AWAY ;
> A sacrifice of nobler name
> And richer blood than they."

This is the life of victory : —

God for us	.....	....	verse 31.
Christ for us	.....	....	verse 34.
The Spirit for us	.....	.....	verse 26.

the whole Triune God, working on behalf of the believer, as well as dwelling in him.

The Spirit-filled life triumphs over everything, until the sufferings of this present time become nothing by comparison with the life that is hid with Christ in God.

The same man, who at the end of chapter vii. said : " O wretched man that I am ! Who shall deliver me . . . ", closes chapter viii., and this doctrinal section, with the triumph of " Nay, in all these things we are more than conquerors through Him that loved us ; for I am persuaded, that neither death, nor life, nor angels, nor principalities, nor powers, nor things present, nor things to come, nor height, nor depth, nor any other creature, shall be able to separate us from the love of God, which is in Christ Jesus our Lord."

(2) DISPENSATIONAL (Chapters ix. - xi.)

ISRAEL AND HIS SOVEREIGNTY. The three chapters now under review are entirely different from those that have preceded them, and also from the chapters that follow. This section is always known as a parenthesis, because in chapter xii. Paul picks up his theme just where he left it in chapter viii.

The Apostle turns, temporarily, from the doctrinal to the dispensational, from the Church to the Jew. This means that these chapters must be interpreted differently. They relate to Israel, not to the Church. In fact, the three chapters survey Israel's history — past, present, and future.

The change of subject is obvious by the change of tone. The last verses of chapter viii. are triumphant, the first verse of chapter ix. is tragic. " I have great heaviness and continual sorrow in my heart, for I could wish that myself were accursed from Christ for my brethren, my kinsmen according to the flesh." This was a passion towards the souls of lost men and also a loyalty toward those of his own nationality. Moses displayed the same devotion to his people when he prayed : " Oh, this people have sinned a great sin, and have made them gods of gold. Yet now, if Thou wilt forgive their sin — ; and if not, blot me, I pray Thee, out of Thy book which Thou hast written " (Exodus xxxii. 31-32).

In the ninth chapter Paul deals with Israel's

PAST, enumerating their many blessings.

(1) *Adoption.* " To whom pertaineth the adoption " (ix. 9). God had said to Pharaoh, " Israel is My son, even My firstborn." This sonship was not by birth, but by adoption, because God chose this nation from all other nations, without any reason other than that He loved them. " The Lord did not set His love upon you, nor choose you, because ye were more in number than any people; for ye were the fewest of all people ; But because the Lord loved you . . . " (Deuteronomy vii. 7-8).

(2) *Glory.* "And the glory" (ix. 4). God had given them the Shekinah Glory of His Presence, had taken it away, but would restore it.

(3) *Covenants.* " and the covenants " (ix. 4). These were made in Abraham, Isaac, and Jacob. They were binding promises to which God had committed Himself. " For when God made promise to Abraham, because He could swear by no greater, He sware by Himself " (Hebrews vi. 13).

(4) *Law.* " and the giving of the law " (ix. 4). This was given at Sinai, and ordained by angels (Galatians iii. 19).

(5) *Service.* " and the service of God " (ix. 4). This embraced the Tabernacle, the Priesthood, the Offerings, and the Feasts.

(6) *Promises.* " and the promises " (ix. 4). This nation commenced in the Dispensation of Promise.

(7) *Fathers.* " Whose are the fathers, and of whom as concerning the flesh Christ came " (ix. 5). These are all found in the genealogies.

In this election of God, He not only called a nation in Abraham, but in

> Isaac as against Ishmael and the Ishmaelites,
> Jacob as against Esau and the Edomites,
> Sarah's children as against Keturah's children and the Midianites,

because this nation was not to be of the children of the flesh, but they were to be the children of promise.

God claims that He has the power and the right to choose whom He will, and to refuse whom He will. If one should question His authority, He will reply: "Hath not the potter power over the clay, of the same lump to make one vessel unto honour, and another unto dishonour?" (ix. 21).

Thus it was that God chose Israel and favoured her above all peoples, "BUT Israel, which followed after the law of righteousness, hath not attained to the law of righteousness. Wherefore ? Because they sought it not by faith, but as it were by the works of the law " (ix. 31-32).

In chapter x. Paul moves into the

PRESENT. As in chapter ix. he opens with a burden because of Israel's sin, so in chapter x. he opens with a prayer for Israel's salvation : " Brethren, my heart's desire and prayer to God for Israel is, that they might be saved. For I bear them record that they have a zeal of God, but not according to knowledge." They had been so concerned with law that they had lost grace. Grace was only to be found in the Christ they had crucified.

The Apostle declares the gospel in terms that are clear and plain : —

> Its acceptance ..... believe in the heart, confess with the mouth.
> Its message ..... the resurrection of Jesus from the dead.
> Its extent ..... whosoever — Jew and Greek alike.

" For whosoever shall call on the Name of the Lord shall be saved " (x. 13).

The Apostle then reasons why the Jewish nation was in such darkness as to these things. It was not because of ignorance ; as some had tried to use this as an excuse. Isaiah and others had declared the truth, the preachers had gone forth with the good news, but the Jews had refused it. The charge, therefore, was disobedience. " All day long I have stretched forth My hands unto a disobedient and gainsaying people " (x. 21).

This leads into chapter xi. which concerns the

FUTURE. The question is asked in the light of the foregoing : " Hath God cast away His people ? God forbid . . . " (xi. 1). His promises cannot be broken. His covenants cannot be disannulled. Many may be rejected because of their rejection ; but as God had seven thousand in Israel who had not bowed the knee to Baal in the days of Elijah, so God will always have a faithful remnant.

We must not disregard the Jew because, in the first place God has not and will not ; and, secondly, through their fall comes our salvation.

The chapter concludes with some grand reasoning. If the fall of Israel brought such riches to the world, what will come through their regathering ? If their casting away meant our reconciliation, what will be the result of their being received ?

The warning to the Gentiles is that they should not be wise in their own conceits, for the blindness of Israel is only in part and is UNTIL . . . . Then all Israel shall be saved (xi. 25/26).

Paul now returns to his former subject, the Church.

(3) PRACTICAL (Chapters xii. - xvi.)

THE SERVANT AND HIS SERVICE. Paul never failed to apply truth. Of what value is doctrine unless it finds its expression in everyday living ? Up to this point nothing has been asked FROM the Christian. It has been an unfolding of the plan of salvation. All that has been asked of us is an acceptance and, in so doing, Christ dwells within. The practical becomes effective as we allow the Christ Who is within to become Lord of our lives, to take over control, and to work out His purpose through us. " I beseech you therefore, brethren, by the mercies of God, that ye present your bodies a living sacrifice, holy, acceptable unto God, which is your reasonable service. And be not conformed to this world : but be ye transformed by the renewing of your mind, that ye may prove what is that good, and acceptable, and perfect, will of God " (xii. 1-2).

In other words, because of all that the Lord has done for us and given to us, now we should give ourselves, which is the most reasonable thing we can do.

Seeing that we have been given a spiritual life and made to become heirs of the world to come, let us be not bound by the things of this world.

Our citizenship is in heaven. Live according to the requirements of that country, not according to the alien world in which we find ourselves. The slogan of the world, " When in Rome do as Rome does ", is not the maxim of the Christian. We are ambassadors for, or the representatives of, the King of kings.

All this in chapter xii. concerns our moral relationships. When it is a matter of legal conduct then chapter xiii. is the answer. We are to be subject to the powers that be because they are ordained of God.

The subject changes again in chapter xiv. from collective relationships to personal and individual relationships, or our fellow-Christian, the man who loves the same Lord but does not see or understand things the same way as we do. To such a man we have to be charitable. God has not made us to be the judge of that man's understanding, any more than He has made the other man to be our judge. Both of us will have to answer to God, Who is the Judge of all the earth, and before Him we shall stand or fall.

We are not to examine the other man's conduct by our standards, neither are we to examine our own conduct by our standards. We are to examine our conduct in relationship to the other man lest we become a stumbling block to him, thereby causing him to fall.

Chapter xv. concerns the matter of ministry. Christ had no selfish ambition in His ministry. To the contrary, He was self-sacrificing, and we must minister similarly. Neither was the Lord partial in His ministry. It belonged to all men. Paul, as a follower of Christ, ministered to Jew and Gentile alike. He tells of the extent of his ministry, seeking to present the Word of God where it had not been heard before, avoiding, so far as possible, taking the message where it had already been lest he build on another man's foundations.

These four chapters have been summarised thus : —

(1)	In relation to self	Self-sacrifice	xii.	1 - 2
(2)	In relation to the Church	Humility	xii.	3 - 8
(3)	In relation to society	Love	xii.	9 - 21
(4)	In relation to government	Submission	xiii.	1 - 14
(5)	In relation to brethren	Consideration	xiv.	1 - 21
(6)	In relation to ministry	Impartial	xv	

In writing this letter to the Romans, Paul tells of the long-standing desire he had to visit that city, but his next journey was to be to Jerusalem. He had uncertainties as to the safety of that journey because of his many enemies. Therefore, he sought the prayers of the saints in Rome for his physical protection so that he might come to them.

Finding someone taking the journey to Rome, he concludes his Epistle with a number of salutations, revealing that personal interest which Paul ever had for the saints.

Then comes a benediction. Every Epistle written by Paul concludes with the mention of the word Grace ; usually, as here in verse 24, " The grace of our Lord Jesus Christ be with you all. Amen."

I CORINTHIANS

CHRISTIAN CONDUCT

"From whence come wars and fightings among you? Come they not hence, even of your lusts that war in your members? Ye lust, and have not; ye kill, and desire to have, and cannot obtain; ye fight and war, yet ye have not; because ye ask not. Ye ask, and receive not, because ye ask amiss, that ye may consume it upon your lusts" (JAMES iv. 1-3)

CORINTH

The city which Paul knew was a second Corinth. The previous powerful city had been destroyed in B.C. 146. It had lain in ruins for a century until Julius Caesar rebuilt it. The city soon became important because of its position. Situated on the Isthmus of Greece, with two large harbours, it was on the main trade route of the Empire. Jews found their way there for trade, the Phoenicians for its commerce, the Romans came for its antiquities, whilst the Greeks became interested in its revived games. Before long it became a great cosmopolitan place of all nationalities, seeking wealth or pleasure. Such conditions soon create a cesspool of sin and moral corruption. Dishonesty, drunkenness, sensuality, were at their worst, intensified by the idolatrous worship of Venus, the goddess of love.

It was into this city that Paul came after his departure from Athens, where he had ministered to the Athenians and preached his great sermon on Mars Hill, as recorded in Acts xvi. Paul's preaching had not been too successful in Athens. "After these things Paul departed from Athens, and came to Corinth" (Acts xviii. 1), one may imagine with a very heavy heart. The Apostle stayed in this latter city for a year and a half.

During the whole of this stay Paul was not chargeable to anyone. Having found Aquila and Priscilla, who were tent makers, he plied his trade with them for a meagre remuneration. It was a requirement of Jewish law that every boy must have a trade, even though he might plan to be a scholar. Jesus learned the trade of a carpenter.

The Gospel had already been preached in Corinth, and churches had been established. It must be understood by the word "churches" that these were just small groups of believers gathering in someone's home, for church buildings, as we know them, did not come into existence until some two hundred years later.

At this time Paul worked through the week, preached in the synagogues on the Sabbath Day, and ministered to the Gentiles whenever he could. When he was excommunicated from the synagogue he moved into the house adjoining, belonging to one called Justus, and there declared the whole counsel of God.

Whilst he ministered in Corinth, Silas and Timotheus came from Philippi, bringing gifts from the Church there. They joined Paul in his ministry, which must have been a comfort to the Apostle for, at that time, he was greatly burdened. This is gleaned from Acts xviii. 5 : "Paul was pressed in the spirit, and testified to the Jews that Jesus was Christ."

Paul's ministry in Corinth was not without fruit. A number of churches were established in the city, and also in Cenchrea. Eventually he took his departure from Corinth, when he sailed to Ephesus on his way to Jerusalem, and thence to Antioch, where he spent three years.

It had been Paul's intention to return to Corinth in order to bring spiritual help to the Church. "And in this confidence I was minded to come unto you before, that ye might have a second benefit" (2 Corinthians i. 15). He changed his plans, however, when he learned of the sin that was abounding in the Church, and wrote to them instead. This is the epistle he wrote.

THE EPISTLE

The book divides itself into two main sections : —

(1) INFORMATION REPORTED TO PAUL — occupying the first five and a half chapters.

(2) INFORMATION DISCOVERED BY PAUL — making up the balance of the book.

Much of the reported information came from Apollos, from the house of Chloe (i. 11), and others.

(1) INFORMATION REPORTED TO PAUL (Chapters i. - v.)
The first nine verses are an

INTRODUCTION. "Paul, called to be an apostle of Jesus Christ through the Will of God . . . " The difference in the salutation from book to book is noteworthy. In both of the epistles to the Corinthians he introduced himself as " an apostle of Jesus Christ through the Will of God." This was because the Corinthians had challenged his right to such a title. He was an apostle to the Corinthians, Galatians, Ephesians, and Colossians ; just Paul to the Thessalonians ; a servant to the Romans, Philippians and Titus, when he was instructing others to serve ; and a prisoner when writing to Philemon concerning a slave.

The Apostle, like the Lord when He wrote to the seven Churches in Asia, commended before he condemned. He rejoiced in all the grace that God had bestowed upon them, and the resulting testimony.

CHURCH DISORDERS. These were several in number. The first was that of

Contention (chapter i.). The Church at Corinth was divided against itself, not on the matter of doctrine but on personality. A party spirit prevailed among the believers, what is sometimes referred to as favouritism. Some followed Paul, because he was the first one they knew and, maybe, he was simple in his delivery and easy to understand. Another section favoured Apollos, because he was eloquent in speech and powerful in style. Such would appeal to the Greeks who boasted of their knowledge and their superior education. Others chose Cephas. These would have been the Jewish converts who had regard for anything that pertained to the law, and Cephas, or Peter, was certainly the apostle of the circumcision.

Another class claimed they were of Christ. These were those who sought to break away from any human agent or any worldly tag. This, of course, was right and proper except, in so doing, they created an enmity, established a partiality, and made their virtue to become a vice.

The Church is to live in the joy of fellowship, not in the spirit of animosity. It is to exercise love, not hate. It is to know the strength of consolidation, not the weakness of division. It is to know a loyalty in the Gospel, not a defence of the Gospel. Doctrinal differences and denominational dogmas have driven more people from Christ and the Church than they have ever drawn to it.

Paul pinpoints the cause of all such factions for then and now in verse 9, " The wisdom of the wise." Why do we argue ? What do we seek to defend ? Is it our devoted love for the Lord ? Or is it our dogged pride in what we think ? The Jews sought a sign, the Greeks wisdom, and we our intellect.

All of these things must be destroyed by the one and only Person — Christ — through the one and only work — the Cross, or Christ and Him crucified.

Worldly Wisdom (chapter ii.). The Apostle develops this last thought as he moves on into chapter ii. with a continuance of his general theme. It is an attack upon those who desired that the wisdom of their philosophy should outweigh the simplicity of the Gospel. He pointed out that it was because the rulers of the people thought they knew everything, that they had crucified the Lord. If they had been ready to learn they would not have done it. " Which none of the princes of this world knew : for had they known it, they would not have crucified the Lord of glory " (ii. 8). Spiritual virtues are not to be comprehended by worldly reasonings. Spiritual things are spiritually discerned. They are hidden from the worldly wise and revealed to babes. Babes do not reason the love of a mother or the protection of a father — they accept.

Carnality (chapter iii.). This was another sin which had been filed against the Corinthian Christians. Fleshly desire, self, pride, and all that belongs to the carnal passions of the flesh, are a hindrance to spiritual growth.

In moral issues, we are to be as babes or children. In practice, we are to be men. These Christians were still babes, but not in the sense of weakness and innocence.

The word " babes " in verse 1 means " immature." They had failed to grow. The time must come when the child is weaned from the breast and learns to eat solid food. If this does not happen at a certain age, then the child is abnormal and growth is stunted.

Paul charged this Church with such immaturity but, alas, they are not alone. Too many Churches to-day are nurseries for immature babes, when they ought to be armouries for battle-hardened soldiers, able to resist the devil and to wrestle against the powers of darkness.

If these Christians had grown in grace and in the knowledge of Christ Jesus the Lord then, instead of comparing ministers, they would have been harmonising ministries. They would have known that ministries are complementary to each other, that one man plants, another waters, but God, and God alone, gives the increase. This should mean that there is no superiority in the various forms of service. Each is dependent upon the other. All labourers in the Church should be workers together with God.

Paul strengthens his argument, from verse 10 onwards, by using the metaphor of a building, where there must be the co-operation of many craftsmen. If the plasterer despises the painter, and the plumber boasts over the electrician, or the carpenter says that he has no need of the bricklayer, where will be the building ? Every tradesman and craftsman must work with his neighbour, and all must obey the architect. Even so, we, as Christians, are labourers together, fellow-labourers with each other. One is a worker with children, another is an able personal worker, some evangelise, others teach. The pianist, soloist, leader, writer, organiser, preacher, all have to obey the great Architect of the Christian faith and of the Church — God Himself — if we are to grow into a holy temple in the Lord. We are to be concerned with foundation not faction, and there is only one foundation — Jesus Christ the Lord.

Having dealt with the matter of workmanship, the Apostle directs the attention of the Corinthian Christians, and of ourselves also, to the matter of material. A good foundation will never justify faulty work or inferior material. Wood, hay, and stubble, are things which grow on top of the earth and are subjected to fire. Gold, silver, and precious stones come from the bosom of the earth. The first grow quickly and disappear quickly. The second are age-long and are precious. They speak of the deep things of life. Ought we not to examine the quality and the motive of our service ? If we were honest, most of us would have to confess that so much is surface or duty, and so little has the depth of devotion. We should not be building for time, but for eternity.

Having thus reproved the Church, the Apostle immediately vindicates himself lest his reproof should be rejected as coming from one who had not the authority to correct others.

His authority was twofold : —

(1) *He was a minister of Christ* (iv. 1), as were also those who laboured with him. The connotation of this word "minister" is "under-rower," and refers to a common sailor pulling on the oars with others under the command of the captain. Those who want to exalt the position of the minister to one of "lords over God's heritage," need to appreciate the definition of the word MINISTER — it means "serving."

Paul is declaring that, whilst they would favour one personality against another, their authority or power was not in themselves. They only possessed that which they had received of the Lord. God alone was the Captain, and unless they, Paul and Cephas and

Apollos, and the rest of Christ's ministers, pulled together, each equally on his own oar, then the boat of the Church would only go round in circles and there would be no progress. Oh, that we, as ministers, knew the same humility and unity as were exercised by Paul !

(2) *Steward of the mysteries of God* (iv. 1). A steward is a trusted agent who handles and dispenses his master's properties. God had entrusted to His servants, the apostles, His Word. He had made known His Truth to them by revelation. They were to handle these things on His behalf, in His Name, and for His glory.

One thing is required of stewards. It is not ability, power, success, or eloquence. A steward may have these things. In fact these were the things which had attracted certain people to certain apostles. The required qualification is faithfulness. "Moreover it is required in stewards, that a man be found faithful" (iv. 2), faithful in discharging his obligations to his master. The approval of satisfaction is not to come from the steward, nor yet from the customer, but from the master. So Paul says, in effect: "You do not judge me — I do not judge myself — but He that judgeth me is the Lord" (v. 4). This judgment will take place in the last days, when the Lord shall set up His Bema, and our works shall be tried as to what sort they are.

The Church at Corinth was about as deceived in its appraisals as is the Church to-day. The cross is making its appearance everywhere. It is being inscribed into modern Church architecture, and figured in stained glass windows. It is being displayed on the pulpit or altar, and is being worn around the necks of women. It is being embossed on the covers of Bibles, and displayed in pictures and on monuments. It is always an empty cross around which man is placing a halo of glory, but to Christ it was a thing of shame. To Him the halo was a crown of thorns. The cry of the Lord was : " Father, let it pass from Me." The gory cross has been changed for a glory symbol, the suffering has been lost for a sanctimoniousness, its reality has been surrendered for a formality.

Likewise the ministry, it has become a coveted position instead of a consecrated condition. It is a profession instead of a calling. It savours authority rather than service. Before a man enters the ministry he ought to read the latter part of this chapter. "For I think that God hath set forth us the apostles last, as it were appointed to death . . . we are fools . . . we are weak . . . we are despised . . . " for Christ's sake. To serve Christ is to suffer, even as He suffered in serving us.

Social Sins (chapter v.). The whole of this chapter is given over to a gross sin found in one of the members of this Church. The sin was one of immorality. It has already been noted that such sin was common in the practices of the city and, seemingly, it was in the Church to a degree, but now one of the members committed the sin in its grossest form. Instead of the Church dealing with this irregularity, it was allowing the member to continue to enjoy all the privileges of its fellowship, without reproof or correction. Failure to deal with misconduct is equal to granting permission to commit it. Such toleration would bring a complete failure to the Christian Church. The influence of the Church in a sinful world would be gone if the sins of the world were permitted to be enjoyed in the Church.

Paul minced no words in this matter. He demanded that the offender be excommunicated from the assembly before the leaven of sin permeated the whole Church and caused it to become a corrupt thing.

Two lessons are to be learned. Firstly, that the laws of the Old Testament, so far as moral issues are concerned, are still binding upon the saints of the New Testament. Grace is not a cloak for sin or maliciousness, neither does it free from the requirements of God's holy law. The second lesson is that a Church should not allow offenders of the laws of God to be partakers in holy things. The Church, as a body, must exercise its discipline.

Too many people are permitted to be members of, and even to be officers in, the Church of to-day, who are divorced and remarried, or are known to be dishonest in business, or are openly engaging in other sins. Such things should never be tolerated. When they are, it means the loss of power and influence on the part of the Church, in which case it might just as well close its doors for, when the salt has lost its savour, it is good for nothing.

Judgment (chapter vi.). Whilst dealing with this sin question, the Apostle took the opportunity to say that not only should the Corinthian Church have dealt with that matter, but also with all matters wherein its members went wrong. It should be a tribunal handling its own problems. His language is strong. " Dare any of you . . . go to law . . . ? " Of course, when it is the world that is in the wrong it may be necessary to seek the protection of

the law, but when it is a brother it is better to suffer the wrong
than to seek the judgment of the world against a fellow-saint.

As Moses, Samuel, and other Old Testament leaders had to
judge the affairs of Israel, so should the Church judge the affairs
of its members.

Other matters are also dealt with in the chapter, under the
subject of lawfulness versus expediency. Many things may appear
right. They may be perfectly legitimate so far as we are personally
concerned, but, as members of the Body of Christ, we are members
one of another and, therefore, have to take into consideration our
influence upon the lives of other people. The world is very selfish.
All it says is, "I can please myself," but the Church should be
selfless. Our concern should be as to how we can please Him Who
hath called us. "What? Know ye not that your body is the
temple of the Holy Ghost which is in you, which ye have of God,
and ye are not your own? For ye are bought with a price:
therefore glorify God in your body, and in your spirit, which are
God's" (vi. 19-20).

(2) INFORMATION DISCOVERED BY PAUL
(Chapters vii. - xvi.)

OUR CONDUCT FOR CHRIST'S SAKE. The matters that
follow were discovered by Paul as a result of a letter he had
received from the Church (vii. 1). The subject still concerns the
conduct of saints in the Church. He is teaching here, and in the
few previous verses, that we are to keep our bodies pure, virile,
strong, and wholesome, because they are the temples of God. All
of our energies are to be devoted to Him because they belong to
Him. We have been purchased by Him, with His Blood. We
have died to self that we may be alive to Him.

Again the Apostle deals with the matter of

MARRIAGE (chapter vii.). Practice is often the outcome of
teaching or non-teaching. False teaching, in turn, brings confused
minds. In Corinth there was the doctrine of loose living which
was coming from the Gnostics (see chapter on I, II, III John), and,
on the other hand, the teaching of celibacy propounded by the
Ascetics. Therefore Paul shows, on the one side, the lawfulness
and rightness of marriage as that which had been ordained by God,
whilst, on the other side, the man or the woman who remained
single for the Gospel's sake could serve the Lord much better
because they would be free from the commitments and obligations
which naturally belong to married life.

MEAT OFFERED TO IDOLS (chapter viii.). Some people considered that an idol was only an inert thing. It was no real god. It had no life and, therefore, it had no influence, which meant that it could do neither good nor evil. Meat offered to it could not in any way be contaminated and so no harm could come in partaking of it. This, of course, would be a fact which we to-day would endorse, but, says Paul, such a reasoning can be a revelation of knowledge which, in turn, can be a display of superiority. It can cause a man to be puffed up. Better that we display the hallmark of charity, which is a consideration of our fellow-man. To him an idol can be a very real thing, with power and influence. To him that meat could have been blessed or sanctified. If I eat that meat, to that idol worshipper I believe the same as he does. I endorse his religion. I encourage him to continue in a way that is not right. Then it is better that, for the sake of my weak brother, I refrain from eating, even although I have a clear conscience.

This principle applies to a host of things in life. It should apply to every action of the believer, and it will if our actions are motivated by love.

The statement in verse 1 " but charity edifieth " reads in the Greek " Love buildeth up." The chapter is telling the Christian that he should not abuse his Christian liberties any more than he should yield his Christian principles.

The Apostle continues to reason this thought in chapter ix. in a personal fashion, declaring that

SELF-DENIAL must be practised for Christ's sake. If this should be done in a real spirit of love it should not be an irksome thing but only a matter of personal adjustment. If one should consider that it comes within the realm of discipline, then that discipline should do us more good than harm. There were many things that Paul could have done, which would have been legal and moral, but from which he refrained for the sake of others.

In the matter of discipline, should a Christian complain of any self-denial he may have to make that might be for the eternal glory of some soul, when men for honours make sacrifices that are only temporary ? Paul points to men who,

SEEKING MASTERY over other contestants in the race, endeavour to control their habits that they might be temperate in all things. In their desire to win the race, or to be victor in the conflict, they never consider that their training, their discipline and denials, are sacrifices. They do those things gladly because their eye is on the reward.

Christ endured the Cross because of the joy that was set before Him. Lord, help me to lift mine eyes from temporal desires and selfish gratifications that I might see the eternal values of that soul who needs my help and example.

EXAMPLES (chapter x.). Paul showed to the Corinthians, and ourselves, the measure to which we are obligated to others. For this he went back to the Old Testament, declaring that the things which happened unto those people were for ensamples, and that they were written for our admonition.

> They were led by a pillar of cloud or fire, which was ever with them in the desert.
> We are led by the Lord throughout the whole of our earthly journey.
> They all passed through the Red Sea and were baptised with Moses.
> We should pass through the waters of baptism, and be baptised into Christ.
> They all ate the same spiritual meat.
> We all feed on the Manna of God's Word.
> They all drank the same spiritual drink — the Smitten Rock.
> We all drink of Him, the Water of Life.
> They lusted after the things of this world, and were punished with serpents.
> We, too, must be punished if we become carnally minded.
> They wandered, they lusted, they murmured, they tempted, and accordingly God dealt with them.
> " Wherefore let him that thinketh he standeth take heed lest he fall."

DRESS AND CONDUCT (chapter xi.). This concerned the behaviour of women within the Church. Strange as it may seem, the writings of Paul have been accepted as the doctrine and conduct of the Christian Church throughout the centuries, he being recognised as a man inspired of God, and yet there have been made some exceptions. It is difficult to discover the grounds for these exceptions, unless it is the desire of so many to be conformed to this world. One of these exceptions is the matter of dress, particularly headdress.

Is it possible to give an honest reason to God why, in the light of the statements of verses 3 to 15, and in the light of our own confession that all Scripture is given by inspiration of God, and also in the light of chapter viii. that we should abstain from anything that offends a brother, women do not wear hats in church ? (The practice has become common in America where choirs sing before the congregation, and women lead certain meetings and auxiliaries, and speak in young people's meetings, without a head covering.)

A difference of opinion has existed in recent days because some will try to excuse their conduct by declaring that their hair is their covering. However, this is not a true interpretation because a woman was forbidden to pray with her head uncovered, and it is obvious that a woman cannot take her hair off and put it on at will.

The Scripture teaches that a woman's hair is her glory. Therefore *it* should be covered.

It must be recognised that a woman in the East who had her hair uncovered or unveiled was a vulgar and sinful woman, and must be avoided. A covering of the hair is obviously referred to in each instance, and not the hair for a covering.

Let us stand on the broadest basis that we can and yet remain consistent with our understanding of Scripture. That basis would be principle, not detail. The principle, which is obvious enough throughout the chapter, is that the covering of the head was an act whereby one acknowledged the presence of a superior. Therefore the woman covered her head as an acknowledgment that she was coming into the presence of a Holy God : likewise the men uncovered their feet. As to the fact that men no longer uncover their feet but, instead, uncover their head, is a point of detail. The principle remains with the men.

This can be carried far beyond the chapter under consideration, and removed entirely from Paul, for some think it was only his idea.

The High Priest of Israel covered his head with a mitre when he was in the presence of God. In the British Law Court a woman must cover her head as an act of respect to the authority of the law being dispensed in that Court. A soldier, when in public, is expected to wear his hat or he dishonours the Queen's uniform. In fact, there is no official uniform or dress which is devoid of a headdress, except an American church choir ! If a woman should be invited to a high social function she would certainly wear a hat. If a man were invited to meet Royalty, or the President, he would

wear his best suit — maybe he would even buy a new one! He
would clean his shoes and feel proud to stand in the presence of
such nobility. He used to go to church in his best clothes. Now
he comes into the presence of God in a sports shirt, or without his
coat, or with dirty shoes, and sits and eats sweets or chews gum
and tries to sing the praises of God. Where is principle? When
deterioration starts we can slip a long way!
The rest of the chapter deals with

THE LORD'S TABLE (vv. 17-34). The Lord had established
this feast as one of commemoration. It was to take the place of
the Passover Feast, which was Jewish both in its rite and remembrance. It belonged to the law; but the Christian Church embraced both Jew and Gentile, and was of grace. The first feast
was national, a reminder of when God delivered a nation from a
nation; the second was universal, remembering the Lord Who
delivered the "whosoever will" from the power of the Devil and
made believing man become one in the Beloved. The feast was
to be sacramental, with one central point of focus — "Himself."
Instead, the people were bringing food and drink with them, and
were following the practices of idolatrous worship in their love
feasts. It started as something communal, then divided into cliques
eating together here and there, and ended in gluttony and drunkenness, the result being that the spirit of worship was lost in the
spirit of wantonness. The supper was overshadowed by their
feast.

The Apostle is putting this matter in order. Men were eating
and drinking damnation to themselves. Nothing was left that was
worthy of God.

The Table of the Lord is an exclusive thing, not exclusive to
certain believers, but exclusive *to* all believers. The exclusion is *of*
the unbeliever.

SPIRITUAL GIFTS (Chapters xii. - xiv.). Three chapters are
given to this subject. In chapter xii the gifts are all dealt with as
a whole. They are many and are diverse, but there is only one
Giver. Although referred to as the Gifts of the Spirit, yet they
come from the whole Triune God. The operations are of God
(verse 6), the administrations are of the Lord (verse 5), and the
manifestations are of the Spirit (verse 4).

There is a great deal of controversy concerning these gifts
as to whether they are still the property of the Church, and should
they be exercised to-day. No one is going to raise a question as
to whether wisdom, knowledge, helps, government, are required;

but, at the same time, the subject of tongues, interpretation, and healings will be debated. This creates a partiality, an acceptance and rejection according to our own feelings.

The Church should accept every one of these gifts, for there appears to be no time in history when any of them was withdrawn. They make a unifying whole in the Church of Jesus Christ, as the many members make one body in the realm of the physical. When a person can show a generation in which God withdrew some of man's members because modern invention has made things less necessary, then one can accept a dispensation in which there came a withdrawal of spiritual gifts.

The tragic situation is that certain people have run riot with the more demonstrative and spectacular gifts, as healings, tongues and interpretation, at the expense of the more important gifts of wisdom, knowledge, and helps, so that the rest of the Church has left the subject strictly alone. The one section can be as guilty as the other.

Paul neither denounces nor denies the operation of any gift of the Spirit. Contrariwise, he declares that many members are required to complete the body, and that the denial of right of any member by any other member, never alters the fact that the member is still there functioning in its own capacity. What Paul does emphasise is that the uncomely members are often the more important members! To use an example, we take great care of our eyes and ears, and are anxious concerning our heart and lungs, but who ever considers his great toes! Surely they would be called uncomely members? However, if they were amputated, not only would one not be able to walk any more, but one could not even stand. The whole equilibrium of the body is dependent upon those two toes.

Tongues and healings have their place, but not necessarily first place.

Whilst all of these gifts have a purpose in the mechanics of Christian life, they will only function rightly and freely whilst operating with the lubricating oil of love, for " Though I speak with the tongues of men and of angels, and have not love, I am become as sounding brass, or a tinkling cymbal."

LOVE (chapter xiii.). This is one of the treasured chapters of the Bible. Halley, in his *Bible Handbook*, uses these potent words : " Love remains. The perfection of human character, the most powerful ultimate force in the universe. The essence of

God's nature. We may all possess it. The Church's most effective weapon. Irresistible. Undying. Eternal."

WOMEN SPEAKING IN THE CHURCH (Chapter xiv.). The whole of this chapter is given to the matter of tongues and prophecy, and particularly to their control in the early Church. What might be the subject of greatest importance is in verse 34 : " Let your women keep silence in the churches : for it is not permitted unto them to speak ; . . . " This statement has been badly abused, especially by certain sections of Christ's Church who forbid a woman to open her lips in any way or for any purpose. This attitude creates a contradiction of the Scriptures, because Paul, in this same Epistle, sanctions women to pray and prophesy in the Church. " But every woman that prayeth or prophesieth with her head uncovered dishonoureth her head " (1 Corinthians xi. 5). This verse cannot be related to the home because Paul is dealing with Church conduct, and neither does a person prophesy or preach at home. Moreover, Philip had daughters who prophesied. Women were the first to carry the message of resurrection.

If we are honest in dividing the Word, the text will not be taken out of its context, and the context concerns speaking in tongues. In relationship to that subject alone Paul says : " Let your women keep silence in the Churches." It has to be admitted that the largest portion of speaking in tongues, as practised in Pentecostal Churches to-day, is done by women. This in itself is contrary to Scripture and makes the practice wrong.

The other reference to the ministry of women, in 1 Timothy ii. 12, is to forbid her to teach or usurp authority over the man. There is a measure of equality but no allowance for superiority. " Let all things be done decently and in order."

RESURRECTION (Chapter xv.)

(a) *Necessity.* Paul never lost an opportunity to preach the subject of resurrection, both of Christ and of the believer. Here in this chapter are the most beautiful and expressive words on this subject. The reasoning is sublime. Here are words that have brought more comfort than any others to thousands of sorrowing hearts. The Gospel is here in a nutshell.

Christ died for our sins, was buried, rose again from the dead, and was seen of many. These things were not the imaginations of a few people, but were " according to the Scriptures."

Having given all the evidence of Christ's resurrection, His victory over death and the grave, Paul moves on to declare that, if Christ rose from the dead, we too shall be raised in Him. This is the great and glorious hope of the Church, the comfort of all sad hearts, the victory which takes away the sting of death, and the light that dispels the gloom of the tomb.

(b) *Manner.* The man who does not believe in the resurrection is of all men most miserable.

The parable the Apostle uses to declare the glorious truth of resurrection is beautiful in its simplicity and perfect in its understanding.

For the physical body to become a participant in the spiritual realm, there must be an adjustment — in fact, a change. It is what is called a metamorphosis, or a transformation.

The seed must be cast into the ground and, as a seed, die, if there is to be a flower, a fruit, or a vegetable. The caterpillar must creep away into the chrysalis and die, if it is ever to be a beautiful butterfly flitting on the wing in the glorious sunshine. Neither the seed nor the caterpillar are beautiful in themselves. Their after-life is more beautiful than the former existence. So it is with the resurrection. As the mourners stand by the open grave, if the one they are laying to rest has died in the Lord then that corpse is just the seed being planted into the ground. It is as the caterpillar creeping away into its sleep, to await a resurrection morn. Believers do not die. They sleep until the morning. Then the corruptible (that decomposing body) shall put on incorruption (endless life), and the mortal (the living who have bodies still subjected to death) shall put on immortality (a deathless body), and together we shall enter into that fuller, more glorious life, when we shall be changed into His likeness.

Because of this blessed hope there is given the challenge : " Therefore, my beloved brethren, be ye stedfast, unmoveable, always abounding in the work of the Lord, forasmuch as ye know that your labour is not in vain in the Lord " (xv. 58).

This would have been a triumphant note upon which to end his Epistle, but from consolations the Apostle moves on to

THE COLLECTION (Chapter xvi.). It is his final matter in Church conduct.

Christian living is not made up entirely of getting, even although our lives should be enriched constantly from day to day out of the abundance of His grace and power. It is also one of giving — giving of our time and worship to the Lord, and giving of our substance to the work of the Lord at home and overseas. This giving should be done unostentatiously.

The pastor sitting in his vestry to receive the annual Thank-offering and writing out the receipt with many thanks to the rich, whilst the poor feel a sense of embarrassment, does not fit into this verse.

A few exhortations and encouragements end the Epistle, which included a promise to visit them personally in due course.

II CORINTHIANS

MINISTERIAL SUFFERING

*" But the Lord said unto him, Go thy way : for he is a chosen
vessel unto Me, to bear My Name before the Gentiles, and
kings, and the children of Israel : For I will shew him how
great things he must suffer for My Name's sake"*

(ACTS ix. 15-16)

INTRODUCTION

It will be remembered that Paul had written his first letter
to the Corinthian church in order to deal with a gross sin which
had been permitted, and to adjust many other matters of church
conduct.

This second epistle followed closely after the first. The
Apostle had written to Corinth with such firmness that he had
many misgivings as to how the letter had been received. Patiently
he was awaiting the reaction. Faithfulness to God, and to duty,
has caused many heartaches and many sleepless nights for the
servants of God, about which faithless church members have never
given a moment of thought.

During this anxious period Paul had become involved in the
riot which took place in Ephesus (Acts xix. 21-41), in which he
nearly lost his life. He tells the Corinthians of this, in the eighth
verse of the first chapter.

When he left Ephesus he began to move toward Corinth (i.
15), but, whilst in Macedonia (i. 16 and ii. 13), he found Titus who
had just returned from Corinth.

From Titus he learned that the Church had received his letter
with charity, and that it had been very effective. Nevertheless
there were those who had become very indignant and, therefore,
were challenging Paul's apostleship and his authority to interfere
in their affairs.

This caused the Apostle to sit down and write to them another
letter, known as Paul's second Epistle to the Corinthians.

It was written from Macedonia and is one of great feeling.
In some places it is joyous and affectionate, in other places it is

passionate and stern, commending here and rebuking there. This was because of the disaffection. The majority had repented as a result of the first letter. These members he was seeking to encourage, but there was the minority which was suspicious and critical, and was seeking to damage the Apostle's character. The letter was written to the Church as a whole and, therefore, to the two factions.

THE EPISTLE

The keyword of the Epistle is " Comfort " and, with it, several associate words, so that the words comfort, consolation, commendation, and confidence are repeated throughout the book no less than thirty-seven times.

The book divides into three parts in the main analysis.

(a) EXPLANATION (Chapters i. - vii.)

(b) EXHORTATION (Chapters vii. - ix.)

(c) VINDICATION (Chapters x. - xiii.)

These divisions also create a past, present, and future.

Past ..... Paul's relationship with Corinth.

Present ..... The Church's immediate duties.

Future ..... Future relationship of Paul's apostleship.

In this present treatise the book will be divided : —

(1) PAUL IN CORRESPONDENCE.

(2) COMFORT AND CONSOLATION.

(3) CHARACTER AS COMMENDATION.

(4) CONCERNING THE COLLECTION.

(5) CONFIDENCE OF HIS CALLING.

(a) EXPLANATION — PAUL'S RELATIONSHIP WITH CORINTH (Chapters i. - vii.)

(1) PAUL IN CORRESPONDENCE

The Apostle was a great letter writer. One may be sure that he wrote many more letters than those which are in the Bible, some that were general and others that were private. His correspondence was very effective ; in fact, at times more effective than his preaching or his person. Such is declared in the Epistle now under consideration. "For his letters, say they, are weighty and powerful ; but his bodily presence is weak, and his speech contemptible " (x. 10). Paul's concern for those at a distance was as real as for those at hand. He was not only concerned for the sinner but he interested himself in the young convert. Philemon is an example. Then, too, the newly established Churches throughout Asia needed to be encouraged, or warned, whilst pastors, as Timothy and Jude, needed instruction. The Apostle's wide vision and concern are spoken of in this Epistle as he says : " Beside those things that are without, that which cometh upon me daily, the care of ALL the churches " (xi. 28).

How many saints have engaged in this ministry since the days of the Apostle ? Some of them have been recorded and are now in our libraries. Such a ministry is dying out and yet is much needed to-day, a letter of consolation or comfort, another of encouragement or commendation, advice here or warning there. Have you ever written to the young convert, the minister, the visiting preacher, the author of that book which helped you so much, or to the lonely missionary on the field, or to that heart-broken mother ? We are exhorted to admonish one another in the faith.

(2) COMFORT AND CONSOLATION

The principal reason why Paul wrote this second Epistle was to bring to the Corinthian Church a measure of comfort and consolation.

The saints were somewhat distressed because Paul had promised to visit them, after which he had changed his mind. They considered this as failure on his part and that he was unreliable. Therefore, he thought it necessary to write and explain his position and to reassure them that it was not a matter of neglect or indifference, but, rather, one of wisdom. The visit had been postponed for their good.

Having heard of the sin that was in their midst, he would have come with a rod of chastisement, which would have grieved both them and him. Words might have been uttered for which they would always be sorry. He had decided that, in these circumstances, it would be better for all concerned if he stayed away and wrote a letter which, of course, was his first Epistle ; but now that the wrong had been righted he was ready to come to them.

In the first chapter he made known to them that, if they had suffered tribulation, so had he ; if they needed comfort and consolation, so did he. Both could find this comfort in the God of all comfort, and both could find it the one in the other, for often to that end did the Lord permit men to suffer, that they might comfort those who were in distress. " Who comforteth us in all our tribulation, that we may be able to comfort them which are in any trouble, by the comfort wherewith we ourselves are comforted of God " (i. 4).

The whole of chapter i. having been given to introduction, chapter ii. becomes a chapter of

Discipline. Paul assured them that, if his first letter had hurt them, it had hurt him more in having to write it, but now that the letter had accomplished its purpose they could all rejoice in it.

Being satisfied that the sinner had been excommunicated, the Apostle gave further advice on the matter, recommending that, if the brother now out of the Church had repented of his sin and had corrected the wrong he had done, the Church should not continue to show a bitter spirit or continue the judgment against him but, rather, forgive him and receive him back into fellowship. This was exactly what the Lord had done for them, and has done for us, for when we confessed our sins, He was faithful and just to forgive us our sins, and to cleanse us from all unrighteousness.

Writing to the Galatians the Apostle said : " Brethren, if a man be overtaken in a fault, ye which are spiritual, restore such an one in the spirit of meekness ; considering thyself, lest thou also be tempted " (Galatians vi. 1).

Should these Corinthian brethren fail in this respect, then the person concerned might be lost entirely to the enemy, and so Satan would get an advantage of them.

This is something which might be given some diligent consideration in the Church to-day. They were not to wait until the guilty party asked for renewed fellowship. He might never do that, for he might have overmuch sorrow and be too shamefaced. He had had his punishment (ii. 6), so now they were to go out and meet him, invite him back, and comfort him with all their love.

It must be emphasised that this does not concern a person living in sin, but one who has repented and corrected his wrong. " And be ye kind one to another, tenderhearted, forgiving one another, even as God for Christ's sake hath forgiven you " (Ephesians iv. 32).

Paul's deep concern for this Church was manifested when he declared that God had opened for him a great door of opportunity in Troas, and that he was enjoying a time of precious ministry, yet it was clouded by his concern for them. He had expected

Titus to bring news of them, but he had not as yet met him. Therefore he went in search of him because he could find no rest in
spirit until he had obtained a first-hand report.

When Paul did find Titus, and had learned the good news,
then he rejoiced in the Lord and in the triumphs of His grace (ii.
14).

(3) CHARACTER AS COMMENDATION

Ministry. The subject changes completely in chapter iii. A
question had been raised by Paul's enemies as to his right of
apostleship, and as to his authority for interfering in local Church
matters. One would imagine that it would be this same group of
people who had been demanding that every preacher should carry
with him his credentials, which should be in the form of a letter
of commendation. This demand was to be imposed upon the
Apostle Paul as well as every would-be preacher. In some cases
it might be a very commendable thing. There are sections of the
Christian Church who make such requests to-day, particularly
regarding the Lord's Table, but such a procedure carries the risk
of abuse. Who makes the commendation, especially for such a
one as Paul ? Some letters of recommendation are no more worthy
than the persons who carry them. People can give such letters as
favours to friends, some make them purely denominational. Many
churches have been disappointed, even hurt, in accepting such
letters. Men have been asked to write letters for people who are
unknown personally, and whose ministry and qualifications have
never been heard nor tested.

The Apostle reasons, and rightly so, that every man ought to
be his own commendation. It should be character, not caricature.
The difference between these two terms is — " Character — the
peculiar qualities impressed by nature or habit on a person, which
distinguish him from others." The word comes from a Latin root
meaning " an engraved mark." The other word " caricature,"
means " to represent in an exaggerated fashion."

Character is that which will always precede a man. If a man
is faithful in his handling of the Word of God, earnest in delivering his message, consistent in his interpretation of truth, and men
are rejoicing in that he led them into a knowledge of salvation
or taught them how to live the victorious life, if his practice is in
accordance with his preaching, what other commendation does
such a man need ? This man is known before he comes to town.

The Apostle appealed to the people themselves. " Need we
. . . epistles of commendation to you, or letters of commendation
from you ? Ye are our epistles written in our hearts, known and
read of all men " (iii. 1-2).

Such epistles and such commendations are the most effective,
written not with ink but in the Spirit, written not on stone, as was
the law, but in fleshy hearts, as is the Gospel.

The Apostle draws a comparison between the two ministries,
that which was of God and that which belonged to the pretender,
or the man without the Divine Call and, therefore, without the
Divine Unction.

Spiritual	*Carnal*
The Gospel of Grace.	A ministry of law.
Written on fleshy hearts.	Written on tables of stone.
Was in the power of the Spirit.	Was in the deadness of the letter.
Was a message of life.	It concerned death.
It was unveiled.	It was veiled by a darkened mind.
Concerned righteousness.	Carried condemnation.
Its message was eternal.	Was only temporary.

Therefore it should be easy for men to discern between
commercialised evangelism and Spirit-filled ministry. The tragedy
of to-day is that, whilst these things can be discerned by the Church,
they are not always acknowledged by the leaders. These are more
anxious to have crowds and increased numbers, which they call
" success," than a deepened work of grace in the hearts and lives
of their people.

Most of chapter iii. illustrates this truth, with Moses as an
example of one who experienced the wonder and the glory of the
presence of God. This effulgence continued to radiate from him
so that it was necessary for him to put a veil over his face because
the people could not behold him.

If this glory were manifested from the mount of the law, what
should be the glory which should radiate from the Gospel of His
grace !

The veil of unbelief is still robbing man of the glory that excelleth. Christ came to remove that veil in order that, by faith, we
might behold His Glory, the glory of the only begotten of the
Father.

As Moses reflected the glory of God, and as a mirror reflects that which comes within its focus, so are we to reflect the Lord until we are changed into the very same image.

The theme continues into chapter iv. with the declaration that, being privileged to enjoy this relationship, we must live a life of strict honesty in handling the Word of God and in preaching the Gospel, making sure that we preach not ourselves, but Jesus Christ the Lord. Note how Paul emphasises the Lordship of Jesus, as well as His saving grace. There is a danger to preach the Saviourhood of Christ at the expense of His Lordship. This does not produce the best Christians because the outlook can be " get " not " give ", and that is already a big weakness in human nature.

We must ever be conscious of our own unworthiness. We are only earthen vessels. His is the excellency of the power.

As to the earthen vessel, the Apostle makes the declaration that, amidst all troubles, perplexities and persecutions, the Christian can always be victorious through His grace, for the afflictions of the moment are as nothing in comparison with the glory that is yet to be. Our troubles are temporal, our triumphs are eternal.

Separation. Paul pursues his reasoning of chapter iv. into the opening verses of chapter v. where he introduces his readers to the matter of life after death. He speaks with absolute certainty. " For we know that if our earthly house of this tabernacle (this temporary abode) were dissolved, we have a building of God, an house not made with hands, eternal in the heavens."

In that day we shall stand before the Judgment Seat of Christ. This is not for the judgment of sins. The unbeliever will stand before the Great White Throne for that condemnation. For the believer sin has already been judged at the Cross and condemnation is past. Paul is referring to the Bema, or the Judgment Seat of Christ, at which the believer will be tried for his service, and from which he will receive reward according to the faithfulness with which the service has been rendered.

Not only are we to anticipate our citizenship in that future realm, but we are to realise that our citizenship has already been established to enjoy in the present for, " if any man be in Christ Jesus, he is a new creature."

As citizens of another realm we are strangers in the present realm. We are here as ambassadors, the representatives of heaven's eternal King, calling upon men to be reconciled to God.

An ambassador holds the greatest and most honourable office in the realm. He represents the king, whilst others represent the government. He must know the mind and will of his sovereign and act accordingly. As ambassadors, therefore, we are representatives of the God of heaven.

Paul goes a step further, a grade higher. All servants of the realm work for their king. We, then, as workers together WITH Him, should not do less. The ambassador in the far-off country sometimes has to make important decisions without opportunity for consultation. The Lord is ever with us and we are with Him. At any time we may have communication through prayer and may know His will.

Paul's sufferings. The Apostle's faithfulness to his Lord, his true representation, sometimes brought him into difficulty and suffering, for he was in an alien land. We, too, shall learn that His enemies are our enemies, but in all of these sufferings we are still more than conquerors through Him Who loved us and gave Himself for us.

The Christian life should be one of separation from the world. Therefore, the command is, " Be ye not unequally yoked together with unbelievers ", which means, be not linked or harnessed into companionship with this world. This present world does not belong to the Christian, and neither does the Spiritual realm belong to this world. This is the world which crucified our Lord, and it would do it again. We should be as foreign to this world as light is to darkness, as Christ is to Belial, and as the Temple is to idols. There are certain elements which will not mix — Christianity and worldliness are two such elements. We are called unto holiness. " Wherefore come out from among them, and be ye separate, saith the Lord " (vi. 17).

(b) EXHORTATION — THE CHURCH'S IMMEDIATE DUTIES (Chapters vii. - ix.)

In chapter vii. the Apostle returns to the subject which had necessitated his first Epistle to this Church. He wished the Church to know that the matter of the sin which had been permitted was not a little thing and that his intervention had not been a matter of petty interference in local Church affairs. The sin was big and grievous and could not possibly remain in a body of people who belonged to a celestial home. It was, therefore, a necessary thing to " cleanse ourselves from all filthiness of the flesh and spirit, perfecting holiness in the fear of God " (vii. 1).

Paul was comforted in the knowledge that they had corrected the wrong.

(4) CONCERNING THE COLLECTION

Chapter viii. brings a complete change in the subject — or is it a complete change ? Paul now is dealing with the matter of the collection. He has been speaking of the glories of the Christian faith, of the riches of His grace, of the inheritance of the saints. With all that the believer has received and is receiving, maybe it is natural to turn to the subject of giving. Two chapters are allocated to a matter for which the Church so often makes an apology.

As a result of a great famine which had stricken Palestine, the people were suffering much privation. Poverty and depression were hitting hard. In such circumstances there comes quite a response from the world. It has happened many times in our own generation, in emergencies that have been created by war, floods, drought, hurricane or famine. Governments take upon themselves the responsibility of relieving the needy. Ofttimes there are minority groups which get left out.

In the time of the Apostle the Jews would help the Jews. The Roman authorities would come to the help of the masses, but the Christians could easily be boycotted. The Jews did not like those who had turned from Judaism, and the Romans looked with disfavour upon those who had turned from their idolatrous system. So Paul made an appeal to the Churches of Asia and Achaia. He told the people of Macedonia of the promise of help which had come from Corinth. He told the Corinthians of the response of the Macedonians, thereby causing the one to encourage the other.

Should a national tragedy hit any part of the world to-day, peoples and governments step in with immediate relief, and we rejoice in such a spirit of brotherhood. In community work there is the same spirit of co-operation — flag days in England, tag days in the United States, public subscriptions for hospitals, clubs, benefits, youth, old age, and other social activities ; but when did the world help a Gospel effort, or come to the aid of a Christian organisation in need ? When did a government contribute to the missionary programme ?

The Church faces financial commitments locally and worldwide. Who is it who meets the need of the missionary on the field, the pastor in his retirement, or the Church in its ministry ? Only the Christian — and the Lord would not have it otherwise. He does not need the unconsecrated money of the world. We have received a commission from the Lord. " Freely ye have received, freely give."

In order that our giving should not be in any way meritorious, and that we should not to seek to purchase for ourselves the favours of the Lord, the Scripture everywhere teaches that we should yield ourselves first in consecration, and afterwards offer our gifts. The Corinthian Church did this very thing. "And this they did, not as we hoped, but first gave their own selves to the Lord, and unto us by the will of God" (viii. 5).

It is on this principle that we should never look to the world for its support. To the world the Lord would say : " Thy money perish with thee."

Giving is part of Christian ministry. Therefore, let it be learned from this letter not how much should be given, but how to give.

(a) *Liberally.* " Abounded unto the riches of their liberality. For to their power, I bear record, yea, and beyond their power they were willing of themselves " (viii. 2-3). The Apostle is writing concerning the self-sacrifice of the Macedonians. They did not give of their abundance but of their poverty ; they did not give according to their ability, but beyond it.

In the next chapter he reverses the tables and tells of the liberality of the Corinthians. And what to those who say that it is asking too much ? Let it be seen that these people gave before they were asked. They gave because they themselves saw the need. The same questioner might reply that it is giving too much. The answer to that is in chapter ix. 6 : " But this I say, He which soweth sparingly shall reap also sparingly ; and he which soweth bountifully shall reap bountifully." God is generous in what He gives in nature. God is generous in His grace and His love. He spared not His only-begotten Son, and He is no man's debtor. Therefore, we can afford to be liberal in giving.

(b) *Proportionately.* This was what had been asked of them in the first Epistle. " Upon the first day of the week let every one of you lay by him in store, *as God hath prospered him* . . . " (1 Corinthians xvi. 2).

This proportionate giving is what is known as tithing. It was basic in Old Testament teaching. Offerings were in excess of the tithe. Whilst the Lord expects from us according to the measure of our prosperity, at the same time the Lord prospers us according to the measure of our giving. Our gifts are accepted " according to that a man hath, and not according to that he hath not " (viii. 12).

(c) *Willingly.* " For if there be first a willing mind . . ." (viii. 12). " Every man according as he hath purposed in his heart, so let him give ; not grudgingly, or of necessity . . . " (ix. 7). Many of us lose the joy of giving because we do it as a duty instead of as a privilege.

(d) *Systematically.* " Upon the first day of the week let every one of you lay by him in store, as God hath prospered him, that there be no gatherings when I come " (1 Corinthians xvi. 2).

Gathering of the gifts was not made weekly as it is in churches to-day, but the gifts had to be put aside weekly, so that they would be waiting when Paul came, and he would not have to make appeals for the collection. Some people only give when they go to church. When they are away on holiday, away for sickness, away because of the weather, or away for any other reason, then they do not give to the Lord either their money or their worship. So the exhortation is to be systematic, to be regular.

(e) *Cheerfully.* "For God loveth a cheerful giver" (ix. 7), giving without a grudge, a complaint, or any dissension. Give as the children of Israel gave for building the Tabernacle. There they had to be stopped because the gifts were greater than the needs on hand. "And they spake unto Moses, saying, The people bring much more than enough for the service of the work, which the Lord commanded to make. And Moses gave commandment, and they caused it to be proclaimed throughout the camp, saying, Let neither man nor woman make any more work for the offering of the sanctuary. So the people were restrained from bringing. For the stuff they had was sufficient for all the work to make it, and too much" (Exodus xxxvi. 5/7).

Against any objection that might be raised, Paul gives a solid reason why we should all be ready and willing givers. " For ye know the grace of our Lord Jesus Christ, that, though He was rich, yet for your sakes He became poor, that ye through His poverty might be rich " (viii. 9).

The Apostle concludes the section with a reminder of the riches of His grace toward us, and culminates the whole with the final verse, " Thanks be unto God for His unspeakable gift " (ix. 15). That gift was His only-begotten Son, the Son of His love. Against His giving, what is ours even at its best ?

(c)   VINDICATION — FUTURE RELATIONSHIP OF PAUL'S
       APOSTLESHIP Chapters x. - xiii.)

(5)   CONFIDENCE OF HIS CALLING

Much of this section is in the form of a defence of his calling.
He was seeking to vindicate his right to his Divine Calling.   The
reason for this was, as has already been seen from his first Epistle,
because of those who had questioned Paul's right to apostleship.
They had disapproved his interference in their Church matters.
Later, these same people had demanded letters of commendation.
They had sought by various means to humiliate Paul, even by
derogative remarks concerning his personal appearance and physical disabilities.

Whilst there was a lack of common courtesy on the part of
these adversaries, there was a great display of Christian courtesy,
blended with a firm adherence to his spiritual calling, on the part
of Paul.

These accusations were coming from false teachers, whose
selfish practices will always be hurt so long as truth has the right
to exercise itself.   When such men cannot deny truth, they will
always seek to pervert or misconstrue it.   If they cannot succeed in
that practice, then they bring false accusations against the servant
of God. What Paul encountered in his day is faced to-day from
the very same adversary.   Let us profit, therefore, from Paul's
handling of the situation.

He was not aggressive but persuasive.   " I beseech you, by
the meekness and gentleness of Christ, who in presence am base
among you, but being absent am bold toward you " (ix. 1).   He
lined up his physical weakness with his spiritual power, and reminded them that, if he had been gentle toward them, it was
because Christ had been gentle.

The enemy had said that his letters were forceful and weighty,
but not his personal presence and preaching. They were weak and
his speech contemptible.

The Apostle assured them that he could be just as forceful
when present, that in the flesh he might be weak, but although he
walked in the flesh and knew its limitations, he did not war after
the flesh.   He warred in the realm of spiritual powers, and there
he would glory in his infirmities that the power of Christ might
rest upon him.

The Apostle uses the word " boast " some twenty times in this argument. Thirteen of these occasions have been translated " glory " in the authorised version. He draws a contrast between a boasting which is after the flesh, and a boasting which is in the Lord, in the One Who could take the weak and the foolish things of this world to bring to naught the mighty man with his worldly wisdom.

If the Apostle had done any boasting, the reason was his jealousy for the Corinthian saints, that they might be the best they could be for the Lord. He had an intense jealousy for the truth of God, lest these people should be beguiled by another gospel.

In his zeal for their spiritual well-being he had taken nothing from them. He had all that they possessed, and more. If they boasted of their Jewish stock, he came from the same seed of Abraham. If they boasted of their Christian ministry, he could boast more because he had suffered more for the Gospel. Whereupon he lists his sufferings (xi. 21-33). As many could boast of the first things and few of the latter things (the sufferings), Paul would gladly make his boast there. " If I must needs glory (boast), I will glory (boast) of the things which concern my infirmities " (xi. 30).

In chapter xii. he tells of one of the occasions of his suffering that came at the hand of man, and of the glory that came out of the same experience granted to him by the Lord. " I knew a man in Christ above fourteen years ago (that man was himself), whether in the body . . . or out of the body, I cannot tell." To understand this statement it is necessary to go back fourteen years in the life of the Apostle. In Acts xiv., during his first missionary tour, the Apostle came to Lystra and there wrought a miracle of healing on a lame man, after which his enemies came down from Antioch and Iconium, stoned him, and then drew him out of the city supposing he had been dead.

It seems evident that this was the unconscious state to which the Apostle referred, when he did not know whether he was in the body or out of the body. His enemies thought he was out of it but, to the joy of his friends, Paul revived and continued his journeyings.

Whilst men sought to do the Apostle physical injury, God was giving him a season of spiritual ecstasy. The revelation was such that he could not make it known to man. It was also such that it could have exalted him into a pride which goes before a fall, so much so that there was given to him a " thorn in the flesh."

Whatever the thorn in the flesh may have been, it would appear that it was a physical disability which might have been painful. A thorn in the finger can be painful. The expression " buffet " has a similar meaning. As the Lord does not afflict His people, what is not in His Sovereign Will is often within His Permissive Will. Therefore, He permits Satan, or a messenger of Satan, to do the buffeting.

When the Apostle sought deliverance from the Lord, he learned that suffering must continue, but that the Lord's grace would prove to be his sufficiency. God promised that His strength would be perfected in Paul's weakness.

The Apostle submitted gladly to Divine Wisdom that he might enjoy Divine Power. Oh, that we might know how to rest in the Lord and to wait patiently for Him.

It is to be noted in verse 2 that Paul was " caught up to the third heaven." Many people refer to being caught up, or taken, into the seventh heaven. There is no such place in Scripture. The idea of seven heavens comes from the Spiritualists, who speak of seven spheres and of the Lord as an advanced spirit who has reached the sixth sphere. He is not even given the honour of the seventh !

The three heavens of the Bible are : —

  (1) The atmosphere immediately surrounding this earth, which is known to be charged with evil spirits and is the realm of the god of this world.

  (2) The heavens above us, known as the solar system, where all the stars or heavenly bodies move in space, the earth being one of those bodies.

  (3) The third heaven, or the abode of God, where the Lord has gone and where He is preparing a place for us. This realm is in eternity.

Men might question Paul's apostleship because he had not seen the Lord in the flesh as had all the other apostles, but here, in defence of his position, he was informing them that he had seen the Lord in His glory, had witnessed what none of the disciples had ever seen, and declared, " for in nothing am I behind the very chiefest apostles, though I be nothing " (xii. 11).

He concludes the chapter by reminding them again that he had never been chargeable to them, even though he had done so much for them, neither had Titus been chargeable to them. He also warned them again of their weaknesses in debates, envyings, wraths, strifes, backbitings, whisperings, swellings, tumults, all of which may mean that he might have to come to them in the spirit of reproof and correction, which might be hurtful to them and to himself. Nevertheless he would not withhold the reproof if it were necessary. Therefore he bade them examine their own lives. God truly had a faithful and stalwart steward in Paul.

The Epistle concludes with the usual gracious benediction of the Apostle.

"Finally, brethren, farewell. Be perfect, be of good comfort, be of one mind, live in peace ; and the God of love and peace shall be with you. Greet one another with an holy kiss. All the saints salute you. The grace of the Lord Jesus Christ, and the love of God, and the communion of the Holy Ghost, be with you all. Amen."

GALATIANS

LAW AND GRACE

" O foolish Galatians, who hath bewitched you, that ye should not obey the truth, before whose eyes Jesus Christ hath been evidently set forth, crucified among you ? " (GALATIANS iii. 1)

INTRODUCTION

The Galatians were a very emotional people. One moment they would worship Paul, the next they would stone him. One day they were under law, the next day under grace. As soon as a few Judaisers came along they were back under law again. This fickle nature may be explained by the fact that they were a group of Gauls, hasty, fighting people, who had broken away from a migration from the North, the main body of these people going to France. The French people to-day, who are Gauls, have the very same characteristics.

Paul moved through this area on his first missionary tour, a journey which included Iconium, Lystra, Derbe, etc. During this itinerary the Apostle had been very successful. A great number of people, especially Gentiles, had been converted to the Christian faith so that churches had been established throughout the whole region.

After Paul's departure certain Jews came in and preached circumcision, declaring that the Christian faith was of no avail unless they had first accepted the Jewish Law and submitted themselves to its ritual. At one time Peter found himself entangled in this doctrine and was severely reprimanded by Paul.

As soon as Paul heard of this trouble in Galatia, he wrote to them, and this is the Epistle. He is very firm on this matter. He must be, for it was condemning the work he had done. In fact, if it continued it would destroy Christianity altogether because they were seeking to make the Church a department of Judaism instead of recognising it as a new order. Law and grace can no more mix than can oil and water or light and darkness.

With this background a profitable approach can be made to the book and its exposition.

THE BOOK

The whole message can be summed up in the words: " Out of the bondage of the flesh into the liberty of the Spirit."

In Romans Paul had declared and expounded the great fundamentals of our faith, Justification and Sanctification. The first is doctrinal, the second practical, or the inworking and outworking of the Gospel of Salvation.

The Epistles were written to Corinth because they had come short in the matter of sanctification. Moral issues had to be corrected.

In Galatia things were different. It was the matter of justification, or their doctrine, that was at fault. Therefore the Apostle found it necessary to clarify these truths.

The book divides into four in its main analysis.

(1) PAUL'S CONVERSION AND COMMISSION (Chapter i.).

(2) PAUL CONTESTING AND CRUCIFIED (Chapter ii.).

(3) BOND SLAVES OR BOND SERVANTS (Chapters iii. and iv.).

(4) FRUIT OF THE SPIRIT OR WORKS OF THE FLESH (Chapters v. and vi.).

(1) PAUL'S CONVERSION AND COMMISSION (Chapter i.)

Paul, as an opponent to these Judaisers, must establish his own position of authority, for it seemed that these Jewish proselytes were trying to discredit Paul's right to apostleship — therefore his introduction, " Paul, an apostle, (not of men, neither by man, but by Jesus Christ, and God the Father, Who raised Him from the dead) " (i. 1).

" *Not of men* ", that would have been the source if it had been bestowed upon him, and " *not by man* " would have been the channel if it were hereditary.

It is true that Paul makes this introduction, "Paul, an apostle" in eight other of his Epistles, but here he reasons out his authority.

They would not accept his apostleship because he had not seen nor heard the Lord and, therefore, was not an eye-witness, as were the twelve. Peter had said, when they appointed two men from whom they were to elect an apostle, " . . . These men which have companied with us all the time that the Lord Jesus went in and out among us, beginning from the baptism of John, unto that same day that He was taken up from us, must one be ordained to be a witness with us of His resurrection " (Acts i. 21 - 22).

They claimed that Paul had followed the apostles and gained
information which was second-hand. Paul opposed their statements by saying that he did not receive it " of men." They were
not the source of his information. Neither did he receive it " by
man." This could refer to the time when Ananias laid his hands
upon him in order that he might receive his sight, at which time
Ananias said : " . . . and be filled with the Holy Ghost." But
Paul never deceived himself that this gave him the right to apostleship.

He claimed that his call was Divine and that it came from
Jesus Christ and the Father. Against the two accusations he says
in verse 12 : " I neither received it of man, neither was I taught
it . . . , " following this with the testimony of his conversion, and
how God gave him a revelation of His Son and a Divine anointing
whilst he was on his way to Damascus. At that time he assures
them that he conferred not with flesh and blood, neither went he up
to Jerusalem to be taught by the apostles ; instead he went into the
solitude of Arabia and back to Damascus.

It was another three years before he made his first visit to
Jerusalem and then only for fifteen days, during which time he saw
none other than Peter and James. After that he remained as a
stranger in Syria and Cilicia. Fourteen more years elapsed before
his second visit to Jerusalem and then he went as an apostle, taking
Barnabas and Timothy with him.

In chapter ii. 9 the Apostle bears witness that the three pillars
of the Church, James, Peter, and John, all recognised his Divine
Calling.

If any other evidence were needed of his right to his apostleship, then they should take into consideration the marks of the
Lord Jesus Christ which he carried in his body, or his sufferings
which he suffered for Christ's sake. He then bade them to trouble
him no more on this matter (vi. 17).

In the same chapter in which the Apostle was defending his
own position, he reproved the Galatians for their position in that
they had so quickly been removed from their faith, saying : " I
marvel that ye are so soon removed from Him that called you into
the Grace of Christ unto another gospel " (i. 6), causing this faithful servant of the Lord then to take up the challenge of the Gospel,
declaring that there was but one Gospel, one message of salvation.

To those who have confused minds to-day, declaring there are
so many truths that they do not know which to believe, here is
their answer. This does not come from a denominational man,
nor from the supporter of any faction. It comes from a man who

has no axe to grind. If anyone, man or angel, preach any kind
of message or propound any theory other than that which is declared in this Book, not only is he wrong but, says the Apostle,
let him be accursed, for such a one is not only failing to help man
but he is a positive hindrance to man's spiritual growth.

(2) PAUL CONTESTING AND CRUCIFIED (Chapter ii.)

Whilst Paul was the Apostle to the Gentiles and Peter was the
Apostle to the Jews, neither was restricted to his sphere for both
sought to lead men into the one common salvation. As the Gospel
moved to the Gentiles so the centre of activity moved to Antioch.
Peter visited this centre. Whilst there, gladly he adjusted his habits.
There were certain requirements of the Jewish faith which had
always been considered a burden. These same things were not
required in Christianity. The Gentile convert was not bound in
any way by such measures, whilst those who came out from
Judaism to Christ were freed from such bondage. Peter was very
happy to be free from this legalism and to enjoy the liberty of the
Spirit. The abolished requirements included circumcision and eating with the Gentiles.

Peter had been eating with these Gentiles and was within his
rights. God had taught him not to call that unclean which He had
cleansed, referring more to the people with whom he ate rather
than the food which he ate. But when certain Jews came to
declare otherwise, Peter withdrew from his new position with saints
to take up his old position with Judaism, and caused that others
should follow his example. This incident is recorded in Acts xv.
Barnabas also became entangled in the same situation. This was
not because Peter did not know which was right and which was
wrong, but because he was afraid of the Judaisers.

As a result of this, Paul rebuked Peter for being responsible
for a dissention. A faction of this kind could have been strong
enough to destroy the whole Christian doctrine.

Paul made it clear, to Jew and Gentile alike, that the matter
of circumcision and other things required by the law had ceased.
The Jew had been dependent upon fulfilling the law for his salvation, but now "by the works of the law can no man be justified."
The new position was " . . . we have believed in Jesus Christ, that
we might be justified by the faith of Christ . . . " (ii. 16).

Paul gave them his own position as an illustration. He had
been brought up strictly according to the law. He had been rigid
in all of its requirements, but now he was dead to it all. " I am

crucified with Christ : nevertheless I live : yet not I, but Christ
liveth in me : and the life which I now live in the flesh I live by
the faith of the Son of God, Who loved me, and gave Himself for
me " (ii. 20).

If the law had been sufficient to meet man's need, then Christ
need not have died. Therefore, by going back to the law it would
appear that Christ's death had been in vain.

Paul, having reminded the Galatian Church of the mistake
Peter had made and how he had to deal with him, then remonstrated with them for similar behaviour, as he said : " O foolish
Galatians, who hath bewitched you, that ye should not obey the
truth . . . having begun in the Spirit, are ye now made perfect by
the flesh ? " (iii. 1-3).

(3) BOND SLAVES OR BOND SERVANTS (Chapters iii. and iv.)

If there were any doubt in the minds of these people as to
which of these two schools had priority or as to which might have
precedence by reason of age, then the Apostle declares Faith came
before Law, contrary to those who declare otherwise. Using
Abraham as his illustration, he shows that Faith preceded Law by
four hundred and thirty years. The Law was given by Moses,
but the Scripture saith : " Even as Abraham believed God, and
it was accounted to him for righteousness." This Paul quotes
from Genesis xv. 6. If Abraham were counted as righteous four
centuries before the Law was given then, obviously, it was not his
by fulfilling the Law. If we have faith in God, so did Abraham.
This teaches that we can be the children of Abraham, not after
the flesh but after the Spirit.

The Law was not of faith. This was inflicted upon man as
a moral code because man had failed to exercise his prerogative
of faith. Keeping the Law brought no particular reward, any
more than a man is rewarded for obeying the laws of his country,
or his club, or anything else with which he associates himself ;
but let that same man break any of those laws and he may find
himself arrested or excommunicated. Thus it was, and thus it is,
with the Law of God. " For as many as are of the works of the
law are under the curse : for it is written, Cursed is every one that
continueth not in all things which are written in the book of the
law to do them. But that no man is justified by the law in the
sight of God, it is evident : for, The just shall live by faith " (iii.
10-11). This last statement comes from the pen of Habakkuk

(ii. 4), is quoted by Paul in Romans i. 17, and is repeated in Hebrews x. 38, with the great faith chapter following (Hebrews xi.). The evidence is, therefore, that in all periods of time it has been faith and not works.

If God's purposes were fulfilled through faith, then the law coming four hundred and thirty years later could not disannul, or make the promise of none effect (iii. 17).

All of this would naturally cause the question to be asked : "Wherefore then serveth the law ? " (iii. 19), but the answer follows, " It was added because of transgressions . . . ".

If the natural heart were not selfish, greedy, and rebellious, men would not be required sitting at Westminster, Washington, or elsewhere, making laws. God would never have said "Thou shalt not steal," or " bear false witness," if man did not want to do such things. God would never have said, "Thou shalt love thy neighbour " if man's heart had been overflowing with love.

When the Law was given, it was only to be a temporary measure. It was to be " till the seed should come to whom the promise was made ", that " seed " being Christ, Who would deliver from that Law by changing our hard, stony, unbelieving hearts into the fleshy hearts of feeling, love, and obedience.

The Apostle, having pointed out that the Law could not justify, declares that " the law was our schoolmaster to bring us unto Christ, that we might be justified by faith " (iii. 24).

The " schoolmaster " had a very different meaning from that which is attached to the word to-day. He was a household servant who, in those days, acted as a guardian over younger members of the family. He was often a trusted slave. He possessed no authority and did no teaching. He was a chaperone who watched, and reported any wrongs back to the father of the child, who alone administered his authority, correction, or instruction. When the child reached maturity of years the servant was taken away and the young man became a free, responsible citizen.

So the Law became the guardian of man's outward conduct until he came to the place where his spirit life developed and he put on Christ, or, should it be said, he put on Christ and his spirit life developed ! Then he was free from the Law because he was in Christ.

So the Apostle continues : " But after that faith is come, we are no longer under a schoolmaster. For ye are all the children of God by faith in Christ Jesus. For as many of you as have been baptised into Christ have put on Christ " (iii. 25-27).

Seeing that faith supersedes all things else, and understanding that the salvation of the Lord Jesus Christ is for the "whosoever will", no longer should man make comparisons, because they do not exist so far as the Christian is concerned, for "There is neither Jew nor Greek, there is neither bond nor free, there is neither male nor female: for ye are all one in Christ Jesus. And if ye be Christ's, then are ye Abraham's seed, and heirs according to the promise" (iii. 28/29).

The Judaisers were desirous of dragging men back to the traditions of the fathers and to the Law of Moses, suggesting that these things were essential to those who claimed to be the seed of Abraham. Paul refuted their argument by reminding the Galatians that God's promise to Abraham was that through him should all the families of the earth be blessed. Abraham was of the line through which the Messiah — the Christ — would come. If, therefore, these people had received Christ, they would be of the seed of Abraham, as Christ was, and they would be heirs through Christ of all that God had promised to Abraham.

The Law was a temporary thing, so why be in bondage to it when Christ came to fulfil that Law, to deliver from its bondage, and to cause men to rejoice in the liberties that have come through the One Who has made us to become heirs of the life that now is and of the Life that is to come according to that promise ?

In chapter iv. the Apostle elaborates the subject of heirship. The definition of the word " heir " is " prospective possessor." A child may be the heir to a great fortune but, whilst a child or a minor, it makes no difference to him whatsoever. He may not even be aware of his possessions.

As a minor he is no different from a servant. Both are subject to the head of the house. From both is expected obedience without reasoning. The child is subject to its parents and to its instructors. This condition remains until the child reaches adulthood, when the father no longer treats him as a child but as a son. He has been a son all the time, so far as human relationship is concerned, but now he enters into the social and business matters of the family, into the sphere of consultation and reason. He is given to know the reasons why the father does certain things or why he does not. He becomes a partaker in business. He begins to understand some of the position and the wealth which is now partially his and will be completely his later.

The argument is that an Israelite under the Law was subject to that Law. It held him in bondage. As a minor he was expected to obey that Law, whether he understood it or not. It was a

period of darkness and limitation. When Christ came He came
to redeem them who were under the Law and to bring them into
the fulness and into the liberty of the Sons of God, a partaker in
His present glory, and an inheritor of all the blessings of the saints
in light.

What man, enjoying the fellowship of his father and knowing
a relationship where the one could speak freely with the other,
would want to return to the days of the nursery, of the school, and
of a rigid discipline ?

The illustration is forceful. In Christ a man is infinitely
better off than when he was under law, and to bring about this
new relationship " God sent forth His Son, made of a woman,
made under the law " (iv. 4), or, His Incarnation and Virgin Birth.

In the light of all this blessedness of the Gospel and the riches
that are to be enjoyed in Christ Jesus, there comes a most natural
question : " How turn ye again to the weak and beggarly elements,
whereunto ye desire again to be in bondage ? " (iv. 9). How can
any man to-day, who has enjoyed the blessings of salvation, revelled
in the abundance of His love, and known something of the life
of sanctification, want to share in carnal things which belong to
a world of sin and death ? The cry must be renewed : " Come
out from among them, and be ye separate, saith the Lord, and
touch not the unclean thing . . . " (2 Corinthians vi. 17).

The evidence that comes out of the next verses is that there
was a strong resentment on the part of some in this Church because
the Apostle reminded them of an earlier relationship, when in the
days of his suffering these people were so loyal to the Apostle and
so concerned for him in his suffering for Christ's sake, although
his body was evidently broken and bruised, yet they never saw
his disfigurement. To them he was an angel. In their devotion
to their friend many of them would have plucked out their eyes
and given them to him, had it been possible.

This is one of the statements which suggests that Paul's thorn
in the flesh, about which he had prayed for deliverance, was
ophthalmic trouble. Other Scriptures strengthen the idea. (See
Galatians vi. 11 and Philemon i. 9).

That zeal had now gone and a feeling against Paul had taken
its place because he had been honest enough to reprove them for
error. However, the yearnings of the Apostle toward them remained unchanged. His desire was that they should be their best
for the Lord, and enjoy the best from the Lord.

He then makes another appeal in the form of an allegory.
This is the only time Paul ever used a story.

The Apostle told these people, who wanted to secure their legal claim as the seed of Abraham, to reread the law with an open ear and hear what it said : " Abraham had two sons, the one by a bondmaid, the other by a free woman." To claim to be of Abraham was one thing, but of which woman would be another thing, for " he who was of the bondwoman was born after the flesh ; but he of the freewoman was by promise."

God had promised to Abraham a seed and a posterity. He had promised that through that seed all the families of the earth should be blessed. Both Abraham and Sarah were advanced in years. In the realm of natural things this promise could not be fulfilled, so Abraham sought to do what many seek to do to-day, thereby always making a tragic mistake. He tried to help God out of a difficulty by taking to himself a younger wife in the person of Sarah's handmaid, but God is never in a difficulty, and never needs man's help. Graciously He permits man to help at times, but still He does not *need* him. The result of this conduct of Abraham was that a child was born of Hagar — Ishmael by name. He was born after the flesh.

Later, God came to His servant, saying in effect : " Abraham, you have had your way and Ishmael has been born, but I am still going to have My way and fulfil My promise, for Sarah shall conceive and bare a son and thou shalt call his name Isaac. He will be a son, not according to the flesh, but according to promise," and thus it was.

The Apostle declared this to be a parable. It had meaning and truth that was beyond the literal, for these two women, with their two sons, represented two covenants. The one, as a bondwoman, stands for Sinai and the Law and tells of bondage. The other is the freewoman who speaks of the Jerusalem which is above, the heavenly Jerusalem, and the work of grace which is performed by God alone.

We know, and they knew, yet had to be reminded, that God's chosen people came through the freewoman and Isaac. Moreover, it soon became obvious that these two women and their offspring could not dwell together. The coming of the latter, which was according to the Will of God, meant casting out the former, which was according to the will of man. Hagar and Ishmael, the Law, were cast out and sent across the desert (not destroyed or annihilated, for they had a place and a purpose), so that Grace might have its rightful place.

Paul had been preaching Grace. The Church was founded on Grace. The dispensation of the Grace of God had been

established and Law had gone out. Who, then, were these Judaisers, and what right had they to seek to establish what God had
removed ?

So the Lord would say to all Christians who have been delivered from sin and the world, who have been delivered from death
and brought into life, "Stand fast therefore in the liberty wherewith Christ hath made us free, and be not entangled again with
the yoke of bondage " (v. 1).

(4) FRUIT OF THE SPIRIT OR WORKS OF THE FLESH
   (Chapters v. and vi.)

Seeing that no man could be justified by the deeds of the
Law, for the Law only temporarily covered sin but could never
remove it, and seeing that Christ had already accomplished this
justification, the Law of Moses was no longer in force. The
Jews had been delivered from the Law. The Gentiles had never
been under it, that is, not under the ceremonial Law. They
would have been under a moral law.

The Christian, having been delivered from the Law and now
standing in the liberty wherewith Christ has made him free, must
know the following : —

(1) He must allow no one to rob him of his privileges or
his spiritual blessings. At the same time he must not allow his
liberty to become licence (v. 13).

Whilst law does not dominate our lives, love should — love
to the Lord and love to our brethren.

(2) He is not at liberty to please himself. He pleases Him.
Love is never selfish. So often Christians use the expression " I
can please myself." That is a declaration of selfishness. Surely
the greatest joy in life is pleasing others. If Jesus could say : " I
seek not Mine own will, but the Will of the Father which hath
sent Me," we can do the same.

(3) He is not at liberty to serve his own desires, but " to
serve one another." He must watch his conduct. So many feel
that because they are not under law they are free to do exactly
what they like, but the truth is that he who is without the law is
a law unto himself. It is not a question of how much less, but
how much more, we submit to His Word.

Because the law says, " Thou shalt not kill " and grace has
delivered us from the law, does that give the right to kill ? Of
course not ! If the world must not kill, how much less the
Christian. Apply that principle to all the smaller moral issues

of life, and the Christian would find himself saying with the Apostle : "Wherefore, if meat make my brother to offend, I will eat no flesh while the world standeth, lest I make my brother to offend" (1 Corinthians viii. 13). That is the law of charity. It knows no punishment, but it knows great reward.

(4) When he was under the law he produced the works of the flesh. Now that he is led of the Spirit he will produce the fruit of the Spirit.

These are contrasted by the Apostle in chapter v. 19-25. As a tree cannot bear good and evil fruit, and as a fountain cannot produce fresh and foul water at the same time, neither can we.

The flesh and the Spirit are opposed the one to the other. In fact, between the two there stands the Cross, creating an impassable barrier. On the negative side of the Cross is the flesh, dwelling in darkness and manifesting its ugly works. On the positive side of the Cross is the life of the Spirit, producing the fruit which is natural to that life.

Note the two words used — Works and Fruit. Works are artificial. They come as a result of effort. They are manufacturies. Nature itself declares that many of the things which the human heart desires to do are wrong. The natural heart is deceitful above all things and desperately wicked. Fruit, however, is natural. It is the outgrowth of the nature of the tree. The apple tree does not need effort to produce apples — it would to produce grapes, because they are foreign to its nature. Such is the Spirit-filled life. To produce fruit of the Spirit should not require effort by the child of God.

An objection may be raised regarding the natural product of the apple tree that, if it is not pruned, fed, etc., it will go back into a wild state and produce crab apples! That is also true of the Christian. Unless Christ dwells in him, and he is Spirit fed, and pruned of unproductive wood, then the fruit will be poor, but the Apostle is dealing with the Spirit-filled life, not the Spirit-impoverished life.

Works. This ugly list, which denotes the behaviour of the unregenerate heart, may appear more ugly, but perhaps more recognisable, if quoted from one of the modern translations which uses the language of to-day. Here is J. B. Phillips' translation : "The activities of the lower nature are obvious. Here is a list : sexual immorality, impurity of mind, sensuality, worship of false gods, witchcraft, hatred, quarrelling, jealousy, bad temper, rivalry,

factions, party spirit, envy, drunkenness, orgies, and things like
that."

What a description of the world! What a portrait of the
generation in which we live!! What a disgrace to a so-called
enlightened age!!! Let it speak for itself. It needs no further
comment.

Fruit. What a luscious combination — love, joy, peace,
longsuffering, gentleness, goodness, faith, meekness, and temperance.

D. L. Moody, referring to the singular word " fruit ", pointed
out that there is but one fruit — LOVE — the rest are its attributes.

> Joy is love rejoicing.
> Peace is love resting.
> Longsuffering is love enduring.
> Gentleness is love in kindness.
> Goodness is love in action.
> Faith is love trusting.
> Meekness is love stooping.
> Temperance is love restraining.

LOVE. Sir Henry Drummond, in his book *The Greatest Thing
in the World,* where he expounds 1 Corinthians xiii., said: " When
a beam of light is passed through a crystal prism, that prism will
break up light into its component colours of violet, indigo, blue,
green, yellow, orange, and red, the colours of the rainbow." So
he called the thirteenth chapter of 1 Corinthians " the spectrum
of love."

Without love we are nothing.

JOY. The world may have pleasure, it may have happiness, but
joy is something deep-seated. It comes from knowing the Lord
and the indwelling of His Spirit. Like love it is self-sacrificing,
and has been wisely expressed in an acrostic : —

> J — Jesus first
> O — Others next
> Y — Yourself last

PEACE is love in repose. The dictionary defines peace as " calm ;
repose ; freedom from war ; quietness of mind ; harmony." What
a blessedness it is to be in harmony with the Will of God, and

to enjoy the peace that passeth all understanding, because our hearts are garrisoned with it.

LONGSUFFERING. We live in an impatient world. It knows nothing of forbearance. James says : " Let patience have her perfect work, that ye may be perfect and entire, wanting nothing " (i. 4). Jesus has been slow to anger and plenteous in mercy to usward. We must produce the same fruit for others to enjoy.

GENTLENESS. Said the Psalmist : " Thy gentleness hath made me great."

Gentleness is a potential force which cannot be manufactured. Nature has some powerful forces at work and can display itself in the hurricane, the blizzard, the drought, etc., and yet these forces are usually met in their gentler form, the rain distilling itself in soft refreshing showers, the snow falling silently flake by flake. The wind is often a balmy breeze cooling the atmosphere. The sun's rays, after travelling ninety million miles in eight minutes, touch the eye so gently that man is not blinded thereby.

Gentleness is not being weak or effeminate. It is a potential quality. Charles V refused to have his tent removed on one occasion because a swallow had built its nest upon it. He left the tent until the young had flown away. That was the gentler side of the hard soldier.

GOODNESS. The better word is " benevolence," which means " a disposition to do good." This is not a goodness which savours works as a means of salvation. It would come into that realm of which David spoke when he said of the Lord : " Thou crownest the year with Thy goodness," and, again, " The earth is full of the goodness of the Lord." This is a goodness which is seen in active, energetic benevolence of the Lord, and should be seen likewise in the Lord's people.

FAITH is both a fruit of the Spirit and a gift of the Spirit. " Without faith it is impossible to please God." Faith is a root and a fruit, a foundation stone and a topstone. As a root and a fruit the Christian life is the product of faith (root) but it also produces faith (fruit). It is the fruit of the trusting heart that rests in the Lord.

MEEKNESS. This is defined as " a virtue which consists in due regulation of the natural passions of anger." Aristotle, the Greek philosopher, said : " The meek man is not given to retaliate injuries, but rather to forgive. It is a slavish thing for a man to take insult calmly," but Jesus said : " Blessed are the meek for they shall inherit the earth." The doctrines of Jesus are more sound than the philosophies of men, although harder to practise. Lord, give us that " ornament of a meek and quiet spirit, which is in the sight of God of great price " (1 Peter iii. 4).

TEMPERANCE is the controlled life, with every passion mastered. "Temperate in *all* things." This is the last in the list and should be the natural result of all the others.

As love weaves itself into the rest, let us use the last of the fruit as the warp of the fabric of Christian living   Without temperance

Love would be devitalised.
Joy would be bloodless.
Peace would be dead.
Longsuffering would be jerky.
Gentleness would be rudeness.
Goodness would be badness.
Faith would be infidelity.
Meekness would disappear.

Each depends on the other. It is the single fruit of the Spirit, the warp and woof of life.

The chapter closes by stating that if we live in the Spirit we shall walk in the Spirit, meaning that if the inner life is Spirit-controlled the outward walk, or conduct, will be lived accordingly. The last chapter reveals that outworking : —

There will be the spirit of forgiveness (vs. 1).
We shall realise our responsibility to other people and so become burden-bearers (vs. 2).
We shall walk humbly before God and man (vs. 3).
We shall share our spiritual blessings (vs. 6).
We shall get out of life the same kind of thing that we put into it, only it will be multiplied, as harvest always is (vs. 7-8).
Reward is promised for all service (vs. 9).

Verse 11 is another indication that Paul's thorn in the flesh might have been eye trouble.

His final boast, as he closes an Epistle in which he has sought to separate Law and Grace, the flesh and the Spirit, is : " But God forbid that I should glory, save in the Cross of our Lord

Jesus Christ, by whom the world is crucified unto me, and I unto the world."

The old life must mean nothing, the new creation must be everything.

The book concludes with a benediction.

EPHESIANS

THE CHURCH — HIS BODY

"Blessed be the God and Father of our Lord Jesus Christ, Who hath blessed us with all spiritual blessings in heavenly places in Christ: According as He hath chosen us in Him before the foundation of the world, that we should be holy and without blame before Him in love"　(EPHESIANS i. 3-4)

INTRODUCTION

This Epistle is one of the " Prison Epistles." It was written by Paul at Rome in the year A.D. 64. The letter is linked closely with those written to the Philippians and the Colossians. Ephesians, Colossians and Philemon were written at the same time and carried by Tychicus to their various destinations.

EPHESUS was an important city of Asia, noted for its great temple and the worship of the goddess Diana. When Paul left Corinth on his first missionary journey he took with him Aquila and Priscilla and came to Ephesus. Having preached there he was invited to stay, but decided against it. Instead, he left Aquila and Priscilla and journeyed toward Jerusalem because there he wanted to keep the feast (Acts xviii. 18-21).

Later, Apollos came to Ephesus and ministered but, whilst he was eloquent in speech, he was not too sound on doctrine, so that Aquila and Priscilla instructed him more perfectly (Acts xviii. 24-28).

Paul returned to Ephesus and remained for three years. It was during this period, after a hard struggle and much disputing, and fighting with beasts, that there came to the city a great revival, during which time the people burned their books and their charms. The outcome of this was the uproar created by the silversmiths, who thought they would lose their livelihood which came from the worship of Diana. Many people worship money. Their gold becomes their god.

In Acts xx. 17, when Paul had no time to make a third visit to this city, he sent for the elders to meet him at Miletus.

713

From Ephesus Paul wrote his first Epistle to the Corinthians. It is understood that John wrote his Gospel and Epistles from the same place. Patmos, from whence he wrote the Revelation, was only sixty miles away.

Ephesus was the first of the seven churches of Asia to whom the Lord wrote in Revelation ii.

THE MESSAGE

The book divides into two parts in its first analysis. Three chapters are DOCTRINAL — they deal with the believer's position, " In Christ ", " In heavenly places ", " We in Him and He in us." The other three chapters are PRACTICAL, and show the believer's responsibility in service and walk in four different realms — The Church, Society, Home, and Warfare.

The theme of the Epistle is " The Church as the Body of Christ." In Colossians the subject is " Christ, the Head of the Church." The two Epistles together portray a full picture. They are very closely related.

The true Church, made up of all believers, is that Body of which He is the Head. God not only prepared a Body in which the Lord should suffer — His human frame — but He prepared a Body for Him in which He should be glorified — the Church. As a Body the Church is not an organisation but an organism. Organisation is mechanical. Everything operates because of the compelling power of something behind it. An organism is life, and functions naturally. Each member of the body operates in its own way and place in obedience to the mind or the head.

This is the reasoning of the first three chapters of this Epistle.

DOCTRINAL — OUR POSITION — " IN HIM " — " IN US "

SALUTATION. The Epistle is broad because its contents were not only the property of the saints in the Church at Ephesus but it was also addressed " to the faithful in Christ Jesus." That would include the saints of the present day.

Paul extended grace to the saints and offered praise to the Lord.

Immediately an introduction is made to

OUR POSITION " IN HIM." Everything we have and are and ever will be is because of this established relationship in Him. Underscore the word IN and discover

" The faithful IN Christ Jesus " (i. 1).
" IN heavenly places IN Christ " (i. 3).
" He hath chosen us IN Him " (i. 4).
" Accepted IN the Beloved ' (i. 6).
" IN Whom we have redemption " (i. 7).
" IN all wisdom and prudence " (i. 8).
" All things IN Christ . . . even IN Him " (i. 10).
" IN Whom also we have obtained an inheritance " (i. 11).
" IN Whom ye also trusted " (i. 13).
" IN Whom also after that ye believed, ye were sealed "
    (i. 13).
" IN the knowledge of Him " (i. 17).
" His mighty power which He wrought IN Christ (i.
    19/20).
" IN heavenly places IN Christ Jesus " (ii. 6).
" That IN the ages to come He might show . . . His grace
    IN His kindness " (ii. 7).
" Created IN Christ Jesus " (ii. 10).
" IN Christ Jesus . . . made nigh " (ii. 13).
" IN Whom all the building fitly framed together " (ii. 21).
" Groweth unto an holy temple IN the Lord " (ii. 21).
" IN Whom ye also are builded together " (ii. 22).
" Partakers of His promise IN Christ " (iii. 6).
" Purpose which He purposed IN Christ Jesus our Lord "
    (iii. 11).
" IN Whom we have boldness and access " (iii. 12).

This, surely, is a place of security, of blessing, and of confidence.

Here men are princes not beggars.

Here men are enriched not poverty-stricken.

Here men are giants not dwarfs and pygmies.

Another repeat word in this Epistle is ACCORDING. None of the blessings of the Lord comes to us according to our deserving, but according to His choosing (i. 4), according to His good pleasure (i. 5), according to His grace (i. 7), according to His predestination (i. 11), according to His power (i. 19), according to His purpose (iii. 11), according to His riches (iii. 16), according to the gift of Christ (iv. 7).

PREDESTINATION (Chapter i. 5-14). Concerning this controversial subject suffice it to say that the word is never associated with the sinner and his salvation, but is always related to the saint and his sanctification. Because we have already been accepted in

716 EPHESIANS

the Beloved (i. 6), and first trusted in Christ (i. 12), God has pre-determined that we should be continuously transformed into the full likeness of His dear Son, that we should be to His praise.

The verses concern those who are IN HIM and, therefore, cannot suggest (as some would) that some men are doomed to a lost perdition.

SEALED BY THE HOLY SPIRIT (Chapter i. 13-14). Another subject of controversy in the Church concerns whether a person receives the Holy Spirit at conversion, or whether it is a " second blessing." In a measure both are right and both are wrong. The Holy Spirit is received at conversion, but not in all the fulness of His power, not a baptism. On the other hand, the expression " second blessing " suggests a limitation. The blessings of the Holy Spirit go on and on and on. " Be being filled " is the correct statement of chapter v., verse 18.

In the verses under consideration it is declared : " In Whom ye also trusted *after* that ye heard the Word of truth, the Gospel of your salvation : in Whom also *after* that ye believed, ye were sealed with that Holy Spirit of promise, which is the earnest (or pledge, or seal) of our inheritance until the redemption of the purchased possession, unto the praise of His glory."

In the Eastern market, when a man purchased a large quantity of grain, as he was not able to remove it immediately, he carried with him a corn seal, which he would plunge into each side of the pile, thus leaving an embossment of identification in the corn. As it was more than a man's life was worth to break a corn seal, the grain stood secure against theft until the carriers came down to remove it from the market floor.

Likewise, when a couple become engaged, the promises of loyalty are made one to the other. As the man cannot marry her immediately, because of various preparations which must be made, he gives to his fiancée an engagement ring, which is a token, or a seal, of contract that marks the girl as his until the day of the wedding.

Even so, when we are purchased by Christ through His Blood, and we become His, He does not take us immediately out of this world. We are left in a strange country, amidst a hostile people. He has gone to prepare a place for us, but His promise is, " I will not leave you comfortless." Therefore, He gives to His Church upon earth His Holy Spirit, which is a pledge, or seal, of identity UNTIL the redemption of the purchased possession, or until He completes His contract by taking us out of this world and unto Himself. In other words, our redemption will not be complete until the second coming of Christ.

PRAYER FOR KNOWLEDGE (Chapter i. 16-21). As one reads these verses it is with a consciousness that we have not even begun to know what our riches are in Christ Jesus. We have to hang our heads in shame when we consider how impoverished we are, when we should be glorying in that Name which is above every name, ministering in that Power which is beyond all powers, and dwelling in that fulness which causes everything else to become a void.

CHRIST THE HEAD (v. 22), not only of the Church and, therefore, of us, but Head over *all* things *to* the Church.

GOD'S GREAT LOVE is the theme of most of the second chapter. There is a small word occurring twice in the chapter which has a great transforming power. It is the word BUT in vv. 4 and 13.

Firstly, the Apostle paints the picture of man by nature — dead in sin, walking according to this world, and according to the will of Satan, bound by fleshly lusts and carnal desires. A benighted picture indeed, BUT — and then follows the transformation. God's great love towards the sinner had changed all this.

> From death, he passes into the fulness of life.
>
> From walking in this world, he is made to sit in heavenly places.
>
> Instead of serving Satan, he is revelling in the riches of the Saviour.

Paul's second picture is one of distance. It concerns the Gentile, far off, alienated, strangers, BUT now made nigh, made fellow citizens, and in family relationship.

HIS POSITION — " IN US ", is in chapter iii.

> " That Christ may dwell *IN your hearts* by faith " (iii. 17).
>
> " That *ye might be filled* with all the fulness of God " (iii. 19).
>
> " According to the power that worketh *IN us* " (iii. 20).

This relationship was summed up by the Lord Himself in His words : " He that abideth in Me, and I in him, the same bringeth forth much fruit : for without Me ye can do nothing " (John xv. 5). The abundance of that fruit is back in Ephesians

iii. 20 : "Now unto Him that is able to do exceeding abundantly above all that we ask or think, according to the power that worketh in us."

The fruit is His ability for the Saint — " able to do."

The extent of that ability is, " all we ask or think," to which is added a list of adverbs.

we ask.

we think.

all we ask or think.

above all we ask or think.

abundantly above all we ask or think.

exceeding abundantly above all we ask or think.

Having expounded the doctrine, the last three chapters declare the

PRACTICAL — OUR RESPONSIBILITY

This is twofold :   (1)   Our walk and service.

(2)   Our walk and warfare.

The section begins by telling us to " walk worthy of the vocation wherewith ye are called."

Walk suggests progress, activity, service. Sitting with Him in heavenly places will be reward, when service is complete.

This walk is defined thus : —

(1)   Walk worthy (iv. 1). ..... in lowliness, meekness, patience, love, unity and peace.

(2)   Walk differently (iv. 17)   not as the Gentiles, not proudly, not ignorantly.

(3)   Walk in love (v. 2). ..... in the love of Christ and free from the love of the world.

(4)   Walk as children of light (v. 8) ..... in the light of Divine revelation.

(5)   Walk circumspectly ..... with great care, watching where (v. 15)   each step is placed.

This practical life operates in four spheres — the Church, society, the family, warfare. Three of these come under

WALK AND SERVICE

(1)   *In the Church* (iv. 1-16). Here it is of unity and yet one of diversity, a unity of faith with a diversity of ministry. In our faith we are exhorted to " keep the unity of the Spirit in the bond

of peace." We are called to one high calling in which " There is one body and one Spirit, even as ye are called in one hope of your calling : One Lord, one faith, one baptism, One God and Father of all, Who is above all, and through all, and in you all " (iv. 3-6).

Most people are agreed on this unity except for the matter of baptism. Then the question arises — which baptism ? The Bible itself speaks of three. There is a baptism of the Spirit, a baptism in water, and a baptism into death, whilst in baptism in water there comes a further division, as some believe in immersion and others in sprinkling. So far as this last point is concerned, the difference is in mode or method. The answer should be clear. The

One baptism is into His death. Jesus once asked the question of two of His disciples : " Are ye able . . . to be baptised with the baptism that I am baptised with ? " (Matthew xx. 22). This was in reference to His death. The Christian life is one in which to learn that we are not our own, we are bought with a price. Therefore we have to die to self and live unto the Lord. Water baptism is only the outward testimony to this inward work. As a person cannot live under water, baptism by immersion is the evidence that our old life is dead and buried. " Buried with Him in baptism " (Colossians ii. 12).

As to the baptism of the Spirit, that is a further blessing which the Lord bestows upon the obedient and surrendered heart which has died to self and is already alive to Him.

The baptism of the Spirit is not *the* baptism, for it is the source of power, not the source of life, and is a gift bestowed upon those who are *in* Christ Jesus.

From unities the Apostle moves to diversities. In doctrine there is oneness and solidarity. In

Service there is diversity. Five gifts were bestowed upon the Church — apostles, prophets, evangelists, pastors and teachers.

One of the weaknesses of man to-day is to compare one person's gifts with another person's ability, then assess likes and dislikes, and create certain evaluations. But all of these gifts come from one Giver, and do not hold a comparative value. Contrariwise, each gift is complementary to the others, and all together create a whole.

It has been pointed out in the book of Exodus that these five ministries may be seen typified in the five bars of the Tabernacle, and that they are set in a perfect order.

The first two — apostles and prophets — are foundational. This is stated in chapter ii. 20 : " And are built upon the foundation of the apostles and prophets." To this statement someone might raise a voice of protest and declare that there is only one foundation, " For other foundation can no man lay than that is laid, which is Jesus Christ " (1 Corinthians iii. 11). This is no contradiction of statements. Jesus Christ is the one and only foundation, so far as salvation is concerned, but Paul is writing to the Ephesians concerning the saints who are enjoying the fulness of Divine blessing, and this chapter is dealing with *service* in the Church. That service is built upon the foundation of the apostles and prophets, for they were the first men to go forth preaching the Word, establishing Churches, opening mission fields, and we continue to do the same things, building on what they commenced.

The third gift is that of the evangelist. His ministry is to go into all the world and preach the Gospel to every creature. When the evangelist has engaged in his special work and led the sinner to Christ, then the pastor shepherds the flock, cares for, protects, leads, instructs, whilst the teacher builds them up in their most holy faith.

As to the purpose of these gifts, it is made clear that they were not given for the exaltation or for the self-satisfaction of the recipient, but for the edifying, building up, and consolidating of the Church of Christ, so that it would be able to resist all the forces of the Evil One, all the deceivableness of fickle man, and all the cunning of crafty man.

These same verses declare a further truth. God distributes His gifts according to His own divine wisdom, each gift contributing its part to the Church as a whole, which is the Body of Christ, even as God has made many members, each functioning according to its own ability, to create a healthy body. A Church with duplicated ministries of one kind, and no ministries of another kind, would be like a body with four arms and no legs, or four eyes and no ears, or too many brains and no heart. Sometimes we see a deformed child and our heart goes out in sympathy. Is not the heart of God grieved in having a deformed Church ? Therefore, do not covet other people's gifts, but remember that the callings and elections are of God, and be more concerned about being in His will than wanting another man's ability.

(2) *In Society* (iv. 17 - v. 9). From conduct in the Church Paul moves to behaviour in the world. We do not walk as other Gentiles. They have been blinded by the god of this world. Their consciences have been seared by the powers of darkness. They are governed by the passions of the flesh. All of these conditions belong to the " old man," but the Child of God is a " new man." He has been taught otherwise. If the attitude of our mind has been changed, then the conduct of our walk must be changed also, so that we will be

> Truthful in all things (iv. 25).
> Disciplined in our temper (iv. 26).
> Honest in our dealings (iv. 28).
> Kindly in our speech (iv. 29).

In the matter of honesty, this is not restricted to money. It concerns every avenue of life — money, time, energy, duty. The world is full of dishonesty, and so is the Church. The Apostle says : " Let him that stole steal no more ; but rather let him labour working with his hands . . . " The Christian should not follow the world which idles away its master's time, demanding high wages but not doing honest work during the hours for which it is paid. The Christian should be recognised by his diligence. His should be a life of giving more than a life of getting.

Maybe the life of the Christian in society is summed up in the last verse of the chapter : " And be ye kind one to another, tenderhearted, forgiving one another, even as God for Christ's sake hath forgiven you."

(3) *In the Family* (v. 19 - vi. 9). In the home the walk is to be one of love in all relationships, husband to wife, wife to husband, children to parents, parents to children, servants to masters, masters to servants. These things will readily be established if, first, our relationships are right with God. "Be ye therefore followers of God as dear children." As in the family the parent can be the source of inspiration to the child, so that the boy wants to be all that his father is, and the girl wants to imitate or mimic her mother, doing the same things in the same way, so should we desire to be followers and imitators of the Lord, revealing the same characteristics. Things that are foreign to His character should be foreign to our lives, not even named amongst us.

It is in this chapter that three references are made as to our walk.

We are to " walk in love as Christ also hath loved us." We are to " walk as children of light," having been delivered from darkness ; and we are to " walk circumspectly," or carefully. Being separate from the contaminations of the world, we should continue to be being filled with the fulness of the Holy Spirit until His life overflows out of us in praise and thanksgiving. The reaction of this Spirit-filled life in the home will be

(a) *"Wives,* submit yourselves unto your own husbands," remembering that God has set the man as the head of the family even as Christ is the Head of the Church. The Church has to submit herself to the Lord.

This is not a submission of cowardice, nor of inferiority, nor yet of slavery, but of respect.

The second family relationship is

(b) " *Husbands,* love your wives, even as Christ also loved the Church." His love was a sacrificial love, counting not the cost. His love is a protective love, as He intercedes for us with the Father and covers us against the enemy. His love is a pro-viding love, meeting our every need along life's way. His love is a permanent love. It never varies, it is steadfast, it is never shared with another — so ought men to love their wives.

Having spoken to the wife and to the husband separately, the Apostle then links them together as one entity. " For this cause shall a man leave his father and mother, and shall be joined unto his wife, and they two shall be one flesh. This is a great mystery, but I speak concerning Christ and the Church." How-ever one reads these words, they reveal the closeness of the bond of holiness and affinity which exists between husband and wife, and Christ and His people.

(c) *"Children,* obey your parents in the Lord." In making this injuction, Paul is but reminding them of' the first command-ment which has a promise of blessing attached to it. This is an oft-repeated command, with many examples of the results of obedience and disobedience. Timothy tells of the last days, when one of the evidences of God-rejection and anarchy will be " dis-obedient to parents."

God has established the family and sanctified its relation-ship. He has bestowed honour upon parenthood and required that children be submissive. Therefore Christian children should never take their example from the people of a godless world. What they do does not give licence to what we do.

There is one condition only to this obedience, and that is " in the Lord." A Christian child must remain obedient to non-Christian parents up to the point where the parent requires something which is contrary to the mind of the Lord, and then one has to decline, not with impudence nor an air of superiority, but graciously and with a sound reason.

He must never disobey nor refuse because he wants his way or desires to please himself. Our submission might be helped if it is remembered that " Though He were a Son, yet learned He obedience by the things which He suffered " (Hebrews v. 8), and He " became obedient unto death, even the death of the cross " (Philippians ii. 8).

The promise that God has made to young people for their submission is long life.

(d) " And, ye *fathers*, provoke not your children to wrath." A great deal is heard to-day concerning the waywardness and the rebellion of children, but maybe not enough concerning the neglect and indifference of parents, those who have done a great injustice to their children and brought a moral tragedy to this generation in their doctrine of self-expression. Such have neglected their own parental responsibility of child training.

These young people, when they reach adulthood and begin to realise how they were wronged by their parents, are going to be provoked with anger toward them. The Apostle is saying to you, Christian father, and God-fearing mother, do not do these things. Find time for your children. Enter into their lives, feelings, and problems. Enter into their confidence and allow them to gain your confidence. Close up that gap of fear, and create that spirit of absolute trust. Get to understand their point of view and then they will understand your viewpoint.

(e) "*Servants*, be obedient to them that are your masters according to the flesh." This is everyday relationship in the business world. The people for whom we work may not be Christians. We are to be subject to these by virtue of the fact that they pay us for the service we render. Let us see to it that we give fully that which is their due. Such service should not be influenced by the pay packet or the trade union, not even with an eye on promotion. The incentive in business should be to serve willingly and not grudgingly, doing it as unto the Lord.

Such service should bring its own promotion and its rewards, both here and hereafter.

(f) "And, ye *masters*, do the same things unto them, forbearing threatening ; knowing that your Master also is in heaven ; neither is there respect of persons with Him."

Christianity, and Christian relationships, could solve all the industrial problems, and put master and men on a platform of mutual understanding.

(4) *In Warfare* (vi. 10-19). This is our walk and conduct in the world where the adversary is. In this realm the Christian is instructed to put on the whole armour of God, for the warfare is not carnal but spiritual. We do not oppose and resist men but spirits, even though at times man is used by the enemy as his tool. " For we wrestle not against flesh and blood, but against principalities, against powers, against the rulers of the darkness of this world, against spiritual wickedness in high places."

God has provided all the equipment needed to combat the enemy ; five pieces of armour for the defensive and one piece for the offensive. In this warfare we are again reminded that we do not belong to this world. We are dead to it. We are in heavenly places. Therefore we encounter spiritual foes.

The armour of God includes : —

The Girdle of Truth. The girdle was that part of a man's clothing which bound everything to him. Into it he tucked the loose ends of his flowing robes so that they would not hinder his progress. On to it would be placed many things. David put his sling there and also his shepherd's lamp. The scribe kept his inkhorn there.

Jesus said : "I am the Truth." Then we must allow Him to surround us, control all the things that are outwardly attached to us. We should bring under His control all the loose ends of our thinking, bring every thought into captivity to the obedience of His will, and gird up the loins of our mind. To be surrounded by Truth is to be delivered from error.

The Breastplate of Righteousness, not our righteousness, which is as filthy rags, but His imputed righteousness which cannot be gainsaid.

This piece of armour protects the heart, that heart which is deceitful above all things and desperately wicked. To be a good soldier of Jesus Christ, to resist the powers of darkness and the forces of evil, there is no doubt that the heart of man needs to be protected, and the provision has been made in Him.

The Shoes of the Gospel of Peace. This statement almost suggests a contradiction of terms. The soldier is being equipped for war. He is putting on his armour, not taking it off. He is preparing to wrestle, not retreat. Maybe that is why there is the word *preparation* of the Gospel of Peace. If we are to enjoy the peace which comes through the Gospel, we must put on those heavy shoes that belong to the soldier, that are suitable to the rough terrain over which he must sometimes march, shoes that will withstand all weathers and conditions, shoes that will allow one to trample underfoot the lion and the adder (Psalm xci. 13), as well as the thorn and the briar.

Equipped by the Lord we overcome the temptations and the tests of life and thereby enjoy " the peace of God that passeth all understanding."

The Shield of Faith through which no fiery dart of the enemy can penetrate. " This is the victory that overcometh the world, even our faith." Said the Lord to Abram in Genesis xv. 1 : " Fear not, Abram, I am thy shield." A shield is different from the other pieces of armour in that it is movable. Wherever the enemy directs his fire the shield can be lifted or dropped, so that it comes between the arrows and the soldier. If the arrows were shot at the eyes, the shield was lifted ; if directed at the heart or any other vital organs, the shield would cover. If the darts were fired at the feet to destroy advancement, then the shield could be dropped.

The main avenues through which the enemy would seek to destroy are the lust of the eye, the lust of the flesh, and the pride of life. Jesus was tempted through each of these avenues when in the wilderness, and won the victory so that the darts fell blunted at His feet. It was thus that He became our shield, and if we would stand behind Him, with a perfect faith in His finished work, we should learn that we are more than victors through Him Who loved us, and gave Himself for us.

The Helmet of Salvation. The head is the seat of the mind, and the mind controls the actions of life. Satan has ever sought to gain the control of that mind and, if not, to confuse it. All false doctrines, all of men's theories, are to this end. Hence we are told to "Gird up the loins of your mind, be sober" (1 Peter i. 13), and to be "renewed in the spirit of your mind" (Ephesians iv. 23). "Let this mind be in you, which was also in Christ Jesus" (Philippians ii. 5). Here the mind of the soldier of Jesus Christ is to be covered and protected with the Helmet of Salvation. His thinking, understanding, discernment, must be under His control, dispelling doubts and fears, and making him strong in the Lord and in the power of His might. Our enemy is neither human nor physical, the battle is spiritual and moral. It was here that Adam and Eve fell. "For God doth know that in the day ye eat thereof, then your eyes shall be opened; and ye shall be as gods, knowing good and evil" (Genesis iii. 5).

The Sword of the Spirit, which is the Word of God. In the list of articles mentioned this is the only one which is a weapon. It is for the offensive and not the defensive. The Sword is the Word of God, and the Holy Spirit is the One Who wields it. Only Spirit-filled, Spirit-controlled ministry is effective ministry.

This sword is sharp and two-edged. It cuts both ways. It commends and condemns, it encourages and reproves. Often people want to apply a truth or a sermon to someone else in the Church, forgetting that there are two sides to every situation, and the Word of God can apply both ways.

This is the sword of the " It is written " from which the Devil retreated when he tempted the Lord in the wilderness of Judæa, and from which he must always retreat. Never substitute this well-proved sword of God's providing by any modern or moral armament. It is the power of God unto salvation to every one who will believe. With David of old, who was offered the sword with which he had beheaded Goliath, we would say : " There is none like that ; give it me " (1 Samuel xxi. 9).

As surely as the uniform of any nation, or the military equipment of any army, is worthless apart from the loyalty of the soldier to his country and his obedience to his captain, even so all this armour of the Lord's providing must be buckled on with prayer and with a complete yieldedness to the Lord. " Praying always with all prayer and supplication in the Spirit, and watching thereunto with all perseverance and supplication for all saints ; And for me, that utterance may be given unto me, that I may open my mouth boldly, to make known the mystery of the Gospel, for which I am an ambassador in bonds ; that therein I may speak boldly, as I ought to speak " (vi. 18-20).

In the light of this glorious message of victorious living, is it not tragic to listen to the words of the Lord, written to this same Church only thirty years later, as through John He said : " I know thy works, and thy labour, and thy patience, and how thou canst not bear them which are evil ; and thou hast tried them which say they are apostles, and are not, and hast found them liars : And hast borne, and hast patience, and for My Name's sake hast laboured, and hast not fainted. Nevertheless I have somewhat against thee, because thou hast left thy first love. Remember therefore from whence thou art fallen, and repent, and do the first works ; or else ——" (Revelation ii. 2-5).

To all of us, and especially the active servant of the Lord, these solemn words say, " Put on the whole armour of God and take heed lest thou fall."

PHILIPPIANS

ALL JOY

*"Holding forth the Word of life; that I may rejoice in the
day of Christ, that I have not run in vain, neither laboured
in vain. Yea, and if I be offered upon the sacrifice and service
of your faith, I joy, and rejoice with you all. For the same
cause also do ye joy, and rejoice with me"*

(PHILIPPIANS ii. 16-18)

INTRODUCTION

The Church at Philippi was the first Church to be established
in Europe. Like many others, it had a very small beginning. The
account of its birth is in the sixteenth chapter of The Acts.

The apostles had planned to go into Asia, but the Spirit
of God forbade them. Then they decided to go into Bithynia
and, again, the Spirit of God restrained them. This did not cause
the apostles to give up and declare that there was nothing for
them to do because all the doors were closed to them. This
should never be the attitude of the child of God although, alas,
too often it is. How quickly do some people become discouraged,
and particularly so in the work of the Lord.

When the Lord restrained them from moving in the direction
they had chosen, quietly they waited on Him in prayer until they
had the revelation of His will. This came to them in a vision
of the night watches, for whilst men sleep He, the Lord, neither
slumbers nor sleeps.

In a vision "There stood a man of Macedonia and prayed
him, saying, Come over into Macedonia and help us." This
was the open door so, without any delay, Paul and his companions
journeyed to Europe. On their arrival they found their way to
Philippi. Then on the Sabbath Day they wended their footsteps
toward the river because they had heard that people met there to
pray.

On reaching the river, Paul found only women so, never
losing an opportunity, he sat down and preached to them. This
resulted in his first European convert, a woman named Lydia of
Thyatira. She was saved and baptised. Not only did she open

728

her heart to the Lord but she opened her house also to the apostles.

A little later Paul met a damsel possessed of an evil spirit. The spirit was cast out and, presumably, the girl followed the Apostle. She would be his second convert.

As a result of this healing both Paul and Silas were cast into prison, and there they sang praises to God, rejoicing that they were counted worthy to suffer for Christ's sake. An earthquake that night set these prisoners free, and also shook the jailor to his senses so that he sought the Lord. Both he and his family were saved and baptised, and so began the Philippian Church.

To this Church Paul wrote his Epistle.

The keyword is " Joy." " Joy " and " rejoicing " are mentioned seventeen times in the four chapters. The word " all " is repeated twenty-four times. The joy of the Apostle, the joy that dominated the Church, should be the possession of every believer. In fact, joy will become the experience of every believer who is a servant, for joy comes through service.

Of the Lord it was said : " Who for the joy that was set before Him endured the Cross, despising the shame." The statement is made in Hebrews xii. 2. The experience of it is unfolded in this Epistle.

THE BOOK

It can be divided according to its four chapters.

Chapter 1.   Joy in living.
Chapter 2.   Joy in service.
Chapter 3.   Joy in fellowship.
Chapter 4.   Joy in rewards.

Again the book divides by chapter as : —

Chapter 1.   Christ, the believer's Life.
Chapter 2.   Christ, the believer's Pattern.
Chapter 3.   Christ, the believer's Object.
Chapter 4.   Christ, the believer's Strength.

(1) CHRIST — THE BELIEVER'S LIFE (Chapter i.)

The book opens with Paul's usual salutation, except that he uses the word " all " as in none other of his Epistles. The constant repetition of this word has already been mentioned.

In the first chapter the Apostle saluted *all* the saints, and he told them how he prayed for them *all*, that God's work was for them *all*, and that they were *all* to be sharers in His grace ; also they were *all* to continue their testimony in *all* places.

There was evidently a unity of spirit in this Church. It knew a freedom from division and partiality which brought great joy to the heart of the Apostle.

Paul then begins to enter into the theme of the Epistle — The Christ Life. If we have fully yielded our lives, and have unreservedly accepted His Life, then we should be free from the cares of this life. The Lord is fully responsible for us, for our life is His Life. Therefore we may be " confident of this very thing, that He which hath begun a good work in you will perform it until the day of Jesus Christ " (i. 6).

With this submission one may even submit joyfully to the trials of life, knowing that " all things work together for good to them that love God." Here the Apostle expresses it in the words: "But I would ye should understand, brethren, that the things which happened unto me have fallen out rather unto the furtherance of the gospel " (i. 12).

At the time when Paul wrote this Epistle he was in prison. As a result of this imprisonment, some of the more timid believers had become encouraged to preach the Word, and so do what Paul could not. This meant a wider spread of the Gospel.

In some cases the motive for preaching was wrong, but the Apostle did not seem to mind the motive so long as the Word was being preached.

If Christ were magnified as a result of his imprisonment then he was happy, for, said he : " For to me to live is Christ, and to die is gain." He longed to be with the Lord, to enjoy His presence, and yet he desired to remain on earth because, in so doing. he could impart blessing to his fellow-men and enrich them in their spiritual life. This is the life that has nothing to lose.

When Christ is thus dwelling in us, and when He is living through us, then only the Christ life will be seen by the world. The Christ life does not mean a religious life, or a pretence life, or a veneer life. That is something put on. The real life is some thing, or some One, coming out. Then the daily walk, or citizenship, shall be as " becometh the Gospel of Christ " (i. 27).

(2) CHRIST — THE BELIEVER'S PATTERN (Chapter ii.)

This is the classic chapter of the book and, possibly, the classic chapter of all literature on the subject of humility. It is certainlv the basic chapter for all the ills of this world.

If Christ means anything, if Christianity is a reality, then here is the sphere of operation. " Let nothing be done through strife or vainglory ; but in lowliness of mind let each esteem other better than themselves. Look not every man on his own things, but every man also on the things of others " (ii. 3-4).

The following verses set forth Christ's humiliation as the example of accomplishment.

If it can be appreciated that we have nothing but what we receive, then we will give everything that others may receive. If we have received everything we possess, then in what do we boast ? Nothing ! This will rob us of vainglory and cause us to think of the other man as better than ourselves and, in turn, will make for the humility which pleases God. " Though the Lord be high, yet hath He respect unto the lowly ; but the proud He knoweth afar off " (Psalm cxxxviii. 6).

If it is hard to be humble and consider the other man first — and who does not find it so — then, says the Apostle : " Let this mind be in you, which was also in Christ Jesus," or, " Take Him as your pattern. Mould your conduct according to His conduct. Think in the same terms for, after all, you have the same life."

The Apostle then enumerates the seven heavy steps which the Lord took in His humiliation on our behalf. Let us remember that when we begin to practise the life of humiliation, we will never start at the height from which He started — " Equal with God " — and neither will we reach as low as He reached — " Even the death of the Cross."

Let us ponder this descent.

He was the only One Who could claim to be equal with God. He was with the Father from before the world was. " In the beginning was the Word, and the Word was with God, and the Word was God " (John i 1). That is a declaration of *His Eternal Existence.* All other beings including the angelic hosts, are created beings. He was a Son for ever, One in the bosom of the Father. That is His Divinity. He participated in the creation of man, " Let *us* make man in *our* image." That is a declaration of *His Authority.* " God, Who at sundry times and in divers manners, spake in times past unto the fathers by the prophets, hath in these last days spoken unto us by His Son, Whom He hath appointed Heir of all things, by Whom also He made the worlds ; Who being the brightness of His glory, and the express image of His Person, and upholding all things by the Word of His Power, when He had by Himself purged our sins, sat down on the right hand of the

Majesty on high " (Hebrews i. 1-3). That is *His Equality*. This
same Jesus made Himself of

No Reputation. Who of men are not proud of their reputation?
Who of us would not be willing to fight in defence of that reputation ? It is a degrading thing to have it said : " His reputation
is doubtful," and worse still to be charged with having no
reputation. A person of no repute is one who is in the lowest
bracket of the social scale. He is the criminal. She is the woman
of the street — the harlot. Jesus was scandalously referred to as
the friend of publicans and sinners. They questioned the legiti-
macy of His Birth. They called Him an imposter, asserting that
He posed to be someone whom He was not.

His Birth was marred with no home, no cradle — only
a stable.

His life was marred with poverty and loneliness.

His ministry was marred by their unbelief.

How many of us would be willing to take this first step in
following Him as our pattern ?

" And took upon Him the

Form of a Servant." In considering this statement it must
be borne in mind that the expression " servant " had a very
different connotation in those bygone days. It did not refer to
a well-paid servant of some Company or Government, nor did it
even refer to the domestic servant, a position which seems to be
despised and beneath the dignity of most to-day. It referred to a
slave, a man who laboured and expected little reward and received
little appreciation for anything he did.

Servants ? To-day we all want to be masters. We all want
to tell the other person what he ought to do, but no one must tell
us what our responsibility is !

He served. He fed the hungry. He healed the sick. He
ministered to the poor. He washed His disciples' feet. And the
reward ? None, save the joy of doing it. The appreciation ?
None. They bade Him leave their coasts when He cast out a
demon. They would not believe in Him when He taught. They
said, " Away with Him " when He offered them a kingdom.

When Jesus washed His disciples' feet He said : " So ought
ye." " I have given you an example, that ye should do as I
have done to you." " He that would be greatest must be servant of
all."

Can we take this step for His sake ?
" And was made in the

Likeness of Men." Man to-day is not anxious to recognise his identity. Whilst some behave as though they were demons, others want to recognise themselves as gods. They teach that there is a spark of divinity in every man. Man must develop his mind and his nature until he becomes his own saviour. They will hail men, such as Buddha, Confucius, Bernard Shaw, and others, as those who attained their goal. They will speak of Jesus as another Man who attained. Man, with this sickening theosophy, reaches upward toward a utopia. Jesus, with all of His heartening Grace, reached downward toward a fallen world.

Can we step down to men of low degree ?
" And being found in

Fashion as a Man." The " likeness " of a man could readily refer to his thoughts, desires, ambitions, his moral being. It has been seen that man desires to be a god, and God desired to become a man, to enter into his fears and heartaches, his passions, love, and devotion, his longings and aspirations. But " fashion " surely means " form," taking upon Himself a physical frame, a human body, with all of its limitations, and those limitations would be many to the One Who filled eternity and knew no limitation. Then it would seem that as we consider the limitation of the fashion or the form of a man, we would discover the limitation of its duration — three score years and ten, and then death. Man, with his evil heart, did not allow the Lord to make half of that span.

The word " fashion " and the limits of the physical or material can be more fully appreciated as Scripture is compared with Scripture. " And they that use this world, as not abusing it ; for the *fashion* of this world passeth away " (1 Corinthians vii. 31), or " For the sun is no sooner risen with a burning heat, but it withereth the grass, and the flower thereof falleth, and the grace of the fashion of it perisheth . . . " (James i. 11).

From these Scriptures it is seen that *fashion* is something transient. It soon passes away, as the fashions of the world pass. Thus Jesus took upon Himself the physical form of a thing that is temporary.

" *He humbled Himself,"* not merely in words but in the fullest sense of action. Such humiliation is costly at any time, but more so when the King of Glory, Who had all heaven at His command, allowed common soldiers to sport Him and set Him up as a false king with a crown of thorns, reed, and scarlet robe — Oh, the injustice and the shame !

" And became obedient

Unto Death." The Prince of Life, the Eternal One, Who of Himself knew no death, " became," that was when He changed His fashion, " obedient," which means He submitted voluntarily unto death. This was the price of sin, the thing He had never committed, a thing His holiness abominated, the thing so contrary to His nature. Death is an enemy. No man welcomes it. It is that from which all men flee, even when it comes in its gentlest form.

But oh, that final step !

" Even the Death of the Cross." Could He, the Lord of Glory, step lower ? He died the death of a criminal. " Cursed is everyone that hangeth on a tree." This was a death which was merciless, a death which was excruciating. What a relief comes to the heart and the mind when He makes the cry " It is finished." He had reached the lowest depths, He could go no lower. " It is finished " — His suffering was finished, His humiliation was finished, the mockery and shame were finished, the work God had given Him to do was finished.

From those hard, cold, painful steps of His humiliation there comes the ascent of the incense of His resurrection and exaltation.

" Wherefore God also hath highly exalted Him ",
Man debases — God exalts.

" And given Him a Name which is above every name ",
Man dragged that Name into the gutter. God has lifted it up to heaven.

" That at the Name of Jesus every knee should bow ",
Men may humble the Lord to-day in their selfishness and disrespect. Presently they are going to be humbled before Him.

" And every tongue should confess that Jesus Christ is Lord."
This restores to Him the glory He laid aside temporarily — " Equal with God." And He shall reign for ever and ever !

Maybe in the light of the foregoing, the next verse may explain itself. The verse, or, rather, a part of it, has been a problem to many minds, and also has become a basis of wrong interpretation. The statement is : " work out your own salvation with fear and trembling."

The wrong interpretation has been a salvation by works and not of Grace. The problem is caused by taking the statement away from its context.

The first word of this twelfth verse is " Wherefore," which links it with that which precedes it. The subject is humility. Christ is the example. The Philippians were instructed to " Let this mind be in you." In the light of this, " work out your own salvation." Having received Christ, now let the world see Him by working out this same life day by day. When one receives Christ, He comes in to abide. From within He works, " For it is God which worketh *in* you both to will and to do of His good pleasure." When He thus controls, then we shall find ourselves living blameless lives in this perverse world. The obvious truth is, therefore, that it is not our effort or our works, but His Grace working through us and out of us.

The chapter is concluded by giving a record of the lives of three men who sought to follow that example.

(1) *Paul*. As Christ had yielded Himself and had become our pattern, and as Peter says, " For even hereunto were ye called: because Christ also suffered for us, leaving us an example, that ye should follow His steps ; " (1 Peter ii. 21), even so Paul, the once-bigoted Pharisee, had never counted the cost of serving Christ — or, had he ? He found the price to be all joy, for writing here he says : " Yea, and if I be offered (or poured out as a libation) upon the sacrifice and service of your faith, I joy, and rejoice with you all"(ii. 17). Paul never counted his life dear unto himself.

(2) *Timothy*. The Apostle said that all men seek their own. No one was willing to sacrifice self for the sake of others, except Timothy. Timothy had served Paul as a son to a father. He had certainly made full proof of his ministry, and now that Paul was in prison, he was hoping to send this fully surrendered man.

(3) *Epaphroditus*. His labour had brought him near to death. He had been a companion in labour, a fellow-soldier, a faithful messenger. Paul was sending him also to the Philippians

for their consolation and joy. The testimony of this self-sacrificing life is in the last verse of the chapter, " Because for the work of Christ he was nigh unto death, not regarding his life, to supply your lack of service toward me."

(3) CHRIST — THE BELIEVER'S OBJECT (Chapter iii)

Before moving into his next subject, there is another call to rejoice from the one who had learned how in all things to be content. " Finally, my brethren, rejoice in the Lord." He feels the urgency to repeat this exhortation because of the tendency of the human heart to move away from such an exercise. Around these people there were enemies, and a sufficiency of the flesh, to draw them into a state of self-complacency, or into a place where their satisfaction could be measured according to the accomplishments of the flesh.

The Apostle enlarges his exhortation with his own testimony. If anyone should have reason to glory in the flesh, it would be himself. He could boast of circumcision, of nationality, of race, of faith, of position, of zeal, and of conduct, according to the law, but all of these things he counted as nothing and less than nothing, that he might win Christ and be found in Him. His whole soul longing was, " That I may know Him, and the power of His resurrection, and the fellowship of His sufferings."

As it was said of the Lord : " Though He were a Son, yet learned He obedience by the things which He suffered " (Hebrews v. 8) and again, the Lord's own words : " I seek not Mine own Will, but the Will of the Father which hath sent Me " (John v. 30), so Paul counted not the cost, neither sought his own, but laid aside every thing of which he made a boast that he might please Him Who had called him.

The Apostle's one great object can be summarised thus : —

That I may win Christ	Verse 8.
That I may be found in Him	Verse 9.
That I may know Him	Verse 10.
That I may know the power of His resurrection	Verse 10.
That I may know the fellowship of His sufferings	Verse 10.
That I may apprehend	Verse 12.
That I may press toward the mark	Verse 14.

Against this the glory of the world is nothing and less than nothing, for he refers to such things as the off-scouring (dung) of the earth.

The Apostle's statements in verses 11 and 12 would possibly be against some erroneous doctrines which had crept into the Church and, strangely enough, are still in the Church to-day. The first was to the effect that the resurrection of the dead had already taken place. This is stated in another of his Prison Epistles — 2 Timothy ii. 18. Paul was declaring that it was still future, and that his desire was to be a partaker in it.

The other doctrine was one of sinless perfection. The Apostle refuted this inasmuch as, although he was the chiefest of the apostles, yet he had not attained. He never expected to be perfect until the resurrection when he would be with his Lord. Therefore he intended ever to be reaching out toward his goal. To do this we must ever forget the things that are behind and only press on for the things that are before us.

Having declared his allegiance to the Lord Jesus Christ and testified that the world with its highest awards meant nothing to him, Paul concludes the chapter with one further testimony of his political standing, reminding all saints that their relationship is the same. "For our conversation (meaning our citizenship) is in heaven." We belong to that Country. We are subject to its King, and we are His ambassadors or representatives here. Therefore we labour here awaiting our recall when He shall come, and take from us the passports of this world which are our "vile bodies." The word "vile" used to mean "common or ordinary," but the original is "the body of our humiliation," and we shall no more be looked upon as foreigners, or strangers, but shall be at home with the Lord, putting on the robes of His glory.

(4) CHRIST — THE BELIEVER'S STRENGTH (Chapter iv.)

In the Philippian Church there was apparently a lack of strength. The cause of the weakness was a division of opinion. The leaders of this division are now named. " I beseech Euodias, and beseech Syntyche, that they be of the same mind in the Lord " (iv. 2). Probably some personal pride was responsible for the one not yielding to the other. To bring about a Divine conviction, as against a personal rebuke which might be resented, was probably the reason why Paul had written so much about humility, saying in chapter ii. 2-3 : " Fulfil ye my joy, that ye be likeminded, having the same love, being of one accord, of one mind. Let nothing be done through strife or vainglory ; but in lowliness of mind let each esteem other better than themselves," and then setting forth the example set by Christ.

Having named the two doctrines, he then makes a further appeal for co-operation with others who had been serving the Lord and helping him.

How can one know the Lord's strength dispelling all one's anxieties and differences ? The key to the book is the answer — " Rejoice in the Lord alway : and again I say, Rejoice." Rejoicing is victory. A man cannot rejoice and complain at the same time. When one is counting his blessings there is no time to count other things.

Another avenue of the Lord's strength is found in the attitude of complete yieldedness, and this is the meaning of the word " moderation " (iv. 5). One is yielded to the Lord when he is in that state of relaxation which brings him to the place of being " careful for nothing." This does not mean carelessness or indifference to prevailing conditions. It means not being full of care and anxiety. He is not worried. He brings his burdens to the Lord. He gives Him thanks that he is privileged so to do. He thanks Him for His interest and love — just leaves the whole situation with Him.

If we can learn to do this, then there will come to the mind and to the soul a peace which is unknown to the world. It is the peace of God, and it will act as a garrison, a military fortification, to heart and mind that all the forces of evil will never be able to penetrate.

Finally, brethren, if you would know the strength of the Lord in your life, if you would know the power of the Lord in your Church, never contemplate the wrongs which exist, the injustices that have been done or the defeats that have been suffered. That is the negative side of life and brings defeat. We must live on the positive side, so

> Whatsoever things are true
> Whatsoever things are honest
> Whatsoever things are just
> Whatsoever things are pure
> Whatsoever things are lovely
> Whatsoever things are of good report

If there be any virtue
If there be any praise —
think on these things.

This is no suggestion of mind over matter. It is feeding the soul upon the food which creates spiritual growth.

The closing verses of the book are personal and material as against the spiritual truth Paul has imparted to the Church. The business matter being dealt with, he acknowledges the Church's goodness to him in supplying those necessities of life, even when other people forgot him, as they did in Thessalonica. The Lord has declared that the labourer is worthy of his hire, but it is not every church which does its duty toward such. God will make up the lack to His servant, as He did to Paul, but the church which fails in its duties loses out sadly in its blessings.

The servant who knows how to trust the Lord has a richness of experience that money can never buy, and he has a knowledge of the Lord of which he can never be robbed.

Rich is the man who can say : " For I have learned, in whatsoever state I am, therewith to be content. I know both how to be abased, and I know how to abound : everywhere and in all things I am instructed both to be full and to be hungry, both to abound and to suffer need. I can do all things through Christ which strengtheneth me " (iv. 11-13).

Having spoken òf the manner in which the Lord had met his own need, and having acknowledged their gifts, Paul reverses the truth by assuring them that " My God shall supply all your need according to His riches in glory by Christ Jesus " (iv. 19).

God has never at any time promised to supply our wants. Therefore we have no claim on Him for these. He has promised, however, to supply our needs, or our essentials. This does not mean that He will not give us some of the things we want, particularly if they are for our good, but what we must learn to avoid is seeking to hold God responsible for certain things for which He has never committed Himself.

The verse also declares that His promise is not according to our needs, but according to His riches in glory — and they are inexhaustible !

The concluding verse is : " The grace of our Lord Jesus Christ be with you all. Amen."

Every Epistle of Paul ends with a benediction and each benediction has the word " grace " in it. Grace almost becomes Paul's signature, for the word is missing from the Epistles written by other men.

One wonders whether such could be a further pointer to the authorship of Hebrews.

COLOSSIANS

HEAD OVER ALL

" Hath in these last days spoken unto us by His Son, Whom He hath appointed heir of all things, by Whom also He made the worlds; Who being the brightness of His glory, and the express image of His Person, and upholding all things by the word of His power, when He had by Himself purged our sins, sat down on the right hand of the Majesty on high"
(HEBREWS i. 2-3)

INTRODUCTION

This Epistle was written to the Church which met in the house of Philemon. The Epistle to Philemon was written at the same time as this was and is closely related.

So far as is known Paul had never visited Colosse. The converts who had made the foundation members of this Church must have heard Paul ministering elsewhere as they had travelled. These included Philemon and his family. It is deduced that Paul had not been in the city because there is no record that he had, and also in chapter i. 4 he says : " Since we *heard* of your faith in Christ Jesus." The thought is strengthened several times in the chapter.

THE MESSAGE

The theme of this Epistle is the Supremacy of Christ as Head over all things. It reveals the relationship of Christ and the Church — He, the Head, and the Church, the Body. As the physical body is subjected to the complete control of the head, so ought also the Body of Christ, the Church, to be subject to Him in all things.

The book divides into two : —

(1) DOCTRINAL (Chapter i.). This deals with the matter of *steadfastness.*

(2) PRACTICAL (Chapters ii. - iv.). This section breaks again into *fellowship* (chapter ii.) and *sanctification* (chapters iii. and iv.).

As in so many of Paul's letters, he expounds doctrine and then applies it to everyday practical living.

(1) DOCTRINAL (Chapter i.) — STEADFASTNESS

In Paul's introductory greeting Timothy is in partnership with Paul, as in four other of the Epistles. Epaphras, one of Paul's friends, had been to this Church. The evidence from verse 7 is that at the particular time he was acting as Pastor of the Church, although from the end of the Epistle it would appear that Archippus had some ministry in this same assembly. Epaphras had sent back to the Apostle some very encouraging reports concerning the saints, of their faith and love, to which Paul makes comment in these eight verses of introduction.

At verse 9 the Apostle enters right into his subject, seeking for these believers that they " might be filled with the knowledge of His Will in all wisdom and spiritual understanding " (i. 9), three things that we might all do well to covet — Knowlelge, Wisdom, and Understanding. We ofttimes refer to the fact that we seek His Will, but here the exhortation is to KNOW His Will, and this is not to be in half measure, thinking we know, but, rather, knowing that we know His Will.

Wisdom and understanding are often associated, part'cularly so in the Proverbs, where there are such statements as : " Incline thine ear unto *wisdom* and apply thine heart to *understanding* " (ii. 2). "*Wisdom* is the principal thing ; therefore get *wisdom ;* and with all thy getting get *understanding* " (iv. 7). " My son, attend unto my *wisdom,* and bow thine ear to my *understanding* " (v. 1). These qualities are essential to

> a walk that is worthy,
> a life that is pleasing,
> a work that is fruitful,
> a knowledge that is increasing,
> a strength that is powerful, and
> a patience that is joyful,

which is a summarisation of verses 10 and 11.

Knowledge brings wisdom, and wisdom develops understanding. These things are sought by all — the student at school and the man in his business or profession. Paul makes it an injunction for the believer in his Christian life, because spiritual understanding is basic to spiritual living. Are we as anxious to understand the Will of God and His Word that we "might walk worthy of the Lord unto all pleasing" (i. 10), as we are ofttimes anxious to understand our profession, vocation, or sport, that we might succeeed therein?

It must be appreciated why the Apostle starts this Epistle with the introduction of knowledge, wisdom, and understanding, and then from it moves into this glorious exaltation of the Person of the Lord Jesus Christ, the great central theme of the book.

A very dangerous error was beginning to creep into the Church, known as "The Colossian Heresy", a doctrine which, later, developed into what was known as Gnosticism, the cult which became prevalent in the days when John wrote his Epistles (see the Epistles of John for a description). The followers of this cult were a people who claimed to have both knowledge (the meaning of Gnostic) and wisdom. At this time it was somewhat philosophical, hence Paul said: "Beware lest any man spoil you through philosophy and vain deceit, after the tradition of men, after the rudiments (elements) of the world, and not after Christ" (ii. 8). It had also an element of Judaism, which required circumcision — so the admonition, "In Whom also ye are circumcised with the circumcision made without hands, in putting off the body of the sins of the flesh by the circumcision of Christ" (ii. 11).

They demanded certain ordinances also, and therefore the Apostle writes: "Blotting out the handwriting of ordinances that was against us, which was contrary to us, and took it out of the way, nailing it to His Cross" (ii. 14). It brought in a legalism which Paul opposed. "Let no man therefore judge you in meat, or in drink, or in respect of a holy day, or of the new moon, or of the sabbath days" (ii. 16). They taught the worship of angels, and so the next statement: "Let no man beguile you of your reward in a voluntary humility and worshipping of angels, intruding into those things which he hath not seen, vainly puffed up by his fleshly mind" (ii. 18).

Much of what has been stated here is with us to-day. Errors which creep into the Church are seldom eliminated.

The errors of that day are those of to-day, and the whole can be summed up in three words that make the Church weak to-day, for we are attacked by

(1) Modernism ..... the traditions of men (ii. 8).
(2) Spiritualism ..... intruding into those things which are not seen (ii. 18).
(3) Materialism ..... subject to ordinances (ii. 20).

It can be readily seen that all of these things, which belong to the worldly-wise, can rob the Lord of His rights. They limit the power and authority of Christ, putting a great chasm between God and man, which could only be bridged in some measure through the medium of angels and spirits. By the help of these spirits man could rise above the sordid and materialistic things of this world to some higher level whilst, at the same time, his body could continue to participate in the social sins and material advantages of the world order. It was the fact of opposing these intermediaries and this materialism that caused Paul to declare all the glories and unlimited authority of Christ as the All in all, the One in Whom dwells " all the fulness of the Godhead bodily."

We do not need the mediation of spirits. We ourselves have been made " meet to be partakers of the inheritance of the saints in light " (i. 12). We have been delivered from the power of darkness and have been translated into the kingdom of His dear Son. We have been redeemed through His Blood. We are rejoicing in the forgiveness of sins, so let us take our eyes and our thoughts off the world and the rudiments thereof, from which we have been delivered, and centre them upon the glories of heaven and upon the Person of the Lord Jesus Christ " Who is the image of the invisible God " (i. 15) ; in other words, the manifestation of God. No man hath seen God at any time because God is a Spirit, yet He was manifested, or revealed Himself to the world, in the Person of His Son. If He is the Son then He is One with the Father and of the Father, thus declaring His eternal Oneness.

" The firstborn of every creature " (i. 15) does not imply that He is a created being but, rather, as the firstborn He is Heir of all that is of the Father. He is Heir before any created being. This makes Him Heir of all things and, therefore, the Heir of creation.

The Apostle closes this relationship still tighter as he declares that everything belongs to Christ by ownership as the Co-Creator. " For by Him were all things created, that are in heaven, and that are in earth ; visible and invisible, whether they be thrones, or dominions, or principalities, or powers ; all things were created by Him, and for Him. And He is before all things, and by Him all things consist " (i. 16-17). These majestic verses suggest that this earth is but a small item in the vast universe in which there are unseen powers, principalities, and governments, all controlled by the might of the Eternal Son. There are principalities and powers in that unseen world which belong to the powers of darkness and are to be subdued, according to Ephesians vi. 12. Therefore we must not limit the reign of the Eternal to the restrictions of time. There is no limitation to which the mind may reach out in seeking to comprehend the eternal glories of the Son of God. When one has reached out as far as the mind will permit in seeing Omnipotence in His relationship with His own creation, when one has pondered His glorious majesty and power, then we may come all the way back into time and read the next verse : " And He is the Head of the body, the Church " (i. 8). We are members of that Church. Therefore this Omnipotent Lord is our Head. Does this not cause us to bow our heads and cry " Love so amazing, so Divine, shall have my life, my soul, my all."

Both the universe and this earth within the universe are an organic unity. The heavenly bodies are so inter-related that there is never a planetary collision. The movements of sun and moon control the tides which, in turn, control the seasons of this earth. When we study the earth scientifically or chemically, in the realm of nature or electronics, it is found to be an organic unity. Everything relates to something else, and all things are controlled by some Master-mind which, of course, is the Creator-God.

Likewise, the body is fearfully and wonderfully made, bone, flesh, muscle, sinew, blood, nerves, organs, limbs, brain, heart — all co-operating each with the other in one organic unity, the whole being controlled by the head, through the nerve centre of our whole being.

As the head controls the body in its every action, so Christ is the Head of the Church, which is His Body. Therefore, every part of that Body should be submissive to Christ.

Every Church organisation should be part of the great organism.

Every Church member should be under the control of the Head of the Church.

Every part of my being, as an individual member, should be submissive to His Will.

> " My spirit, soul, and body,
> Jesus, I give to Thee :
> A consecrated offering,
> Thine evermore to be."

Take my life, my heart, my hands, my feet, my will ; take my moments and my days, my silver and my gold, not a mite would I withhold that in all things He might have the pre-eminence.

In the Universe — all is held together by His Creative Power.

In the Church — all are welded together by His Sovereign Lordship.

Heaven and earth have been reconciled. The things seen and unseen have been harmonised — God and man united — but not by the display of power and authority such as we have just pondered. There is something which is greater than the power of God. It is the love of God, " That *great* love wherewith He hath loved us." So the Apostle, having declared that " it pleased the Father that in Him should all fulness dwell " (i. 19), makes it known in the next verse how He emptied Himself for mankind, " having made peace through the Blood of His Cross, by Him to reconcile all things unto Himself," that we, in turn, might be filled with the fulness of God — " Christ in you, the hope of glory."

Having dealt with the matter of doctrine, the Apostle moves to the

(2) PRACTICAL (Chapters ii. - iv.)

(a) FELLOWSHIP (Chapter ii.). This sets forth the Believer's relationship with these glories, part of which has already been covered in the approach to the subject as a whole.

What an insignificant creature of dust and of time is man ! He is brought to the place where, with the Psalmist, he says: "What is man, that Thou art mindful of him? And the son of man that Thou visitest him?" (Psalm viii. 4), and, at the same time, with Isaiah he cries: "Woe is me! For I am undone; because I am a man of unclean lips . . . " (Isaiah vi. 5). If a retreat be made with a sense of shame, then it is an evidence that we are being drawn by cords of love, for we are "in Him" and "with Him."

" For IN HIM dwelleth all the fulness of the Godhead bodily, and ye are complete IN HIM . . . " (ii. 9-10).

" IN WHOM (Him) are hid all the treasures of wisdom and knowledge " (ii. 3). This means one must find Christ before he can find wisdom and knowledge, for they are hidden in Him.

Walk in Him (ii. 6). When people take a long journey they may board a train or a ship. That vehicle is responsible for bringing them to their destination, but the passenger needs exercise in order that he may keep fresh and agile. Therefore, he walks the corridor of the train or the deck of the ship. Although he is walking, he is asserting no power to bring himself on his journey or to his destination. Even so, the Lord has promised to take us from earth to heaven. That becomes His responsibility. We can do nothing in the matter but trust Him. However, spiritual exercise is needed for the development of faith and character, so we walk in Him and in His Will. To get away from Him is to get out of fellowship with Him.

Rooted in Him (ii. 7). This is a picture of establishment. The English oak is able to weather every storm. It can resist these because its roots spread as far underground as its branches do above ground. They also dig deep for food supply. The elm is the first tree to fall in the storm because its roots are only just under the surface of the ground. Rooted in the Lord and in His Word also enables us to bring forth fruit in its season.

Built up in Him (ii. 7). Here the mind travels from the English oak to the American skyscraper. New York City has the tallest buildings in the world ; reaching to one hundred and two floors, or a quarter of a mile high. The reason for such tall buildings is the sure foundation. Between the Hudson River and the North River is a seam of solid granite, known as Manhattan Island. Christ is the sure, the solid, the immovable foundation upon which we may build our whole spiritual being.

Complete in Him (ii. 10). No man is complete out of Christ because God made man for Himself. We are spirit, soul, and body, and if we neglect to develop any one of these we are incomplete. To have all that the soul longs after of this world, and to have bodies which are pampered and allowed to engage in everything which appeals to the flesh, and to neglect the things of the Spirit, means an incomplete man.

It is every part of my being yielded to the dictates of the Head of my life.

Buried with Him (ii. 12). Seeing that the whole of our being is to be surrendered, we are brought to the place of our own nothingness. As a symbol to ourselves, and a testimony to the world that we no longer live to ourselves, we obey the Lord's command in baptism — that is, baptism by immersion. There can be no other way because there is nothing else that would suggest burial. Sprinkling a few drops of water has no association with death and burial. The infant knows nothing of a surrendered life, because it knows nothing of life. The illustration cannot be made more clear than it is in this chapter, and in this book, which is recognising the Lordship of Christ. Immersed beneath waters would certainly denote death. Only a few minutes there and it would be actual and physical death, but, as it is a symbol of a life which has died to self, there comes the immediate sequence, which is

Risen with Him (ii. 12) in newness of life. The power that God uses to transform our lives is the same power which He used to raise Jesus from the dead, the power through which our sins are forgiven.

Verse 14 is a further rebuke to the Judaisers. " Blotting out the handwriting of ordinances," or cancelling the bond written in ordinances, which had always been a burden to the people. This law had been brought to an end by nailing it to His Cross.

The picture is Eastern. If a person had a bill which it was impossible for him to discharge, a last recourse would be to nail that bill to the doorpost of the house, hoping some rich Pharisee would see the bill, understand the reason why it was there, and so take pity upon the occupant and pay the account for him ; but the Pharisee never paid it because of any pity he had for the debtor. He did it so that other people, seeing his charity, would praise him. This custom accounts for the words of the Lord to the Pharisees : " Let not thy left hand know what thy right hand doeth " (Matthew vi. 3).

When man could not meet the requirements of the law and became a debtor to keep them, Jesus, in love for helpless man, took that law, nailed it to His Cross, paid the price to the full — death — and thereby delivered him from death and from him that hath the power of death, even the Devil.

Therefore, we are free from the law. No man has a right to judge us in such matters. The question is now asked: "If the law has no more control over my life, then I can do as I please and none can condemn me?" The answer to this often-asked question is that, whilst we are not bound by the law, as the Body of Christ we are subject to Him as the Head, which means how much more, not how much less, should our lives be disciplined to that which pleases Him, rather than that which pleases ourselves.

This is the reasoning of the last section, which is :

(b) SANCTIFICATION (Chapters iii. and iv.). " If ye then be risen with Christ, seek those things which are above, where Christ sitteth on the right hand of God " (iii. 1).

The old life is dead and buried. Therefore there is no more relationship so far as this world is concerned. Our life is now a heavenly life, with heavenly desires and interests, and so we should " set your affection on things above, and not on things of the earth " (iii. 2).

The old life was full of carnal desires and fleshly lusts, such as fornication, uncleanness, inordinate affection, evil concupiscence, covetousness, idolatry, anger, wrath, malice, blasphemy, filthy communication, and lies. All of these have to be mortified, meaning they must be destroyed. They should have died with the old man.

Having put on the new man, which is the life of Christ, and bearing His image, we should naturally perform the actions and conduct of that life, which include compassion, kindness, humility, meekness, patience and forgiveness.

Because our life has become the Christ life, everything else becomes subservient to that life, so that all other identities are surrendered, for in Him " there is neither Greek nor Jew, circumcision nor uncircumcision, Barbarian, Scythian, bond nor free : but Christ is all, and in all " (iii. 11).

Our Christian relationship toward the world and man can be established if we have much of the lubricating oil of love, here called " the bond of perfectness."

When the love of God is flowing free from us toward the world, then the peace of God will be flowing into us, controlling our spirit.

We will appreciate that this is life, real life, victorious living, but some may say that this is their longing and desire but not their experience, and so they would ask how to enter into such fulness. The next verses point out that our relationship with the Lord affects our relationship with each other, whilst our relationship with each other affects our relationship with the Lord. These things are inter-related.

Firstly, " let the word of Christ dwell in you richly." There is nothing casual in this statement. It does not mean to read your Bible every day. So doing, you might find that the Word of Christ will visit you, but this does not refer to visitation. It is dwelling. It means permanent residence. The Word must be the controlling factor of the whole being, controlling, counselling, comforting, commissioning, and not in partiality. It must be there " richly " — deep-seated. To know this relationship is to know the joy and ecstasy which was the experience of David, and which bubbled out of him in the 119th Psalm and elsewhere. He could say : " Thy Word have I hid in my heart, that I might not sin against Thee " (vs. 11). " I have rejoiced in the way of Thy testimonies, as much as in all riches " (vs. 14). " Thy testimonies also are my delight and my counsellors " (vs. 24). " Behold, I have longed after Thy precepts " (vs. 40). " The law of Thy mouth is better unto me than thousands of gold and silver " (vs. 72). " O how I love Thy law ! it is my meditation all the day " (vs. 97). " I have more understanding than all my teachers : for Thy testimonies are my meditation " (vs. 99). " How sweet are Thy words unto my taste ! yea, sweeter than honey to my mouth ! " (vs. 103). " Great peace have they which love Thy law ; and nothing shall offend them " (vs. 165).

On this subject the tongue of the Psalmist was as the pen of a ready writer. The note of rejoicing is throughout this Psalm, as in verse 54 : " Thy statutes have been my songs in the house of my pilgrimage."

In Colossians the Apostle is expressing the same thought. When the Word of Christ dwells in us richly, then our lives will be filled with praise and we shall be " teaching and admonishing one another in psalms and hymns and spiritual songs, singing with grace in your hearts to the Lord " (iii. 16).

> " Fill Thou my life, O Lord my God,
> In every part with praise,
> That my whole being may proclaim
> Thy being and Thy ways.
> Not for the lip of praise alone,
> Nor e'en the praising heart
> I ask, but for a life made up
> Of praise in every part."

When the Word of Christ is established within, then the work of the Lord will be manifested without, not in some restricted sphere, but in everyday action, so that " whatsoever ye do in word or deed, do all in the Name of the Lord Jesus, giving thanks to God and the Father by Him " (iii. 17), and " whatsoever ye do, do it heartily, as to the Lord, and not unto man " (iii. 23).

The intervening verses (18-22) are a repetition of Ephesians v. and vi., but what the Apostle is making known here is the fact that this new relationship, which is established with the Father and with His Son, also affects the relationship of the home. If anger, wrath, and malice have been put off, and kindness, humbleness, and meekness have been put on, and we have learned to forbear and forgive, then wives will be submitting to their husbands, not because they are afraid of them or humiliated by them, but because they know that that is the Will of the Lord. A servile subjection cannot be the attitude, because the husband has learned to love the wife with a holy love, which has now taken the place of a sentimental love. Sentimental love is a temperamental love, as the world has painfully learned. It has so often reacted in bitterness and disappointment, but the Apostle says: "and be not bitter against them" (iii. 19).

In this atmosphere it will be easier for children to learn to obey their parents in all things.

Fathers are to be tolerant and understanding toward their children, not neglectful of them, socially, morally, or spiritually, and yet not so firm and hard as to bring them into a place of discouragement. Parents must learn to understand their children and train them (not drive them) in the fear of the Lord.

Servants, likewise, must learn subjection, for the joy and the fulness of the Christian life belongs to them as it belongs to the master or the mistress. The service rendered should not be limited to what reward might be given by the master, nor should it be measured as against the wages given, but should be done as unto the Lord, remembering that, if the earthly master fails in his reward, the Heavenly Master is the One really served, and He will not fail. If we are dilatory in our service, we are depriving ourselves of our eternal inheritance.

The first verse of chapter iv. belongs to chapter iii., and adds to the list of relationships, the master toward the servant, " Masters, give unto your servants that which is just and equal," or, show justice and equity, remembering that you will be expecting the same from your Master in heaven.

If we were to measure the Church to-day by this yardstick, it would be discovered that she comes a long way short, which should teach that we are not yet buried with Him and, therefore, have not risen with Him in newness of life.

The last chapter is rather miscellaneous and it is made up of exhortations, commendations, and salutations.

The *exhortations* include a call to prayer at all times, and especially on behalf of Paul and his companions that they would have freedom of thought and utterance in their ministry, so that their preaching might be effective toward the hearers. This is a prayer which all preachers might covet, and a prayer in which all saints should engage.

As our ministry should not be in word only but also in deed, the second exhortation is that we may be wise in our walk before the ungodly (those who are without), and that we might buy up every opportunity of living our testimony. The next verse (6) continues the thought, for the word " speech " means " manner of life." This should be seasoned with salt. Salt keeps food free from corruption, and thus must it be with our lives. Salt was used to establish covenants, as in Numbers xviii. 19. " All the heave offerings of the holy things, which the children of Israel offer unto the Lord, have I given thee, and thy sons and thy daughters with thee, by a statute for ever : it is a covenant of salt for ever before the Lord unto thee and to thy seed with thee," and 2 Chronicles xiii. 5 : " Ought ye not to know that the Lord God of Israel gave the kingdom over Israel to David for ever, even to him and to his sons by a covenant of salt ? " This means that our lives and our conduct before the world should be such as to cause the world to understand that we are a people who are in a covenant relationship with the Lord and, therefore, must live accordingly.

Verses 7-9 are *commendations*. From the footnote at the end of the Epistle it will be observed that the two men commended in these verses were the two men who carried the letter to Colosse. Tychicus was a faithful friend of Paul. Onesimus was the runaway slave of Philemon, who was being sent back to his master, no longer a slave but a brother (see the chapter on Philemon.)

The book concludes with a number of *salutations* coming from Aristarchus, who was also in bonds for the sake of the gospel.

Marcus.	This was Mark who, at one time, parted from Paul and travelled with Barnabas because Paul would not trust him. They were in fellowship again.
Justus.	It is the only time this fellow-worker is referred to in Scripture.
Epaphras	was a native of Colosse, and had a great concern for his fellow-townsmen.
Luke	was ever a faithful companion to Paul, and
Demas	was the one who later forsook the Apostle causing him much grief.

The final word was one of encouragement addressed to Archippus. He is mentioned in Philemon, in whose house the Church at Colosse met, and is generally believed to be the son of Philemon. He was commanded to be faithful in the ministry to which he had been called, as each of us must be faithful to the revelation or ministry given to us.

The whole of this Epistle may be summarised in its practical teaching thus : —

Let us meditate His fulness until we become empty.

Let us contemplate His sufficiency until we realise our nothingness.

Let us ponder the height of His glory until we lie in the dust of our own humility.

Then, having died to self and having been buried with Him, may we rise in the power of His Life to ascend to the heights of that life which is hid with Christ in God until our souls are lost in wonder, love, and praise.

I THESSALONIANS

THE COMING OF THE LORD IN GLORY

*"And when He had spoken these things, while they beheld,
He was taken up; and a cloud received Him out of their
sight. And while they looked stedfastly toward heaven as He
went up, behold, two men stood by them in white apparel,
which also said, Ye men of Galilee, why stand ye gazing up
into heaven? This same Jesus, which is taken from you into
heaven, shall so come in like manner as ye have seen Him
go into heaven"* (ACTS i. 9-11)

INTRODUCTION

It has been stated that Philippi was the first Church to be
established in Europe. Paul, in the company of Silas and Timothy,
journeyed from Philippi to Thessalonica, where was a synagogue
of the Jews, and there Paul ministered the Word. Whilst a division
was caused among the Jews, as a few believed and many resisted,
yet of the Gentiles a great number believed and, as a result, a
second Church was established in Europe (Acts xvii.). It was
to this Church that Paul wrote this Epistle.

Owing to an uproar, the apostles were advised to leave
Thessalonica, and they were sent to Berea, but the incensed Jews
followed them to that city. Again Paul journeyed on and went
to Athens, Silas and Timothy following later. It was from
Athens that the letter was written, according to the footnote at
the end. Although Paul had been driven out of Thessalonica,
yet he did not forget the saints there. He had a great desire to
return to them. In fact, he had made two attempts but was
hindered by Satan.

His concern was that, as the Church was young and persecution was strong, would such babes in Christ be able to resist
the forces of evil. Paul himself was not finding it easy at Athens
and was in need of the moral support of his companions. Nevertheless he sent Timothy back to Thessalonica to help these babes
in the faith and to establish them. This he states in 1 Thessalonians iii. 1-2. What relief came to the Apostle when Timothy

returned with the report of their steadfastness! However, there were one or two weak points in the Church which needed to be strengthened, most particularly in relationship to the matters of the dead and of the coming of the Lord. In these circumstances Paul wrote this Epistle, which was closely followed by the second.

THE MESSAGE

The theme of the first Epistle is the coming of the Lord in glory. The key phrase is, " To wait for His Son." The book divides into two sections : —

(1) PERSONAL (Chapters i. - iii.), dealing with the Church, the Servant, the Brother — one in each chapter.

(2) PRACTICAL (Chapters iv. and v.), concerning the believer's walk.

(1)   PERSONAL (Chapters i. - iii.)

(a) *The Church* (Chapter i.). Greetings are extended from the three servants of God — Paul, Silas, Timothy — who together had been responsible for founding this Church, and who would be equally loved and honoured by the saints. The three were also united in their prayers for the Church.

The theme of the first chapter is the natural outcome of salvation, and is threefold — past, present, and future. All three tenses are in verses 3 and 9-10.

(1)   PAST — saved from sin by the Blood of the Cross.
   vs. 3 — " Your work of faith."
   vs. 9 — " How ye turned to God from idols."
As to their acceptance of the Gospel there was no question.

(2)   PRESENT — kept in service by the power of His Spirit.
   vs. 3 — " And labour of love."
   vs. 9 — " To serve the living and true God."

The Apostle assures them that the Gospel came to them, not in word only, but also in power. It became practical in their everyday living, so much so that the knowledge of their lives and testimony, and their service rendered in the power of the Holy Ghost, had spread throughout the world, enabling them to become ensamples to all believers everywhere.

(3) FUTURE — waiting for the Lord's return.
  vs. 3 — "And patience of hope in our Lord Jesus Christ."
  vs. 10 — "To wait for His Son from heaven."

The whole theme of Paul's two Epistles to the Thessalonians is the second coming of Christ.

Maybe it would be profitable here to present the truth of the Second Advent of Christ in order to show the difference between the messages of these Epistles.

The coming of Christ is in two phases. Firstly, the Lord comes in *the air for His saints,* to take away from the world His waiting Church. It is the glorious appearing of our great God and Saviour Jesus Christ. This phase is generally known as the Rapture, and is the theme of the first Epistle.

The second phase is when the Lord comes to *the earth.* On that occasion He comes *with His saints,* and in judgment, to deal with a God-rejecting world. This is known as the Revelation, and is the subject of the second Epistle.

Returning to the first Epistle and the Lord coming for His saints, it is to be noted that the end of each chapter concerns His coming. To put the five verses together is profitable : —

"And to wait for His Son from heaven, Whom He raised from the dead, even Jesus, which delivered us from the wrath to come" (i. 10). This is WAITING FOR HIS COMING.

"For what is our hope, or joy, or crown of rejoicing ? Are not even ye in the presence of our Lord Jesus Christ at His coming ? " (ii. 19). Here is REJOICING AT HIS COMING.

"To the end He may stablish your hearts unblameable in holiness before God, even our Father, at the coming of our Lord Jesus Christ with all His saints" (iii. 13). We are to be ESTABLISHED FOR HIS COMING.

" . . . Then we which are alive and remain shall be caught up together with them in the clouds, to meet the Lord in the air : and so shall we ever be with the Lord. Wherefore comfort one another with these words" (iv. 17-18), or COMFORTED IN HIS COMING.

"And the very God of peace sanctify you wholly : and I pray God your whole spirit and soul and body be preserved blameless unto the coming of our Lord Jesus Christ" (v. 23). We are to be BLAMELESS UNTO HIS COMING.

(b) *The Servant* (Chapter ii.). The Lord said : "In the world ye shall have tribulation : but be of good cheer ; I have

overcome the world " (John xvi. 33). This statement does not
say that we shall pass through a period of time called The
Tribulation.   The Lord is telling us that we shall not be immune
from trouble.   This second chapter of 1 Thessalonians foretells
suffering and tribulation.   Paul suffered, the saints will suffer —
but we may all look up and rejoice !

Many were the accusations which were laid against Paul.
They concerned his ministry, his practices, and his person, but all
of them were false.

He reminded the Thessalonians of his physical suffering at
Philippi, when he was cast into prison for the Gospel's sake.
Notwithstanding he was still ready to preach that same Gospel,
despite the fact that there were enemies in Thessalonica who were
prepared to treat him in the same shameful way.

Paul had no intention of being less faithful because of enemies.
He was a servant of God, not of men, and must please God even
though he might offend some men.   As to his determination not
to compromise in preaching the Gospel, he declared that, if
necessary, he was prepared to surrender his life.

Another accusation which had been laid against the apostles
was that their ministry was for material gain.   This might have
been true so far as some of the Pharisees and other religionists
of Paul's day were concerned, and could be true of some preachers
in our day ; but there are those who have made great sacrifices
in their love for God and for mankind.   Paul answered this
accusation by reminding the Church that they had worked day
and night with their hands in order that they might not be chargeable to any.   Yea, in every respect they had sought to live above
reproach, and had encouraged the saints to do the same, that they,
too, might be ensamples.

However, evil men can never see goodness, and so misconstrue the goodness of others.   As the apostles had suffered,
so had this Church.   " For ye, brethren, became followers of the
churches of God which in Judæa are in Christ Jesus : for ye
also have suffered like things of your own countrymen, even as
they have of the Jews " (ii. 14).

Paul, being aware of the sufferings of this young Church,
had been very anxious to return to them and encourage them,
but had been hindered, so he informed them that, although he
had been absent in body, he had been very much present in spirit.

In the midst of misunderstanding, misinterpretation, and false
accusation, they were to keep an upward look, seeing only the
Saviour, not the sufferings.

The Apostle's anticipation, and hope, was that these saints would so live their lives here upon earth, and should so serve the Lord that, when the Lord returned to take His saints to Himself and they all stood before Him, their presence would be Paul's crown of rejoicing, or to him heaven would be the happier place because they were sharing it with him.

(c) *The Brother* (Chapter iii.). Timothy was the link which connected Paul and this Church. The Apostle was at Athens but, being concerned for the well-being of these people, he sent Timothy to them. Timothy had a twofold ministry. Firstly, he was to *establish them*. Establishment is the theme of the third chapter. In verse 2 he had to *establish them in their faith*. Suffering in one form or another seemed almost to be the norm of Christian living, due to the fact that they were strangers in an alien country and were, therefore, surrounded by enemies. Timothy was to encourage the saints, to the end that they should not be moved from their faith. Paul had warned them, when he was present, that they would know tribulation, but he was fearful lest, in his absence, they would succumb. Timothy had reported back to Paul that these saints were standing steadfast, which brought great comfort and encouragement to God's servant.

In verse 13 Timothy had to *establish their hearts*. " To the end he may stablish your hearts unblameable in holiness before God . . . "

The first half of this verse reveals that faith was their inward strength, whilst the second statement declares their outward walk — " unblameable in holiness." By these their lives would testify to the Lord's grace.

Added to this they were to be *established* FOR *His coming,* in order that they might not be ashamed *at* His coming.

The second thing Timothy had to do in his ministry was *to comfort them*. This also is in verse 2. " And to comfort you concerning your faith." It is a ministry which should never cease. The Church of Jesus Christ to-day needs to be encouraged and established in its service for God and, at the same time, needs to be comforted in its sufferings for Jesus' sake. If the suggestion should be made that it does not suffer, then it needs to be borne in mind that the Church is world-wide and, whilst there may be little suffering where we are located, there is immense suffering in other parts.

So much for the personal section of this Epistle, but the greater emphasis is on the practical side, and the Epistle as a whole will be better understood in the light of the contents of the next two chapters.

(1) PRACTICAL (Chapters iv. and v.)

This concerned the believer's walk, and is made very emphatic in the opening verse. " Furthermore then we beseech you, brethren, and exhort you by the Lord Jesus, that as ye have received of us *how ye ought to walk* and to please God, so ye would abound more and more."

The Lord has ever required a life of sanctification, but somehow people are ever seeking to excuse themselves from this full surrender. Each generation has faced its own problems in this respect. So far as the Thessalonian Christians were concerned, they had come out from a world of idolatry where fornication and similar sins were not frowned upon but were commonplace to the extent that such conditions were almost natural to them ; in fact, such sin was practised in the name of some of the idolatrous worship. To-day Christians want to attend films and movies because they are popular, and because their friends in the world do so, and they seem to have no thought of the vice, the sex, the drinking, the shooting, the murdering, and all other evils associated with such things, yet the Lord has called us to come out from this very life, which is opposed to every principle of holiness, and to be separate.

If such things hold an interest in our lives, there will always be the tendency to pull away from the things of God. Obviously, such interests are no aid to spiritual growth or to victorious living. Moreover, such careless living for God always fosters doubts as to the Word of God, due to an attitude in which we are ever seeking to justify ourselves in our carnal desires. To justify self will aiways mean to condemn the Lord, whether one is conscious of it or not.

So the Apostle says : " He therefore that despiseth, despiseth not man, but God, Who hath also given unto us His Holy Spirit " (iv. 8).

As surely as a man begins to lose his sanctification and becomes slack in his Christian practice, so surely does that same man begin to question the doctrines. If he can find fault with the Word of God, then its power and authority are weakened. He feels that its authority to condemn him in his conduct is lessened, and thereby he seeks to ease his own conscience.

The doctrine that was open to abuse, so far as the Thessalonians were concerned, was that of the Second Advent of Christ, with its relative subject of the resurrection.

The same opposition continues to come from the unsanctified lives of to-day.

It is to be remembered that in the days of the Apostle there were a great many Sadducees who sought to use their influence. Amongst other things, the Sadducees did not believe in the fact of the resurrection of the dead. They had tried to entangle the Lord Jesus with their belief, but without success; but, of course, their teaching would influence the lives of some people. Whilst some would deny any resurrection, there would be those who would seek to establish a compromise between resurrection and no resurrection. Thus came about the teaching that only those who died with the knowledge of the resurrection would be raised in the last day. Others believed that those who died could not enjoy the same privileges as those who would be alive at the coming of the Lord. Either their joy would be delayed to some later period, or they would have an inferior position. This would almost make a man responsible for the time of his death, as though he had some control over whether he died or lived, and would be rewarded accordingly.

It can readily be seen that such teachings would add sorrow to the already sorrowful hearts of those who had been bereaved.

Paul writes to correct these fallacies and so bring comfort to the distressed. The revelation which God gave to the Apostle Paul at that time has brought comfort to countless multitudes ever since. These are the words that it is a delight to repeat when standing by the open grave of some child of God who has responded to the call of the Lord to leave this world and his loved ones. To those broken, aching, sorrowing hearts, we say: "But I would not have you to be ignorant, brethren, concerning them which are asleep" (iv. 13). Our Authorized Version of the Bible presents this statement in the negative form: "I would not have you to be ignorant . . . ", but the statement in its original form is more positive than negative, and reads, "I would have you fully informed." It is lack of information, or a condition of ignorance, which becomes the breeding ground of anything that is evil. No hope means no comfort. That is the tragic portion of the world, not the lot of the brethren. The sinner is dead. The Christian can never die. He is the possessor of eternal life. Jesus came to destroy death and him that hath the power of death, even the Devil. Death is the penalty of sin. A penalty can only be exacted once and, as Jesus paid the penalty of our sin upon the Cross and we have accepted His work on our behalf, we cannot die.

The Apostle, therefore, refers to " them which are *asleep.*" If the believer sleeps, then know that sleep is only a temporary state at any time. We rise out of it. So also is the resurrection. Christ's resurrection has secured our resurrection. What a delightful expression it is to " sleep in Jesus." Jesus said : " I am the resurrection and the life." Therefore, to sleep in Jesus is to sleep in resurrection and to sleep in the arms of life. Death is not defeat. It is victory.

To those who believed that the person who had died might have some inferior or delayed blessing in the future world, Paul points out that Jesus had died but He rose again. Death had robbed Him of nothing, so why should it rob anyone else who had died in the Lord? When Jesus comes back again those who sleep in Him will come with Him. Their reward will be a full one. Again, as to any sense of inferiority, in point of fact there was more likely to be a superiority. "For this we say unto you by the Word of the Lord, (so this was not Paul's reasoning but the Lord's revelation) that we which are alive and remain unto the coming of the Lord shall not prevent (hinder, or get into the way of) them which are asleep. For the Lord Himself shall descend from heaven with a shout, with the voice of the archangel, and with the trump of God; and the dead in Christ shall rise *first*" (iv. 15/16). The dead are going to be raised before the living are translated, even though the time element may only be a matter of moments, for we shall meet together in the air.

Any who are troubled about death and its power, if they are believers in the Lord Jesus Christ, can safely and confidently look death in the face and say: " O death, where is thy sting ? O grave, where is thy victory ? The sting of death is sin ; and the strength of sin is the law. But thanks be to God, which giveth us the victory through our Lord Jesus Christ " (1 Corinthians xv. 55-57).

Having straightened out the order of the resurrection of the dead, the Apostle gives some information as to the method of the Lord's coming.

(1) " *The Lord Himself shall descend.*" This hardly suggests a coming in faith or in spirit. Many would seek to tell us that the Lord's second coming is when He comes into the heart at salvation. So far as experience proves, none of us would agree that at the moment of our salvation had we any sense of the arrival

of the Lord in any personal form, neither were we conscious of a great shout having taken place, nor yet did we hear the blast of a trumpet. Such reasoning certainly does not take into account the facts of the case as stated here and elsewhere.

Luke and Paul confirm each other, for Luke declares : " . . . While they beheld, He was taken up ; and a cloud received Him out of their sight. And while they looked stedfastly toward heaven as He went up, behold, two men stood by them in white apparel ; which also said, Ye men of Galilee, why stand ye gazing up into heaven ? This same Jesus, which is taken up from you into heaven, shall so come in like manner *as ye have seen Him go into heaven* " (Acts i. 9-11). He went in personal form, He will come again in personal form — HIMSELF.

(2) "*With a shout.*" The Hebrew word occurs but once in the whole of the New Testament and means " a cry of excitement, an urging on, a clamour or shout as of sailors at the oar, of soldiers rushing into battle, of huntsmen to their dogs, or of a multitude of people." The thought is that the shout does not come from the Lord, nor is it the shout of the redeemed. They have not yet been raised or caught up. This is a prelude to that event. Therefore, it suggests that the Lord will be accompanied by angelic hosts who are excited and thrilled at the realisation that, at long last, their Master, the One Whom they serve day and night, is now on His way to take to Himself the triumphs of the Cross in receiving that great army of the redeemed for whom He died.

If heaven be excited at the thought of the Lord receiving to Himself His Church, what should be the excitement of the Church herself! One is left to imagine also the thrill of anticipation, then becoming realisation, in the heart of the glorified Lord, Who is about to experience the full accomplishment of the sufferings which He endured at Calvary.

(3) "*The voice of the archangel.*" There are many angelic beings. Angels, Cherubim and Seraphim, are in their myriads, but there is only one archangel. His name is Michael. He has always been associated with the deliverance of God's people, the Jews, and with resurrection. These two responsibilities of his can be gleaned from various parts of the Scriptures but the two are found linked together in the last chapter of Daniel. "And at that time shall Michael stand up, the great prince which standeth for the children of thy people: and there shall be a time of

trouble, such as never was since there was a nation even to that
same time : and at that time thy people shall be delivered, every
one that shall be found written in the book. And many of them
that sleep in the dust of the earth shall awake, some to everlasting life, and some to shame and everlasting contempt " (Daniel
xii. 1 - 2).

It was Michael who contended with the Devil for the body
of Moses, recorded in Jude v.6, which may be the first resurrection
of the dead. It is the voice of the same archangel which summons
the dead in Christ to arise and meet their coming Lord.

(4) " *The trump of God.*" The trumpet called men to solemn
assemblies. The first trumpet was at Mount Sinai and was
sounded when the Law was given. That trumpet ushered in the
dispensation of Law. This trump, which the Apostle calls " the
last trump " (1 Corinthians xv. 52), brings to a close the dispensation of the Grace of God, as the complete Church of God, past
and present, dead or alive, is gathered together " to meet the Lord
in the air," and " so shall we ever be with the Lord."

(5) " *In the clouds.*" This statement reads in the Greek as " In
clouds." " In the clouds " would cause one to think of the clouds
which are above us. Those clouds belong to the realm of earth.
They are usually linked with the idea of storms, of judgment,
or of trouble in some form or another. In the Greek the thought
would be " in clouds," which could mean clouds of light, of glory,
or clouds of angelic beings.

What might be even more correct is that it will be the redeemed of the Lord who, themselves, will be caught up in clouds,
or in hosts. Hebrews xii. 1 makes use of the same word: " Wherefore seeing we also are compassed about with so great a *cloud*
of witnesses."

With this joyous anticipation and such an absolute confidence
as to the events of the last days, the Apostle has removed the
doubts and the fears from sorrowing hearts. Therefore, he concludes the chapter with " Wherefore comfort one another with
these words," and this we have continued to do throughout the
whole of the Church period.

Chapter v. begins with the time element of the Lord's coming.
This is the only uncertainty of the whole subject. We are not to
concern ourselves in working out times and seasons. Our responsibility is so to live that we shall be both ready and unashamed
if the Lord should come in the next minute of our lives, for He

will come as a thief in the night. As to the signs of the times, they are general, not specific. The spirit of the age in which we find ourselves is one of greed, lawlessness, and fear. Robberies, violence, and murder are on the increase, but that is no indication as to whether, or when, your house might be broken into or your business robbed. The thief gives no notice of his coming, and neither does the Lord. It is " at an hour when ye think not " that the Lord will come.

This suddenness, which should be the purifying hope of the believer, not only means sudden glory for the child of God, but it also means sudden calamity for the sinner. Paul expounds this in his second Epistle.

If the coming of the Lord is to be so sudden, should not all men make preparation for it ? The sinner should be seeking salvation, and the saint establishing his sanctification. A man insures himself against old age or robbery because either of these things *might* befall him. Then should we not prepare ourselves for the coming of the Lord seeing that such an event *must* be, and that it will affect us whether we be in life or in death.

The book concludes with a number of

ADMONITIONS

(1) A recognition of God's servants (v. 12-13). These are to be loved, encouraged, honoured, and rewarded, not in the sense of hero-worship, nor man-worship, but, rather, as a recognition of the service rendered and the work performed in the Name of the Lord.

(2) A reasoning peaceably with each other (v. 13). This might possibly refer to differences of opinion among the saints on the matter of doctrine and its interpretation. It is certainly a weakness in the churches to-day, and particularly so among Evangelicals who ought to know better.

(3) A responsibility toward all men (v. 14), meeting them on their own ground, warning the unruly, comforting the troubled mind, strengthening the weak, and being patient·to all.

(4) A retaliation that was to be unknown (v. 15), or doing only that which is good.

All these appear to be man's relationship to man. The next verses would be the believer's conduct in his relationship to the Lord.

Rejoice evermore.
Pray without ceasing.
In every thing give thanks.
Quench not the Spirit.
Despise not prophesyings.
Prove all things.
Abstain from all forms of evil.

All of these add up to a God-centred, fully consecrated life, which, at every point of the way, we should be living to the glory of His Name. It is what the Apostle says elsewhere " is your reasonable service " (Romans xii. 1).

Paul links this life to the truth of the second advent as in verse 23 he says : " And the very God of peace sanctify you wholly ; and I pray God your whole spirit and soul and body be preserved blameless unto the coming of our Lord Jesus Christ." This would make us to be blameless unto His coming.

The Apostle wrote to correct error and misunderstanding among the saints in the Thessalonian Church. If the saints of this twentieth century Church would take heed to all that is written here concerning the Lord's imminent return, it would make a deal of difference in their living, service, and witness.

We must not excuse ourselves because of problems, or justify ourselves because of the times in which we live, for we live in the Church age, the only era for which these things were written. To all the admonition there is added in the next verse (24) a reassuring promise : " Faithful is He that calleth you, Who also will do it."

Sanctification is not something which has to be acquired through some sacrificial spirit. It is something that He will perform in us, if we are willing.

The book closes with a benediction, in which Paul asks for the prayers of the saints on behalf of himself and his companions, and also gives a charge to the elders of the Church : " I charge you by the Lord that this Epistle be read unto all the holy brethren " (vs. 27).

II THESSALONIANS

THE LORD'S COMING IN JUDGMENT

*"And in the latter time of their kingdom, when the trans-
gressors are come to the full, a king of fierce countenance,
and understanding dark sentences, shall stand up. And his
power shall be mighty, but not by his own power: and he
shall destroy wonderfully, and shall prosper, and practise,
and shall destroy the mighty and the holy people. And
through his policy also he shall cause craft to prosper in his
hand; and he shall magnify himself in his heart, and by
peace shall destroy many; he shall also stand up against the
Prince of princes; but he shall be broken without hand"*
(DANIEL viii. 23-25)

INTRODUCTION

There is sufficient evidence to reveal that the second Epistle
was written not long after the first. Its purpose appears to be
that of clearing up some misunderstandings which had been created
by Paul's first letter to this Church. Some think that the difficulties were because of a letter written by an unknown person and
forged in the name of Paul. This is gleaned from chapter ii.,
verse 2 : " That ye may be not soon shaken in mind or be troubled,
neither by spirit, nor by word, nor by letter *as from us*, as that
the day of Christ is at hand."

It is asserted that some people had given up work, had
relinquished their responsibilities, and were just waiting, believing
that the end of the world was imminent. Others were saying that
the Lord had come already. As a result of this, faith and confidence were being shaken.

Paul wrote the Epistle to clarify this situation.

THE MESSAGE

It is one that is entirely of judgment, not of the Church (that
had already gone) but of the Christ-rejector.

The book divides according to its three chapters. There is

CONSOLATION CONCERNING A FUTURE GLORY
(Chapter i.).

INSTRUCTION CONCERNING A COMING APOSTASY
(Chapter ii.).

EXHORTATION CONCERNING PRESENT LIVING
(Chapter iii.).

CONSOLATION CONCERNING A FUTURE GLORY
Chapter i.)

The book opens with Paul's usual style of introduction of himself and his associates in the Gospel, followed by commendation to the Church.

The Church as a whole was flourishing, like a fruitful tree bringing forth its fruit in its season. They had love one toward another, and they were exercising patience and faith amidst persecution and tribulation.

Paul was rejoicing in the fact that these trials were an evidence of a close relationship with the Lord, because, on the one hand, the Lord chastens those whom He loves so that they may become better fruit-bearers and presently enjoy greater rewards; on the other hand, the Devil never bothers those who are cold and indifferent. He is concerned with those who are loyal.

The day would come when these things would be reversed, " seeing it is a righteous thing with God to recompense tribulation to them that trouble you " (i. 6). Our afflictions are temporary, theirs will be eternal.

Seemingly it was a minority within the Church who had created the disturbance concerning the immediate return of the Lord. The Apostle was consoling the Church that, when that day of judgment comes, they, as all of the apostles, will be resting in the Lord. In his first Epistle he had spoken of the coming of the Lord in glory to receive unto Himself His saints. The critical element in the Church had altered the meaning of his words and were speaking of the end of the world, and the day of judgment, but Paul had not mentioned judgment. Now he does. He is taking up the statements of the worldly-wise, and says : " . . . the Lord Jesus shall be revealed from heaven with His mighty angels, in flaming fire taking vengeance on them that know not God, and that obey not the Gospel of our Lord Jesus Christ : who shall

be punished with everlasting destruction from the presence of
the Lord, and from the glory of His power " (i. 7-9). This coming
of the Lord does not concern the saint, but only the sinner. The
saint will already be at rest.

The solemn truth still holds — the Lord will come for His
saints, and He will come with vengeance to deal with the rejectors.
Let us not overlook the solemnity of such a day !

It must be recognized that two classes of people are included
in this judgment, (1) "them that know not God," which include
all who have rejected Him; (2) "that obey not the Gospel of our
Lord Jesus Christ," embracing all who have neglected Him. It
is not sufficient to say that one believes God. The devils believe
and tremble. It is not sufficient to say, "I accept the Lord and
the Bible." There are many things in the world which are
accepted because their existence cannot be denied, but accepting
a thing is not necessarily approving or endorsing it. What the Lord
is requiring of us is obedience — "To obey is better than
sacrifice." This judgment is upon those who obey not the
Gospel.

Everlasting destruction does not mean annihilation, which is
total destruction. It is a destruction which is everlasting — a condition of continual existence, and is as eternal as eternal life.

This great event, which will prove so disastrous to the God-
rejector, will be one of unsurpassable glory to the children of God,
as well as to the Lord Himself, for in that day He is " to be
admired in all them that believe " (i. 10). It is an established
fact that these words should read " to be wondered at."

We know that one of the names given to the Lord was
" Wonderful." We have marvelled at the wonder of His grace
and power. We have wondered at the power He displayed at
Creation. We have marvelled at the extent of His love revealed
at the Cross. We have contemplated the glories of His eternal
existence as One with the Father, and have anticipated with joy
His coming again to receive us unto Himself.

Now has come the day when contemplation has ceased, when
anticipation has become realisation. The saint has already been
translated, and transformed into His likeness. That took place
when He came *for us*, but now He has come back in glory and
power to reveal Himself as a God of justice. It is the day when
" we shall be like Him ; for we shall see Him as He is " (1 John
iii. 2), and " We all, with open face beholding as in a glass the
glory of the Lord, are changed into the same image from glory
to glory even as by the Spirit of the Lord " (2 Corinthians iii. 18),

because we, who have borne the image of the earthy, are now bearing the image of the heavenly.

In the midst of all this we are going to stand in wonderment at the glory of His Person, and admire Him above and beyond all things else, for we are discovering that the half has never yet been told.

The saint, or the sinner who believed the message of salvation whilst on earth and recognised the Lordship of Christ, has been glorified and is now glorifying the Lord of glory. How transcendent!

This is a scene before which we should sit in holy contemplation until we are assured as to which part of it will be our portion, and then move forward praying that God would count us worthy of our calling, making the last verse of the chapter to become practical in our lives down here, " That the Name of our Lord Jesus Christ may be glorified in you, and ye in Him, according to the grace of our God and the Lord Jesus Christ " (i. 12).

INSTRUCTION CONCERNING A COMING APOSTASY
(Chapter ii.)

What has been considered in chapter i., glorious as it is, is only introduction. The Apostle now moves into the purpose of the letter. In his first Epistle to this Church he had taught them concerning the coming of the Lord, when He would receive to Himself His own, but he had given no indication as to when that might be. The things which were disturbing this Church, therefore, were read into his letter, suggested by other people, or given to them in some false manner (as a forged letter).

In clarifying the matter, Paul indicates that the final coming of the Lord and the day of judgment, so far as they were concerned, were a long way off because certain things would have to take place first.

This, of course, does not apply to the Church to-day. Nearly two millenniums have passed since Paul wrote his letter.

The statement used by Paul " that the day of Christ is at hand " reads differently according to marginal notes, where it is " the day of the Lord is come." " The day of the Lord " refers to that period of time which embraces both the Tribulation and the Millennium. It is a period of time which succeeds " The day of grace." The coming of the Lord for His saints terminates the day of Grace. The coming of the Lord with His saints is in " the Day of the Lord." This makes clear the fact that the

Apostle is now dealing with the time when the Lord will come to this earth at the end of the Tribulation, judge the wicked, cast Satan into the Bottomless Pit, and will establish a reign of righteousness which shall endure for one thousand years.

"Let no man deceive you by any means: for that day shall not come, except there come a falling away first, and that man of sin be revealed, the son of perdition" (ii. 3). The first part of the verse has already been fulfilled, in what is commonly called the Apostasy, a word which means "total destruction of principles of faith once acknowledged." This desertion has taken the form of open denial with some, whilst others have so corrupted the doctrines by their theories as to render them insufficient for the salvation of a soul or for the consecration of a life.

We are living in a day when the Church which was founded upon the doctrines of the Bible, has become divided, and much of it is now denying the authority of that Bible as the inspired Word of God. It denies the Virgin Birth of the Lord, the efficacy of the Blood of Jesus, the Personal Return of the Lord, and many, many other truths.

Following this moving away from the things which are spiritual there is naturally a moving toward things which are material, hence conditions are created for the final scenes of time.

When one refuses the Lord of righteousness, he finds himself accepting the *man of sin*.

When one turns his back upon the Son of God, he finds himself facing the *son of perdition*.

When one does not embrace the Mystery of Godliness, he is embraced by the *mystery of iniquity*.

When one closes his eyes to Holiness, then the *Wicked One* is revealed.

When one disbelieves the Truth as it is in Christ Jesus, then he will believe *Satan* who will come with all power and signs and lying wonders. Those who have refused to follow Christ will find themselves following the Antichrist.

All of these names belong to one great personality who is to appear after the Church has been taken away and before the Lord returns with His saints. The period during which this person controls the affairs of men is known as the Tribulation. The person is Antichrist. He is anti to Christ, and will be the personification of the Devil himself, even as Jesus was God manifest in the flesh.

Although he is a deceiver and the father of lies, yet all the world will rally to his standard and, when he sets himself up as God, all the world will worship him. Such a situation seems unreasonable to our present thinking, but it must be remembered that God is exceedingly jealous of His Name and His Word, and is ever ready to vindicate both. Seeing men have refused His Word, the Apostle says : " . . . because they received not the love of the truth, that they might be saved. And for this cause God shall send them strong delusion, that they should believe a lie (or the lie) ; that they all might be damned who believed not the truth, but had pleasure in unrighteousness " (ii. 10-12).

By the Word of God the earth, and all that is therein, was created. " And God said " (Genesis i.).

By the Word of God the world continues. " Upholding all things by the Word of His Power " (Hebrews i. 3).

By the Word of God man is saved. " Being born again, not of corruptible seed, but of incorruptible, by the Word of God, which liveth and abideth for ever " (1 Peter i. 23).

That Word is eternal. Many are the Scriptures to prove this. Peter says : " But the Word of the Lord endureth for ever. And this is the Word which by the gospel is preached unto you " (1 Peter i. 25).

Because this Word has been refused, men are being condemned ; but the next verse confirms that, because this Word has been received, men have been blessed. " But we are bound to give thanks alway to God for you, brethren beloved of the Lord, because God hath from the beginning chosen you to salvation, through sanctification of the Spirit and belief of the *truth* " (ii. 13).

If there be one great outstanding truth in this chapter, it is the power and authority of the Word of God and man's relationship to it.

There is an unfortunate approach given to this chapter. Many people have seen the Antichrist standing forth so prominently that they have failed to see the Christ. They have so occupied themselves with " the lie," who is introduced, that they have lost " the truth " which is taught. No wonder we are exhorted rightly to divide the Word of Truth ! According to our relationship with the Word of God to-day will be His relationship with us in the day to come.

EXHORTATION CONCERNING PRESENT LIVING
(Chapter iii.)

The emphasis shown in chapter ii continues in the opening verses of chapter iii. " Finally, brethren." When you have considered the events of the last days, when you have been enlightened concerning the conduct of the Antichrist, when you have appreciated the meaning of the Coming of the Lord, there will still remain one great and important fact which must never be forgotten. It is "that the Word of the Lord may have free course, and be glorified." To this end the Apostle asks the prayers of the saints.

Because it is the work of the enemy to hinder its progress with signs, lying wonders, deceit, human pride, unbelief, indifference, and every other conceivable thing, it becomes our responsibility to advance the Word, by reading, study, testimony, ministry, example, and faith. Brethren, pray that this may be so in your life and in the lives of those who name the Name of Christ. In so doing, we have been promised deliverance from wicked men.

These wicked men are not the sinners, in the ordinary sense of the word, who are living corrupt lives, but men who are wicked because they are deceiving so many by having a form of godliness but denying the power thereof. This is gleaned from the next statement, "for all men have not faith," which reads in the margin of the Bible, "for all men have not THE faith."

These were the people who were troubling the Thessalonian Church, not from without but from within. They have been in every Church. They are with us to-day. The Apostle said: "But the Lord is faithful, Who shall stablish you, and keep you from evil" (iii. 3). "And the Lord direct your hearts into the love of God, and into the patient waiting for Christ" (iii. 5). This is the same patience that belonged to the husbandman, referred to by James when he said: "Be patient therefore, brethren, unto the coming of the Lord. Behold, the husbandman waiteth for the precious fruit of the earth, and hath long patience for it, until he receive the early and latter rain. Be ye also patient; stablish your hearts: for the coming of the Lord draweth nigh" (James v. 7-8).

The Apostle concludes the Epistle with some exhortations as to conduct in the Church. There were some brethren who were walking disorderly, or out of order. One must conclude that it was those people who were out of step with the doctrines which had been taught them, and who had been responsible for the misunderstanding of the truth of the second advent. This may be gathered from two statements — (1) They were not following after the tradition received from Paul. This word "tradition" does not mean the oral and unwritten laws or beliefs passed down through many generations, but the message of truth as it had come to them from the lips of Paul, and (2) "For we hear that there are some which walk among you disorderly, working not at all, but are busybodies" (iii. 11). These were the people who had stopped working and had sat down to wait the immediate return of the Lord.

Even to-day there are those who will not plan for the future and will not make preparations for old age because they believe that the Lord must come in their lifetime. This is contrary to the teaching of Scripture, which declares that "in such an hour as ye think not the Son of man cometh" (Matthew xxiv. 44), and "Occupy till I come" (Luke xix. 13). From such people the true child of God must withdraw himself but, at the same time, must not treat them as enemies, for such need to be delivered from their heresy. This may be done by admonishing them, but not by abusing them.

The word "admonish" means "to counsel or reprove a person because of a fault," but to do it kindly and mildly. What a need there is for such a ministry!

The Epistle is concluded with a Pauline benediction — "The grace of our Lord Jesus Christ be with you all. Amen."

I TIMOTHY

MY SON IN THE FAITH

" Take heed therefore unto yourselves, and to all the flock, over the which the Holy Ghost hath made you overseers, to feed the church of God, which He hath purchased with His own blood " (ACTS xx. 28)

INTRODUCTION

The Epistles of Paul to Timothy and Titus are different from all his other letters. The nine already considered are called Church Epistles because they were written to Churches. The next three are known as Pastoral Epistles because they were written by Paul to men who had the oversight of Churches. It is to be observed that the burden of each letter is the conduct, care, and ministry of the Pastor in the Church. Two of these letters were written to Timothy and one to Titus. One other Epistle came from the pen of Paul — it was a private letter written to Philemon.

TIMOTHY

More is known about this man than most of the friends of Paul, and certainly more than is known of any man whose name appears as a title of a book. He was a native of Lystra. His mother was a Jewess by the name of Eunice, whilst his father was a Greek. His grandmother, Lois, is mentioned as having part in the Christian training and the moral background of the young man.

He accompanied Paul a great deal and became a very close friend. He is mentioned as being with Paul in Troas, Philippi, Thessalonica, Berea, Athens, Macedonia, and Rome. He journeyed with Paul part of the way to Rome. On several occasions Paul sent Timothy out on special missions, including those to Thessalonica, Corinth, and Ephesus. In this latter place Timothy spent a great deal of his time because he was appointed Pastor of the Church which Paul had founded there. Paul, it will be remembered, ministered for about four years in Ephesus, where he faced and overcame a great amount of opposition. As a result, a strong and vigorous Church had been established. Multitudes had been added to the Church, to the extent of badly damaging the heathen temples, which were emptying. The city had become a centre of Christianity.

When Timothy, Titus, and others, are referred to as Pastors of Churches, one must not think of the Pastor as he is known to-day, ministering to the group of people who assemble in some ornate building set apart for the worship of God. There were no church buildings in those early days. The Church met in small groups in the homes, each group being ministered to by men called " elders " or " pastors," " . . . when they had ordained them elders in every church . . . " (Acts xiv. 23).

THE MESSAGE

The book concerns THE SERVANT OF GOD.

The analysis divides into three sections : —

(1)   A COMMISSION (Chapter i.).

(2)   PRAYER (Chapter ii. 1 - 8).

(3)   CONDUCT (Chapters ii. 9 - vi. 21).

(1)   A COMMISSION (Chapter i.)

Paul had a great love for this convert whom he called MY SON IN THE FAITH. He often longed for his companionship. It is a beautiful picture to have hanging in the gallery of one's mind — the old, strong, forthright, experienced Paul, and the young, fearful, hesitant, inexperienced Timothy, as companions in travel. God so often brings opposite characters together into the close bond of friendship, one a complement to the other, one constraining, the other restraining, as in Peter and John, Elijah and Elisha, and now Paul and Timothy.

If one could advise the young student coming out of college, or the energetic churchworker, it would be that they seek the counsel and companionship of the sound and experienced pastor or leader. To be an assistant to a good pastor in a large church can mean so much as against taking charge of a church without practical experience in leadership. In the latter so many mistakes can be made because a pastor cannot too well consult the people he is expected to lead, whilst to have the counsel of a senior can often prevent a pitfall.

It was whilst Timothy was the Pastor of the Church at Ephesus that Paul wrote to him these two Epistles.

The early Church, in fact the Church of all time, has been subjected to intruders, those who ever seek to introduce their own theories. So the Apostle warns the Pastor to avoid fables, endless genealogies, and all such things as would harm the Christian faith and gender strife. In warning Timothy, the Scriptures have warned all young preachers to be as assured of their calling as Paul was, and to be as steadfast to the truth as he proved to be.

Paul declares his unworthiness for such a ministry in chapter i. 13. He tells of the grace of God that enabled him, in verses 12 and 14, and of the Gospel that transformed him, in verse 15 : " This is a faithful saying, and worthy of all acceptation, that Christ Jesus came into the world to save sinners ; of whom I am chief."

From his own unworthiness he moves into a crescendo of praise to THE ETERNAL GOD Who was the All-worthy One : " Now unto the King eternal, immortal, invisible, the only wise God, be honour and glory for ever and ever. Amen " (i. 17).

The first chapter, and the commission, ends with A CHARGE TO TIMOTHY. From the language of this charge, and of the two Epistles as a whole, it would appear that there was an amount of fear and timidity in Timothy which needed to be overcome, hence the constant exhortations to hold fast. He is told : —

" War a good warfare "	1 Timothy	i. 18
" Let no man despise thy youth "	,,	iv. 12
" Neglect not the gift that is in thee "	,,	iv. 14
" Fight the good fight of faith "	,,	vi. 12
" For God hath not given us the spirit of fear "	2 Timothy	i. 7
" Be not thou therefore ashamed of the testimony of our Lord "	,,	i. 8
" That good thing which was committed unto thee keep by the Holy Ghost . . . "	,,	i. 14
" Thou therefore, my son, be strong "	,,	ii. 1
" Thou therefore endure hardness, as a good soldier "	,,	ii. 3
" I charge thee . . . preach the Word "	,,	iv. 1-2

This constant encouragement is needed to-day as much as it has been needed in any generation. In the past it was needed because of the opposition of the enemy and the persecutions inflicted. To-day it is needed because of the cunning of the enemy and the half-heartedness of the servant of God. So many are wanting to take the path of least resistance, the result of which is that too much has already been yielded to the enemy. In our generation we are conscious of our inabilities because of what has been yielded by the generation which has passed. To the extent that we yield to the opponents of truth to-day, so shall we make it that much harder for the generation which is to follow. Therefore, the challenge must be echoed and re-echoed.

Timothy was charged to hold tenaciously to the faith because some had made shipwreck of it, and of themselves.

Two classes of people made up this element of opposition against which Timothy had to " war a good warfare." Firstly, there were those who had never accepted the faith, but were adherents to other dogmas. Secondly, there was the more harmful group of those who had made a profession of the Christian faith and had then become desirous of being teachers instead of learners. These, not being established in the faith, introduced every kind of theory and interpretation. They are referred to in chapter iv. 1. " Now the Spirit speaketh expressly, that in the latter times some shall depart from the faith, giving heed to seducing spirits, and doctrines of devils. Speaking lies in hypocrisy; having their conscience seared with a hot iron." Also in chapter i. Paul had said: " From which some having swerved have turned aside unto vain jangling : Desiring to be teachers of the law ; understanding neither what they say, nor whereof they affirm " (i. 6-7).

It was against these unlawful teachers that Timothy, a man ordained of God, was to raise his voice, and not he alone but he must encourage all the brethren to oppose error, found in the words : " If thou put the brethren in remembrance of these things, thou shalt be a good minister of Jesus Christ, nourished up in the words of faith and of good doctrine, whereunto thou hast attained " (iv. 6).

Before a person can become an exponent of the Word of God he must first learn to be a student of that Word, and allow the Spirit of God to instruct him.

Two expressions were used by the old warrior of the faith, which must have come out of his own practical experience. They are : —

(1)   Give attendance to reading (iv. 13).

(2)   Meditate upon these things (iv. 15).

There is a third expression but it is used in the second Epistle and will be dealt with there.

(3)   Study to show thyself approved (2 Timothy ii. 15).

(1) *Give attendance to reading* (iv. 13).   This included exhortation and doctrine.   Ignorance is a tragedy of the first order. All nations are now aware of this fact, and the fight against illiteracy is being waged everywhere.   Error can only be suppressed by truth, and truth is that which makes a man free.   Man needs to know the world in which he lives.   He needs to know the God Who made this world.   He needs to know the adverse powers that are around him.   He needs to know his fellow-man — and he needs to know himself.   Failure in any of these brings a life of disaster and disappointment.   These things are recognised in the economic and social world.   Education is a prime factor in the strength of a nation.   Therefore, it stands to reason that the same must apply to the realm of moral and spiritual life.

Nominal Christians consider it the duty of the Christian ministry to do the reading and the studying, whilst they do the listening.   This may be true to an extent, but the man in the pew ought also to do his reading.   The greater number of church members never knows whether the preacher is right or wrong. It could be said of them as it was said by Paul when he was addressing the Athenians : " Whom therefore ye ignorantly worship " (Acts xvii. 23).   If we are to be the followers of Jesus Christ, if our lives are to be effective, if we are to be an influence for good in the world, if we are going to be a blessing to our neighbours, then we must give attendance to reading.

To know the world in which we live, it is necessary to read the book of nature.   To know our fellow-man, one must know how to read the book of human character. To know God, the adversary and ourselves, we must read the Bible — the Word of God.

The influence that reading has upon the lives of men, the potential force that lies behind the printed page, may be ascertained by contemplating the fact that to-day the bulk of reading matter is fiction, comics, sex, and films, and the result is that it is producing an immoral world.   Newspapers, advertisements, and almost everything which our young people set their eyes upon, are corrupt, sensational, and suggestive.

The Word of God says : "Give attendance to reading." Christian, are you reading ? What are you reading ? How much are you reading ? Why are you reading ? Have you read the Word of God to-day ? The Bible has become a neglected book. Christian litrature has not the place in the Christian home that it should have. Knowledge dispels ignorance, but knowledge only comes through contact.

Reading can be for pleasure, it can be a pastime, but it should be more. Reading should be for profit.

Paul moves on from his exhortation to read and uses another statement : —

(2) *Meditate upon these things* (iv. 15). "Meditate upon these things ; give thyself wholly to them ; that thy profiting may appear to all."

The dictionary defines the word "meditate" as "Fix the mind upon," or "To think with a view to a plan of action." This thought is expressed elsewhere in the pages of Scripture, for James says : "But be ye doers of the Word, and not hearers only, deceiving your own selves " (i. 22). It is one thing to read, it is yet another thing to apply what is read to the everyday practical life.

Every time one reads the Word of God he should meditate as to how the particular injunctions or information can fit into the life to make it more effective for God.

The word "meditate" is derived from the same root as that which means "to chew the cud." The cow continues to chew until its food is thoroughly masticated. Such a thought is precious, but here is something more. The animal which chews the cud never assimilates the poisonous weeds. It would be natural for the grazing animal to pick up some poison with its fodder, but to be provided with the ability to discharge (or to nullify) that poison, by the process of regurgitation, is remarkable.

The lesson is clear and potent. If we are diligent and faithful in feeding upon the Word of the Lord, if we give it all the due consideration to which it has the right, we should never be affected or troubled by any of the poisons of doubt and unbelief which must be picked up at times in our general reading.

When the servant of God has devoted himself to preparation, it is natural that it will work itself out in the practical everyday life. This is the reasoning of the rest of the Epistle.

(2) PRAYER (Chapter ii. 1-8)

(a)* *Prayer.* " I exhort therefore, that, first of all, supplications, prayers, intercessions, and giving of thanks, be made for all
men ; For kings, and for all that are in authority ; that we may
lead a quiet and peaceable life in all godliness and honesty " (ii.
1-2. The effective life begins with a prayer life — " First of
all."

This prayer life should be neither selfish nor narrow. Prayers
should be for all men. So often they are for ourselves, our
families, our friends, our Church. The Lord instructed us to pray
for our enemies, for those who despitefully use us, for sinners.
Secondly, prayers should be national. We are to pray for those in
authority, whether we like them or not, whether they are our party
or not. The fact is they are in authority. They are making our
laws. They are directing our lives, and governing our nation. The
decisions of men in high office affect our lives. Their decisions
make for peace or war, for righteousness or for evil, for honesty
or for corruption ; and " righteousness exalteth a nation : but sin
is a reproach to any people " (Proverbs xiii. 34). Therefore, pray
that they may be directed in their decisions in order that we, as
Christians, may be permitted to live a quiet and peaceable life.
Further, prayers should not only be for their guidance but also for
their salvation. Paul would have all men, high and low, king and
subject, ruler and ruled, to know that there is one Supreme Ruler
and He is God, and that there is but ONE MEDIATOR between
God and men, the Man Christ Jesus (ii. 5).

(3) CONDUCT (Chapters ii. 9 - vi. 21)

This conduct concerns all kinds of people, both outside and
inside the Church. It is important because conduct is

(b) *Example.* Firstly, Paul writes concerning the women.
In dress they are to be modest. So much to-day is for appeal.
This should not be so with Christian women. They are not to
use attire or make-up in order to attract others to themselves. That
does not mean they are to be dowdy, indifferent, or old-fashioned.
It does mean they are to be smart, tidy, modest, and by so doing
attract others to their Lord and Saviour.

Secondly, he deals with their behaviour in the Church. Here
it was a matter of subjection, but that must not be interpreted as

* NOTE.   (a), (b), (c), (d) concern four results of study shown in the
synthesis of the Chart, and noted at the end of this chapter.

servitude. This does not say that a woman cannot speak in the
Church. That matter has been dealt with in the Corinthian
Epistle, and it was learned that there it related to the matter of
speaking in tongues. In this Epistle it concerns exercising authority.
She must not teach, which is a matter of instruction in the Word
of God, and is very different from preaching, which means making
known the good news. A woman has never been permitted leadership in the Church. God made man first and has intended to keep
him thus.

In chapter ii. the Apostle instructs the Pastor concerning his
character, and also that of his deacons. Every person who holds
office should be an example of the honour of that office. The
Pastor should be blameless, not a divorcee, self-controlled, hospitable, able to teach, not given to social sins, neither given to a desire
for worldly gain. All this is summed up in one who is able to
control his own passions and his own life.

Furthermore, such a person must also know how to control
his family. If a man cannot exercise his authority as the head
of his own family, how can he expect to direct the Church of Jesus
Christ ? He must never tell other people to do what he is not
prepared to do himself. We are called to be examples so that,
like Paul, we can say : " Be ye followers of me, even as I also
am of Christ " (1 Corinthians xi. 1).

The Pastor must live so that he is respected by those outside
the Church, as well as by those inside. The next door neighbours
and the tradesmen are important witnesses.

" If a man desire the office of a bishop, he desireth a good
work " (iii. 1), but such an office needs more than a desire, it must
know a Divine Call. Therefore the statement in verse 6 must be
underscored, " Not a novice." This ministry is a high calling.
Therefore it is not to be played with but to be handled seriously.
The pulpit is not the place for humour, it is a place of honour.
It is ever to be remembered that the Call comes from God, and
to God we shall have to give an account of our stewardship.

Linked with the bishop (or Pastor) are the deacons. " Likewise
must the deacons " (iii. 8). They must be unselfish men, men who
are sound in the faith, men who have first been proved and found
blameless. They, too, must be men who know how to rule their
own children and their household.

If these conditions were enforced to-day more than half of
the deacons of Churches would have to retire. If the Bible is
true then we are wrong, and it is high time some of us began to
put our house in order ! How can the blessing of the Lord be

expected in the Church, or souls saved, if leaders are disobedient to His instruction. So important is the office of the deacon that even his wife is not excluded from the qualifications which should be considered by the Church meeting before it makes its appointments. She must be serious, honest, self-controlled, and faithful in all things.

All of this touches the physical and moral life.

Lest there should be any reasoning as to the importance of this ministry, or the high standard of qualifications demanded of its ministers, in the last verse of the chapter the Apostle reveals the whole content of the message. John iii. 16 has been referred to by many as " The Gospel in a nutshell." That may be true in the simplicity of the message manward ; but here, in a classic verse, is the whole message of redemption in its sublimity Godward. " And without controversy great is the mystery of Godliness : God was manifest in the flesh, justified in the Spirit, seen of angels, preached unto the Gentiles, believed on in the world, received up into glory.' The sublime and the simple are so blended that such a verse should need no comment if man would but sit and ponder.

Here is revelation beyond contradiction or argument. Men may seek to deny, but will never disprove, they will try to denounce, but will never destroy, the validity of the Gospel. It is beyond controversy. All the secrets of the Godly life, all the mysteries of how the Gospel can transform a man from a life of sin to one of holiness, have been declared publicly before the world, " for this thing was not done in a corner " (Acts xxvi. 26).

(1) " God was manifest in the flesh." This was the Virgin Birth, the story of the incarnation. It is not only a historical record coming from the past but a fact which is kept alive year by year in the acceptation of Christmas.

(2) " Justified in the Spirit." The evidence that Jesus was no imposter is the fact that the Spirit of God justified His claims all along the way. When He was baptised in the Jordan, the Spirit of God descended upon Him and a voice declared : " Thou art My Beloved Son, in Whom I am well pleased " (Mark i. 11).

(3) " Seen of angels." Angels announced His birth, and at the end of the temptation in the wilderness " angels came and ministered unto Him " (Matthew iv. 11). In Gethsemane " . . . there appeared an angel unto Him from heaven, strengthening

Him " (Luke xxii. 43). Angels were witnesses of His resurrection and His ascension, and they will accompany Him on His return to this earth.

(4) " Preached unto the Gentiles." This statement was made by Paul, the great Apostle to the Gentiles. The Gospel has been preached to all nations ever since, and its message is still being proclaimed to the " whosoever will."

(5) " Believed on in the world." To any who would reason against the Gospel there stands a great cloud of witnesses, the true Church of Jesus Christ world-wide, the great assembly of believers of all ages and all climes. There is an army of believing saints whose impact cannot be denied.

(6) " Received up into glory " — the testimony of His ascension which was also witnessed by many.

The fact that the Gospel has withstood the opposition of nearly two millenniums, and is still the power of God unto salvation, is an evidence that it cannot be destroyed.

The Apostle moves on to speak about the dangerous class of people who depart from the faith, and to whom reference has already been made. These people are not a danger to the Gospel, but they are a potential danger to their fellow-men. They must be exposed, their doctrines refused, and the brethren warned.

The New Testament has given many warnings of these apostates who would appear in the last days, and are truly in the world to-day.

Christian, you should not be discouraged by the things you see but, instead, challenged to become " . . . an example of the believers, in word, in conversation, in charity, in spirit, in faith, in purity " (iv. 12), and also to " Take heed unto thyself, and unto the doctrine ; continue in them : for in doing this thou shalt both save thyself, and them that hear thee " (iv. 16). This, of course, means to save ourselves from falling into their snares. We cannot save ourselves from sin.

(c) *Service.* From the Acts of the Apostles it is learned that the early Church had a ministry which was social as well as one which was spiritual. There was no relief for the poor, no care for the aged, no ministry to the sick, no pensions for the infirmed, no education for the masses. It was the Church which first interested itself in these things. After much opposition, the values of such care began to be appreciated so that local authorities, social services, and governments, have taken over these responsibilities, but it should never be forgotten that the world owes most of its blessings and privileges to Christendom and the Church. Where the Christian faith has never found its way in the world, suppression, illiteracy, and suffering still abound.

Although much of the social responsibility has been taken away from the Church, yet it still has the privilege of meeting man's needs. Much of this is now continued in the realm of overseas missionary activity and home missions.

It appears from this fifth chapter that then, as now, there had been people who were ready to defraud, to obtain under false pretences, and also those who were ready to relieve themselves of their own personal responsibilities, if they could see the opportunity to saddle someone else with them. Paul, therefore, gave instruction to Timothy as to how to handle such a situation. There are always those who will come to the Church and seek charity. Some people consider the duty of a Christian is to help all and sundry without asking questions. This cannot be a proper procedure. It is taking money, which could be the sacrificial giving of some Church members, and gifts which have become sacred in that they have been given to the Lord, and handing them to sinners to squander in their sin and selfishness. If there is any difference of opinion on this matter, then Paul has clarified it in this Epistle as it concerns widows.

He differentiates between widows and "widows that are widows indeed" (v. 3). A widow is a person who has lost her main support. A widow indeed is one who has lost her complete support. If a woman has lost her husband and has grown children, or nephews, they are responsible for her need, not the Church. If a woman has lost her husband and she is still young and is supported by charity, she could become lazy and a busybody in other people's affairs. Her duty is to remarry and become responsible in family duties.

If believers lose their father and the mother is left a widow, they are responsible for that parent, as individuals, and not the Church. The reason for this is "that it (the Church) may relieve them that are widows indeed" (v. 16). She is the widow who has no relative to whom she may turn, and no interested friend who is able to assist her. She is a woman who is " . . . desolate, trusteth in God, and continueth in supplications and prayers night and day" (v. 5).

The Church, therefore, is responsible for helping the desolate widow, and the godly widow. It is no more right to take the Lord's money and give it to sinners, allowing them to continue in their sin, than it is to cast pearls before swine.

Having declared the duties and prerogatives of the Pastor and the deacon toward the Church, the next point of conduct is the responsibility of the Church toward the Pastor and the elders. Such men are worthy of double honour, but especially the man who has yielded his whole life to the Church and the Gospel, who has surrendered business life and every source of income (v. 17). This man is worthy of his hire, and is entitled to the full support of the Church. " Even so hath the Lord ordained that they which preach the gospel should live of the gospel " (1 Corinthians xi. 14).

As, under the law, an " ox that treadeth out the corn " was not allowed to be muzzled, so a servant of the Lord should not be muzzled, or restrained ; neither must he be unjustly accused (v. 19).

A few generalities, concerning all who are in the Church, conclude this chapter.

The Christian is expected to be
    (1)   Obedient in all these things (vs. 21).
    (2)   Not given to partiality (vs. 21).
    (3)   Not hasty in his decisions (vs. 22).
    (4)   Separate from the sins of others (vs. 22).

Verse 23 has ofttimes been used as a permission to partake of wines and liquor. An honest reading of the verse makes it amply clear that no permission was given to a person to take wine as an indulgence but, rather, to use wine as a medicine.

(d) *Faithfulness.* In this last chapter (vi.), it would appear that the instruction concerns the life lived outside the Church, the everyday living of the child of God.

In business, the Christian is instructed to do an honest day's work and to respect his master, so that the world will never be able to point the finger and say : " That is a Christian not doing his duty, or not being honest with his master's property or time ", and thereby cause it to blaspheme God (vi. 1).

The Christian who has the privilege of having a Christian master should never seek to take advantage of that privilege, nor attempt to put the master on his own level. Because they are brethren in the Lord and are equal in the Church, that does not make them brethren in the flesh, or give them equality in the business life (vi. 2).

Anyone who opposes this instruction and seeks to teach otherwise is both proud and ignorant and is the cause of strife and envy. With such there is to be no companionship, for his one desire is to seek his own advantage always. " To get " is his god, but it is the man who is content and happy in the Lord who really has the advantage. His contentment is his enrichment. He is gaining in spiritual stature. After all, what is a man profited even if he gain the whole world, " For we brought nothing into this world, and it is certain we can carry nothing out " (vi. 7). To gain riches is to gain trouble, for the love of money is the root of all evil and, as a result of it, many a man has lost his soul.

The Christian must flee from these carnal ambitions and desires and, instead of expending his energy upon material possessions, use it in fighting the good fight of faith. This statement of verse 12 does not refer to warfare and subduing our enemy but, rather, to the sports arena, where gladiators met in duels, and where boxing, racing, and other contests took place. There men fought good, honest fights, meaning that they obeyed all the rules of the contest.

It was customary to hang the prize, usually a crown of laurels, within the sight of the contestants, as an encouragement. It was within sight but not within reach, but it was a coveted possession. Every man wanted it, but he must prove himself in every way as being worthy of the trophy, not only to the judge, but also to the spectators.

There is laid up for the child of God a crown of life, and he must fight who wins, so the whole verse says : " Fight the good fight of faith (in the arena of this world), lay hold on eternal life (reaching after the prize), whereunto thou art also called (as a contestant), and hast professed a good profession before many witnesses (the spectators)."

Here is a similar picture from the pen of the same Apostle: " Know ye not that they which run in a race run all, but one receiveth the prize ? So run, that ye may obtain. And every man that striveth for the mastery is temperate in all things. Now they do it to obtain a corruptible crown ; but we an incorruptible. I therefore so run, not as uncertainly ; so fight I, not as one that beateth the air : But I keep under my body, and bring it into subjection : lest that by any means, when I have preached to others, I myself should be a castaway " (1 Corinthians ix. 24-27).

One other important reminder was submitted to Timothy as the contestant. Not only was he, and not only are we, to be

faithful before many witnesses, but also before the Judge, and
our Judge is the One Who quickeneth, or giveth life to, all things.
He, when on earth, was faithful in witnessing before Pontius
Pilate, and we are to stand before Him, the greatest of all judges
and Who is the only Potentate, the King of kings, and Lord of
lords, and Whose glory supersedes all other glories.

Two admonitions remain, one for the Church and the other
for Timothy. The first concerned the rich in the Church. It
must be noted that neither here nor anywhere else was man condemned because he was rich. On one occasion the Lord said:
" The poor ye always have with you " (John xii. 8), which infers
that the rich will always be with us also. The condemnation was
the deceitfulness of riches.

The instruction is for the rich in order that they might know
how they should behave themselves. They should not become
proud and should not rely on their wealth, because money is a
very uncertain thing. It can be lost more easily than it can be
made. The advice to the rich is that their trust should be in the
Lord. He is the only sure foundation and, because He is the
source of all true riches, He giveth us all things richly to enjoy.
" All things " embraces more than wealth. It includes health,
friends, virtues, graces, the beautiful world in which we live, the
sunshine and the rain, and everything else which is ours physically,
morally, mentally, socially, and spiritually.

In the same way as this bountiful God has poured out of His
wealth, even so the rich are encouraged to share their possessions
with others and, by so doing, they will enrich themselves for the
Life to come.

The second admonition was a final reminder of a constant
challenge to Timothy to keep himself free from the wranglings
of the false teachers. We must do likewise.

II TIMOTHY

THE SCRIPTURE OF TRUTH

" Beloved, when I gave all diligence to write unto you of the common salvation, it was needful for me to write unto you, and exhort you that ye should earnestly contend for the faith which was once delivered unto the saints. For there are certain men crept in unawares, who were before of old ordained to this condemnation, ungodly men, turning the grace of our God into lasciviousness, and denying the only Lord God, and our Lord Jesus Christ " (JUDE 3-4)

INTRODUCTION

This second Epistle to Timothy was written by Paul toward the end of a very noble life. The Apostle was in prison for the second time and he was not expecting any mercy nor yet any more liberty.

It is believed that Nero, with his desire to build a better Rome and not sure how he was going to accomplish it, in one of his nights of debauchery, gave orders to have the city set on fire, then sat and, with delight, watched it burn whilst he played on his fiddle. Having fired the city, he must put the blame on to someone else so that he might justify himself. Thus it was that he accused the Christians, and then punished them with inhuman tortures. Night after night many Christians were soaked in oil and set alight that they might become torches to light up his palace grounds. Paul, as a leader of the Christians, was probably cast into prison in these circumstances. He was aware of the suffering, he was also aware that there was little chance to escape such suffering. Therefore he wrote to Timothy to encourage him to continue in the things that he had been taught from his childhood.

In the light of these dreadful conditions it should inspire our hearts to hear this old warrior of the Gospel saying : " For I am now ready to be offered, and the time of my departure is at hand. I have fought a good fight, I have finished my course, I have kept the faith " (iv. 6-7).

The expression " the time of my departure is at hand " is interesting because it really is " the time of my unyoking is at hand." From the time Paul received his commission from the Lord and allowed Him to place upon his shoulders the yoke of Christian service, he never once shirked that ministry. The Lord placed the yoke and only the Lord would remove it.

It was in these circumstances, which could have brought despair, that he uttered such triumphant words of faith as " I know Whom I have believed, and am persuaded that He is able to keep that which I have committed unto Him against that day " (i. 12), and " The Lord shall deliver me from every evil work, and will preserve me unto His heavenly kingdom ; to Whom be glory for ever and ever. Amen " (iv. 18). It is easy to use such expressions of confidence when everything is going well, or even when the trouble is behind and the believer is in victory, but the Apostle expressed his confidence whilst he faced his earthly condemnation.

THE MESSAGE

It concerns THE SCRIPTURE OF TRUTH, the thing for which many of them might have to sacrifice their lives. Therefore it was essential that they should be fully persuaded that it was The Truth, and that they should be firmly established in that Truth.

Notice the prominence that the Apostle gives to the Word of God. In his opening salutation he comments on the faithfulness of Timothy's mother and grandmother in bringing up this child in the faith and establishing him in the truth. Later he said : " From a child thou hast known the holy scriptures " (iii. 15). What a blessing to be instructed in the Word of God whilst the mind is young, susceptible, and capable of remembering. Christian parent, this is the greatest blessing that you can bestow upon your child. It is something that will remain throughout life, and will also influence that life — but, this word of advice ! Do not force the Word of God into that life. Do not compel your child to go to church and to pray. The day will come when he will resent it, and presently " kick the traces." Many parents to-day have broken hearts because of this very thing. Do not compel, but encourage. Let your thrill for the Truth encourage him to want to know. Let your keenness whet his appetite. Learn to discuss things on his level, and he will grow to your level.

Notice the encouragement Paul gave to his " son in the Faith." It was pointed out in the first Epistle that there was a timidity on the part of Timothy which needed to be challenged. Now there is a defence of the Truth in the face of persecution, which needs to be strengthened. The emphasis is toward the Word of God : —

> " Be not thou therefore ashamed of the testimony of our Lord " (i. 8).
> " Hold fast the form of sound words, which thou hast heard of me " (i. 13).
> " Study to show thyself approved unto God, a workman that needeth not to be ashamed, rightly dividing the Word of Truth " (ii. 15).
> " But continue thou in the things which thou hast learned and hast been assured of, knowing of whom thou hast learned them ; and that from a child thou hast known the Holy Scriptures " (iii. 14-15).
> " All Scripture is given by inspiration of God, and is profitable for doctrine, for reproof, for correction, for instruction in righteousness " (iii. 16).
> " Preach the Word " (iv. 2).

Wherever the Word of God has been acknowledged there has been blessing, whether individually or nationally.

Wherever the same Word has been neglected or pushed aside, calamity has befallen that community or nation. Look at the nations to-day in the light of these things. All revivals have been based upon the Word of God, but churches and nations are made up of individuals. In exhorting Timothy, the young preacher, to successful ministry, Paul suggests four things, which are found in chapter ii., and yet which summarise the whole Epistle.

They are a call to

DILIGENCE (Chapters ii. and iii.)

(1) *A Good Soldier* (ii. 3-5). " Thou therefore endure hardness, as a good soldier . . . "

In all of the characters which are introduced an adjective is used to declare the quality, for only the best is acceptable to God.

There are many men who are compelled to join an army by conscription. Most of them are unwilling. Many of them never see war. Such are ever complaining. Some only look for what they can get out of it in the form of pensions and privileges, as though they were heroes. They may be called soldiers, but they are not *good* soldiers. A *good* soldier volunteers. He has a pride and a patriotism. He endures hardness without a murmur. He is not wronged. That is his calling. He was ready for hardness and inconvenience when he volunteered. He does not ask for leave. Absenteeism is foreign to his vocabulary. There is a battle to fight, and a victory to win. There is a country to defend, and an honour to maintain. His calling becomes his first and last consideration. He gives himself to his training and he learns thoroughly all army regulations.

Says the Apostle to his " son in the faith " : " Thou therefore endure hardness, as a *good* soldier of Jesus Christ. No man that warreth entangleth himself with the affairs of this life ; that he may please Him Who hath chosen him to be a soldier " (ii. 3 - 4).

British soldiers make great sacrifices and endure some of the toughest training for the honour of being one of the Queen's Guards. We have been called of God. There is an enemy to fight. Evil has to be subdued. The integrity of the Church has to be maintained. The Name of the Lord has to be honoured. None of these things can be done by a crowd of quarrelling babies in a nursery, and yet the Church is often just that, when it should be an armoury. Christian, have you put on the whole armour of God ? Are you studying the articles of war committed to you ? Have you sworn your allegiance to the King of kings ? Have you pledged your loyalty to the Blood-stained banner of the Cross ? If so, then the commission is, " Be not entangled with the affairs of this life," or, as the Apostle put it to the Corinthians : " Come out from among them, and be ye separate " (2 Corinthians vi. 17).

" And if a man also strive for masteries, yet is he not crowned, except he strive lawfully " (ii. 5). This would apply to the soldier who desires promotion, or seeks to gain an award. It also applies to a man who enters a race, or engages in a combat, or becomes a contestant in some sport. If he desires to be master over his opponent, or if he expects to gain the crown of laurels, then he must study the rules and regulations, and obey them. It must be a lawful combat if it is to be the victor's crown. Our Christian service must be according to the requirements of God's Word or our labour is in vain.

(2) *A Patient Husbandman* (ii. 6). " The husbandman that laboureth must be first partaker of the fruits." The man who diligently labours is the man who is not only entitled to, but must receive, the firstfruits of the harvest. There is no fruit without labour, no reward without service, no victory without battle. This verse is made a little clearer by James who, using the same illus-

tration, wrote : " Be patient therefore, brethren, unto the coming of the Lord. Behold, the husbandman waiteth for the precious fruit of the earth, and hath long patience for it, until he receive the early and latter rain " (James v. 7).

Timothy must not expect to reap the fruit until he had put in labour, and a lot of patient labour, for harvest cannot be hurried ; and every Christian worker must learn the same truth and then he will not so quickly become disappointed. The seasons take their course, rain and sunshine, frosts and dews, sowing and reaping, fertilising, weeding, and patient waiting, BUT the man who has been diligent in labour will be the first to appreciate the fruit of that labour.

Thus it is in relationship to the Scriptures. Some people are very quick in saying that they do not understand the Bible, but there are many things in life that one does not understand when they are first met. To know the Bible means that it must be read, meditated upon, and inwardly digested. The farmer does not sow seed to-day and then sit down and watch a harvest develop to-morrow, and we must not expect such a miracle to happen in our Christian service. We must read, reread, pray, compare, enquire, ponder, investigate, wait, pray again. We must testify, set examples, and speak again and again, ever waiting on the Lord, remembering that the husbandman has long patience, but the harvest is sure. The reward has been promised by the Lord of the harvest. " So shall My Word be that goeth forth out of My mouth: it shall not return unto Me void, but it shall accomplish that which *I* please, and it shall prosper in the thing whereto *I* sent it " (Isaiah lv. 11).

God has never promised that our service will ever fulfil *our* desires. Maybe many have been disappointed and frustrated because they did not understand this.

The promise is : " It shall accomplish that which *I* please," not " you please." " It shall prosper in the thing whereto *I* sent it," not " you planned it."

Let us get our perspectives right, and be *patient* husbandmen.

(3) *An Unashamed Workman* (ii. 15). " Study to show thyself approved unto God, a workman that needeth not to be ashamed, rightly dividing the Word of Truth."

According to the dictionary the word " study " means " To devote oneself to the mastery of." Is this the way we read the Word of God ? Is our reading for pleasure or for profit ? As we seek to master the things of God so shall we discover that the things of God are mastering us. Then shall we be living unto

all well pleasing. "Study to show thyself approved unto God."
Better to be approved unto God than approved unto men.

There are two kinds of workmen in the world to-day. There
is the man who works for pay, and the man who is paid for work.
The first works because it is necessary. He cannot escape it. He
does not do one stroke more than he has to do. This man has
no interest in his work whatever. The result is that his products
are inferior. No one would be proud to be the owner of anything
which he makes, and he himself has nothing about which he
might boast.

The other workman works for the sheer joy of accomplishing. When he has finished his task he is proud of it. He is ready
to exhibit it. He is prepared for anyone to give it a thorough
examination. He is unashamed. He pleases his master, and he
pleases the customer.

We are to study the Word of God so that, as Christians, we
can live a life and bear a testimony that will bring glory to the
Name of the Lord.

We are to study the Word of God so that, as teachers,
preachers, or pastors, we may present well-ordered, God-inspired,
effective messages which will honour the Lord and bring blessing
to His people.

Were you proud of that action of yours ? Did you feel that
your Sunday School lesson accomplished its purpose ? Was that
sermon the finest thing you could produce for your Master, or
could you have done better ? Were you ashamed, or unashamed?

(4) *A Vessel of Honour* (ii. 20-21). "But in a great house
there are not only vessels of gold and of silver, but also of wood
and of earth ; and some to honour, and some to dishonour. If
a man therefore purge himself from these, he shall be a vessel
unto honour, sanctified, and meet for the Master's use, and prepared unto every good work."

This verse might readily suggest to some minds the idea of
the beautiful vases holding flowers, or the bowls of art which
contain the fruit, or even the ornaments, all of which adorn the
best rooms of the great house, and exist for the admiration of
all, as against the less beautiful vessels to be found in the kitchen
which had their daily and common use and, therefore, were made
of common material. However, man would be without his food
but for such things. Upon further reflection it may be observed
that the previous verses of the chapter refer to " profane and vain
babblings " that are like a canker, something that eats into the very

substance of things. It is also stated that these people had erred from the truth, particularly in the matter of the resurrection. These had disturbed the faith of some. When Paul said in verse 21 : " If a man therefore purge himself from these, he shall be a vessel unto honour . . . ", " these " must have referred to the teachers of error which were in the world, and also in the Church.

In the light of this context may we suggest that the vessels of dishonour would refer to the containers used in the kitchen to take all of the waste, trash, and unwanted garbage of the house.

In the Church are to be found people who have ears and hearts wide open for every evil doctrine, every unholy rumour, every false and unfounded statement, every kind of lie or fable that some newcomer might propound. From these we must keep ourselves free, for such things and people are unsanctified. We are to be vessels into which the Master may place the precious gifts of His love, the beautiful fruit of His Spirit, and the fragrant bouquets of His grace.

The Lord make us all to become *good* soldiers, *patient* husbandmen, *unashamed* workmen, and *sanctified* vessels !

Chapter iii. is given to signs of the last days, and how accurate was the description given.

Many people in these days want to give up their faith in God, suggesting that the Church has let them down, the Bible is not trustworthy, and everything has failed, because the world is full of corruption, the Church is full of hypocrisy, and the Bible is full of contradictions. The fact is that the Bible is full of declarations, none of which can be denied. Had the Bible promised that the world would continually improve until man found himself in a wonderful Utopia, and then things proved to be in the reverse, man would have cause for complaint. However, the fact is that the Word of God declared " . . . that in the last days perilous times shall come. For men shall be lovers of their own selves, covetous, boasters, proud, blasphemers, disobedient to parents, unthankful, unholy, without natural affection, trucebreakers, false accusers, incontinent, fierce, despisers of those that are good, traitors, heady, highminded, lovers of pleasures more than lovers of God " (iii. 1-4). There is not a single statement that could be removed from these verses as not belonging to this present day. Nothing is wrong with the Bible. It has declared the exact truth. This then is what must be expected. Therefore, instead of present conditions driving us away from the Lord, His Word and His Church, they should draw us much nearer to the Lord because they reveal His truth, also our complete helplessness, and so our utter dependence upon Him if we are to avoid the errors of others.

Not only was the condition of man in his moral life accurately defined, but also in his spiritual life. "Having a form of godliness, but denying the power thereof" (iii. 5). Was there anything so contradictory as man in his religious outlook! Many preachers read the Bible, go to school to study it, are paid to preach it, and all they do is to deny it.

People go to Church most religiously, put their money into the collection, listen to the preacher, and neither believe nor practise anything he teaches. Surely the heart is deceitful above all things!

Another class of people is that cult which goes from door to door, seeks to have what it calls Bible classes, but in the name of religion introduces every kind of philosophy in which it leads astray many women who, desiring to know everything, know nothing.

"Jannes and Jambres," two men named in verse 8, are recognised by most scholars as two of the magicians who withstood Moses in Exodus vii. 11, and performed some of the same miracles as wrought by Moses. Their ability, which soon proved to be limited, deceived some of the people, who were made to believe that Moses, as the servant of God, had no more power or authority than they. So, in the last days, godless men will exercise so much power and usurp so much authority that men will believe that the Bible must give place to science, and creation yield to evolution, and that the Church will be silenced by the voice of advanced education, but the day will come when "they shall proceed no further: for their folly shall be manifest unto all men" (iii. 9), when the God of all wisdom shall appear.

Paul reminded Timothy that he had suffered for Christ's sake, and that the last days will be no better than his day because "evil men and seducers shall wax worse and worse, deceiving and being deceived" (iii. 13). We must be prepared for these conditions, and also brace ourselves against them by remembering that, although men deny, yet the fact remains that "ALL Scripture is given by inspiration of God." When man has said his last word, performed his last act, and moves off the scene of time, it will be learned in eternity, by those who would not learn in time, that the Word of the Lord abideth for ever.

For the believer this Word will be his stronghold, his city of refuge in the day of opposition. By it he will be perfected.

In the light of the foregoing, the Apostle concludes his Epistle with a charge, a testimony, and a salutation.

A CHARGE (iv. 1-5). This was given in the Name of the Coming Lord Who, in the day of His appearing, will sit as the Great Judge and will judge both the living and the dead, as all will have to stand before Him and give an account of their stewardship.

The charge was " Preach the Word," not what others think, nor yet what they like ; not what we think, not even our own experiences, even though they may be helpful. Of course, this does not mean that a testimony must never be given, nor experiences related. It means that such things must not take the place of the preaching of the Word. The promise is " MY WORD . . . shall not return unto Me void " (Isaiah lv. 11).

Recently some Churches have adopted the use of films for departmental work, and some Sunday Schools have put on plays, particularly at Christmas (the rights or wrongs will not be discussed here), but now these same things are being used in the Sunday night service in place of the sermon, and so have become a substitute for preaching the Word. God has promised no blessing on such substitutes. Pastor, preach the Word and nothing but the Word. When shall we preach ? Always, " In season, out of season," whenever the opportunity affords itself. The reason for the urgency is that the time will come when men will not endure sound doctrine. The god of this world is blinding the eyes and deceiving the mind, so that men prefer to believe the lie rather than the truth.

Because this condition is fast coming upon the world, and much of it is already with us, we must be diligent in reproving, rebuking, and exhorting, so making full proof of our ministry.

A TESTIMONY (iv. 6-8). "For I am now ready to be offered, and the time of my departure is at hand. I have fought a good fight, I have finished my course, I have kept the faith : Henceforth there is laid up for me a crown of righteousness, which the Lord, the righteous judge, shall give me at that day : and not to me only, but unto all them also that love his appearing."

Paul's faithfulness, declared in the first two verses, has already been considered. He goes on to testify that God had prepared a reward for him, and also for all who will remain steadfast to the Truth.

Is it not better to suffer affliction and to be despised for the moment, because of our love for the Truth, and then to enjoy the eternal reward which comes from a righteous Judge, than to enjoy the popularity of the present and lose the blessings of the Lord in the hereafter ?

SALUTATIONS (iv. 10-22). In the loneliness of Paul's prison life Luke was the only companion he had. He asks Timothy to visit him and to bring Mark with him. It is good to see how Paul was appreciating the value of Mark's ministry. Paul and Barnabas had parted from each other because of a difference of opinion as to Mark's faithfulness.

Paul had always longed for the fellowship of other saints. He had had many companions in travel. Most of them had been very loyal. Here he mentions two who had failed him — Demas, who had gone back into the world, and Alexander, who had opposed him.

He requests some material things, asking for his cloak in order to bring him some added comfort, but, more particularly, the parchments, for these were his delight day and night.

His final word of assurance was that, though all men might forsake him, he was confident that the Lord would never leave him nor forsake him.

TITUS

BISHOP OF CRETE

*" Pure religion and undefiled before God and the Father is
this, To visit the fatherless and widows in their affliction, and
to keep himself unspotted from the world"* (JAMES i. 27)
*" And let us not be weary in well doing : for in due season
we shall reap, if we faint not. As we have therefore opportunity, let us do good unto all men, especially unto them
who are of the household of faith"* (GALATIANS vi. 9-10)

INTRODUCTION

THE MAN. This is the fourth and last of the Pastoral Epistles,
and is one of four addressed to individuals — two to Timothy,
one to Philemon, and this one to Titus.

Little is known of this man because he is not mentioned in
the Acts of the Apostles. He appears to have been a man of great
ability, and was a close and active friend of Paul.

He was a Greek by birth. This is learnt from Paul at the
time when he took him with Barnabas to Jerusalem. " Then fourteen years after I went up again to Jerusalem with Barnabas, and
took Titus with me also . . . But neither Titus who was with me,
being a Greek, was compelled to be circumcised " (Galatians
ii. 1-3).

Titus was brought into the Christian faith through the ministry
of Paul, so that the Apostle refers to him in similar language to
that which he uses concerning Timothy, for he calls him " mine
own son after the common faith " (Titus i. 4). Paul had a great
heart-yearning for this young man who was so full of possibilities
that, when he (Paul) had come to Troas, even though there was
a wide open door of service, he could not tarry there because he
could not find Titus. The result was that Paul went on into
Macedonia in search of him. This he states in his second letter
to the Corinthians. " I had no rest in my spirit, because I found
not Titus my brother : but taking my leave of them, I went from
thence into Macedonia " (2 Corinthians ii. 13). Paul had a great
concern for the Corinthians, but this was shared by Titus, as

declared in 2 Corinthians viii. 16 : " But thanks be to God, which put the same earnest care into the heart of Titus for you." In fact, Paul sent his Epistle to Corinth by the hands of Titus and Luke, and he told the Corinthians that, if they wanted to know who Titus was, then " he is my partner and fellow-helper concerning you " (2 Corinthians viii. 23).

Titus spent quite a time ministering to the saints at Corinth.

For a while he was with Paul in Rome during the period of the Apostle's imprisonment for, when Paul wrote from prison to Timothy, he said : " For Demas hath forsaken me, having loved this present world, and is departed unto Thessalonica ; Crescens to Galatia, Titus unto Dalmatia. Only Luke is with me . . . " (2 Timothy iv. 10-11).

Later Titus was sent to take charge of the work in the island of Crete and, according to the footnote at the end of this Epistle, he became the first Bishop of Crete. " It was written to Titus, ordained the first Bishop of the Church of the Cretians, from Nicopolis of Macedonia."

THE MESSAGE

The subject matter is good works, and the reasoning is that man is not saved by good works but is saved unto good works.

The words " sound ", " sober ", and " good works " are each repeated five times.

The book is a letter by Paul written to a Bishop concerning the matter of Christian conduct. The keyword of the book is " Godliness," and in this subject Titus was to show himself a pattern.

The three chapters make a natural division : —

GODLINESS IN THE CHURCH, or, the character of ministers (Chapter i.)

GODLINESS IN THE HOME, or, the character of believers (Chapter ii.).

GODLINESS IN THE WORLD, or, the conduct of believers (Chapter iii.).

In the greeting Paul introduces himself as " A servant of God." In two Epistles he introduces himself as " Paul " ; in eight he is " An Apostle " ; in three " A servant " ; and in one " A prisoner." In this Epistle he is " A servant and an Apostle." All of these titles relate to the particular Epistles. In this letter Paul is writing to one who was to be a servant of the Church, so he takes the same status and introduces himself as a servant. This is the meaning of Paul's testimony, " I became all things to all men."

Whilst a servant, however, he is also an Apostle. In fact, all Church leaders, pastors, bishops, and deacons, should learn that they are servants of God and of the Church, and not lords of God's heritage. Their task is to serve, but to serve with authority.

" To Titus, mine own son after the common faith " (i. 4). There is an interesting comparison between this salutation and the one addressed to Timothy. Both were converts of Paul's ministry, and he looked upon them as his children. Timothy, who was a Jew, is referred to as " my own son in the faith," but Titus, being a Gentile, is addressed as " mine own son after the common faith," meaning that the faith which is in Christ Jesus is not an exclusive faith, which is the right of a certain race, but it is an inclusive faith which embraces all men who will believe, irrespective of nationality and all else.

Paul had not only had the privilege of leading this young man into salvation, but he had also done much in developing his Christian character, until he felt that Titus was so established in the faith that he could ordain him as a Bishop and give him the oversight of the Churches which were on the island of Crete.

Certain things were out of order in these Churches, and missing in the lives of the professing Christians, which were to be corrected — and summed up in the word, Godliness. As there were a number of Churches on the island, there was also the need to appoint elders who would have local responsibilities and would be, to some extent, local pastors, whilst Titus had general oversight of all the Churches. Hence his title of Bishop, as declared in the footnote at the end of the Epistle.

One thought more from the introductory verses. In verse 2 Paul uses the phrase : " . . . God, that cannot lie . . . " This statement, as it appears in our Authorised Version, is in the negative form, but in the Greek it is in the positive : " . . . God, Who is absolute truth . . . " This introduction of the Lord is appreciated when one remembers that truth was a missing quality of the Cretians, as stated in verse 12 : " One of themselves, even a prophet of their own, said, The Cretians are always liars." Satan is a liar and the father of lies, but the Lord is absolute truth. He cannot lie.

Turn now to the main theme of the book.

(1) GODLINESS IN THE CHURCH, or, the Character of Ministers (Chapter i.)

This book gives guidance as to the election of officers and their eligibility. It applies to ministers, to deacons, to elders, and to anyone who would serve the Church of God in the realm of leadership, and thereby establishes conditions of Church government.

We are in the same Church that was established at Pentecost and continues until the Second Advent of Christ, so what applied to the Church when Paul wrote to Titus should apply to us to-day.

An elder or officer should be

BLAMELESS, or above reproach in everyday living, and above criticism in everyday ministry. It would be to great advantage, when a Church is electing officers, that this chapter be read. It would also be to the enrichment of the Church if elders and deacons were ordained. It would help the man to realise the solemnity of the office he undertakes and, also, it would give the Church members a greater respect for these offices.

Too many men are appointed because they have money, influence, or because there is no one else, or because it might prevent someone from being upset. This attitude is unscriptural and dangerous. The Church is not a social club. It is the Body of Christ, and the Bride of Christ, and for it Christ died. Everything connected with that Church is sacred and holy. Everyone who works in it will have to give an account of his stewardship to the Lord of the Church. These matters, therefore, are weighty and serious. An elder must be blameless.

THE HUSBAND OF ONE WIFE. This cannot refer to polygamy because it was not practised in those days. What was common at that time were divorce and remarriage, so the injunction becomes obvious. A divorcé should not hold office in the Church of Christ. He has failed in respect of the laws of God. The Bible is clear and emphatic on this matter of divorce, so it is no use trying to make excuses and soothe consciences when, inwardly, we know they will not hold with God.

Many people want to justify themselves by putting the blame on to the other person, and calling themselves the " innocent party." If such are innocent to the extent of justifying divorce, it does not justify remarriage. The so-called " innocent party " must remember that usually it takes two people to make a quarrel.

The only cause for which the Lord permitted divorce was adultery, and then there should be no remarriage.

FAITHFUL AT HOME. An elder's children must be disciplined and obedient for, if a man cannot rule his own house, how can he lead the Church of God ? Not only must he control his children, but also himself, his temper, his appetite, and his desires. He must be a man who seeks not his own desires but those of others because, as a leader, the Church must come first.

He also must not be a man who has a passionate desire for money, because the love of money is the root of all evil. This means that after he has been appointed to his office, he must resist any craving for money.

HOSPITABLE. He must be a lover of hospitality and of good men, a person whose home is always open to the people of God, and who ever finds it a delight to be in the company of those who are of like precious faith.

It is essential for a servant of the Lord to watch his company, for it can influence him for good or ill. It must not be forgotten that the world assesses our character by our company, for there is a proverb which says : " Birds of a feather flock together."

From personal character the Apostle moves to

PUBLIC MINISTRY. This is declared to be threefold : —

(1) *Holding fast to the Word.* Titus had been taught the truth in all faithfulness. In the same way he must deliver it.

(2) *Expounding sound Doctrine.* The Church badly needs to understand doctrine. It is not what others think but what God has laid down as the basic things of our faith. Then, too, the Church needs exposition. Applications may be good, comparisons may be useful, theories have little value, but to open up the Word of God, to lay bare the great principles, to let the Book speak for itself, are the all-important things. By so doing there is an

(3) *Exposing of false teachers.* These are men who have received no Divine Call, and have had no revelation, but will teach anything because they like to hear their own voices. They love publicity, and they see a means whereby they may make money. Truth is the greatest weapon for the exposure of error.

The chapter ends with a declaration that " Unto the pure all things are pure ; but unto them that are defiled and unbelieving

is nothing pure; but even their mind and conscience is defiled"
(i. 15), which means that, if godliness be manifested in the life
and ministry of God's servants, then godly people will recognise
it and rejoice in it. If the other man wishes to criticise, find fault,
and condemn, do not worry about it, or allow it to affect one's
holiness, because the minds of such men are so defiled that nothing
is right. They are reprobates.

(2) GODLINESS IN THE HOME, or, the Character of Believers (Chapter ii.)

God has placed man in the family circle. He has made us
male and female. He has caused to be established the phases
of life known as childhood, youth, manhood, and old age. He
recognises the master and the servant. He has said : "The poor
always ye have with you," thereby recognising the rich and the
poor. Nothing is wrong in being rich, but a great deal is wrong
in being greedy and unjust, and not recognising the existence of
the poor. All of these things come within the economy of God
and, therefore, are termed natural things.

The Lord does not expect the fig tree to bear olives, but figs.
He does not look for figs from the vine, but grapes. He does not
expect a corrupt tree to bring forth good fruit, or a good tree to
bear corrupt fruit. Even so, in the family He does not expect
the young to display the maturity of the old, neither does He look
for a man to be a keeper of the home, but each person functioning
rightly in his own office, according to his own position.

There was but one thing that the Lord did require from all,
and still does, and that was godliness.

God's expectations from the different classes are now
enumerated.

From the aged men He expects maturity. "That the aged men
be sober, grave, temperate, sound in faith, in charity, in patience"
(ii. 2). Age brings with it experience, experience develops
maturity, and maturity should create a well-balanced godly life,
to which others might look for guidance. Frivolity is not becoming
to those of advanced years, and certainly not foolishness. The
word "sound" in verses 1 and 2 comes from a medical term
meaning "free from taint or disease." Faith can be tainted by
doubt, and sin and selfishness are both a disease. The aged men
in the Church are expected to be free from such things. "Sound
in faith" reads in the Greek as "sound in THE faith."

From the aged women He expects holiness. "The aged women likewise, that they be in behaviour as becometh holiness, not false accusers, not given to much wine, teachers of good things; That they may teach the young women to be sober, to love their husbands, to love their children, to be discreet, chaste, keepers at home, good, obedient to their own husbands, that the Word of God be not blasphemed" (ii. 3-5).

Every woman in the Church should become "a mother in Israel." Her demeanour, or bearing and conduct, should display that calm, peaceful, well-ordered life of a saint, which is so becoming to the aged, that they can instruct the younger generation in the ways of holy living.

From the young women He expects chastity. The verses are included in the instruction given to the aged women, verses 4 and 5.

This younger generation was not to spend its time gadding around flippantly, spending time in the homes of other people, with loose talk, gossiping, backbiting, things which gender strife, but, contrariwise, they were to remain at home, remembering that their first duty and obligation was that of wife and mother. Therefore, they were to love their husbands and their children, and display such behaviour that the world would never have the opportunity to point the finger of scorn at them, saying: "That is a Christian," and thereby cause the Word of God to be blasphemed.

From the young men He expects soundness. "Young men likewise exhort to be sober minded. In all things showing thyself to be a pattern of good works: in doctrine showing uncorruptness, gravity, sincerity. Sound speech, that cannot be condemned; that he that is of the contrary part may be ashamed, having no evil thing to say of you" (ii. 6-8).

The call is for soundness in doctrine, in life, in speech, and in good works. Christian men should ever be a pattern of good, manly living, with energy, power, and ability consecrated, so as to put all other men to shame because they can find no fault in their living and yet their living is exposing the failures of the others, thus leaving them confounded.

From servants He expects obedience. "Exhort servants to be obedient unto their own masters, and to please them well in all things; not answering again; not purloining, but shewing all good fidelity ; that they may adorn the doctrine of God our Saviour in all things " (ii. 9 -10).

This is sound admonition for all time. It is good policy for the world, how much more for the Christian ! Obedience to their *own* masters, and the master is the one who pays the wages. To-day men are wanting to draw their wages from one source, and pledge their loyalty to, and receive their instruction from, another source. This is contrary to the teaching of Scripture. The servant must serve his master well, not abusing him by working against him and acting contrary to instructions ; not purloining, which means stealing, the materials and doing jobs for one's self, such as writing letters in the firm's time and using the firm's stationery and stamps, and not stealing the master's time by idleness.

By these things God is dishonoured, but by honesty the doctrine of God our Saviour is adorned.

Thus the matter of the believer's conduct is covered.

The closing verses of the chapter deal with that unmerited favour of God which has already been bestowed upon us, redeeming us from all of these sinful tendencies, and enabling us to live to His glory.

In the three verses 11-13 there is a summarisation of the Gospel as it applies to the past, present, and future of the Christian life.

THE PAST. " For the grace of God that bringeth salvation *hath* appeared to all men." This is our salvation which has already been effected.

THE PRESENT. " Teaching us that, denying ungodliness and worldly lusts, we should live soberly, righteously, and godly, in this *present* world." This is our sanctification and is operative here and now.

THE FUTURE. " *Looking* for that blessed hope, and the glorious appearing of the great God and our Saviour Jesus Christ." This is our consummation, and our anticipation of the to-morrow.

Paul points out in verse 14 that the Lord gave Himself for us, and redeemed us that we might be a peculiar people. The word " peculiar " comes from the word " peculiam," and refers to that which is particularly personal. It could mean a private purse, in which personal money is kept separate from household allowances. It also refers to a locket, carried around the necks of Roman soldiers, in which they had some priceless treasure reminding them of home, as some people will carry a cutting of hair of someone they love, or a photograph, in a locket.

It is the idea of something personal and precious. The Lord has set us apart from all the people of the world to be His precious treasure.

(3) GODLINESS IN THE WORLD, or, the Believer's Conduct (Chapter iii.)

In the world we are

Subjected to Powers (iii. 1). Although the Christian is not of this world, he is in it and has an important role to play, for he is the salt of the earth. He is here in order to be a check to the corruption that abounds, and to be a witness for God. These he can never be if he becomes an isolationist. Wherever he can help the world by communicating good, he is expected so to do.

Therefore we are " to be subject to principalities and powers, to obey magistrates, to be ready to every good work."

Gentle to all men (iii. 2-3). Men may be foolish in their attitude toward spiritual things. They may be living in malice and envy, seeking only pleasure and fulfilling selfish desires, but this does not mean that we must oppose them or fight them. We must not speak evil of them. Instead, we are to be gentle toward them, gracious and patient, remembering that there was a time when we were as stupid and as deceived ; that we, too, sought our own pleasures, and were not willing to listen to any one who might have suggested otherwise. It was the love and the grace of God which wrought the transformation.

Not our works, His mercy (iii. 5). As to the blessings of salvation which belong to us, we have nothing of which to boast. We did nothing to obtain them. We are no better than the other people. " Not by works of righteousness which we have done, but according to His mercy He saved us, by the washing of regeneration, and renewing of the Holy Ghost."

Justification (iii. 6-7). This has come to us as the gift of God through Jesus Christ our Saviour. Therefore, we should be careful always to maintain good works in the world, avoiding all things that are contentious and unprofitable and tend only to strife.

The Epistle closes with a few personal comments and a final salutation, followed with what appears to be Paul's signature : " Grace be with you all. Amen." Every Epistle written by Paul ends with the word " Grace " in the benediction. The same word is missing in each of the General Epistles. It is found at the conclusion of the Epistle to the Hebrews, which might be an indication of Pauline authorship.

PHILEMON

THE RUNAWAY SLAVE

" Let as many servants as are under the yoke count their own masters worthy of all honour, that the Name of God and His doctrine be not blasphemed. And they that have believing masters, let them not despise them, because they are brethren; but rather do them service, because they are faithful and beloved, partakers of the benefit. These things teach and exhort " (1 TIMOTHY vi. 1-2)

INTRODUCTION

The Epistles of Paul to the Colossians and Philemon are very closely related, for they were written at the same time by the same person. Both were carried by the same person to the same destination. All of this is learned from the footnotes at the end of the two Epistles.

The difference between the two Epistles is that the first was a general letter addressed to the Church at Colosse, which met in the house of Philemon and of which he was a member, and the other was a private letter written personally to Philemon.

This Epistle is the only private letter coming from the pen of Paul of which there is any record. That does not mean that it was the only letter of this nature which Paul ever wrote. It is known that he was a great letter writer. Most of the letters would have served their purpose, and then have been destroyed.

Letter writing is a great ministry in which many people could engage, especially those who are conscious that they have no public ministry. A letter of congratulation, of encouragement, or of sympathy, and also letters of guidance, counsel, or warning, can bring much blessing, but beware of the letter of criticism which can be so damaging.

This letter of the Apostle is a masterpiece. It has been considered " a model of tact and delicacy." Luther called it " a charming and masterly example of Christian love." Alexander McLaren said : " I do not know that anywhere else in literature one can find such a gem, so admirably adapted for the purpose on hand."

The background of the letter is that of a slave who, having stolen some of his master's property, fled to Rome. There, coming under the influence of Paul's ministry, he was gloriously saved. As a Christian he was sent back to his master to make good the wrong he had done, but, lest there should be any doubt on the part of the master as to the genuineness of the conversion, Paul wrote a letter of explanation with an appeal for the slave's reinstatement — and this is the letter.

Three characters are interwoven into the episode.

Philemon — the Master.

Onesimus — the Runaway Slave.

Paul — the Prisoner.

THE MESSAGE

(1) *Paul — the Prisoner.* In his introduction Paul does not refer to himself as an apostle but as a prisoner of Jesus Christ. It has already been pointed out that Paul made various introductions according to the nature of the circumstances in which he wrote. In this Epistle he was writing on behalf of a slave. He was seeking mercy for him, so he reminded the recipient that he himself was a prisoner and, therefore, able to speak on behalf of a prisoner. Paul became all things to all men that he might win some.

It is of importance to notice that, throughout Paul's ministry, he was not only interested in the salvation of sinners but also concerned for the development of the new life — the consecration of the saint. Too many men to-day are only evangelistic in desire. They seek the salvation of the lost and work for the increase of their church membership but, to them, it is the beginning and the end. The saints are not nurtured. They are not built up in their most holy faith. Socials are held to keep them coming to church, but there is little Bible study or spiritual development which will enable converts to become conquerors, and saints to become soldiers, so that every Christian might be an asset and not a liability.

(2) *Philemon — the Master.* This is the person to whom the letter was addressed. He was a man of standing who lived at Colosse. He had become a convert to the Christian faith through the ministry of Paul. As Paul had never visited Colosse, it is considered that he must have met the Apostle elsewhere, possibly at Ephesus, as it was not far distant, and Paul had ministered in that city for three years.

The whole family of Philemon was evidently Christian because, not only does Paul salute Philemon as a fellow-labourer, but he includes Apphia, who is recognised as Philemon's wife, and also Archippus, who is acknowledged by tradition to be their son. He is called a fellow soldier, and a soldier is one who fights, so he was a man prepared to "contend for the faith once delivered." According to the letter to Colosse, Archippus had a ministry in the Church (Colossians iv. 17).

There was a number of other Christians in this town, so that a Church was formed and it met in the home of Philemon. When a man opens his heart to the Gospel, he often opens his house and his pocket to the Lord.

From these things it is learned that Philemon was a man of means and of influence. Moreover, he possessed slaves. How many is not indicated, but it was one of those slaves who caused the letter to be written.

In the days of the early Church it was common for men to have slaves, and it was not considered to be wrong. Paul never reproved Philemon, nor anyone else, for possessing slaves. In fact, he would have kept Onesimus, because he could have been useful to him. He only declined because he was the property of another man, purchased with money.

One is not seeking to justify slavery — it is positively wrong. The Church has come a long way since those days.

The Apostle, in his introduction, commends this family for their devotion to the Lord, and for their ministry to the saints of God. In verses 8 and 9 the Apostle is again speaking of himself. He is making a very tactful approach as he moves toward the purpose of his letter. His boldness is because of his love for the Lord. His approach is not a matter of duty but one of love for his fellow-man, and his authority none other than the fact that he was an old man seeking to advise or guide a young man, and a prisoner who himself had suffered and was suffering whilst others enjoyed their freedom. "I beseech thee for my son" (vs. 10).

(3) *Onesimus — the Runaway Slave.* Although he was in a Christian household, with a good master, and under the sound of the gospel as the Church met together in that house, yet he was a man who apparently stole some of his master's goods and ran away. Where is the person who declares that right environment is conducive to Christian profession! It may help, but certainly is not decisive.

Such conduct often subjected slaves to severe punishment, and masters were not always kind to their slaves.

This man fled to Rome, which would be considered a safe place. It was the metropolis of the world. Therefore, a person could soon be lost in the crowds of nationals. Here he enjoyed his freedom, on the strength of the stolen money. However, he made the same mistake as the Prodigal Son and many others have made — he forgot that money has a way of disappearing!

What happened to Onesimus in the city is not related. There are many conjectures. Some think he was arrested and cast into prison and, as a result, met Paul. Such an idea is not in harmony with what is known. Paul, during his first imprisonment, had his own hired house where people were permitted to come and go. Therefore he was not in the common ward where many a runaway slave might be cast. If Onesimus had been a prisoner he would not have had the liberty to go to Paul.

Two things could have happened. Firstly, this man could have met Paul accidentally. Secondly, like the Prodigal, he had spent all and had come to an end of himself. What should he do? Where could he go? Who could help him now in his dire need? Whilst in Rome it was possible that he had heard of Paul, and now would remember that he had heard a great deal about him when he was back in Colosse. Paul was a friend of his master. The family often spoke about him, and so did all of the people who attended Church there. Paul was a valued friend to all of them. Everyone spoke kindly about him, and no one said anything against him. He had helped them, so could Paul help him? Would he help? At least he could go and see.

If this were so, there is no evidence as to whether Onesimus sought Paul because of a conviction, or as a matter of convenience. So many people do seek the help of the Church as a convenient way out of their own self-imposed problems. In this story the motive is not given, and it does not matter, for no one ever came into the presence of Paul without hearing the Gospel. He could bid Timothy to preach the Word in season and out of season because it was something which he himself practised.

The result of this meeting was that Onesimus was born again. He passed from death unto life. His conversion was so genuine, his change of life so obvious, and his testimony so useful, that the one-time " unprofitable " became " profitable," according to his name. Paul would have kept him as a fellow-labourer in the Gospel but for the fact that, in the eyes of the law, he was another man's property. The Christian must live honestly. Even although slavery might be wrong, the only man who has the power to release a slave is the owner.

Another beautiful picture to be seen in this incident is the wonderful grace of God. Onesimus would have heard of Christ and His salvation whilst a slave working in the home of Philemon, but he had never accepted. Instead, he had gone the opposite way and absconded as a thief, but the grace of God pursued him all the way to Rome and found him. Some people have to be brought very low before they recognise their need.

It was in Rome that the slave of man became the freeman of Christ, the servant became a brother beloved, the unprofitable became profitable, and the sinner became a saint. This is the transforming power of Calvary.

Paul was aware of the equalising power of that Gospel. It could lift the slave and humble the master. It was the Gospel which freed the bound, and bound the free. Onesimus had been saved and belonged to the world to come, but he still lived in the world that now is. His sin demanded punishment, a punishment that was cruel in those days. That sin had been confessed to God, and had been forgiven by God. It must now be confessed to man and, if possible, man's forgiveness must be obtained, and especially so in this instance, because now this master and slave have become related — they are brethren in Christ.

It would be difficult for the slave to tell this to the wronged master. It might be more difficult for the master to believe it in the circumstances of a guilty man seeking mercy. Yet something must be done for this new " son in the faith."

In these circumstances Paul wrote this particular letter, and with it another to the Church at Colosse that they should receive Onesimus into Church fellowship.

Here was a letter that needed tact and skill, a letter of courtesy and persuasiveness, of pathos and love.

Paul did not enter into the rights and wrongs of the situation. He was not concerned with the past, only the present. He was writing on behalf of a brother, and Christian relationship rises above social standing. It is here, in Christ Jesus, that master and servant, bond and free, rich and poor, learned and unlearned, become one.

What he did tell Philemon was that the Lord has a wonderful way of turning losses into gain, and of making our disappointments to become His appointments. It is not the same Onesimus who is being sent back. It is a better one. The departure was temporary, just for a season, but receiving him back would be permanent, not now as a servant but above a servant, a brother beloved. Is it not true that " whosoever will lose his life for My sake shall find it " ? (Matthew xvi. 25).

When we were unprofitable to the Lord and dead in sin, He had mercy on us and, because we have been the recipients of His grace, we must learn to be gracious.

The letter, in its conclusion,

> Reasons for grace on the part of Philemon.
>
> Rests with confidence in the character of Onesimus.
>
> Reveals full confession and repentance on the part of Onesimus.
>
> Requests that the debt should be put to Paul's account.
>
> Requires that Onesimus should be received as graciously as they would receive Paul himself.
>
> Reminds Philemon that all are in debt, each to the other.
>
> **Reserves accommodations with Philemon for a future visit.**

The statement in verse 18: "If he hath wronged thee, or oweth thee aught, put that on mine account," is beautifully rendered by Scofield as: "Reckon to him my merit, reckon to me his demerit." That is exactly what the Lord has done for us.

Onesimus carried this letter back to his master. One wonders sometimes whether there were any misgivings on the part of this man as to the effectiveness of the letter and the reactions of his master. Paul made provision for this. The law required that everything should be established in the mouth of two or three witnesses. Therefore, he sent with Onesimus a companion, Tychicus, who carried the letter to the Church. This is gleaned from the footnote at the end of the Epistle to the Colossians, as well as the statement Paul made in that letter : " All my state shall Tychicus declare unto you, who is a beloved brother, and a faithful minister and fellow-servant in the Lord : Whom I have sent unto you for the same purpose, that he might know your estate, and comfort your hearts : With Onesimus a faithful and beloved brother, who is one of you . . . " (Colossians iv. 7-9).

Onesimus returned, resting in his two companions in travel — the precious document and the faithful Tychicus.

As to the results, nothing is stated because this is a letter and not a historical record.

Did Philemon receive his servant back again ? Did he restore him or promote him ? No one has any misgivings about it. We believe that such a letter as this could not have been unfruitful.

Tradition has it that Onesimus became a diligent servant of the Church, but that be as it may. The letter is placed within the sacred record for our admonition and profit.

Man, who was created in the likeness of God and made that God might have fellowship with him, has robbed God and run away.

God required of man obedience, loyalty, and worship. Instead, man has disobeyed the Lord, robbed God of loyalty and worship, despised His Word, rejected His Day, and fled to the world, selfishly to enjoy himself, spending the health, the time, and every other thing on which God has a claim, in his own pleasure.

Into that world God sent His only begotten Son, and many of us have met with Jesus and have learned the truth of our lost estate. We have been made aware that the pleasures of sin are only for a season. As a result, we have repented of those sins, and have been made desirous of returning to God. Our journey is a homeward one. We have an assurance that God will accept us at the end because the Lord has given us a letter. It is His Holy Word, the Bible. Not only so, but He has given to us a companion in travel, the Holy Spirit. " But when the Comforter is come, Whom I will send unto you from the Father, even the Spirit of truth, which proceedeth from the Father, He shall testify of Me " (John xv. 26).

As to our future, much is still veiled from human eyes which will be enjoyed in the day of His Revelation, when all will be Yea and Amen in Christ Jesus the Lord.

HEBREWS

FROM SHADOW TO SUBSTANCE

"Now all these things happened unto them for ensamples: and they are written for our admonition, upon whom the ends of the world are come" (1 CORINTHIANS x. 11)

"For the vision is yet for an appointed time, but at the end it shall speak, and not lie: though it tarry, wait for it; because it will surely come, and will not tarry" (HABAKKUK ii. 3)

INTRODUCTION

The Author. This must be considered because of the amount of reasoning and the differences of opinion that exist. The negative side can be left. Just two reasons why one accepts Paul as the penman of the Holy Spirit. Firstly, every Epistle which has the name of Paul attached to it ends with grace. All of the other Epistles end differently. Hebrews closes with " Grace be with you all. Amen."

Secondly, all of Paul's letters were written to the Church, except this one which was written to the Hebrews. To some people this makes it to be non-Pauline, but Scripture must be compared with Scripture. When it is, then it will be discovered that, when Peter wrote to these same Hebrews, he said : " And account that the longsuffering of our Lord is salvation ; even as our beloved brother Paul also according to the wisdom given unto him hath written unto you ; as also in all his epistles, speaking in them of these things ; in which are some things hard to be understood, which they that are unlearned and unstable wrest, as they do also the other Scriptures, unto their own destruction " (2 Peter iii. 15-16). When did Paul write to the Hebrews ? From the Acts of the Apostles and from Paul's Epistles it will be seen that, whilst the Gentiles received Paul graciously and with open arms, the Jews never did. They were ever sceptical, often hostile. His Apostleship they doubted, and his opposition to Moses and the Law they feared. Therefore, in writing to those whom he longed to win, one can see the advisability of keeping his name out of the narrative.

The author reasons from the Old to the New in unsurpassed skill.

THE BOOK

Hebrews has readily been called the commentary of Leviticus, as Leviticus has been known as the commentary of Hebrews. Whilst this is true, yet it is more, for the author does not limit himself to Leviticus for his types. He goes back beyond Moses to Melchisedec, to Abraham, to angels, and to Eternal Sonship.

The message seems to have been written to Christians who had come out from Judaism but, for some reason, were not progressing in their Christian faith. This can be appreciated to some extent. The Jews were deeply established in their faith and their traditions. It had been no easy move for them to leave a faith which they understood was God-given and accept another faith which was also claimed to be of God. Their enthusiasm would be curbed by a desire to accept the new, and yet hang on to the old. This would tend toward half-heartedness which, in turn, would bring neglect, which also would lead into a condition of backsliding. Thus it was that such expressions as these are found in the book : " How shall we escape if we neglect so great salvation ? ", and " ye are become such as have need of milk, and not of strong meat," and " refusing Him Who speaks from heaven." In this connection it may be possible to find an answer to the problem of Hebrews vi. 4-6, which will be handled later.

As these Jewish Christians sought to keep their Christianity and, at the same time, reach back into their Judaism, thus hindering progress, so to-day many people want to enjoy the blessings of Christian life and also reach back for some of the old life of carnalism. The result is a tendency to backsliding. The message of the book, therefore, is very timely.

THE MESSAGE

The purpose of the book is to reveal the glories of the Christian faith and the transcendency of Christ, until the old life fades into nothingness by comparison. The subject of the book is Faith, and the keyword is " Better."

There are several ways in which the book may be divided. The analysis chosen for this treatise is

(1) THE FOUNDATION OF FAITH, which is that of Doctrine (Chapters i. 1 - x. 18)

(2) THE FRUITFULNESS OF FAITH, which is the practical application (Chapters x. 19 - xii. 29)

(3) A CONCLUSION (Chapter xiii.)

The keyword, "Better,' is found thirteen times in the book, and can be summarised thus : —

Although these are the actual occurrences of the word " better ", there are many more in principle.

(1)   THE FOUNDATION OF FAITH (Chapters i. - x.)

(a)   *Christ's Pre-eminence* (Chapters i. - iv.).   The approach made by the author is a technique which it might be as well to follow. He commences with a subject acceptable to all concerned — GOD. The authority of Christ was a question with some, whilst with others the matter of religion caused a division of opinion. These were the concern of the Apostle in this book. It is always policy to begin at a point of agreement. God has revealed Himself twice to mankind — through the patriarchs and the prophets — but, later, there was a greater manifestation in the Person of His only begotten Son. This was the Messiah rejected by the Jews, and the Jesus refused by the Gentiles. The foundation, the faith, and the future of the Church were in Him. Therefore His pre-eminence must be established and His authority accepted.

Firstly, as to His eternal existence, God hath appointed Him Heir of all things. He shared in the creation of the world. He was the express image of God. By His Word were all things maintained. All this means He was with God — He was God. He was before all things because He created all things. This same Jesus at the Cross became the Redeemer of man and, afterward, the Intercessor for man as He sat down on the right hand of the Majesty on high. This is Deity.

Secondly, a comparison is drawn between Jesus, the uncreated One, and a number of created beings, each of whom had a pre-eminence in their own realm, but Jesus is pre-eminent over them all. He was

Compared with Angels, and His superiority was manifested in that

They were created	.....	He was begotten
They were servants	.....	He was a Son
They were worshippers	.....	He was worshipped
They were ministers	.....	He was a Monarch

If Christ be above the angels, and they are His servants, then man should take heed to the things that were spoken by Christ.

Compared with Men. The Apostle proceeds to show that man is just a little lower than the angels, and yet higher than the angels, for angels are ministering spirits. They serve God and they serve man. " Are they not all ministering spirits, sent forth to minister for them who shall be heirs of salvation ? " (i. 14). To none of these will the Lord say : " Sit on My right hand ", but this is to be the reward of men — that is, men who, through faith, have become the sons of God.

" But we see Jesus Who was made a little lower than the angels for the suffering of death, crowned with glory and honour . . . " (ii. 9). There were two reasons why Jesus " took not on Him the nature of angels." The first was " for the suffering of death." Angels are not mortal, but men are. Secondly, " Wherefore in all things it behoved Him to be made like unto His brethren, that He might be a merciful and faithful High Priest . . . " (ii. 17), or, an Intercessor.

Having revealed that Jesus came into the realm of the human so that He might bring Divine Life into human life, the Apostle then proceeds to make known that, whilst Jesus was made lower than the angels, yet He was greater than man. In this connection he lines up for comparison the men who, for their work's sake, were most highly esteemed by the Jews. The first was

MOSES (Chapter iii.). Moses was their Law-giver. He was their deliverer and leader. He brought them out from the bondage of Egypt and led them for forty years toward the Promised Land. They revered the name of Moses. The reasoning used here is that he was only a servant, but a faithful servant who was doing the will of God. " This Man " is worthy of more honour than Moses because He is a Son, and Master over His own house.

Concerning Moses as a leader, the people had continually murmured against him. They had rebelled and hardened their hearts, provoking the anger of God. The author of the Epistle is warning this present generation not to harden their hearts against the Lord and thereby bring upon themselves similar tragedies. The people whom Moses led entered into their rest. " Let us labour therefore to enter into that rest, lest any man fall after the same example of unbelief. For the Word of God is quick (alive), and powerful, and sharper than any two-edged sword, piercing even to the dividing asunder of soul and spirit, and of the joints and marrow, and is a discerner of the thoughts and intents of the heart " (iv. 11-12).

In moving on to the next men, there is also a moving on into another of the attributes of the Lord.

(b) *The Priesthood of Christ* (Chapters v. - x.). The introduction to this subject is from verses 14 to 16 of chapter iv. : " Seeing then that we have a Great High Priest, that is passed into the heavens, Jesus the Son of God, let us hold fast our profession. For we have not an High Priest which cannot be touched with the feeling of our infirmities ; but was in all points tempted like as we are, yet without sin. Let us therefore come boldly unto the throne of grace, that we may obtain mercy, and find grace to help in time of need."

Leaving the Priesthood of Christ for the moment, attention is drawn to

AARON, and the Aaronic priesthood established in the book of Exodus where, in chapters xxviii. and xxix., Aaron was called, cleansed, clothed, and consecrated. This priesthood had been questioned in Numbers chapter xvi., but qualified in chapter xvii., since when there had never been further questioning concerning that priesthood.

One great fault weakened the Aaronic priesthood — it was ever changing, the cause of the changes being that men were not able to continue by reason of death. One priest might be kind and understanding, the next hard and indifferent.

One of the Jewish historians informs us that between Aaron, the first, and Caiaphas, the last, some eighty men held the position.

There was no self-election in this priesthood. It was hereditary, and the calling was of God. Jesus, in His priestly ministry, was also called of God. However, Jesus did not inherit His office from Aaron. In fact, He could never be a priest of this changing

order because He was not a Levite. Jesus was born of the tribe
of Judah from whence no priests could come. Therefore, the
Apostle took a step back to another priesthood, and declared that
Jesus was greater than

MELCHISEDEC. An introduction is made to him who was the
priest of the Most High God, and who appeared to Abraham on
his return from the battle with Chedorlaomer. This priesthood
was an unchanging one. It is enlarged upon in chapter vii.

As to the statement in verse 3 of that chapter, an explanation
is needed. The verse is : " Without father, without mother, without descent, having neither beginning of days, nor end of life ;
but made like unto the Son of God ; abideth a priest continually."

The problem is — how can a person be without parentage,
and how can there be an existence without a beginning and an
end ?

Firstly, it must be observed that this statement is in the book
of Hebrews, but is not found in the book of Genesis. In Genesis,
where there is a record of history, every statement is historical
and logical, but Hebrews is not history. It is doctrine built upon
history.

In the records of births and deaths, the name of this king of
Salem cannot be found. If his birth were not registered, then, of
course, the names of his parents could not appear. In this case
the question would be, if his parents were not known, then it is
not known from whom he received his priesthood, and if there
is no record of his death, then there is no record as to who inherited his priesthood. From what is known, he received his
priesthood from no one and passed it on to no one. Therefore,
he stands as a priest of an endless order. Melchisedec lived before
the time of Jew or Gentile. Therefore, if Christ is of the Melchisedec order, He has an endless priesthood and a universal priesthood which belongs to Jew and Gentile alike if they are in Christ
Jesus. Thus this Jesus was greater than Aaron.

Before proceeding further with the subject of priesthood, it
is necessary to return to these verses again for they are exceedingly
important ones.

In chapter v., verse 11 onwards, these saints were warned,
yea, reproved, because they were not in a position to enter into
the truth which was now brought to them. The Aaronic priesthood
they could appreciate, but the Melchisedec priesthood they could
not because they were dull of hearing. The difference between
the two priesthoods in question might be that the Aaronic order

was earthly, Aaron and his successors stood on earth with men and interceded with God, but in the Melchisedec order Christ was seated in heaven, interceding for believers. Many people can and do accept the message of the Gospel so far as salvation is concerned, but their salvation ofttimes amounts to no more than that *from which* they have been saved. There is little appreciation as *to what* they have been saved. Are we not making a big mistake in our preaching to-day by making known the Saviour-hood of Christ without the Lordship of Christ? Do not the Scriptures declare Him to be Lord and Saviour? To ask people to receive the gift of salvation without accepting the Giver of salvation is creating the unhealthy atmosphere in the Church of salvation without sanctification. This leads to a form of godliness which denies the power thereof. Christianity is a life, and where there is life there cannot be stagnation. Lack of growth means early death. In life the babe must develop into childhood, and childhood must progress to manhood. "When I became a man, I put away childish things . . . " (1 Corinthians xiii. 11).

The complaint in these verses is that of no growth. One has to impart the things learned because the time must come when Christians become teachers as well as learners. When we are babes we need milk and have to be spoon-fed because we have not the skill or the ability to feed ourselves, but the day must come when the milk gives way to solid food — likewise for spiritual growth.

The elementary things of the Word of God belong only to the young convert, the babe in Christ. The Church is not a nursery for babies. That may be the function of the Sunday school. The Church is an armoury for training soldiers. It is a school for instructing saints.

The greatest weakness of the Church, and of Christendom, is the appalling ignorance of the Word of God, which has created a shallowness that has almost left the Church stripped of spirituality and caused it to become not much more than a social institution.

There is one solution to this condition, and that is growth. "Therefore leaving the principles of the doctrine of Christ, let us go on unto perfection . . . " (vi. 1), which means, leaving behind the first principles of our salvation, there must be a building up of the fuller and deeper life in the Lord. As to the people to whom this letter was addressed, it would mean leaving the early truths, as taught in the Old Testament, for the fulness of the New Testament life.

The next statement conveys the same thought : " Not laying again the foundation of repentance from dead works (old formalities), and of faith toward God. Of the doctrine of baptisms, and of laying on of hands, and of the resurrection of the dead, and of eternal judgment " (vi. 1-2). All this has been accepted. A builder does not keep working on his foundations. Having truly laid them, he commences to erect his structure. So with the saint, having accepted the Gospel, he must then build Christian character. Unless this is done there will necessarily be a falling back. Look at nature. Should there be no continual cultivation, there will be a return to the wild nature. The high grade apple tree can return to the crab apple, the beautiful prize rose can go back to the briar.

Even so is it in the spiritual life. To come into the light of truth, to taste the fruit of salvation, to learn of the power of the Holy Ghost, to prove the Word of God, to know that there is a future life, and contentedly to leave it all there, is a dangerous situation because, as surely as nature abhors a vacuum, so surely does it resist stagnation. When there is not a going on unto perfection, then there is a falling back in depreciation. This is what is commonly called backsliding. The truth is solemn, but that is all the more reason why it should be faced. Profession will get a man nowhere. Such a man, who has been satisfied with a head knowledge of all these things, because they never brought him complete satisfaction, if he falls away he is hard to win back — in fact, it is almost impossible to bring him to a place of true repentance. Knowing the truth without growing in the truth brings the Lord into an open shame.

That such conditions can exist is established in the next verses, 7 and 8.

The earth can receive the same rain and the same gracious showers, and yet one field can produce herbs and another thorns and briars. The difference between the two is cultivation or non-cultivation.

From warning, the theme changes to encouragement. "But, beloved, we are persuaded better things of you . . . " (vi. 9). If man will not yield to indolence but will press on in the Spirit, although life will have its problems, he may be assured that the God Who has promised is the God Who is able and faithful. God, Who made promises to Abraham under oath, will not allow things to fail which He has promised us. Therefore, we look not at the things which *are* but at those which are *to be*. That is the hope which is like an anchor. When the storm rages, the ship can drop anchor. The waves on top may be boisterous, but the rocks at the bottom are steadfast. They cannot be seen, but the anchor lays hold of them and the ship can ride out the storm. Likewise with the saint, the anchor is made secure within the veil where Christ is, as our great Intercessor and High Priest. With faith made sure, and the soul in His keeping, we may be more than conquerors.

Still laying the foundation of our faith, the next two chapters (viii. and ix.) summarise that which has already been related concerning the priesthood and, at the same time, they move away from personalities, whom the Jews had respected, and whose lives and ministries were but shadows of the greater ministry of Christ, to types, of which Christ was greater.

The High Priest of Israel ministered in the Tabernacle. The Great High Priest intercedes in the true tabernacle of heaven. The High Priest offered gifts and sacrifices according to the Law. Jesus gave Himself an offering for sin, once for all. The Priest of Israel entered into the Holy of Holies once a year on the Day of Atonement. Our Great High Priest has entered the heavenly sanctuary, a Priest for ever. The High Priest of the Old Testament never finished, but we have such an High Priest Who, having finished the work God gave Him to do, ascended on high and sat down, so that it can be said : " Now of the things which we have spoken this is the sum : We have an High Priest, Who is set on the right hand of the throne of the Majesty in the heavens " (viii. 1). There He sits as a Mediator of a better covenant.

The old covenant was full of ordinances, none of which made the offerer or the observer to be perfect, and none of which could remove sin. Therefore it was at fault. This made it necessary to bring in a New Covenant, one that would meet man's need, not temporarily, but permanently and completely. The establishment of this New Covenant, plus the fact that Jesus was the One Who would mediate it, caused that the old one must vanish away.

This old covenant embraced the Tabernacle, a temporary and worldly sanctuary which met the need of man whilst he was a pilgrim in the wilderness, but was later superseded by the Temple when the people became permanent residents in their own land.

Every detail of that Tabernacle and every function in its ordinances were types. The full significance of this subject is found in the book of Exodus.*

---

* See author's book *Made According to Pattern*.

One difference in detail should be explained. In Exodus it is stated that a golden candlestick, a table of shewbread, and a golden altar, made the furniture of the Holy Place, whilst the Ark of the Covenant had the sole occupancy of the Holy of Holies. Here in Hebrews ix. 3-4 it is stated that " After the second veil, the Tabernacle which is called the Holiest of all: Which had the golden censer, and the ark of the covenant overlaid round about with gold." Was the golden altar outside the veil, or the censer (golden altar) inside ? To understand a difference of this kind, it must be remembered that the book of Exodus is history and the book of Hebrews is doctrine. History is a record of facts, so what Exodus says must be accepted. The golden altar was outside.

A further explanation is that between Exodus and Hebrews stands a Cross, and that Cross, or the work that was accomplished upon it, was revolutionary. Reading verse 8 of the ninth chapter, one is informed : " The Holy Ghost this signifying, that the way into the holiest of all was not yet made manifest, while as the first tabernacle was yet standing : Which was a figure for the time then present." Whilst the Tabernacle stood, representing the old economy, the High Priest ministered outside, but when Christ died the veil of the Temple was rent in twain, and He opened a new and living way whereby we have access unto the Father. No longer is an earthly priest needed but, with a censer in hand, we can enter right into His immediate presence and make our own requests.

The Tabernacle was but a type. Jesus has entered the heavenly tabernacle. He has carried within a better Blood. The blood of animals only sanctified the flesh, and had to be offered repeatedly because the flesh continued to sin, but the Blood of Christ, through the eternal Spirit, has purged our consciences from dead works to serve the living God.

These two chapters can be summed up thus. The crucified, resurrected and ascended Lord has given to His people a *better hope*, that has been made by a *better covenant*, which has been based upon *better promises*, because of a *better sacrifice*.

In the closing verses of chapter ix., the Lord's ministry is expanded to its fullest capacity as the three tenses of time are used, and a threefold attribute is declared.

(1) " For then must he often have suffered since the foundation of the world : but now once in the end of the world (age) *hath He appeared* to put away sin by the sacrifice of Himself " (ix. 26).

This declares that in the PAST He appeared as the PROPHET for man's SALVATION.

(2) " For Christ is not entered into the Holy places made with hands, which are the figures of the true ; but into heaven itself, *now to appear* in the presence of God for us " (ix. 24).

This verse is in the PRESENT tense and declares that the Lord is now officiating as a PRIEST for our SANCTIFICATION.

(3) " So Christ was once offered to bear the sins of many ; and unto them that look for Him *shall He appear* the second time without sin unto salvation " (ix. 28).

Christ is coming again in the near FUTURE. He will come to reign as a KING, which will be for our GLORIFICATION.

The last verse states that He Who came the first time for sin and as sin, will come the second time without sin unto salvation. In the original this is " unto the *fulness* of salvation," because salvation will not be complete until the second coming of Christ. We have already been saved from the penalty of sin, which is death. We are being saved day by day from the power of sin by His Holy Spirit. We are yet to be saved from the presence of sin when He comes to take from the world His own.

Having reasoned out, and made comparisons between, the Aaronic priesthood and the Melchisedec priesthood, in the tenth chapter the Apostle gives a picture of the completeness of this office and work.

The Law, perfect though it was, came a long way short of God's final purposes. It was only a shadow " and not the very image." The difference between these two things is considerable. An image is a recognisable thing, whether it be a photograph, a piece of sculpture, or an impression on a coin. There is always likeness, but a shadow can be long and lean, or short and stumpy, and constantly changing in its shape, according to the movement of the light or the object, so that nothing can be recognised. One cannot have shadow without substance. Therefore reality is somewhere.

These offerings of the Old Testament were continual because they were inadequate. All they did was to cover sin. They could not remove it. Jesus came and made one offering, once for all, which took man's sin and removed it for ever. Having completed that work He " sat down on the right hand of God."

As a result, the veil has been rent, and we have " boldness to enter into the holiest by the Blood of Jesus, by a new and living way, which He hath consecrated for us, through the veil (the rent veil), that is to say, His flesh " (x. 19-20).

The exhortation is to hold fast to this glorious truth because, if we despise it and wilfully push it aside for something we may consider better, we shall lose all. Then comes a warning — there is no alternative, there is no other salvation. To reject His finished work is to expose oneself to fearful judgment, from which there is no escape.

The foundation of faith being laid, the second part of the book deals with

(2) THE FRUITFULNESS OF FAITH (Chapters xi. and xii.)

This is moving from " carnal ordinances imposed on them until the time of reformation " (ix. 10), and from the things seen and legal ceremonies, " to the things not seen, eternal in the heavens." It is moving from form to faith. It is the entrance of the new and living way which had been opened by His Blood. It is drawing near with a full assurance of faith.

The author reminds his readers that all the saints of the past came through great trials and with great confidence; through faith we must do the same. The prophet Habakkuk had declared it, he must repeat it, and so must we in our generation — "The just shall live by faith."

A definition of faith is given as the great Faith chapter opens (xi.). " Now faith is the substance of things hoped for, the evidence of things not seen." Faith is the substance, or ground, or confidence, of things hoped for. What is hope ? " For we are saved by hope ; but hope that is seen is not hope ; for what a man seeth, why doth he yet hope for ? But if we hope for that we see not, then do we with patience wait for it " (Romans viii. 24/25). Faith, then, is a natural principle of the mind, not an act. All men exercise faith, for apart from it we cannot live a natural life.

" Through faith we understand " (xi. 3). The maxim of the world is " seeing is believing." That is reversed in the spiritual realm. There it is " believing is seeing." Jesus said to Martha : " If thou wouldest *believe* thou shouldest *see* the glory of God " (John xi. 40).

The chapter is known as Faith's Picture Gallery. Wonderful portraits and glorious scenes hang upon its walls, which are worthy of hours of meditation. Here only the catalogue of the titles can be given.

By faith the elders obtained a good report.
Through faith all Christians accept the creation record.
By faith Abel offered unto God.
By faith Enoch was translated.
By faith we believe in the existence of God.
By faith Noah built an ark.
By faith Abram went out.
Through faith Sarah conceived.
By faith Abram offered up Isaac.
By faith Isaac blessed Jacob and Esau.
By faith Jacob blessed his sons.
By faith Joseph requested his burial place.
By faith Jochebed hid Moses.
By faith Moses refused royal privileges.
By faith Moses forsook Egypt.
Through faith Moses kept the Passover.
By faith Israel crossed the Red Sea.
By faith Jericho was taken.
By faith Rahab found deliverance.
By faith the Judges ruled Israel.
Through faith saints endured sufferings.

" And these all, having obtained a good report through faith, received not the promise : God having provided some better thing for us, that they without us should not be made perfect " (xi. 39 - 40).

If these people, who had never had the revelation of Christ Jesus the Lord, could accomplish so much through faith, and endure so much for their faith, then what should be the accomplishments of those who belong to the dispensation of Grace ! We have been caused to know the manifestation of God's love as demonstrated at Calvary. We have knowledge, revelation, and the help of the Holy Spirit, which they knew not.

The Great Race (Chapter xii.). Life is likened to a race in which the children of God become the contestants. The course is lined on either side with spectators, some are interested that we should reach the goal, and some are not. The world looks on sceptically. The angels look on wonderingly. Satan looks on anxiously, and all the saints of past ages look on encouragingly, whilst God looks on lovingly. "Wherefore seeing we also are compassed about with so great a cloud of witnesses, let us lay aside every weight (every hindrance, burden, or care), and the sin which doth so easily beset us (which would be that besetting sin of unbelief which is antagonistic to faith), and let us run with patience . . . " (xii. 1), not giving up at any stumble which may be made, or at any criticism from a hostile world, or because someone else overtakes us on some particular lap, but, rather, let us get our eyes off everything around us and cause our attention to be fixed undividedly upon the Judge Who sits at the end of the race, waiting with the reward. The Judge is the same Person Who, at the beginning, set us forward in the race. It is Jesus, the Author and Finisher of our faith.

He has already run the course of life as our example. He was surrounded by those who sought to deviate Him from the path that meant sacrifice, but He was able to endure the Cross, despise the shame, suffer the contradiction of sinners, and reach His goal, and with His help so may we.

Our race will never be as hard as His. He endured unto Blood.

The race may prove to be somewhat costly. We may weary, we may know exhaustion, we may get sore feet and stiff limbs. There may be many knocks, and blows. We may get hurt, for this is not a flat race. It is an obstacle race, with things to get through, over, and under, but, remember, God has never promised an easy road for the Christian, but He has promised grace sufficient, so He says : " My son, despise not thou the chastening of the Lord, nor faint when thou art rebuked of Him : For whom the Lord loveth He chasteneth, and scourgeth every son whom He receiveth. If ye endure chastening, God dealeth with you as with sons ; for what son is he whom the Father chasteneth not ? " (xii. 5-7).

The Great Goal. The Lord makes an appeal for steadfastness, for diligence, and for earnestness, reminding the contestants that " no chastisement for the present seemeth to be joyous, but grievous : nevertheless afterward . . . " (xii. 11). The " afterward " is the goal and the reward. " But ye are come unto Mount Sion, and unto the city of the living God, the heavenly Jerusalem, and to an innumerable company of angels. To the general assembly and church of the firstborn, which are written in heaven, and to God the Judge of all, and to the spirits of just men made perfect. And to Jesus the Mediator of the New Covenant, and to the Blood of sprinkling, that speaketh better things than that of Abel " (xii. 22-24).

The chapter ends with a warning.

CONCLUSION (Chapter xiii.)

A number of admonitions bring the great Epistle to a close. These include

The continuance of brotherly love	..... verse	1
An encouragement to hospitality	..... verse	2
A statement of chastity	..... verse	4
A promise of His unfailing supply	..... verse	5
A reminder of His changelessness	..... verse	8
A warning against strange doctrines	..... verse	9
A call to identify ourselves with the Lord in His reproach	..... verses	10-13
A command to submit ourselves to rulers	verse	17

Then there is a benediction : " Now the God of peace, that brought again from the dead our Lord Jesus, that great Shepherd of the sheep, through the Blood of the everlasting covenant, make you perfect in every good work to do His will, working in you that which is well-pleasing in His sight, through Jesus Christ, to Whom be glory for ever and ever. Amen " (xii. 20-21).

JAMES

FAITH AND WORKS

*" Knowing that a man is not justified by the works of the law,
but by the faith of Jesus Christ, even we have believed in
Jesus Christ, that we might be justified by the faith of Christ,
and not by the works of the law ; for by the works of the
law shall no flesh be justified"* (GALATIANS ii. 16).

INTRODUCTION

This Epistle is the first of what are known as General
Epistles. It was written by James, two others were written by
Peter, three by John, and one by Jude. James was the " brother "
of the Lord, inasmuch as he was a son of Mary (Galatians i. 19).
He was also called " James the Just." He was an apostle and
held a very prominent position in the early Church. Paul at one
time called him a " pillar of the Church " (Galatians ii. 9). His
prominence and his ability were revealed when he controlled a very
stormy church meeting and guided it into an acceptable decision.
This is recorded in Acts xv. 6-35. Paul called on James to
convene a business meeting, in Acts xxi. 18.

In date the Epistle is older than any written by Paul. It is
thought by some to be the first Epistle written to Christians.
There are two reasons for the suggestion : —
(1) The Epistle does not make any reference to the complications
of doctrine, which arose later with Paul's ministry.
(2) Tradition holds that James was martyred in A.D. 62. This
letter was written some considerable time before that ; it is generally accepted as between A.D. 45 and 49. Most of Paul's epistles
were written between A.D. 59 and 64.

The theme of the book is Christian Ethics, rather than
Christian Doctrine. It deals with conduct rather than faith, and
declares that Faith is revealed by Works.

The early Church at that time was suffering a great deal
because of persecution. Christians, some from Judaism and some
from the Gentile nations, were being scattered abroad. James

seems to have remained at Jerusalem but, feeling that he had a responsibility toward those who had come out of Jewry, he wrote this letter, addressing it " to the twelve tribes which are scattered abroad " (i. 1).

THE MESSAGE

This book differs from most of the other books by reason of the fact that it has no particular analysis. It is more a series of admonitions. James was very conscious of the weaknesses of those Jewish people. He knew their desire for wealth, their partiality, their pride, things that are in us as well as in them. Therefore he warned them, and us, of the impending dangers, and bade men to watch the little details of everyday life.

Because of these many admonitions, it is possible to see a likeness between this book and the book of Wisdom. We have chosen, therefore, to call it " The Proverbs of the New Testament."

As the text of the book is entered, the first verse would cause a reflection on the earlier statement that James was a brother of the Lord. In his humility he does not mention this fact. There may be an honour, but certainly no merit, in having a relationship with the Lord in the bonds of the flesh, for greater is the privilege of being a servant of the Lord Jesus Christ in the Spirit than a brother in the flesh.

Entering straight into his admonitions, the first subject for consideration is

TEMPTATIONS (Chapter i.)

" My brethren, count it all joy when ye fall into divers temptations ; Knowing this, that the trying of your faith worketh patience. But let patience have her perfect work, that ye may be perfect and entire, wanting nothing " (i. 2-4).

"My brethren " is a well used expression by James. It is found fifteen times in these five chapters. For ministers to meet their fellow-Christians and talk to them as brethren, and not as subordinates, produces a far more effective ministry, because we are not lords of God's heritage but servants of Jesus Christ.

The word " temptations " in this verse means " trials," the difference between the two words being that trials are from without and temptations are from within. James makes this clear a little later when he says that a man is tempted when he is drawn away by his own lusts (i. 14).

The Apostle is not suggesting that there is joy in temptation or trial. Everyone knows differently. The joy comes from the result of the trial, for it worketh patience which, in turn, brings one into a life of victory. His reasoning is that trial is not something of which we are to be afraid, but that which we should receive manfully because, by it, character is strengthened, trust is enlivened, faith is proved, patience is developed, so that, as the oak tree is strengthened by the storm, the Christian life is developed and matured.

Peter had something similar to say in the words : " That the trial of your faith, being much more precious than of gold " (1 Peter i. 7). It is not faith but the trial of your faith that is acceptable to God.

These are the things which bring joy. If this is difficult to comprehend then we are to seek WISDOM. " If any of you lack wisdom, let him ask of God, that giveth to all men liberally, and upbraideth not ; and it shall be given him " (i. 5).

God has no desire that men should be ignorant either of Himself or of the Devil. " Blind unbelief is sure to err, and scan His works in vain." Therefore the Lord is anxious that we should be fully informed. For that reason He has given us His Word, and also the Holy Spirit, to lead us into all Truth.

The Lord is desirous that we should be as wise as serpents and as harmless as doves. God was so pleased when Solomon asked for wisdom that He granted it to him in full measure, and everything else for which he might have asked.

Christians are encouraged to make the same request, and are given the promise that wisdom will be bestowed in no small measure, and they shall never be reproved for asking. Many are the encouragements to seek wisdom. In the book of Proverbs it is declared : " Happy is the man that findeth wisdom . . . , she is more precious than rubies . . . , length of days is in her right hand ; and in her left hand riches and honour " (iii. 13-16). " Wisdom is the principal thing ; therefore get wisdom : and with all thy getting get understanding " (iv. 7).

To obtain wisdom or any other blessing which God has promised and man needs, James says : " Let him ask in faith, nothing wavering. For he that wavereth is like a wave of the sea driven with the wind and tossed " (i. 6). Having doubts is to have double interests, and such a person has no stability.

None of us is in this world for long and, if we have possessions, they will not last for long. Everything on earth is no more than a fading flower, so seek those things that are above.

Reward for Endurance. " Blessed is the man that endureth temptation : for when he is tried, he shall receive the crown of life, which the Lord hath promised to them that love Him " (i. 12).

The Apostle returns to his subject of trial, and again encourages man to endure, because trials are sent that he might not only enjoy the sense of victory in the present life but also rejoice in the reward that will be his in the life to come, for God has promised the crown of life.

God is the Source of all Good. " Every good gift and perfect gift is from above, and cometh down from the Father of lights, with Whom is no variableness, neither shadow of turning " (i. 17).

If this be true, then no evil can proceed from God and no dark shadow can fall from Him. Therefore " let no man say when he is tempted, I am tempted of God : for God cannot be tempted with evil, neither tempteth He any man " (i. 13).

God is not the Author of temptation. The Devil is the tempter, and man's evil heart is deceitful above all things and desperately wicked, and these things are the sources of sin. However, God does, in His Permissive Will, cause all things to work together for our good, so that the wrath of man can be turned into His praise, and the temptations of life used for the development of character.

With the movements and revolutions of the planetary system of sun, moon, and stars, there come shadows, but He Who created these things never changes. Therefore He cannot shine upon us in goodness to-day, and cast the shadow of trouble upon us to-morrow. However, we are capable of turning our backs upon Him, and thereby bringing ourselves into the gloom of despair.

Among the many good and perfect gifts which are bestowed upon us is the blessing of

Receiving God's Word. " . . . and receive with meekness the engrafted Word, which is able to save your souls " (i. 21). The chapter from verse 18 on deals with the Word of God. By that Word we were saved. " Of His own Will begat He us with the Word of Truth . . . " (i. 18). Through the Word we are made wise. By it we are sanctified. Until we have received it we are ignorant. The Word of God has to be engrafted. Many people can talk about religion, about the church, and even about the Bible, and sometimes they can become very boring ! Religion can be no more than the sour crab-apple. It was in the name of religion that Jesus was crucified. Many holy crusades have been carried out in the name of religion, which have brought much bloodshed.

If the Word of God be engrafted into our lives and allowed to grow, then a great transformation will take place. The beautiful fruit of His Word will be produced, religion will drop off and, instead of talking about the Church, God Himself will do the talking, making known through us the wonders of His grace.

This is not all the truth because, from receiving God's Word, we move to the place of being

Doers of God's Word. " But be ye doers of the Word, and not hearers only, deceiving your own selves " (i. 22).

There is a body of water in Palestine which is ever receiving a great volume of water, as hourly and daily the River Jordan pours itself into it, but it has no outlet. The result is that it is known as the Dead Sea. It contains 25% salt as against 4% to 6% in the oceans. Anything which receives and never gives is dead. Discharge must be equal to intake. If a warehouse had a loading dock and kept receiving from the factory but had no unloading dock on the other side to distribute to the consumer, it would soon be choked until it could not receive. Thus it is with the Christian. If we receive the Word of God and never share its blessings with other people, then we are like a man who looks hastily into the mirror and moves on to forget what he looks like. To take a hasty and casual glance at the Bible, just when it suits us, is not very useful. One has to look steadily and continuously into the Word until its Truth impresses mind and heart. Then we go forth to live it, and others with us will enjoy the blessing.

TRUE RELIGION (Chapter ii.)

This subject is introduced in chapter i., verse 27, and developed in chapter ii.

Pure Religion. " Pure religion and undefiled before God and the Father is this, To visit the fatherless and widows in their affliction, and to keep himself unspotted from the world " (i. 27).

Christianity is not a set of precepts. It is an every day practice. Too many people make the responsibility of the visitation of the sick and needy the exclusive duty of Ministers, but this verse says that it belongs to all who know anything of a pure religion.

No Partiality. " For if there come unto your assembly a man with a gold ring, in goodly apparel, and there come in also a poor man in vile raiment ; and ye have respect to him that weareth the gay clothing, and say unto him, Sit thou here in a good place ; and say to the poor, Stand thou here, or sit here under my footstool : Are ye not then partial in yourselves, and are become judges of evil thoughts ? " (ii. 2-4).

God is no respecter of persons, and the Christian should be the same ; to honour the rich and despise the poor is sin, to minister to the poor and neglect the rich in spiritual things is also sin. All men are equal in the sight of God because all men have souls for whom Christ died. It is true that some men are great and many are not, but greatness is not defined by material possessions or by social status. It is character which should differentiate. God does not separate the rich from the poor, or the learned from the unlearned. He separates the just from the unjust, the saint from the sinner, and that is character. God finds people poor in pocket but rich in faith, and uses them. Therefore we are bidden to fulfil the " Royal Law " — " Thou shalt love thy neighbour as thyself."

One offence equal to all. Lest some should consider the matter of partiality just a minor sin which could be overlooked, and only think of adultery, murder, and other major issues, as sin, James points out that sin is a transgression of the law, irrespective of its particular form, by saying : " For whosoever shall keep the whole law, and yet offend in one point, he is guilty of all " (ii.10).

Living Faith. " What doth it profit, my brethren, though a man say he hath faith, and have not works ? Can faith save him ? " (ii.14).

This is the key to the whole Epistle — Faith versus Works. Works without faith will not save, but faith without works has no evidence of salvation and is dead. James uses three illustrations:

(a) There is nothing logical, pious, or Christian, in saying to a ragged man " Be clothed," or to a hungry child " Be fed." One has to do something about it. He has to put his hand into his pocket and make the necessary provision, and then experience the resultant joy that comes, for it is more blessed to give than to receive.

(b) Abraham had to do more than believe God's ability to deliver. He was called upon to do something about it, and only by going all the way, in offering his son, learned the perfection of faith.

(c)   When Rahab hid the spies she did so at the risk of her life because, had they been found, she would have died as a traitor but, in risking her life, because she believed that the God of the Israelites would prevail, she saved it and the lives of her family when all else perished.

Thus it is with faith.   It is only as it is put into action that it produces the fruit which man can enjoy.

THE TONGUE (Chapter iii.)

The subject has not changed in this chapter.   It is still the matter of declaring our faith by our works, but the medium has changed to the tongue.

The first warning concerns the many people who love to hear their own voices, who are better at talking than in doing.   The word " master " in verse 1 is " teacher."   So many want to teach rather than learn.   Whether they have the call or the ability does not concern them.   The warning is that leadership brings with it a grave responsibility, and particularly so with the teacher, for the tongue is the most treacherous thing a man possesses.   It can bless or curse.   A slip of the tongue can do untold harm.   Hence man is told to bridle it.

The preacher in the pulpit, through his ministry, is going to help men and women nearer to God, to salvation, and to eternal verities, or he is going to confuse, deceive, and drive a soul away from God.   He can confuse a mind by lack of clarity in doctrinal issues, or deceive a man by making him believe he is saved when he is not, satisfying a soul because he is a church member but damning that same soul because he has not led him into divine sonship.

The solemnity of the power of this little member, the tongue, is painted in no uncertain way by a number of apt illustrations, in which it is declared that the tongue is the most uncontrollable and untamable thing there is.

The BIT is a small thing, but placed inside the mouth of the horse, that great creature is immediately under the control of man and is subject to obedience.

The HELM is a very small thing, and yet by it mighty liners are steered, and kept on any course the captain desires, despite the power of the waves and the force of the winds.

Yet, whilst the tongue is but a small thing, man cannot control his own life or his thoughts with it. The tongue will run riot and say the things one did not desire to say.

Only a match dropped by the wayside, only a few smouldering embers left by someone in the forest, but from what was considered an insignificant and little thing comes the forest fire, when thousands of acres of trees, which have taken generations to grow and which have a thousand potential uses for man's good, come crashing to the ground, whilst multitudes of scared animals flee in every direction for safety, but they perish in the flames.

Only a word of the tongue and someone's character is ruined. Only an unkind word and someone dies with a broken heart. The tongue is only a small member but it can break up a family, split a church, bring a business into bankruptcy, or set the world ablaze in war. Well might we pray with the Psalmist : " Guard thou the words of my lips."

Man has proved himself clever in every department of life. He can tame the beasts of the field, the birds of the air, and the fish of the sea. He can harness the powers of nature and find his way into outer space, but the tongue is beyond him.

Not only is the tongue uncontrollable, and untamable, but James moves on in his reasoning to show that it is a paradox. It is divided against itself and, therefore, has no dependability. It acts contrary to the very laws of nature. A fountain cannot bring forth sweet water and bitter at the same place. A fig tree cannot bear figs and olives, neither a vine produce grapes and figs, nor can salt water and fresh water come from the same source ; yet the tongue can bless God and curse man at the same time.

Beloved, these things ought not to be.

How often has the Word of God warned us ? Said the Lord : " . . . Swear not at all . . . " Matthew v. 34), and " Let your communication be, Yea, yea ; Nay, nay : for whatsoever is more than these cometh of evil " (Matthew v. 37). James said later : " But above all things, my brethren, swear not, neither by heaven, neither by earth, neither by any other oath : but let your yea be yea ; and your nay, nay ; lest ye fall into condemnation " (v. 12).

If there is one thing above all others which should be surrendered to the Lord for His control it is the slanderous, back-biting, gossiping, complaining, bitter tongue.

CARNALITY OR WORLDLINESS (Chapters iii. 14 - iv.)

Worldly Wisdom (Chapter iii. 15/17). In the closing verses of chapter iii. the Apostle tells of two kinds of wisdom. One comes from beneath, the other from above. The evidence is that wisdom is not acquired. Knowledge is that which comes as a result of giving oneself to diligent study. Wisdom is a gift received either from the Lord above or from the Devil beneath.

The Devil can make men wise in the wisdom of the world. Such is earthly, sensual, devilish. Dr. W. B. Riley, speaking of this wisdom, said : " Take it in science ; how much of it is earthly; how much of it is sensual ? God is not regarded. The attempt is to frame His universe without Him, to rule Him out of the world of His own creation. It is not only ' earthly ' then, but it is also ' devilish ' for that has been the desire of the Devil from the beginning."

Dr. Riley said similar things about art, with its suggestive immorality, modern music with its sentimentality, the theatre with its sensuality, schools with their rationalism, and homes with their desire for pleasure.

" But the wisdom that is from above is first pure, then peaceable, gentle, and easy to be intreated, full of mercy and good fruits, without partiality, and without hypocrisy " (iii. 17). What a contrast !

Lusts (Chapter iv. 1-4). " From whence come wars and fightings among you ? Come they not hence, even of your lusts that war in your members ? Ye lust, and have not : ye kill, and desire to have, and cannot obtain : ye fight and war, yet ye have not, because ye ask not."

In those days the word " lust " meant " a longing for possession," or " a craving after." In their longings the people resorted to crime. This is all the manifestation of the flesh. Such things are listed in the works of the flesh in Galatians v. 19-21.

This passion for fleshly things in the hearts of too many Christians is that which prevents God answering so many prayers. We ask God for things, not that His Name might be glorified, not that His Church might be blessed, not that we might be the better Christians, but that we might satisfy a carnal desire.

Pride (iv. 5/10). This is something which God resists. It is pride that is always a prelude to a fall. The Lord draws near to those who humbly draw near to Him with a consciousness of their own unworthiness. "Humble yourselves in the sight of the Lord, and He shall lift you up."

Evil Speaking (iv. 11-12). " Speak not evil one of another, brethren. He that speaketh evil of his brother, and judgeth his brother, speaketh evil of the law, and judgeth the law : but if thou judge the law, thou art not a doer of the law, but a judge. There is one lawgiver, Who is able to save and to destroy : who art thou that judgest another ? "

This is a reminder of that evil tongue again. God alone has the right to pass judgment on the other person's conduct. Let us be concerned that our own conduct is above reproach.

Selfishness (iv. 13-17). " For that ye ought to say, If the Lord will, we shall live, and do this, or that."

All of these things have been said to believers, and all are guilty to some degree, large or small. In these particular verses most of us come a long way short of the mark. We plan for to-day, to-morrow, and next year, as though we were sure of this life. Seldom is God taken into account or His counsel sought. It might be when it concerns the church, but not in the matter of business, private affairs, vacation, and a thousand other things. James is reminding us that, seeing our times are in His hands and that in Him we live and move and have our being, we are ever dependent upon Divine power. Nothing should be planned apart from God. Therefore all things should be " If the Lord will."

Having been thus reminded of the rights and wrongs of Christian living, he ends the chapter with these heart-searching words : " Therefore to him that knoweth to do good, and doeth it not, to him it is sin."

CONDUCT (Chapter v.)

Injustice (v. 1-6). From the prophets of the Old Testament there have come many revelations of the cruel way in which the rich oppressed the poor. They withheld wages, they sold them and their children. The prophets were not the only voices raised against such violence. The Lord Himself ofttimes spoke in defence of the poor.

For some reason man has always had a great love for money. Gold has become his god, causing him to become selfish and mean. To such James writes : " Go to now, ye rich men, weep and howl for your miseries that shall come upon you. Your riches are corrupted, and your garments are moth-eaten. Your gold and silver is cankered ; and the rust of them shall be a witness against you . . . Behold, the hire of the labourers who have reaped down your fields, which is of you kept back by fraud, crieth : and the cries of them which have reaped are entered into the ears of the Lord of sabaoth."

The Christian to-day is not always the honest man he should be. Paul said : " Render therefore to all their dues : . . . Owe no man anything . . . " (Romans xiii. 7-8), and Solomon wrote in the Proverbs : " Withhold not good from them to whom it is due, when it is in the power of thine hand to do it. Say not unto thy neighbour, Go, and come again, and to-morrow I will give ; when thou hast it by thee " (iii. 27-28).

As a Bible Teacher spending many years travelling Britain and the United States, the author has known churches which have taken a love-offering as a remuneration for the preacher and, although the people have given on that understanding, the whole offering has not been passed on to the preacher. In one instance, some of the money was drafted into a building fund, and often the cheque has arrived two or three weeks later. In the meantime one has struggled to pay travelling expenses to the next place, and has had to eat meagrely on the road.

If such a church has not seen a resultant blessing from the Conference, then the members consider that the preacher was not so good after all, and they have failed to see that they have robbed themselves because they have displeased the Lord in their dishonesty toward the Lord's people who gave and the Lord's servant who is worthy of his hire.

May one be permitted to add another dishonesty of the church, particularly the American churches. An Evangelist, or Conference Speaker, is booked for certain meetings, assured that it is the Will of the Lord, and then, a few weeks before the engagement is due, is cancelled without reason, without reimbursement, without the offer of an alternative date, or another engagement elsewhere. Sometimes a reason is given which is so weak that the Lord would never be able to accept it ! The author and his wife have been in some very embarrassing situations as, for ten years, they travelled the United States, without a home. If it were the Lord's will when the engagement was made, it must still be the Lord's will when the time of its fulfilment has arrived !

Patience (v. 7-11). " Be patient therefore, brethren, unto the coming of the Lord. Behold, the husbandman waiteth for the precious fruit of the earth, and hath long patience for it, until he receive the early and latter rain. Be ye also patient : stablish your hearts : for the coming of the Lord draweth nigh."

If one is to understand these verses aright, then the word " therefore " links them with what has gone immediately before, and that was the matter of injustice. These, then, would be addressed to the Lord's " brethren " who have been wronged. He tells them to be patient, for the coming of the Lord is at hand, and when He comes wrongs will be righted.

One may have to wait a long time, but then the husbandman has to wait until the harvest for the reward of his spring labour but, when it comes, he enjoys it to the full. Those who are wronged must have the same patience and, in the meantime, must hold no grudge lest, in so doing, they, too, become condemned with those who are unjust. A reminder of some of God's servants who endured suffering and displayed patience is given as an encouragement.

The Ministry of Prayer (v. 13-18). The ministry of Divine Healing also comes within these verses and must be given honest consideration. The details in the verses are precise but they are also unique.

" Is any among you afflicted ? Let HIM PRAY." Afflictions refer to the problems, distresses, burdens, and cares of life. They are moral and material, but not necessarily physical. In these troubles a man is exhorted to pray.

" Is any merry ? Let HIM SING psalms." This is the man who is in blessing, enjoying the goodness of the Lord. He must render praise to God.

" Is any sick among you ? Let HIM CALL for the elders of the church."

Firstly, it is learned that a man can pray for himself in all matters in life except his sickness. Then he is instructed to call for the elders of the church. By this means he exercises his faith.

Secondly, when a person is sick, " let him call." That does not suggest that a pastor, elder, evangelist, or anyone else, has the right to hold a so-called healing meeting, and call the public to come out, not even the church members. Such is the practice of many Pentecostal churches, but it is a reversal of the teaching of God's Word. " For my thoughts are not your thoughts, neither are your ways My ways, saith the Lord " (Isaiah lv. 8).

Thirdly, James says : " Let him call for the *elders* of the church," not an elder, not the pastor, not an individual at all. If a group of men should lay their hands on the sick and together pray, neither the restored sufferer nor yet the elders could give the glory to any save the Lord Himself.

There is a deal of difference between what is known as faith healing and Divine Healing. A person can have faith in the waters of Lourdes, in the skill of a doctor, or in the power of a preacher. He can believe in mind over matter and accept the teaching of Christian Science. All of these things are within the realm of Faith and yet all of them could be far removed from God. In the matter of Divine Healing, there comes a recognition of the power and ability of God as prayer is offered to Him. Then there is an exercise of faith in God as the sick person is anointed with oil, knowing that there is no medical quality in the oil, or any virtue in the hands which are laid upon him. Oil in the Bible is so often a symbol of the Holy Spirit so, in obeying this command, it is understood that the anointing of the Holy Spirit is sought, remembering the words of Romans viii. 11: "But if the Spirit of Him that raised up Jesus from the dead dwell in you, He that raised up Christ from the dead shall also quicken your mortal bodies by His Spirit that dwelleth in you." So, "The prayer of faith shall save the sick, and the LORD shall raise him up."

The conditions of Divine Healing seem to be a right relationship with the Lord and with our fellow-men. If we want to be forgiven, then we must know how to forgive.

As to the matter of prayer, this is not quantity but quality — the quality of the pray-er (a righteous man), and the quality of the prayer (effectual and fervent). Elijah was a man just as we are, with the same passions, and the same weaknesses, yet his prayers prevailed with God, and so can our prayers.

Ministry of Salvation (v. 19-20), a ministry that is greater than that which concerns the physical body and its temporary ailments. " Brethren, if any of you do err from the truth, and one convert him ; Let him know, that he which converteth the sinner from the error of his way, shall save a soul from death, and shall hide a multitude of sins."

To bring a soul to Christ that he might receive salvation is one of the greatest ministries of man, because its result belongs to the life to come.

I PETER

TO A PERSECUTED CHURCH

" We are troubled on every side, yet not distressed; we are perplexed, but not in despair; persecuted, but not forsaken; cast down, but not destroyed: Always bearing about in the body the dying of the Lord Jesus, that the life also of Jesus might be made manifest in our body. For we which live are alway delivered unto death for Jesus' sake, that the life also of Jesus might be made manifest in our mortal flesh"

(2 CORINTHIANS iv. 8-11)

INTRODUCTION

Peter, who was the author of this Epistle and the one which follows, had been the impetuous disciple during the Lord's ministry, but now is known as one of the pillars of the Church. Well did the Lord say to him : " When thou art converted." Pentecost and the outpouring of the Holy Spirit had transformed that life, even as all lives are transformed when they have had real personal dealings with the Holy Spirit.

Peter, who presently was to prove himself faithful unto death, wrote this first Epistle at a time when the Christian Church was suffering tremendous persecution. The Church was only thirty-five years old. It is true that it had known opposition, suffering, and trial, from the time of its inception, but now it was facing its worst experiences in a universal persecution, organized by the reigning monarch, which gave licence to all minorities to do their worst, in addition to that which was organized.

The period is the same as that which is mentioned in the second chapter of Revelation, known as the Smyrnan Period, in which the Lord said : " And ye shall have tribulation ten days," which may have referred to ten different sources of persecution.

In most of Paul's Epistles the foe was within, in the believer's half-heartedness and his allowing of certain sins, or his failure to make full surrender, but here the Church was meeting an external foe.

Peter, in addressing himself to the " strangers," uses the word " sojourners." He is not writing to those who were strangers to the faith, but to the dispersion who had been scattered because of their faith, and who, therefore, found themselves as strangers in the various countries where they were then sojourning, throughout Pontus, Galatia, Cappadocia, Asia, and Bithynia. They were both Jews and Gentiles.

From chapter v. 13 it is gathered that the letter was written from Babylon. It is not certain whether this actually refers to the city of Babylon, or whether Rome is indicated, for Rome is often called Babylon metaphorically, as it is in the book of Revelation. Mark was there at that time, and it is known that Mark was in Rome.

At this particular period in Church history Nero was persecuting the Christians in Rome. Every night they were being burned in his garden. False charges were being laid against them as a pretext for the justification of such persecution.

This background accounts for the language of the Epistle and helps one to understand such terms as :

> " Though now for a season, if need be, ye are in heaviness through manifold temptations " (i. 6).
> " The trial of your faith " (i. 7).
> " Submit yourselves to every ordinance of man " (ii. 13).
> " If a man for conscience toward God endure grief, suffering wrongfully " (ii. 19).
> " And who is he that will harm you, if ye be followers of that which is good ? " (iii. 13).
> " But and if ye suffer for righteousness' sake, happy are ye ; and be not afraid of their terror, neither be troubled " (iii. 14).
> " They may be ashamed that falsely accuse your good conversation in Christ " (iii. 16).
> " For it is better, if the Will of God be so, that ye suffer for well doing, than for evil doing " (iii. 17).
> " Beloved, think it not strange concerning the fiery trial which is to try you, as though some strange thing happened unto you : " (iv. 12).

THE MESSAGE

The Apostle was seeking to encourage a church which was faced with persecution. The book divides into three. Chapter i. concerns the Believer's inheritance, and the next two chapters the

Christian's pilgrimage; in other words, the first chapter is the Christian's privilege, followed by the Christian's duties. Duties grow out of privileges. The book concludes with two chapters on trials.

(1) THE BELIEVER'S INHERITANCE (Chapter i.)

Although we may be strangers in our earthly relationships, we are elect of God and have a citizenship in heaven. Election and freewill are difficult for our puny minds to comprehend or harmonise, but they do not seem to clash in God's purposes and economy.

The Apostle seeks to comfort the people by diverting their thoughts from the things which were immediate to the things which were future, from the things that belonged to sense and time to those that related to the spirit and eternity. They had been begotten to a lively hope. Peter had witnessed the resurrection of his Lord, and that had continued to be the joy of his life. As a result of it, his eyes were always toward the future resurrection, as he says here: " Begotten us again unto a lively hope." Peter has often been referred to as the Apostle of hope.

The next verses state his anticipated hope of the resurrection. " To an inheritance incorruptible, and undefiled, and that fadeth not away, reserved in heaven for you who are kept by the power of God through faith unto salvation ready to be revealed in the last time " (i. 4-5). This anticipated blessing is not a reward, neither is it a wage, nor remuneration. Such things are earned or merited, but an inheritance is a free gift. One does nothing for it. Ofttimes it comes as a complete surprise to the one who inherits. An inheritance can include money, land, property, or an estate. The one which awaits the child of God includes all the riches of God, an eternal home, and the glories of heaven. Such an inheritance comes through the death of the testator, and Jesus died that we might have these things.

Our heavenly inheritance supersedes anything that could come to man on earth.

Firstly, it is incorruptible. That is not true of the things of earth. Everything wears out. Constant repair is needed to all kinds of property.

Secondly, it is undefiled. In this realm one might be left monies or properties which have been acquired by many injustices or illegal pursuits, such as gambling, dishonesty, unfair labour, or through the brewery business which has brought tragedy to many lives and homes. These are the things that are defiled.

Thirdly, it does not fade away. Death duties, inheritance taxes, spendings, and riches, have wings and take their flight! The inheritance of the Believer knows none of these things. It is eternal, pure, holy, and constantly increasing. It is not ours for immediate enjoyment, but it is the lively hope; for the present we live in the joy of anticipation. As to the full realisation, " For since the beginning of the world men have not heard, nor perceived by the ear, neither hath the eye seen, O God, beside Thee, what He hath prepared for him that waiteth for Him " (Isaiah lxiv. 4), and as to the assurance of these blessings, there is the promise that they are reserved in heaven. God has already made His will. The names are already placed beside the blessings. They are the properties of those who are kept by the power of God. There are some blessings which belong to overcomers, there are some rewards for service given, but this inheritance is the free gift of God with our salvation. Because of this we should count our present problems as light, and rejoice even in manifold temptations.

This leads into a further truth. Temptation is the atmosphere and soil in which faith grows best. Faith is not an action whereby we receive all that for which we ask. It is a condition of heart and mind which believes in the faithfulness of God in every condition of life, but especially when we do not receive the thing for which we ask. So the Apostle bade these scattered saints to rejoice in their manifold temptations knowing " That the TRIAL of your faith, being much more precious than of gold that perisheth, though it be tried with fire, might be found unto praise and honour and glory at the appearing of Jesus Christ " (i. 7).

There is a present inheritance as well as a future one. It includes our REDEMPTION. How the Old Testament prophets would have delighted to know the significance and the fulness of that salvation! They could not discern between the sufferings and the glory of Christ, and yet it was on our behalf that they ministered, but we are going to share together the blessing.

This Redemption has come to us at tremendous cost, not with silver or gold, but with the precious Blood of Christ.

Included in our present inheritance is the Word of God. By it we were brought into this new life: " Being born again, not of corruptible seed, but of incorruptible, by the Word of God, which liveth and abideth for ever " (i. 23). There is nothing in this world which is enduring. Man himself is only as the grass of the field, which is a fading thing, but the Word of the Lord endures for ever.

(2) THE CHRISTIAN'S PRIVILEGES (Chapters ii. and iii)

In the light of the infallible, incorruptible, enduring Word of God, we should watch our own words and lay aside all evil speakings with their accompanying sins and, as young babes, feed regularly on the sincere milk of the Word, that we may grow thereby. Then, when growth has taken place, the milk should be left for the meat.

Not only is the child of God nourished by Him through the Word, but he is builded into Him as a spiritual house, every member being a living stone, whilst the Lord, Who was despised and rejected by the world because He was the Stone which never fitted into their planning, is the foundation stone, corner stone, and top stone; or, He is the key stone which binds all the other stones into a wonderful solidarity, known as the Church.

As part of the Church the believers are not just ornate stones but living stones. They have a vital part in the Divine structure. " Ye are a chosen generation, a royal priesthood, an holy nation, a peculiar people . . . " (ii. 9), set apart as distinct from the world that they might show forth His praise.

The Church itself, whilst in this world, must remain separate from it in relationship. We, too, are " strangers and pilgrims " — strangers because we are away from home, and pilgrims because we are on the way home.

Whilst the Christian is not of this world, he is in it, and must be an example of holy living. Therefore, the next instructions concern his duties.

Firstly, to the State — he is expected to submit to the powers that be, to obey the laws, and show himself a worthy citizen, so that he will not give the other man any occasion to find fault. The whole is summed up in the one verse : " Honour all men. Love the brotherhood. Fear God. Honour the king " (ii. 17).

Secondly, to the employer — a man, having been engaged by one who pays him wages, as an employee he is expected by God to be submissive and obedient, performing the best service he knows, even though the employer might not be a kindly man. Jesus was wronged often but showed no retaliation, and, in so doing, set an example.

Thirdly, to marital relationship — this is in chapter iii. It has been dealt with as a subject by the Apostle Paul. It suggests a mutual understanding between husband and wife, and a recognition of the rights and privileges of each.

Before looking into the last two chapters, a beautiful picture of the Christian life upon earth might be discovered by consideration of the little word " BE ", which occurs so many times — ten in all. These have been referred to as " Be's without stings." They are " Be's " which should produce some sweetness in the Christian life to help counteract the bitterness which is to be found in the world. That has been stung by a different swarm of " Be's ", such as

" BE sure your sin will find you out" (Numbers xxxii. 23).
" BE not deceived ; God is not mocked ; " (Galatians vi. 7).
" BE ye not unequally yoked together with unbelievers " (2 Corinthians vi. 14).

The only immunity from these stings is to be in Christ Jesus.

BE'S WITHOUT STINGS

(1) *Be Sober* (i. 13 ; iv. 7 ; v. 8). " Wherefore gird up the loins of your mind, be sober, and hope to the end for the grace that is to be brought unto you at the revelation of Jesus Christ " (i. 13).

It is an easy thing for a Christian to get his eyes on the things which are around him and his mind confused with the problems of life, and so, like David, begin to ask why the ungodly prosper ; or, like Habakkuk, to ask why God's people are punished for little things, whilst the world escapes punishment for the big crimes it commits ; or, like many other people, to ask — Why this adversity ? Why that problem ? Has God forgotten ? Is God just ? These are things which Satan delights to crowd into the minds of God's children. They hinder faith and hold back Christian progress.

In the East all people wear ankle-length, loose garments. These impede rapid movement. If men were called upon to engage in some activity, such as walk, work, or war, where these garments would become a hindrance, then they picked up the loose ends, tucked them inside the girdle around their waist and tightened it up. By this means the legs were free from the knees downward, which created freedom of movement and an unhindered advance.

In the same way, when the Christian allows loose thoughts, doubts, and misgivings to flow from the mind, they become a positive hindrance to progress. It is necessary, therefore, to bring all such thoughts under a self-control. They must be girded up.

We must be sober, or disciplined, not looking at the things around us, but looking off unto Jesus, and anticipating the coming of the Lord.

Not only our thoughts but also our actions must be controlled, therefore

(2) *Be Holy* (i. 15-16). " But as He which hath called you is holy, so be ye holy in all manner of conversation ; because it is written, Be ye holy ; for I am holy."

In the whole course of daily life, in all its details as it is lived before men, the pattern of that life must be the Holiness of God. Men can only see Him in the everyday lives of His children, who are His ambassadors. It is to be remembered always that " ye are a chosen generation, a royal priesthood, an holy nation, a peculiar people." The last expression " a peculiar people " does not mean " strange " or " funny." It is the word " Peculiam " which means " a priceless treasure."

(3) *Be of one mind* (iii. 8). " Finally, be ye all of one mind, having compassion one of another . . . " Schisms have ever rent the Church. Divisions are always weakening the cause of Christ. The Apostle was reiterating a truth taught by the Lord in the Beatitudes : " Love your enemies . . . , bless them that curse you . . . " (Luke vi. 27-28). This cannot be done unless our relationship with the brethren is right. There must be unity within the Church if we are going to do anything toward winning those who are outside the Church.

If we all have the same mind, it will mean rejoicing with those who rejoice, and sorrowing with those who sorrow. It will mean that we are one in the principles of Faith, even although there may be variation in some methods of practice. There should be the same exalted opinion of Christ, Who is Lord of all, also the same dislike for sin. We are to love one another. Paul reproved the Corinthians because of the contentions that were among them (1 Corinthians i. 11), and David said : " Behold, how good and how pleasant it is for brethren to dwell together in unity ! " (Psalm cxxxiii. 1).

(4) *Be Pitiful* (iii. 8). This word means " tender-hearted." The same injunction is in Ephesians iv. 32 : " And be ye kind one to another, tenderhearted, forgiving one another, even as God for Christ's sake hath forgiven you." This is a quality of character which Jesus was ever exhibiting, being moved with compassion.

Tenderheartedness is not a symptom of weakness, as youth would desire to interpret it. In truth, it is the very reverse. The Psalmist said : "Thy gentleness hath made me great" (xviii. 35). This is a quality of character much needed by all of us. It would eliminate backbiting, slander, criticism, jealousy, and all the other damaging disaffections.

(5) *Be Courteous* (iii. 8). The meaning of this word is "court-like in manner, polite." As the children of God good manners should be natural. The little things, such as thank you, excuse me, I beg your pardon, if you do not mind, if I may, please; these make up the language of a gentleman, and Christianity should make ladies and gentlemen of all of us. There is nothing common or coarse about the things of the Lord. This should not apply only in words but also actions — the little acts of giving way, taking a back seat, respecting the aged, giving up a seat to an older person. They are little things which add up to high moral and spiritual character. They become the oil which makes everything run smoothly, the lubrication that takes away the friction.

(6) *Be Imitators* (iii. 13). "And who is he that will harm you, if ye be followers of that which is good ? " (or, the Good One). Paul said : "Be ye followers of me even as I am of Christ" (1 Corinthians xi. 1). There are three different ways in which to copy someone else — to mimic, to ape, or to imitate.

A parrot will mimic. It will repeat what it hears, but has no reason for so doing.

A monkey is an ape. It will copy man's actions up to a point and if it so desires, but it has no moral reason for its conduct, and no objective in its actions. It neither wants to be good, clever, nor equal.

A child imitates. He will put on father's hat and coat, take his brief bag, do what he does ; or the little girl will put on an apron and become mother, wash the dolly, put it to bed, become a nurse and care for it. Children will conduct meetings, lead, sing, and preach. They will do other things also, whatever father or mother does. Why ? They have reason. Father is the little boy's hero. Father is big. Mother is right. In the child's mind he wants to be like father, and she reasons that mother is the great ideal. This is the thought in " Be ye followers of the Good One." Let Christ be your ideal, your pattern, your objective. Mould your life according to His. Paul said : "Be ye therefore followers of God, as dear children " (Ephesians v. 1).

(7) *Be Ready* (iii. 15). " But sanctify the Lord God in your hearts : and be ready always to give an answer to every man that asketh you a reason of the hope that is in you with meekness and fear." One sometimes sings : " Blind unbelief is sure to err, and scan His works in vain " — but blind faith is a dangerous thing also. There are those who make a profession but have no testimony. They claim to believe the Word of God but, when questioned, do not know the Word of God. It is true that faith is believing where one cannot see, but that does not make a Christian useful in helping the other man with his doubts and problems.

Whatever man may claim for himself, the world demands proof, and rightly so. If we claim the knowledge of salvation, if we declare a confidence for present day provision, if we claim an assurance as to our future life, if we are to have victory over the enemies of the Gospel, if we are going to win men for Christ, then it is necessary that

(1) The Lord should have His rightful place in the heart. " But sanctify the Lord God in your hearts."

(2) We should be fully persuaded in our own hearts. " And be ready always to give an answer."

(3) We should have meekness and fear, because it is not argument or force that will bring conviction. " A reason of the hope that is in you with meekness and fear."

(8) *Be Watchful* (iv. 7). " But the end of all things is at hand : be ye therefore sober, and watch unto prayer." This is a call to alertness. There are times of distress when we find ourselves looking for the way out of the trials and temptations. As a Londoner, one remembers the longings that were in the heart for a cessation of hostilities and a termination of the air-raids with, possibly, only one thought in mind — a relief from the constant tension and a sense of personal deliverance and safety. It is so easy for our prayers to become selfish and circumscribed. Here the exhortation is to get our thoughts off the immediate and the selfish, and allow the desires and the prayers to be moulded in the light of " the end of all things " and of the coming of the Lord. Watch for every opportunity of service, watch for every object for prayer, watch for every occasion to witness. Watch in all things. " Watch ye and pray, lest ye enter into temptation " (Mark xiv. 38).

(9) *Be Humble* (v. 5). "Likewise, ye younger, submit your-selves unto the elder. Yea, all of you, be subject one to another, and be clothed with humility : for God resisteth the proud, and giveth grace to the humble." "Be clothed with humility" comes from a word found nowhere else in the Scriptures. It means "Put on the apron of humility." It was the slave's dress and was a mark of servitude. Was it possible that, whilst Peter was writing to these saints, his mind went back to that memorable day when the Lord girded Himself with a towel to wash His disciples' feet, teaching them that he who would be master must learn to be a servant ? Peter, at the beginning, resisted this action of the Lord, not knowing the lesson the Lord was teaching. "Thou shalt never wash my feet," said he ; to which the Lord's response was that, unless He did, there was no relationship. Peter submitted. He is now teaching the lesson he learned that day and practised thereafter.

In his second Epistle he introduces himself as a servant (slave). Servitude is something human pride resents, but something the Christian must receive. For service there is reward, for humility there is exaltation. The proud, God resists, or opposes like an army. The Psalmist said : "The Lord . . . hath respect unto the lowly : but the proud He knoweth afar off " (cxxxviii. 6).

(10) *Be Vigilant* (v. 8). "Be sober, be vigilant ; because your adversary the devil, as a roaring lion, walketh about, seeking whom he may devour."

In this fifth chapter Peter is exhorting the elders that they, as faithful under-shepherds, should feed the flock of God and do it with a willing mind and with a single eye. He reminds them that Christ, as the Chief Shepherd, is coming back and will reward them according to their faithfulness. This shepherd picture must still have been in the mind of the Apostle as he wrote this partic-ular verse. A good shepherd must always be vigilant, always on the watch for wild animals which would prowl around. David, as a shepherd, had dealt with the lion and the bear. Amos, the herdman, wrote similarly : "Therefore thus saith the Lord God : an adversary there shall be even round about the land ; and he shall bring down thy strength from thee, and thy palaces shall be spoiled. Thus saith the Lord ; As the shepherd taketh out of the mouth of the lion two legs, or a piece of an ear ; so shall the children of Israel be taken out that dwell in Samaria in the corner of a bed, and in Damascus in a couch " (iii. 11 -12).

We, too, must be vigilant, always alert, always on the watch tower, because we have an adversary who is ever active, sometimes as a roaring lion and sometimes as an angel of light. He is to be found inside the Church as well as outside.

(3) THE CHRISTIAN'S TRIALS (Chapters iv. and v.)

Having warned the Church of the fiery trials, and also encouraged it, the Apostle then gave some admonition which will ever stand as sound advice. Instead of looking at one's own suffering, and thus becoming overwhelmed with self-pity, let us consider Christ's suffering, remembering that it was not only voluntary but also on our behalf, and we will gladly endure light afflictions, and will arm ourselves both to resist and oppose all those things that are done by the ungodly Gentiles. They may think us strange because we refuse to engage in their ways, but they must know that we are not of them and neither will we have to give an account to them. The accounting will be to God, to the One Who is ready to judge both the living and the dead.

If, instead of counting trial as some strange thing, it be considered a natural thing that those who hated and crucified the Lord of Glory will do the same thing to His followers, and if the Christian will count it a joy to suffer for Christ's sake, then he will learn that presently the Lord is going to count it a joy to share with him the fulness of His Glory.

Man has never been promised immunity from suffering. Therefore it is better that one suffer for righteousness' sake than suffer as an evil-doer.

If the Lord permits His own children to suffer for the strengthening of their character, " What shall the end be of them that obey not the Gospel of Christ ? " (iv. 17).

In the last chapter Peter calls upon the

Elders to be faithful. Three things are stated in this faithfulness :

(1) Their responsibility was to feed the flock of God. Jesus is the Good Shepherd. These are the under-shepherds, who have been called upon to care for the sheep of His pasture. The elder is not chosen to be a social leader, nor yet elected to become an entertainer. He is to feed the flock, leading them into the green pastures of God's Word, feeding the young with the sincere milk of the Word, and ministering to the established saint the strong meat of the Word. There is no question in the Scriptures as to

the first duty of any Church leader — feed the flock, and be faithful in doing it.

(2) They are not to render their service as a duty, nor yet for material reward. Service must be willing and spontaneous. It must be given in the spirit of love, as Paul had said : " For the love of Christ constraineth us " (2 Corinthians v. 14).

Peter is not suggesting that those who give themselves to full time service should not be financially cared for, because Scripture teaches otherwise. The thought is that money should not be the motive of service, only the temporary reward.

(3) " Neither as being lords over God's heritage, but being ensamples to the flock " (v. 3). This would be a very difficult passage for the Roman Catholic Church to interpret, who have taken the author of the statement and made him to become the first pope of an hierarchy which makes a great distinction between the priesthood and the laity. The elder or leader is never to be a lord or a master, for One is our Master. He is ever to be an example.

If we will humble ourselves now, Christ will exalt us in due season. To-day we should put on the apron of humility and, presently, when the Chief Shepherd shall appear, we shall wear with comfort and satisfaction the unfading crown which He will place upon the head.

Peter then calls upon the

Younger to be humble. ' ' Likewise, ye younger, submit yourselves unto the elder " (v. 5). Submission is a grace which is becoming to young people, and can be a precious adornment in the eyes of other people.

Finally he calls upon

All to be vigilant. Pride goes before a fall. Therefore all must walk humbly, watchful against every move of the adversary who is ever seeking to overthrow.

In this world, which is alienated from the Lord and which is adverse to all that becometh to holiness, we must necessarily expect opposition and suffering. If we will courageously meet this situation and resist the world, the flesh and the devil, there is the promise that "The God of all grace, Who hath called us into His eternal glory by Christ Jesus, after that ye have suffered a while, make you perfect, stablish, strengthen, settle you" (v. 10).

The book concludes with a benediction.

II PETER

AN APOSTATE CHURCH

*" And the world passeth away, and the lust thereof: but he
that doeth the will of God abideth for ever. Little children,
it is the last time : and as ye have heard that antichrist shall
come, even now are there many antichrists ; whereby we know
that it is the last time. They went out from us but they were
not of us ; for if they had been of us, they would no doubt
have continued with us : but they went out, that they might
be made manifest that they were not all of us "*

(1 JOHN ii. 17-19)

INTRODUCTION

This second Epistle followed closely after the first, because
they were written very near to the end of Peter's life. In fact,
it was in the consciousness that his days were numbered and that
his death would be sudden that he wrote the words : " Yea, I
think it meet, as long as I am in this tabernacle, to stir you up
by putting you in remembrance ; knowing that shortly I must put
off this my tabernacle, even as our Lord Jesus Christ hath shewed
me " (i. 13-14).

The word " remembrance " is the keyword of the book. It
is mentioned four times in the three chapters.

In the first Epistle Peter wrote to a Persecuted Church, and
encouraged them to stand united against an external foe. In this
Epistle he wrote to an Apostate Church, and warned the believers
to withstand an internal foe who was in their midst in the form of
false teachers.

This second letter is wider in its scope than the first, which
was to the strangers in Pontus, Galatia, Cappadocia, Asia, and
Bithynia. The second is addressed to all who have obtained the
same precious faith, wherever they might be, and whoever they
might be, whether they were from the stock of Israel, or whether
they had come from the Gentiles. Because of the wideness of his
appeal, he introduces himself as Simon Peter. In the first Epistle it
was just Peter. Simon was the old name. It belonged to his old

life and to his Judaism. Peter was his new name, given to him by the Lord, the name which meant " a stone." This combined name introduces him to the Church which is made up of Jew and Gentile, of all who are of " like precious faith."

In his first Epistle he calls himself an Apostle ; in the second Epistle " a servant and an apostle."

The nearer Peter came to his Lord the more humble became his nature. The church that boasts of Peter as its head is as far removed from these qualities of Peter as it is possible to be.

THE BOOK

There is no ready analysis in so short a book, but a title could be given to each of the three chapters :

- (1) Precious Promises.
- (2) Seducers.
- (3) The Second Advent.

(1) PRECIOUS PROMISES (Chapter i.)

The Apostle refers to *our* faith and *His* promises as being precious. Faith is precious because we cannot live without it. The writer to the Hebrews said: "But without faith it is impossible to please Him" (xi. 6). Without faith our works are dead, and without works our faith is dead. A thing can become precious by its rarity. Diamonds are precious because they are not abundant like pebbles. Food became precious in the days of rationing because it was difficult to obtain. Faith can become precious in the same way. Concerning the last days it was said: " . . . Nevertheless when the Son of Man cometh, shall He find faith on the earth?" (Luke xviii. 8).

The promises of God are also precious because, apart from them, we are an impoverished people. Yea, apart from them we cannot live. Salvation is a promise made to those who will believe in the redeeming work of Christ upon the Cross. We claim His promises for every need and step of life. He has promised strength, wisdom, guidance, provision, companionship, comfort, and every other spiritual and physical blessing for the present. He has also promised to come back again, to receive us to Himself, to give us reward for service rendered, and much more that belongs to the future. It is by His great and precious promises that we become partakers of the Divine nature, and by them we know deliverance from the corruption of this world, according to verse four.

The Apostle concludes this Epistle with the instruction : "But grow in grace." In verses 5 to 8 of chapter i. is some evidence of growth. It is the greatest additional sum in all arithmetic. Faith may be a precious thing. It is a gift from God, but one has to exercise that gift until it fills the whole life.

FAITH is a gift from God. Through faith man becomes the recipient of all the other good gifts. After that it is a matter of man's doing. He has to add to the gift of faith certain graces, or he must permit some choice fruits to grow from the root of faith. To change the metaphor, he must shape and build the stones of character upon the foundation of faith. The first of these is

VIRTUE. The word is " manliness, or manly vigour," a manliness that will shake off all the surrounding vices of the world, which would seek to cling to a man as a parasite to a tree. A Christian, in his virtue, must stand head and shoulders above all others in noble living. The woman must produce the same qualities as the virtuous woman of Proverbs xxx.

To virtue is added

KNOWLEDGE, or discernment. Ignorance is the root of much evil, and ignorance is ofttimes wilful. From the root of faith should come the power to discern between right and wrong, to discern the Will of God from the will of self, and to know when the Devil is tempting and when the Lord is testing. Knowledge teaches one how to divide rightly the Word of God.

To knowledge must be added

TEMPERANCE, or self-control, so that one does not take advantage of the knowledge gained and use it in his own self-interest. Passions, desires, ambitions, yea, self, must be brought into subjection, and everything under control, for the life of faith is a life of discipline, not licence.

Add to temperance

PATIENCE. This is not a hardy fruit. It is often difficult to rear, knowing how to abide His time. James gives some details for the cultivation of this grace.

Add to patience

GODLINESS. The thought is Godly reverence, or a fear of God which will create a fellowship with God. When the relationship is rightly and strongly established Godward, then it reaches out into a right relationship manward until it is discovered that to Godliness has been added

BROTHERLY KINDNESS. John clarified this truth when he said : " Every one that loveth Him that begat, loveth him also that is begotten of Him " (1 John v. 1). If we love God we will love the brethren also.

Add to brotherly kindness

CHARITY, or love, the capstone of the building, the choicest of all fruits, the lubricating oil of all machinery. This is a love which not only moves to God and to the brethren but, like the love of the Lord, reaches out toward our enemies.

When all of these additions are put together they create the grand total of

FRUITFULNESS. We have been called upon to be fruitful in all things. The barren fruit tree is unprofitable to the farmer who seeks to cultivate it. He grew the tree that it might be profitable to himself, and Christ saved us that we might live unto His praise and His glory, that we might be fruitful unto all good works.

It is not sufficient that man should go through life hoping he is saved. " Rather, brethren, give diligence to make your calling and election sure " (i. 10) — that is, sure to yourself.

The author remembers well the day he went into a jeweller's shop and purchased a diamond. That diamond was of great value to him for two reasons — firstly, it had cost him a lot of hard-earned savings, and, secondly, the next day it was going to seal for him the bonds of an engagement with someone he loved. Having made the purchase, he put it into his vest pocket. When he left the shop he felt to see if it were still there. When he boarded the bus he felt again. When he alighted from the bus there was another check that the diamond had not fallen from his pocket. Owing to its value he was ever assuring himself that it was there. Beloved, with the same diligence we must satisfy ourselves that salvation is ours. It is the most precious gift. We cannot afford to hope. Hope is a companion of doubt ; assurance is the confidence of living. " If ye do these things, ye shall never fall." To be assured of salvation from sin is the incentive to fruitbearing which, in turn, becomes the confidence that presently,

when life has terminated on earth, there will be an abundant
entrance into the everlasting kingdom of our Lord and Saviour,
Jesus Christ.

Three times in the next four verses he used the word "remembrance." In view of the apostasy that he declared would come
upon the Church in the last days, he was anxious to assure and
reassure the believers of their standing so that they should not
be resting upon him, because the time of his departure was at hand.
He himself would soon be in the presence of his Lord.

Christians must not rest upon the testimony, nor the ministry,
of saints, but upon the unchanging, infallible Word of God. The
Apostate Church would seek to deny God's Word and bring into
disrepute the testimony of God's servants. Before they could
inject their poison of doubt, Peter declared that they had not
followed cunningly devised fables, but were eye-witnesses of the
things they testified. The same Voice which had come out of
heaven at the time of Christ's baptism at Jordan, which had
declared : " This is My Beloved Son in Whom I am well pleased,"
was the very same Voice which he had heard when, with James
and John, he was on the Mount of Transfiguration and saw Jesus
transfigured before them, and that Voice uttered the same words :
" This is My Beloved Son, in Whom I am well pleased ; hear
ye Him " (Matthew xvii. 5).

Against those who might question the veracity of Peter's
experience, he added : " We have also a more sure word of
prophecy ; whereunto ye do well that ye take heed, as unto a
light that shineth in a dark place, until the day dawn, and the
day star arise in your hearts : " (i. 19).

There are two approaches to this verse. Firstly, the marginal
reference is " and we have the word of prophecy confirmed."
This would give it a retrospective look. The Apostle would
think of all the Old Testament prophecies concerning the glory
of the Lord, His power and dominion, His coming to earth, and
His return to glory. These prophecies were now more sure
because he had seen Him in the flesh, fulfilling the Will of God,
and he had also seen Him in the effulgence of His glory and had
heard the approving voice of the Father. He and the other
apostles had been eye-witnesses both of Christ's earthly life and
His heavenly glory.

The second approach would be more prospective. So far as
Peter himself was concerned he had had this glorious revelation
that to him would ever be an all-sufficiency. It was something
that could never be taken from him. In this Epistle, however,

he is not thinking of himself but of his readers, those who had not had his confirmation. To them he said, and here is another translation : " And still stronger is the surety we have in the prophetic Word." Peter had this great witness of the Transfiguration which could only be confirmed by James and John, but we have many, many witnesses which make the Word of God more sure. The truth as we have it came from many sources, over a long period of time, and yet everything is harmonious. We have the testimony of past witnesses. We may see the transforming power of the Word in lives around us. We have the inner realisation that His Spirit witnesseth with our spirits that we are the children of God.

The Bible is the light of the mind, the guide to the feet, and the assurance of our faith. We must take heed to its instructions, cherish its precepts, obey its commands. This written Word will be our sure portion, lighting up this dark valley of sin until the Author of the Book, the Living Word, shall appear and so dispel all darkness.

Before a man can take heed to the Scriptures and allow his life to be moulded according to its precepts, he must be fully persuaded that this Book is Divine in its origin and, therefore, authoritative and trustworthy. Peter removed any doubts in this respect as he said : " Knowing this first, that no prophecy of the Scripture is of any private interpretation " (i. 20).

No portion of the Bible contains the mind of man, his feelings, his ideas, or his imaginations. Moses declared this in Numbers xvi. 28 : " And Moses said, Hereby ye shall know that the Lord hath sent me to do all these works ; for I have not done them of my own mind." Every prophet spoke or wrote what was the mind of God. " For the prophecy came not in old time by the will of man : but holy men of God spake as they were moved by the Holy Ghost " (i. 21).

One of the most potent pictures concerns Balaam, who was engaged by Balak, king of the Moabites, to curse Israel. Although Balaam was offered an attractive reward, yet the only thing he could say to the king was : " Lo, I am come unto thee : have I now any power at all to say any thing ? The word that God putteth in my mouth, that shall I speak " (Numbers xxii. 38).

Holy men wrote as they were moved, or were borne along like a boat before the wind, carried by a power independent of and greater than themselves.

Matthew Henry expressed it thus : " The Holy Spirit so wisely and carefully assisted and directed them in the delivery of what

they had received from Him that they were effectually secured
from any the least mistake in expressing what they revealed ;
so that the very words of Scripture are to be accounted the
words of the Holy Ghost, and all the plainness and simplicity,
all the power and virtue, all the elegance and propriety, of the
very words and expressions are to be regarded by us as proceeding
from God. Mix faith, therefore, with what you find in the
Scriptures ; esteem and reverence your Bible as a book written by
holy men, inspired, influenced, and assisted by the Holy Ghost."

This causes one to add a further thought. Although God
did not take away from Moses, Elijah, Isaiah, Peter, Paul, John,
or any other of these holy men, their individuality, yet He uttered
through them words, the significance of which these men never
appreciated. They would have known something of the immediate
meaning. Isaiah did not know the full implication of his declarations
of the sufferings of the Son of God.

We may, therefore, with complete confidence and without
any reservations, accept the Bible in its entirety as the Divine
Word of the Living God.

This emphasis that Peter used concerning the truth is quickly
appreciated as one enters into the next chapter which deals with

(2) SEDUCERS, OR FALSE PROPHETS (Chapter ii.)

As already stated, the Church has never been free from
malicious enemies. Peter went back farther. He had been speaking
about the prophecy of old time, and then said : " But there were
false prophets also," thus declaring that from the beginning there
have been those who have denied the truth or have risen in
opposition to it. Satan in the Garden said : " Hath God said ? "
In Genesis man said : " Let us make us a name," and thereby
rejected God's Name. In Exodus they rebelled against the
message of Moses. In Judges " every man did that which was
right in his own eyes," and thus it is through every book of the
Old and New Testament. So shall it be to the end of time, except
that in the latter days they shall wax worse and worse. In the
past denial was open, now it is subtle. They come in pretending
to possess the truth. Craftily they catch the young and the weak
in their net, and then change their methods until they move into
open denial. We have it all around us to-day, false cults which
are ever springing up with what is suggested as a new interpretation
or a new approach, but before long it is no interpretation at all
but complete denial.

There is one fundamental reason for every new group which has an interpretation, and it is to beguile mankind and make money out of them. Peter said : " through covetousness shall they with feigned words make merchandise of you . . . " (ii. 3).

Opposition to God is not even limited to man nor yet to time. The Apostle brings to notice that even the angels did the same thing before time was counted.

God has never countenanced such conduct. The angels which followed Lucifer in his rebellion were cast out of their first estate, and were, and are still, reserved for judgment.

The world that turned against God in the days of Noah perished in the Flood of that time.

The men of Sodom and Gomorrah never escaped judgment. Nevertheless, in every instance, God did provide an escape for those who were faithful. " The Lord knoweth how to deliver the godly out of temptations . . . . " (ii. 9).

These false prophets of the last days, the days of declension, will not only seduce men in relationship to the truth as it is taught in doctrine, but their characters declare them to be opposed to every moral issue as taught by God.

They are given to moral uncleanness, yet excuse themselves. The lives of the founders of several of the stronger cults of to-day do not stand investigation in this respect. In their selfish pride and over-confidence they despise any form of authority. In their presumption they know no subjection, but criticise all superiors, speaking evil of dignitaries. They seek to exercise powers that not even angels would seek to use.

The Lord's instruction is that we are to pray for those in authority over us. We are not to touch the Lord's anointed or do His servants any harm.

It is necessary that the Church continues to warn mankind of these false prophets, because they go about as angels of light. They are deceived and deceivers but, because of their air of superiority, because of their display of seeming authority, because of their swelling words, because they promise men liberty, because the things they offer do not call for sanctification and sacrifice, there are crowds who are ready to follow, but they are going to learn too late that what they thought was superiority will be an inferiority, that the display of authority was nothing but emptiness, that the swelling words were idle words, and that the promised liberty has only brought them into hopeless bondage.

To have known the truth and then to turn from it and follow false teachers, to be dragged down by them into an entanglement of truth and error which cannot be unravelled, is like the dog that turns to its own vomit, or to the washed sow that goes straight back to her wallowing in the mire. The Apostle says it would have been better if they had never known the truth. These are solemn words. Therefore, take heed, for the army of seducers is increasing every day. Remember it has been said, concerning the coming of the Lord : " Shall He find faith on the earth ? " (Luke xviii. 8).

The third chapter is given to the subject of Christ's

(3) SECOND COMING (Chapter iii.)

Four times in the chapter is the occurrence of the word " Beloved," an endearing term used because Peter is still giving them warnings as well as reminders. The Apostle uses an amount of discretion lest he cause offence and thereby drive away the people he longs to win.

The four expressions are : —

(1)	Beloved . . . remember	(iii. 1).
(2)	Beloved, be not ignorant	(iii. 8).
(3)	Beloved, . . . be diligent	(iii. 14).
(4)	Beloved, . . . beware	(iii. 17).

The chapter can be summarised under these four headings.

(1) *Beloved, . . . remember.* This would take the mind back over the things he had declared already. " This second epistle, beloved, I now write unto you ; in both which I stir up your minds by way of remembrance."

They must remember not only the things that he had just stated, but all that had been spoken by the other apostles — Paul, John, James, and Jude, and also the prophets who had been the mouthpieces of God before them.

Each of them in turn had declared the condition which would prevail in the last days. They had warned the Church of the scoffing, unbelieving, and lustful element which would pervade the hearts of men.

Men have ever rejected, and still do openly reject, the truth of the Lord's second coming. They will seek to explain it away as a spiritual experience, as a coming into the heart, as anything save a Personal return to this earth.

They will seek to justify their position by declaring that this doctrine has been propounded for hundreds of years, that each generation has believed that the Lord would come in its time, but that they were all deceived, and that life goes on just the same as from the beginning. So, presumably, it always will. To such teaching, Peter said : " Beloved, remember."

That is exactly the way in which men spoke long ago, and they defied, ignored, and ridiculed all that Noah declared for a hundred and twenty years, *but* it happened. Man's unbelief and his rejection can never alter facts. Even leaving God out for a moment, men of the past prophesied concerning the coming of cars, electricity, radio, television, and now the control of outer space. All have been scorned, but they have happened.

God destroyed the world once by a flood. He is going to destroy it again, by fire, but, before He does, He is going to take out of it all who love Him, as He protected Noah and his family.

Amidst all the false doctrines of these days BELOVED, REMEMBER !

The Apostle's second instruction was

(2) *Beloved, be not ignorant.* " But, beloved, be not ignorant of this one thing, that one day is with the Lord as a thousand years, and a thousand years as one day " (iii. 8). Men are working out their theories. They are adding their thoughts here and subtracting God's Word there, and juggling with ideas as mathematicians do with figures, but their arithmetic is all wrong because they have lost true values. They are trying to measure the Eternal God with a human yardstick, and fail to see that their yardstick is inadequate. Therefore, they charge God with slackness. The Apostle is correcting this ignorance by reminding them " that one day is with the Lord as a thousand years, and a thousand years as one day." The Psalmist had long before declared the same thing : " A thousand years in Thy sight are but as yesterday ' (xc. 4). God is not bound by the limitations of time on the one hand ; whilst we, the creatures of time, cannot comprehend the infinite and the eternal. In the light of the eternal it becomes evident that what appears to be delay in the mind of man is not slackness on the part of God. " The Lord is not slack concerning His promise, as some men count slackness ; but is longsuffering to usward, not willing that any should perish " (iii. 9).

Be not ignorant of the Lord's coming, for the Day of the Lord WILL come.

Be not ignorant of the Lord's judgment, when He will deal with this world in righteousness and all that has been marred by sin will be burned up and then remade. The earth has had its baptism in water — it is yet to have a baptism in fire.

To those who look at these verses and enquire as to whether the melting of the elements in fervent heat refers to the atomic bomb or some other nuclear weapon, it is fairly safe to make the reply — No! The evidence is that God will not give man the privilege of burning up the earth that He has created. It will remain under His power because He is also going to remake it.

It may also be stated that the medium of destruction will probably be atomic energy, but it must be borne in mind that atomic energy is one thing and an atomic bomb is another thing. God created this earth with matter. It is known that all matter is made up of atoms. When the atom is split it becomes energy. Energy is an unseen force. Said the writer to the Hebrews: " Through faith we understand that the worlds were framed by the Word of God, so that things which are seen (matter) were not made of things which do appear (energy) " (xi. 3). BELOVED, BE NOT IGNORANT.

(3) *Beloved, . . . be diligent.* " Wherefore, beloved, seeing that ye look for such things, be diligent that ye may be found of Him in peace, without spot, and blameless " (iii. 14). This is a call to sanctification which becomes the safeguard against the dangers of the closing days of time. The Apostle has already enlarged on this subject in his first chapter, as he requested that men should make their calling and election sure. The delay of the Lord's return is not indifference, but, rather, an opportunity that we may prove Him and prove ourselves here, so that we shall not be ashamed at His appearing.

Some have abused this situation. They have wrested the Scriptures out of their real context and meaning, but to their own harm.

Owing to the fact that others have gone astray, and because the Adversary is busy seeking to confuse and entangle all he can, there comes the last word of admonition

(4) *Beloved, . . . beware.* " Ye therefore, beloved, seeing ye know these things before, beware lest ye also, being led away with the error of the wicked, fall from your own stedfastness " (iii. 17), and the thought is not a sudden tragedy or a total about-turn. The word " fall " means " to fade as a flower." It is the same expression which the Apostle uses in his first Epistle. " The grass withereth, and the flower thereof falleth away." (i. 24).

Peter had the right to give this warning. He had been too sure of himself at one time and had painfully learned the truth, " Let him that thinketh he standeth take heed lest he fall " (1 Corinthians x. 12).

The only sure way of not falling into this evil is

(1) Grow in grace.

(2) Grow in the knowledge of our Lord and Saviour Jesus Christ.

This is done by taking heed to His Word.

I, II, III JOHN

"THAT YE MIGHT KNOW"

" In the beginning was the Word, and the Word was with God, and the Word was God. The same was in the beginning with God. All things were made by Him; and without Him was not anything made that was made. In Him was life; and the life was the light of men. And the light shineth in darkness; and the darkness comprehended it not " (JOHN i. 1-5)

INTRODUCTION

Although no name is given in the text as to who was the author of these Epistles, yet there appears to be no doubt that John, whose name gives a title to the books, was the person.

It is a strange situation that many scholars who question the authorship of the fourth Gospel, which bears the same name, never raise a question as to the Epistles. The strangeness is that, whoever wrote the one, must have written the other. There is a great deal of sameness of subject and similarity of expression in both the Gospel and the Epistles.

The following is an example : —

Gospel	*Epistles*
i. 1 " In the beginning was the Word, and the Word was with God."	i. 1. " That which was from the beginning, which we have heard."
i. 4-9. The Light of life.	i. 5-7. " God is light, and in Him is no darkness at all . . . Walk in the light."
ix. 5. " I am the Light of the world."	
iii. 16. " For God so loved the world . . . "	iv. 8. " God is love."
	iv. 19. " We love Him, because He first loved us."

Gospel	Epistles
iv. 24. "God is a Spirit : and they that worship Him must worship Him in spirit and in truth."	iv. 2. "Hereby know ye the Spirit of God : Every Spirit that confesseth that Jesus Christ is come in the flesh is of God."
xiv. 6. "I am the way, the truth, and the life."	v. 6. "And it is the Spirit that beareth witness, because the Spirit is truth."
viii. 32. "And ye shall know the truth, and the truth shall make you free."	
v. 31-32. "If I bear witness of Myself, My witness is not true. There is another that beareth witness of Me ; and I know that the witness which He witnesseth of Me is true."	v. 9. "If we receive the witness of men, the witness of God is greater."
The witnesses were : — John, His works, the Father, the Word.	The witnesses were : — The Father, the Word, the Holy Ghost. The Spirit, the Water, the Blood.

To appreciate the message of these Epistles it is necessary to discover the conditions which were prevailing at that time, for thereby the purpose of the books is made known, and then the interpretation becomes clear.

Throughout history the Church has had to contend with enemies. The false has always counterfeited the true. Opposite the truth has ever been error. Against right has always stood wrong. Counteracting the light of revelation have come the forces of darkness. The philosophies of men have ever crossed swords with the faith of God.

At the time when John wrote, the Church was being troubled with a pagan cult known as Gnosticism. This name is derived from a Greek word meaning "To know." These Gnostics claimed to know all the mysteries of the Universe. They taught that material things belonged to one realm and spiritual things to another realm, and that there was no immediate point of contact between them. They also taught that the physical could live in a physical world, engage in its pursuits and sins, follow its lusts and desires, but the spirit could be allowed to rise above them. This, of course, was an opening to carnality, and would pull down and destroy all Christian morals.

Such a doctrine could not accept the Deity of Christ, because God, Who is a Spirit, could not enter the human realm, and neither could men partake of the nature of God.

This same doctrine is prevalent in the world to-day, denying Divinity and the Virgin Birth, calling evil good, sanctioning loose living and free love, and propounding the tenets of materialism.

It was in the light of such error creeping into the Church that John wrote these Epistles, and in the same light they must be read.

THE MESSAGE

The subject of the Epistles is Fellowship; that is, Fellowship with the Father and with the Son, the thing which the Gnostics denied, for only as man knows fellowship with the Divine can he know real fellowship with his fellow man.

The key-phrase of the Epistles is " That ye might know." The Gnostics claimed to know all things, but John is declaring to the Christian Church that we should be the people of knowledge because we have a Divine revelation.

In the first Epistle the Apostle expounds : —

The Fellowship of light	.....	Chapter i.
The Fellowship of love	.....	Chapters ii.-iv.
The Fellowship of witness	.....	Chapter v.
The Fellowship of life	.....	Chapter v.

The introductory verse is powerful and convincing, and concerns, on the one hand, the truth of Deity, and, on the other hand, John's own authority for writing on such a matter. " That which was from the beginning (Deity), which we have heard, which we have seen with our eyes, which we have looked upon, and our hands have handled, of the Word of life." This is the Word which became flesh and dwelt amongst us.

John, as an Apostle, had heard the teachings of Jesus with his own ears. He had witnessed the ministry of Jesus with his own eyes, and had made contact with the Person of Jesus with his own hands and body. He had leaned on Jesus' breast at the supper table and had enjoyed His fellowship. Therefore he knew from experience, as did others, that God can and does manifest Himself to human beings, and also that man in the flesh can enjoy God in the spirit. Experience can always be a death-blow to theory. The blind man might be uneducated as compared with the scribes and the rulers, but he could speak with undeniable authority when he said: " One thing I know, that, whereas I was blind, now I see " (John ix. 25). Christians to-day must have this same assurance of faith. The work of the Lord should be so transforming in the life, and love for Him should be so established, that the testimony of experience should silence the theories and speculations of all liberal reasoning.

Again, this cult claimed that they knew all things, and called themselves " to know." John, therefore, told the Church that it should not be ignorant concerning spiritual things, neither should it be blind to the life that now is, nor yet to the life that is to come. Twenty-six times he says : " We know " or " Ye know." The first one is very forceful : " And hereby we do know that we know Him " (ii. 3). Too many people think they know. How often are the expressions used : " I think I know the way," " I think I know where it is," " I think I know them." All such statements are doubts. It is not sufficient to suggest that we think we are saved, think we are going to heaven, think that all is well. Joseph and Mary thought that Jesus was in the company, but they were wrong. The Christian position must always be one of complete assurance. " We do know that we know."

Some of the other statements John uses to strengthen the Christians against this materialism are : —

" Hereby *know* we that we are in Him " (ii. 5).

" We *know* that it is the last time " (ii. 18).

" Ye *know* the truth . . . " (ii. 21).

" Ye *know* that He is righteous " (ii. 29).

" Ye *know* that every one that doeth righteousness is born of Him " (ii. 29).

" Ye *know* that He was manifested to take away our sins " (iii. 5).

" We *know* that we have passed from death unto life " (iii. 14).

" We *know* that He abideth in us " (iii. 24).

" We *know* that we have the petitions that we desired of Him " (v. 15).

" We *know* that the Son of God is come " (v. 20).

" Ye *know* that our record is true " (3 John xii.).

Every one of these statements, with others, was in direct opposition to the teachings of Gnosticism, and these same words are as vital to-day as they were when John picked up his pen and wrote, for they are in direct opposition to all that liberalism now teaches.

If the Christian be assured of the things which John declared, if he knows this is truth, then, obviously, he has fellowship with the Father and with His Son, Jesus Christ.

Having established a firm foundation of faith, John proceeds to enlighten the believer with an understanding of the One with Whom he is to enjoy this fellowship, so that their joy might be full.

(1) THE FELLOWSHIP OF LIGHT (Chapter i.)

" This then is the message which we have heard of Him, and declare unto you, that GOD IS LIGHT, and in Him is no darkness at all " (i. 5).

It is not that God is *a* light, nor that He dwells in light, but He is light itself, light which is independent of the sun or of physics. God *is* light. Therefore He can know no darkness. He changes not. He is the Father of lights and knows no variableness neither shadow of turning. Because He casts no shadows, knows no pause, and knows no setting, it is not possible for man to claim fellowship with God and yet to walk in darkness.

Light is an all-pervading thing. It fills the earth, it fills everything. A little hole or crack and light will penetrate the darkness. Darkness never penetrates the light. Photographers are very aware of this. The light of the Gospel is able to penetrate the darkest heart, and transform heathendom. The light of knowledge is able to dispel ignorance, doubt, and superstition.

When light falls upon the prism it is broken into beams of colour, which is called the spectrum of light. In these three Epistles the nature of God is broken into four great attributes. They are

GOD IS LIGHT	.....	Chapters i. and ii.
GOD IS LOVE	.....	Chapters iii. and iv.
GOD IS SPIRIT	.....	Chapters iv. and v.
GOD IS TRUTH	.....	Epistles 2 and 3.

These qualities, which essentially belong to God, are radiated to the children of God and they, in turn, are expected to reveal them to the world.

GOD IS LIGHT. The first creative act of God in the first chapter of Genesis was " Let there be light, and there was light." Apart from light nothing lives, except the very lowest forms of life. John said, when writing the Gospel : " That was the true Light, which lighteth every man that cometh into the world " (i. 9).

In the book of the Revelation John again was writing and said : " And the city had no need of the sun, neither of the moon, to shine in it : for the glory of God did lighten it, and the Lamb is the light thereof " (xxi. 23). He is the light of time and of eternity. This light is to be the enjoyment of the believer. Therefore he is exhorted to

Walk in the Light. The light of the Gospel has brought salvation to mankind. The light of understanding has come to His people through His Word, and the light of sanctification has come from the Holy Spirit. Walk in that light and, by so doing, enjoy fellowship with each other, and the full realisation that the ever-cleansing power of the Blood is keeping the soul clean from day to day.

This walking in the light of the Lord will cause His people to become reflectors of that light, even as the moon reflects the light of the sun in the hours of darkness when the sun cannot be seen.

Let your light shine in this dark world of sin. " He that loveth his brother abideth in the light, and there is none occasion of stumbling in him " (ii. 10). This means that he himself will not stumble, and neither will he become a stumbling-block to another. The world is to see Christ through Christian behaviour. " Ye are the light of the world. A city that is set on an hill cannot be hid. Neither do men light a candle, and put it under a bushel, but on a candlestick ; and it giveth light unto all that are in the house. Let your light so shine before men, that they may see your good works, and glorify your Father which is in heaven " (Matthew v. 14-16). *This is the light of life.*

(2) THE FELLOWSHIP OF LOVE (Chapters ii. - iv.)

GOD IS LOVE. This is more than attribute. Neither light nor love are qualities. They are essence — GOD IS — He is the source and the supply. It has often been said that love is not easily defined. That is true. The reason why man is not able to define love is because God is love, and man cannot define God.

There is a great deal of sensual and sentimental emotion in the world which is referred to as love, but it is as far removed from love as it is possible for anything to be. True love is sacred, carnal love is sordid.

John, who has ever been known as the disciple of love, said: " God is love ; and he that dwelleth in love dwelleth in God, and God in him " (iv. 16).

God's love was manifested in His creative power, for He made the world for man and He made it exceedingly beautiful. It was sin which marred that beauty. A further manifestation of that love was made when God gave His only begotten Son to be the Saviour of fallen man. " Hereby perceive we the love of God, because He laid down His life for us : " (iii. 16). This is in harmony with the same chapter and verse in John's Gospel narrative.

Any love which is possessed by man is no credit to him. " We love Him because He first loved us." The outworking of His love in man is expressed in the words : " Behold, what manner of love the Father hath bestowed upon us, that we should be called the sons of God " (iii. 1).

This love of God is imparted to the believer.

Love in your hearts. Paul said : " . . . the love of God is shed abroad in our hearts by the Holy Ghost which is given unto us " (Romans v. 5).

The Christian is the possessor of that for which the world ever craves and never knows — that is, peace and quietness, a sense of security. The more the world talks about security the less it knows of it. Peace and security are the fruits of love. " There is no fear in love ; but perfect love casteth out fear : because fear hath torment. He that feareth is not made perfect in love " (iv. 18).

A husband and a wife, who are confident of the complete love of each other, never worry when they are apart as to how the other might be behaving. Such thoughts never enter their minds. They have no fear. They know that love " doth not behave itself unseemly, seeketh not her own, is not easily provoked, thinketh no evil ; rejoiceth not in iniquity, but rejoiceth in the truth ; beareth all things, believeth all things, hopeth all things, endureth all things. Love never faileth " (1 Corinthians xiii. 5-8). This is the love of God that passeth all understanding. The source of this love is God. The course of the love is in or through the believer, and its influence should be poured into the restless, turbulent ocean of the world. Hence the command is to

Love one another. " We love the brethren." " If a man say I love God and hateth his brother, he is a liar." " And this commandment have we from Him that he who loveth God loveth his brother also." " Love your enemies, pray for them that despitefully use you." The Word of God is full of such instruction.

The Christian must not love the world, nor the things of the world, but he is to love the sinner with a Calvary love. *This is the light of love.* GOD IS A SPIRIT. The world is full of spirits, good and bad. There is the Holy Spirit and there is a Satanic spirit. There is the Spirit of Christ and the spirit of antichrist. Therefore John says : " Beloved, believe not every spirit, but try the spirits whether they are of God : because many false prophets are gone out into the world. Hereby know ye the Spirit of God : Every spirit that confesseth that Jesus Christ is come in the flesh is of God : And every spirit that confesseth not that Jesus Christ is come in the flesh is not of God : and this is that spirit of antichrist . . . " (iv. 1-3).

It is to be noted that every false cult and every diverse creed deny the Virgin Birth or that Jesus Christ is come in the flesh. These are the spirit of antichrist.

God is a Trinity —Father, Son, and *Spirit.*

Man is a Trinity — body, soul, and *spirit.*

The point of contact between the two is *spirit.* It is in this realm that God and man are able to have fellowship. John declared this in the Gospel. " God is a Spirit : and they that worship Him must worship Him in spirit and in truth " (iv. 24).

The Spirit of God has become the inheritance of the believer. " And hereby we know that He abideth in us, by

The Spirit which He hath given us" (iii. 24). The Spirit which confesseth that Jesus Christ is come in the flesh is the Spirit which dwelleth in us. Before the Lord left this earthly scene He bade His disciples tarry at Jerusalem until they were endued with power from on high (Luke xxiv. 29). This they did until the Day of Pentecost was fully come, and then the Holy Spirit descended upon them. Thus they became equipped for Christian service. Without that same equipment the Church to-day will never produce effective spiritual service. The more the Church moves away from the truth of Pentecost the more social it becomes in its activities. We need to dispense with those socials, suppers, and banquets, which are becoming such a prominent part in the

Church. We need to substitute the modern kitchen by the old-fashioned prayer room, and supper tables by the spread of the meat of God's Word.

When the evidence of the work of the Holy Spirit becomes manifest in the Church life, then will the same power move out from the Church into the needy world through the agency of the church member, for

" *Ye are My witnesses,*" or, as John has declared it: " Hereby know we that we dwell in Him, and He in us, because He hath given unto us of His Spirit. And we have seen and do testify that the Father sent the Son to be the Saviour of the world " (iv. 13-14).

Our testimony in the world is not to be our self effort, but our dying to self, for " It is the Spirit that beareth witness, because the Spirit is truth " (v. 6). *This is the light of power.*

(3) THE FELLOWSHIP OF WITNESS (Chapter v.)

GOD IS TRUTH. Truth has to be established in the mouth of witnesses, according to God's own law. " One witness shall not rise up against a man for any iniquity, or for any sin in any sin that he sinneth : at the mouth of two witnesses, or at the mouth of three witnesses, shall the matter be established " (Deuteronomy xix. 15).

Before declaring this fourth quality of God, the Apostle brings forward the witnesses who declare His authority and who give assurance to the believer of his standing in Christ.

There are three witnesses in heaven — the Father, the Word, and the Holy Ghost. This is the Trinity which is united and satisfied " that God hath given to us eternal life."

Then there are three witnesses on earth — " The Spirit, and the water, and the blood " (v. 8) — the Spirit, because His Spirit witnesseth with our spirit that we are the sons of God.

The water and the blood might refer to outward and inward cleansing, washing the hands and the feet to be cleansed from daily defilements. Jesus did say to Peter : " If I wash thee not, thou hast no part with Me " (xiii. 8). Then there are other Scriptures, such as : " Christ also loved the Church, and gave Himself for it ; that He might sanctify and cleanse it with the washing of water by the Word, that He might present it to Himself a glorious church . . . " (Ephesians v. 25-27). Yet this cleansing was insufficient without the blood, for " The Blood of Jesus Christ, His Son, cleanseth us from all sin " (1 John i. 7).

Another thought for consideration is that those who are washed in the Blood are commanded to be baptised in water. Yet again, when Christ died upon the Cross, it was John who recorded : " But one of the soldiers with a spear pierced His side, and forthwith came there out blood and water " (John xix. 34). These, with the Spirit, were certainly witnesses on earth. Apart from them, man has the inward witness of his own heart. " He that believeth on the Son of God hath the witness in himself " (v. 10).

All of this is manifested to the children of God that they might *know* and be fully assured of their salvation. He who believes on the Son of God should never have doubts in his heart or mind. If he has, then he may question the fact that he has believed.

Having reasoned out the confidence of the believer in his God, the Apostle then declares that God is Truth. " That we may know Him that is true, and we are in Him that is true, even in His Son Jesus Christ. This is the true God, and eternal life " (v. 20). Jesus said to Thomas : " I am the Truth." John reasons this subject also in his Gospel narrative. " And the Word was made flesh, and dwelt among us . . . the only begotten of the Father, full of grace and truth " (i. 14). Again, he said : " For the law was given by Moses, but grace and truth came by Jesus Christ " (i. 17).

This Truth is the Eternal Word, the Creative Word. How the Bible always exalts and extols the Word of Truth ! " My Word shall not return unto Me void." The Psalmist said that God created the world by the Word of His power. " He spake and it was done." " Thy Word is true from the beginning."

Meditate the 119th Psalm concerning the Word of Truth. The believer is exhorted again and again to

Walk in the Truth, as in the second Epistle, verse 4 : " I rejoiced greatly that I found of thy children walking in truth, as we have received a commandment from the Father " ; and in the third Epistle, verses 3 and 4 : " For I rejoiced greatly, when the brethren came and testified of the truth that is in thee, even as thou walkest in the truth. I have no greater joy than to hear that my children walk in the truth."

The exhortation to walk in the truth, continued in the second Epistle, is addressed to " the elect lady and her children." There is an amount of disputation as to who this elect lady was. No one can be sure. As John wrote his first Epistle to the saints, estab-

lishing them that they might meet the inroads of a false cult, and
as he continues his subject into the second book, let the title be
accepted as belonging to the Church. The Church has always
been referred to in the feminine gender, which is correct because
she is the Bride of Christ, presently to be united to Him in the
great heavenly marriage. The children are those who are begotten
of the Holy Spirit and born again through the ministry of that
same Church.

Man walks in the truth as he obeys the commandments of his
Lord. This is spelt out in the word " obedience."

It is exceedingly essential for the child of God to be fully
surrendered and completely submissive to the Lord, walking in
the truth, because of the Deceiver, the Antichrist, whom the Lord
declared was the father of lies, and a liar from the beginning.
He is going about seeking whom he may deceive ; and he is not
the only enemy, but his adherents, too, deceive those who abide not
in the doctrine of Christ. This is expressed in verse 9 : " Whosoever transgresseth, and abideth not in the doctrine of Christ, hath
not God. He that abideth in the doctrine of Christ, he hath both
the Father and the Son."

This is followed by a very definite and deliberate instruction
concerning the Christian's attitude toward false teachers. " If
there come any unto you, and bring not this doctrine, receive him
not into your house, neither bid him God speed : For he that
biddeth him God speed is partaker of his evil deeds " (2 John
10-11). It is a declaration that those who teach the Truth must
always have an open house, but that hospitality must never be
given to any who are teachers of error. " Jehovah's Witnesses "
are ever requesting that they may come into homes and give
Bible Studies. They must be refused. Any person who desires
to know truth must be welcomed, but any who desire to teach
their " truth " must be kept on the doorstep. The door must be
politely closed against them !

Moreover, when such are refused, whilst it is necessary to be
polite, they must never be wished God speed. Never say " God
bless you," because God cannot bless those who are in error.
God is jealous of His Name and He is jealous of His Word.
Therefore He cannot share these things with those who are
opposed to Him.

Only as man abides faithfully in the Truth will that Truth
reach the world.

He who receives must also give, so we become

Witnesses to the Truth, being always ready to give a reason of the hope that is within us. The Church must preach the Word, in season and out of season.

The third Epistle contains the same instruction concerning the truth, written to an individual, Gaius.

Gaius was a companion of Paul and came from Derbe, and was one of the very few who were baptised by Paul.

Whether it be the Church as a whole, or whether it be an individual in that Church, the command remains the same — faithfulness to the Truth and open denial of all error. *This is the light of revelation.*

The Epistles can be summarised : —

    (1) Man must seek to know God, His Will, and His purposes.

    (2) Man must adjust his life and conduct accordingly.

    (3) Man must manifest it to the world in practical Christian living.

The Epistles together make a book of principles and practices, of faith and ethics, things that are ever inseparable.

JUDE

CONTENDING FOR THE FAITH

" Only let your conversation be as it becometh the gospel of Christ : that whether I come and see you, or else be absent, I may hear of your affairs, that ye stand fast in one spirit, with one mind striving together for the faith of the gospel ; And in nothing terrified by your adversaries : which is to them an evident token of perdition, but to you of salvation, and that of God. For unto you it is given in the behalf of Christ, not only to believe on Him, but also to suffer for His sake ; having the same conflict which ye saw in me, and now hear to be in me " (PHILIPPIANS i. 27-30)

INTRODUCTION

This Epistle was written by Jude, the brother of James, according to the first verse. James was a brother of the Lord. Paul gave this information to the Galatians : " But other of the apostles saw I none, save the Lord's brother " (i. 19). This would mean that Jude was also a brother of the Lord. Neither of these men made any claim of human relationship with the Lord. The question might well be asked : Why not ? Two suggestions are made : —

(1) Jesus had said : " Who is my mother and who are my brethren ? " To be a servant of Christ in spiritual ministry was far greater than being a brother in the flesh. Human relationships are temporary. Divine relationships and results are eternal.

(2) Maybe these men would not be too anxious to make known their identity seeing that, in the early days of Christ's ministry, they had not believed in Him.

All of the apostles, as Jude, James, Paul, and Peter, spoke of themselves as " the servants of Jesus Christ." This was a wonderful calling, but such is the calling of every child of God. We are called to be workers together with Him. All that is required on the part of the saint is yieldedness. Jude faced what every genera- tion has faced, and we face today — a great horde of enemies. Some are indifferent to the truth, some opponents to the common salvation, whilst others are antagonists to Divine Revelation. The Apostle, therefore, challenged the people of his day, and those who live in this day, to " earnestly contend for the faith which was once delivered unto the saints " (vs. 3).

This is more than the mere acceptance of A faith which brings a sense of personal comfort and consolation. It is THE faith, ONCE delivered, never to be withdrawn, amended, or adjusted in any way to meet the desires or the fancies of men. It is to be CONTENDED in the midst of all opposition. This calls for action, not retraction; for challenge, not resignation ; and all must be done EARNESTLY, with zeal and determination. The fact that he called it a COMMON salvation was because it was for all men, Jew and Gentile alike.

His reason for exhorting them to earnestly contend for the faith was because there had come into the Church many who were deniers of the faith, which is seen in

THE MESSAGE

Although there is only one chapter, yet the book divides into two sections. The first sixteen verses concern
AN APOSTATE CHURCH,
and the remaining nine verses
THE TRUE CHURCH.
The one is set against the other, and the whole relates to faith.

(1) AN APOSTATE CHURCH (verses 1 - 16)

Apostasy is always resultant upon a falling away from the faith. Jude declared that there were certain men who had crept in unawares (vs. 4), but why unawares ? The answer appears to be obvious. The Church was not alert, not watchful, not awake to the activities of the enemy, and the enemy is never asleep to his opportunities. These conditions are prevailing everywhere today. Apathy and indifference have thrown doors wide open for materialism, liberalism, and socialism, until the enemy has established himself inside the church, and he has done it so insidiously that many of the churches are not aware of their position. Liberality of thought quickly leads to denial of the things once held. Man would not say it is denial. He would declare that he is broadminded, and believes that every man is entitled to his opinion. The fact is that we are not entitled to anything ! God is God, or He is not. Either we believe Him, or we are denying Him, and thereby turning the grace of God into lasciviousness and denying the only Lord God, and our Lord Jesus Christ.

Disavowing the Lord Jesus Christ does not mean a repudiation of His existence. That would be too blatant, and the Devil knows exactly how far he can go with man. It is a denial of His Divinity, His Virgin Birth, the Efficacy of His Blood, His Second Advent.

As to this apostate condition, Jude uses Israel as an example, in verse 5. This people had been saved nationally as God brought them out of Egypt with a strong hand and with mighty power, having wrought great miracles on their behalf; yet He had to punish them because, afterwards, they forsook Him, set up idols and worshipped other gods, denying the very God Who had delivered. As a result, these very people, whom God delivered from Egypt, He destroyed in the wilderness because of their unbelief — that was, all except Joshua and Caleb who had remained faithful, and also their children who had not partaken in their sins. The God Who did it once will do it again. The great host of religious professors, and the unregenerate church members, will die in their sins, but God has a remnant, the faithful God-believing, Bible-loving saints, whom He will take to Himself.

The Apostle moves further, and declares that not even angels can escape the judgment of God if they, like man, will rebel against His sovereign Will and purpose. When God created the world in Genesis i. 1 (that is, the original earth, created millions of years back), He gave selected angels certain privileges, for angels, as created beings, are His ministering spirits. Lucifer, one of the supreme beings, became discontented with his appointment, and in pride rebelled against His Creator and Master, saying : " I will be like the Most High " (Isaiah xiv. 14). Rebels always find malcontents who will be their supporters, and so a rebellion broke out in the heavenlies, and God, in His supremacy, cast out Lucifer and his adherents and turned the earth upside down, accounting for the statement in Genesis i. 2. These are the fallen angels who kept not their first estate. No longer angels to serve God, they became demons, the servants of the Devil. Instead of being free angels of light, they had become bound demons of darkness, " reserved in everlasting chains under darkness unto the judgment of the great day " (vs. 6).

Peter referred to this same incident in II Peter i. 4, when he said : " For if God spared not the angels that sinned, but cast them down to hell (Tartarus) . . . " If God spared not angels, how can man expect to escape if he, too, is wilful in rejecting the Word of the Lord ?

In the next verse Jude tells how God meted out His judgment upon the cities of Sodom and Gomorrha because of their fornication, and those cities exist no more.

Another class of people is mentioned in verse 8, those who refuse to recognise authority. They disobey laws, having neither time nor place for them. They defile the flesh, or are governed by their own passions. A man cannot abuse that which is in the realm of the flesh without affecting that which is in the realm of the spirit, and thereby he injures his own soul.

The dominion and the dignitaries which they despise may refer to rulers and magistrates, to governments and lawmakers, because man is instructed both to obey them and pray for them, but it is also possible that reference is made to church leaders, to those who would seek to instruct them in their moral and spiritual behaviour, and whose interference they abhor. There are multitudes of people who consider that the Church is a concern which interferes with their freedom and personal rights. That is one of the underlying factors which causes the Bible to be banned from the schools of America. The argument used is separation of the State and the Church, but that is a mere pretext. The Bible is not the Church. The Bible is a book and the Church is an organisation. The Bible is not the property of any one faith. It is the property of the people. The Church might be a medium of interpretation and, as such, should be kept distinct from the schools, but the Bible is a code of morals. It is the food of the soul. It is the guide-post of life and, therefore, is essentially a vital part of general education.

Man today is despising the Church and speaking evil of its leaders, many of whom are God-ordained and Divinely-inspired men. Jude said that even Michael, the archangel, would not usurp such authority. There is but one archangel, who is above all angels. He has been given great privileges. He is the protector of God's people, the Jews, according to Daniel. He also is closely associated with resurrection. It will be at his voice that the dead in Christ shall rise (I Thessalonians iv. 16). In this ninth verse of Jude he is sent by God to obtain the body of Moses in resurrection and, later, he is going to lead the angels in that war against the dragon, when Satan will be overcome and cast out (Revelation xii. 7). Yet, with all of his authority, he would not lift his voice against the Devil.

Moses had died on Mount Nebo and had been buried by God, but he was to be one of the two witnesses on the Mount of Transfiguration and, probably, in other events, so God wanted Moses to be raised from the dead. Therefore He sent Michael to get his body. Seemingly, Satan intervened and refused to surrender that body, for Satan is the god of this world and the prince of death. He knows that, as one who has already been defeated at the Cross, the day is coming when he will have to surrender the bodies of the believers which are buried in the graveyards of this world, but he is not going to yield anything a day before he has to, so he sought to retain the body of Moses until the resurrection morn. In the struggle that ensued Michael would not speak out of turn and rebuke the enemy, but said : " The Lord rebuke thee " Let us be careful in our day as to how we speak of the Devil, remembering that, although he is not all powerful, yet he is powerful, and does dominate this world. We are only protected from his power inasmuch as we are covered by the Blood of Jesus Christ. We triumph only in the triumphs of the Cross.

Cain, Balaam, and Korah, all had rebellious spirits, and all brought tragedy not only upon themselves but upon whole nations. Such characters are deceivers, forerunners of others who in the last days would, if it were possible, deceive even the elect.

These characters are as deceptive as : —

Clouds that have no water.

Trees that produce no fruit.

Waves that are ever restless.

Wandering stars that cannot give guidance to travellers.

Eternal punishment is their doom, even though they may prosper in this world's goods, and pose as worthy leaders and teachers before those who are easily beguiled.

Enoch, the seventh from Adam, back in his day foretold such conditions as one of the many signs of Christ's return. We are living in those days. These men of God made no mistakes, for they wrote and spoke as they were moved by the Holy Ghost.

We are surrounded by those who are walking after their own lusts, are speaking swelling words, and are seeking worldly advantages from holy pretences.

They run showy campaigns for worldly gain (Balaam).

They deny the inspiration of the Word of God (Core).

They deny the work of the Cross (Cain).

They are murmurers and complainers who seek only the praises of men.

Against these things the child of God is given the following instruction : " But ye, beloved, building up yourselves on your most holy faith, praying in the Holy Ghost, keep yourselves in the love of God, looking for the mercy of our Lord Jesus Christ unto eternal life " (vss. 21-22).

In view of these devastating conditions, the Christian is called upon to " earnestly contend for the faith which was once delivered unto the saints " (vs. 3).

What is this " Faith . . . once delivered " which men resist ? It is : —

(1) The revelation that man himself is a sinner, and that there is no good in him. This they will not admit.

(2) That in man's helpless estate, the Eternal God, Who is Creator of all things, has provided a remedy. This God they will not acknowledge, because they would sooner accept their own theories of evolution and their scientific research.

(3) That the remedy for sin is the acceptance by faith of the work of God's Son upon the Cross bringing redemption. This they will not confess, because man has no part in it. Therefore, they say that they cannot accept what they cannot see.

(4) That this faith demands a full allegiance to Christ as Lord and Saviour, but men do not want to acknowledge the Lordship of another. They desire to be their own masters and please themselves.

Every one of these objections can be spelled in cne word — PRIDE. This has been man's downfall from the beginning.

Having looked at the sinner's opposition to the Faith, which is the negative side, a consideration of the saint's acceptance, or the positive side, would be timely. This will be done by considering its position in the Word of God and seeing its operation throughout the ages.

Note then

(1) THE FAITH ENVISAGED

(2) THE FAITH DELIVERED

(3) THE FAITH CONTENDED

(1) THE FAITH ENVISAGED

This Faith was seen, and appropriated by faith, long before it became an accepted code of ethics. A great number of the Old Testament saints saw it. In fact, one can go back farther and find this Faith envisaged in a past eternity. "Him, being delivered by the determinate counsel and foreknowledge of God . . ." (Acts ii. 23), and again : " According as He hath chosen us in Him before the foundation of the world . . . " (Ephesians i. 4). God planned man's salvation long before he sinned. After man's arrival on this earth and his fall, God began to make known to man His plan of Salvation. Jesus said : " These are the words which I spake unto you, while I was yet with you, that all things must be fulfilled, which were written in the law of Moses, and in the prophets, and in the Psalms, concerning Me " (Luke xxiv. 44).

This Faith was envisaged in

> THE LAW, in what are commonly called types and shadows, such as : —
>
> The coats of skin to Adam.
>
> The bow in the sky to Noah.
>
> The altar of sacrifice to Abram.
>
> The blood on the doorposts to Israel.
>
> The sacrifices, the Tabernacle, the Priesthood, the Offerings, and a multitude of other things given to Moses, the lawgiver.

All these were shadows of good things to come.

THE PSALMS, which give praise to God as the Creator of all things, and which call upon every thing in nature to bear witness to the power of God. Many of these are called Prophetic Psalms because they tell of the Gospel of God's grace.

> Psalm 22 tells of the sufferings of Christ.
>
> Psalm 32 tells of the forgiveness of sin.
>
> Psalms 40 and 68 tell of our salvation.

Many declare Him as the God of Salvation, the Rock of Salvation — in fact, the references are too many to enumerate.

THE PROPHETS. Moses, Elijah, Elisha, Jeremiah, Isaiah, Amos, Joel, Jonah, all preached salvation, maybe none so much as Isaiah. The key of that whole book is Salvation, with such wonderful chapters as liii. and lv. The Apostle said, concerning these Old Testament saints : " These all died in faith, not having received the promises, but having seen them afar off, and were persuaded of them, and embraced them, and confessed that they were strangers and pilgrims on the earth. For they that saw such things declare plainly that they seek a country " (Hebrews xi.

13-14). In fact, the whole of the eleventh chapter of Hebrews is a citation of those who, in the past, envisaged this Faith and conducted themselves accordingly.

(2) THE FAITH DELIVERED

This is the message of the New Testament. It is the whole story of the Gospel, which Paul summed up in the words : " And without controversy great is the mystery of Godliness : God was manifest in the flesh, justified in the Spirit, seen of angels, preached unto the Gentiles, believed on in the world, received up into glory " (I Timothy iii. 16).

HIS LIFE. He was born to be a Saviour. Hence He was given the Name of Jesus, " for He shall save His people from their sins." His whole life's ministry was to that end. His teaching was : " I come not to call the righteous but sinners to repentance," " Christ Jesus came into the world to save sinners." His Life proved His right and ability to do this because it was a perfect Life, free from any sin. He knew no sin. He did no sin. Therefore He could die for sin, the Just for the unjust that He might bring us to God.

Although His Life was perfect and His work beyond reproach, yet this was not sufficient because man is not saved by works, neither his own nor those of any one else. Man is saved by

HIS DEATH. This is the thing against which man rebels so much. For some reason he takes a great dislike to the fact that salvation is not of works. He is willing to accept any faith which does not embrace the Death of Jesus, and yet it is the only Faith. It was the very thing that had created the apostate Church to which Jude was writing, but the truth remains — He died :—

> " He died that we might be forgiven,
> He died to make us good ;
> That we might go at last to heaven
> Saved by His precious Blood."

HIS RESURRECTION. In order to make known to the world the fact that Jesus did not die as a martyr of a faith, but that He might establish a Faith, there comes the great declaration that the third day God raised Him from the dead.

The early Church ever declared His Death and Resurrection. Paul constantly faced the opposition of the religionists of his day when he preached the resurrection of Christ.

This was THE FAITH once delivered. The " once " does not mean that there was no continuation of the message, but that there has never been an amendment to the original declaration. An apostate church, which seeks to move away from that first declaration, should take heed to the words of Galatians i. 6-8: " I marvel that ye are so soon removed from Him that called you into the grace of Christ unto another gospel; which is not another; but there be some that trouble you, and would pervert the gospel of Christ. But though we, or an angel from heaven, preach any other gospel unto you than that which we have preached unto you, let him be accursed."

(3) THE FAITH CONTENDED

Jude, having exposed the apostate church, then enjoins the true Church. He is anxious that, not only shall they be kept free from contamination, but that they shall be strong enough to resist it. This is to be done in three different ways.

By Study (vs. 20). " But ye, beloved, building up yourselves on your most holy faith . . . " Study of the Word is the only way to grow in the Word, and growth in the Word is the only means whereby one can be strong in the Faith — " . . . ready always to give an answer to every man that asketh you a reason of the hope that is in you with meekness and fear " (1 Peter iii. 15).

A man who would be physically strong must eat regularly and carefully. Eating everything and anything causes a man to put on excess weight which, in turn, becomes a strain on the heart, as well as causing other ailments. Should he fail in respect of his appetite, then he ceases to be the strong, robust, vigorous man he desires.

Thus in spiritual life, we must feed if we would grow, but we must also feed regularly and *carefully*. Man has been instructed by the Word of God to " Believe not every spirit," and to " prove the spirits." The Bereans searched the Scriptures daily. Our strength depends upon our study, for the output depends entirely upon the intake — no intake, no output — poor intake, poor output. Jacob said to Asher : " His bread shall be fat, and he shall *yield* royal dainties " (Genesis xlix. 20). So " receive with meekness the engrafted Word, which is able to save your souls " (James i. 21).

This modern age is producing a great deal of mediocre preaching because men are not giving themselves to study like the old giants of the Faith.

By Prayer (vs. 20). " Praying in the Holy Ghost." The Holy Ghost was given to us to be the Interpreter of Scripture. The Lord promised that He, the Spirit of Truth, should lead us into all Truth. It is necessary, therefore, to seek His guidance in all study.

Contending does not mean taking up the battle-axe and fighting all who do not see exactly the same as we do. The constructive is always better than the destructive. The conference table is more profitable than the battlefield. Instead of fighting those who are different in their outlook, one would gain by praying for them. " More things are wrought through prayer than this world dreams of."

What one must not do is to yield ground to the enemy.

By Service (vs. 21). " Keep yourselves in the Love of God." James said : " Faith without works is dead." We are saved to serve. Therefore, as good husbandmen, let us labour in God's vineyard to gather the grapes, or in the harvest field to bring in the sheaves.

Let us, as good soldiers, put on the whole armour of God and fight a good fight of faith. God does not want parade ground soldiers who put on a great show. He wants battlefield soldiers, wearing the battledress of prayer and service.

Let us, as good stewards, engage in a faithful ministry, rightly dividing the Word of Truth.

Let us, as dear children, bear a faithful testimony to the God of our salvation, and thereby ascribe to Him this glorious benediction : " Now unto Him that is able to keep you from falling, and to present you faultless before the presence of His glory with exceeding joy ; To the only wise God our Saviour, be glory and majesty, dominion and power, both now and ever. Amen."

REVELATION

THE CONSUMMATION

*" And at that time shall Michael stand up, the great prince
which standeth for the children of thy people: and there
shall be a time of trouble, such as never was since there
was a nation even to that same time: and at that time
thy people shall be delivered, every one that shall be found
written in the book. And many of them that sleep in
the dust of the earth shall awake, some to everlasting life,
and some to shame and everlasting contempt. And they that
be wise shall shine as the brightness of the firmament; and
they that turn many to righteousness as the stars for ever
and ever"* (DANIEL xii. 1-3)

INTRODUCTION

It has been mentioned before that the titles of the books of
the Bible are not part of the Inspired text, and many of them are
at fault. This is one of them — the fault is obvious because it
has created a contradiction of statements. The title says : " The
Revelation of St. John the Divine," whilst the text begins with :
" The revelation of Jesus Christ." The possessive pronoun " of "
should not be in the title. The full title might read : " The
revelation of Jesus Christ TO St. John the Divine."

Many people speak of this book as a book of mysteries.
That is exactly what it is not. Another title given to this concluding book is " The Apocalypse," which is derived from two
Greek words, " Apo " which means " To take away " and
" Kalypto " meaning " Veil." So long as a thing is covered and
hidden from view it can be a mystery, a thing of uncertainty,
but at the moment of unveiling everything is revealed, the doubts
are gone — it is a revelation.

Concerning the things which belonged to the time of the end,
it would appear that Jesus Himself did not possess full knowledge
of them whilst He was in the flesh. We know that such was true
of other phases of His life.

Although He was Omnipotent, Omniscient, and Omnipresent, yet some of these qualities were forfeited whilst He was man, for He knew hunger, thirst and weariness. He was never in two places at the same time, but ever remained within the limits of the human frame. With regard to knowledge, there are the somewhat startling words of Mark xiii. 32 : " But of that day and that hour knoweth no man, no, not the angels which are in heaven, *neither the Son,* but the Father."

When Christ had completed His redemptive work upon earth, and had ascended to the Father, then God made known to Him the final consummation of all things. Thus it is that the book opens with the words : " The Revelation of Jesus Christ which God gave unto Him." One cannot give to a person that which he already possesses. This knowledge Jesus was to communicate to man whom He had redeemed — " To shew unto His servants things which must shortly come to pass."

Daniel had desired to understand these things but God had said to him : " But thou, O Daniel, shut up the words, and seal the book, even to the time of the end " (Daniel xii. 4). " And He said, Go thy way, Daniel : for the words are closed up and sealed till the time of the end " (Daniel xii. 9). Note, not the end of time.

Of all the apostles who had walked and worked with Jesus upon earth, John may have been the only one still alive. He outlived all of the others. Many of them had suffered martyrdom. John had been put into exile on the Isle of Patmos, shut away from all contacts with man but not cut off from communication with God. So Jesus sent an angel to him with the revelation, and John, under Divine Inspiration, recorded for our information.

Another important point for consideration, before dealing with the exposition, is that of time element. It is a known fact that Christendom is divided into main schools of interpretation, plus several smaller groups. It is also recognised that there are good and trustworthy scholars in both schools, with the result that one has to come to his own decision as to which interpretation is to be accepted. The two major schools are known as Historicists and Futurists. We seek to show the point of departure, and state the reason for our own decision.

The Historicists believe that most of the book has already had its fulfilment, and they seek to fit all of its details into past history.

The Futurists believe that none of the Revelation has had a fulfilment yet, other than it is now the end of the Church period described in chapters ii. and iii.

The point of separation is on the interpretation of the words " The things which are, and the things which shall be hereafter " (i. 19). In the case of the Historicists, the " hereafter " would be after the death of John, or at the completion of the Revelation which was given to him. That, of course, would cause the interpretation to begin at that point.

The Futurists, however, cannot accept that such big issues can swing on such a small hinge as an individual — John.

John, who outlived his Master by many years (over half a century), witnessed the first fifty years of Church history. Therefore he lived and wrote in the Church period. We ourselves live in that same Church period, known as the Dispensation of the Grace of God. Consequently, the words " After this " (iv. 1) mean after the Church period which, of course, is still in the future — hence the term " futurists."

This is the interpretation being accepted here.

INTERPRETATION

The book can be divided into three in a first analysis. It was Dr. Graham Scroggie who used the three words GRACE, GOVERNMENT, GLORY. This is very comprehensive.

GRACE would be chapters i. - v., and takes in the period of the Church.

GOVERNMENT embraces chapters vi. - xix., and deals with God's judgments upon the world.

GLORY includes chapters xx. - xxii., or the final consummation — Satan cast out, the Great White Throne, The Millennium, and Eternity.

GRACE (Chapters i. - v.)

(a) THE CHURCH ON EARTH

This covers the period of the Church both in time and eternity, the Church militant and the Church triumphant. It commences with : " John to the seven churches which are in Asia." Here the point is raised, in favour of a historic interpretation, that the " hereafter " would refer to the time of the seven churches of Asia, churches which have long since ceased to exist.

Several things must be noted. (1) The number seven is used as a symbol of completeness and would, therefore, represent the complete Church of all time. This can be established by the fact that there were more than seven Churches in Asia which are mentioned in Scripture. It was not the principal churches which were addressed, because the church at Smyrna was small whilst a large church at Hierapolis is not mentioned. They were chosen, as will be seen later, because of their particular characteristics. (2) The seven letters are to be read collectively rather than individually, as ascertained from Chapter i., verse 11 : " What thou seest, write in A book and send IT unto the seven churches which are in Asia . . . " As this book travelled around, each church read what God had to say to it, and what He had to say to the other six. The whole Church must know what God stated about each, because what He said to one church concerned the whole.

Having named the seven churches which made up " the things which are," one is caused to step back to see the things which were. It is a vision of the Son of man in the midst of the seven candlesticks. He is in the attire of the Priest of Israel. Each description declares an attribute or a characteristic of the Lord, and each separate description is applied to one or other of the seven churches.

As previously stated, these seven messages embrace the whole Church period.

Ephesus — Pentecost to A.D.70. Lost Love

Within thirty-five years of the birth of the Church, with all of the power and wonder of Pentecost, it had lost its first love and was suffering a slow deterioration, so that the call is made : " Nevertheless I have somewhat against thee, because thou hast left thy first love. Remember therefore from whence thou art fallen, and repent, and do thy first works : or else . . . " (ii. 4-5).

Smyrna — A.D.70 - A.D.312. Persecution

The repentance asked by God did not come, and so the " or else " did. The Church suffered a long period of persecution when there was much martyrdom, but the losses sustained by the faithful in this life earned for them great rewards in the life to come.

Pergamos — A.D.312 - A.D.606. Licentiousness

Many evil doctrines were introduced into the Church during this era, including many of the Roman Catholic practices, such as idolatry, confessions, penance, purgatory, Mariolatry, etc. Here it is referred to as the doctrine of the Nicolaitanes, meaning the domination of the priests over the laity or the people. This condition worsened in the following period described in the message to

Thyatira — A.D.606 - A.D.1520. Illicit Marriage

In A.D. 606 Boniface was crowned first Universal Bishop. The Catholic Church became a State Church, so that the Church and State married, when the Lord had said: "Come out from among them, and be ye separate" (2 Corinthians vi. 17). This Church system, with its domination, became the "Mother Church," and that is why the Lord said: " . . . because thou sufferest that woman Jezebel, which calleth herself a prophetess . . . " (ii. 20). This period is known as Mediaeval history, or the Dark Ages.

Sardis — A.D. 1520 - A.D. 1750. Dead

" . . . that thou hast a name that thou livest and art dead " (iii. 1). Ritual and formality had taken the place of the Gospel. The Church was a Church by name and nothing more. All of the great doctrines had been lost, and yet there were a few individuals left who were the salt of the Church. It was during these conditions that Martin Luther raised his voice, protested the practices which had been imposed, and declared that the just should live by faith. So came the Reformation, a renewal of the doctrines which had been lost, and an ushering in of the period of Church history covered by the message to

Philadelphia — A.D. 1750 - A.D. 1900. Brotherly Love

This was a time of great spiritual revival. The demands of Romanism were suppressed, the power of the hierarchy subdued, and the freedom of the Gospel permitted.

During the period the Church enjoyed the blessing of the great preachers and revivalists, such as the Wesleys, Whitfield, Finney, Spurgeon, Moody, Sankey, and many others. It was in this same period that all of the Missionary Societies were established and the Mission field opened ; also great religious institutions and organisations found their birth.

How different to-day ! Mission fields are closing, church doors are closing, great preachers are scarce, the Bible is rejected. And why ?

Laodicea — A.D. 1900 - ?. Lukewarm

We are living in a period of indifference. We are not cold in our denial, but we are not hot in our testimony. It is an attitude that every man has a right to think what he will and do what he will, and we must not interfere with man's liberty.

The fact is that many people do not think, and others think wrongly, or there would not be such an amount of crime. Therefore, man's thinking must be guided. The politician seeks to guide or influence man's thoughts, and so does the commercial world. Then it is right for the Church to direct the thoughts of men, morally and spiritually. If it does not, it is shelving its responsibility. The Lord is outside the door, and the Church is not aware of it. No wonder it was said of the last days of the Church Dispensation : " Shall He find faith on the earth ? "

Some of the deciding points of interpretation are found here. Having been brought along through the Church period to this lukewarm condition that was declared to be indicative of the last days, the next words are : " After this . . . Come up hither, and I will shew thee things which must be hereafter " (iv. 1), or, after the Church period.

(b) THE CHURCH IN HEAVEN

It is to be noted that there is no mention in the book of Revelation of the Coming of the Lord, nor of the departure of the Church. However, in chapters ii. and iii. the Church is on earth, and in chapters iv. and v. it is in heaven, which means that this unrecorded event took place between chapters iii. and iv.

John did not see the Person of God sitting upon the throne, for no man hath seen God at any time. What the Apostle saw was the character of God, represented by a yellow, transparent jasper, speaking of God's holiness, and a red, sardine stone, which denoted His justice. Holiness and Justice are inseparable qualities of the Divine character. The complete rainbow tells of the covenant-keeping God Whose promises will then be complete.

The four and twenty elders and the four living creatures are representative of the redeemed because, in the next chapter, all of them are engaged in singing the new song, in which they claim themselves to have been redeemed by the Blood of the Lamb (v. 8-9).

The elders could represent the *saints* of all time, twelve patriarchs representing the Old Testament saints, and twelve apostles being the symbol of the New Testament saints. Now they are united into twenty-four, because in Christ there is neither Jew nor Gentile. They are seated, as though satisfied that they have gained their reward.

The four living creatures are not sitting. Their eyes are alert in every direction, and their wings are ready to go into action to do His bidding. These could readily represent the *servants* of God as against the *saints* of God. We are all saved to serve, but not all who are saved do serve. Some are content to sit. The characteristics of these creatures are such as belong to the servants of the Lord.

The lion speaks of power and tenacity.
The calf speaks of humility and service.
The face of a man speaks of consecrated intellect.
The eagle is the creature which can climb high and look into the face of the sun.

Whether saints or servants, all are engaged in worship.

The sealed book, in the hand of Him Who sat upon the throne, could have been the book which Daniel was commanded to seal in Daniel xii. 4.

The only qualification for breaking these seals was worthiness, and John wept because, whilst heaven was full of power, glory, might, and majesty, there was no one worthy. The Apostle was quickly encouraged to wipe away his tears as the Worthy One was there. It was Christ, the Son of God, the Lion of the tribe of Judah, the Root of David, the Lamb that had been slain. At His appearing everyone and everything in heaven, on earth, and under the earth, bowed in reverence and worshipped Him.

This is the time to which reference was made that the trees of the fields will clap their hands, the mountains and hills will rejoice together, whilst everything that has breath will praise the Lord.

We shall join in that praise of eternity. The Lord help us to praise Him now and tune our hearts for that great day.

With this scene the Dispensation of Grace closes.

GOVERNMENT (Chapters vi. - xix.)

SEVEN SEALS BROKEN (chapters vi. - vii)

Whilst heaven is full of worship to the Lord, earth is full of woes because the Lord is about to avenge the blood of His saints.

The cry "come and see" in verses 1, 3, 5, and 7, which comes from the lips of the Living Creatures, is really the one word "Come," and is not an invitation to John to come and see what is happening, but is a command to whatever was behind the seals to come forth.

The First Seal — A White Horse. It has been suggested by some that the rider of this horse was Christ, but that cannot be seeing that Christ is the One Who is breaking the seals, and Who is releasing that which has been bound up. Christ is on the white horse in chapter xix., but the description is very different there. Here it is the counterfeit — Antichrist. The result of the reign of Antichrist is revealed in the breaking of

The Second Seal — A Red Horse. The rider had power to take peace from the earth — in other words, to create war. In the first seal the rider had a bow but no arrows. Antichrist comes posing as a friend, but soon declares himself the enemy of mankind.

The Third Seal — A Black Horse, whose rider carried a balance and measured out the food, thus denoting a time of famine so severe that a measure of wheat, or three measures of inferior barley, would be sold for a penny, or a day's pay (see Matthew xx. 2). "And see thou hurt not the oil and the wine" (vi. 6). The war will have taken all labour, so that men will have to rely on that which grows wild and needs little cultivation — the oil and the wine.

The Fourth Seal — A Pale Horse. Death was the rider and Hell followed with him. Each horse is a natural follower of the other. Antichrist brings war, war brings famine, famine brings death. Here the death is both physical and spiritual.

The Fifth Seal — The Martyred Saints. Under the altar of sacrifice were seen the disembodied spirits of those who had died for the cause of Christ. They were awaiting the final resurrection.

They were demanding justice to be meted out upon their adversaries. This cannot be done until the cup of indignation is full and the day of suffering for the Church of Christ is complete. When our sufferings have ended, those of the God-rejectors will only be beginning. Their day is yet to come.

The Sixth Seal — Physical Changes. Such physical upheavals will take place that all men remaining on the earth, both small and great, will know that the great day of His wrath has come. Then they will seek death but shall not find it.

Interval. This interval is to be seen between the sixth and seventh seals, the sixth and seventh trumpets, and the sixth and seventh vials.

During the interval the judgments are held, whilst one hundred and forty-four thousand are sealed. These are an elect number of Israel who are going to be protected from an impending catastrophe. At the same time a multitude of the redeemed is seen by John in a place of security around the throne, rejoicing in God their salvation. This new vision of the redeemed is shown immediately before the great tribulation breaks, and thereby reveals in a positive way that the Church does not go through the tribulation.

After this comes the breaking of

The Seventh Seal — Seven Trumpeters. This act was preceded by a period of silence. The book, which was in the process of being opened, was sealed with seven seals. Although six of these had been broken, the contents of the book remain a secret. It would be this final break which would unfold its hidden mysteries. Awful things had already transpired, so what would come as this seal was broken ? It was this which caused the great suspense. As there comes a great hush over nature before the breaking of a storm, when the birds seek refuge and the wild animal retreats to his lair, so here was a tenseness when everything and everyone held their breath, as it were, in awe and wonderment.

The book opened with the appearance of seven angels, each having a trumpet. These were accompanied by an eighth angel who stood by the golden altar, the place of intercession. This angel had in his hand a golden censer, and with it he exercised a twofold ministry.

Firstly, he placed upon it much incense, which typified the acceptance of the prayers of the saints.

Secondly, he filled his censer with the fire off the altar, and then tipped it down to earth, thus declaring the judgment of God upon the sinner because of his rejection of the Saviour.

THE SOUNDING OF THE SEVEN TRUMPETS
(Chapters viii. - xi.)

The First Trumpet. A third part of all trees and green grass was destroyed as the result of a fearful hailstorm.

The Second Trumpet. This brought destruction to a third part of the sea as it was turned into blood, bringing death to the third part of life in the sea and destruction to the third part of ships. The blood was not that of the slain. Life perished because of the blood.

The Third Trumpet. Wormwood embittered a third part of the water of the rivers and fountains. That would be the domestic supply, the drinking water, so that men died from this contamination.

The Fourth Trumpet. At its sounding a third part of the solar system was darkened, including the sun, moon, and stars.

With this an angel flew through heaven, crying, Woe, Woe, Woe, for conditions worsen in the sounding of the remaining trumpets. Up to the moment nature has been affected, but now man himself is going to be touched.

The Fifth Trumpet, and First Woe. From the bottomless pit a great plague of infernal locusts is released by an angel who unlocks the pit. These are commanded not to touch the vegetation, which is the natural thing for ordinary locusts. Instead, they are to torment men for five months, but not to kill any. They must be a host of evil spirits released by the permissive Will of God. For years men had refused the appeals of the Holy Spirit. Now they would suffer an attack from the evil spirit, until they long for death as a way of escape. Remember, Paul had warned that it would be a " fearful thing to fall into the hands of the living God " (Hebrews x. 31).

The Sixth Trumpet, and Second Woe. An infernal army of horsemen is released from the Euphrates, and a third of men die at the advance of this host. These horsemen had been reserved for this particular time, for verse 15 should read : " Which were prepared for the hour of the day of the month of the year." It is a particular moment of time rather than a period of time, as is suggested in the text. God has ever worked according to a timetable. He has appointed a time in which He will judge the world.

As there was an interval between the sixth and seventh seals, so there was an

Interval before the sounding of the seventh trumpet. In it the Apostle saw another vision. *A mighty angel clothed in a cloud,* and hallowed with a rainbow. His face was as the sun, and his feet as pillars of fire. This is similar to the vision in chapter i., which was of the Lord, the rainbow reminding us that He is the Covenant-keeping God. There was a little book in the hand of the angel, the word in the Greek meaning " miniature Bible ", or, the Word of God. He stood in the attitude of swearing or taking an oath, as he lifted his hand toward heaven (vs. 5). His position was possessive, placing one foot on the sea and the other upon the earth (vs. 2). His cry was " that there should be time no longer " (vs. 6), or, as the margin quotes it, there should be " no more delay." The souls under the altar had cried : " O Lord, how long ? ", to which He had replied : " Yet a little while." Now the delay is ending, and also the day of His rejection. The Lord is making a formal claim of sea and earth. Satan is to be cast out — Jesus, Whose right it is, is about to reign.

In this same interval there appear

The Two Witnesses. These are undoubtedly Moses and Elijah. They are described in verse 6. They have " power to shut heaven, that it rain not in the days of their prophecy." Elijah alone had that power. They also have power over waters to turn them into blood, and to smite the earth with all plagues, as often as they will. Moses alone had that power. Elijah was translated, and Moses was raised from the dead (Jude vi.), in order that they might become His witnesses. These two men were together on the Mount of Transfiguration, as witnesses. They are named together in the closing verses of the Old Testament, and there is no reason why it should not be believed that they were the two men in shining apparel at the tomb witnessing His resurrection, and also witnessing His ascension, and declaring His coming again.

The Seventh Trumpet. With it we are brought into the middle of the week, known as the Tribulation, and into the half of the week known as the Great Tribulation. It was mentioned in the previous chapter that the Lord was formally taking possession of all that was His. Verse 15 of this eleventh chapter confirms the act.

At the sounding of this trumpet two wonders, or two signs or symbols, appear. A sign cannot give any time element. This may be illustrated in the Union Jack and the Stars and Stripes, which are the flags, or symbols, of two great nations. Both of these flags could tell a great story because both have grown over the years. The three crosses of the Union Jack used to be separate flags ; in fact, they still are, but at different time elements they have grown into the present Union. The Stars and Stripes started with thirteen stars, in the days of Abraham Lincoln, and have grown over the years to the present stars for the fifty States in the Union and the thirteen stripes for the thirteen Colonies. A development of history is interwoven in these two flags. In a similar manner must these two wonders be interpreted.

(1) A woman clothed with the sun. This is a symbol of Israel, resplendent in her glory. The sun, moon, and stars, are all Jewish symbols. The moon is sometimes a picture of the Church. That moon is under the woman's feet, signifying that the Church has run its course, and has been removed from the earth. Israel has become the leading nation of the world. " Travailing in birth " denotes that she is a married woman. The Church is the Bride of Christ, Israel the wife of Jehovah — " Thy maker is thine husband " (Isaiah liv. 5). The Manchild is Christ, born of that nation.

(2) The Dragon. This is the Devil, a murderer from the beginning. When Satan failed to prevent Christ from dying on the Cross, he then centred his evil designs upon the nation of Israel, and will continue to do so, but God is providing a way of escape for them.

In the second half of the chapter there is

WAR IN HEAVEN. Michael and his angels fight against the Devil and his angels. It is a battle in which no armaments will be used and no blood shed. It is true of some of the great battles of the past. Battles do not belong exclusively to battlefields and military personnel. Some of the greatest battles have been fought in Law Courts, where the ammunition has been words. Counsel and Defence hurl words one against the other in a desperate endeavour to win the case. Thus it is here. On the one side is the

Accuser of the brethren, charging, accusing, condemning. On the other side are the brethren who overcome by the *word of their testimony* and the Blood of the Lamb. " Who shall lay anything to the charge of God's elect ? It is God that justifieth. Who is he that condemneth ? " (Romans viii. 33-34). The Dragon is cast out and defeated, bringing rejoicing in heaven, but woe to the inhabiters of the earth. It is at this juncture that God makes provision for His people's safety as the Devil makes his last attack upon the earth.

A SATANIC TRINITY (Chapter xiii.). God is a Trinity — Father, Son, and Spirit. Man is a trinity — body, soul, and spirit, and Satan is also a trinity. The Dragon is Anti-god. The Beast is Antichrist, and the False Prophet is Anti-spirit.

The Antichrist is referred to in verses 1-3, and is seen as the Beast that rose up from the sea. He possessed all the same characteristics of the Beast in the book of Daniel. The Beast receives his power from the Dragon (verses 4-10), as Christ received His power and authority from His Father. He went forth to *make war against* the saints, as Christ *brought peace to* the saints.

The lamb-like creature, who becomes the False Prophet (verses 11-18), is the Anti-spirit. Like the Holy Spirit, he never speaks of himself but always exalts the Antichrist. He caused an image to be set up to the Beast, and required that all men should worship it and receive its mark.

Six is the number of man, created on the sixth day. Six hundred and sixty-six is the number of the superman who will control the lives of those who have refused to bow the knee to the Man, Christ Jesus.

From the lamb-like creature of the earth, the thoughts are directed to the

LAMB ON MOUNT SION (Chapter xiv.), Who is in the midst of those who have received the mark of His Father, those who have been delivered out of the Tribulation but do not belong to the Church (that does not go through the Tribulation). These are Israelites, because there are twelve thousand from each of the twelve tribes of Israel.

SIX ANGELS (Chapter xiv.)

First Angel (vs. 6 and 7), preaches the Everlasting Gospel. This is not to be confused with the Gospel of the Grace of God, which is preached by the Church to sinners unto eternal life. The burden of the Everlasting Gospel is to fear God (not love Him), and worship Him as Creator (not as a Redeemer), for the hour of His judgment is come (not the day of His Grace).

Second Angel (vs. 8). He announces the fall of the great city of Babylon.

Third Angel (vs. 9-15). This angel pronounces the wrath of God which is to fall on the followers of Antichrist. So appalling will be those days of judgment that a Voice is heard from heaven saying : " Blessed are the dead which die in the Lord *from henceforth,"* or, happy is the man who, by reason of death, escapes those dreadful days.

Christ then appears as a reaper, whilst a

Fourth Angel (vs. 15-16) bids Him cast in the sickle and reap, because the sins of the people are ripe and ready for judgment.

Fifth Angel (vs. 17-20). He thrusts in his sickle and gathers in the vintage of the earth.

Sixth Angel (vs. 18). He comes from the golden altar and gives command to the fifth angel.

In chapter xv. those who are saved through the Tribulation Period are seen separated and standing on a sea of glass and singing the song of Moses and the Lamb. This song is not the song of redemption, for they are not part of the Church. Instead of worshipping a Saviour, they are worshipping a King. " Great and marvellous are Thy works, Lord God Almighty ; just and true are Thy ways, Thou King of Saints " (vs. 3).

THE SEVEN VIALS (Chapters xvi. - xvii.)

These vials are poured out upon the earth by seven other angels.

First Vial brings grievous sores upon the followers of Antichrist.

Second Vial turns the sea into blood, bringing death.

Third Vial turns the rivers into blood.

Fourth Vial is poured upon the sun, causing men to be burned with heat.

Fifth Vial brings darkness and pain.

Sixth Vial is poured upon the River Euphrates, causing it to dry up.
Then comes the interval which is found between the sixth and seventh in each series.
Following this interval three unclean spirits, likened to frogs, emanate from the Satanic Trinity. Frogs are croaking creatures that make a great deal of noise in the evening time, spoiling man's peace and quietness. These evil spirits appear in the evening of the age, taking peace from the world. They will be responsible for gathering the armies of the world together for the battle of Armageddon.
The outpouring of the

Seventh Vial brings about the greatest earthquake of all time, which destroys the cities of the world.
None of these judgments brings repentance on the part of men but, instead, further blasphemy.

THE FALL OF ECCLESIASTICAL BABYLON (Chapter xvii.)

Babylon represents a church and a city, a religion and a commercial system, both of which come to a sudden end. Christ has a Bride; that Bride is a Church, and that Church is a City. " Come hither, I will shew thee the bride, the Lamb's wife. And he carried me away in the spirit to a great and high mountain, and shewed me that great city, the holy Jerusalem, descending out of heaven from God " (xxi. 9-10). Antichrist also has a wife. That wife is a church, Ecclesiastical Babylon or the Roman Catholic Church (Revelation xvii.), and that church is a city, commercial Babylon (Revelation xviii.).
The religious system of Rome is fully described in the seventeenth chapter, and is comparable throughout with the Roman Catholic Church. This church, which has always sought world domination, will be carried to the apex of her power by the Antichrist. " . . . I saw a woman sit upon a scarlet coloured beast . . . " (vs. 3), " . . . the beast that carrieth her " (vs. 7). At the beginning, he poses to be a friend of the church but, later,

breaks that friendship, for in verse 16 the woman is hated and burned.

The sudden change will be appreciated as it is realised that, after the Antichrist has helped the Roman church to world domination, which, of course, is after the true Church has been taken away, an image will be set up to the Beast. The False Prophet then commands that all men must worship that image at pain of death. As man cannot worship two things, there will be a sudden swing from Romanism to the Beast, thus the whore will be hated.

At this particular time Babylon will have been rebuilt as a city. It will be the centre of commerce and the seat of Antichrist. It, too, is going to fall, and those who had enriched themselves from her merchandise are going to bewail her. As to the completeness of her destruction, that is expressed in chapter xviii., verse 21 : "And a mighty angel took up a stone like a great millstone, and cast it into the sea, saying, Thus with violence shall that great city Babylon be thrown down, and shall be found no more at all."

TWO SUPPERS (Chapter xix.)

As a result of the overthrow of Babylon, there is to be a great rejoicing amongst all the saints of God, in which a vast multitude joins them in singing the Alleluia chorus. They rejoice because, in the first place, God has avenged the blood of His servants who had died at her hand and, secondly, the day had come for the Church to be united to the Lord at the great

MARRIAGE SUPPER OF THE LAMB. The Church for whom Christ had died, the Church, made up of all true believers for whom He had made constant intercession as their Great High Priest, and whom He had loved as His Bride on earth, is becoming His Wife in heaven.

The believer is now in the fulness of his glory, feasting with his Lord.

The second half of the chapter tells of the unbeliever who has come to the finality of his judgments, for the Lord prepares His second supper, called the

SUPPER OF THE GREAT GOD (Chapter xix. 17). The Lord rides forth on a white horse, followed by all the armies of heaven. He rides as King of kings, and Lord of lords. His only weapon of warfare is the sharp, two-edged sword of His Word, that Word which had been rejected by the world. This is the battle of Armageddon, when the great men of the earth, led by the Antichrist, gather against the Lord, but He destroys them all and calls upon the fowls of the air to come and feast upon their flesh.

At the end of this conflict, the Antichrist and the False Prophet are cast *alive* into the lake of fire, and meet their final doom.

GLORY (Chapters xx. - xxii.)

The Bottomless Pit (Chapter xx. 3). The Devil himself is bound, and cast into the bottomless pit for a period of one thousand years.

Concerning the bottomless pit, so many people cannot conceive the idea of such a place, thinking of a constant falling without reaching the bottom, but if one took a ball, placed inside it a pea, and then spun the ball, the pea would jump, bounce, and toss, because there would be no bottom to the spinning ball. This earth is a spinning globe, which means that the very centre of it could be a bottomless pit, for the nearer one comes to the centre the faster are the revolutions.

The Millennium (Chapter xx. 4-10). The saints live and reign with Christ, for the resurrection of the just has already taken place. Satan is bound, sin is removed, death is vanquished, and peace reigns. There are still nations of people upon the earth over whom the saints reign.

At the end of the thousand years Satan is loosed and permitted to go forth to deceive the four quarters of the earth, and again men gather themselves together against the saints of God, thus establishing a fact that a perfect environment, even of a thousand years' duration, does not change the human heart. Sin is still there even though it may have been dormant.

The result of this battle, known as Gog and Magog, is that Satan is committed to his final doom, the lake of fire.

For those who do not believe in eternal fire and eternal punishment, may it be pointed out that it was a thousand years earlier that the Beast and False Prophet were cast into it *alive* (xix. 20). Now Satan is cast into the same lake of fire where the Beast and the False Prophet *are* (xx. 10). That is not annihilation.

As to eternal fire, no one questions the scientists that fire ever burns within the heart of this earth, and that volcanoes, like Mount Etna, are caused by the fire breaking through where the crust of the earth is thinnest. If one believes the scientists who discover, why not believe the God Who created ?

THE GREAT WHITE THRONE (Chapter xx. 11-15). This is the final resurrection, when the people who have died without accepting Christ Jesus as their personal Saviour from sin, shall be raised from the dead to stand before the Lord. This is the place where man must take the judgment of his own sin. The Book of Life will be opened to find the record of when that person was born again through faith in Christ. This is not the Church membership book, which means nothing up there. Seeing that everything must be established in the mouth of two witnesses, other books will be opened. These contain all the works which have been performed, good and bad, the motives which controlled the actions, all the wrongs done to men, and all the sins committed against the Holy God Who will be sitting upon that Throne, the God Who was forgotten in life, Whose Book was rejected, Whose worship was despised, the God Who blessed mankind in so many ways but for Whom man had no time, not even on Sundays.

According to those records men will be judged, and not a single excuse will be made. Every soul whose name is missing from that Book of Life will be cast out into the lake of fire, which is the second death. The first death is when the soul is separated from the body. The second death is when that soul is separated from God, from all that is pure and holy — alone for ever.

After this comes the establishment of

A NEW HEAVEN AND A NEW EARTH

Old things have passed away. Sin and sorrow are no more. The Lord is the centre, the glory, and the light, and His people are basking in the fulness of His love.

How can man enjoy the blessings of an eternity with the Lord? Here it is — " And the Spirit and the bride say, Come. And let him that heareth say, Come. And let him that is athirst come. And whosoever will, let him take of the water of life freely " (xxii. 17).

See that thou add nothing thereto, and take nothing therefrom.